The Complete Book of
Bible Quotations from

THE OLD
TESTAMENT

Also edited by Mark L. Levine and Eugene Rachlis:

The Complete Book of Bible Quotations
The Complete Book of Bible Quotations
from the New Testament

Published by POCKET BOOKS

The Complete Book of Bible Quotations from

THE OLD TESTAMENT

Edited by MARK L. LEVINE
and EUGENE RACHLIS

POCKET BOOKS
New York   London   Toronto   Sydney   Tokyo   Singapore

This edition incorporates material from
The Complete Book of Bible Quotations.

An *Original* Publication of POCKET BOOKS

POCKET BOOKS, a division of Simon & Schuster Inc.
1230 Avenue of the Americas, New York, NY 10020

Library of Congress Cataloging-in-Publication Data

The complete book of Bible quotations from the Old Testament / edited
  by Mark L. Levine and Eugene Rachlis.
     p.   cm.
  Originally published as part of The complete book of Bible
quotations.
    ISBN 0-671-53796-2
    1. Bible—Quotations.   I. Levine, Mark L.   II. Rachlis, Eugene.
III. Complete book of Bible quotations.
BS416.C66   1996
221.5′2036—dc20   95-38500
                                                           CIP

First Pocket Books trade paperback printing April 1996

10 9 8 7 6 5 4 3 2 1

POCKET and colophon are registered trademarks of
Simon & Schuster Inc.

Cover design by Tom McKeveny

Printed in the U.S.A.

INTRODUCTION

Most books of quotations—Bartlett's and H.L. Mencken's come immediately to mind—contain only the most familiar quotations from the Bible, the popular phrases and verses that virtually everyone knows and is fond of. The Bible, however, contains thousands of additional phrases and verses that are just as beautiful and just as significant, yet are not as well known or used as often because they haven't been identified as "quotations."

The Old Testament and New Testament editions of *The Complete Book of Bible Quotations* contain not only the Bible's famous lines and phrases, but also those phrases that *should be* famous—by virtue of what is said or the way it is said. These editions are the definitive source books of quotations from the Bible, truly a "Bartlett's of the Bible."

"Quotability"—how the phrase sounds, in speech and on paper—was an essential element in every selection. We carefully reread the entire Bible and chose only those verses and phrases that we believed to be of such style, beauty and brevity that individuals would readily repeat them to make a point or illustrate an image in conversation, sermons, speeches, and in writing.

In preparing the Old Testament and New Testament editions, we selected over 6,000 different quotations and classified them into more than 800 categories. There are quotations from every one of the Bible's books in these editions. Each quotation has been placed into an average of two categories (though some may only be in one and a handful in as many as five). Cross-references to related categories with pertinent quotations are indicated where applicable.

Categorizing the quotations was difficult. We took particular care to make sure that each quotation was properly categorized and in context. We not only used our own judgment but consulted with clergy and Biblical scholars and availed ourselves of numerous translations and Biblical commentaries.

If not limited by space, we could have put each quotation into far more categories than we did. But of necessity, we made choices and selected only those that we considered most appropriate and most likely to be helpful to you; we also included in certain categories quotations about both the topic and its antonym. Please keep in mind that, because of the criteria used in selecting these quotations, the book is not intended to be a compilation of everything the Bible says on each subject.

We have given the chapter and verse citation for every quotation in the book and urge you to refer to the Bible for the full context in which each phrase appears. In the chapter and verse references, we have used *"e.g."* to indicate that the phrase appears several times in the Bible even though we have generally listed only one reference. We have used *"see also"* to indicate a verse similar but not identical to the one quoted where we thought you might want to consult that verse too.

We also compiled an extensive Index which gives the key words in every quotation in the book, together with a few adjacent words to provide the context. This serves both as a supplement to the main categories in the book and to help readers find a quotation when they remember a word or two but not the entire quotation.

In addition, we have provided in an Appendix to this volume the full text of three lengthier passages from the Old Testament that we consider particularly beautiful, meaningful and quotable in their entirety. Many more could, of course, have been included.

The translation used is the King James Version, universally renowned for its poetic and beautiful language. The only changes from the King James Version made in this Old Testament edition were to capitalize first-, second- and third-person pronouns which refer to God.

Mark L. Levine
Eugene Rachlis

ACKNOWLEDGMENTS

No book of this size can be prepared without the assistance of a great many people.

In particular, we wish to thank Diana Bryant, Howard Cutler, Nick Egleson, Diana Finch, Sophie Greenblatt, Sheila Heyman, Sydny Miner, Katherine Romaine, Charles Salzberg, Jan Stone, Anna Van and Stephanie von Hirschberg.

We are also deeply indebted to Professor Douglas Stuart, chairman of the Biblical Studies Department and Professor of Old Testament at Gordon-Conwell Theological Seminary in South Hamilton, Massachusetts, and to Dr. Gregory K. Beale, Professor of New Testament at Gordon-Conwell, for reviewing the categorization of the quotations. Any errors in final placement, however, are not their fault but ours.

CONTENTS

Bravery—*See* Courage
Bribery
Brotherhood
Brothers—*See* Siblings
Building
Burial
Business

Calling—*See* Mission
Candor
Capacity
Capital Punishment
Captivity
Care—*See* Comfort, Devotion
Carnage
Caution—*See* Prudence, Vigilance,
  Warning
Celebration
Census
Certainty
Challenges
Chance
Change
Chaos
Character
Charity
Chastisement
Cheating—*See* Honesty, Lies
Child-Rearing
Childbirth—*See* Birth
Childlessness
Children
Choice
Chosen People
Church Governance—*See* Clergy,
  Leadership
Churches
Circumcision
Clarity
Clergy
Comfort
Commandments
Commitment
Common Sense—*See* Wisdom
Communication
Companions
Compassion
Competition
Complaints
Compromise
Conceit

Conduct—*See* Behavior
Conduct toward God
Confession
Confidence
Confusion
Conquest
Conscience
Consecration
Consequences
Conspiracy—*See* Betrayal, Crime
Contamination
Contempt
Contentment
Continuity
Contrition
Conversion
Cooperation
Corruption
Courage
Courtesy
Covenant
Cowardice
Creation
Creativity—*See* Achievement,
  Building, Planning
Credibility
Crime
Criminals
Criticism
Cruelty
Cultivation
Curses
Cynicism

Damnation—*See* Salvation
Dance
Danger
Darkness—*See* Enlightenment,
  Light and Darkness
Death
Debt—*See* Borrowing
Decadence
Deception
Decisions
Deeds
Defeat
Defiance—*See* Arrogance, Audacity,
  Rebellion
Delay—*See* Laziness, Patience,
  Procrastination
Deliverance

Denial

Dependence—*See* God's Protection, Reliance

Depravity

Depression

Deprivation

Desecration—*See* Holiness, Sacrilege

Desire

Desolation

Despair

Destiny

Destruction

Determination

Devotion

Diligence

Diplomacy—*See* Tact

Disappointment

Disarmament—*See* War and Peace, Weapons

Disbelief—*See* Doubt, Godlessness, Skepticism

Discernment

Discipline

Discontent—*See* Contentment, Satisfaction

Discretion—*See* Prudence, Silence, Understanding

Dishonesty

Disobedience

Distance

Diversity

Doctrine

Doom

Doubt

Dreams

Drunkenness

Duty

Duty, Neglect of

Earth

Education

Effort

Ego—*See* Arrogance, Conceit, Humility

Eloquence

Embarrassment—*See* Shame

Emotions—*See* Fear, Happiness, Hatred, Love, Sorrow

Empathy

Employees

Employers—*See* Business, Work

Encouragement

End Days

Endings

Endurance—*See* Diligence, Fortitude, Perseverance, Strength

Enemies

Enlightenment

Enthusiasm

Environment—*See* Nature

Envy

Ephemera

Equality

Escape

Estrangement

Eternal Life

Eternity

Ethics—*See* Behavior, Honesty, Law

Evangelism

Evidence—*See* Capital Punishment, Judging, Perjury, Proof

Evil

Exaltation

Exasperation

Excess

Excuses

Exile

Expectation

Experience

Exposure

Failure

Fairness

Faith

Faithfulness

Faithlessness

False Gods

False Prophets

Fame

Family

Famine

Farming—*See* Animals, Cultivation, Growth

Fashion—*See* Appearance, Beauty

Fasting

Favoritism

Fear

Fear of God

Fellowship

Fertility

Fidelity—*See* Commitment,
  Faithfulness, Loyalty
Finance—*See* Borrowing
Firstborn
Flattery
Flavor
Floods
Folly
Food
Fools
Foreigners
Forgiveness
Fortitude
Frailty
Freedom
Friendship
Frustration
Fulfillment
Futility
Future

Generosity
Gifts
Gloating
Glory
Gluttony
Goals
God
God's Anger
God's Glory
God's Goodness—*See* Goodness
God's Greatness
God's Knowledge
God's Love
God's Mercy
God's People
God's Power
God's Presence
God's Protection
God's Support
God's Temple
God's Uniqueness
God's Will
God's Word
God, Names of
God, Traits of
Godlessness
Godliness
Good and Evil
Goodness
Gossip

Government
Grandchildren
Gratitude
Greatness
Greed
Greetings—*See* Salutations
Grief
Growth
Grudges
Guidance
Guilt

Habit
Handicapped
Hanging
Happiness
Hatred
Healing
Health—*See* Handicapped, Healing
Heaven
Heaven and Earth
Heedfulness
Height—*See* Size
Hell
Help—*See* Assistance, Deliverance
Heresy
Heritage
Heroism—*See* Courage, Leadership
Hierarchy—*See* Authority,
  Leadership
History
Holidays
Holiness
Homage
Home
Homeless—*See* Exile, Poverty
Homosexuality
Honesty
Honor—*See* Glory, Respect
Hope
Hospitality
Human Nature
Humiliation
Humility
Hunger
Husband and Wife—*See* Marriage
Hypocrisy

Idolatry
Idols
Ignorance

Imagination—*See* Dreams, Future,
  Visions
Imminence
Immorality
Immortality—*See* Death, Eternal
  Life, Resurrection
Impartiality
Impatience
Impenitence
Impossibility—*See* God's Power,
  Possibility
Imprisonment
Incest
Indecision
Independence
Individual, Importance of
Inevitability—*See* Certainty, Death,
  Mortality
Infinity
Ingratitude
Inheritance
Injustice
Innocence
Innovation
Insanity—*See* Madness
Insincerity—*See* Hypocrisy,
  Sincerity
Inspiration
Instability
Instigation
Instinct
Instruction
Insults
Integrity
Intelligence—*See* Education,
  Ignorance, Knowledge,
  Understanding
Intentions
Intercession
Intermarriage
Intoxication—*See* Drunkenness,
  Liquor, Pleasure
Israel

Jealousy
Jerusalem
Jews—*See* Chosen People
Joy—*See* Happiness, Laughter,
  Tears
Judging
Judgment

Judgment Day
Justice

Kindness
Kings—*See* Monarchy
Knowledge
Knowledge of God

Labor—*See* Business, Work
Lament
Language—*See* Communication,
  Eloquence, Speech
Last Judgment—*See* Apocalypse,
  Judgment Day
Laughter
Law
Lawlessness
Laziness
Leadership
Leniency—*See* Compassion,
  Forgiveness, Punishment
Lies
Life
Life and Death
Light and Darkness
Liquor
Listening—*See* Heedfulness
Loneliness
Longevity—*See* Age, Mortality
Loss
Love
Love of God
Loyalty
Luck—*See* Chance
Lust

Madness
Man and Woman
Management—*See* Business,
  Leadership
Mankind
Manners—*See* Courtesy
Marriage
Martyrdom
Materialism
Maturity—*See* Age, Experience,
  Growth
Medicine—*See* Healing
Meekness
Memorials—*See* Burial,
  Remembrance

Prejudice—*See* Brotherhood, Equality
Preparedness—*See* Readiness, Vigilance
Pride
Priesthood
Principles—*See* Integrity
Priorities—*See* Goals, Values
Prison—*See* Imprisonment
Procrastination
Profanity—*See* Blasphemy
Profit
Progress—*See* Success
Promises
Proof
Property
Prophecy
Proselytization—*See* Evangelism
Prosperity
Prostitution
Protection—*See* Deliverance, God's Protection, Safety, Vigilance
Provocation
Prudence
Public Opinion
Publicity
Punishment
Purity
Purpose

Quality
Quantity
Questioning—*See* Authority, Skepticism
Quotations

Rain
Rainbow
Rashness
Readiness
Rebellion
Reciprocity
Redemption
Refuge—*See* Safety, Sanctuary
Regret
Rehabilitation—*See* Renewal
Rejection
Reliability
Reliance
Remembrance
Renewal

Repentance
Representatives—*See* Reliability, Spokesmen
Reputation
Rescue—*See* Assistance, Danger, Deliverance
Respect
Responsibility
Restitution
Restoration
Restraint
Resurrection
Retribution
Revelation
Revenge
Reverence
Reversal
Revolution—*See* Rebellion, Strife
Reward
Riddles
Righteousness
Risk
Rituals
Robbery
Romance

Sabbath
Sacrifice—*See* Martyrdom
Sacrifices
Sacrilege
Safety
Salutations
Salvation
Sanctuary
Sarcasm—*See* Mockery
Satisfaction
Scapegoat
Scheming
Scorn
Scripture
Searching
Seas—*See* Oceans
Seasons
Secrecy
Security
Seduction—*See* Temptation
Self-Awareness
Self-Confidence—*See* Confidence
Self-Control
Self-Deception
Self-Denial

THE BOOKS OF THE OLD TESTAMENT

Genesis
Exodus
Leviticus
Numbers
Deuteronomy
Joshua
Judges
Ruth
I Samuel
II Samuel
I Kings
II Kings
I Chronicles
II Chronicles
Ezra
Nehemiah
Esther
Job
Psalms
Proverbs

Ecclesiastes
Song of Solomon
Isaiah
Jeremiah
Lamentations
Ezekiel
Daniel
Hosea
Joel
Amos
Obadiah
Jonah
Micah
Nahum
Habakkuk
Zephaniah
Haggai
Zechariah
Malachi

ABBREVIATIONS

Amos	Amos
1 Chron.	I Chronicles
2 Chron.	II Chronicles
Dan.	Daniel
Deut.	Deuteronomy
Eccl.	Ecclesiastes
Esther	Esther
Ex.	Exodus
Ezek.	Ezekiel
Ezra	Ezra
Gen.	Genesis
Hab.	Habakkuk
Hag.	Haggai
Hos.	Hosea
Isa.	Isaiah
Jer.	Jeremiah
Job	Job
Joel	Joel
Jonah	Jonah
Josh.	Joshua
Judg.	Judges
1 Kings	I Kings
2 Kings	II Kings
Lam.	Lamentations
Lev.	Leviticus
Mal.	Malachi
Mic.	Micah
Nah.	Nahum
Neh.	Nehemiah
Num.	Numbers
Obad.	Obadiah
Prov.	Proverbs
Ps.	Psalms
Ruth	Ruth
1 Sam.	I Samuel
2 Sam.	II Samuel
Song	Song of Solomon
Zech.	Zechariah
Zeph.	Zephaniah

ABANDONMENT

He will not forsake thee, neither destroy thee, nor forget the covenant of thy fathers which He sware unto them.
Deut. 4:31

How should one chase a thousand, and two put ten thousand to flight, except their Rock had sold them, and the Lord had shut them up?
Deut. 32:30

I will not fail thee, nor forsake thee.
(I: God)
Josh. 1:5
See also Deut. 31:6, Heb. 13:5

The Lord will not forsake His people for His great name's sake.
1 Sam. 12:22

And when Saul enquired of the Lord, the Lord answered him not.
1 Sam. 28:6

God is departed from me, and answereth me no more, neither by prophets, nor by dreams.
Saul to Samuel
1 Sam. 28:15

Let Him not leave us, nor forsake us.
1 Kings 8:57

I will forsake the remnant of Mine inheritance, and deliver them into the hand of their enemies.
2 Kings 21:14

Thus saith the Lord, Ye have forsaken Me, and therefore have I also left you.
2 Chron. 12:5

If ye forsake Him, He will forsake you.
2 Chron. 15:2

God will not cast away a perfect man, neither will He help the evil doers.
Job 8:20

Wherefore hidest Thou Thy face, and holdest me for Thine enemy?
Job 13:24

How long wilt Thou forget me, O Lord? for ever? how long wilt Thou hide Thy face from me?
Ps. 13:1

My God, my God, why hast Thou forsaken me?
Ps. 22:1, Matt. 27:46,
Mark 15:34

When my father and my mother forsake me, then the Lord will take me up.
Ps. 27:10

I have been young, and now am old; yet have I not seen the righteous forsaken.
Ps. 37:25

Forsake me not, O Lord: O my God, be not far from me.
Ps. 38:21
See also Ps. 71:12

God my rock, Why hast Thou forgotten me?
Ps. 42:9

Wilt Thou hide Thyself for ever?
Ps. 89:46

Wherefore should the heathen say, Where is now their God?
Ps. 115:2
See also Ps. 79:10

I have done judgment and justice: leave me not to mine oppressors.
Ps. 119:121

If I forget thee, O Jerusalem, let my right hand forget her cunning.
Ps. 137:5

When ye spread forth your hands, I will hide Mine eyes from you.
Isa. 1:15

For a small moment have I forsaken thee; but with great mercies will I gather thee.
Isa. 54:7

I have forsaken Mine house, I have left Mine heritage; I have given the dearly beloved of My soul into the hand of her enemies.
Jer. 12:7

Among all her lovers she hath none to comfort her.
(her: Jerusalem)
Lam. 1:2

Wherefore dost Thou forget us for ever, and forsake us so long time?
Lam. 5:20

[*See also* Rejection]

ABILITY

Seest thou a man diligent in his business? he shall stand before kings.
Prov. 22:29

[*See also* Achievement, Character, Competition]

ABSENCE

The Lord watch between me and thee, when we are absent one from another.
Gen. 31:49

ABUNDANCE

I will make thy seed as the dust of the earth: so that if a man can number the dust of the earth, then shall thy seed also be numbered.
God to Abram
Gen. 13:16
See also Gen. 28:14

And ye shall eat the fat of the land.
Gen. 45:18

Who can count the dust of Jacob, and the number of the fourth part of Israel?
Num. 23:10

Their camels were without number, as the sand by the sea side for multitude.
Judg. 7:12
See also 1 Sam. 13:5, 2 Sam. 17:11

My cup runneth over.
Ps. 23:5

They are more than the hairs of mine head.
(they: iniquities)
Ps. 40:12

[*See also* Excess, Infinity, Quantity]

ACCEPTANCE

But I must die in this land, I must not go over Jordan.
Moses
Deut. 4:22

Do to me according to that which hath proceeded out of thy mouth.
Judg. 11:36

It is the Lord: let Him do what seemeth Him good.
1 Sam. 3:18
See also 2 Sam. 15:26

Hearken unto their voice, and make them a king.
God to Samuel
1 Sam. 8:22

Now he is dead, wherefore should I fast? can I bring him back again?
David, about his son
2 Sam. 12:23

Let him alone, and let him curse; for the Lord hath bidden him.
2 Sam. 16:11

Fear not to be the servants of the Chaldees.
2 Kings 25:24

Naked came I out of my mother's womb, and naked shall I return thither.
Job 1:21

The Lord gave, and the Lord hath taken away; blessed be the name of the Lord.
Job 1:21

Shall we receive good at the hand of God, and shall we not receive evil?
Job 2:10

If I be wicked, woe unto me.
Job 10:15

If I hold my tongue, I shall give up the ghost.
Job 13:19

Acquaint now thyself with Him, and be at peace: thereby good shall come unto thee.
Job 22:21

The hypocrites in heart heap up wrath: they cry not when He bindeth them.
Job 36:13

Let the righteous smite me; it shall be a kindness.
Ps. 141:5

That which is crooked cannot be made straight: and that which is wanting cannot be numbered.
Eccl. 1:15

A time to get, and a time to lose.
Eccl. 3:6

Who can make that straight, which He hath made crooked?
Eccl. 7:13

Serve the king of Babylon, and live.
Jer. 27:17

Whether it be good, or whether it be evil, we will obey the voice of the Lord.
Jer. 42:6

[*See also* Contentment, Restraint]

ACCOUNTABILITY

See Responsibility.

ACCURACY

Every one could sling stones at an hair breadth, and not miss.
Judg. 20:16

Their arrows shall be as of a mighty expert man; none shall return in vain.
Jer. 50:9

ACCUSATIONS

Ye are spies; to see the nakedness of the land ye are come.
Joseph to his brothers
Gen. 42:9

Wherefore have ye rewarded evil for good?
Gen. 44:4

How long wilt thou be drunken? put away thy wine from thee.
Eli to Hannah
1 Sam. 1:14

And Nathan said to David, Thou art the man.
2 Sam. 12:7

My desire is, that the Almighty would answer me, and that mine adversary had written a book.
Job 31:35

The stone shall cry out of the wall, and the beam out of the timber shall answer it.
Hab. 2:11

[*See also* Criticism]

ACHIEVEMENT

If thou doest well, shalt thou not be accepted?
God to Cain
Gen. 4:7

The dead which he slew at his death were more than they which he slew in his life.
(he: Samson)
Judg. 16:30

Except the Lord build the house, they labour in vain that build it.
Ps. 127:1

The desire accomplished is sweet to the soul.
Prov. 13:19

Through wisdom is an house builded; and by understanding it is established.
Prov. 24:3

There is nothing better, than that a man should rejoice in his own works.
Eccl. 3:22

A good name is better than precious ointment; and the day of death than the day of one's birth.
Eccl. 7:1

[*See also* Deeds, Success, Victory]

ACKNOWLEDGMENT

In all thy ways acknowledge Him.
Prov. 3:6

Hear, ye that are far off, what I have done; and, ye that are near, acknowledge My might.
Isa. 33:13

They shall all know Me, from the least of them unto the greatest.
> *Jer. 31:34*
> *See also Heb. 8:11*

I will say, It is My people: and they shall say, The Lord is my God.
> *Zech. 13:9*

[*See also* Knowledge of God]

ACTION

See Deeds.

ADULTERY

Thou shalt not commit adultery.
> *Seventh Commandment*
> *Ex. 20:14, Matt. 5:27*
> *See also, e.g., Deut. 5:18,*
>   *Mark 10:19*

Thou shalt not covet thy neighbour's wife.
> *Ex. 20:17*

The adulterer and the adulteress shall surely be put to death.
> *Lev. 20:10*

Her belly shall swell, and her thigh shall rot: and the woman shall be a curse among her people.
> *Num. 5:27*

Wherefore hast thou despised the commandment of the Lord, to do evil in His sight?
> *(thou: David)*
> *2 Sam. 12:9*

It is a fire that consumeth to destruction.
> *Job 31:12*

The lips of a strange woman drop as an honeycomb, and her mouth is smoother than oil.
> *Prov. 5:3*

Drink waters out of thine own cistern, and running waters out of thine own well.
> *Prov. 5:15*

Lust not after her beauty in thine heart; neither let her take thee with her eyelids.
> *Prov. 6:25*

Can a man take fire in his bosom, and his clothes not be burned?
> *Prov. 6:27*

Can one go upon hot coals, and his feet not be burned?
> *Prov. 6:28*

Whoso committeth adultery with a woman lacketh understanding: he that doeth it destroyeth his own soul.
> *Prov. 6:32*

His reproach shall not be wiped away.
> *Prov. 6:33*

He goeth after her straightway, as an ox goeth to the slaughter.
> *Prov. 7:22*

Let not thine heart decline to her ways, go not astray in her paths.
> *Prov. 7:25*

She hath cast down many wounded: yea, many strong men have been slain by her.
> *Prov. 7:26*

Her house is the way to hell.
> *Prov. 7:27*

She eateth, and wipeth her mouth, and saith, I have done no wickedness.
> *(She: adulteress)*
> *Prov. 30:20*

I will be a swift witness against the sorcerers, and against the adulterers, and against false swearers, and against those that oppress the hireling in his wages.
> *Mal. 3:5*

ADVERSITY

The more they afflicted them, the more they multiplied and grew.
> *(them: Hebrews in Egypt)*
> *Ex. 1:12*

God hath delivered me to the ungodly, and turned me over into the hands of the wicked.
> *Job 16:11*

Princes have persecuted me without a cause: but my heart standeth in awe of Thy word.
> *Ps. 119:161*

[*See also* Prosperity]

Consider of it, take advice, and speak your minds.
Judg. 19:30

Blessed be thy advice, and blessed be thou, which hast kept me this day from coming to shed blood.
1 Sam. 25:33

I hate him; for he doth not prophesy good concerning me, but evil.
1 Kings 22:8

Speak that which is good.
1 Kings 22:13

Tell me nothing but that which is true in the name of the Lord.
1 Kings 22:16

If the prophet had bid thee do some great thing, wouldest thou not have done it?
2 Kings 5:13

But he forsook the counsel which the old men gave him.
2 Chron. 10:8

Your remembrances are like unto ashes.
Job 13:12

Receive my sayings; and the years of thy life shall be many.
(thy: children)
Prov. 4:10

Hear instruction, and be wise, and refuse it not.
Prov. 8:33

Give instruction to a wise man, and he will be yet wiser: teach a just man, and he will increase in learning.
Prov. 9:9

The lips of the righteous feed many.
Prov. 10:21

In the multitude of counsellors there is safety.
Prov. 11:14, Prov. 24:6

The thoughts of the righteous are right: but the counsels of the wicked are deceit.
Prov. 12:5

The way of a fool is right in his own eyes:

but he that hearkeneth unto counsel is wise.
Prov. 12:15

A word spoken in due season, how good is it!
Prov. 15:23

Hear counsel, and receive instruction, that thou mayest be wise in thy latter end.
Prov. 19:20

With good advice make war.
Prov. 20:18

Speak not in the ears of a fool: for he will despise the wisdom of thy words.
Prov. 23:9

A flattering mouth worketh ruin.
Prov. 26:28

Better is a poor and a wise child than an old and foolish king, who will no more be admonished.
Eccl. 4:13

The poor man's wisdom is despised, and his words are not heard.
Eccl. 9:16

Thou art wearied in the multitude of thy counsels.
Isa. 47:13

They shall be as stubble; the fire shall burn them.
(They: false advisers)
Isa. 47:14

Hearken not ye to your prophets, nor to your diviners, nor to your dreamers, nor to your enchanters.
Jer. 27:9

Where are now your prophets which prophesied unto you, saying, The king of Babylon shall not come?
Jer. 37:19

If I declare it unto thee, wilt thou not surely put me to death?
Jer. 38:15

Is counsel perished from the prudent? is their wisdom vanished?
Jer. 49:7

[*See also* Candor, Criticism, Guidance]

AGE

And all the days of Methuselah were nine hundred sixty and nine years.
> *Gen. 5:27*

Thou shalt be buried in a good old age.
> *Gen. 15:15*

Behold now, I am old, I know not the day of my death.
> *Abraham*
> *Gen. 27:2*

Honour the face of the old man.
> *Lev. 19:32*

Thou art old and stricken in years, and there remaineth yet very much land to be possessed.
> *God to Joshua*
> *Josh. 13:1*

Can I hear any more the voice of singing men and singing women?
> *2 Sam. 19:35*

With the ancient is wisdom; and in length of days understanding.
> *Job 12:12*

Art thou the first man that was born? or wast thou made before the hills?
> *Job 15:7*

They that are younger than I have me in derision, whose fathers I would have disdained to have set with the dogs of my flock.
> *Job 30:1*

Great men are not always wise: neither do the aged understand judgment.
> *Job 32:9*

I have been young, and now am old; yet have I not seen the righteous forsaken.
> *Ps. 37:25*

Cast me not off in the time of old age; forsake me not when my strength faileth.
> *Ps. 71:9*

When I am old and greyheaded, O God, forsake me not.
> *Ps. 71:18*

My soul is full of troubles: and my life draweth nigh unto the grave.
> *Ps. 88:3*

The hoary head is a crown of glory, if it be found in the way of righteousness.
> *Prov. 16:31*

Despise not thy mother when she is old.
> *Prov. 23:22*

All things have I seen in the days of my vanity.
> *Eccl. 7:15*

Even to your old age I am He; and even to hoar hairs will I carry you.
> *Isa. 46:4*

[*See also* Life, Mortality, Youth]

AGGRESSIVENESS

The young lions roar after their prey, and seek their meat from God.
> *Ps. 104:21*

They shall roar like young lions: yea, they shall roar, and lay hold of the prey.
> *Isa. 5:29*

AGREEMENT

Did not I serve with thee for Rachel?
> *Jacob to Laban*
> *Gen. 29:25*

If thou utter this our business, then we will be quit of thine oath.
> *Josh. 2:20*

The Lord be witness between us, if we do not so according to thy words.
> *Judg. 11:10*

They shall see eye to eye.
> *Isa. 52:8*

[*See also* Arguments, Negotiation]

ALCOHOL

See Drunkenness, Liquor.

ALIENATION

See Abandonment, Betrayal.

ALLEGIANCE

Who is on the Lord's side? let him come unto me.
Moses
Ex. 32:26

Him shalt thou serve, and to Him shalt thou cleave, and swear by His name.
Deut. 10:20

As I was with Moses, so I will be with thee.
God to Joshua
Josh. 1:5, Josh. 3:7

Swear unto me by the Lord.
Josh. 2:12

Art thou for us, or for our adversaries?
Josh. 5:13

I am with thee according to thy heart.
Armor-bearer to Jonathan
1 Sam. 14:7

Is this thy kindness to thy friend?
Absalom to Hushai
2 Sam. 16:17

If I do not remember thee, let my tongue cleave to the roof of my mouth.
Ps. 137:6

Unto Me every knee shall bow, every tongue shall swear.
Isa. 45:23
See also Rom. 14:11

Circumcise yourselves to the Lord.
Jer. 4:4

They shall be My people, and I will be their God.
E.g., Jer. 24:7

The Lord is good unto them that wait for Him, to the soul that seeketh Him.
Lam. 3:25

Ye shall be My people, and I will be your God.
E.g., Ezek. 36:28

[*See also* Betrayal, Faithfulness, Loyalty]

ALLIES

The Lord shall fight for you, and ye shall hold your peace.
Ex. 14:14

I will be an enemy unto thine enemies, and an adversary unto thine adversaries.
God
Ex. 23:22

Slack not thy hand from thy servants; come up to us quickly, and save us.
Josh. 10:6

I am as thou art, my people as thy people, my horses as thy horses.
1 Kings 22:4, 2 Kings 3:7
See also 2 Chron. 18:3

Shouldest thou help the ungodly, and love them that hate the Lord?
2 Chron. 19:2

The battle is not your's, but God's.
2 Chron. 20:15
See also 1 Sam. 17:47

Our help is in the name of the Lord.
Ps. 124:8

I have trodden the winepress alone; and of the people there was none with me.
Isa. 63:3

[*See also* Allegiance, Enemies, Loyalty]

ALTERNATIVES

See Choice, Compromise.

ALTRUISM

I was eyes to the blind, and feet was I to the lame.
Job 29:15

The cause which I knew not I searched out.
Job 29:16

He that hath pity upon the poor lendeth

unto the Lord; and that which he hath given will He pay him again.
Prov. 19:17

Cast thy bread upon the waters: for thou shalt find it after many days.
Eccl. 11:1

[*See also* Charity, Generosity, Selfishness]

AMBITION

Now nothing will be restrained from them, which they have imagined to do.
Gen. 11:6

Seek ye the priesthood also?
Moses to Korah the Levite
Num. 16:10

Should I forsake my sweetness, and my good fruit, and go to be promoted over the trees?
Fig tree to other trees
Judg. 9:11

Should I leave my wine, which cheereth God and man, and go to be promoted over the trees?
Vine to trees
Judg. 9:13

What can he have more but the kingdom?
Saul about David
1 Sam. 18:8

The desire of the wicked shall perish.
Ps. 112:10

His breath goeth forth, he returneth to his earth; in that very day his thoughts perish.
Ps. 146:4

The desire accomplished is sweet to the soul.
Prov. 13:19

The foolishness of man perverteth his way.
Prov. 19:3

Labour not to be rich.
Prov. 23:4

Hell and destruction are never full; so the eyes of man are never satisfied.
Prov. 27:20

He that maketh haste to be rich shall not be innocent.
Prov. 28:20

The eye is not satisfied with seeing, nor the ear filled with hearing.
Eccl. 1:8

Better is an handful with quietness, than both the hands full with travail and vexation of spirit.
Eccl. 4:6

All the labour of man is for his mouth, and yet the appetite is not filled.
Eccl. 6:7

Seekest thou great things for thyself? seek them not.
Jer. 45:5

[*See also* Goals, Leadership, Satisfaction]

ANARCHY

See Chaos, Lawlessness.

ANCESTRY

See Heritage.

ANGER

They be chafed in their minds, as a bear robbed of her whelps in the field.
2 Sam. 17:8

Wrath killeth the foolish man, and envy slayeth the silly one.
Job 5:2

Cease from anger, and forsake wrath.
Ps. 37:8

The king's favour is toward a wise servant: but his wrath is against him that causeth shame.
Prov. 14:35

A soft answer turneth away wrath.
Prov. 15:1

He that is slow to anger appeaseth strife.
Prov. 15:18

The wrath of a king is as messengers of death.
Prov. 16:14

He that is slow to anger is better than the mighty.
Prov. 16:32

The king's wrath is as the roaring of a lion; but his favour is as dew upon the grass.
Prov. 19:12

A gift in secret pacifieth anger.
Prov. 21:14

Make no friendship with an angry man.
Prov. 22:24

Wrath is cruel, and anger is outrageous; but who is able to stand before envy?
Prov. 27:4

Wise men turn away wrath.
Prov. 29:8

An angry man stirreth up strife.
Prov. 29:22

Anger resteth in the bosom of fools.
Eccl. 7:9

In wrath remember mercy.
Hab. 3:2

[*See also* Arguments, Exasperation, God's Anger, Provocation, Restraint, Temper]

ANGUISH

Hast thou not reserved a blessing for me?
Esau to Isaac
Gen. 27:36

Hast thou but one blessing, my father?
Esau to Isaac
Gen. 27:38

Are there yet any more sons in my womb, that they may be your husbands?
Naomi to Ruth and Orpah
Ruth 1:11

The hand of the Lord is gone out against me.
Ruth 1:13

Call me Mara: for the Almighty hath dealt very bitterly with me.
Ruth 1:20

Anguish is come upon me, because my life is yet whole in me.
2 Sam. 1:9

I rent my garment and my mantle, and plucked off the hair of my head and of my beard.
Ezra 9:3

How can I endure to see the evil that shall come unto my people?
Esther 8:6

Wherefore is light given to him that is in misery, and life unto the bitter in soul?
Job 3:20

My sighing cometh before I eat, and my roarings are poured out like the waters.
Job 3:24

The arrows of the Almighty are within me, the poison whereof drinketh up my spirit.
Job 6:4

When I looked for good, then evil came unto me: and when I waited for light, there came darkness.
Job 30:26

Be not far from me; for trouble is near; for there is none to help.
Ps. 22:11

The plowers plowed upon my back: they made long their furrows.
Ps. 129:3

The heart knoweth his own bitterness.
Prov. 14:10

We roar all like bears, and mourn sore like doves.
Isa. 59:11

How is the gold become dim!
Lam. 4:1

Woe is me!
E.g., Mic. 7:1

[*See also* Depression, Despair, Grief, Mourning, Sorrow, Suffering, Torment]

ANIMALS

Let them have dominion over the fish of the sea, and over the fowl of the air, and over the cattle, and over all the earth, and over every creeping thing that creepeth.
(them: mankind)
Gen. 1:26

Of every living thing of all flesh, two of

every sort shalt thou bring into the ark, to keep them alive with thee.
Gen. 6:19

Every moving thing that liveth shall be meat for you.
Gen. 9:3

Be ye not as the horse, or as the mule, which have no understanding.
Ps. 32:9

Thou takest away their breath, they die, and return to their dust.
(they: animals)
Ps. 104:29

A righteous man regardeth the life of his beast.
Prov. 12:10

The wolf also shall dwell with the lamb, and the leopard shall lie down with the kid; and the calf and the young lion and the fatling together.
Isa. 11:6

[*See also* Snakes]

ANNIHILATION

I would make the remembrance of them to cease from among men.
Deut. 32:26

Slay both man and woman, infant and suckling, ox and sheep, camel and ass.
Samuel to Saul
1 Sam. 15:3

I beat them as small as the dust of the earth, I did stamp them as the mire of the street.
2 Sam. 22:43

I will bring evil upon thee, and will take away thy posterity.
1 Kings 21:21

Their memorial is perished with them.
Ps. 9:6

They shall have no pity on the fruit of the womb; their eye shall not spare children.
Isa. 13:18

Spare ye not her young men; destroy ye utterly all her host.
Jer. 51:3

They shall not take of thee a stone for a corner, nor a stone for foundations; but thou shalt be desolate for ever, saith the Lord.
Jer. 51:26

He that is far off shall die of the pestilence; and he that is near shall fall by the sword; and he that remaineth and is besieged shall die by the famine.
Ezek. 6:12

Though thou be sought for, yet shalt thou never be found again.
Ezek. 26:21

[*See also* Carnage, Desolation, Destruction]

ANXIETY

See Worry.

APOCALYPSE

At the time appointed the end shall be.
Dan. 8:19
See also Dan. 11:27

[*See also* End Days, Judgment Day]

APPEARANCE

The Lord seeth not as man seeth, for man looketh on the outward appearance, but the Lord looketh on the heart.
1 Sam. 16:7

Thou art but a youth, and he a man of war.
Saul to David about Goliath
1 Sam. 17:33

[*See also* Deception, Ostentation, Status]

APPRECIATION

And they shall know that I am the Lord their God, that brought them forth out of the land of Egypt.
Ex. 29:46

Thou art good in my sight, as an angel of God.
> *1 Sam. 29:9*

[*See also* Contentment, Gratitude, Satisfaction]

APPROVAL

And God saw the light, that it was good.
> *Gen. 1:4*

And God saw every thing that He had made, and, behold, it was very good.
> *Gen. 1:31*

[*See also* God's Support]

ARCHITECTURE

See Building.

ARGUMENTS

Strive not with a man without cause, if he have done thee no harm.
> *Prov. 3:30*

Hatred stirreth up strifes: but love covereth all sins.
> *Prov. 10:12*

It is an honour for a man to cease from strife.
> *Prov. 20:3*

Debate thy cause with thy neighbour himself; and discover not a secret to another.
> *Prov. 25:9*

A soft tongue breaketh the bone.
> *Prov. 25:15*

Wise men turn away wrath.
> *Prov. 29:8*

An angry man stirreth up strife.
> *Prov. 29:22*

Produce your cause, saith the Lord; bring forth your strong reasons.
> *Isa. 41:21*

[*See also* Anger, Peace, Strife, Temper]

ARMIES

See Peace, War, War and Peace.

ARROGANCE

Who is the Lord, that I should obey His voice to let Israel go?
> *Pharaoh*
> *Ex. 5:2*

How long wilt thou refuse to humble thyself before Me? let My people go.
> *God to Pharaoh*
> *Ex. 10:3*

Let not arrogancy come out of your mouth: for the Lord is a God of knowledge, and by Him actions are weighed.
> *1 Sam. 2:3*

Thine eyes are upon the haughty, that Thou mayest bring them down.
> *2 Sam. 22:28*

Which way went the Spirit of the Lord from me to speak unto thee?
> *1 Kings 22:24*

On whom dost thou trust, that thou rebellest against me?
> *King of Assyria to King of Judah*
> *2 Kings 18:20, Isa. 36:5*

Have the gods of the nations delivered them which my fathers have destroyed?
> *Sennacherib to Hezekiah*
> *2 Kings 19:12, Isa. 37:12*

Thy rage against Me and thy tumult is come up into Mine ears.
> *2 Kings 19:28*
> *See also Isa. 37:29*

Canst thou by searching find out God?
> *Job 11:7*

What knowest thou, that we know not? what understandest thou, which is not in us?
> *Eliphaz to Job*
> *Job 15:9*

Is it any pleasure to the Almighty, that thou art righteous?
> *Job 22:3*

Have the gates of death been opened unto

thee? or hast thou seen the doors of the shadow of death?
God to Job
Job 38:17

Hast thou perceived the breadth of the earth? declare if thou knowest it all.
God to Job
Job 38:18

Gavest thou the goodly wings unto the peacocks?
God to Job
Job 39:13

Him that hath an high look and a proud heart will not I suffer.
Ps. 101:5

Let not the proud oppress me.
Ps. 119:122

These six things doth the Lord hate: yea, seven are an abomination unto Him: A proud look, a lying tongue, and hands that shed innocent blood, An heart that deviseth wicked imaginations, feet that be swift in running to mischief, A false witness that speaketh lies, and he that soweth discord among brethren.
Prov. 6:16–19

The bricks are fallen down, but we will build with hewn stones.
Isa. 9:10

I will cause the arrogancy of the proud to cease, and will lay low the haughtiness of the terrible.
Isa. 13:11

We have made a covenant with death, and with hell are we at agreement.
Isa. 28:15

According to all that she hath done, do unto her: for she hath been proud against the Lord, against the Holy One of Israel.
Jer. 50:29

I am against thee, O thou most proud, saith the Lord God of hosts.
Jer. 50:31

The most proud shall stumble and fall, and none shall raise him up.
Jer. 50:32

Thou art a man, and not God.
Ezek. 28:2

Wilt thou yet say before him that slayeth thee, I am God?
Ezek. 28:9

Thou shalt be a man, and no God, in the hand of him that slayeth thee.
Ezek. 28:9

[*See also* Audacity, Boasting, Conceit, Gloating, Humility, Pride]

ASSASSINATION

Cursed be he that taketh reward to slay an innocent person.
Deut. 27:25

I have a message from God unto thee.
Ehud to King of Moab
Judg. 3:20

Turn in, my lord, turn in to me; fear not.
Jael to Sisera
Judg. 4:18

Where he bowed, there he fell down dead.
Judg. 5:27

Who can stretch forth his hand against the Lord's anointed, and be guiltless?
David to his servant
1 Sam. 26:9

[*See also* Murder]

ASSISTANCE

I sent the hornet before you.
Josh. 24:12

They fought from heaven; the stars in their courses fought against Sisera.
Judg. 5:20

Wherefore then dost thou ask of me, seeing the Lord is departed from thee, and is become thine enemy?
Samuel to Saul
1 Sam. 28:16

If the Lord do not help thee, whence shall I help thee?
2 Kings 6:27

Call now, if there be any that will answer thee.
Job 5:1

Unto God would I commit my cause.
Job 5:8

Why standest Thou afar off, O Lord? why hidest Thou Thyself in times of trouble?
Ps. 10:1

Lighten mine eyes, lest I sleep the sleep of death.
Ps. 13:3

Lord, be Thou my helper.
Ps. 30:10

Save me for Thy mercies' sake.
E.g., Ps. 31:16

O Lord: keep not silence: O Lord, be not far from me.
Ps. 35:22

O Lord, make haste to help me.
Ps. 40:13

Call upon Me in the day of trouble: I will deliver thee, and thou shalt glorify Me.
Ps. 50:15

As for me, I will call upon God; and the Lord shall save me.
Ps. 55:16

Vain is the help of man.
Ps. 60:11

Save me, O God; for the waters are come in unto my soul.
Ps. 69:1

Hide not Thy face from Thy servant; for I am in trouble.
Ps. 69:17
See also Ps. 102:2

I am poor and needy: make haste unto me, O God.
Ps. 70:5
See also Ps. 40:17

O God, be not far from me.
Ps. 71:12
See also Ps. 22:11

There is none upon earth that I desire beside Thee.
Ps. 73:25

Keep not Thou silence, O God: hold not Thy peace.
Ps. 83:1

Unless the Lord had been my help, my soul had almost dwelt in silence.
Ps. 94:17

Help me, O Lord my God: O save me according to Thy mercy.
Ps. 109:26

I was brought low, and He helped me.
Ps. 116:6

I will lift up mine eyes unto the hills, from whence cometh my help.
Ps. 121:1

My help cometh from the Lord, which made heaven and earth.
Ps. 121:2

The Lord is nigh unto all them that call upon Him, to all that call upon Him in truth.
Ps. 145:18

Better is a neighbour that is near than a brother far off.
Prov. 27:10

Incline Thine ear, O Lord, and hear; open Thine eyes, O Lord, and see.
Isa. 37:17
See also 2 Kings 19:16

In Me is thine help.
Hos. 13:9

Whosoever shall call on the name of the Lord shall be delivered.
Joel 2:32
See also, e.g., Acts 2:21

He knoweth them that trust in Him.
Nah. 1:7

They shall call on My name, and I will hear them.
Zech. 13:9

[*See also* Deliverance, God's Protection, Prayer, Safety, Trouble]

■ 13 ■

ASTROLOGY

Let now the astrologers, the stargazers, the monthly prognosticators, stand up, and save thee from these things.
Isa. 47:13

They shall be as stubble; the fire shall burn them.
(They: false advisers)
Isa. 47:14

Be not dismayed at the signs of heaven; for the heathen are dismayed at them.
Jer. 10:2

ASYLUM

See Sanctuary.

ATHEISM

The fool hath said in his heart, There is no God.
Ps. 14:1, Ps. 53:1

[*See also* Godlessness]

AUDACITY

Wherefore do ye tempt the Lord?
Moses
Ex. 17:2

Who is this uncircumcised Philistine, that he should defy the armies of the living God?
David, about Goliath
1 Sam. 17:26

What is the Almighty, that we should serve Him?
Job 21:15

What profit should we have, if we pray unto Him?
Job 21:15

Where wast thou when I laid the foundations of the earth?
God to Job
Job 38:4

I will ascend above the heights of the clouds; I will be like the most High.
Isa. 14:14

Shall the clay say to him that fashioneth it, What makest thou?
Isa. 45:9
See also, e.g., Isa. 29:16, Rom. 9:20

Wherefore will ye plead with Me? ye all have transgressed against Me.
Jer. 2:29

As I live, saith the Lord God, I will not be enquired of by you.
Ezek. 20:3, 31

[*See also* Arrogance]

AUTHENTICITY

What is the chaff to the wheat? saith the Lord.
Jer. 23:28

If they be prophets, and if the word of the Lord be with them, let them now make intercession to the Lord of hosts.
Jer. 27:18

[*See also* Deception, False Prophets, Proof]

AUTHORITY

And God made two great lights; the greater light to rule the day, and the lesser light to rule the night.
Gen. 1:16

Let them have dominion over the fish of the sea, and over the fowl of the air, and over the cattle, and over all the earth, and over every creeping thing that creepeth.
(them: mankind)
Gen. 1:26

Be fruitful, and multiply, and replenish the earth, and subdue it.
Gen. 1:28

Thy desire shall be to thy husband, and he shall rule over thee.
God to Eve
Gen. 3:16

Unto him ye shall hearken.
Deut. 18:15
See also Acts 3:22

Thus saith the Lord.
E.g., 2 Chron. 34:24

A people whom I have not known shall serve me.
Ps. 18:43
See also 2 Sam. 22:44

Where the word of a king is, there is power.
Eccl. 8:4

The ox knoweth his owner, and the ass his master's crib: but Israel doth not know, My people doth not consider.
Isa. 1:3

He shall open, and none shall shut; and he shall shut, and none shall open.
Isa. 22:22

Shall the clay say to him that fashioneth it, What makest thou?
Isa. 45:9
See also, e.g., Isa. 29:16, Rom. 9:20

Who is like Me? and who will appoint Me the time? and who is that shepherd that will stand before Me?
Jer. 49:19, Jer. 50:44

And ye shall know that I am the Lord.
E.g., Ezek. 25:5

For I have spoken it, saith the Lord God.
E.g., Ezek. 28:10

[*See also* God's Power, Government, Leadership, Obedience]

AVARICE

See Greed.

AWE

I have seen God face to face, and my life is preserved.
Jacob
Gen. 32:30

Who is like unto Thee, O Lord, among the gods? who is like Thee, glorious in holiness, fearful in praises, doing wonders?
Ex. 15:11

Speak thou with us, and we will hear: but let not God speak with us, lest we die.
Israelites to Moses
Ex. 20:19

What hath God wrought!
Num. 23:23

Did ever people hear the voice of God speaking out of the midst of the fire, as thou hast heard, and live?
Deut. 4:33

We shall surely die, because we have seen God.
Judg. 13:22

The mountains skipped like rams, and the little hills like lambs.
Ps. 114:4

Mine eyes have seen the King, the Lord of hosts.
Isa. 6:5

Fear ye not Me? saith the Lord: will ye not tremble at My presence?
Jer. 5:22

Let all the inhabitants of the land tremble: for the day of the Lord cometh, for it is nigh at hand.
Joel 2:1

Who may abide the day of his coming? and who shall stand when he appeareth?
Mal. 3:2

Unto you that fear My name shall the Sun of righteousness arise with healing in his wings.
Mal. 4:2

[*See also* Fear of God, Reverence, Wonders]

B

BACKSLIDING

If ye forsake the Lord, and serve strange gods, then He will turn and do you hurt.
Josh. 24:20

They turned quickly out of the way which their fathers walked in.
Judg. 2:17

And the children of Israel remembered not the Lord their God.
Judg. 8:34

And the children of Israel did evil again in the sight of the Lord.
E.g., Judg. 13:1

His heart was not perfect with the Lord his God.
E.g., 1 Kings 11:4

He forsook the Lord God of his fathers, and walked not in the way of the Lord.
2 Kings 21:22

If thou forsake Him, He will cast thee off for ever.
1 Chron. 28:9

If ye forsake Him, He will forsake you.
2 Chron. 15:2

His power and His wrath is against all them that forsake Him.
Ezra 8:22

They that are far from Thee shall perish.
Ps. 73:27

Correction is grievous unto him that forsaketh the way.
Prov. 15:10

The ox knoweth his owner, and the ass his master's crib: but Israel doth not know, My people doth not consider.
Isa. 1:3

They that forsake the Lord shall be consumed.
Isa. 1:28

Woe to the rebellious children, saith the Lord, that take counsel, but not of Me.
Isa. 30:1

All we like sheep have gone astray.
Isa. 53:6

It is an evil thing and bitter, that thou hast forsaken the Lord thy God.
Jer. 2:19

Can a maid forget her ornaments, or a bride her attire? yet My people have forgotten Me days without number.
Jer. 2:32

Thou hast played the harlot with many lovers; yet return again to Me, saith the Lord.
Jer. 3:1

All that forsake Thee shall be ashamed.
Jer. 17:13

Go not after other gods to serve them.
Jer. 25:6, Jer. 35:15

How long wilt thou go about, O thou backsliding daughter?
Jer. 31:22

They have turned unto Me the back, and not the face.
Jer. 32:33

My people hath been lost sheep: their shepherds have caused them to go astray.
Jer. 50:6

The righteousness of the righteous shall not deliver him in the day of his transgression.
Ezek. 33:12

When the righteous turneth from his righteousness, and committeth iniquity, he shall even die thereby.
Ezek. 33:18

Woe unto them! for they have fled from Me: destruction unto them! because they have transgressed against Me.
Hos. 7:13

Thou hast gone a whoring from thy God.
Hos. 9:1

[*See also* Disobedience, Estrangement, Godlessness, Idolatry, Obedience]

BARGAINING

See Agreement, Negotiation, Reciprocity.

BATTLE CALLS

Who is on the Lord's side? let him come unto me.
Moses
Ex. 32:26

Shout; for the Lord hath given you the city.
Joshua, at Jericho
Josh. 6:16

The Spirit of the Lord came upon Gideon, and he blew a trumpet.
Judg. 6:34

The sword of the Lord, and of Gideon.
Judg. 7:18, 20

Remember the Lord, which is great and terrible, and fight for your brethren, your sons, and your daughters.
Neh. 4:14

Set ye up a standard in the land, blow the trumpet among the nations, prepare the nations against her.
Jer. 51:27

BATTLES

See War.

BEAUTY

The sons of God saw the daughters of men that they were fair.
Gen. 6:2

How goodly are thy tents, O Jacob, and thy tabernacles, O Israel!
Num. 24:5

As thou art, so were they; each one resembled the children of a king.
Judg. 8:18

From the sole of his foot even to the crown of his head there was no blemish in him.
(him: Absalom)
2 Sam. 14:25

As a jewel of gold in a swine's snout, so is a fair woman which is without discretion.
Prov. 11:22

Favour is deceitful, and beauty is vain: but a woman that feareth the Lord, she shall be praised.
Prov. 31:30

I am black, but comely, O ye daughters of Jerusalem.
Song 1:5

I am the rose of Sharon, and the lily of the valleys.
Song 2:1

As the lily among thorns, so is my love among the daughters.
Song 2:2

Thy two breasts are like two young roes that are twins, which feed among the lilies.
Song 4:5
See also Song 7:3

Fair as the moon, clear as the sun.
Song 6:10

The joints of thy thighs are like jewels, the work of the hands of a cunning workman.
Song 7:1

Thy navel is like a round goblet, which wanteth not liquor.
Song 7:2

Though thou deckest thee with ornaments of gold, though thou rentest thy face with painting, in vain shalt thou make thyself fair.
Jer. 4:30

But thou didst trust in thine own beauty.
Ezek. 16:15

[*See also* Appearance, Body]

BEGINNINGS

In the beginning God created the heaven and the earth.
Gen. 1:1

When I begin, I will also make an end.
God to Samuel
1 Sam. 3:12

The wicked are estranged from the womb: they go astray as soon as they be born, speaking lies.
Ps. 58:3

A time to be born, and a time to die; a time to plant, and a time to pluck up that which is planted.
Eccl. 3:2

A time to break down, and a time to build up.
Eccl. 3:3

[*See also* Creation, Endings]

BEHAVIOR

Ye shall not steal, neither deal falsely, neither lie one to another.
Lev. 19:11

Be ye holy.
Lev. 20:7

Take heed to thyself, and keep thy soul diligently, lest thou forget the things which thine eyes have seen.
Deut. 4:9

Ye shall walk in all the ways which the Lord your God hath commanded you, that ye may live, and that it may be well with you.
Deut. 5:33

Ye shall not tempt the Lord your God.
Deut. 6:16

Do that which is right and good in the sight of the Lord.
Deut. 6:18

Walk in all His ways.
E.g., Deut. 10:12

I have set before thee this day life and good, and death and evil.
Deut. 30:15

Take good heed therefore unto yourselves, that ye love the Lord your God.
Josh. 23:11
See also Deut. 4:15

Turn ye from your evil ways, and keep My commandments and My statutes.
2 Kings 17:13

Stand up and bless the Lord your God for ever and ever.
Neh. 9:5

Shall mortal man be more just than God? shall a man be more pure than his maker?
Job 4:17

If iniquity be in thine hand, put it far away.
Job 11:14

Trust in the Lord, and do good.
Ps. 37:3

The steps of a good man are ordered by the Lord: and He delighteth in his way.
Ps. 37:23

Teach me Thy way, O Lord; I will walk in Thy truth.
Ps. 86:11

Fear the Lord, and depart from evil.
Prov. 3:7
See also Ps. 34:14, Ps. 37:27

Enter not into the path of the wicked, and go not in the way of evil men.
Prov. 4:14

These six things doth the Lord hate: yea, seven are an abomination unto Him: A proud look, a lying tongue, and hands that shed innocent blood, An heart that deviseth wicked imaginations, feet that be swift in running to mischief, A false witness that speaketh lies, and he that soweth discord among brethren.
Prov. 6:16–19

When a man's ways please the Lord, he maketh even his enemies to be at peace with him.
Prov. 16:7

A man's heart deviseth his way: but the Lord directeth his steps.
Prov. 16:9

Be not over much wicked, neither be thou foolish: why shouldest thou die before thy time?
Eccl. 7:17

Learn to do well.
Isa. 1:17

He will teach us of His ways, and we will walk in His paths.
Isa. 2:3, Mic. 4:2

Come ye, and let us walk in the light of the Lord.
Isa. 2:5

This is the way, walk ye in it.
Isa. 30:21

My thoughts are not your thoughts, neither are your ways My ways, saith the Lord.
Isa. 55:8

Keep ye judgment, and do justice.
Isa. 56:1

Learn not the way of the heathen.
Jer. 10:2

Break off thy sins by righteousness, and

thine iniquities by showing mercy to the poor.
Dan. 4:27

Sow to yourselves in righteousness, reap in mercy.
Hos. 10:12

The ways of the Lord are right, and the just shall walk in them: but the transgressors shall fall therein.
Hos. 14:9

Hate the evil, and love the good, and establish judgment in the gate.
Amos 5:15

What doth the Lord require of thee, but to do justly, and to love mercy, and to walk humbly with thy God?
Mic. 6:8

Consider your ways.
Hag. 1:5, 7

Execute true judgment, and show mercy and compassions every man to his brother.
Zech. 7:9

[*See also* Conduct toward God, Deeds, Good and Evil, Love, Sin, and the Appendix at p. 272]

BELIEF

Thou shalt find Him, if thou seek Him with all thy heart and with all thy soul.
Deut. 4:29

If ye will hear His voice, Harden not your heart.
Ps. 95:7–8
See also, e.g., Heb. 3:15

If ye will not believe, surely ye shall not be established.
Isa. 7:9

He that believeth shall not make haste.
Isa. 28:16

Come, and let us join ourselves to the Lord.
Jer. 50:5

[*See also* Doubt, Faith, Prayer, Sincerity, Skepticism]

BELIEVERS

They that trust in the Lord shall be as mount Zion, which cannot be removed.
Ps. 125:1

They that wait upon the Lord shall renew their strength; they shall mount up with wings as eagles; they shall run, and not be weary.
Isa. 40:31

[*See also* Chosen People, God's People]

BENEVOLENCE

See Altruism, Charity.

BESTIALITY

See Sodomy.

BETRAYAL

Entice thy husband, that he may declare unto us the riddle.
(he: Samson)
Judg. 14:15
See also Judg. 16:5

If ye had not plowed with my heifer, ye had not found out my riddle.
Samson to Philistines
Judg. 14:18

Tell me, I pray thee, wherein thy great strength lieth.
Delilah
Judg. 16:6

The Philistines be upon thee, Samson.
Delilah
E.g., Judg. 16:20

Set ye Uriah in the forefront of the hottest battle.
David, about Bathsheba's husband
2 Sam. 11:15

He that speaketh flattery to his friends, even the eyes of his children shall fail.
Job 17:5

They whom I loved are turned against me.
Job 19:19

Thy tongue deviseth mischiefs; like a sharp razor, working deceitfully.
Ps. 52:2

It was not an enemy that reproached me; then I could have borne it.
Ps. 55:12

Devise not evil against thy neighbour.
Prov. 3:29

Discover not a secret to another.
Prov. 25:9

Confidence in an unfaithful man in time of trouble is like a broken tooth, and a foot out of joint.
Prov. 25:19

Mine heritage is unto Me as a lion in the forest; it crieth out against Me: therefore have I hated it.
Jer. 12:8

Her friends have dealt treacherously with her, they are become her enemies.
Lam. 1:2

To subvert a man in his cause, the Lord approveth not.
Lam. 3:36

Keep the doors of thy mouth from her that lieth in thy bosom.
Mic. 7:5

Why do we deal treacherously every man against his brother?
Mal. 2:10

[*See also* Allegiance, Deception, Loyalty, Treachery]

BIRTH

In sorrow thou shalt bring forth children.
God to Eve
Gen. 3:16

For this child I prayed; and the Lord hath given me my petition.
Hannah
1 Sam 1:27

In sin did my mother conceive me.
Ps. 51:5

A time to be born, and a time to die.
Eccl. 3:2

Before I formed thee in the belly I knew thee.
Jer. 1:5

Before thou camest forth out of the womb I sanctified thee.
God to Jeremiah
Jer. 1:5

The anguish as of her that bringeth forth her first child.
Jer. 4:31

Cursed be the day wherein I was born: let not the day wherein my mother bare me be blessed.
Jer. 20:14

[*See also* Fertility]

BITTERNESS

Their grapes are grapes of gall, their clusters are bitter.
Deut. 32:32

Call me Mara: for the Almighty hath dealt very bitterly with me.
Ruth 1:20

Knowest thou not that it will be bitterness in the latter end?
2 Sam. 2:26

The heart knoweth his own bitterness.
Prov. 14:10

He hath filled me with bitterness, He hath made me drunken with wormwood.
Lam. 3:15

[*See also* Anguish]

BLAME

The woman whom Thou gavest to be with me, she gave me of the tree, and I did eat.
Adam
Gen. 3:12

The serpent beguiled me, and I did eat.
Eve
Gen. 3:13

Upon me be thy curse, my son: only obey my voice.
Rebekah to Jacob
Gen. 27:13

His blood shall be upon him.
Lev. 20:9

Let not mine hand be upon him, but let the hand of the Philistines be upon him.
Saul about David
1 Sam. 18:17

Art thou he that troubleth Israel?
Ahab to Elijah
1 Kings 18:17

If thou wert pure and upright; surely now He would awake for thee.
Job 8:6

He hath borne our griefs, and carried our sorrows: yet we did esteem him stricken, smitten of God, and afflicted.
Isa. 53:4

Hast thou not procured this unto thyself, in that thou hast forsaken the Lord thy God?
God to Jews
Jer. 2:17

The fathers have eaten sour grapes, and the children's teeth are set on edge.
Ezek. 18:2
See also Jer. 31:29

What shall we do unto thee, that the sea may be calm unto us?
Sailors to Jonah
Jonah 1:11

Lay not upon us innocent blood: for thou, O Lord, hast done as it pleased Thee.
Sailors to God
Jonah 1:14

Mine anger was kindled against the shepherds, and I punished the goats.
Zech. 10:3

[*See also* Guilt, Responsibility, Scapegoat]

BLASPHEMY

Who is the Lord, that I should obey His voice to let Israel go?
Pharaoh
Ex. 5:2

Thou shalt not take the name of the Lord thy God in vain.
Third Commandment
Ex. 20:7, Deut. 5:11

Whosoever curseth his God shall bear his sin.
Lev. 24:15

The Lord will not hold him guiltless that taketh His name in vain.
Deut. 5:11, Ex. 20:7

Let not thy God in whom thou trustest deceive thee.
2 Kings 19:10, Isa. 37:10

What is the Almighty, that we should serve Him?
Job 21:15

It profiteth a man nothing that he should delight himself with God.
Job 34:9

How long shall the adversary reproach? shall the enemy blaspheme Thy name for ever?
Ps. 74:10

Whoso mocketh the poor reproacheth his Maker.
Prov. 17:5

Jerusalem is ruined, and Judah is fallen: because their tongue and their doings are against the Lord.
Isa. 3:8

I will ascend above the heights of the clouds; I will be like the most High.
Isa. 14:14

My name continually every day is blasphemed.
Isa. 52:5
See also Rom. 2:24

Pollute ye My holy name no more with your gifts, and with your idols.
Ezek. 20:39

And who is that God that shall deliver you out of my hands?
Nebuchadnezzar
Dan. 3:15

It is vain to serve God: and what profit is it that we have kept His ordinance?
Mal. 3:14

[*See also* Heresy]

In thee shall all families of the earth be blessed.
> *God to Abram*
> *Gen. 12:3*
> *See also Gen. 28:14*

Cursed be every one that curseth thee, and blessed be he that blesseth thee.
> *Isaac to Jacob*
> *Gen. 27:29*
> *See also Num. 24:9*

Hast thou not reserved a blessing for me?
> *Esau to Isaac*
> *Gen. 27:36*

I will not let thee go, except thou bless me.
> *Jacob to Angel*
> *Gen. 32:26*

A nation and a company of nations shall be of thee, and kings shall come out of thy loins.
> *Gen. 35:11*

And God Almighty give you mercy before the man.
> *Jacob to his sons*
> *Gen. 43:14*

Go in peace.
> *E.g., Ex. 4:18*

The Lord bless thee, and keep thee: The Lord make His face shine upon thee, and be gracious unto thee: The Lord lift up His countenance upon thee, and give thee peace.
> *Num. 6:24–26*

Behold, I set before you this day a blessing and a curse; A blessing, if ye obey the commandments of the Lord your God, which I command you this day: And a curse, if ye will not obey.
> *Deut. 11:26–28*

Blessed shalt thou be in the city, and blessed shalt thou be in the field.
> *Deut. 28:3*

As thy days, so shall thy strength be.
> *Deut. 33:25*

The Lord thy God be with thee, as He was with Moses.
> *Josh. 1:17*

The Lord deal kindly with you, as ye have dealt with the dead, and with me.
> *Naomi*
> *Ruth 1:8*

The Lord be with you.
> *Ruth 2:4*
> *See also 1 Sam. 17:37*

The Lord bless thee.
> *Ruth 2:4*

The Lord our God be with us, as He was with our fathers.
> *1 Kings 8:57*

Peace be unto thee, and peace be to thine helpers; for thy God helpeth thee.
> *1 Chron. 12:18*

Think upon me, my God, for good.
> *Neh. 5:19*
> *See also Neh. 12:31*

Thou preparest a table before me in the presence of mine enemies: Thou anointest my head with oil; my cup runneth over.
> *Ps. 23:5*

Surely goodness and mercy shall follow me all the days of my life: and I will dwell in the house of the Lord for ever.
> *Ps. 23:6*

God be merciful unto us, and bless us; and cause His face to shine upon us.
> *Ps. 67:1*

The curse of the Lord is in the house of the wicked: but He blesseth the habitation of the just.
> *Prov. 3:33*

God giveth to a man that is good in His sight wisdom, and knowledge, and joy.
> *Eccl. 2:26*

The sure mercies of David.
> *Isa. 55:3, Acts 13:34*

Blessed be the name of God for ever and ever.
> *Dan. 2:20*
> *See also Ps. 145:1*

[*See also* Curses, Reward]

Cursed be he that maketh the blind to wander out of the way.
Deut. 27:18

I was eyes to the blind, and feet was I to the lame.
Job 29:15

The Lord openeth the eyes of the blind.
Ps. 146:8

The eyes of the blind shall be opened, and the ears of the deaf shall be unstopped.
Isa. 35:5

[*See also* Enlightenment, Handicapped, Sight, Stubbornness]

BLOOD

It is the blood that maketh an atonement for the soul.
Lev. 17:11

The life of all flesh is the blood thereof.
Lev. 17:14

[*See also* Guilt, Murder, Punishment]

BOASTING

Where is now thy mouth?
Judg. 9:38

I will give thy flesh unto the fowls of the air, and to the beasts of the field.
Goliath to David
1 Sam. 17:44

Let not him that girdeth on his harness boast himself as he that putteth it off.
1 Kings 20:11

A prudent man concealeth knowledge: but the heart of fools proclaimeth foolishness.
Prov. 12:23

For men to search their own glory is not glory.
Prov. 25:27

Boast not thyself of to morrow; for thou knowest not what a day may bring forth.
Prov. 27:1

Let not the wise man glory in his wisdom, neither let the mighty man glory in his might, let not the rich man glory in his riches.
Jer. 9:23

Rejoice not against me, O mine enemy: when I fall, I shall arise.
Mic. 7:8

[*See also* Arrogance, Gloating, Publicity]

BODY

Dust thou art, and unto dust shalt thou return.
Gen. 3:19

Thy two breasts are like two young roes that are twins, which feed among the lilies.
Song 4:5
See also Song 7:3

His legs are as pillars of marble, set upon sockets of fine gold.
Song 5:15

Thy navel is like a round goblet, which wanteth not liquor.
Song 7:2

Thy neck is as a tower of ivory; thine eyes like the fishpools in Heshbon.
Song 7:4

Thy nose is as the tower of Lebanon which looketh toward Damascus.
Song 7:4

Thy stature is like to a palm tree, and thy breasts to clusters of grapes.
Song 7:7

[*See also* Appearance, Beauty, Speech]

BOOKS

Oh that my words were now written! oh that they were printed in a book!
Job 19:23

My desire is, that the Almighty would

answer me, and that mine adversary had written a book.
>*Job 31:35*

Of making many books there is no end.
>*Eccl. 12:12*

[*See also* History]

BOREDOM

See Pleasure.

BORROWING

Thou shalt lend unto many nations, but thou shalt not borrow.
>*Deut. 15:6*
>*See also Deut. 28:12*

The wicked borroweth, and payeth not again: but the righteous showeth mercy, and giveth.
>*Ps. 37:21*

He that is surety for a stranger shall smart for it.
>*Prov. 11:15*

The borrower is servant to the lender.
>*Prov. 22:7*

Better is it that thou shouldest not vow, than that thou shouldest vow and not pay.
>*Eccl. 5:5*

As with the buyer, so with the seller; as with the lender, so with the borrower; as with the taker of usury, so with the giver of usury to him.
>*Isa. 24:2*

[*See also* Generosity, Usury]

BRAVERY

See Courage.

BRIBERY

Thou shalt not respect persons, neither take a gift.
>*Deut. 16:19*
>*See also Deut. 1:17*

A gift doth blind the eyes of the wise, and pervert the words of the righteous.
>*Deut. 16:19*
>*See also Ex. 23:8*

Fire shall consume the tabernacles of bribery.
>*Job 15:34*

A gift in secret pacifieth anger.
>*Prov. 21:14*

A gift destroyeth the heart.
>*Eccl. 7:7*

[*See also* Corruption, Greed]

BROTHERHOOD

Am I my brother's keeper?
>*Cain*
>*Gen. 4:9*

Thou shalt love thy neighbour as thyself.
>*E.g., Lev. 19:18, Matt. 19:19*

Love ye therefore the stranger: for ye were strangers in the land of Egypt.
>*Deut. 10:19*

Did not He that made me in the womb make him?
>*Job 31:15*

Behold, how good and how pleasant it is for brethren to dwell together in unity!
>*Ps. 133:1*

If two lie together, then they have heat: but how can one be warm alone?
>*Eccl. 4:11*

The wolf and the lamb shall feed together, and the lion shall eat straw like the bullock.
>*Isa. 65:25*

Execute true judgment, and show mercy and compassions every man to his brother.
>*Zech. 7:9*

Let none of you imagine evil against his brother in your heart.
>*Zech. 7:10*
>*See also Zech. 8:17*

Have we not all one father? hath not one God created us?
>*Mal. 2:10*

Why do we deal treacherously every man against his brother?
Mal. 2:10

[*See also* Enemies, Equality, Friendship, Hatred, Love, Peace]

BROTHERS

See Siblings.

BUILDING

Let the foundations thereof be strongly laid.
Ezra 6:3

Except the Lord build the house, they labour in vain that build it.
Ps. 127:1

Through wisdom is an house builded; and by understanding it is established.
Prov. 24:3

By much slothfulness the building decayeth.
Eccl. 10:18

[*See also* Planning]

BURIAL

Bury me not, I pray thee, in Egypt.
Jacob to Joseph
Gen. 47:29

The carcase of Jezebel shall be as dung upon the face of the field.
2 Kings 9:37

They shall not say, This is Jezebel.
2 Kings 9:37

[*See also* Death, Remembrance]

BUSINESS

Because thou art my brother, shouldest thou therefore serve me for nought? tell me, what shall thy wages be?
Laban to Jacob
Gen. 29:15

Ye shall do no unrighteousness in judgment, in meteyard, in weight, or in measure.
Lev. 19:35

Thou shalt not oppress an hired servant that is poor and needy.
Deut. 24:14

Thou shalt not have in thy bag divers weights, a great and a small.
Deut. 25:13

All that do unrighteously, are an abomination unto the Lord thy God.
Deut. 25:16

A false balance is abomination to the Lord: but a just weight is His delight.
Prov. 11:1

He that withholdeth corn, the people shall curse him: but blessing shall be upon the head of him that selleth it.
Prov. 11:26

Divers weights, and divers measures, both of them are alike abomination to the Lord.
Prov. 20:10
See also Prov. 20:23

It is naught, it is naught, saith the buyer: but when he is gone his way, then he boasteth.
Prov. 20:14

Seest thou a man diligent in his business? he shall stand before kings.
Prov. 22:29

Ye shall have just balances.
Ezek. 45:10

He is a merchant, the balances of deceit are in his hand: he loveth to oppress.
Hos. 12:7

[*See also* Employees, Honesty, Leadership, Work]

CALLING

See Mission.

CANDOR

How long shall this man be a snare unto us? let the men go.
Advisers to Pharaoh
Ex. 10:7

Knowest thou not yet that Egypt is destroyed?
Pharaoh's servants to Pharaoh
Ex. 10:7

I will speak in the anguish of my spirit; I will complain in the bitterness of my soul.
Job 7:11

Let me alone, that I may speak, and let come on me what will.
Job 13:13

He that hideth hatred with lying lips, and he that uttereth a slander, is a fool.
Prov. 10:18

Open rebuke is better than secret love.
Prov. 27:5

A time to keep silence, and a time to speak.
Eccl. 3:7

This man seeketh not the welfare of this people, but the hurt.
(man: Jeremiah)
Jer. 38:4

If I declare it unto thee, wilt thou not surely put me to death?
Jer. 38:15

Whatsoever thing the Lord shall answer you, I will declare it unto you; I will keep nothing back.
Jer. 42:4

[*See also* Advice, Honesty, Prudence, Truth]

CAPACITY

All the rivers run into the sea; yet the sea is not full.
Eccl. 1:7

CAPITAL PUNISHMENT

He that smiteth a man, so that he die, shall be surely put to death.
Ex. 21:12

He that smiteth his father, or his mother, shall be surely put to death.
Ex. 21:15

He that killeth a man, he shall be put to death.
Lev. 24:21
See also Lev. 24:17

One witness shall not testify against any person to cause him to die.
Num. 35:30

Ye shall take no satisfaction for the life of a murderer, which is guilty of death: but he shall be surely put to death.
Num. 35:31

At the mouth of two witnesses, or three witnesses, shall he that is worthy of death be put to death; but at the mouth of one witness he shall not be put to death.
Deut. 17:6

[*See also* Murder, Punishment]

CAPTIVITY

Behold, I am in your hand: do with me as seemeth good and meet unto you.
Jer. 26:14

Thou hast broken the yokes of wood; but thou shalt make for them yokes of iron.
Jer. 28:13

[*See also* Exile, Freedom, Imprisonment, Outcast, Slavery]

See Comfort, Devotion.

CARNAGE

In the place where dogs licked the blood of Naboth shall dogs lick thy blood, even thine.
(thy: Ahab)
1 Kings 21:19

The dogs shall eat Jezebel by the wall of Jezreel.
1 Kings 21:23

When they arose early in the morning, behold, they were all dead corpses.
2 Kings 19:35, Isa. 37:36

The sword shall devour, and it shall be satiate and made drunk with their blood.
Jer. 46:10

[*See also* Violence, War]

CAUTION

See Prudence, Vigilance, Warning.

CELEBRATION

To every one a loaf of bread, and a good piece of flesh, and a flagon of wine.
1 Chron. 16:3

Go your way, eat the fat, and drink the sweet.
Neh. 8:10

The joy of Jerusalem was heard even afar off.
Neh. 12:43

Let the heavens rejoice, and let the earth be glad; let the sea roar, and the fulness thereof.
Ps. 96:11
See also 1 Chron. 16:31–32

Make a joyful noise unto the Lord, all the earth: make a loud noise, and rejoice, and sing praise.
Ps. 98:4
See also Ps. 100:1

This is the day which the Lord hath made; we will rejoice and be glad in it.
Ps. 118:24

Let us eat and drink; for to morrow we shall die.
Isa. 22:13, 1 Cor. 15:32

[*See also* Happiness, Pleasure]

CENSUS

Number ye the people, that I may know the number of the people.
2 Sam. 24:2

CERTAINTY

When I begin, I will also make an end.
God to Samuel
1 Sam. 3:12

He is not a man, that He should repent.
1 Sam. 15:29

As the Lord liveth, the Lord shall smite him.
1 Sam. 26:10

How long halt ye between two opinions?
1 Kings 18:21

Boast not thyself of to morrow; for thou knowest not what a day may bring forth.
Prov. 27:1

I have spoken it, I will also bring it to pass.
Isa. 46:11

I the Lord have spoken it.
Ezek. 5:13, 17

[*See also* Chance, Decisions, Indecision]

CHALLENGES

Ye shall not tempt the Lord your God.
Deut. 6:16

Give me a man, that we may fight together.
Goliath
1 Sam. 17:10

Call ye on the name of your gods, and I will call on the name of the Lord.
Elijah
1 Kings 18:24

Come, let us see one another in the face.
2 Chron. 25:17

Touch all that he hath, and he will curse
Thee to Thy face.
Satan to God, about Job
Job 1:11

All that he hath is in thy power; only upon
himself put not forth thine hand.
God to Satan, about Job
Job 1:12

[*See also* Competition, Testing]

CHANCE

The lot is cast into the lap; but the whole
disposing thereof is of the Lord.
Prov. 16:33

The race is not to the swift, nor the battle
to the strong, neither yet bread to the
wise, nor yet riches to men of understanding, nor yet favour to men of skill; but
time and chance happeneth to them all.
Eccl. 9:11

CHANGE

Can the Ethiopian change his skin, or the
leopard his spots? then may ye also do
good, that are accustomed to do evil.
Jer. 13:23

[*See also* Conversion, Habit]

CHAOS

The earth was without form, and void;
and darkness was upon the face of the
deep.
Gen. 1:2

They shall fight every one against his
brother, and every one against his neighbour; city against city, and kingdom
against kingdom.
Isa. 19:2

The fathers shall eat the sons in the midst

of thee, and the sons shall eat their fathers.
Ezek. 5:10

[*See also* Confusion]

CHARACTER

The excellency of dignity.
Gen. 49:3

Unstable as water, thou shalt not excel.
Gen. 49:4

What doth the Lord thy God require of
thee, but to fear the Lord thy God, to walk
in all His ways, and to love Him, and to
serve the Lord thy God with all thy heart
and with all thy soul.
Deut. 10:12

As the man is, so is his strength.
Judg. 8:21

As his name is, so is he.
1 Sam. 25:25

Be thou strong therefore, and show thyself
a man.
David to Solomon
1 Kings 2:2

What, is thy servant a dog, that he should
do this great thing?
2 Kings 8:13

Dost thou still retain thine integrity?
curse God, and die.
Job's wife to Job
Job 2:9

Surely men of low degree are vanity, and
men of high degree are a lie.
Ps. 62:9

Let not mercy and truth forsake thee: bind
them about thy neck.
Prov. 3:3

He that walketh uprightly walketh surely.
Prov. 10:9

A false witness will utter lies.
Prov. 14:5

Even a child is known by his doings.
Prov. 20:11

Iron sharpeneth iron; so a man sharpeneth the countenance of his friend.
Prov. 27:17

Better is the poor that walketh in his

uprightness, than he that is perverse in his ways, though he be rich.
Prov. 28:6

[*See also* Ability, Behavior, Honesty, Integrity]

CHARITY

Thou shalt not harden thine heart, nor shut thine hand from thy poor brother.
Deut. 15:7

Thou shalt open thine hand wide unto thy brother, to thy poor, and to thy needy, in thy land.
Deut. 15:11

Every man shall give as he is able, according to the blessing of the Lord thy God which He hath given thee.
Deut. 16:17

Thou shalt not bring the hire of a whore, or the price of a dog, into the house of the Lord.
Deut. 23:18

Send portions unto them for whom nothing is prepared.
Neh. 8:10

The cause which I knew not I searched out.
Job 29:16

Blessed is he that considereth the poor: the Lord will deliver him in time of trouble.
Ps. 41:1

The sacrifice of the wicked is an abomination to the Lord: but the prayer of the upright is His delight.
Prov. 15:8

Whoso stoppeth his ears at the cry of the poor, he also shall cry himself, but shall not be heard.
Prov. 21:13

He that giveth unto the poor shall not

lack: but he that hideth his eyes shall have many a curse.
Prov. 28:27

Will a man rob God? Yet ye have robbed Me.
Mal. 3:8

Wherein have we robbed Thee? In tithes and offerings.
Mal. 3:8

[*See also* Altruism, Generosity, Poverty, Tithe, Underprivileged]

CHASTISEMENT

Art thou come unto me to call my sin to remembrance?
1 Kings 17:18

Hast thou killed, and also taken possession?
(thou: Ahab)
1 Kings 21:19

Happy is the man whom God correcteth.
Job 5:17

Rebuke me not in Thine anger, neither chasten me in Thy hot displeasure.
Ps. 6:1
See also Ps. 38:1

Despise not the chastening of the Lord: neither be weary of His correction.
Prov. 3:11

Whom the Lord loveth He correcteth.
Prov. 3:12

Lift up thy voice like a trumpet, and show My people their transgression.
Isa. 58:1

Prophesy against them, prophesy, O son of man.
Ezek. 11:4

[*See also* Discipline, Guidance, Punishment]

See Honesty, Lies.

He that spareth his rod hateth his son: but he that loveth him chasteneth him betimes.
Prov. 13:24

Chasten thy son while there is hope, and let not thy soul spare for his crying.
Prov. 19:18

Train up a child in the way he should go: and when he is old, he will not depart from it.
Prov. 22:6

Foolishness is bound in the heart of a child; but the rod of correction shall drive it far from him.
Prov. 22:15

Withhold not correction from the child: for if thou beatest him with the rod, he shall not die.
Prov. 23:13

Thou shalt beat him with the rod, and shalt deliver his soul from hell.
Prov. 23:14

A child left to himself bringeth his mother to shame.
Prov. 29:15

Even the sea monsters draw out the breast, they give suck to their young ones.
Lam. 4:3

[*See also* Children, Parents]

See Birth.

Give me children, or else I die.
Rachel to Jacob
Gen. 30:1

The Lord had shut up her womb.
(her: Hannah)
1 Sam. 1:5

Am not I better to thee than ten sons?
(I: Hannah's husband)
1 Sam. 1:8

I am a woman of a sorrowful spirit.
Hannah
1 Sam. 1:15

Sing, O barren, thou that didst not bear; break forth into singing, and cry aloud, thou that didst not travail with child: for more are the children of the desolate than the children of the married wife, saith the Lord.
Isa. 54:1
See also Gal. 4:27

[*See also* Fertility]

Be fruitful, and multiply.
E.g., Gen. 1:28

Be fruitful, and multiply, and replenish the earth.
God to Noah, after the flood
Gen. 9:1

The smell of my son is as the smell of a field which the Lord hath blessed.
Gen. 27:27

Thy seed shall be as the dust of the earth.
God to Jacob
Gen. 28:14
See also Gen. 13:16

Israel loved Joseph more than all his children, because he was the son of his old age.
Gen. 37:3

If I be bereaved of my children, I am bereaved.
Gen. 43:14

The males shall be the Lord's.
Ex. 13:12

Do not prostitute thy daughter, to cause her to be a whore; lest the land fall to

whoredom, and the land become full of wickedness.
Lev. 19:29

Ye are the children of the Lord your God.
Deut. 14:1

He walked in all the sins of his father.
E.g., 1 Kings 15:3

Out of the mouth of babes and sucklings.
Ps. 8:2, Matt. 21:16

Children are an heritage of the Lord: and the fruit of the womb is His reward.
Ps. 127:3

As arrows are in the hand of a mighty man; so are children of the youth. Happy is the man that hath his quiver full of them.
Ps. 127:4-5

A wise son maketh a glad father: but a foolish son is the heaviness of his mother.
Prov. 10:1

A fool despiseth his father's instruction.
Prov. 15:5

A wise son maketh a glad father: but a foolish man despiseth his mother.
Prov. 15:20

A foolish son is a grief to his father, and bitterness to her that bare him.
Prov. 17:25

A foolish son is the calamity of his father.
Prov. 19:13

He that begetteth a wise child shall have joy of him.
Prov. 23:24

A little child shall lead them.
Isa. 11:6

The seed of evildoers shall never be renowned.
Isa. 14:20

More are the children of the desolate than the children of the married wife, saith the Lord.
Isa. 54:1

[*See also* Birth, Child-Rearing, Fertility, Firstborn, Grandchildren, Parents, Youth]

CHOICE

If thou wilt take the left hand, then I will go to the right; or if thou depart to the right hand, then I will go to the left.
Gen. 13:9

Behold, I set before you this day a blessing and a curse; A blessing, if ye obey the commandments of the Lord your God, which I command you this day: And a curse, if ye will not obey.
Deut. 11:26-28

I have set before thee this day life and good, and death and evil.
Deut. 30:15

Choose life, that both thou and thy seed may live.
Deut. 30:19

Choose you this day whom ye will serve.
Josh. 24:15

But as for me and my house, we will serve the Lord.
Josh. 24:15

Ye are witnesses against yourselves that ye have chosen you the Lord, to serve Him.
Josh. 24:22

I offer thee three things; choose thee one of them, that I may do it unto thee.
*God to David
2 Sam. 24:12, 1 Chron. 21:10*

How long halt ye between two opinions? if the Lord be God, follow Him: but if Baal, then follow him.
*Elijah to Israelites
1 Kings 18:21*

Serve the king of Babylon, and live.
Jer. 27:17

Seek good, and not evil, that ye may live.
Amos 5:14

[*See also* Battle Calls, Good and Evil, Indecision, Loyalty]

CHOSEN PEOPLE

I will make of thee a great nation.
*God to Abram
Gen. 12:2*

In thy seed shall all the nations of the

earth be blessed; because thou hast obeyed My voice.
God to Abraham
Gen. 22:18

Thus saith the Lord, Israel is My son, even My firstborn.
Ex. 4:22

I will take you to Me for a people, and I will be to you a God.
Ex. 6:7

Ye shall be a peculiar treasure unto Me above all people: for all the earth is Mine.
Ex. 19:5

And they shall know that I am the Lord their God, that brought them forth out of the land of Egypt.
Ex. 29:46

I will walk among you, and will be your God, and ye shall be My people.
Lev. 26:12
See also 2 Cor. 6:16

Who can count the dust of Jacob, and the number of the fourth part of Israel?
Num. 23:10

He lay down as a lion, and as a great lion: who shall stir him up?
Num. 24:9

Blessed is he that blesseth thee, and cursed is he that curseth thee.
Num. 24:9

Surely this great nation is a wise and understanding people.
Deut. 4:6

Did ever people hear the voice of God speaking out of the midst of the fire, as thou hast heard, and live?
Deut. 4:33

The Lord made not this covenant with our fathers, but with us, even us, who are all of us here alive this day.
Deut. 5:3

Thou art an holy people unto the Lord thy God.
E.g., Deut. 7:6

The Lord thy God hath chosen thee to be a special people unto Himself.
Deut. 7:6

The Lord did not set His love upon you, nor choose you, because ye were more in number than any people; for ye were the fewest of all people: But because the Lord loved you.
Deut. 7:7–8

All people of the earth shall see that thou art called by the name of the Lord; and they shall be afraid of thee.
Deut. 28:10

The Lord's portion is His people.
Deut. 32:9

The apple of His eye.
Deut. 32:10

They are a nation void of counsel, neither is there any understanding in them.
Deut. 32:28

It hath pleased the Lord to make you His people.
1 Sam. 12:22

They shall dwell in their place, and shall be moved no more.
1 Chron. 17:9

He reproved kings for their sakes.
Ps. 105:14, 1 Chron. 16:21

Touch not Mine anointed, and do My prophets no harm.
Ps. 105:15, 1 Chron. 16:22

He that keepeth Israel shall neither slumber nor sleep.
Ps. 121:4

The Lord hath chosen Jacob unto Himself, and Israel for His peculiar treasure.
Ps. 135:4

The ox knoweth his owner, and the ass his master's crib: but Israel doth not know, My people doth not consider.
Isa. 1:3

The vineyard of the Lord of hosts is the house of Israel.
Isa. 5:7

They shall be My people, and I will be their God.
E.g., Jer. 24:7

Again I will build thee, and thou shalt be built, O virgin of Israel.
Jer. 31:4

He that scattered Israel will gather him,

and keep him, as a shepherd doth his flock.
Jer. 31:10

The number of the children of Israel shall be as the sand of the sea, which cannot be measured nor numbered.
Hos. 1:10

[*See also* Believers, Circumcision, Covenant, God's People]

CHURCH GOVERNANCE

See Clergy, Leadership.

CHURCHES

Let them make Me a sanctuary; that I may dwell among them.
Ex. 25:8

I dwell in an house of cedar, but the ark of God dwelleth within curtains.
David
2 Sam. 7:2

I have surely built Thee an house to dwell in, a settled place for Thee to abide in for ever.
Solomon to God
1 Kings 8:13

Who is able to build Him an house, seeing the heaven and heaven of heavens cannot contain Him?
2 Chron. 2:6

Heaven and the heaven of heavens cannot contain Thee; how much less this house which I have built!
Solomon
2 Chron. 6:18
See also 1 Kings 8:27

I will not give sleep to mine eyes, or slumber to mine eyelids, Until I find out a place for the Lord.
Ps. 132:4–5

Mine house shall be called an house of prayer for all people.
Isa. 56:7

The heaven is My throne, and the earth is My footstool: where is the house that ye build unto Me?
Isa. 66:1
See also Acts 7:49, Matt. 5:34–35

I will be glorified, saith the Lord.
Hag. 1:8

[*See also* God's Presence, God's Temple, Prayer, Worship]

CIRCUMCISION

Ye shall circumcise the flesh of your foreskin; and it shall be a token of the covenant betwixt Me and you.
Gen. 17:11

Circumcise therefore the foreskin of your heart, and be no more stiffnecked.
Deut. 10:16

Circumcise yourselves to the Lord.
Jer. 4:4

[*See also* Chosen People, Covenant]

CLARITY

They are all plain to him that understandeth, and right to them that find knowledge.
Prov. 8:9

Write the vision, and make it plain.
Hab. 2:2

[*See also* Communication, Eloquence, Speech]

CLERGY

The Lord is their inheritance.
Deut. 18:2

I will raise Me up a faithful priest.
1 Sam. 2:35

Ye are holy unto the Lord.
Ezra 8:28

They shall teach My people the difference between the holy and profane.
Ezek. 44:23

The priest's lips should keep knowledge.
Mal. 2:7

[*See also* Ministry, Preaching, Priesthood]

Fear not, for I am with thee, and will bless thee, and multiply thy seed.
>*God to Isaac*
>*Gen. 26:24*

Peace be unto thee; fear not: thou shalt not die.
>*Judg. 6:23*

Ye are forgers of lies, ye are all physicians of no value.
>*Job to his friends*
>*Job 13:4*

Miserable comforters are ye all.
>*Job to his friends*
>*Job 16:2*

Thou, O Lord, art a shield for me; my glory, and the lifter up of mine head.
>*Ps. 3:3*

He maketh me to lie down in green pastures: He leadeth me beside the still waters. He restoreth my soul.
>*Ps. 23:2–3*

Thy rod and Thy staff they comfort me.
>*Ps. 23:4*

I looked for some to take pity, but there was none; and for comforters, but I found none.
>*Ps. 69:20*

Thy statutes have been my songs in the house of my pilgrimage.
>*Ps. 119:54*

Trouble and anguish have taken hold on me: yet Thy commandments are my delights.
>*Ps. 119:143*

Comfort ye, comfort ye My people, saith your God.
>*Isa. 40:1*

When thou passest through the waters, I will be with thee; and through the rivers, they shall not overflow thee: when thou walkest through the fire, thou shalt not be burned.
>*Isa. 43:2*

I, even I, am He that comforteth you.
>*Isa. 51:12*

As one whom his mother comforteth, so will I comfort you.
>*Isa. 66:13*

Is there no balm in Gilead? is there no physician there?
>*Jer. 8:22*

Mine eye runneth down with water, because the comforter that should relieve my soul is far from me.
>*Lam. 1:16*

Do not My words do good to him that walketh uprightly?
>*Mic. 2:7*

My spirit remaineth among you: fear ye not.
>*Hag. 2:5*

[*See also* Anguish, Fear, Grief, Mourning, Sympathy]

COMMANDMENTS

If a soul sin, and commit any of these things which are forbidden to be done by the commandments of the Lord; though he wist it not, yet is he guilty.
>*Lev. 5:17*

Do them, that ye may live.
>*Deut. 4:1*
>*See also Luke 10:28*

Keep therefore and do them; for this is your wisdom and your understanding in the sight of the nations.
>*Deut. 4:6*

And thou shalt teach them diligently unto thy children, and shalt talk of them when thou sittest in thine house, and when thou walkest by the way, and when thou liest down, and when thou risest up.
>*Deut. 6:7*
>*See also Deut. 11:19*

Thou shalt keep the commandments of the Lord thy God, to walk in His ways, and to fear Him.
>*Deut. 8:6*

Behold, I set before you this day a blessing and a curse; A blessing, if ye obey the commandments of the Lord your God,

which I command you this day: And a curse, if ye will not obey.
Deut. 11:26–28

What thing soever I command you, observe to do it: thou shalt not add thereto, nor diminish from it.
Deut. 12:32

Do them, that ye may prosper in all that ye do.
Deut. 29:9

The word is very nigh unto thee, in thy mouth, and in thy heart.
Deut. 30:14
See also Rom. 10:8

It is not a vain thing for you; because it is your life.
Deut. 32:47

Turn not from it to the right hand or to the left, that thou mayest prosper whithersoever thou goest.
Josh. 1:7

Keep His commandments.
E.g., Josh. 22:5

Let it be done according to the law.
Ezra 10:3

Lay up His words in thine heart.
Job 22:22

The testimony of the Lord is sure, making wise the simple.
Ps. 19:7

More to be desired are they than gold, yea, than much fine gold: sweeter also than honey and the honeycomb.
Ps. 19:10

Thy word have I hid in mine heart, that I might not sin against Thee.
Ps. 119:11

Teach me, O Lord, the way of Thy statutes; and I shall keep it unto the end.
Ps. 119:33

Thy statutes have been my songs in the house of my pilgrimage.
Ps. 119:54

Give me understanding, that I may learn Thy commandments.
Ps. 119:73
See also Ps. 119:34

Thy law is my delight.
Ps. 119:77, 174
See also Ps. 119:143

Thy law is the truth.
Ps. 119:142

Great peace have they which love Thy law.
Ps. 119:165

He that keepeth the commandment keepeth his own soul; but he that despiseth His ways shall die.
Prov. 19:16

He that keepeth the law, happy is he.
Prov. 29:18

He will teach us of His ways, and we will walk in His paths.
Isa. 2:3, Mic. 4:2

Out of Zion shall go forth the law, and the word of the Lord from Jerusalem.
Isa. 2:3

This is the way, walk ye in it.
Isa. 30:21

Remember ye the law of Moses My servant.
Mal. 4:4

[*See also* God's Word, Law, Obedience, Scripture, Sin, Ten Commandments, and the Appendix at p. 272]

COMMITMENT

With all thy heart and with all thy soul.
E.g., Deut. 10:12
See also Deut. 11:13

I am my beloved's, and my beloved is mine.
Song 6:3

I am my beloved's, and his desire is toward me.
Song 7:10

[*See also* Devotion, Impartiality, Neutrality, Perseverance, Sincerity]

COMMON SENSE

See Wisdom.

COMMUNICATION

Let us go down, and there confound their language, that they may not understand one another's speech.
Gen. 11:7

Babel; because the Lord did there confound the language.
Gen. 11:9

Come now, and let us reason together, saith the Lord.
Isa. 1:18

[*See also* Clarity, Eloquence, News, Publicity, Speech]

COMPANIONS

Put not thine hand with the wicked to be an unrighteous witness.
Ex. 23:1

Thou shalt not follow a multitude to do evil.
Ex. 23:2

Blessed is the man that walketh not in the counsel of the ungodly, nor standeth in the way of sinners, nor sitteth in the seat of the scornful.
Ps. 1:1

If sinners entice thee, consent thou not.
Prov. 1:10

Forsake the foolish, and live.
Prov. 9:6

He that walketh with wise men shall be wise: but a companion of fools shall be destroyed.
Prov. 13:20

He that is a companion of riotous men shameth his father.
Prov. 28:7

Thou dwellest in the midst of a rebellious house.
Ezek. 12:2

[*See also* Cooperation, Fellowship, Friendship]

COMPASSION

Thou shalt not harden thine heart, nor shut thine hand from thy poor brother.
Deut. 15:7

Thou shalt open thine hand wide unto thy brother, to thy poor, and to thy needy, in thy land.
Deut. 15:11

Remember that thou wast a bondman in the land of Egypt, and the Lord thy God redeemed thee.
Deut. 15:15
See also Deut. 5:15, Deut. 24:22

Blessed be ye of the Lord; for ye have compassion on me.
Saul
1 Sam. 23:21

Deal gently for my sake with the young man, even with Absalom.
2 Sam. 18:5

This day thou shalt bear no tidings, because the king's son is dead.
2 Sam. 18:20

O my Lord, give her the living child, and in no wise slay it.
1 Kings 3:26

Thine eyes shall not see all the evil which I will bring upon this place.
2 Kings 22:20

Have pity upon me, O ye my friends; for the hand of God hath touched me.
Job 19:21

I was eyes to the blind, and feet was I to the lame.
Job 29:15

According to the greatness of Thy power preserve Thou those that are appointed to die.
Ps. 79:11

The Lord is merciful and gracious, slow to anger, and plenteous in mercy.
Ps. 103:8

As a father pitieth his children, so the Lord pitieth them that fear Him.
Ps. 103:13

He knoweth our frame; He remembereth that we are dust.
Ps. 103:14

He raiseth up the poor out of the dust, and lifteth the needy out of the dunghill.
Ps. 113:7
See also 1 Sam. 2:8

Let Thy tender mercies come unto me, that I may live.
Ps. 119:77

Though the Lord be high, yet hath He respect unto the lowly.
Ps. 138:6

The Lord is gracious, and full of compassion; slow to anger, and of great mercy.
Ps. 145:8

He that hath mercy on the poor, happy is he.
Prov. 14:21

He that honoureth Him hath mercy on the poor.
Prov. 14:31

He that hath pity upon the poor lendeth unto the Lord; and that which he hath given will He pay him again.
Prov. 19:17

Relieve the oppressed, judge the fatherless, plead for the widow.
Isa. 1:17

I have heard thy prayer, I have seen thy tears: behold, I will add unto thy days fifteen years.
God to Hezekiah
Isa. 38:5
See also 2 Kings 20:5–6

Can a woman forget her sucking child, that she should not have compassion on the son of her womb?
Isa. 49:15

Is it not to deal thy bread to the hungry, and that thou bring the poor that are cast out to thy house?
Isa. 58:7

In My wrath I smote thee, but in My favour have I had mercy on thee.
Isa. 60:10

Thou art a gracious God, and merciful,

slow to anger, and of great kindness, and repentest Thee of the evil.
Jonah 4:2

Love mercy.
Mic. 6:8

Show mercy and compassions every man to his brother.
Zech. 7:9

Oppress not the widow, nor the fatherless, the stranger, nor the poor.
Zech. 7:10

[*See also* Charity, Comfort, Empathy, God's Mercy, Kindness, Mercy, Suffering, Sympathy, Understanding]

COMPETITION

The race is not to the swift, nor the battle to the strong, neither yet bread to the wise, nor yet riches to men of understanding, nor yet favour to men of skill; but time and chance happeneth to them all.
Eccl. 9:11

If thou hast run with the footmen, and they have wearied thee, then how canst thou contend with horses?
Jer. 12:5

[*See also* Loss]

COMPLAINTS

Ye have wept in the ears of the Lord.
Num. 11:18

Doth the wild ass bray when he hath grass?
Job 6:5

I will speak in the anguish of my spirit; I will complain in the bitterness of my soul.
Job 7:11

Should thy lies make men hold their peace?
Job 11:3

As for me, is my complaint to man?
Job 21:4

Why dost thou strive against Him? for He giveth not account of any of His matters.
>   *Job 33:13*

Wilt thou condemn Him that is most just?
>   *Job 34:17*

[*See also* Acceptance, Contentment]

COMPROMISE

If thou wilt take the left hand, then I will go to the right; or if thou depart to the right hand, then I will go to the left.
>   *Gen. 13:9*

Peradventure there shall lack five of the fifty righteous: wilt Thou destroy all the city for lack of five?
>   *Gen. 18:28*

Do with them what seemeth good unto you: but unto this man do not so vile a thing.
>   *Judg. 19:24*

Divide the living child in two, and give half to the one, and half to the other.
>   *1 Kings 3:25*

[*See also* Arguments]

CONCEIT

To whom would the king delight to do honour more than to myself?
>   *Haman*
>   *Esther 6:6*

Art thou the first man that was born? or wast thou made before the hills?
>   *Job 15:7*

Hast thou heard the secret of God?
>   *Job 15:8*

Seest thou a man wise in his own conceit? there is more hope of a fool than of him.
>   *Prov. 26:12*

The sluggard is wiser in his own conceit than seven men that can render a reason.
>   *Prov. 26:16*

He that trusteth in his own heart is a fool.
>   *Prov. 28:26*

Be not righteous over much; neither make thyself over wise.
>   *Eccl. 7:16*

Woe unto them that are wise in their own eyes.
>   *Isa. 5:21*
>   See also *Prov. 3:7*

Thy wisdom and thy knowledge, it hath perverted thee; and thou hast said in thine heart, I am, and none else beside me.
>   *Isa. 47:10*

Thy terribleness hath deceived thee, and the pride of thine heart.
>   *Jer. 49:16*

But thou didst trust in thine own beauty.
>   *Ezek. 16:15*

Thou hast corrupted thy wisdom by reason of thy brightness.
>   *Ezek. 28:17*

The pride of thine heart hath deceived thee.
>   *Obad. 3*

[*See also* Arrogance, Boasting, Gloating, Humility, Pride, Self-Righteousness]

CONDUCT

See Behavior.

CONDUCT TOWARD GOD

Walk before Me, and be thou perfect.
>   *God to Abram*
>   *Gen. 17:1*

What doth the Lord thy God require of thee, but to fear the Lord thy God, to walk in all His ways, and to love Him, and to serve the Lord thy God with all thy heart and with all thy soul.
>   *Deut. 10:12*

Thou shalt fear the Lord thy God; Him shalt thou serve, and to Him shalt thou cleave, and swear by His name.
>   *Deut. 10:20*
>   See also *Deut. 6:13*

Thou shalt be perfect with the Lord thy God.
Deut. 18:13

How should man be just with God?
Job 9:2

[*See also* Behavior, Fear of God, Love of God, Service to God, and the Appendix at p. 272]

CONFESSION

I have sinned against the Lord.
David
2 Sam. 12:13

We have sinned, and have done perversely, we have committed wickedness.
1 Kings 8:47

We have sinned, we have done amiss, and have dealt wickedly.
2 Chron. 6:37

My sin is ever before me.
Ps. 51:3

My sins are not hid from Thee.
Ps. 69:5

We have sinned with our fathers, we have committed iniquity, we have done wickedly.
Ps. 106:6

Acknowledge thine iniquity, that thou hast transgressed against the Lord.
Jer. 3:13

We have sinned against the Lord our God, we and our fathers, from our youth even unto this day.
Jer. 3:25

We have sinned, we have done wickedly.
Dan. 9:15

[*See also* Acknowledgment, Contrition, Forgiveness, Repentance]

CONFIDENCE

Let us go up at once, and possess it; for we are well able to overcome it.
(it: Canaan)
Num. 13:30

Is not the Lord gone out before thee?
Judg. 4:14

There is no restraint to the Lord to save by many or by few.
Jonathan
1 Sam. 14:6

The Lord that delivered me out of the paw of the lion, and out of the paw of the bear, He will deliver me out of the hand of this Philistine.
David
1 Sam. 17:37

This day will the Lord deliver thee into mine hand.
David to Goliath
1 Sam. 17:46

The battle is the Lord's.
1 Sam. 17:47

Be strong, and of good courage; dread not, nor be dismayed.
E.g., 1 Chron. 22:13

Our God shall fight for us.
Neh. 4:20

Let me be weighed in an even balance, that God may know mine integrity.
Job 31:6

Yea, though I walk through the valley of the shadow of death, I will fear no evil: for Thou art with me.
Ps. 23:4

Be of good courage, and He shall strengthen your heart, all ye that hope in the Lord.
Ps. 31:24
See also Ps. 27:14

He only is my rock and my salvation: He is my defence; I shall not be moved.
Ps. 62:6

In Thee, O Lord, do I put my trust.
Ps. 71:1
See also, e.g., 1 Sam. 22:3

The Lord is on my side; I will not fear: what can man do unto me?
Ps. 118:6
See also Heb. 13:6

He that walketh uprightly walketh surely.
Prov. 10:9

Lift up thy voice with strength; lift it up, be not afraid.
Isa. 40:9

Thy God whom thou servest continually, He will deliver thee.
Dan. 6:16

The flight shall perish from the swift, and the strong shall not strengthen his force, neither shall the mighty deliver himself.
Amos 2:14

Rejoice not against me, O mine enemy: when I fall, I shall arise.
Mic. 7:8

[*See also* Courage, Faith, Pride, Reliability, Timidity]

CONFUSION

Let us go down, and there confound their language, that they may not understand one another's speech.
Gen. 11:7

Babel; because the Lord did there confound the language.
Gen. 11:9

[*See also* Chaos]

CONQUEST

If the Lord delight in us, then He will bring us into this land.
Joshua and Caleb
Num. 14:8

There shall not a man of them stand before thee.
God to Joshua
Josh. 10:8

The hill is not enough for us.
Josh. 17:16

Ye shall possess their land, as the Lord your God hath promised unto you.
Josh. 23:5

Behold, I have delivered the land into his hand.
Judg. 1:2

Whomsoever the Lord our God shall drive out from before us, them will we possess.
Judg. 11:24

We will light upon him as the dew falleth on the ground.
2 Sam. 17:12

There was none that moved the wing, or opened the mouth, or peeped.
Isa. 10:14

They are cruel, and have no mercy; their voice roareth like the sea.
Jer. 6:23

She that was great among the nations, and princess among the provinces, how is she become tributary!
Lam. 1:1

Our inheritance is turned to strangers, our houses to aliens.
Lam. 5:2

[*See also* War]

CONSCIENCE

Thou knowest all the wickedness which thine heart is privy to.
1 Kings 2:44

My righteousness I hold fast, and will not let it go: my heart shall not reproach me so long as I live.
Job 27:6

The wicked flee when no man pursueth.
Prov. 28:1

[*See also* Guilt, Honesty, Integrity, Soul]

CONSECRATION

Sanctify unto Me all the firstborn.
Ex. 13:2

The males shall be the Lord's.
Ex. 13:12

The firstborn of thy sons shalt thou give unto Me.
Ex. 22:29

The tabernacle shall be sanctified by My glory.
Ex. 29:43

[*See also* Holiness]

CONSEQUENCES

His wife looked back from behind him, and she became a pillar of salt.
Gen. 19:26

Because ye are turned away from the Lord, therefore the Lord will not be with you.
Num. 14:43

Because thou hast rejected the word of the Lord, He hath also rejected thee from being king.
Samuel to Saul
1 Sam. 15:23

Thus saith the Lord, Ye have forsaken Me, and therefore have I also left you.
2 Chron. 12:5

Let me alone, that I may speak, and let come on me what will.
Job 13:13

His mischief shall return upon his own head.
Ps. 7:16

The labour of the righteous tendeth to life: the fruit of the wicked to sin.
Prov. 10:16

[*See also* Punishment, Reciprocity, Retribution, Revenge, Reward]

CONSPIRACY

See Betrayal, Crime.

CONTAMINATION

Shall one man sin, and wilt Thou be wroth with all the congregation?
Num. 16:22

Keep yourselves from the accursed thing, lest ye make yourselves accursed.
Josh. 6:18

[*See also* Corruption, Purity]

CONTEMPT

Am I a dog, that thou comest to me with staves?
Goliath to David
1 Sam. 17:43

If thou wilt give me half thine house, I will not go in with thee, neither will I eat bread nor drink water in this place.
1 Kings 13:8

They that are younger than I have me in derision, whose fathers I would have disdained to have set with the dogs of my flock.
Job 30:1

[*See also* Hatred, Scorn]

CONTENTMENT

Would to God we had been content, and dwelt on the other side Jordan!
Josh. 7:7

Should I forsake my sweetness, and my good fruit, and go to be promoted over the trees?
Fig tree to other trees
Judg. 9:11

Should I leave my wine, which cheereth God and man, and go to be promoted over the trees?
Vine to trees
Judg. 9:13

Doth the wild ass bray when he hath grass?
Job 6:5

Better is little with the fear of the Lord than great treasure and trouble therewith.
Prov. 15:16

Give me neither poverty nor riches; feed me with food convenient for me.
Prov. 30:8

The eye is not satisfied with seeing, nor the ear filled with hearing.
Eccl. 1:8

Better is an handful with quietness, than

both the hands full with travail and vexation of spirit.
Eccl. 4:6

[*See also* Greed, Happiness, Satisfaction, Serenity]

CONTINUITY

As I was with Moses, so I will be with thee.
God to Joshua
Josh. 1:5, Josh. 3:7

The sun also ariseth.
Eccl. 1:5

Unto the place from whence the rivers come, thither they return again.
Eccl. 1:7

A time to be born, and a time to die; a time to plant, and a time to pluck up that which is planted.
Eccl. 3:2

The morning cometh, and also the night.
Isa. 21:12

CONTRITION

Thou art more righteous than I: for thou hast rewarded me good, whereas I have rewarded thee evil.
Saul to David
1 Sam. 24:17

I have sinned.
Saul to David
1 Sam. 26:21

Behold, I have played the fool, and have erred exceedingly.
1 Sam. 26:21

I beseech Thee, O Lord, take away the iniquity of Thy servant; for I have done very foolishly.
David to God
2 Sam. 24:10

Because he humbleth himself before Me, I will not bring the evil in his days: but in his son's days will I bring the evil.
1 Kings 21:29

Thou hast done right, but we have done wickedly.
Israelites to God
Neh. 9:33

Behold, I am vile; what shall I answer Thee?
Job to God
Job 40:4

A broken and a contrite heart, O God, Thou wilt not despise.
Ps. 51:17

I have gone astray like a lost sheep; seek Thy servant.
Ps. 119:176
See also Isa. 53:6

[*See also* Confession, Humility, Regret]

CONVERSION

Thy people shall be my people, and thy God my God.
Ruth 1:16

I am sought of them that asked not for Me; I am found of them that sought Me not.
Isa. 65:1
See also Rom. 10:20

[*See also* Evangelism]

COOPERATION

Now nothing will be restrained from them, which they have imagined to do.
Gen. 11:6

Is not the hand of Joab with thee in all this?
2 Sam. 14:19

I am as thou art, and my people as thy people.
2 Chron. 18:3
See also 1 Kings 22:4

Shouldest thou help the ungodly, and love them that hate the Lord?
2 Chron. 19:2

Through wisdom is an house builded; and by understanding it is established.
Prov. 24:3

Two are better than one; because they have a good reward for their labour.
Eccl. 4:9

Woe to him that is alone when he falleth; for he hath not another to help him up.
Eccl. 4:10

If two lie together, then they have heat: but how can one be warm alone?
Eccl. 4:11

A threefold cord is not quickly broken.
Eccl. 4:12

Can two walk together, except they be agreed?
Amos 3:3

[*See also* Brotherhood, Planning, Unity]

CORRUPTION

Thou canst not stand before thine enemies, until ye take away the accursed thing from among you.
Josh. 7:13

Wherefore kick ye at My sacrifice and at Mine offering?
1 Sam. 2:29

I will raise Me up a faithful priest.
1 Sam. 2:35

His sons walked not in his ways, but turned aside after lucre.
1 Sam. 8:3

Hast thou killed, and also taken possession?
(thou: Ahab)
1 Kings 21:19

Who can bring a clean thing out of an unclean? not one.
Job 14:4

Fire shall consume the tabernacles of bribery.
Job 15:34

There is none that doeth good, no, not one.
Ps. 14:3, Ps. 53:3, Rom. 3:12

Lord, how long shall the wicked, how long shall the wicked triumph?
Ps. 94:3

The profit of the earth is for all: the king himself is served by the field.
Eccl. 5:9

One sinner destroyeth much good.
Eccl. 9:18

From the least of them even unto the greatest of them every one is given to covetousness; and from the prophet even unto the priest every one dealeth falsely.
Jer. 6:13
See also Jer. 8:10

Woe unto him that buildeth his house by unrighteousness, and his chambers by wrong.
Jer. 22:13

All that honoured her despise her, because they have seen her nakedness.
Lam. 1:8

Woe be to the shepherds of Israel that do feed themselves! should not the shepherds feed the flocks?
Ezek. 34:2

They sold the righteous for silver, and the poor for a pair of shoes.
Amos 2:6

Ye have turned judgment into gall, and the fruit of righteousness into hemlock.
Amos 6:12

The best of them is as a brier: the most upright is sharper than a thorn hedge.
Mic. 7:4

[*See also* Bribery, Decadence, Good and Evil, Honesty, Injustice, Lawlessness, Purity, Wickedness]

COURAGE

Be strong, and quit yourselves like men.
1 Sam. 4:9

Let no man's heart fail because of him; thy servant will go and fight with this Philistine.
David, about Goliath
1 Sam. 17:32

They were swifter than eagles, they were stronger than lions.
2 Sam. 1:23

Let us play the men for our people.
2 Sam. 10:12

Is not this the blood of the men that went in jeopardy of their lives?
2 Sam. 23:17

With the jeopardy of their lives they brought it.
1 Chron. 11:19

Be of good courage.
E.g., 1 Chron. 19:13

Should such a man as I flee?
Neh. 6:11

He mocketh at fear, and is not affrighted; neither turneth he back from the sword.
Job 39:22

The Lord is the strength of my life; of whom shall I be afraid?
Ps. 27:1

Be of good courage, and He shall strengthen your heart, all ye that hope in the Lord.
Ps. 31:24
See also Ps. 27:14

The voice of him that crieth in the wilderness.
Isa. 40:3
See also, e.g., Matt. 3:3

I have trodden the winepress alone; and of the people there was none with me.
Isa. 63:3

Be not afraid of them, neither be afraid of their words.
Ezek. 2:6

When my soul fainted within me I remembered the Lord.
Jonah 2:7

Fear not, but let your hands be strong.
Zech. 8:13

[*See also* Confidence, Encouragement, Fear]

COURTESY

The poor useth intreaties; but the rich answereth roughly.
Prov. 18:23

[*See also* Behavior, Hospitality]

COVENANT

Neither shall there any more be a flood to destroy the earth.
Gen. 9:11

I do set My bow in the cloud, and it shall be for a token of a covenant between Me and the earth.
God to Noah
Gen. 9:13

I will make of thee a great nation.
God to Abram
Gen. 12:2

In thee shall all families of the earth be blessed.
God to Abram
Gen. 12:3
See also Gen. 28:14

My covenant is with thee, and thou shalt be a father of many nations.
God to Abram
Gen. 17:4

Ye shall circumcise the flesh of your foreskin; and it shall be a token of the covenant betwixt Me and you.
Gen. 17:11

I will multiply thy seed as the stars of the heaven, and as the sand which is upon the sea shore.
God to Abraham
Gen. 22:17

Thy seed shall be as the dust of the earth.
God to Jacob
Gen. 28:14
See also Gen. 13:16

It is a covenant of salt for ever before the Lord.
Num. 18:19

He will not forsake thee, neither destroy

thee, nor forget the covenant of thy fathers which He sware unto them.
Deut. 4:31

The Lord made not this covenant with our fathers, but with us, even us, who are all of us here alive this day.
Deut. 5:3

There hath not failed one word of all His good promise.
1 Kings 8:56

The covenant that I have made with you ye shall not forget; neither shall ye fear other gods.
2 Kings 17:38

Unto thee will I give the land of Canaan, the lot of your inheritance.
1 Chron. 16:18, Ps. 105:11

I will ordain a place for My people Israel.
1 Chron. 17:9

He will ever be mindful of His covenant.
Ps. 111:5
See also 1 Chron. 16:15

Cursed be the man that obeyeth not the words of this covenant.
Jer. 11:3

Remember, break not Thy covenant with us.
Jer. 14:21

Ye shall be My people, and I will be your God.
E.g., Jer. 30:22
See also Jer. 24:7

Come, and let us join ourselves to the Lord.
Jer. 50:5

[*See also* Chosen People, Circumcision]

COWARDICE

The sound of a shaken leaf shall chase them.
Lev. 26:36

We be not able to go up against the people; for they are stronger than we.
Num. 13:31

The hearts of the people melted, and became as water.
Josh. 7:5

O Lord, what shall I say, when Israel turneth their backs before their enemies!
Josh. 7:8

As people being ashamed steal away when they flee in battle.
2 Sam. 19:3

Should such a man as I flee?
Neh. 6:11

Their might hath failed; they became as women.
Jer. 51:30

[*See also* Defeat, Fear, Timidity]

CREATION

In the beginning God created the heaven and the earth.
Gen. 1:1

The earth was without form, and void; and darkness was upon the face of the deep.
Gen. 1:2

And God said, Let there be light: and there was light.
Gen. 1:3

And God made two great lights; the greater light to rule the day, and the lesser light to rule the night.
Gen. 1:16

God created man in His own image, in the image of God created He him; male and female created He them.
Gen. 1:27
See also Gen. 5:1–2

And God saw every thing that He had made, and, behold, it was very good.
Gen. 1:31

The Lord God formed man of the dust of the ground, and breathed into his nostrils the breath of life.
Gen. 2:7

The rib, which the Lord God had taken from man, made He a woman.
Gen. 2:22

Male and female created He them; and blessed them.
Gen. 5:2

It repented the Lord that He had made man on the earth.
Gen. 6:6

Who hath made man's mouth? or who maketh the dumb, or deaf, or the seeing, or the blind? have not I the Lord?
Ex. 4:11

In six days the Lord made heaven and earth, the sea, and all that in them is.
Ex. 20:11

In six days the Lord made heaven and earth, and on the seventh day He rested, and was refreshed.
Ex. 31:17

Hast Thou not poured me out as milk, and curdled me like cheese?
Job 10:10

He stretcheth out the north over the empty place, and hangeth the earth upon nothing.
Job 26:7

Who laid the corner stone thereof?
Job 38:6

By the word of the Lord were the heavens made.
Ps. 33:6

He spake, and it was done; He commanded, and it stood fast.
Ps. 33:9

It is He that hath made us, and not we ourselves.
Ps. 100:3

I will praise Thee; for I am fearfully and wonderfully made.
Ps. 139:14

The Lord hath made all things for Himself: yea, even the wicked for the day of evil.
Prov. 16:4

I have created him for My glory, I have formed him; yea, I have made him.
Isa. 43:7

He hath established it, He created it not in vain, He formed it to be inhabited.
Isa. 45:18

We are the clay, and Thou our potter.
Isa. 64:8

We all are the work of Thy hand.
Isa. 64:8

I create new heavens and a new earth: and the former shall not be remembered, nor come into mind.
Isa. 65:17

He hath made the earth by His power.
Jer. 10:12

He hath established the world by His wisdom, and hath stretched out the heavens by His discretion.
Jer. 10:12

He hath made the earth by His power, He hath established the world by His wisdom.
Jer. 51:15

[*See also* Beginnings]

CREATIVITY

See Achievement, Building, Planning.

CREDIBILITY

Is the Lord's hand waxed short?
Num. 11:23

I have not said in vain that I would do this evil unto them.
Ezek. 6:10

[*See also* Belief, Doubt, Skepticism]

CRIME

Thou shalt not steal.
Eighth Commandment
Ex. 20:15
See also Lev. 19:11, Deut. 5:19,
  Matt. 19:18

Ye shall not pollute the land wherein ye are.
Num. 35:33

Defile not therefore the land which ye shall inhabit.
Num. 35:34

Why hast thou troubled us? the Lord shall trouble thee this day.
Joshua to Achan
Josh. 7:25

Wickedness proceedeth from the wicked: but mine hand shall not be upon thee.
1 Sam. 24:13

Enter not into the path of the wicked, and go not in the way of evil men.
Prov. 4:14

Men do not despise a thief, if he steal to satisfy his soul when he is hungry.
Prov. 6:30

Treasures of wickedness profit nothing.
Prov. 10:2

He that pursueth evil pursueth it to his own death.
Prov. 11:19

Whoso is partner with a thief hateth his own soul.
Prov. 29:24

Woe to the bloody city! it is all full of lies and robbery.
(it: Nineveh)
Nah. 3:1

[*See also* Depravity, Evil, Lawlessness, Restitution, Scheming, Wicked People, Wickedness]

CRIMINALS

He taketh the wise in their own craftiness.
Job 5:13

They are of those that rebel against the light.
Job 24:13

The morning is to them even as the shadow of death.
Job 24:17

There is no darkness, nor shadow of

death, where the workers of iniquity may hide themselves.
Job 34:22

They say, Who shall see them?
Ps. 64:5

As a cage is full of birds, so are their houses full of deceit.
Jer. 5:27

They consider not in their hearts that I remember all their wickedness.
Hos. 7:2

Woe to them that devise iniquity, and work evil upon their beds!
Mic. 2:1

Woe to him that increaseth that which is not his!
Hab. 2:6

[*See also* Crime, Depravity, Evil, Lawlessness, Restitution, Scheming, Wicked People, Wickedness]

CRITICISM

Ye are forgers of lies, ye are all physicians of no value.
Job to his friends
Job 13:4

The foolish man reproacheth Thee daily.
Ps. 74:22

Reprove not a scorner, lest he hate thee: rebuke a wise man, and he will love thee.
Prov. 9:8

He that refuseth reproof erreth.
Prov. 10:17

Whoso loveth instruction loveth knowledge: but he that hateth reproof is brutish.
Prov. 12:1

A wise son heareth his father's instruction: but a scorner heareth not rebuke.
Prov. 13:1

A fool despiseth his father's instruction.
Prov. 15:5

He that hateth reproof shall die.
Prov. 15:10

A scorner loveth not one that reproveth him.
Prov. 15:12

A reproof entereth more into a wise man than an hundred stripes into a fool.
Prov. 17:10

Faithful are the wounds of a friend; but the kisses of an enemy are deceitful.
Prov. 27:6

It is better to hear the rebuke of the wise, than for a man to hear the song of fools.
Eccl. 7:5

Take no heed unto all words that are spoken; lest thou hear thy servant curse thee.
Eccl. 7:21

He hath made my mouth like a sharp sword.
Isa. 49:2

Fear ye not the reproach of men, neither be ye afraid of their revilings.
Isa. 51:7

They hate him that rebuketh in the gate, and they abhor him that speaketh uprightly.
Amos 5:10

[*See also* Accusations, Chastisement, Discipline, Guidance, Public Opinion, Scorn, Slander]

CRUELTY

I will harden his heart, that he shall not let the people go.
Ex. 4:21

Let me not fall into the hand of man.
1 Chron. 21:13, 2 Sam. 24:14

In my thirst they gave me vinegar to drink.
Ps. 69:21

The merciful man doeth good to his own soul: but he that is cruel troubleth his own flesh.
Prov. 11:17

The tender mercies of the wicked are cruel.
Prov. 12:10

They shall have no pity on the fruit of the womb; their eye shall not spare children.
Isa. 13:18

They are cruel, and have no mercy; their voice roareth like the sea.
Jer. 6:23

They sold the righteous for silver, and the poor for a pair of shoes.
Amos 2:6

[*See also* Oppression, Persecution, Tyrants]

CULTIVATION

Six years thou shalt sow thy land, and shalt gather in the fruits thereof: But the seventh year thou shalt let it rest and lie still; that the poor of thy people may eat.
Ex. 23:10–11

He causeth the grass to grow for the cattle, and herb for the service of man.
Ps. 104:14

They that sow in tears shall reap in joy.
Ps. 126:5

He that goeth forth and weepeth, bearing precious seed, shall doubtless come again with rejoicing, bringing his sheaves with him.
Ps. 126:6

A time to plant, and a time to pluck up.
Eccl. 3:2

[*See also* Growth, Nature]

CURSES

Upon thy belly shalt thou go, and dust shalt thou eat all the days of thy life.
God to serpent
Gen. 3:14

A fugitive and a vagabond shalt thou be in the earth.
Gen. 4:12

How shall I curse, whom God hath not cursed? or how shall I defy, whom the Lord hath not defied?
Balaam to Balak
Num. 23:8

Cursed be the man before the Lord, that riseth up and buildeth this city Jericho.
Josh. 6:26

The sword shall never depart from thine house.
(thine: David)
2 Sam. 12:10

Get thee to thine own house: and when thy feet enter into the city, the child shall die.
1 Kings 14:12

Touch all that he hath, and he will curse Thee to Thy face.
Satan to God, about Job
Job 1:11

Dost thou still retain thine integrity? curse God, and die.
Job's wife to Job
Job 2:9

Let their way be dark and slippery.
Ps. 35:6

Let his children be fatherless, and his wife a widow.
Ps. 109:9

I will prepare thee unto blood, and blood shall pursue thee.
Ezek. 35:6

Give them, O Lord: what wilt Thou give? give them a miscarrying womb and dry breasts.
Hos. 9:14

Thou shalt eat, but not be satisfied.
Mic. 6:14

I will curse your blessings.
God to wayward priests
Mal. 2:2

[*See also* Blasphemy, Blessing, Disobedience, Punishment, Speech]

CYNICISM

The sword devoureth one as well as another.
David, about Bathsheba's husband
2 Sam. 11:25

Vanity of vanities; all is vanity.
Eccl. 1:2
See also Eccl. 12:8

Behold, all is vanity and vexation of spirit.
Eccl. 1:14
See also, e.g., Eccl. 2:17

He that increaseth knowledge increaseth sorrow.
Eccl. 1:18

What hath man of all his labour, and of the vexation of his heart, wherein he hath laboured under the sun?
Eccl. 2:22

What profit hath he that hath laboured for the wind?
Eccl. 5:16

A man hath no better thing under the sun, than to eat, and to drink, and to be merry.
Eccl. 8:15

Money answereth all things.
Eccl. 10:19

[*See also* Doubt, Skepticism]

DAMNATION

See Salvation.

DANCE

Let them praise His name in the dance: let them sing praises unto Him with the timbrel and harp.
Ps. 149:3
See also Ps. 150:4

A time to mourn, and a time to dance.
Eccl. 3:4

[*See also* Music, Song]

DANGER

Thou shalt fear day and night, and shalt have none assurance of thy life.
Deut. 28:66

The Philistines be upon thee, Samson.
E.g., Judges 16:9

Let all thy wants lie upon me; only lodge
not in the street.
   Judg. 19:20

There is but a step between me and death.
   1 Sam. 20:3

He that seeketh my life seeketh thy life.
   David to Abiathar
   1 Sam. 22:23

The wicked watcheth the righteous, and
seeketh to slay him.
   Ps. 37:32

We are counted as sheep for the slaughter.
   Ps. 44:22

We went through fire and through water.
   Ps. 66:12

A thousand shall fall at thy side, and ten
thousand at thy right hand; but it shall not
come nigh thee.
   Ps. 91:7

Though I walk in the midst of trouble,
Thou wilt revive me.
   Ps. 138:7

Sharp as a twoedged sword.
   Prov. 5:4

Can a man take fire in his bosom, and his
clothes not be burned?
   Prov. 6:27

Can one go upon hot coals, and his feet
not be burned?
   Prov. 6:28

Let a bear robbed of her whelps meet a
man, rather than a fool in his folly.
   Prov. 17:12

Go not forth into the field, nor walk by
the way; for the sword of the enemy and
fear is on every side.
   Jer. 6:25

The sword is without, and the pestilence
and the famine within.
   Ezek. 7:15

Our God whom we serve is able to deliver
us from the burning fiery furnace.
   Dan. 3:17

[*See also* Safety, Traps, Trouble]

DARKNESS

See Enlightenment, Light and Darkness.

DEATH

Dust thou art, and unto dust shalt thou
return.
   Gen. 3:19

Then Abraham gave up the ghost, and
died in a good old age.
   Gen. 25:8

Now let me die, since I have seen thy face,
because thou art yet alive.
   Jacob to Joseph
   Gen. 46:30

Your carcases shall fall in this wilderness.
   God to Israelites
   Num. 14:29

Let me die the death of the righteous, and
let my last end be like his!
   Num. 23:10

Alas, who shall live when God doeth this!
   Balaam
   Num. 24:23

He that is hanged is accursed of God.
   Deut. 21:23
   See also Gal. 3:13

This day I am going the way of all the
earth.
   Josh. 23:14

Why tarry the wheels of his chariots?
   Judg. 5:28

And Samson said, Let me die with the
Philistines.
   Judg. 16:30

Where thou diest, will I die, and there will
I be buried.
   Ruth 1:17

I went out full, and the Lord hath brought
me home again empty.
   Ruth 1:21

To morrow shalt thou and thy sons be
with me.
   Samuel, after his death, to Saul
   1 Sam. 28:19

In their death they were not divided.
   (they: Saul and Jonathan)
   2 Sam. 1:23

The sword devoureth one as well as another.
David, about Bathsheba's husband
2 Sam. 11:25

Can I bring him back again?
David, about his son
2 Sam. 12:23

I shall go to him, but he shall not return to me.
David, about his son
2 Sam. 12:23

I go the way of all the earth.
1 Kings 2:2

I will not put thee to death with the sword.
1 Kings 2:8

Set thine house in order; for thou shalt die, and not live.
2 Kings 20:1, Isa. 38:1

Thou shalt be gathered into thy grave in peace.
2 Kings 22:20

He died in a good old age, full of days, riches, and honour.
(He: David)
1 Chron. 29:28

There the wicked cease from troubling; and there the weary be at rest.
Job 3:17

The small and great are there; and the servant is free from his master.
Job, speaking of death
Job 3:19

He that goeth down to the grave shall come up no more.
Job 7:9

He destroyeth the perfect and the wicked.
Job 9:22

Before I go whence I shall not return, even to the land of darkness and the shadow of death.
Job 10:21

Man dieth, and wasteth away: yea, man giveth up the ghost, and where is he?
Job 14:10

If a man die, shall he live again?
Job 14:14

My breath is corrupt, my days are extinct, the graves are ready for me.
Job 17:1

I have said to corruption, Thou art my father: to the worm, Thou art my mother, and my sister.
Job 17:14

Though after my skin worms destroy this body, yet in my flesh shall I see God.
Job 19:26

They shall lie down alike in the dust, and the worms shall cover them.
Job 21:26

Drought and heat consume the snow waters: so doth the grave those which have sinned.
Job 24:19

The worm shall feed sweetly on him; he shall be no more remembered.
(him: the wicked)
Job 24:20

Have the gates of death been opened unto thee? or hast thou seen the doors of the shadow of death?
God to Job
Job 38:17

In death there is no remembrance of Thee: in the grave who shall give Thee thanks?
Ps. 6:5

Lighten mine eyes, lest I sleep the sleep of death.
Ps. 13:3

Yea, though I walk through the valley of the shadow of death, I will fear no evil: for Thou art with me.
Ps. 23:4

Like sheep they are laid in the grave; death shall feed on them.
Ps. 49:14

They that are far from Thee shall perish.
Ps. 73:27

What man is he that liveth, and shall not see death?
Ps. 89:48

Thou takest away their breath, they die, and return to their dust.
(they: animals)
Ps. 104:29

The dead praise not the Lord.
Ps. 115:17

Righteousness delivereth from death.
Prov. 10:2, Prov. 11:4

When the wicked perish, there is shouting.
Prov. 11:10

There are three things that are never satisfied, yea, four things say not, It is enough: The grave; and the barren womb; the earth that is not filled with water; and the fire that saith not, It is enough.
Prov. 30:15–16

How dieth the wise man? as the fool.
Eccl. 2:16

That which befalleth the sons of men befalleth beasts.
Eccl. 3:19

All go unto one place.
Eccl. 3:20
See also Eccl. 6:6

As he came forth of his mother's womb, naked shall he return.
Eccl. 5:15

It is better to go to the house of mourning, than to go to the house of feasting: for that is the end of all men; and the living will lay it to his heart.
Eccl. 7:2

There is no man that hath power over the spirit to retain the spirit.
Eccl. 8:8

All things come alike to all.
Eccl. 9:2

Remember the days of darkness; for they shall be many.
Eccl. 11:8

The spirit shall return unto God who gave it.
Eccl. 12:7

Hell hath enlarged herself, and opened her mouth without measure.
Isa. 5:14

Hell from beneath is moved for thee to meet thee at thy coming.
Isa. 14:9

The worm is spread under thee, and the worms cover thee.
Isa. 14:11

He will swallow up death in victory.
Isa. 25:8

We have made a covenant with death, and with hell are we at agreement.
Isa. 28:15

The grave cannot praise Thee, death cannot celebrate Thee: they that go down into the pit cannot hope for Thy truth.
Isa. 38:18

He is brought as a lamb to the slaughter.
Isa. 53:7
See also Jer. 11:19, Acts 8:32

The righteous is taken away from the evil to come.
Isa. 57:1

They shall sleep a perpetual sleep.
Jer. 51:57

Abroad the sword bereaveth, at home there is as death.
Lam. 1:20

They that be slain with the sword are better than they that be slain with hunger.
Lam. 4:9

I have no pleasure in the death of him that dieth, saith the Lord God.
Ezek. 18:32

I have no pleasure in the death of the wicked.
Ezek. 33:11

Turn ye, turn ye from your evil ways; for why will ye die?
Ezek. 33:11
See also Jonah 3:8

I will prepare thee unto blood, and blood shall pursue thee.
Ezek. 35:6

O death, I will be thy plagues; O grave, I will be thy destruction.
Hos. 13:14
See also 1 Cor. 15:55

[*See also* Annihilation, Burial, Despair, Destruction, Eternal Life, Hanging, Life, Life and Death, Martyrdom, Mortality, Mourning, Punishment, Resurrection]

See Borrowing.

Sodom and Gomorrah.
Gen. 18:20, Gen. 19:28

Thou art waxen fat, thou art grown thick, thou art covered with fatness.
Deut. 32:15

[*See also* Corruption, Depravity, Evil, Immorality, Wickedness]

Why didst thou not tell me that she was thy wife?
Pharaoh to Abram
Gen. 12:18

And Jacob said unto his father, I am Esau thy firstborn.
Gen. 27:19

The voice is Jacob's voice, but the hands are the hands of Esau.
Isaac
Gen. 27:22

Did not I serve with thee for Rachel?
Jacob to Laban
Gen. 29:25

Wherefore have ye beguiled us?
Josh. 9:22

I have a secret errand unto thee, O king.
Ehud to King of Moab
Judg. 3:19

Turn in, my lord, turn in to me; fear not.
Jael to Sisera
Judg. 4:18

He asked water, and she gave him milk.
(she: Jael)
Judg. 5:25

Thou dost but hate me, and lovest me not.
Samson's wife
Judg. 14:16

What meaneth then this bleating of the sheep in mine ears?
1 Sam. 15:14

Wherefore then layest thou a snare for my life, to cause me to die?
1 Sam. 28:9

I am a prophet also as thou art; and an angel spake unto me by the word of the Lord.
1 Kings 13:18

Why feignest thou thyself to be another?
1 Kings 14:6

Ahab served Baal a little; but Jehu shall serve him much.
2 Kings 10:18

Let us build with you: for we seek your God, as ye do.
Ezra 4:2

As one man mocketh another, do ye so mock Him?
Job 13:9

The workers of iniquity, which speak peace to their neighbours, but mischief is in their hearts.
Ps. 28:3

Saying, Peace, peace; when there is no peace.
Jer. 6:14, Jer. 8:11
See also Ezek. 13:10

Let not your prophets and your diviners, that be in the midst of you, deceive you.
Jer. 29:8

Ye say, The Lord saith it; albeit I have not spoken.
Ezek. 13:7

Cursed be the deceiver.
Mal. 1:14

[*See also* Appearance, Dishonesty, Hypocrisy, Lies, Self-Deception, Truth]

Do what seemeth good unto thee.
Israelites to Saul
1 Sam. 14:40

Let us choose to us judgment: let us know among ourselves what is good.
Job 34:4

A time to keep, and a time to cast away.
Eccl. 3:6

A time to keep silence, and a time to speak.
Eccl. 3:7

[*See also* Certainty, Choice, Compromise, Indecision, Procrastination, Time, and the Appendix at p. 274]

DEEDS

The Lord is a God of knowledge, and by Him actions are weighed.
1 Sam. 2:3

Even a child is known by his doings.
Prov. 20:11

God shall bring every work into judgment.
Eccl. 12:14

[*See also* Achievement, Ministry]

DEFEAT

Knowest thou not yet that Egypt is destroyed?
Pharaoh's servants to Pharaoh
Ex. 10:7

How should one chase a thousand, and two put ten thousand to flight, except their Rock had sold them, and the Lord had shut them up?
Deut. 32:30

Thus shall the Lord do to all your enemies against whom ye fight.
Josh. 10:25

Whithersoever they went out, the hand of the Lord was against them for evil.
Judg. 2:15

How are the mighty fallen, and the weapons of war perished!
2 Sam. 1:27

Their gods are gods of the hills; therefore they were stronger than we.
1 Kings 20:23

He shall not come into this city, nor shoot an arrow there.
2 Kings 19:32, Isa. 37:33

By the way that he came, by the same shall he return.
2 Kings 19:33, Isa. 37:34

All the men of war fled by night.
2 Kings 25:4

They cried, but there was none to save them: even unto the Lord, but He answered them not.
Ps. 18:41

How art thou fallen from heaven, O Lucifer, son of the morning!
Isa. 14:12

Their might hath failed; they became as women.
Jer. 51:30

Babylon shall become heaps, a dwelling-place for dragons, an astonishment, and an hissing, without an inhabitant.
Jer. 51:37

They shall sleep a perpetual sleep.
Jer. 51:57

How doth the city sit solitary, that was full of people! how is she become as a widow!
Lam. 1:1
See also Lam. 1:2–22

I will deliver thee into the hand of them whom thou hatest.
Ezek. 23:28

Lament like a virgin girded with sackcloth for the husband of her youth.
Joel 1:8

The flight shall perish from the swift, and the strong shall not strengthen his force, neither shall the mighty deliver himself.
Amos 2:14

He that is courageous among the mighty shall flee away naked in that day.
Amos 2:16

[*See also* Desolation, Destruction, Humiliation, Success, Victory]

DEFIANCE

See Arrogance, Audacity, Rebellion.

DELAY

See Laziness, Patience, Procrastination.

DELIVERANCE

I am the Lord thy God, which have brought thee out of the land of Egypt, out of the house of bondage.
Ex. 20:2
See also, e.g., Ex. 29:46, Deut. 5:6

The Lord brought us forth out of Egypt with a mighty hand, and with an outstretched arm.
Deut. 26:8

Slack not thy hand from thy servants; come up to us quickly, and save us.
Josh. 10:6

Ye cried to Me, and I delivered you out of their hand.
Judg. 10:12

He raiseth up the poor out of the dust, and lifteth up the beggar from the dunghill.
1 Sam. 2:8
See also Ps. 113:7

I will call on the Lord, who is worthy to be praised: so shall I be saved from mine enemies.
2 Sam. 22:4
See also Ps. 18:3

He shall deliver you out of the hand of all your enemies.
2 Kings 17:39

He shall hear a rumour, and shall return to his own land.
(He: Sennacherib)
2 Kings 19:7
See also Isa. 37:7

Save Thou us out of his hand, that all the kingdoms of the earth may know that Thou art the Lord God, even Thou only.
2 Kings 19:19
See also Isa. 37:20

Deliver us from the heathen, that we may give thanks to Thy holy name.
1 Chron. 16:35

He delivereth the poor in his affliction.
Job 36:15

The Lord blessed the latter end of Job more than his beginning.
Job 42:12

I sought the Lord, and He heard me, and delivered me from all my fears.
Ps. 34:4

Unto God the Lord belong the issues from death.
Ps. 68:20

Deliver me because of mine enemies.
Ps. 69:18

Deliver me in Thy righteousness, and cause me to escape.
Ps. 71:2

Incline Thine ear unto me, and save me.
Ps. 71:2

How long, Lord?
Ps. 79:5, Ps. 89:46

He saved them for His name's sake, that He might make His mighty power to be known.
Ps. 106:8

They cry unto the Lord in their trouble, and He saveth them out of their distresses.
Ps. 107:19

Save with Thy right hand, and answer me.
Ps. 108:6
See also Ps. 60:5

I will lift up mine eyes unto the hills, from whence cometh my help.
Ps. 121:1

Bring my soul out of prison, that I may praise Thy name.
Ps. 142:7

The righteousness of the upright shall deliver them.
Prov. 11:6

Through knowledge shall the just be delivered.
Prov. 11:9

They shall cry unto the Lord because of

the oppressors, and He shall send them a saviour.
Isa. 19:20

To proclaim liberty to the captives, and the opening of the prison to them that are bound.
Isa. 61:1

He that scattered Israel will gather him, and keep him, as a shepherd doth his flock.
Jer. 31:10

Their Redeemer is strong; the Lord of hosts is His name.
Jer. 50:34

My God hath sent His angel, and hath shut the lions' mouths.
Dan. 6:22

He delivereth and rescueth, and He worketh signs and wonders in heaven and in earth.
Dan. 6:27

Whosoever shall call on the name of the Lord shall be delivered.
Joel 2:32
See also, e.g., Acts 2:21

The earth with her bars was about me for ever: yet hast Thou brought up my life from corruption.
Jonah 2:6

The Lord shall yet comfort Zion, and shall yet choose Jerusalem.
Zech. 1:17

[*See also* Escape, Exile, Freedom, Safety, Salvation]

DENIAL

Shall the work say of him that made it, He made me not?
E.g., Isa. 29:16
See also, e.g., Isa. 45:9, Rom. 9:20

[*See also* Atheism, Blasphemy, Godlessness, Self-Denial]

DEPENDENCE

See God's Protection, Reliance.

DEPRAVITY

Do with them what seemeth good unto you: but unto this man do not so vile a thing.
Judg. 19:24

There was no such deed done nor seen from the day that the children of Israel came up out of the land of Egypt unto this day.
Judg. 19:30

He that is of a perverse heart shall be despised.
Prov. 12:8

[*See also* Decadence, Evil, Immorality, Sin, Wickedness]

DEPRESSION

Why is thy countenance sad, seeing thou art not sick?
Neh. 2:2

My soul is weary of my life.
Job 10:1

I have said to corruption, Thou art my father: to the worm, Thou art my mother, and my sister.
Job 17:14

God my rock, Why hast Thou forgotten me?
Ps. 42:9

Save me, O God; for the waters are come in unto my soul.
Ps. 69:1

My soul is full of troubles: and my life draweth nigh unto the grave.
Ps. 88:3

My days are like a shadow that declineth; and I am withered like grass.
Ps. 102:11

A merry heart doeth good like a medicine: but a broken spirit drieth the bones.
Prov. 17:22

A wounded spirit who can bear?
Prov. 18:14

Behold, all is vanity and vexation of spirit.
Eccl. 1:14
See also, e.g., Eccl. 2:17

Therefore I hated life.
Eccl. 2:17

[*See also* Despair, Sorrow]

DEPRIVATION

He satisfieth the longing soul, and filleth the hungry soul with goodness.
Ps. 107:9

To the hungry soul every bitter thing is sweet.
Prov. 27:7

Every one that thirsteth, come ye to the waters, and he that hath no money; come ye, buy, and eat.
Isa. 55:1

[*See also* Famine, Hunger, Thirst]

DESECRATION

See Holiness, Sacrilege.

DESIRE

Get her for me; for she pleaseth me well.
Samson to his father
Judg. 14:3

The desire accomplished is sweet to the soul.
Prov. 13:19

Better is the sight of the eyes than the wandering of the desire.
Eccl. 6:9

In the broad ways I will seek him whom my soul loveth.
Song 3:2

I am my beloved's, and his desire is toward me.
Song 7:10

[*See also* Jealousy, Lust]

DESOLATION

Jerusalem is ruined, and Judah is fallen: because their tongue and their doings are against the Lord.
Isa. 3:8

The land shall be utterly emptied, and utterly spoiled: for the Lord hath spoken this word.
Isa. 24:3

Babylon shall become heaps, a dwelling-place for dragons, an astonishment, and an hissing, without an inhabitant.
Jer. 51:37

How doth the city sit solitary, that was full of people! how is she become as a widow!
Lam. 1:1
See also Lam. 1:2–22

I shall make thee a desolate city, like the cities that are not inhabited.
Ezek. 26:19

They shall be desolate in the midst of the countries that are desolate.
Ezek. 30:7

When the whole earth rejoiceth, I will make thee desolate.
Ezek. 35:14

All they that look upon thee shall flee from thee.
(thee: Nineveh)
Nah. 3:7

Nineveh is laid waste: who will bemoan her?
Nah. 3:7

[*See also* Annihilation, Destruction, Loneliness]

DESPAIR

Behold, I am at the point to die: and what profit shall this birthright do to me?
Esau to Jacob
Gen. 25:32

Give me children, or else I die.
Rachel to Jacob
Gen. 30:1

Hast thou taken us away to die in the wilderness?
Israelites to Moses
Ex. 14:11
See also Num. 21:5

What shall I do unto this people? they be almost ready to stone me.
Moses
Ex. 17:4

Would God that we had died in the land of Egypt!
Num. 14:2

O that they were wise, that they understood this, that they would consider their latter end!
Deut. 32:29

Would to God we had been content, and dwelt on the other side Jordan!
Josh. 7:7

Now shall I die for thirst, and fall into the hand of the uncircumcised?
Judg. 15:18

I have drunk neither wine nor strong drink, but have poured out my soul before the Lord.
1 Sam. 1:15

God is departed from me, and answereth me no more, neither by prophets, nor by dreams.
Saul to Samuel
1 Sam. 28:15

I, even I only, am left; and they seek my life, to take it away.
1 Kings 19:10, 14
See also Rom. 11:3

This day is a day of trouble, and of rebuke, and blasphemy.
2 Kings 19:3, Isa. 37:3

Let the day perish wherein I was born.
Job 3:3

Why died I not from the womb? why did I not give up the ghost when I came out of the belly?
Job 3:11

What is mine end, that I should prolong my life?
Job 6:11

Is my strength the strength of stones? or is my flesh of brass?
Job 6:12

My days are swifter than a weaver's shuttle, and are spent without hope.
Job 7:6

Where, and who is He?
Job 9:24

If I be wicked, why then labour I in vain?
Job 9:29

My soul is weary of my life.
Job 10:1

Wherefore then hast Thou brought me forth out of the womb? Oh that I had given up the ghost, and no eye had seen me!
Job 10:18

God hath delivered me to the ungodly, and turned me over into the hands of the wicked.
Job 16:11

O that one might plead for a man with God, as a man pleadeth for his neighbour!
Job 16:21

My breath is corrupt, my days are extinct, the graves are ready for me.
Job 17:1

If I wait, the grave is mine house: I have made my bed in the darkness.
Job 17:13

Where is now my hope?
Job 17:15

I cry aloud, but there is no judgment.
Job 19:7

Mine hope hath He removed like a tree.
Job 19:10

I cry unto Thee, and Thou dost not hear me: I stand up, and Thou regardest me not.
Job 30:20

I am a brother to dragons, and a companion to owls.
Job 30:29

It profiteth a man nothing that he should delight himself with God.
Job 34:9

How long wilt Thou forget me, O Lord? for ever? how long wilt Thou hide Thy face from me?
Ps. 13:1

There is none that doeth good, no, not one.
Ps. 14:3, Ps. 53:3, Rom. 3:12

My God, my God, why hast Thou forsaken me?
Ps. 22:1, Matt. 27:46,
Mark 15:34

I cry in the daytime, but Thou hearest not; and in the night season, and am not silent.
Ps. 22:2

I am forgotten as a dead man out of mind: I am like a broken vessel.
Ps. 31:12

I am poor and needy: make haste unto me, O God.
Ps. 70:5
See also Ps. 40:17

Wilt Thou hide Thyself for ever?
Ps. 89:46

Out of the depths have I cried unto Thee, O Lord.
Ps. 130:1

Bring my soul out of prison, that I may praise Thy name.
Ps. 142:7

Let him drink, and forget his poverty, and remember his misery no more.
Prov. 31:7

Vanity of vanities; all is vanity.
Eccl. 1:2

This also is vanity.
Eccl. 2:15

All his days are sorrows, and his travail grief; yea, his heart taketh not rest in the night.
Eccl. 2:23

All that cometh is vanity.
Eccl. 11:8

Vanity of vanities, saith the preacher; all is vanity.
Eccl. 12:8

I sought him, but I found him not.
Song 3:1, 2

Let us be called by thy name, to take away our reproach.
Isa. 4:1

Fear, and the pit, and the snare, are upon thee, O inhabitant of the earth.
Isa. 24:17

Mine eyes fail with looking upward: O Lord, I am oppressed.
Isa. 38:14

Is not the Lord in Zion?
Jer. 8:19

The harvest is past, the summer is ended, and we are not saved.
Jer. 8:20

Cursed be the day wherein I was born: let not the day wherein my mother bare me be blessed.
Jer. 20:14

Wherefore came I forth out of the womb to see labour and sorrow?
Jer. 20:18

O earth, earth, earth, hear the word of the Lord.
Jer. 22:29

They have cut off my life in the dungeon, and cast a stone upon me.
Lam. 3:53

I called upon Thy name, O Lord, out of the low dungeon.
Lam. 3:55

It is better for me to die than to live.
Jonah 4:3, 8

[*See also* Abandonment, Anguish, Death, Depression, Faith, Hope, Self-Pity]

DESTINY

It was not you that sent me hither, but God.
Joseph to his brothers
Gen. 45:8

Such as are for death, to death; and such as are for the sword, to the sword; and such as are for the famine, to the famine; and such as are for the captivity, to the captivity.

Jer. 15:2

As the clay is in the potter's hand, so are ye in Mine hand, O house of Israel.

Jer. 18:6
See also Rom. 9:21

[*See also* Chance]

DESTRUCTION

Neither shall there any more be a flood to destroy the earth.

Gen. 9:11

Wilt Thou also destroy the righteous with the wicked?

Abraham to God
Gen. 18:23

Alas, who shall live when God doeth this!

Balaam
Num. 24:23

As a consuming fire He shall destroy them, and He shall bring them down before thy face.

Deut. 9:3

The sword without, and terror within, shall destroy both the young man and the virgin, the suckling also with the man of gray hairs.

Deut. 32:25

Cursed be the man before the Lord, that riseth up and buildeth this city Jericho.

Josh. 6:26

Joshua drew not his hand back, wherewith he stretched out the spear.

Josh. 8:26

Why wilt thou swallow up the inheritance of the Lord?

2 Sam. 20:19

I will wipe Jerusalem as a man wipeth a dish, wiping it, and turning it upside down.

2 Kings 21:13

The way of the Lord is strength to the upright: but destruction shall be to the workers of iniquity.

Prov. 10:29

A time to break down, and a time to build up.

Eccl. 3:3

A time to rend, and a time to sew.

Eccl. 3:7

Take us the foxes, the little foxes, that spoil the vines: for our vines have tender grapes.

Song 2:15

Howl ye; for the day of the Lord is at hand.

Isa. 13:6

Her time is near to come, and her days shall not be prolonged.

(Her: Babylon)
Isa. 13:22

As with the people, so with the priest; as with the servant, so with his master; as with the maid, so with her mistress; as with the buyer, so with the seller; as with the lender, so with the borrower; as with the taker of usury, so with the giver of usury to him.

Isa. 24:2

The moth shall eat them up like a garment, and the worm shall eat them like wool.

Isa. 51:8

I have created the waster to destroy.

Isa. 54:16

I will not pity, nor spare, nor have mercy, but destroy them.

Jer. 13:14

That which I have built will I break down, and that which I have planted I will pluck up, even this whole land.

Jer. 45:4

Destruction cometh; it cometh out of the north.

Jer. 46:20

I will bring them down like lambs to the slaughter, like rams with he goats.

Jer. 51:40

Abroad the sword bereaveth, at home there is as death.

Lam. 1:20

In the day of the Lord's anger none escaped nor remained.
Lam. 2:22

Your altars shall be desolate, and your images shall be broken: and I will cast down your slain men before your idols.
Ezek. 6:4

He that is in the field shall die with the sword; and he that is in the city, famine and pestilence shall devour him.
Ezek. 7:15

They shall seek peace, and there shall be none.
Ezek. 7:25

Though these three men, Noah, Daniel, and Job, were in it, they should deliver but their own souls by their righteousness.
Ezek. 14:14

The suburbs shall shake at the sound of the cry of thy pilots.
Ezek. 27:28

That which the locust hath left hath the cankerworm eaten; and that which the cankerworm hath left hath the caterpillar eaten.
Joel 1:4

Shall there be evil in a city, and the Lord hath not done it?
Amos 3:6

I will make thy grave; for thou art vile.
(thy: Nineveh)
Nah. 1:14

All the earth shall be devoured with the fire of My jealousy.
Zeph. 3:8

[*See also* Annihilation, Carnage, Defeat, Desolation, Doom, Restoration, Terror, Violence]

DETERMINATION

I will not let thee go, except thou bless me.
Jacob to Angel
Gen. 32:26

Joshua drew not his hand back, wherewith he stretched out the spear.
Josh. 8:26

Intreat me not to leave thee.
Ruth 1:16

He turned not to the right hand nor to the left.
2 Sam. 2:19

If thou seek Him, He will be found of thee.
1 Chron. 28:9
See also 2 Chron. 15:2

Waters wear the stones.
Job 14:19

I shall not die, but live, and declare the works of the Lord.
Ps. 118:17

Let not your eye spare, neither have ye pity.
Ezek. 9:5

I will do it; I will not go back, neither will I spare, neither will I repent.
Ezek. 24:14

[*See also* Diligence, Effort, Fortitude, Perseverance, Work]

DEVOTION

Serve the Lord thy God with all thy heart and with all thy soul.
Deut. 10:12
See also, e.g., Josh. 22:5

Whither thou goest, I will go; and where thou lodgest, I will lodge: thy people shall be my people, and thy God my God.
Ruth 1:16

Where thou diest, will I die, and there will I be buried.
Ruth 1:17

Prepare your hearts unto the Lord, and serve Him only.
Samuel to Israelites
1 Sam. 7:3

Turn not aside from following the Lord.
1 Sam. 12:20

Fear the Lord, and serve Him in truth with all your heart.
1 Sam. 12:24

As the Lord liveth, and as thy soul liveth, I will not leave thee.
E.g., 2 Kings 2:2

Set your heart and your soul to seek the Lord your God.
1 Chron. 22:19

With a perfect heart and with a willing mind.
1 Chron. 28:9

If ye seek Him, He will be found of you.
2 Chron. 15:2
See also 1 Chron. 28:9

My soul thirsteth for Thee.
Ps. 63:1

Seek the Lord, and His strength: seek His face evermore.
Ps. 105:4
See also 1 Chron. 16:11

I will not give sleep to mine eyes, or slumber to mine eyelids, Until I find out a place for the Lord.
Ps. 132:4–5

With my soul have I desired Thee in the night; yea, with my spirit within me will I seek Thee early.
Isa. 26:9

Circumcise yourselves to the Lord.
Jer. 4:4

Ye shall seek Me, and find Me, when ye shall search for Me with all your heart.
Jer. 29:13

Come, and let us go up to the mountain of the Lord, and to the house of the God of Jacob.
Mic. 4:2

Seek ye the Lord, all ye meek of the earth.
Zeph. 2:3

They shall be My people, and I will be their God.
E.g., Zech. 8:8

[*See also* Allegiance, Commitment, Faithfulness, Love, Love of God, Loyalty, Service to God, Sincerity, Worship]

DILIGENCE

He that goeth forth and weepeth, bearing precious seed, shall doubtless come again with rejoicing, bringing his sheaves with him.
Ps. 126:6

Go to the ant, thou sluggard; consider her ways, and be wise.
Prov. 6:6

Seest thou a man diligent in his business? he shall stand before kings.
Prov. 22:29

He that tilleth his land shall have plenty of bread.
Prov. 28:19

The ants are a people not strong, yet they prepare their meat in the summer.
Prov. 30:25

In the morning sow thy seed, and in the evening withhold not thine hand.
Eccl. 11:6

Cursed be he that keepeth back his sword from blood.
Jer. 48:10

They pursued us upon the mountains, they laid wait for us in the wilderness.
Lam. 4:19

By thy great wisdom and by thy traffick hast thou increased thy riches.
Ezek 28:5

[*See also* Effort, Laziness, Perseverance]

DIPLOMACY

See Tact.

DISAPPOINTMENT

Behold it with thine eyes: for thou shalt not go over this Jordan.
God to Moses
Deut. 3:27

But I must die in this land, I must not go over Jordan.
Moses
Deut. 4:22

Thou shalt see the land before thee; but thou shalt not go thither.
God to Moses
Deut. 32:52

When I looked for good, then evil came unto me: and when I waited for light, there came darkness.
Job 30:26

Or ever the silver cord be loosed, or the golden bowl be broken.
Eccl. 12:6

He looked that it should bring forth grapes, and it brought forth wild grapes.
Isa. 5:2

He looked for judgment, but behold oppression; for righteousness, but behold a cry.
Isa. 5:7

As when an hungry man dreameth, and, behold, he eateth; but he awaketh, and his soul is empty: or as when a thirsty man dreameth, and, behold, he drinketh; but he awaketh, and, behold, he is faint.
Isa. 29:8

They shall not be ashamed that wait for Me.
Isa. 49:23

We wait for light, but behold obscurity; for brightness, but we walk in darkness.
Isa. 59:9

How is the gold become dim!
Lam. 4:1

Ye have built houses of hewn stone, but ye shall not dwell in them; ye have planted pleasant vineyards, but ye shall not drink wine of them.
Amos 5:11
See also Zeph. 1:13

Ye looked for much, and, lo, it came to little.
Hag. 1:9

[*See also* Effort, Expectation, Failure, Frustration, Futility, Hope]

DISARMAMENT

See War and Peace, Weapons.

DISBELIEF

See Doubt, Godlessness, Skepticism.

DISCERNMENT

Give therefore Thy servant an understanding heart to judge Thy people, that I may discern between good and bad.
Solomon
1 Kings 3:9

Let us choose to us judgment: let us know among ourselves what is good.
Job 34:4

As a jewel of gold in a swine's snout, so is a fair woman which is without discretion.
Prov. 11:22

A wise man's heart discerneth both time and judgment.
Eccl. 8:5

Butter and honey shall he eat, that he may know to refuse the evil, and choose the good.
Isa. 7:15

[*See also* Folly, Understanding]

DISCIPLINE

As a man chasteneth his son, so the Lord thy God chasteneth thee.
Deut. 8:5

Let the righteous smite me; it shall be a kindness.
Ps. 141:5

A rod is for the back of him that is void of understanding.
Prov. 10:13

He that spareth his rod hateth his son: but he that loveth him chasteneth him betimes.
Prov. 13:24

Correction is grievous unto him that forsaketh the way.
Prov. 15:10

He that refuseth instruction despiseth his own soul.
Prov. 15:32

Chasten thy son while there is hope, and let not thy soul spare for his crying.
Prov. 19:18

Foolishness is bound in the heart of a child; but the rod of correction shall drive it far from him.
Prov. 22:15

Withhold not correction from the child: for if thou beatest him with the rod, he shall not die.
Prov. 23:13

A whip for the horse, a bridle for the ass, and a rod for the fool's back.
Prov. 26:3

A child left to himself bringeth his mother to shame.
Prov. 29:15

I was chastised, as a bullock unaccustomed to the yoke.
Jer. 31:18

[*See also* Chastisement, Criticism, Punishment, Self-Control]

DISCONTENT

See Contentment, Satisfaction.

DISCRETION

See Prudence, Silence, Understanding.

DISHONESTY

Put not thine hand with the wicked to be an unrighteous witness.
Ex. 23:1

With flattering lips and with a double heart do they speak.
Ps. 12:2

He that worketh deceit shall not dwell within my house.
Ps. 101:7

He that telleth lies shall not tarry in my sight.
Ps. 101:7

Deceit is in the heart of them that imagine evil.
Prov. 12:20

Better is a little with righteousness than great revenues without right.
Prov. 16:8

He that hath a perverse tongue falleth into mischief.
Prov. 17:20

He that speaketh lies shall perish.
Prov. 19:9

A poor man is better than a liar.
Prov. 19:22

Divers weights, and divers measures, both of them are alike abomination to the Lord.
Prov. 20:10
See also Prov. 20:23

We have made lies our refuge, and under falsehood have we hid ourselves.
Isa. 28:15

Woe unto them that seek deep to hide their counsel from the Lord.
Isa. 29:15

Trust ye not in lying words.
Jer. 7:4

They bend their tongues like their bow for lies.
Jer. 9:3

He that getteth riches, and not by right, shall leave them in the midst of his days.
Jer. 17:11

With lies ye have made the heart of the righteous sad.
Ezek. 13:22

He is a merchant, the balances of deceit are in his hand: he loveth to oppress.
Hos. 12:7

[*See also* Candor, Honesty, Lies, Truth]

DISOBEDIENCE

She took of the fruit thereof, and did eat.
(She: Eve)
Gen. 3:6

His wife looked back from behind him, and she became a pillar of salt.
Gen. 19:26

How long wilt thou refuse to humble thyself before Me? let My people go.
God to Pharaoh
Ex. 10:3

How long refuse ye to keep My commandments and My laws?
Ex. 16:28

Wherefore do ye tempt the Lord?
Moses
Ex. 17:2

Moses lifted up his hand, and with his rod he smote the rock.
Num. 20:11

Ye have been rebellious against the Lord from the day that I knew you.
Deut. 9:24

Because thou hast rejected the word of the Lord, He hath also rejected thee from being king.
Samuel to Saul
1 Sam. 15:23

Wherefore hast thou despised the commandment of the Lord, to do evil in His sight?
(thou: David)
2 Sam. 12:9

His heart was not perfect with the Lord his God.
E.g., 1 Kings 11:4

Great is the wrath of the Lord that is kindled against us, because our fathers have not hearkened unto the words of this book.
2 Kings 22:13

He did that which was evil in the sight of the Lord his God.
E.g., 2 Chron. 36:12

A stubborn and rebellious generation; a generation that set not their heart aright, and whose spirit was not stedfast with God.
Ps. 78:8

Rivers of waters run down mine eyes, because they keep not Thy law.
Ps. 119:136

Stolen waters are sweet, and bread eaten in secret is pleasant.
Prov. 9:17

This is a rebellious people, lying children, children that will not hear the law of the Lord.
Isa. 30:9

When I called, ye did not answer; when I spake, ye did not hear.
Isa. 65:12

This is a nation that obeyeth not the voice of the Lord.
Jer. 7:28

The stork in the heaven knoweth her appointed times; and the turtle and the crane and the swallow observe the time of their coming; but My people know not the judgment of the Lord.
God to Jews
Jer. 8:7

Cursed be the man that obeyeth not the words of this covenant.
Jer. 11:3

I have spoken unto them, but they have not heard; and I have called unto them, but they have not answered.
Jer. 35:17

Thou dwellest in the midst of a rebellious house.
Ezek. 12:2

They hear thy words, but they do them not.
God to Ezekiel
Ezek. 33:32

We obeyed not His voice.
Dan. 9:14

They made their hearts as an adamant stone, lest they should hear the law.
Zech. 7:12

[*See also* Backsliding, Blame, Curses, Obedience, Punishment, Rebellion, Rejection, Sin]

DISTANCE

From Dan even to Beersheba.
Judg. 20:1

DIVERSITY

All the people, both small and great.
2 Kings 23:2

DOCTRINE

My doctrine shall drop as the rain, my speech shall distil as the dew.
Deut. 32:2

DOOM

If thou return at all in peace, the Lord hath not spoken by me.
1 Kings 22:28
See also 2 Chron. 18:27

Out of the serpent's root shall come forth a cockatrice, and his fruit shall be a fiery flying serpent.
Isa. 14:29

Howl, O gate; cry, O city; thou, whole Palestina, art dissolved.
Isa. 14:31

He who fleeth from the noise of the fear shall fall into the pit; and he that cometh up out of the midst of the pit shall be taken in the snare.
Isa. 24:18
See Jer. 48:44

I will bring My words upon this city for evil, and not for good.
Jer. 39:16

In vain shalt thou use many medicines; for thou shalt not be cured.
Jer. 46:11

They hunt our steps, that we cannot go in our streets: our end is near, our days are fulfilled.
Lam. 4:18

The time is come, the day of trouble is near.
Ezek. 7:7
See also Ezek. 7:12

Let not the buyer rejoice, nor the seller

mourn: for wrath is upon all the multitude.
Ezek. 7:12

Woe, woe unto thee! saith the Lord God.
Ezek. 16:23

The day of the Lord is near.
Ezek. 30:3

[*See also* Apocalypse, Destruction, Punishment, Terror]

DOUBT

Lord, wherefore hast Thou so evil entreated this people?
Moses
Ex. 5:22

Is the Lord among us, or not?
Ex. 17:7

Moses lifted up his hand, and with his rod he smote the rock.
Num. 20:11

If the Lord be with us, why then is all this befallen us?
Judg. 6:13

Where be all His miracles which our fathers told us of?
Judg. 6:13

[*See also* Belief, Faith, Hope, Skepticism]

DREAMS

They hated him yet the more for his dreams, and for his words.
(They: Joseph's brothers)
Gen. 37:8

Do not interpretations belong to God?
Gen. 40:8

What God is about to do He showeth unto Pharaoh.
Gen. 41:28

Thou scarest me with dreams, and terrifiest me through visions.
Job 7:14

When deep sleep falleth upon men, in slumberings upon the bed; Then He

openeth the ears of men, and sealeth their instruction.
Job 33:15–16

I sleep, but my heart waketh: it is the voice of my beloved that knocketh.
Song 5:2

As when an hungry man dreameth, and, behold, he eateth; but he awaketh, and his soul is empty: or as when a thirsty man dreameth, and, behold, he drinketh; but he awaketh, and, behold, he is faint.
Isa. 29:8

The prophet that hath a dream, let him tell a dream; and he that hath My word, let him speak My word faithfully.
Jer. 23:28

Show me the dream, and the interpretation thereof.
Nebuchadnezzar
Dan. 2:6

There is a God in heaven that revealeth secrets.
Dan. 2:28

Your old men shall dream dreams, your young men shall see visions.
Joel 2:28
See also Acts 2:17

DRUNKENNESS

I have drunk neither wine nor strong drink, but have poured out my soul before the Lord.
1 Sam. 1:15

The drunkard and the glutton shall come to poverty.
Prov. 23:21

Woe unto them that rise up early in the morning, that they may follow strong drink.
Isa. 5:11

As a drunken man staggereth in his vomit.
Isa. 19:14

They are drunken, but not with wine; they stagger, but not with strong drink.
Isa. 29:9

Woe unto him that giveth his neighbour drink.
Hab. 2:15

[*See also* Liquor]

DUTY

What doth the Lord thy God require of thee, but to fear the Lord thy God, to walk in all His ways, and to love Him, and to serve the Lord thy God with all thy heart and with all thy soul.
Deut. 10:12

Fear God, and keep His commandments: for this is the whole duty of man.
Eccl. 12:13

Say not, I am a child: for thou shalt go to all that I shall send thee, and whatsoever I command thee thou shalt speak.
God to Jeremiah
Jer. 1:7

What doth the Lord require of thee, but to do justly, and to love mercy, and to walk humbly with thy God?
Mic. 6:8

[*See also* Goals, Mission, Responsibility]

DUTY, NEGLECT OF

Why abodest thou among the sheepfolds, to hear the bleatings of the flocks?
Judg. 5:16

Curse ye bitterly the inhabitants thereof; because they came not to the help of the Lord.
Judg. 5:23

This thing is not good that thou hast done.
David to Abner
1 Sam. 26:16

As the Lord liveth, ye are worthy to die.
1 Sam. 26:16
See also 1 Sam. 26:10

What doest thou here, Elijah?
God
E.g., 1 Kings 19:9

The stork in the heaven knoweth her appointed times; and the turtle and the crane and the swallow observe the time of their coming; but My people know not the judgment of the Lord.

God to Jews
Jer. 8:7

Cursed be he that doeth the work of the Lord deceitfully.

Jer. 48:10

Woe be to the shepherds of Israel that do feed themselves! should not the shepherds feed the flocks?

Ezek. 34:2

My flock was scattered upon all the face of the earth, and none did search or seek after them.

Ezek. 34:6

EARTH

And God called the dry land Earth; and the gathering together of the waters called He Seas.

Gen. 1:10

All the earth is Mine.

Ex. 19:5

The pillars of the earth are the Lord's, and He hath set the world upon them.

1 Sam. 2:8

Who laid the corner stone thereof?

Job 38:6

The earth is the Lord's, and the fulness thereof; the world, and they that dwell therein.

Ps. 24:1
See also 1 Cor. 10:26

The earth is full of the goodness of the Lord.

Ps. 33:5

One generation passeth away, and another generation cometh: but the earth abideth for ever.

Eccl. 1:4

He hath established it, He created it not in vain, He formed it to be inhabited.

Isa. 45:18

He hath made the earth by His power, He hath established the world by His wisdom.

Jer. 51:15

[*See also* Creation, God's Presence, Heaven and Earth, Nature, Oceans]

EDUCATION

And thou shalt teach them diligently unto thy children, and shalt talk of them when thou sittest in thine house, and when thou walkest by the way, and when thou liest down, and when thou risest up.

Deut. 6:7
See also Deut. 11:19

Teach them the good way wherein they should walk.

1 Kings 8:36

Fools despise wisdom and instruction.

Prov. 1:7

Let her not go: keep her; for she is thy life.
(her: instruction)
Prov. 4:13

Receive my instruction, and not silver; and knowledge rather than choice gold.

Prov. 8:10

Hear instruction, and be wise, and refuse it not.

Prov. 8:33

Give instruction to a wise man, and he will be yet wiser: teach a just man, and he will increase in learning.

Prov. 9:9

When the scorner is punished, the simple is made wise.

Prov. 21:11

Train up a child in the way he should go: and when he is old, he will not depart from it.

Prov. 22:6

Much study is a weariness of the flesh.

Eccl. 12:12

Precept must be upon precept, precept upon precept; line upon line, line upon line; here a little, and there a little.

Isa. 28:10

All thy children shall be taught of the

Lord; and great shall be the peace of thy children.
Isa. 54:13

[*See also* Child-Rearing, Enlightenment, Guidance, Instruction, Knowledge, Teaching, Wisdom]

EFFORT

Let not your hands be weak: for your work shall be rewarded.
2 Chron. 15:7

Thou shalt eat the labour of thine hands.
Ps. 128:2

Where no oxen are, the crib is clean: but much increase is by the strength of the ox.
Prov. 14:4

Whatsoever thy hand findeth to do, do it with thy might.
Eccl. 9:10

Cast thy bread upon the waters: for thou shalt find it after many days.
Eccl. 11:1

Blessed are ye that sow beside all waters.
Isa. 32:20

Sow ye, and reap.
Isa. 37:30, 2 Kings 19:29

They have sown the wind, and they shall reap the whirlwind.
Hos. 8:7

Thou shalt sow, but thou shalt not reap.
Mic. 6:15

Ye have sown much, and bring in little; ye eat, but ye have not enough; ye drink, but ye are not filled.
Hag. 1:6

[*See also* Diligence, Patience, Work]

EGO

See Arrogance, Conceit, Humility.

ELOQUENCE

I am slow of speech, and of a slow tongue.
Moses
Ex. 4:10

Go, and I will be with thy mouth, and teach thee what thou shalt say.
God to Moses
Ex. 4:12

My speech shall distil as the dew, as the small rain upon the tender herb, and as the showers upon the grass.
Deut. 32:2

The words of his mouth were smoother than butter, but war was in his heart.
Ps. 55:21

His words were softer than oil, yet were they drawn swords.
Ps. 55:21

The lips of the wise shall preserve them.
Prov. 14:3

The heart of the wise teacheth his mouth, and addeth learning to his lips.
Prov. 16:23

Excellent speech becometh not a fool: much less do lying lips a prince.
Prov. 17:7

A word fitly spoken is like apples of gold in pictures of silver.
Prov. 25:11

I will make My words in thy mouth fire, and this people wood.
Jer. 5:14

[*See also* Silence, Speech, Verbosity]

EMBARRASSMENT

See Shame.

EMOTIONS

See Fear, Happiness, Hatred, Love, Sorrow.

EMPATHY

As thou livest, and as thy soul liveth, I will not do this thing.
Uriah to David
2 Sam. 11:11

[*See also* Compassion, Sympathy]

Thou shalt not oppress an hired servant that is poor and needy.
Deut. 24:14

Thou shalt not muzzle the ox when he treadeth out the corn.
Deut. 25:4
See also 1 Cor. 9:9

A wicked messenger falleth into mischief: but a faithful ambassador is health.
Prov. 13:17

The king's favour is toward a wise servant: but his wrath is against him that causeth shame.
Prov. 14:35

I will be a swift witness against the sorcerers, and against the adulterers, and against false swearers, and against those that oppress the hireling in his wages.
Mal. 3:5

[*See also* Reward, Wages, Work]

EMPLOYERS

See Business, Work.

ENCOURAGEMENT

Fear ye not, stand still, and see the salvation of the Lord, which He will show to you to-day.
Ex. 14:13

The Lord shall fight for you, and ye shall hold your peace.
Ex. 14:14

Rebel not ye against the Lord, neither fear ye the people of the land.
Num. 14:9

Fear not, neither be discouraged.
E.g., Deut. 1:21

Dread not, neither be afraid of them. The Lord your God which goeth before you, He shall fight for you.
Deut. 1:29–30

Be strong and of a good courage.
E.g., Deut. 31:6

Fear not, neither be dismayed.
E.g., Deut. 31:8

Get thee up; wherefore liest thou thus upon thy face?
God to Joshua
Josh. 7:10

Go up; for to morrow I will deliver them into thine hand.
God to Israelites
Judg. 20:28

Do all that is in thine heart; for the Lord is with thee.
2 Sam. 7:3

Be not afraid of the words which thou hast heard.
2 Kings 19:6
See also Isa. 37:6

Let not your hands be weak: for your work shall be rewarded.
2 Chron. 15:7

Be not afraid nor dismayed by reason of this great multitude; for the battle is not your's, but God's.
2 Chron. 20:15

Be strong and courageous, be not afraid nor dismayed.
E.g., 2 Chron. 32:7

Be of good courage, and do it.
Ezra 10:4

Fear not, neither be fainthearted.
Isa. 7:4

It shall not stand, neither shall it come to pass.
Isa. 7:7

Strengthen ye the weak hands, and confirm the feeble knees.
Isa. 35:3

Be strong, fear not: behold, your God will come with vengeance.
Isa. 35:4

Be not afraid of their faces: for I am with thee to deliver thee, saith the Lord.
Jer. 1:8

Be not afraid of him, saith the Lord: for I am with you to save you.
> *Jer. 42:11*

Do not My words do good to him that walketh uprightly?
> *Mic. 2:7*

[*See also* Courage, Fear, God's Protection, God's Support, Hope]

END DAYS

The wolf also shall dwell with the lamb, and the leopard shall lie down with the kid; and the calf and the young lion and the fatling together.
> *Isa. 11:6*

At the time of the end shall be the vision.
> *Dan. 8:17*

Many of them that sleep in the dust of the earth shall awake, some to everlasting life, and some to shame and everlasting contempt.
> *Dan. 12:2*

[*See also* Apocalypse, Judgment Day]

ENDINGS

He that goeth down to the grave shall come up no more.
> *Job 7:9*

The words of Job are ended.
> *Job 31:40*

Better is the end of a thing than the beginning thereof.
> *Eccl. 7:8*

[*See also* Apocalypse, Beginnings, Death, Permanence]

ENDURANCE

See Diligence, Fortitude, Perseverance, Strength.

ENEMIES

His hand will be against every man, and every man's hand against him.
> *(him: Ishmael)*
> *Gen. 16:12*

Ye shall chase your enemies, and they shall fall before you by the sword.
> *Lev. 26:7*

Let them that hate Thee flee before Thee.
> *Num. 10:35*

Dread not, neither be afraid of them. The Lord your God which goeth before you, He shall fight for you.
> *Deut. 1:29–30*

Ye shall not fear them: for the Lord your God He shall fight for you.
> *Deut. 3:22*

They shall be as thorns in your sides, and their gods shall be a snare unto you.
> *Judg. 2:3*

Who is this uncircumcised Philistine, that he should defy the armies of the living God?
> *David, about Goliath*
> *1 Sam. 17:26*

He that seeketh my life seeketh thy life.
> *David to Abiathar*
> *1 Sam. 22:23*

If a man find his enemy, will he let him go well away?
> *Saul to David*
> *1 Sam. 24:19*

The souls of thine enemies, them shall He sling out.
> *1 Sam. 25:29*

They prevented me in the day of my calamity: but the Lord was my stay.
> *2 Sam. 22:19, Ps. 18:18*

Save Thou us out of his hand, that all the kingdoms of the earth may know that Thou art the Lord God, even Thou only.
> *2 Kings 19:19*
> *See also Isa. 37:20*

I will subdue all thine enemies.
> *1 Chron. 17:10*

Because thou didst rely on the Lord, He delivered them into thine hand.
2 Chron. 16:8

They that hate thee shall be clothed with shame; and the dwelling place of the wicked shall come to nought.
Job 8:22

Destroy Thou them, O God; let them fall by their own counsels.
Ps. 5:10

They cried, but there was none to save them: even unto the Lord, but He answered them not.
Ps. 18:41

Thine hand shall find out all Thine enemies: Thy right hand shall find out those that hate Thee.
Ps. 21:8

Thou preparest a table before me in the presence of mine enemies: Thou anointest my head with oil; my cup runneth over.
Ps. 23:5

Let me not be ashamed, let not mine enemies triumph over me.
Ps. 25:2

Let them be as chaff before the wind: and let the angel of the Lord chase them.
Ps. 35:5

Let their way be dark and slippery.
Ps. 35:6

Let not them that are mine enemies wrongfully rejoice over me.
Ps. 35:19

Deliver me from mine enemies, O my God.
Ps. 59:1

They that hate me without a cause are more than the hairs of mine head.
Ps. 69:4

Deliver me because of mine enemies.
Ps. 69:18

Let them be blotted out of the book of the living, and not be written with the righteous.
Ps. 69:28

Let his prayer become sin.
Ps. 109:7

Let mine adversaries be clothed with shame, and let them cover themselves with their own confusion.
Ps. 109:29

Rejoice not when thine enemy falleth, and let not thine heart be glad when he stumbleth.
Prov. 24:17

If thine enemy be hungry, give him bread to eat; and if he be thirsty, give him water to drink.
Prov. 25:21
See also Rom. 12:20

They that war against thee shall be as nothing, and as a thing of nought.
Isa. 41:12

They shall fight against thee; but they shall not prevail against thee; for I am with thee, saith the Lord.
Jer. 1:19

Let me see Thy vengeance on them: for unto Thee have I opened my cause.
Jeremiah to God
Jer. 20:12
See also Jer. 11:20

Our persecutors are swifter than the eagles of the heaven: they pursued us upon the mountains, they laid wait for us in the wilderness.
Lam. 4:19

Thus saith the Lord God; Behold, I, even I, am against thee.
Ezek. 5:8

[*See also* Allies, Brotherhood, Gloating, God's Protection, Hatred, Persecution, Revenge]

ENLIGHTENMENT

Your eyes shall be opened, and ye shall be as gods, knowing good and evil.
Gen. 3:5

The Lord will lighten my darkness.
2 Sam. 22:29

Lord, I pray Thee, open his eyes, that he may see.
2 Kings 6:17

The testimony of the Lord is sure, making wise the simple.
Ps. 19:7

Thy word is a lamp unto my feet, and a light unto my path.
Ps. 119:105

The people that walked in darkness have seen a great light.
Isa. 9:2
See also Matt. 4:16, Luke 1:79

I will bring the blind by a way that they knew not; I will lead them in paths that they have not known.
God
Isa. 42:16

I will make darkness light before them, and crooked things straight.
Isa. 42:16

[*See also* Education, Knowledge, Light and Darkness, Spirituality]

ENTHUSIASM

With all thy heart and with all thy soul.
E.g., Deut. 10:12
See also Deut. 11:13

What ye shall say, that will I do for you.
2 Sam. 21:4

Thou shouldest have smitten five or six times.
2 Kings 13:19

[*See also* Contentment, Zeal]

ENVIRONMENT

See Nature.

ENVY

Thou shalt not covet.
Tenth Commandment
Ex. 20:17, Rom. 13:9
See also Deut. 5:21

Thou shalt not covet thy neighbour's house, thou shalt not covet thy neighbour's wife, nor his manservant, nor his maidservant, nor his ox, nor his ass, nor any thing that is thy neighbour's.
Ex. 20:17
See also Deut. 5:21

Enviest thou for my sake?
Moses to Joshua
Num. 11:29

Hath the Lord indeed spoken only by Moses?
Num. 12:2

Make us a king to judge us like all the nations.
1 Sam. 8:5

Give me thy vineyard, that I may have it for a garden of herbs.
Ahab to Naboth
1 Kings 21:2

Wrath killeth the foolish man, and envy slayeth the silly one.
Job 5:2

A little that a righteous man hath is better than the riches of many wicked.
Ps. 37:16

Be not thou afraid when one is made rich, when the glory of his house is increased; For when he dieth he shall carry nothing away.
Ps. 49:16–17

I was envious at the foolish, when I saw the prosperity of the wicked.
Ps. 73:3

[*See also* Contentment, Greed, Jealousy]

EPHEMERA

Riches certainly make themselves wings; they fly away as an eagle toward heaven.
Prov. 23:5

They shall be as the morning cloud, and as the early dew that passeth away, as the chaff that is driven with the whirlwind out of the floor, and as the smoke out of the chimney.
Hos. 13:3

[*See also* Mortality, Permanence]

EQUALITY

One law shall be to him that is homeborn, and unto the stranger that sojourneth among you.
Ex. 12:49

Ye shall have one ordinance, both for the stranger, and for him that was born in the land.
Num. 9:14
See also Lev. 24:22

The Lord commanded Moses to give us an inheritance among our brethren.
(us: Zelophehad's daughters)
Josh. 17:4

Are they not all my lord's servants?
1 Chron. 21:3

They shall lie down alike in the dust, and the worms shall cover them.
Job 21:26

Did not He that made me in the womb make him?
Job 31:15

They all are the work of His hands.
Job 34:19

The rich and poor meet together: the Lord is the maker of them all.
Prov. 22:2

That which befalleth the sons of men befalleth beasts.
Eccl. 3:19

All are of the dust, and all turn to dust again.
Eccl. 3:20

All things come alike to all.
Eccl. 9:2

As is the good, so is the sinner; and he that sweareth, as he that feareth an oath.
Eccl. 9:2

The race is not to the swift, nor the battle to the strong, neither yet bread to the wise, nor yet riches to men of understanding, nor yet favour to men of skill; but time and chance happeneth to them all.
Eccl. 9:11

As with the people, so with the priest; as with the servant, so with his master; as with the maid, so with her mistress; as with the buyer, so with the seller; as with the lender, so with the borrower; as with the taker of usury, so with the giver of usury to him.
Isa. 24:2

[*See also* Brotherhood, Foreigners, Humility, Impartiality]

ESCAPE

The children of Israel walked upon dry land in the midst of the sea; and the waters were a wall unto them on their right hand, and on their left.
Ex. 14:29

Arise, and let us flee.
2 Sam. 15:14

I am escaped with the skin of my teeth.
Job 19:20

There is no darkness, nor shadow of death, where the workers of iniquity may hide themselves.
Job 34:22

Oh that I had wings, like a dove! for then would I fly away, and be at rest.
Ps. 55:6

If I ascend up into heaven, Thou art there: if I make my bed in hell, behold, Thou art there.
Ps. 139:8

The darkness hideth not from Thee; but the night shineth as the day.
Ps. 139:12

Enter into the rock, and hide thee in the dust, for fear of the Lord.
Isa. 2:10

To whom will ye flee for help? and where will ye leave your glory?
Isa. 10:3

There is no peace, saith the Lord, unto the wicked.
Isa. 48:22
See also Ps. 57:21

Can any hide himself in secret places that I shall not see him? saith the Lord. Do not I fill heaven and earth?
Jer. 23:24

Thy life I will give unto thee for a prey in all places whither thou goest.
Jer. 45:5

He that fleeth from the fear shall fall into the pit; and he that getteth up out of the pit shall be taken in the snare.
Jer. 48:44
See also Isa. 24:18

Though thou shouldest make thy nest as high as the eagle, I will bring thee down from thence, saith the Lord.
Jer. 49:16

Flee out of the midst of Babylon, and deliver every man his soul.
Jer. 51:6

They pursued us upon the mountains, they laid wait for us in the wilderness.
Lam. 4:19

They shall go out from one fire, and another fire shall devour them.
Ezek. 15:7

Shall he escape that doeth such things?
Ezek. 17:15

He that taketh warning shall deliver his soul.
Ezek. 33:5

And who is that God that shall deliver you out of my hands?
Nebuchadnezzar
Dan. 3:15

Our God whom we serve is able to deliver us from the burning fiery furnace.
Dan. 3:17

He that is swift of foot shall not deliver himself: neither shall he that rideth the horse.
Amos 2:15

He that fleeth of them shall not flee away, and he that escapeth of them shall not be delivered.
Amos 9:1

Though they dig into hell, thence shall Mine hand take them; though they climb up to heaven, thence will I bring them down.
Amos 9:2

[*See also* Defeat, Deliverance, Safety, Sanctuary, Survival]

ESTRANGEMENT

Because ye have forsaken the Lord, He hath also forsaken you.
2 Chron. 24:20
See also 2 Chron. 15:2

Why standest Thou afar off, O Lord? why hidest Thou Thyself in times of trouble?
Ps. 10:1

I am become a stranger unto my brethren, and an alien unto my mother's children.
Ps. 69:8

I have gone astray like a lost sheep; seek Thy servant.
Ps. 119:176
See also Isa. 53:6

What iniquity have your fathers found in Me, that they are gone far from Me?
Jer. 2:5

[*See also* Abandonment, Backsliding]

ETERNAL LIFE

Thou wilt not leave my soul in hell; neither wilt Thou suffer Thine Holy One to see corruption.
Ps. 16:10

[*See also* Resurrection]

ETERNITY

The Lord shall reign for ever and ever.
E.g., Ex. 15:18

This God is our God for ever and ever: He will be our guide even unto death.
Ps. 48:14

But Thou, O Lord, shalt endure for ever.
Ps. 102:12
See also, e.g., Ps. 9:7

Thou art the same, and Thy years shall have no end.
Ps. 102:27

Thou, O Lord, remainest for ever; Thy throne from generation to generation.
Lam. 5:19

[*See also* Eternal Life, Permanence]

ETHICS

See Behavior, Honesty, Law.

EVANGELISM

I will publish the name of the Lord: ascribe ye greatness unto our God.
Deut. 32:3

Declare His glory among the heathen; His marvellous works among all nations.
1 Chron. 16:24
See also Ps. 96:3

Say among the heathen that the Lord reigneth.
Ps. 96:10

Make known His deeds among the people.
Ps. 105:1, 1 Chron. 16:8

I shall not die, but live, and declare the works of the Lord.
Ps. 118:17

Praise the Lord, call upon His name, declare His doings among the people, make mention that His name is exalted.
Isa. 12:4

The voice of him that crieth in the wilderness.
Isa. 40:3
See also, e.g., Matt. 3:3

I am sought of them that asked not for Me; I am found of them that sought Me not.
Isa. 65:1
See also Rom. 10:20

They shall declare My glory among the Gentiles.
Isa. 66:19

Hear the word of the Lord, O ye nations, and declare it in the isles afar off.
Jer. 31:10

My name shall be great among the heathen, saith the Lord of hosts.
Mal. 1:11

[*See also* Ministry, Mission, Praise of God, Preaching, Testimony]

EVIDENCE

See Capital Punishment, Judging, Perjury, Proof.

EVIL

The imagination of man's heart is evil from his youth.
Gen. 8:21

Sodom and Gomorrah.
Gen. 18:20, Gen. 19:28

I will not justify the wicked.
God
Ex. 23:7

Thou knowest the people, that they are set on mischief.
Aaron to Moses
Ex. 32:22

Put the evil away from the midst of thee.
Deut. 13:5

Sons of Belial.
E.g., Judg. 19:22

The thing that David had done displeased the Lord.
2 Sam. 11:27

Thou knowest all the wickedness which thine heart is privy to.
1 Kings 2:44

There was none like unto Ahab, which did sell himself to work wickedness in the sight of the Lord.
1 Kings 21:25

Keep me from evil, that it may not grieve me!
1 Chron. 4:10

The triumphing of the wicked is short, and the joy of the hypocrite but for a moment.
Job 20:5

To depart from evil is understanding.
Job 28:28

Far be it from God, that He should do wickedness.
Job 34:10

God will not do wickedly, neither will the Almighty pervert judgment.
Job 34:12

Keep thy tongue from evil, and thy lips from speaking guile.
Ps. 34:13
See also 1 Pet. 3:10

Depart from evil.
E.g. Ps. 34:14
See also Prov. 3:7, Prov. 16:6

Spreading himself like a green bay tree.
Ps. 37:35

Ye that love the Lord, hate evil.
Ps. 97:10

Avoid it, pass not by it, turn from it, and pass away.
Prov. 4:15

The fear of the Lord is to hate evil.
Prov. 8:13

He that pursueth evil pursueth it to his own death.
Prov. 11:19

Evil pursueth sinners.
Prov. 13:21

A wise man feareth, and departeth from evil: but the fool rageth, and is confident.
Prov. 14:16

The thoughts of the wicked are an abomination to the Lord.
Prov. 15:26

The heart of the sons of men is full of evil, and madness is in their heart while they live.
Eccl. 9:3

He that diggeth a pit shall fall into it.
Eccl. 10:8

Wickedness burneth as the fire.
Isa. 9:18

I will punish the world for their evil, and the wicked for their iniquity.
Isa. 13:11

Out of the serpent's root shall come forth a cockatrice, and his fruit shall be a fiery flying serpent.
Isa. 14:29

How long shall thy vain thoughts lodge within thee?
Jer. 4:14

The heart is deceitful above all things, and desperately wicked: who can know it?
Jer. 17:9

They have sown the wind, and they shall reap the whirlwind.
Hos. 8:7

Woe to them that devise iniquity, and work evil upon their beds!
Mic. 2:1

Turn ye now from your evil ways, and from your evil doings.
Zech. 1:4

Let none of you imagine evil in your hearts against his neighbour.
Zech. 8:17
See also Zech. 7:10

[*See also* Behavior, Depravity, Godlessness, Good and Evil, Immorality, Purity, Righteousness, Sin, Wicked People, Wickedness]

EXALTATION

Thou, Lord, art high above all the earth: Thou art exalted far above all gods.
Ps. 97:9

EXASPERATION

How long refuse ye to keep My commandments and My laws?
Ex. 16:28

How long will this people provoke Me?
Num. 14:11

Ye have forsaken Me, and served other gods: wherefore I will deliver you no more.
Judg. 10:13

Have I need of mad men, that ye have brought this fellow to play the mad man in my presence?
1 Sam. 21:15

They have done that which was evil in My sight, and have provoked Me to anger, since the day their fathers came forth out of Egypt.
2 Kings 21:15

Am I a sea, or a whale, that Thou settest a
watch over me?
Job 7:12

Hast Thou eyes of flesh? or seest Thou as
man seest?
Job 10:4

How long will ye vex my soul, and break
me in pieces with words?
Job 19:2

O ye sons of men, how long will ye turn
My glory into shame?
Ps. 4:2

Is it a small thing for you to weary men,
but will ye weary my God also?
Isa. 7:13

I am weary with repenting.
God to Jeremiah
Jer. 15:6

Ye have wearied the Lord with your
words.
Mal. 2:17

[*See also* Anger, God's Anger, Impatience, Patience, Temper]

EXCESS

Thou wilt surely wear away, both thou,
and this people that is with thee.
Jethro to Moses
Ex. 18:18

After whom dost thou pursue? after a
dead dog, after a flea.
David to Saul
1 Sam. 24:14

The king of Israel is come out to seek a
flea, as when one doth hunt a partridge in
the mountains.
1 Sam. 26:20

Be not righteous over much; neither make
thyself over wise.
Eccl. 7:16

Much study is a weariness of the flesh.
Eccl. 12:12

[*See also* Abundance, Gluttony]

EXCUSES

I was afraid, because I was naked.
Adam
Gen. 3:10

The serpent beguiled me, and I did eat.
Eve
Gen. 3:13

I did but taste a little honey with the end
of the rod.
1 Sam. 14:43

I feared the people, and obeyed their
voice.
Saul to Samuel
1 Sam. 15:24

Their gods are gods of the hills; therefore
they were stronger than we.
1 Kings 20:23

The slothful man saith, There is a lion
without, I shall be slain in the streets.
Prov. 22:13
See also Prov. 26:13

Say not, I am a child: for thou shalt go to
all that I shall send thee, and whatsoever I
command thee thou shalt speak.
God to Jeremiah
Jer. 1:7

They say, The Lord seeth us not; the Lord
hath forsaken the earth.
Ezek. 8:12

EXILE

He made them wander in the wilderness
forty years, until all the generation, that
had done evil in the sight of the Lord, was
consumed.
Num. 32:13

The Lord shall scatter you among the
nations, and ye shall be left few in number
among the heathen.
Moses to Israelites
Deut. 4:27

The children of Israel walked forty years
in the wilderness.
Josh. 5:6
See also Num. 14:33

Let him turn to his own house, and let
him not see my face.
(him: Absalom)
2 Sam. 14:24

How shall we sing the Lord's song in a strange land?
Ps. 137:4

My people are gone into captivity, because they have no knowledge.
Isa. 5:13

As ye have forsaken Me, and served strange gods in your land, so shall ye serve strangers in a land that is not your's.
Jer. 5:19

Weep sore for him that goeth away: for he shall return no more, nor see his native country.
Jer. 22:10

To the land whereunto they desire to return, thither shall they not return.
Jer. 22:27

Ye have sinned against the Lord, and have not obeyed His voice, therefore this thing is come upon you.
Jer. 40:3

I will scatter thee among the heathen, and disperse thee in the countries.
Ezek. 22:15

I will sow them among the people: and they shall remember Me in far countries.
Zech. 10:9

[*See also* Freedom, Outcast]

EXPECTATION

The desire of the righteous is only good: but the expectation of the wicked is wrath.
Prov. 11:23

We looked for peace, but no good came; and for a time of health, and behold trouble!
Jer. 8:15

The harvest is past, the summer is ended, and we are not saved.
Jer. 8:20

Ye looked for much, and, lo, it came to little.
Hag. 1:9

[*See also* Disappointment, Hope]

EXPERIENCE

Thou mayest be to us instead of eyes.
Moses to Hobab
Num. 10:31

Remember the days of old, consider the years of many generations: ask thy father, and he will show thee; thy elders, and they will tell thee.
Deut. 32:7

Let not him that girdeth on his harness boast himself as he that putteth it off.
1 Kings 20:11

With the ancient is wisdom; and in length of days understanding.
Job 12:12

Days should speak, and multitude of years should teach wisdom.
Job 32:7

Hast thou perceived the breadth of the earth? declare if thou knowest it all.
God to Job
Job 38:18

Hast thou entered into the treasures of the snow? or hast thou seen the treasures of the hail?
Job 38:22

I understand more than the ancients, because I keep Thy precepts.
Ps. 119:100

The glory of young men is their strength: and the beauty of old men is the grey head.
Prov. 20:29

All things have I seen in the days of my vanity.
Eccl. 7:15

Thou hast not remembered the days of thy youth, when thou wast naked and bare.
Ezek. 16:22

[*See also* Age, Wisdom, Youth]

EXPOSURE

The voice of thy brother's blood crieth unto Me from the ground.
Gen. 4:10

The morning is to them even as the shadow of death.
Job 24:17

[*See also* Criminals, Secrecy]

FAILURE

If thou doest not well, sin lieth at the door.
Gen. 4:7

By the way that he came, by the same shall he return.
2 Kings 19:33, Isa. 37:34

He that trusteth in his riches shall fall.
Prov. 11:28

Pride goeth before destruction, and an haughty spirit before a fall.
Prov. 16:18

[*See also* Acceptance, Defeat, Success, Victory]

FAIRNESS

Wilt Thou also destroy the righteous with the wicked?
Abraham to God
Gen. 18:23

He that gathered much had nothing over, and he that gathered little had no lack.
Ex. 16:18

God do so and more also: for thou shalt surely die, Jonathan.
1 Sam. 14:44

He shall not judge after the sight of his eyes, neither reprove after the hearing of his ears.
Isa. 11:3

As with the buyer, so with the seller; as with the lender, so with the borrower; as with the taker of usury, so with the giver of usury to him.
Isa. 24:2

Is not My way equal? are not your ways unequal?
God to Israelites
Ezek. 18:25

[*See also* Impartiality, Judging, Justice]

FAITH

Is any thing too hard for the Lord?
Gen. 18:14

If the Lord delight in us, then He will bring us into this land.
Joshua and Caleb
Num. 14:8

How long will it be ere they believe Me, for all the signs which I have showed among them?
Num. 14:11

Speak ye unto the rock before their eyes; and it shall give forth his water.
God to Moses
Num. 20:8

He will not fail thee, neither forsake thee: fear not, neither be dismayed.
Deut. 31:8

The Lord that delivered me out of the paw of the lion, and out of the paw of the bear, He will deliver me out of the hand of this Philistine.
David
1 Sam. 17:37

Thou comest to me with a sword, and with a spear, and with a shield: but I come to thee in the name of the Lord of hosts.
David to Goliath
1 Sam. 17:45

This day will the Lord deliver thee into mine hand.
David to Goliath
1 Sam. 17:46

The Lord saveth not with sword and spear: for the battle is the Lord's.
David to Goliath
1 Sam. 17:47
See also 2 Chron. 20:15

There was no sword in the hand of David.
1 Sam. 17:50

Thou art my lamp, O Lord.
2 Sam. 22:29

Let the Lord do that which is good in His sight.
1 Chron. 19:13

If thou seek Him, He will be found of thee.
1 Chron. 28:9
See also 2 Chron. 15:2

Believe in the Lord your God, so shall ye be established; believe His prophets, so shall ye prosper.
2 Chron. 20:20

The Lord gave, and the Lord hath taken away; blessed be the name of the Lord.
Job 1:21

Though He slay me, yet will I trust in Him.
Job 13:15

My friends scorn me: but mine eye poureth out tears unto God.
Job 16:20

I know that my redeemer liveth, and that He shall stand at the latter day upon the earth.
Job 19:25

When Thou saidst, Seek ye My face; my heart said unto Thee, Thy face, Lord, will I seek.
Ps. 27:8

Be of good courage, and He shall strengthen your heart, all ye that hope in the Lord.
Ps. 31:24
See also Ps. 27:14

Many sorrows shall be to the wicked: but he that trusteth in the Lord, mercy shall compass him about.
Ps. 32:10

A mighty man is not delivered by much strength.
Ps. 33:16

Those that wait upon the Lord, they shall inherit the earth.
Ps. 37:9

Trust in Him at all times.
Ps. 62:8

Pour out your heart before Him: God is a refuge for us.
Ps. 62:8

Whom have I in heaven but Thee?
Ps. 73:25

Blessed is the man whose strength is in Thee.
Ps. 84:5

Let me not be ashamed of my hope.
Ps. 119:116

Happy is he that hath the God of Jacob for his help, whose hope is in the Lord his God.
Ps. 146:5

Whoso putteth his trust in the Lord shall be safe.
Prov. 29:25

God is my salvation; I will trust, and not be afraid.
Isa. 12:2

In quietness and in confidence shall be your strength.
Isa. 30:15

Blessed are all they that wait for Him.
Isa. 30:18

My judgment is with the Lord, and my work with my God.
Isa. 49:4

They shall not be ashamed that wait for Me.
Isa. 49:23

Let him that glorieth glory in this, that he understandeth and knoweth Me, that I am the Lord.
Jer. 9:24
See also, e.g., 1 Cor. 1:31

The Lord is good unto them that wait for Him, to the soul that seeketh Him.
Lam. 3:25

I called upon Thy name, O Lord, out of the low dungeon.
Lam. 3:55

Our God whom we serve is able to deliver us from the burning fiery furnace.
Dan. 3:17

The people that do know their God shall be strong.
Dan. 11:32

Turn thou to thy God: keep mercy and judgment, and wait on thy God continually.
Hos. 12:6

When my soul fainted within me I remembered the Lord.
Jonah 2:7

I will look unto the Lord; I will wait for the God of my salvation.
Mic. 7:7

When I sit in darkness, the Lord shall be a light unto me.
Mic. 7:8

The just shall live by his faith.
Hab. 2:4
See also, e.g., Rom. 1:17

[*See also* Belief, Doubt, Fear of God, Healing, Monotheism, Sin, Trust]

FAITHFULNESS

Hath He said, and shall He not do it? or hath He spoken, and shall He not make it good?
Num. 23:19

Beware lest thou forget the Lord.
Deut. 6:12
See also Deut. 8:11

Him shalt thou serve, and to Him shalt thou cleave, and swear by His name.
Deut. 10:20

Cleave unto the Lord your God, as ye have done unto this day.
Josh. 23:8
See also Josh. 22:5

But as for me and my house, we will serve the Lord.
Josh. 24:15

God forbid that we should forsake the Lord, to serve other gods.
Josh. 24:16

Thy people shall be my people, and thy God my God.
Ruth 1:16

There hath not failed one word of all His good promise.
1 Kings 8:56

Remember now how I have walked before Thee in truth and with a perfect heart.
2 Kings 20:3
See also Isa. 38:3

Walk after the Lord.
2 Kings 23:3

Be ye mindful always of His covenant.
1 Chron. 16:15

Are they not all my lord's servants?
1 Chron. 21:3

As for us, the Lord is our God, and we have not forsaken Him.
2 Chron. 13:10

The Lord is with you, while ye be with Him.
2 Chron. 15:2

Touch all that he hath, and he will curse Thee to Thy face.
Satan to God, about Job
Job 1:11

Shall we receive good at the hand of God, and shall we not receive evil?
Job 2:10

The Lord preserveth the faithful, and plentifully rewardeth the proud doer.
Ps. 31:23

The Lord loveth judgment, and forsaketh not His saints.
Ps. 37:28

This God is our God for ever and ever: He will be our guide even unto death.
Ps. 48:14

I am small and despised: yet do not I forget Thy precepts.
Ps. 119:141

The earth shall be full of the knowledge of the Lord, as the waters cover the sea.
Isa. 11:9

Thy counsels of old are faithfulness and truth.
Isa. 25:1

They may forget, yet will I not forget thee.
God, about parents
Isa. 49:15

[*See also* Allegiance, Devotion, Faith, Loyalty]

FAITHLESSNESS

We be not able to go up against the people; for they are stronger than we.
Num. 13:31

He will not be slack to him that hateth Him, He will repay him to his face.
Deut. 7:10

They would not hearken unto their judges, but they went a whoring after other gods.
Judg. 2:17
See also 1 Chron. 5:25

He forsook the Lord God of his fathers, and walked not in the way of the Lord.
2 Kings 21:22

The hypocrite's hope shall perish.
Job 8:13

If I forget thee, O Jerusalem, let my right hand forget her cunning.
Ps. 137:5

Who art thou, that thou shouldest be afraid of a man that shall die, and of the son of man which shall be made as grass; And forgettest the Lord thy maker.
Isa. 51:12–13

Can a maid forget her ornaments, or a bride her attire? yet My people have forgotten Me days without number.
Jer. 2:32

[*See also* Atheism, Godlessness]

FALSE GODS

Take heed to yourselves, that your heart be not deceived.
Deut. 11:16

If he be a god, let him plead for himself, because one hath cast down his altar.
Judg. 6:31

Go and cry unto the gods which ye have chosen; let them deliver you.
God to Israelites
Judg. 10:14

Call ye on the name of your gods, and I will call on the name of the Lord.
Elijah
1 Kings 18:24

There was no voice, nor any that answered.
1 Kings 18:26

Have the gods of the nations delivered them which my fathers have destroyed?
Sennacherib to Hezekiah
2 Kings 19:12, Isa. 37:12

All the gods of the people are idols: but the Lord made the heavens.
1 Chron. 16:26
See also Ps. 96:5

To whom then will ye liken Me, or shall I be equal? saith the Holy One.
Isa. 40:25
See also Isa. 46:5

They that observe lying vanities forsake their own mercy.
Jonah 2:8

[*See also* Idolatry, Idols]

FALSE PROPHETS

Thou shalt not hearken unto the words of that prophet, or that dreamer of dreams: for the Lord your God proveth you, to know whether ye love the Lord your God with all your heart and with all your soul.
Deut. 13:3

When a prophet speaketh in the name of the Lord, if the thing follow not, nor come to pass, that is the thing which the Lord hath not spoken.
Deut. 18:22

I am a prophet also as thou art; and an angel spake unto me by the word of the Lord.
1 Kings 13:18

I will go forth, and I will be a lying spirit in the mouth of all his prophets.
1 Kings 22:22

If thou return at all in peace, the Lord hath not spoken by me.
1 Kings 22:28
See also 2 Chron. 18:27

By sword and famine shall those prophets be consumed.
Jer. 14:15

They speak a vision of their own heart, and not out of the mouth of the Lord.
Jer. 23:16

I have not sent these prophets, yet they ran: I have not spoken to them, yet they prophesied.
Jer. 23:21

The prophet that hath a dream, let him tell a dream; and he that hath My word, let him speak My word faithfully.
Jer. 23:28

I am against the prophets, saith the Lord, that use their tongues, and say, He saith.
Jer. 23:31

Hearken not ye to your prophets, nor to your diviners, nor to your dreamers, nor to your enchanters.
Jer. 27:9

If they be prophets, and if the word of the Lord be with them, let them now make intercession to the Lord of hosts.
Jer. 27:18

They prophesy falsely unto you in My name: I have not sent them, saith the Lord.
Jer. 29:9

Woe unto the foolish prophets, that follow their own spirit, and have seen nothing!
Ezek. 13:3

Ye say, The Lord saith it; albeit I have not spoken.
Ezek. 13:7

Will ye pollute Me among My people for handfuls of barley and for pieces of bread?
Ezek. 13:19

With lies ye have made the heart of the righteous sad.
Ezek. 13:22

Thou speakest lies in the name of the Lord.
Zech. 13:3

The prophets shall be ashamed every one of his vision.
Zech. 13:4

[*See also* Prophecy]

FAME

His fame was noised throughout all the country.
Josh. 6:27

Saul hath slain his thousands, and David his ten thousands.
E.g., 1 Sam. 18:7

Riches and honour come of Thee.
1 Chron. 29:12

His remembrance shall perish from the earth, and he shall have no name in the street.
(His: wicked people)
Job 18:17

I am forgotten as a dead man out of mind: I am like a broken vessel.
Ps. 31:12

His name shall endure for ever: his name shall be continued as long as the sun.
Ps. 72:17

The seed of evildoers shall never be renowned.
Isa. 14:20

Make sweet melody, sing many songs, that thou mayest be remembered.
Isa. 23:16

I will make you a name and a praise among all people of the earth, when I turn back your captivity before your eyes.
Zeph. 3:20

[*See also* Boasting, Deeds, Glory, God's Glory, Modesty, Reputation, Respect, Shame]

FAMILY

Be fruitful, and multiply.
E.g., Gen. 1:28

In thee and in thy seed shall all the families of the earth be blessed.
God to Jacob
Gen. 28:14

He that troubleth his own house shall inherit the wind.
Prov. 11:29

[*See also* Building, Children, Incest, Parents, Siblings, Strife]

FAMINE

The famine shall consume the land.
Gen. 41:30

Famine was over all the face of the earth.
Gen. 41:56

When the poor and needy seek water, and there is none, and their tongue faileth for thirst, I the Lord will hear them, I the God of Israel will not forsake them.
Isa. 41:17

The young children ask bread, and no man breaketh it unto them.
Lam. 4:4

They that be slain with the sword are better than they that be slain with hunger.
Lam. 4:9

They shall eat bread by weight, and with care; and they shall drink water by measure, and with astonishment.
Ezek. 4:16

The fathers shall eat the sons in the midst of thee, and the sons shall eat their fathers.
Ezek. 5:10

He that is far off shall die of the pestilence; and he that is near shall fall by the sword; and he that remaineth and is besieged shall die by the famine.
Ezek. 6:12

The sword is without, and the pestilence and the famine within.
Ezek. 7:15

That which the locust hath left hath the cankerworm eaten; and that which the cankerworm hath left hath the caterpillar eaten.
Joel 1:4

I will send a famine in the land, not a famine of bread, nor a thirst for water, but of hearing the words of the Lord.
Amos 8:11

[*See also* Deprivation, Food, Hunger, Thirst]

FARMING

See Animals, Cultivation, Growth.

FASHION

See Appearance, Beauty.

FASTING

I humbled my soul with fasting.
Ps. 35:13

In the day of your fast ye find pleasure.
Isa. 58:3

Is not this the fast that I have chosen? to loose the bands of wickedness, to undo the heavy burdens, and to let the oppressed go free.
Isa. 58:6

When they fast, I will not hear their cry.
Jer. 14:12

FAVORITISM

He was the son of his old age.
(He: Joseph)
Gen. 37:3

He made him a coat of many colours.
Gen. 37:3

Thou shalt not respect the person of the poor, nor honour the person of the mighty.
Lev. 19:15

Though he was not the firstborn, yet his father made him the chief.
1 Chron. 26:10

[*See also* Equality, Impartiality]

Fear not, for I am with thee, and will bless thee, and multiply thy seed.
> *God to Isaac*
> *Gen. 26:24*

Deliver me, I pray Thee, from the hand of my brother.
> *Jacob to God, about Esau*
> *Gen. 32:11*

It had been better for us to serve the Egyptians, than that we should die in the wilderness.
> *Ex. 14:12*

Ye shall flee when none pursueth you.
> *Lev. 26:17*

We were in our own sight as grasshoppers.
> *Num. 13:33*

Ye shall not fear them: for the Lord your God He shall fight for you.
> *Deut. 3:22*

Be not afraid, neither be thou dismayed: for the Lord thy God is with thee whithersoever thou goest.
> *Josh. 1:9*

Whosoever is fearful and afraid, let him return and depart early.
> *Gideon to his soldiers*
> *Judg. 7:3*

Thou seest the shadow of the mountains as if they were men.
> *Judg. 9:36*

Do what seemeth good unto thee.
> *Israelites to Saul*
> *1 Sam. 14:40*

The hair of my flesh stood up.
> *Job 4:15*

Let not Thy dread make me afraid.
> *Job 13:21*

Yea, though I walk through the valley of the shadow of death, I will fear no evil: for Thou art with me.
> *Ps. 23:4*

The Lord is my light and my salvation; whom shall I fear? the Lord is the strength of my life; of whom shall I be afraid?
> *Ps. 27:1*

In God I have put my trust; I will not fear what flesh can do unto me.
> *Ps. 56:4*
> *See also Ps. 56:11*

Thou shalt not be afraid for the terror by night; nor for the arrow that flieth by day.
> *Ps. 91:5*

The Lord is on my side; I will not fear.
> *Ps. 118:6*
> *See also Heb. 13:6*

The wicked flee when no man pursueth.
> *Prov. 28:1*

Every man hath his sword upon his thigh because of fear in the night.
> *Song 3:8*

Woe is me! for I am undone.
> *Isa. 6:5*

Let Him be your fear, and let Him be your dread.
> *Isa. 8:13*

One thousand shall flee at the rebuke of one.
> *Isa. 30:17*

Who art thou, that thou shouldest be afraid of a man that shall die, and of the son of man which shall be made as grass?
> *Isa. 51:12*

Be not afraid of him, saith the Lord: for I am with you to save you.
> *Jer. 42:11*

Fear them not, neither be dismayed at their looks, though they be a rebellious house.
> *Ezek. 3:9*

[*See also* Courage, Cowardice, Encouragement, God's Protection, Terror, Timidity]

FEAR OF GOD

O that there were such an heart in them, that they would fear Me, and keep all My commandments always.
Deut. 5:29

Fear the Lord thy God.
E.g., Deut. 10:12

Fear before Him, all the earth.
1 Chron. 16:30

The fear of the Lord, that is wisdom.
Job 28:28

The secret of the Lord is with them that fear Him.
Ps. 25:14

When He slew them, then they sought Him.
Ps. 78:34

God is greatly to be feared in the assembly of the saints.
Ps. 89:7

He is to be feared above all gods.
Ps. 96:4

The fear of the Lord is the beginning of wisdom.
Ps. 111:10, Prov. 9:10

Blessed is the man that feareth the Lord.
Ps. 112:1

Ye that fear the Lord, trust in the Lord: He is their help and their shield.
Ps. 115:11

Blessed is every one that feareth the Lord; that walketh in His ways.
Ps. 128:1

The fear of the Lord is the beginning of knowledge.
Prov. 1:7

The fear of the Lord is to hate evil.
Prov. 8:13

The fear of the Lord prolongeth days: but the years of the wicked shall be shortened.
Prov. 10:27

The fear of the Lord is a fountain of life.
Prov. 14:27

By the fear of the Lord men depart from evil.
Prov. 16:6

Be thou in the fear of the Lord all the day long.
Prov. 23:17

Favour is deceitful, and beauty is vain: but a woman that feareth the Lord, she shall be praised.
Prov. 31:30

Fear ye not Me? saith the Lord: will ye not tremble at My presence?
Jer. 5:22

[*See also* Awe, Reverence]

FELLOWSHIP

Behold, how good and how pleasant it is for brethren to dwell together in unity!
Ps. 133:1

Have we not all one father? hath not one God created us?
Mal. 2:10

[*See also* Brotherhood, Companions, Friendship]

FERTILITY

Be fruitful, and multiply.
E.g., Gen. 1:28

I will make thy seed as the dust of the earth: so that if a man can number the dust of the earth, then shall thy seed also be numbered.
God to Abram
Gen. 13:16
See also Gen. 28:14

Shall a child be born unto him that is an hundred years old? and shall Sarah, that is ninety years old, bear?
Gen. 17:17

Thou art barren, and bearest not: but thou shalt conceive, and bear a son.
Angel to Samson's mother
Judg. 13:3

The Lord make the woman that is come into thine house like Rachel and like Leah.
Ruth 4:11

■ **87** ■

Elkanah knew Hannah his wife; and the Lord remembered her.
1 Sam. 1:19

Nay, my lord, thou man of God, do not lie unto thine handmaid.
2 Kings 4:16

He maketh the barren woman to keep house, and to be a joyful mother of children.
Ps. 113:9

Give them, O Lord: what wilt Thou give? give them a miscarrying womb and dry breasts.
Hos. 9:14

[*See also* Birth, Childlessness]

FIDELITY

See Commitment, Faithfulness, Loyalty.

FINANCE

See Borrowing.

FIRSTBORN

The elder shall serve the younger.
Gen. 25:23, Rom. 9:12

His younger brother shall be greater than he.
Gen. 48:19

My firstborn, my might, and the beginning of my strength.
Gen. 49:3

I will pass through the land of Egypt this night, and will smite all the firstborn in the land of Egypt, both man and beast.
Ex. 12:12

Sanctify unto Me all the firstborn.
Ex. 13:2

The males shall be the Lord's.
Ex. 13:12

The firstborn of thy sons shalt thou give unto Me.
Ex. 22:29

All the firstborn are Mine.
Num. 3:13

Though he was not the firstborn, yet his father made him the chief.
1 Chron. 26:10

FLATTERY

As thou art, so were they; each one resembled the children of a king.
Judg. 8:18

The half was not told me.
Queen of Sheba to Solomon
1 Kings 10:7

With flattering lips and with a double heart do they speak.
Ps. 12:2

He that hideth hatred with lying lips, and he that uttereth a slander, is a fool.
Prov. 10:18

Meddle not with him that flattereth with his lips.
Prov. 20:19

A flattering mouth worketh ruin.
Prov. 26:28

Faithful are the wounds of a friend; but the kisses of an enemy are deceitful.
Prov. 27:6

A man that flattereth his neighbour spreadeth a net for his feet.
Prov. 29:5

It is better to hear the rebuke of the wise, than for a man to hear the song of fools.
Eccl. 7:5

FLAVOR

Can that which is unsavoury be eaten without salt?
Job 6:6

Is there any taste in the white of an egg?
Job 6:6

Eat thou honey, because it is good; and

the honeycomb, which is sweet to thy taste.
Prov. 24:13

FLOODS

Of every living thing of all flesh, two of every sort shalt thou bring into the ark, to keep them alive with thee.
Gen. 6:19

And the rain was upon the earth forty days and forty nights.
Gen. 7:12

Neither shall there any more be a flood to destroy the earth.
Gen. 9:11

FOLLY

But he forsook the counsel which the old men gave him.
2 Chron. 10:8

In his disease he sought not to the Lord, but to the physicians.
2 Chron. 16:12

Forsake the foolish, and live.
Prov. 9:6

The foolishness of fools is folly.
Prov. 14:24

He that is hasty of spirit exalteth folly.
Prov. 14:29

Folly is joy to him that is destitute of wisdom.
Prov. 15:21

The foolishness of man perverteth his way.
Prov. 19:3

Wisdom excelleth folly, as far as light excelleth darkness.
Eccl. 2:13

My people is foolish, they have not known Me.
Jer. 4:22

[*See also* Fools, Wisdom]

FOOD

Every moving thing that liveth shall be meat for you.
Gen. 9:3

Eat, that thou mayest have strength, when thou goest on thy way.
Spiritualist to Saul
1 Sam. 28:22

He hath given meat unto them that fear Him.
Ps. 111:5

It is good and comely for one to eat and to drink, and to enjoy the good of all his labour.
Eccl. 5:18
See also Eccl. 3:13

Eat thy bread with joy, and drink thy wine with a merry heart.
Eccl. 9:7

[*See also* Celebration, Deprivation, Famine, Flavor, Gluttony, Hunger, Materialism, Pleasure, Thirst]

FOOLS

The fool hath said in his heart, There is no God.
Ps. 14:1, Ps. 53:1

The foolish man reproacheth Thee daily.
Ps. 74:22

Fools despise wisdom and instruction.
Prov. 1:7

Scorners delight in their scorning, and fools hate knowledge.
Prov. 1:22

He that walketh with wise men shall be wise: but a companion of fools shall be destroyed.
Prov. 13:20

A wise man feareth, and departeth from evil: but the fool rageth, and is confident.
Prov. 14:16

A reproof entereth more into a wise man than an hundred stripes into a fool.
Prov. 17:10

Let a bear robbed of her whelps meet a man, rather than a fool in his folly.
Prov. 17:12

The father of a fool hath no joy.
Prov. 17:21

A foolish son is a grief to his father, and bitterness to her that bare him.
Prov. 17:25

Even a fool, when he holdeth his peace, is counted wise.
Prov. 17:28

A fool's mouth is his destruction, and his lips are the snare of his soul.
Prov. 18:7

Every fool will be meddling.
Prov. 20:3

As snow in summer, and as rain in harvest, so honour is not seemly for a fool.
Prov. 26:1

A whip for the horse, a bridle for the ass, and a rod for the fool's back.
Prov. 26:3

Answer not a fool according to his folly, lest thou also be like unto him.
Prov. 26:4

Answer a fool according to his folly, lest he be wise in his own conceit.
Prov. 26:5

As a dog returneth to his vomit, so a fool returneth to his folly.
Prov. 26:11
See also 2 Pet. 2:22

Though thou shouldest bray a fool in a mortar among wheat with a pestle, yet will not his foolishness depart from him.
Prov. 27:22

The wise man's eyes are in his head; but the fool walketh in darkness.
Eccl. 2:14

A fool's voice is known by multitude of words.
Eccl. 5:3

For He hath no pleasure in fools.
Eccl. 5:4

The heart of the wise is in the house of mourning; but the heart of fools is in the house of mirth.
Eccl. 7:4

[*See also* Folly]

FOREIGNERS

I have been a stranger in a strange land.
Moses
Ex. 2:22

One law shall be to him that is homeborn, and unto the stranger that sojourneth among you.
Ex. 12:49
See also Lev. 24:22, Num. 9:14

Thou shalt neither vex a stranger, nor oppress him: for ye were strangers in the land of Egypt.
Ex. 22:21
See also Ex. 23:9

Thou shalt love him as thyself.
Lev. 19:34

Love ye therefore the stranger: for ye were strangers in the land of Egypt.
Deut. 10:19

Unto a stranger thou mayest lend upon usury; but unto thy brother thou shalt not lend upon usury.
Deut. 23:20

Learn not the way of the heathen.
Jer. 10:2

FORGIVENESS

Hear Thou in heaven Thy dwelling place: and when Thou hearest, forgive.
1 Kings 8:30
See also, e.g., 1 Kings 8:39

Render unto every man according unto all his ways, whose heart Thou knowest.
2 Chron. 6:30

They have humbled themselves; therefore I will not destroy them.
2 Chron. 12:7

Nevertheless there are good things found in thee.
2 Chron. 19:3

Serve the Lord your God, that the fierce-

ness of His wrath may turn away from you.
2 Chron. 30:8

The good Lord pardon every one That prepareth his heart to seek God.
2 Chron. 30:18–19

Remember not the sins of my youth.
Ps. 25:7

According to Thy mercy remember Thou me for Thy goodness' sake.
Ps. 25:7

Blessed is he whose transgression is forgiven.
Ps. 32:1

He remembered that they were but flesh; a wind that passeth away, and cometh not again.
Ps. 78:39

Wilt Thou be angry for ever? shall Thy jealousy burn like fire?
Ps. 79:5

He will not always chide: neither will He keep His anger for ever.
Ps. 103:9

Hatred stirreth up strifes: but love covereth all sins.
Prov. 10:12

A brother offended is harder to be won than a strong city.
Prov. 18:19

Though your sins be as scarlet, they shall be as white as snow.
Isa. 1:18

Thou hast played the harlot with many lovers; yet return again to Me, saith the Lord.
Jer. 3:1

I am merciful, saith the Lord, and I will not keep anger for ever.
God to Jews
Jer. 3:12

I will forgive their iniquity, and I will remember their sin no more.
Jer. 31:34
See also, e.g., Heb. 8:12

I repent Me of the evil that I have done unto you.
Jer. 42:10

I will pardon them whom I reserve.
Jer. 50:20

Though they cry in Mine ears with a loud voice, yet will I not hear them.
Ezek. 8:18

In his righteousness that he hath done he shall live.
Ezek. 18:22

O Lord, hear; O Lord, forgive; O Lord, hearken and do.
Dan. 9:19

Defer not, for Thine own sake, O my God: for Thy city and Thy people are called by Thy name.
Dan. 9:19

Spare Thy people, O Lord, and give not Thine heritage to reproach.
Joel 2:17

I will restore to you the years that the locust hath eaten.
Joel 2:25

Who can tell if God will turn and repent, and turn away from His fierce anger?
Jonah 3:9

God repented of the evil, that He had said that He would do unto them; and He did it not.
Jonah 3:10

He retaineth not His anger for ever, because He delighteth in mercy.
Mic. 7:18

[*See also* Anger, Confession, God's Anger, Repentance, Retribution, Revenge, Sin]

FORTITUDE

Thou wilt surely wear away, both thou, and this people that is with thee.
Jethro to Moses
Ex. 18:18

I am as strong this day as I was in the day that Moses sent me.
Josh. 14:11

As my strength was then, even so is my strength now.
Josh. 14:11

God is my strength and power: and He maketh my way perfect.
2 Sam. 22:33

O God, strengthen my hands.
Neh. 6:9

Is my strength the strength of stones? or is my flesh of brass?
Job 6:12

God is our refuge and strength, a very present help in trouble.
Ps. 46:1

God is the strength of my heart, and my portion for ever.
Ps. 73:26

They go from strength to strength.
Ps. 84:7

They that wait upon the Lord shall renew their strength; they shall mount up with wings as eagles; they shall run, and not be weary.
Isa. 40:31

If thou hast run with the footmen, and they have wearied thee, then how canst thou contend with horses?
Jer. 12:5

[See also Diligence, Patience, Perseverance, Strength, Temptation]

FRAILTY

Remember, I beseech Thee, that Thou hast made me as the clay.
Job 10:9

Have mercy upon me, O Lord; for I am weak.
Ps. 6:2

Every man at his best state is altogether vanity.
Ps. 39:5

If thou faint in the day of adversity, thy strength is small.
Prov. 24:10

We all do fade as a leaf.
Isa. 64:6

[See also Fortitude, Mortality, Strength]

FREEDOM

When ye go, ye shall not go empty.
God to Moses
Ex. 3:21

Thus saith the Lord God of Israel, Let My people go.
E.g., Ex. 5:1
See also, e.g., Ex. 8:20

It is a night to be much observed unto the Lord.
Ex. 12:42

Remember this day, in which ye came out from Egypt, out of the house of bondage.
Ex. 13:3

It had been better for us to serve the Egyptians, than that we should die in the wilderness.
Ex. 14:12

Proclaim liberty throughout all the land unto all the inhabitants thereof.
Lev. 25:10

The Lord brought us forth out of Egypt with a mighty hand, and with an outstretched arm.
Deut. 26:8

The small and great are there; and the servant is free from his master.
Job, speaking of death
Job 3:19

He bringeth out those which are bound with chains.
Ps. 68:6

They shall take them captives, whose captives they were.
Isa. 14:2

The ransomed of the Lord shall return, and come to Zion with songs and everlasting joy.
Isa. 35:10

Ye shall not go out with haste, nor go by flight: for the Lord will go before you.
Isa. 52:12

Behold, all the land is before thee: whither it seemeth good and convenient for thee to go, thither go.
Jer. 40:4

I will make you a name and a praise among all people of the earth, when I turn back your captivity before your eyes.
Zeph. 3:20

[*See also* Captivity, Deliverance, Exile, Imprisonment, Slavery]

FRIENDSHIP

The Lord do so to me, and more also, if ought but death part thee and me.
Ruth 1:17

The soul of Jonathan was knit with the soul of David, and Jonathan loved him as his own soul.
1 Sam. 18:1

Whatsoever thy soul desireth, I will even do it for thee.
Jonathan to David
1 Sam. 20:4

He loved him as he loved his own soul.
(spoken of Jonathan and David)
1 Sam. 20:17

Thy love to me was wonderful, passing the love of women.
David, about Jonathan
2 Sam. 1:26

Thou lovest thine enemies, and hatest thy friends.
2 Sam. 19:6

As the Lord liveth, and as thy soul liveth, I will not leave thee.
E.g., 2 Kings 2:2

Miserable comforters are ye all.
Job to his friends
Job 16:2

My friends scorn me: but mine eye poureth out tears unto God.
Job 16:20

It was not an enemy that reproached me; then I could have borne it.
Ps. 55:12

A talebearer revealeth secrets: but he that is of a faithful spirit concealeth the matter.
Prov. 11:13

The poor is hated even of his own neighbour: but the rich hath many friends.
Prov. 14:20

A friend loveth at all times, and a brother is born for adversity.
Prov. 17:17

There is a friend that sticketh closer than a brother.
Prov. 18:24

Wealth maketh many friends; but the poor is separated from his neighbour.
Prov. 19:4

Every man is a friend to him that giveth gifts.
Prov. 19:6

Make no friendship with an angry man.
Prov. 22:24

Faithful are the wounds of a friend; but the kisses of an enemy are deceitful.
Prov. 27:6

Thine own friend, and thy father's friend, forsake not.
Prov. 27:10

Better is a neighbour that is near than a brother far off.
Prov. 27:10

Iron sharpeneth iron; so a man sharpeneth the countenance of his friend.
Prov. 27:17

Woe to him that is alone when he falleth; for he hath not another to help him up.
Eccl. 4:10

[*See also* Brotherhood, Companions]

FRUSTRATION

The Lord bringeth the counsel of the heathen to nought.
Ps. 33:10

They have sown wheat, but shall reap

thorns: they have put themselves to pain, but shall not profit.
Jer. 12:13

She shall follow after her lovers, but she shall not overtake them.
Hos. 2:7

Thou shalt eat, but not be satisfied.
Mic. 6:14

Thou shalt sow, but thou shalt not reap.
Mic. 6:15

They shall also build houses, but not inhabit them; and they shall plant vineyards, but not drink the wine thereof.
Zeph. 1:13
See also Amos 5:11

[*See also* Disappointment, Futility]

FULFILLMENT

He satisfieth the longing soul, and filleth the hungry soul with goodness.
Ps. 107:9

Surely as I have thought, so shall it come to pass; and as I have purposed, so shall it stand.
God
Isa. 14:24

Every one that thirsteth, come ye to the waters, and he that hath no money; come ye, buy, and eat.
Isa. 55:1

[*See also* Contentment, Reward, Satisfaction]

FUTILITY

Ye shall sow your seed in vain, for your enemies shall eat it.
Lev. 26:16

Wherefore then dost thou ask of me, seeing the Lord is departed from thee, and is become thine enemy?
Samuel to Saul
1 Sam. 28:16

Knowest thou not that it will be bitterness in the latter end?
2 Sam. 2:26

The Lord hath said unto him, Curse

David. Who shall then say, Wherefore hast thou done so?
2 Sam. 16:10

Fight ye not against the Lord God of your fathers; for ye shall not prosper.
2 Chron. 13:12

Call now, if there be any that will answer thee.
Job 5:1

If I be wicked, why then labour I in vain?
Job 9:29

Your remembrances are like unto ashes.
Job 13:12

They cried, but there was none to save them: even unto the Lord, but He answered them not.
Ps. 18:41

Vain is the help of man.
Ps. 60:11

The Lord knoweth the thoughts of man, that they are vanity.
Ps. 94:11
See also 1 Cor. 3:20

Vanity of vanities; all is vanity.
Eccl. 1:2
See also Eccl. 12:8

What profit hath a man of all his labour which he taketh under the sun?
Eccl. 1:3

Behold, all is vanity and vexation of spirit.
Eccl. 1:14
See also, e.g., Eccl. 2:17

What hath man of all his labour, and of the vexation of his heart, wherein he hath laboured under the sun?
Eccl. 2:22

As he came forth of his mother's womb, naked shall he return to go as he came, and shall take nothing of his labour.
Eccl. 5:15

What profit hath he that hath laboured for the wind?
Eccl. 5:16

All that cometh is vanity.
Eccl. 11:8

In vain is salvation hoped for from the

hills, and from the multitude of mountains.
Jer. 3:23

Though thou deckest thee with ornaments of gold, though thou rentest thy face with painting, in vain shalt thou make thyself fair.
Jer. 4:30

They have sown the wind, and they shall reap the whirlwind.
Hos. 8:7

He that is swift of foot shall not deliver himself: neither shall he that rideth the horse.
Amos 2:15

They shall run to and fro to seek the word of the Lord, and shall not find it.
Amos 8:12

Ye have sown much, and bring in little; ye eat, but ye have not enough; ye drink, but ye are not filled.
Hag. 1:6

They shall build, but I will throw down.
God, about Edom
Mal. 1:4

[*See also* Disappointment, Frustration]

FUTURE

What God is about to do He showeth unto Pharaoh.
Gen. 41:28

Hast thou not heard long ago how I have done it, and of ancient times that I have formed it?
God
2 Kings 19:25, Isa. 37:26

Boast not thyself of to morrow; for thou knowest not what a day may bring forth.
Prov. 27:1

Shut thou up the vision; for it shall be for many days.
Dan. 8:26

[*See also* Ambition, Dreams, Posterity, Visions, Worry]

GENEROSITY

Every man shall give as he is able, according to the blessing of the Lord thy God which He hath given thee.
Deut. 16:17

Let her glean even among the sheaves, and reproach her not.
Ruth 2:15

Ask what I shall give thee.
God to Solomon
1 Kings 3:5, 2 Chron. 1:7

Send portions unto them for whom nothing is prepared.
Neh. 8:10

The righteous showeth mercy, and giveth.
Ps. 37:21

A good man showeth favour, and lendeth.
Ps. 112:5

He that watereth shall be watered also himself.
Prov. 11:25

[*See also* Altruism, Charity, Selfishness, Selflessness, Sharing]

GIFTS

He made him a coat of many colours.
Gen. 37:3

A gift in secret pacifieth anger.
Prov. 21:14

[*See also* Altruism, Bribery, Generosity]

GLOATING

Let not them that are mine enemies wrongfully rejoice over me.
Ps. 35:19

Rejoice not when thine enemy falleth, and let not thine heart be glad when he stumbleth.
Prov. 24:17

All mine enemies have heard of my trouble; they are glad that Thou hast done it.
Lam. 1:21

[*See also* Arrogance, Boasting, Conceit, Humility, Pride]

GLORY

The journey that thou takest shall not be for thine honour.
Judg. 4:9

Let them that love Him be as the sun when he goeth forth in his might.
Judg. 5:31

A chariot of fire.
2 Kings 2:11

He died in a good old age, full of days, riches, and honour.
(He: David)
1 Chron. 29:28

In Thy light shall we see light.
Ps. 36:9

In God is my salvation and my glory.
Ps. 62:7

Not unto us, O Lord, not unto us, but unto Thy name give glory.
Ps. 115:1

The wise shall inherit glory: but shame shall be the promotion of fools.
Prov. 3:35

For men to search their own glory is not glory.
Prov. 25:27

[*See also* Fame, God's Glory, Respect]

GLUTTONY

Put a knife to thy throat, if thou be a man given to appetite.
Prov. 23:2

The drunkard and the glutton shall come to poverty.
Prov. 23:21

Let us eat and drink; for to morrow we shall die.
Isa. 22:13, 1 Cor. 15:32

[*See also* Food]

GOALS

The Lord thy God hath set the land before thee: go up and possess it.
Deut. 1:21

Give me now wisdom and knowledge.
Solomon to God
2 Chron. 1:10

[*See also* Ambition, Duty, Mission, Values]

GOD

I am the God of thy father, the God of Abraham, the God of Isaac, and the God of Jacob.
Ex. 3:6
See also, e.g., Mark 12:26

I Am That I Am.
Ex. 3:14

I am the Lord.
E.g., Ex. 6:2

The Lord shall reign for ever and ever.
E.g., Ex. 15:18

I am the Lord thy God, which have brought thee out of the land of Egypt, out of the house of bondage.
Ex. 20:2
See also, e.g., Ex. 29:46, Deut. 5:6

Thou shalt find Him, if thou seek Him with all thy heart and with all thy soul.
Deut. 4:29

He is thy praise.
Deut. 10:21

He is thy life, and the length of thy days.
Deut. 30:20

He is the Rock, His work is perfect.
Deut. 32:4

The Lord liveth.
2 Sam. 22:47, Ps. 18:46

The Lord is God.
1 Kings 8:60

Him shall ye fear, and Him shall ye worship, and to Him shall ye do sacrifice.
2 Kings 17:36

Lord, Thou art God.
1 Chron. 17:26

If thou seek Him, He will be found of thee.
1 Chron. 28:9
See also 2 Chron. 15:2

The Lord shall endure for ever.
Ps. 9:7
See also, e.g., Ps. 102:12

As for God, His way is perfect.
Ps. 18:30, 2 Sam. 22:31

Blessed be the Lord.
E.g., Ps. 31:21

Blessed be God.
E.g., Ps. 68:35

Thou art my father, my God, and the rock of my salvation.
Ps. 89:26

Blessed be the name of the Lord from this time forth and for evermore.
Ps. 113:2

Remember now thy Creator in the days of thy youth.
Eccl. 12:1

The Lord is our judge, the Lord is our lawgiver, the Lord is our king; He will save us.
Isa. 33:22

I am the Lord thy God, that divided the sea, whose waves roared: The Lord of hosts is His name.
Isa. 51:15

I the Lord am thy Saviour and thy Redeemer.
Isa. 60:16

O Lord, Thou art our Father.
Isa. 64:8

The Lord is the true God, He is the living God, and an everlasting king.
Jer. 10:10

All that forsake Thee shall be ashamed.
Jer. 17:13

The Lord, the fountain of living waters.
Jer. 17:13

Behold, all souls are Mine.
Ezek. 18:4

Blessed be the name of God for ever and ever.
Dan. 2:20
See also Ps. 145:1

He giveth wisdom unto the wise, and knowledge to them that know understanding.
Dan. 2:21

The Lord our God is righteous in all His works which He doeth.
Dan. 9:14

The ways of the Lord are right, and the just shall walk in them: but the transgressors shall fall therein.
Hos. 14:9

I am the Lord, I change not.
Mal. 3:6

[*See also* Conduct toward God, Fear of God, Goodness, Holiness, Knowledge of God, Love of God, Praise of God, Reverence, Service to God, Sovereignty, Trust, and the categories which follow]

GOD'S ANGER

How long will it be ere they believe Me, for all the signs which I have showed among them?
Num. 14:11

Shall one man sin, and wilt Thou be wroth with all the congregation?
Num. 16:22

Let not Thine anger be hot against me, and I will speak but this once.
Judg. 6:39

They provoked Him to jealousy with their sins.
1 Kings 14:22

Great is the wrath of the Lord that is kindled against us, because our fathers have not hearkened unto the words of this book.
2 Kings 22:13

The anger of the Lord was kindled against Uzza, and He smote him.
1 Chron. 13:10

His power and His wrath is against all them that forsake Him.
Ezra 8:22

He shall drink of the wrath of the Almighty.
Job 21:20

Rebuke me not in Thine anger, neither chasten me in Thy hot displeasure.
Ps. 6:1
See also Ps. 38:1

His anger endureth but a moment.
Ps. 30:5

Wilt Thou be angry for ever? shall Thy jealousy burn like fire?
Ps. 79:5

Wilt Thou be angry with us for ever? wilt Thou draw out Thine anger to all generations?
Ps. 85:5

He will not always chide: neither will He keep His anger for ever.
Ps. 103:9

For all this His anger is not turned away, but His hand is stretched out still.
E.g., Isa. 9:12

His hand is stretched out, and who shall turn it back?
Isa. 14:27

Lest My fury come forth like fire, and burn that none can quench it.
Jer. 4:4
See also 2 Kings 22:17, Jer. 7:20

The whirlwind of the Lord goeth forth with fury, a continuing whirlwind: it shall fall with pain upon the head of the wicked.
Jer. 30:23

Ye provoke Me unto wrath with the works of your hands.
Jer. 44:8
See also Jer. 25:6

Behold, I will watch over them for evil, and not for good.
Jer. 44:27

In the day of the Lord's anger none escaped nor remained.
Lam. 2:22

Thus saith the Lord God; Behold, I, even I, am against thee.
Ezek. 5:8

I will cause My fury to rest upon them, and I will be comforted.
Ezek. 5:13

I will execute great vengeance upon them with furious rebukes.
Ezek. 25:17

I will pour out My wrath upon them like water.
Hos. 5:10

I will execute vengeance in anger and fury upon the heathen, such as they have not heard.
Mic. 5:15

He reserveth wrath for His enemies.
Nah. 1:2

Who can stand before His indignation? and who can abide in the fierceness of His anger?
Nah. 1:6

His fury is poured out like fire.
Nah. 1:6

Neither their silver nor their gold shall be able to deliver them in the day of the Lord's wrath.
Zeph. 1:18
See also Ezek. 7:19

All the earth shall be devoured with the fire of My jealousy.
Zeph. 3:8

[*See also* Exasperation, Forgiveness, Judgment]

GOD'S GLORY

As truly as I live, all the earth shall be filled with the glory of the Lord.
God
Num. 14:21

Declare His glory among the heathen; His marvellous works among all nations.
1 Chron. 16:24
See also Ps. 96:3

O ye sons of men, how long will ye turn My glory into shame?
Ps. 4:2

The heavens declare the glory of God; and the firmament showeth His handywork.
Ps. 19:1

I will be exalted among the heathen, I will be exalted in the earth.   .
Ps. 46:10

The heavens declare His righteousness, and all the people see His glory.
Ps. 97:6

He saved them for His name's sake, that He might make His mighty power to be known.
Ps. 106:8

Great is the glory of the Lord.
Ps. 138:5

The whole earth is full of His glory.
Isa. 6:3

I am the Lord: that is My name: and My glory will I not give to another.
Isa. 42:8

Do not abhor us, for Thy name's sake, do not disgrace the throne of Thy glory.
Jer. 14:21

I wrought for My name's sake, that it should not be polluted before the heathen.
Ezek. 20:9, 14

I do not this for your sakes, O house of Israel, but for Mine holy name's sake, which ye have profaned.
Ezek. 36:22
See also Ezek. 36:32

I will set My glory among the heathen, and all the heathen shall see My judgment that I have executed.
Ezek. 39:21

I will be glorified, saith the Lord.
Hag. 1:8

My name shall be great among the heathen, saith the Lord of hosts.
Mal. 1:11

GOD'S GOODNESS

See Goodness.

GOD'S GREATNESS

I know that the Lord is greater than all gods.
Ex. 18:11

What God is there in heaven or in earth, that can do according to Thy works?
Deut. 3:24

Thou art great, O Lord God: for there is none like Thee, neither is there any God beside Thee.
2 Sam. 7:22

Let it be known this day that Thou art God in Israel, and that I am Thy servant.
Elijah
1 Kings 18:36

Thine, O Lord, is the greatness, and the power, and the glory, and the victory, and the majesty.
1 Chron. 29:11

The house which I build is great: for great is our God above all gods.
Solomon
2 Chron. 2:5

Heaven and the heaven of heavens cannot contain Thee; how much less this house which I have built!
Solomon
2 Chron. 6:18
See also 1 Kings 8:27

Canst thou by searching find out God?
Job 11:7

Is not God in the height of heaven?
Job 22:12

God is great.
Job 36:26

Great things doeth He, which we cannot comprehend.
Job 37:5

Who is like unto Thee, which deliverest the poor from him that is too strong for him?
Ps. 35:10

Great is the Lord, and greatly to be praised.
E.g., Ps. 48:1

Who is so great a God as our God?
Ps. 77:13

Our Lord is above all gods.
Ps. 135:5

Great is our Lord, and of great power: His understanding is infinite.
Ps. 147:5

Hear, ye that are far off, what I have done; and, ye that are near, acknowledge My might.
Isa. 33:13

Have ye not known? have ye not heard? hath it not been told you from the beginning?
Isa. 40:21

GOD'S KNOWLEDGE

Thou, even Thou only, knowest the hearts of all the children of men.
1 Kings 8:39

I know thy abode, and thy going out, and thy coming in, and thy rage against Me.
2 Kings 19:27, Isa. 37:28

The Lord searcheth all hearts.
1 Chron. 28:9

Doth not He see my ways, and count all my steps?
Job 31:4

His eyes are upon the ways of man, and He seeth all his goings.
Job 34:21

The Lord knoweth the way of the righteous: but the way of the ungodly shall perish.
Ps. 1:6

He that teacheth man knowledge, shall not He know?
Ps. 94:10

There is not a word in my tongue, but, lo, O Lord, Thou knowest it altogether.
Ps. 139:4

The ways of man are before the eyes of the Lord, and He pondereth all his goings.
Prov. 5:21

I know the things that come into your mind, every one of them.
Ezek. 11:5

[*See also* God's Presence, Secrecy]

GOD'S LOVE

The Lord did not set His love upon you, nor choose you, because ye were more in number than any people; for ye were the fewest of all people: But because the Lord loved you.
Deut. 7:7–8

I know that Thou favourest me, because mine enemy doth not triumph over me.
Ps. 41:11

Thy mercy is great unto the heavens, and Thy truth unto the clouds.
Ps. 57:10
See also Ps. 108:4

Thy lovingkindness is better than life.
Ps. 63:3

Cause Thy face to shine; and we shall be saved.
Ps. 80:3, 7, 19

Whoso is wise, and will observe these things, even they shall understand the lovingkindness of the Lord.
Ps. 107:43

The Lord loveth the righteous.
Ps. 146:8

Whom the Lord loveth He correcteth.
Prov. 3:12

The mountains shall depart, and the hills be removed; but My kindness shall not depart from thee.
Isa. 54:10

[*See also* God's Mercy, Love]

GOD'S MERCY

Shall not the Judge of all the earth do right?
Abraham to God
Gen. 18:25

I have looked upon My people, because their cry is come unto Me.
1 Sam. 9:16

My mercy shall not depart away from him.
God to David, about Solomon
2 Sam. 7:15

The Lord your God is gracious and merciful, and will not turn away His face from you, if ye return unto Him.
2 Chron. 30:9

Thou art a God ready to pardon.
Neh. 9:17

Spare me according to the greatness of Thy mercy.
Neh. 13:22

Thou, O Lord, art a God full of compassion, and gracious, longsuffering, and plenteous in mercy and truth.
Ps. 86:15

His mercy is everlasting.
Ps. 100:5

As the heaven is high above the earth, so great is His mercy toward them that fear Him.
Ps. 103:11

His mercy endureth for ever.
E.g., Ps. 118:1

With the Lord there is mercy.
Ps. 130:7

I will not pity, nor spare, nor have mercy, but destroy them.
Jer. 13:14

[*See also* Compassion, God's Love, Mercy]

GOD'S PEOPLE

In thee shall all families of the earth be blessed.
God to Abram
Gen. 12:3
See also Gen. 28:14

Ye are the children of the Lord your God.
Deut. 14:1

The Lord will not forsake His people for His great name's sake.
1 Sam. 12:22

Thou didst separate them from among all the people of the earth, to be Thine inheritance.
1 Kings 8:53

Blessed is the nation whose God is the Lord.
Ps. 33:12

We are the people of His pasture, and the sheep of His hand.
Ps. 95:7
See also Ps. 100:3

As the mountains are round about Jerusalem, so the Lord is round about His people.
Ps. 125:2

The Lord taketh pleasure in His people.
Ps. 149:4

Thou art My servant; I have chosen thee, and not cast thee away.
Isa. 41:9

Fear not: for I have redeemed thee, I have called thee by thy name; thou art Mine.
Isa. 43:1

I have created him for My glory, I have formed him; yea, I have made him.
Isa. 43:7

I have chosen thee in the furnace of affliction.
Isa. 48:10

The redeemed of the Lord shall return, and come with singing unto Zion.
Isa. 51:11

As the days of a tree are the days of My people, and Mine elect shall long enjoy the work of their hands.
Isa. 65:22

Obey My voice, and I will be your God, and ye shall be My people.
Jer. 7:23

Though I make a full end of all nations

whither I have scattered thee, yet will I not make a full end of thee.
Jer. 30:11

Ye My flock, the flock of My pasture, are men, and I am your God.
Ezek. 34:31

They shall be as the stones of a crown, lifted up as an ensign upon His land.
Zech. 9:16

I will say, It is My people: and they shall say, The Lord is my God.
Zech. 13:9

[*See also* Believers, Chosen People]

GOD'S POWER

And God said, Let there be light: and there was light.
Gen. 1:3

Is any thing too hard for the Lord?
Gen. 18:14

Fear ye not, stand still, and see the salvation of the Lord, which He will show to you to-day.
Ex. 14:13

Is the Lord's hand waxed short?
Num. 11:23

Speak ye unto the rock before their eyes; and it shall give forth his water.
God to Moses
Num. 20:8

Alas, who shall live when God doeth this!
Balaam
Num. 24:23

As a consuming fire He shall destroy them, and He shall bring them down before thy face.
Deut. 9:3

The Lord brought us forth out of Egypt with a mighty hand, and with an outstretched arm.
Deut. 26:8

There is no god with Me: I kill, and I make alive; I wound, and I heal: neither is there any that can deliver out of My hand.
Deut. 32:39

The sun stood still in the midst of heaven, and hasted not to go down about a whole day.
Josh. 10:13

The Lord killeth, and maketh alive: He bringeth down to the grave, and bringeth up.
1 Sam. 2:6

The Lord maketh poor, and maketh rich: He bringeth low, and lifteth up.
1 Sam. 2:7

Who is able to stand before this holy Lord God?
1 Sam. 6:20

There is no restraint to the Lord to save by many or by few.
Jonathan
1 Sam. 14:6

I exalted thee out of the dust, and made thee prince over My people Israel.
1 Kings 16:2

Hast thou not heard long ago how I have done it, and of ancient times that I have formed it?
God
2 Kings 19:25, Isa. 37:26

In Thine hand is power and might.
1 Chron. 29:12

The cause was of God, that the Lord might perform His word.
2 Chron. 10:15

God hath power to help, and to cast down.
2 Chron. 25:8

He disappointeth the devices of the crafty, so that their hands cannot perform their enterprise.
Job 5:12

He maketh sore, and bindeth up: He woundeth, and His hands make whole.
Job 5:18

He taketh away, who can hinder Him? who will say unto Him, What doest Thou?
Job 9:12

Speak to the earth, and it shall teach thee: and the fishes of the sea shall declare unto thee.
Job 12:8

What His soul desireth, even that He doeth.
Job 23:13

Hell is naked before Him, and destruction hath no covering.
Job 26:6

The thunder of His power who can understand?
Job 26:14

Whatsoever is under the whole heaven is Mine.
Job 41:11

He maketh the deep to boil like a pot.
Job 41:31

I know that Thou canst do every thing, and that no thought can be withholden from Thee.
Job to God
Job 42:2

Who is this King of glory? The Lord strong and mighty, the Lord mighty in battle.
Ps. 24:8

He spake, and it was done; He commanded, and it stood fast.
Ps. 33:9

The world is Mine, and the fulness thereof.
Ps. 50:12
See also Ex. 19:5

The Lord on high is mightier than the noise of many waters, yea, than the mighty waves of the sea.
Ps. 93:4

The Lord reigneth; let the earth rejoice.
Ps. 97:1

He saved them for His name's sake, that He might make His mighty power to be known.
Ps. 106:8

Our God is in the heavens: He hath done whatsoever He hath pleased.
Ps. 115:3

Who can stand before His cold?
Ps. 147:17

Who can make that straight, which He hath made crooked?
Eccl. 7:13

Surely as I have thought, so shall it come to pass; and as I have purposed, so shall it stand.
God
Isa. 14:24

He shall cry, yea, roar; He shall prevail against His enemies.
Isa. 42:13

I have spoken it, I will also bring it to pass.
Isa. 46:11

I will cause them to know Mine hand and My might; and they shall know that My name is The Lord.
Jer. 16:21

As the clay is in the potter's hand, so are ye in Mine hand, O house of Israel.
Jer. 18:6
See also Rom. 9:21

I am the Lord, the God of all flesh: is there any thing too hard for Me?
Jer. 32:27

Like as I have brought all this great evil upon this people, so will I bring upon them all the good that I have promised.
Jer. 32:42

That which I have built will I break down, and that which I have planted I will pluck up, even this whole land.
Jer. 45:4

Who is like Me? and who will appoint Me the time? and who is that shepherd that will stand before Me?
Jer. 49:19, Jer. 50:44

He doeth according to His will in the army of heaven, and among the inhabitants of the earth: and none can stay His hand.
Dan. 4:35

None can stay His hand, or say unto Him, What doest Thou?
Dan. 4:35

He hath torn, and He will heal us; He hath smitten, and He will bind us up.
Hos. 6:1

The Lord is His name.
E.g., Amos 9:6

The Lord hath His way in the whirlwind

and in the storm, and the clouds are the dust of His feet.
Nah. 1:3

[*See also* God's Knowledge]

GOD'S PRESENCE

And the Spirit of God moved upon the face of the waters.
Gen. 1:2

Surely the Lord is in this place; and I knew it not.
Gen. 28:16

I have seen God face to face, and my life is preserved.
Jacob
Gen. 32:30

Behold, the bush burned with fire, and the bush was not consumed.
Ex. 3:2

There shall no man see Me, and live.
Ex. 33:20

I will walk among you, and will be your God, and ye shall be My people.
Lev. 26:12
See also 2 Cor. 6:16

We have seen this day that God doth talk with man, and he liveth.
Deut. 5:24

The Lord thy God is among you, a mighty God and terrible.
Deut. 7:21

The Lord thy God is with thee whithersoever thou goest.
Josh. 1:9

The Lord your God, He is God in heaven above, and in earth beneath.
Josh. 2:11

We shall surely die, because we have seen God.
Judg. 13:22

The Lord our God be with us, as He was with our fathers.
1 Kings 8:57

Let Him not leave us, nor forsake us.
1 Kings 8:57

Mine eyes and Mine heart shall be there perpetually.
1 Kings 9:3

Who is able to build Him an house, seeing the heaven and heaven of heavens cannot contain Him?
2 Chron. 2:6

The eyes of the Lord run to and fro throughout the whole earth.
2 Chron. 16:9

Upon whom doth not His light arise?
Job 25:3

He hideth His face, who then can behold Him?
Job 34:29

The voice of the Lord is upon the waters.
Ps. 29:3

He that planted the ear, shall He not hear? He that formed the eye, shall He not see?
Ps. 94:9

He is the Lord our God: His judgments are in all the earth.
Ps. 105:7, 1 Chron. 16:14

If I ascend up into heaven, Thou art there: if I make my bed in hell, behold, Thou art there.
Ps. 139:8

The Lord is nigh unto all them that call upon Him, to all that call upon Him in truth.
Ps. 145:18

The eyes of the Lord are in every place, beholding the evil and the good.
Prov. 15:3

The Spirit of the Lord God is upon me.
Isa. 61:1

The heaven is My throne, and the earth is My footstool.
Isa. 66:1
See also Acts 7:49

Am I a God at hand, saith the Lord, and not a God afar off?
Jer. 23:23

Can any hide himself in secret places that I shall not see him? saith the Lord. Do not I fill heaven and earth?
Jer. 23:24

My spirit remaineth among you: fear ye not.
Hag. 2:5

Lo, I come, and I will dwell in the midst of thee, saith the Lord.
Zech. 2:10

[*See also* Awe, Churches, God's Temple]

GOD'S PROTECTION

Whosoever slayeth Cain, vengeance shall be taken on him sevenfold.
Gen. 4:15

The Lord set a mark upon Cain.
Gen. 4:15

I will bless them that bless thee, and curse him that curseth thee.
God to Abram
Gen. 12:3

I am thy shield, and thy exceeding great reward.
God to Abram
Gen. 15:1

Deliver me, I pray Thee, from the hand of my brother.
Jacob to God, about Esau
Gen. 32:11

Against any of the children of Israel shall not a dog move his tongue.
Ex. 11:7

The Lord went before them by day in a pillar of a cloud, to lead them the way; and by night in a pillar of fire, to give them light.
Ex. 13:21
See also, e.g., Num. 14:14

Let us flee from the face of Israel; for the Lord fighteth for them.
Ex. 14:25

I will be an enemy unto thine enemies, and an adversary unto thine adversaries.
God
Ex. 23:22

The Lord thy God is among you, a mighty God and terrible.
Deut. 7:21

All people of the earth shall see that thou art called by the name of the Lord; and they shall be afraid of thee.
Deut. 28:10

As I was with Moses, so I will be with thee.
God to Joshua
Josh. 1:5, Josh. 3:7

The Lord saveth not with sword and spear: for the battle is the Lord's.
David to Goliath
1 Sam. 17:47
See also 2 Chron. 20:15

He is my shield, and the horn of my salvation, my high tower, and my refuge.
David
2 Sam. 22:3

They prevented me in the day of my calamity: but the Lord was my stay.
2 Sam. 22:19, Ps. 18:18

He is a buckler to all them that trust in Him.
2 Sam. 22:31
See also Ps. 18:30

He shall deliver you out of the hand of all your enemies.
2 Kings 17:39

On whom dost thou trust, that thou rebellest against me?
King of Assyria to King of Judah
2 Kings 18:20, Isa. 36:5

He shall not come into this city, nor shoot an arrow there.
2 Kings 19:32, Isa. 37:33

I will defend this city, to save it, for Mine own sake, and for My servant David's sake.
2 Kings 19:34, Isa. 37:35
See also 2 Kings 20:6

I will subdue all thine enemies.
1 Chron. 17:10

The hand of our God is upon all them for good that seek Him.
Ezra 8:22

Hast not Thou made an hedge about him, and about his house?
Satan to God, of Job
Job 1:10

He saveth the poor from the sword, from

their mouth, and from the hand of the mighty.
Job 5:15

Am I a sea, or a whale, that Thou settest a watch over me?
Job 7:12

Thou, O Lord, art a shield for me; my glory, and the lifter up of mine head.
Ps. 3:3

O God, lift up Thine hand: forget not the humble.
Ps. 10:12

In the Lord put I my trust.
Ps. 11:1
See also, e.g., Ps. 71:1

Thou wilt not leave my soul in hell; neither wilt Thou suffer Thine Holy One to see corruption.
Ps. 16:10

Keep me as the apple of the eye, hide me under the shadow of Thy wings.
Ps. 17:8

The Lord is my rock, and my fortress, and my deliverer; my God, my strength, in whom I will trust.
Ps. 18:2

Be not far from me; for trouble is near; for there is none to help.
Ps. 22:11

The Lord is my shepherd; I shall not want.
Ps. 23:1

Thy rod and Thy staff they comfort me.
Ps. 23:4

The Lord is my strength and my shield.
Ps. 28:7

The eye of the Lord is upon them that fear Him.
Ps. 33:18

The eyes of the Lord are upon the righteous, and His ears are open unto their cry.
Ps. 34:15

Who is like unto Thee, which deliverest the poor from him that is too strong for him?
Ps. 35:10

The Lord loveth judgment, and forsaketh not His saints.
Ps. 37:28

Deliver me from the deceitful and unjust man.
Ps. 43:1

God is my defence.
Ps. 59:17
See also Ps. 94:22

Give us help from trouble: for vain is the help of man.
Ps. 60:11

He only is my rock and my salvation: He is my defence; I shall not be moved.
Ps. 62:6

His truth shall be thy shield and buckler.
Ps. 91:4

Thou shalt not be afraid for the terror by night; nor for the arrow that flieth by day.
Ps. 91:5

A thousand shall fall at thy side, and ten thousand at thy right hand; but it shall not come nigh thee.
Ps. 91:7

He suffered no man to do them wrong.
Ps. 105:14, 1 Chron. 16:21

Touch not Mine anointed, and do My prophets no harm.
Ps. 105:15, 1 Chron. 16:22

Sit thou at My right hand, until I make thine enemies thy footstool.
Ps. 110:1
See also, e.g., Matt. 22:44

Ye that fear the Lord, trust in the Lord: He is their help and their shield.
Ps. 115:11

He that keepeth thee will not slumber.
Ps. 121:3

The Lord is thy keeper.
Ps. 121:5

The sun shall not smite thee by day, nor the moon by night.
Ps. 121:6

Our help is in the name of the Lord.
Ps. 124:8

Thy right hand shall save me.
Ps. 138:7

My goodness, and my fortress; my high

tower, and my deliverer; my shield, and
He in whom I trust.
Ps. 144:2

The name of the Lord is a strong tower:
the righteous runneth into it, and is safe.
Prov. 18:10

He is a shield unto them that put their
trust in Him.
Prov. 30:5

Awake, awake, put on strength, O arm of
the Lord; awake, as in the ancient days, in
the generations of old.
Isa. 51:9

He that scattered Israel will gather him,
and keep him, as a shepherd doth his
flock.
Jer. 31:10

I will surely deliver thee.
Jer. 39:18

Come not near any man upon whom is the
mark.
Ezek. 9:6

I will feed My flock, and I will cause them
to lie down, saith the Lord God.
Ezek. 34:15

My God hath sent His angel, and hath
shut the lions' mouths.
Dan. 6:22

The Lord is good, a strong hold in the day
of trouble.
Nah. 1:7

Thy strong holds shall be like fig trees with
the firstripe figs: if they be shaken, they
shall even fall into the mouth of the eater.
Nah. 3:12

His arrow shall go forth as the lightning:
and the Lord God shall blow the trumpet.
Zech. 9:14

[See also Assistance, Enemies, Fear,
God's Presence, God's Support, Reliance,
Security, Trust, and the Appendix at p.
273]

GOD'S SUPPORT

The Lord bless thee, and keep thee.
Num. 6:24

Go not up, neither fight; for I am not
among you.
Deut. 1:42

He will not fail thee, nor forsake thee.
Deut. 31:6
See also Josh. 1:5, Heb. 13:5

Be not afraid, neither be thou dismayed:
for the Lord thy God is with thee whithersoever thou goest.
Josh. 1:9

The living God is among you.
Josh. 3:10

The sun stood still, and the moon stayed,
until the people had avenged themselves
upon their enemies.
Josh. 10:13

The Lord fought for Israel.
Josh. 10:14

The Lord your God, He it is that fighteth
for you.
Josh. 23:10
See also Josh. 23:3

Is not the Lord gone out before thee?
Judg. 4:14

They fought from heaven; the stars in
their courses fought against Sisera.
Judg. 5:20

I will deliver thine enemy into thine hand,
that thou mayest do to him as it shall seem
good unto thee.
God to David
1 Sam. 24:4

I will be his father, and he shall be My
son.
God to David about Solomon
2 Sam. 7:14, 1 Chron. 17:13

Fear not: for they that be with us are more
than they that be with them.
2 Kings 6:16

Go up; for I will deliver them into thine
hand.
1 Chron. 14:10

Seek His face continually.
1 Chron. 16:11

O Lord, Thou art our God; let not man
prevail against Thee.
2 Chron. 14:11

Forbear thee from meddling with God, who is with me, that He destroy thee not.
  2 Chron. 35:21

Our God shall fight for us.
  Neh. 4:20

Their clothes waxed not old, and their feet swelled not.
  Neh. 9:21

God will not cast away a perfect man, neither will He help the evil doers.
  Job 8:20

My witness is in heaven, and my record is on high.
  Job 16:19

Thou preparest a table before me in the presence of mine enemies: Thou anointest my head with oil; my cup runneth over.
  Ps. 23:5

Into Thine hand I commit my spirit.
  Ps. 31:5

Thou art the God of my strength: why dost Thou cast me off?
  Ps. 43:2

God is our refuge and strength, a very present help in trouble.
  Ps. 46:1

Cast thy burden upon the Lord, and He shall sustain thee.
  Ps. 55:22

Thou art my help and my deliverer; O Lord, make no tarrying.
  Ps. 70:5
  See also Ps. 40:17

Whom have I in heaven but Thee?
  Ps. 73:25

He is my refuge and my fortress: my God; in Him will I trust.
  Ps. 91:2
  See also Ps. 71:3

When I said, My foot slippeth; Thy mercy, O Lord, held me up.
  Ps. 94:18

The Lord preserveth the simple.
  Ps. 116:6

The Lord upholdeth all that fall, and raiseth up all those that be bowed down.
  Ps. 145:14

The Lord is far from the wicked: but He heareth the prayer of the righteous.
  Prov. 15:29

Strengthen ye the weak hands, and confirm the feeble knees.
  Isa. 35:3

He giveth power to the faint; and to them that have no might He increaseth strength.
  Isa. 40:29

I am thy God: I will strengthen thee; yea, I will help thee; yea, I will uphold thee with the right hand of My righteousness.
  Isa. 41:10

I will help thee, saith the Lord.
  Isa. 41:14

When the poor and needy seek water, and there is none, and their tongue faileth for thirst, I the Lord will hear them, I the God of Israel will not forsake them.
  Isa. 41:17

Even to your old age I am He; and even to hoar hairs will I carry you.
  Isa. 46:4

O Israel, thou hast destroyed thyself; but in Me is thine help.
  Hos. 13:9

I am with you, saith the Lord.
  Hag. 1:13, Hag. 2:4

[*See also* Abandonment, Encouragement, Faith, God's Protection]

GOD'S TEMPLE

He is my God, and I will prepare Him an habitation; my father's God, and I will exalt Him.
  Ex. 15:2

Mine eyes and Mine heart shall be there perpetually.
  1 Kings 9:3

Let her not be slain in the house of the Lord.
  2 Kings 11:15
  See also 2 Chron. 23:14

He shall build Me an house, and I will stablish his throne for ever.
  (He: Solomon)
  1 Chron. 17:12

The house which I build is great: for great is our God above all gods.
Solomon
2 Chron. 2:5

But will God in very deed dwell with men on the earth?
2 Chron. 6:18
See also 1 Kings 8:27

Whatsoever is commanded by the God of heaven, let it be diligently done for the house of the God of heaven.
Ezra 7:23

The Lord is in His holy temple: let all the earth keep silence before Him.
Hab. 2:20

[*See also* Churches]

GOD'S UNIQUENESS

There is none like Me in all the earth.
Ex. 9:14

Who is like unto Thee, O Lord, among the gods? who is like Thee, glorious in holiness, fearful in praises, doing wonders?
Ex. 15:11

What God is there in heaven or in earth, that can do according to Thy works?
Deut. 3:24

The Lord He is God in heaven above, and upon the earth beneath: there is none else.
Deut. 4:39

See now that I, even I, am He.
Deut. 32:39

There is no god with Me: I kill, and I make alive; I wound, and I heal: neither is there any that can deliver out of My hand.
Deut. 32:39

Who is God, save the Lord?
2 Sam. 22:32, Ps. 18:31

There is no God like Thee, in heaven above, or on earth beneath.
1 Kings 8:23

Thou, even Thou, art Lord alone.
Neh. 9:6

O God, who is like unto Thee!
Ps. 71:19

To whom then will ye liken God? or what likeness will ye compare unto Him?
Isa. 40:18
See also, e.g., Isa. 46:5

I, even I, am the Lord; and beside Me there is no saviour.
Isa. 43:11

I am the first, and I am the last; and beside Me there is no God.
Isa. 44:6
See also Isa. 48:12

I am God, and there is none else; I am God, and there is none like Me.
E.g., Isa. 46:9

I am He; I am the first, I also am the last.
Isa. 48:12

Who is like Me? and who will appoint Me the time? and who is that shepherd that will stand before Me?
Jer. 49:19, Jer. 50:44

[*See also* Monotheism]

GOD'S WILL

It is the Lord: let Him do what seemeth Him good.
1 Sam. 3:18
See also 2 Sam. 15:26

[*See also* Certainty]

GOD'S WORD

The word is very nigh unto thee, in thy mouth, and in thy heart.
Deut. 30:14
See also Rom. 10:8

Thus saith the Lord.
E.g., 1 Kings 12:24

Good is the word of the Lord which thou hast spoken.
2 Kings 20:19, Isa. 39:8

In His word do I hope.
Ps. 130:5

The grass withereth, the flower fadeth: but the word of our God shall stand for ever.
Isa. 40:8
See also 1 Pet. 1:24–25

Every one that thirsteth, come ye to the

waters, and he that hath no money; come ye, buy, and eat.
Isa. 55:1

I the Lord have spoken it.
Ezek. 5:13, 17

They shall run to and fro to seek the word of the Lord, and shall not find it.
Amos 8:12

[*See also* Commandments, Scripture]

GOD, NAMES OF

I am God Almighty.
E.g., Gen. 35:11

I Am That I Am.
Ex. 3:14

The Lord your God is God of gods, and Lord of lords.
Deut. 10:17

The Most High.
Deut. 32:8

Lord God of Israel.
1 Chron. 29:10

The Lord of hosts, He is the King of glory.
Ps. 24:10

Thou, whose name alone is JEHOVAH.
Ps. 83:18

Know ye that the Lord He is God.
Ps. 100:3
See also 1 Kings 18:39

The Lord of hosts is His name.
Jer. 31:35

Their Redeemer is strong; the Lord of hosts is His name.
Jer. 50:34

The Lord is His name.
E.g., Amos 9:6

GOD, TRAITS OF

The Lord is a man of war: the Lord is His name.
Ex. 15:3

Who is like unto Thee, O Lord, among the

gods? who is like Thee, glorious in holiness, fearful in praises, doing wonders?
Ex. 15:11

I the Lord thy God am a jealous God.
E.g., Ex. 20:5

The Lord, The Lord God, merciful and gracious, longsuffering, and abundant in goodness and truth.
Ex. 34:6

The Lord, whose name is Jealous, is a jealous God.
Ex. 34:14

God is not a man, that He should lie; neither the son of man, that He should repent: hath He said, and shall He not do it? or hath He spoken, and shall He not make it good?
Num. 23:19

The Lord thy God is a consuming fire, even a jealous God.
Deut. 4:24
See also Heb. 12:29

The Lord thy God is a merciful God.
Deut. 4:31

A God of truth and without iniquity, just and right is He.
Deut. 32:4

He is an holy God; He is a jealous God; He will not forgive your transgressions nor your sins.
Josh. 24:19

With the merciful Thou wilt show Thyself merciful, and with the upright man Thou wilt show Thyself upright.
2 Sam. 22:26
See also Ps. 18:25

The Lord is righteous.
2 Chron. 12:6

God will not do wickedly, neither will the Almighty pervert judgment.
Job 34:12

All the paths of the Lord are mercy and truth unto such as keep His covenant.
Ps. 25:10

Thy mercy is great unto the heavens, and Thy truth unto the clouds.
Ps. 57:10
See also Ps. 108:4

The Lord is good; His mercy is everlast-

ing; and His truth endureth to all generations.
Ps. 100:5

Thou art the same, and Thy years shall
have no end.
Ps. 102:27

The Lord is merciful and gracious, slow to
anger, and plenteous in mercy.
Ps. 103:8

The works of His hands are verity and
judgment; all His commandments are
sure.
Ps. 111:7

The Lord is gracious, and full of compassion; slow to anger, and of great mercy.
Ps. 145:8

The Lord is righteous in all His ways, and
holy in all His works.
Ps. 145:17

The Lord is a God of judgment: blessed
are all they that wait for Him.
Isa. 30:18

To the Lord our God belong mercies and
forgivenesses, though we have rebelled
against Him.
Dan. 9:9

He is gracious and merciful, slow to anger,
and of great kindness.
Joel 2:13
See also Jonah 4:2

GODLESSNESS

I know not the Lord, neither will I let
Israel go.
Pharaoh
Ex. 5:2

Come not among these nations, these that
remain among you.
Josh. 23:7

There arose another generation after
them, which knew not the Lord.
Judg. 2:10

What profit should we have, if we pray
unto Him?
Job 21:15

The hypocrites in heart heap up wrath:
they cry not when He bindeth them.
Job 36:13

The way of the ungodly shall perish.
Ps. 1:6

The wicked shall be turned into hell, and
all the nations that forget God.
Ps. 9:17

How long shall the adversary reproach?
shall the enemy blaspheme Thy name for
ever?
Ps. 74:10

The foolish man reproacheth Thee daily.
Ps. 74:22

The tumult of those that rise up against
Thee increaseth continually.
Ps. 74:23

A stubborn and rebellious generation; a
generation that set not their heart aright,
and whose spirit was not stedfast with
God.
Ps. 78:8

Wherefore should the heathen say, Where
is now their God?
Ps. 115:2
See also Ps. 79:10

It is time for Thee, Lord, to work: for they
have made void Thy law.
Ps. 119:126

The ox knoweth his owner, and the ass his
master's crib: but Israel doth not know,
My people doth not consider.
Isa. 1:3

Seeing many things, but thou observest
not; opening the ears, but he heareth not.
Isa. 42:20
See also, e.g., Matt. 13:13

Of whom hast thou been afraid or feared,
that thou hast lied, and hast not remembered Me?
Isa. 57:11

My people is foolish, they have not known
Me.
Jer. 4:22

Shall not My soul be avenged on such a nation as this?
Jer. 5:9

Learn not the way of the heathen.
Jer. 10:2

Pour out Thy fury upon the heathen that know Thee not, and upon the families that call not on Thy name.
Jer. 10:25

Walk ye not in the statutes of your fathers, neither observe their judgments, nor defile yourselves with their idols.
Ezek. 20:18

I will send a famine in the land, not a famine of bread, nor a thirst for water, but of hearing the words of the Lord.
Amos 8:11

The day of the Lord is near upon all the heathen.
Obad. 15

I will execute vengeance in anger and fury upon the heathen, such as they have not heard.
Mic. 5:15

The good man is perished out of the earth: and there is none upright among men.
Mic. 7:2

[*See also* Atheism, Backsliding, Faith, Godliness, Idolatry, Rebellion, Sin]

GODLINESS

Happy is that people, whose God is the Lord.
Ps. 144:15

Though a sinner do evil an hundred times, and his days be prolonged, yet surely I know that it shall be well with them that fear God.
Eccl. 8:12

[*See also* Righteousness]

Of every tree of the garden thou mayest freely eat: But of the tree of the knowledge of good and evil, thou shalt not eat.
Gen. 2:16–17

Your eyes shall be opened, and ye shall be as gods, knowing good and evil.
Gen. 3:5

The Lord God said, Behold, the man is become as one of us, to know good and evil.
Gen. 3:22

I have set before thee this day life and good, and death and evil.
Deut. 30:15

Give therefore Thy servant an understanding heart to judge Thy people, that I may discern between good and bad.
Solomon
1 Kings 3:9

When I looked for good, then evil came unto me: and when I waited for light, there came darkness.
Job 30:26

They have rewarded me evil for good, and hatred for my love.
Ps. 109:5
See also 1 Sam. 25:21

The eyes of the Lord are in every place, beholding the evil and the good.
Prov. 15:3

Whoso rewardeth evil for good, evil shall not depart from his house.
Prov. 17:13

Woe unto them that call evil good, and good evil.
Isa. 5:20

Butter and honey shall he eat, that he may know to refuse the evil, and choose the good.
Isa. 7:15

I make peace, and create evil: I the Lord do all these things.
Isa. 45:7

They are wise to do evil, but to do good they have no knowledge.
Jer. 4:22

Can the Ethiopian change his skin, or the

leopard his spots? then may ye also do good, that are accustomed to do evil.
Jer. 13:23

I have set My face against this city for evil, and not for good, saith the Lord.
(city: Jerusalem)
Jer. 21:10

Out of the mouth of the most High proceedeth not evil and good?
Lam. 3:38

Seek good, and not evil, that ye may live.
Amos 5:14

Hate the evil, and love the good, and establish judgment in the gate.
Amos 5:15

Discern between the righteous and the wicked, between him that serveth God and him that serveth Him not.
Mal. 3:18

[*See also* Corruption, Evil, Wickedness]

GOODNESS

Thou art not a God that hath pleasure in wickedness.
Ps. 5:4

Surely goodness and mercy shall follow me all the days of my life: and I will dwell in the house of the Lord for ever.
Ps. 23:6

The earth is full of the goodness of the Lord.
Ps. 33:5

The Lord is good.
Ps. 100:5

Give thanks unto the Lord; for He is good: for His mercy endureth for ever.
E.g., Ps. 106:1

Your goodness is as a morning cloud, and as the early dew it goeth away.
Hos. 6:4

The good man is perished out of the earth: and there is none upright among men.
Mic. 7:2

The Lord is good, a strong hold in the day of trouble.
Nah. 1:7

[*See also* Altruism, Good and Evil, Kindness, Righteousness, Virtue]

GOSSIP

Thou shalt not go up and down as a talebearer among thy people.
Lev. 19:16

A talebearer revealeth secrets.
Prov. 11:13

A whisperer separateth chief friends.
Prov. 16:28

The words of a talebearer are as wounds.
Prov. 18:8, Prov. 26:22

Meddle not with him that flattereth with his lips.
Prov. 20:19

Where no wood is, there the fire goeth out: so where there is no talebearer, the strife ceaseth.
Prov. 26:20

[*See also* Secrecy, Slander, Speech]

GOVERNMENT

Provide out of all the people able men, such as fear God, men of truth, hating covetousness.
Jethro to Moses
Ex. 18:21

Thou shalt not revile the gods, nor curse the ruler of thy people.
Ex. 22:28
See also Acts 23:5

They are a nation void of counsel, neither is there any understanding in them.
Deut. 32:28

I will not rule over you, neither shall my son rule over you: the Lord shall rule over you.
Gideon
Judg. 8:23

He that ruleth over men must be just, ruling in the fear of God.
2 Sam. 23:3

The kingdom is the Lord's.
Ps. 22:28

Blessed is the nation whose God is the Lord.
Ps. 33:12

It is better to trust in the Lord than to put confidence in princes.
Ps. 118:9

By me kings reign, and princes decree justice. By me princes rule, and nobles, even all the judges of the earth.
(me: wisdom)
Prov. 8:15–16

In the multitude of people is the king's honour: but in the want of people is the destruction of the prince.
Prov. 14:28

Righteousness exalteth a nation: but sin is a reproach to any people.
Prov. 14:34

When the righteous are in authority, the people rejoice: but when the wicked beareth rule, the people mourn.
Prov. 29:2

Woe unto them that decree unrighteous decrees.
Isa. 10:1

The nations are as a drop of a bucket, and are counted as the small dust of the balance.
Isa. 40:15

All nations before Him are as nothing.
Isa. 40:17

Woe to him that buildeth a town with blood.
Hab. 2:12

[*See also* Independence, Leadership, Monarchy, Obedience, Rebellion]

GRANDCHILDREN

He shall be unto thee a restorer of thy life, and a nourisher of thine old age.
Ruth 4:15

A good man leaveth an inheritance to his children's children.
Prov. 13:22

Children's children are the crown of old men.
Prov. 17:6

[*See also* Children]

GRATITUDE

Remember this day, in which ye came out from Egypt, out of the house of bondage.
Ex. 13:3

What goodness the Lord shall do unto us, the same will we do unto thee.
Num. 10:32

Praise ye the Lord for the avenging of Israel.
Judg. 5:2

If thou wilt offer a burnt offering, thou must offer it unto the Lord.
Judg. 13:16

Let me find favour in thy sight, my lord; for that thou hast comforted me.
Ruth 2:13

Blessed be ye of the Lord; for ye have compassion on me.
Saul
1 Sam. 23:21

When the Lord had delivered me into thine hand, thou killedst me not.
Saul to David
1 Sam. 24:18

When the Lord shall have dealt well with my lord, then remember thine handmaid.
Abigail to David
1 Sam. 25:31

Whatsoever thou shalt require of me, that will I do for thee.
2 Sam. 19:38

Let them be of those that eat at thy table.
1 Kings 2:7

Blessed be the Lord, that hath given rest unto His people Israel.
1 Kings 8:56

Good is the word of the Lord which thou hast spoken.
2 Kings 20:19, Isa. 39:8

My cup runneth over.
Ps. 23:5

Blessed be the Lord, because He hath heard the voice of my supplications.
Ps. 28:6

Give unto the Lord the glory due unto His name.
Ps. 29:2

O Lord my God, I will give thanks unto Thee for ever.
Ps. 30:12

Blessed be the Lord.
E.g., Ps. 31:21

I will praise the name of God with a song, and will magnify Him with thanksgiving.
Ps. 69:30

It is a good thing to give thanks unto the Lord.
Ps. 92:1

Give thanks unto the Lord; call upon His name.
Ps. 105:1, 1 Chron. 16:8

Give thanks unto the Lord; for He is good: for His mercy endureth for ever.
E.g., Ps. 106:1

In all thy ways acknowledge Him.
Prov. 3:6

Withhold not good from them to whom it is due, when it is in the power of thine hand to do it.
Prov. 3:27

[*See also* Appreciation, Ingratitude, Praise of God]

GREATNESS

Great men are not always wise: neither do the aged understand judgment.
Job 32:9

God is greater than man.
Job 33:12

[*See also* God's Greatness, Size, Status]

GREED

There shall cleave nought of the cursed thing to thine hand.
Deut. 13:17

Is it a time to receive money?
2 Kings 5:26

Will ye even sell your brethren?
Neh. 5:8

Better is a little with righteousness than great revenues without right.
Prov. 16:8

Hell and destruction are never full; so the eyes of man are never satisfied.
Prov. 27:20

He that maketh haste to be rich shall not be innocent.
Prov. 28:20

The horseleach hath two daughters, crying, Give, give.
Prov. 30:15

He that loveth silver shall not be satisfied with silver; nor he that loveth abundance with increase.
Eccl. 5:10

Will ye pollute Me among My people for handfuls of barley and for pieces of bread?
Ezek. 13:19

[*See also* Ambition, Contentment, Envy, Jealousy, Satisfaction]

GREETINGS

See Salutations.

GRIEF

If I be bereaved of my children, I am bereaved.
Gen. 43:14

How long wilt thou mourn for Saul, seeing I have rejected him?
God to Samuel
1 Sam. 16:1

They had no more power to weep.
1 Sam. 30:4

Tell it not in Gath, publish it not in the streets of Askelon.
2 Sam. 1:20

Would God I had died for thee, O Absalom, my son, my son!
2 Sam. 18:33

The victory that day was turned into mourning.
2 Sam. 19:2

O my son Absalom, O Absalom, my son, my son!
2 Sam. 19:4

My friends scorn me: but mine eye poureth out tears unto God.
Job 16:20

The Lord is nigh unto them that are of a broken heart; and saveth such as be of a contrite spirit.
Ps. 34:18

Pour out your heart before Him: God is a refuge for us.
Ps. 62:8

Thou feedest them with the bread of tears.
Ps. 80:5

To the sinner He giveth travail, to gather and to heap up.
Eccl. 2:26

Teach your daughters wailing, and every one her neighbour lamentation.
Jer. 9:20

Her sun is gone down while it was yet day.
Jer. 15:9

Behold, and see if there be any sorrow like unto my sorrow.
Lam. 1:12

Ye shall pine away for your iniquities, and mourn one toward another.
Ezek. 24:23

Lament like a virgin girded with sackcloth for the husband of her youth.
Joel 1:8

I will wail and howl, I will go stripped and naked.
Mic. 1:8

[*See also* Anguish, Mourning, Sorrow, Tears]

GROWTH

Can the rush grow up without mire? can the flag grow without water?
Job 8:11

Spreading himself like a green bay tree.
Ps. 37:35

The righteous shall flourish like the palm tree: he shall grow like a cedar in Lebanon.
Ps. 92:12

Thou hast multiplied the nation, and not increased the joy.
Isa. 9:3

A little one shall become a thousand, and a small one a strong nation.
Isa. 60:22

Being planted, shall it prosper?
Ezek. 17:10

[*See also* Cultivation]

GRUDGES

He that repeateth a matter separateth very friends.
Prov. 17:9

[*See also* Anger, Arguments, Forgiveness, Temper]

GUIDANCE

The Lord went before them by day in a pillar of a cloud, to lead them the way; and by night in a pillar of fire, to give them light.
Ex. 13:21
See also, e.g., Num. 14:14

If I have found grace in Thy sight, show me now Thy way, that I may know Thee.
Moses to God
Ex. 33:13

Thou mayest be to us instead of eyes.
Moses to Hobab
Num. 10:31

Thou art my lamp, O Lord.
2 Sam. 22:29

Enquire of the Lord for me, and for the people.
2 Kings 22:13

He maketh me to lie down in green pastures: He leadeth me beside the still waters. He restoreth my soul.
Ps. 23:2–3

Show me Thy ways, O Lord; teach me Thy paths.
Ps. 25:4

The meek will He guide in judgment: and the meek will He teach His way.
Ps. 25:9

The steps of a good man are ordered by the Lord: and He delighteth in his way.
Ps. 37:23

Send out Thy light and Thy truth: let them lead me.
Ps. 43:3

This God is our God for ever and ever: He will be our guide even unto death.
Ps. 48:14

Teach me Thy way, O Lord; I will walk in Thy truth.
Ps. 86:11

Thy word is a lamp unto my feet, and a light unto my path.
Ps. 119:105

Cause me to know the way wherein I should walk.
Ps. 143:8

Attend to my words; incline thine ear unto my sayings.
(thine: children)
Prov. 4:20

The commandment is a lamp; and the law is light.
Prov. 6:23

Where no counsel is, the people fall.
Prov. 11:14

Where there is no vision, the people perish.
Prov. 29:18

The words of the wise are as goads.
Eccl. 12:11

This is the way, walk ye in it.
Isa. 30:21

I will also give thee for a light to the Gentiles.
Isa. 49:6
See also Acts 13:47

The Lord shall be unto thee an everlasting light.
Isa. 60:19

O Lord, correct me, but with judgment.
Jer. 10:24

When I sit in darkness, the Lord shall be a light unto me.
Mic. 7:8

[*See also* Advice, Behavior, Instruction]

GUILT

Who told thee that thou wast naked?
Gen. 3:11

The voice of thy brother's blood crieth unto Me from the ground.
Gen. 4:10

I have sinned this time: the Lord is righteous, and I and my people are wicked.
Pharaoh
Ex. 9:27

Thy blood be upon thy head.
2 Sam. 1:16

Hast thou killed, and also taken possession?
(thou: Ahab)
1 Kings 21:19

Every man shall be put to death for his own sin.
E.g., 2 Kings 14:6

If I be wicked, woe unto me.
Job 10:15

Thy mouth uttereth thine iniquity.
Job 15:5

Thine own mouth condemneth thee, and not I.
Job 15:6

Thine own lips testify against thee.
Job 15:6
See also 2 Sam. 1:16

Your hands are full of blood.
Isa. 1:15

The show of their countenance doth witness against them.
Isa. 3:9

Our sins testify against us.
Isa. 59:12

Though thou wash thee with nitre, and take thee much soap, yet thine iniquity is marked before Me.
Jer. 2:22

His blood shall be upon him.
E.g., Ezek. 18:13

The stone shall cry out of the wall, and the beam out of the timber shall answer it.
Hab. 2:11

[*See also* Blame, Innocence, Justice, Responsibility, Restitution, Self-Incrimination]

HABIT

As a dog returneth to his vomit, so a fool returneth to his folly.
Prov. 26:11
See also 2 Pet. 2:22

Can the Ethiopian change his skin, or the leopard his spots? then may ye also do good, that are accustomed to do evil.
Jer. 13:23

HANDICAPPED

Who hath made man's mouth? or who maketh the dumb, or deaf, or the seeing, or the blind? have not I the Lord?
Ex. 4:11

Thou shalt not curse the deaf, nor put a stumblingblock before the blind.
Lev. 19:14

[*See also* Blindness, Healing, Sight]

HANGING

He that is hanged is accursed of God.
Deut. 21:23
See also Gal. 3:13

HAPPINESS

My heart rejoiceth in the Lord.
1 Sam. 2:1

Happy is the man whom God correcteth.
Job 5:17

The triumphing of the wicked is short, and the joy of the hypocrite but for a moment.
Job 20:5

Let all those that put their trust in Thee rejoice: let them ever shout for joy.
Ps. 5:11

Surely goodness and mercy shall follow me all the days of my life: and I will dwell in the house of the Lord for ever.
Ps. 23:6

Weeping may endure for a night, but joy cometh in the morning.
Ps. 30:5

Be glad in the Lord.
Ps. 32:11

Shout for joy, all ye that are upright in heart.
Ps. 32:11

Blessed is that man that maketh the Lord his trust.
Ps. 40:4
See also, e.g., Ps. 34:8

Shout unto God with the voice of triumph.
Ps. 47:1

Blessed is the man whom Thou choosest, and causest to approach unto Thee.
Ps. 65:4

Light is sown for the righteous, and gladness for the upright in heart.
Ps. 97:11

Glory ye in His holy name.
Ps. 105:3, 1 Chron. 16:10

Let the heart of them rejoice that seek the Lord.
Ps. 105:3

Thy law is my delight.
Ps. 119:77, 174
See also Ps. 119:143

They that sow in tears shall reap in joy.
Ps. 126:5

Happy is that people, whose God is the Lord.
Ps. 144:15

Happy is he that hath the God of Jacob for his help, whose hope is in the Lord his God.
Ps. 146:5

Happy is the man that findeth wisdom, and the man that getteth understanding.
Prov. 3:13

When it goeth well with the righteous, the city rejoiceth.
Prov. 11:10

When the wicked perish, there is shouting.
Prov. 11:10

A merry heart maketh a cheerful countenance.
Prov. 15:13

He that is of a merry heart hath a continual feast.
Prov. 15:15

Whoso trusteth in the Lord, happy is he.
Prov. 16:20

A merry heart doeth good like a medicine: but a broken spirit drieth the bones.
Prov. 17:22

A time to weep, and a time to laugh; a time to mourn, and a time to dance.
Eccl. 3:4

Blessed is the man that trusteth in the Lord, and whose hope the Lord is.
Jer. 17:7

Their soul shall be as a watered garden; and they shall not sorrow any more at all.
Jer. 31:12

I will rejoice in the Lord, I will joy in the God of my salvation.
Hab. 3:18

[*See also* Celebration, Contentment, Laughter, Pleasure, Satisfaction]

HATRED

My soul shall abhor you.
Lev. 26:30

Let them that hate Thee flee before Thee.
Num. 10:35

The hatred wherewith he hated her was greater than the love wherewith he had loved her.
2 Sam. 13:15

They that hate me without a cause are more than the hairs of mine head.
Ps. 69:4

They have sharpened their tongues like a serpent; adders' poison is under their lips.
Ps. 140:3
See also Rom. 3:13

He that hideth hatred with lying lips, and he that uttereth a slander, is a fool.
Prov. 10:18

He that despiseth his neighbour sinneth.
Prov. 14:21

A time to love, and a time to hate.
Eccl. 3:8

[*See also* Brotherhood, Contempt, Enemies, Love, Persecution, Self-Hatred]

HEALING

There is no god with Me: I kill, and I make alive; I wound, and I heal: neither is there any that can deliver out of My hand.
Deut. 32:39

Am I God, to kill and to make alive?
2 Kings 5:7

If the prophet had bid thee do some great thing, wouldest thou not have done it?
2 Kings 5:13

In his disease he sought not to the Lord, but to the physicians.
2 Chron. 16:12

He maketh sore, and bindeth up: He woundeth, and His hands make whole.
Job 5:18

A merry heart doeth good like a medicine: but a broken spirit drieth the bones.
Prov. 17:22

A time to kill, and a time to heal; a time to break down, and a time to build up.
Eccl. 3:3

A time to rend, and a time to sew.
Eccl. 3:7

Then shall the lame man leap as an hart, and the tongue of the dumb sing.
Isa. 35:6

I have heard thy prayer, I have seen thy tears: behold, I will add unto thy days fifteen years.
God to Hezekiah
Isa. 38:5
See also 2 Kings 20:5–6

With his stripes we are healed.
Isa. 53:5

Is there no balm in Gilead? is there no physician there?
Jer. 8:22

Heal me, O Lord, and I shall be healed; save me, and I shall be saved.
Jer. 17:14

In vain shalt thou use many medicines; for thou shalt not be cured.
Jer. 46:11

I will seek that which was lost, and bring again that which was driven away, and will bind up that which was broken, and will strengthen that which was sick.
Ezek. 34:16

He hath torn, and He will heal us; He hath smitten, and He will bind us up.
Hos. 6:1

[*See also* Faith, Restoration]

HEALTH

See Handicapped, Healing.

HEAVEN

If I ascend up into heaven, Thou art there: if I make my bed in hell, behold, Thou art there.
Ps. 139:8

[*See also* Creation, Eternal Life, God's Presence]

HEAVEN AND EARTH

And God called the firmament Heaven.
Gen. 1:8

In six days the Lord made heaven and earth, the sea, and all that in them is.
Ex. 20:11

All that is in the heaven and in the earth is Thine.
1 Chron. 29:11

The heavens declare the glory of God; and the firmament showeth His handywork.
Ps. 19:1

The world is Mine, and the fulness thereof.
Ps. 50:12
See also Ex. 19:5

The heavens are Thine, the earth also is Thine.
Ps. 89:11

The heavens declare His righteousness, and all the people see His glory.
Ps. 97:6

They shall perish, but Thou shalt endure.
Ps. 102:26

The heaven, even the heavens, are the Lord's: but the earth hath He given to the children of men.
Ps. 115:16

He telleth the number of the stars; He calleth them all by their names.
Ps. 147:4

The heaven is My throne, and the earth is My footstool.
Isa. 66:1
See also Acts 7:49

He hath established the world by His wisdom, and hath stretched out the heavens by His discretion.
Jer. 10:12

[*See also* Creation, Earth]

HEEDFULNESS

Speak, Lord; for Thy servant heareth.
1 Sam. 3:9

Hold thy peace, and I shall teach thee wisdom.
Job 33:33

A wise man will hear, and will increase learning.
Prov. 1:5

I spake unto thee in thy prosperity; but thou saidst, I will not hear.
Jer. 22:21

I have spoken unto them, but they have not heard; and I have called unto them, but they have not answered.
Jer. 35:17

They hearkened not, nor inclined their ear to turn from their wickedness.
Jer. 44:5

Thus saith the Lord God; He that heareth, let him hear; and he that forbeareth, let him forebear.
Ezek. 3:27

They hear thy words, but they do them not.
God to Ezekiel
Ezek. 33:32

Hear the word of the Lord, ye children of Israel.
Hos. 4:1

[*See also* Obedience, Pleas, Prayer, Preaching, Warning]

HEIGHT

See Size.

HELL

Hell and destruction are never full.
Prov. 27:20

Hell hath enlarged herself, and opened her mouth without measure.
Isa. 5:14

Hell from beneath is moved for thee to meet thee at thy coming.
Isa. 14:9

[*See also* Death, Torment]

HELP

See Assistance, Deliverance.

HERESY

Thou shalt not hearken unto the words of that prophet, or that dreamer of dreams: for the Lord your God proveth you, to know whether ye love the Lord your God with all your heart and with all your soul.
Deut. 13:3

Put the evil away from the midst of thee.
Deut. 13:5

Woe unto him that striveth with his Maker!
Isa. 45:9

I am against the prophets, saith the Lord, that use their tongues, and say, He saith.
Jer. 23:31

Thou shalt die, because thou hast taught rebellion against the Lord.
Jer. 28:16

[*See also* Blasphemy, False Prophets]

HERITAGE

My covenant is with thee, and thou shalt be a father of many nations.
God to Abram
Gen. 17:4

In thee and in thy seed shall all the families of the earth be blessed.
God to Jacob
Gen. 28:14

I am the God of thy father, the God of Abraham, the God of Isaac, and the God of Jacob.
Ex. 3:6
See also, e.g., Mark 12:26

He is my God, and I will prepare Him an habitation; my father's God, and I will exalt Him.
Ex. 15:2

Why should the name of our father be done away from among his family, because he hath no son?
Num. 27:4

The Lord made not this covenant with

our fathers, but with us, even us, who are all of us here alive this day.
Deut. 5:3

Let a double portion of thy spirit be upon me.
Elisha to Elijah
2 Kings 2:9

The lines are fallen unto me in pleasant places; yea, I have a goodly heritage.
Ps. 16:6

Who shall declare his generation?
Isa. 53:8

As is the mother, so is her daughter.
Ezek. 16:44

The fathers have eaten sour grapes, and the children's teeth are set on edge.
Ezek. 18:2
See also Jer. 31:29

[*See also* Character, Inheritance, Tradition]

HEROISM

See Courage, Leadership.

HIERARCHY

See Authority, Leadership.

HISTORY

Remember the days of old, consider the years of many generations: ask thy father, and he will show thee; thy elders, and they will tell thee.
Deut. 32:7

Write it before them in a table, and note it in a book, that it may be for the time to come for ever and ever.
Isa. 30:8

Have ye forgotten the wickedness of your fathers?
Jer. 44:9

[*See also* Testimony]

HOLIDAYS

It is a night to be much observed unto the Lord.
Ex. 12:42

This day is holy unto the Lord your God; mourn not, nor weep.
Neh. 8:9

[*See also* Celebration, Sabbath]

HOLINESS

Put off thy shoes from off thy feet, for the place whereon thou standest is holy ground.
Ex. 3:5
See also Josh. 5:15

I will be sanctified in them that come nigh Me.
Lev. 10:3

Ye shall be holy: for I the Lord your God am holy.
E.g., Lev. 19:2
See also 1 Pet. 1:16

Every devoted thing is most holy unto the Lord.
Lev. 27:28

There is none holy as the Lord.
1 Sam. 2:2

Who shall ascend into the hill of the Lord? or who shall stand in His holy place? He that hath clean hands, and a pure heart; who hath not lifted up his soul unto vanity, nor sworn deceitfully.
Ps. 24:3–4

Holy, holy, holy, is the Lord of hosts: the whole earth is full of His glory.
Isa. 6:3

Before thou camest forth out of the womb I sanctified thee.
God to Jeremiah
Jer. 1:5

They shall teach My people the difference between the holy and profane.
Ezek. 44:23

Holiness unto the Lord.
Zech. 14:20

[*See also* Consecration]

He that sacrificeth unto any god, save unto the Lord only, he shall be utterly destroyed.
Ex. 22:20

What shall be done unto the man whom the king delighteth to honour?
Esther 6:6

Give unto the Lord the glory due unto His name.
Ps. 29:2

Worship Him, all ye gods.
Ps. 97:7

Come ye, and let us go up to the mountain of the Lord.
Isa. 2:3

I am sought of them that asked not for Me; I am found of them that sought Me not.
Isa. 65:1
See also Rom. 10:20

[*See also* Fear of God, Respect]

HOME

Bury me not, I pray thee, in Egypt.
Jacob to Joseph
Gen. 47:29

How goodly are thy tents, O Jacob, and thy tabernacles, O Israel!
Num. 24:5

By the rivers of Babylon, there we sat down, yea, we wept, when we remembered Zion.
Ps. 137:1

Every wise woman buildeth her house: but the foolish plucketh it down with her hands.
Prov. 14:1

[*See also* Building, Children, Family, Marriage]

See Exile, Poverty.

HOMOSEXUALITY

Thou shalt not lie with mankind, as with womankind: it is abomination.
Lev. 18:22
See also Lev. 20:13

They shall surely be put to death.
Lev. 20:13

Sons of Belial.
E.g., Judg. 19:22

HONESTY

If thou meet thine enemy's ox or his ass going astray, thou shalt surely bring it back to him again.
Ex. 23:4

Keep thee far from a false matter.
Ex. 23:7

Ye shall not steal, neither deal falsely, neither lie one to another.
Lev. 19:11

Ye shall do no unrighteousness in judgment, in meteyard, in weight, or in measure.
Lev. 19:35

Must I not take heed to speak that which the Lord hath put in my mouth?
Num. 23:12

A gift doth blind the eyes of the wise, and pervert the words of the righteous.
Deut. 16:19
See also Ex. 23:8

Thou shalt not have in thy bag divers weights, a great and a small.
Deut. 25:13

All that do unrighteously, are an abomination unto the Lord thy God.
Deut. 25:16

Serve Him in sincerity and in truth.
Josh. 24:14

Walk before Me, as David thy father

walked, in integrity of heart, and in uprightness.
1 Kings 9:4

How forcible are right words!
Job 6:25

He that hath clean hands, and a pure
heart.
Ps. 24:4

Keep thy tongue from evil, and thy lips
from speaking guile.
Ps. 34:13
See also 1 Pet. 3:10

The wicked borroweth, and payeth not
again: but the righteous showeth mercy,
and giveth.
Ps. 37:21

He that walketh uprightly walketh surely.
Prov. 10:9

The tongue of the just is as choice silver:
the heart of the wicked is little worth.
Prov. 10:20

A false balance is abomination to the
Lord: but a just weight is His delight.
Prov. 11:1
See also Prov. 20:10, 23

He that speaketh truth showeth forth
righteousness.
Prov. 12:17

A true witness delivereth souls.
Prov. 14:25

The just man walketh in his integrity.
Prov. 20:7

Be not a witness against thy neighbour
without cause.
Prov. 24:28

Deceive not with thy lips.
Prov. 24:28

Better is the poor that walketh in his
uprightness, than he that is perverse in his
ways, though he be rich.
Prov. 28:6

Ye shall have just balances.
Ezek. 45:10

Speak ye every man the truth to his neighbour.
Zech. 8:16

The law of truth was in his mouth, and
iniquity was not found in his lips.
Mal. 2:6

[*See also* Candor, Corruption, Dishonesty, Integrity, Lies, Truth]

HONOR

See Glory, Respect.

HOPE

The poor hath hope.
Job 5:16

The hypocrite's hope shall perish.
Job 8:13

The needy shall not always be forgotten:
the expectation of the poor shall not perish for ever.
Ps. 9:18

Those that wait upon the Lord, they shall
inherit the earth.
Ps. 37:9

Thou art my hope, O Lord God: Thou art
my trust from my youth.
Ps. 71:5

I will lift up mine eyes unto the hills, from
whence cometh my help.
Ps. 121:1

I wait for the Lord, my soul doth wait.
Ps. 130:5

In His word do I hope.
Ps. 130:5

My soul waiteth for the Lord more than
they that watch for the morning.
Ps. 130:6

In Thee is my trust; leave not my soul
destitute.
Ps. 141:8

The eyes of all wait upon Thee.
Ps. 145:15

Hope deferred maketh the heart sick: but when the desire cometh, it is a tree of life.
Prov. 13:12

A living dog is better than a dead lion.
Eccl. 9:4

Awake and sing, ye that dwell in dust.
Isa. 26:19

Fear thou not; for I am with thee: be not dismayed; for I am thy God.
Isa. 41:10

Be not a terror unto me: Thou art my hope in the day of evil.
Jer. 17:17

Ye prisoners of hope.
Zech. 9:12

[*See also* Depression, Despair, Disappointment, Encouragement, Expectation, Prayer, Restoration]

HOSPITALITY

Thou shalt neither vex a stranger, nor oppress him: for ye were strangers in the land of Egypt.
Ex. 22:21
See also Ex. 23:9

Comfort thine heart with a morsel of bread, and afterward go your way.
Judg. 19:5

Let all thy wants lie upon me; only lodge not in the street.
Judg. 19:20

Eat, that thou mayest have strength, when thou goest on thy way.
Spiritualist to Saul
1 Sam. 28:22

The stranger did not lodge in the street: but I opened my doors to the traveller.
Job 31:32

Withdraw thy foot from thy neighbour's house; lest he be weary of thee, and so hate thee.
Prov. 25:17

[*See also* Brotherhood, Kindness]

HUMAN NATURE

The imagination of man's heart is evil from his youth.
Gen. 8:21

The heart of the sons of men is full of evil, and madness is in their heart while they live.
Eccl. 9:3

[*See also* Behavior, Mankind, Sin]

HUMILIATION

Upon thy belly shalt thou go, and dust shalt thou eat all the days of thy life.
God to serpent
Gen. 3:14

Thus shall the Lord do to all your enemies against whom ye fight.
Josh. 10:25

Draw thy sword, and slay me, that men say not of me, A woman slew him.
Judg. 9:54

The glory is departed from Israel: for the ark of God is taken.
1 Sam. 4:22

He shall lie with thy wives in the sight of this sun.
(He: David's neighbor)
2 Sam. 12:11

Thou didst it secretly: but I will do this thing before all Israel, and before the sun.
God to David
2 Sam. 12:12

The carcase of Jezebel shall be as dung upon the face of the field.
2 Kings 9:37

I will put My hook in thy nose, and My bridle in thy lips, and I will turn thee back by the way by which thou camest.
2 Kings 19:28, Isa. 37:29

They shall be eunuchs in the palace of the king of Babylon.
2 Kings 20:18, Isa. 39:7

They shall become a prey and a spoil to all their enemies.
2 Kings 21:14

His enemies shall lick the dust.
Ps. 72:9

The mean man shall be brought down, and the mighty man shall be humbled.
Isa. 5:15

Thy pomp is brought down to the grave, and the noise of thy viols.
Isa. 14:11

Thy nakedness shall be uncovered, yea, thy shame shall be seen.
Isa. 47:3

He was despised, and we esteemed him not.
Isa. 53:3

Though thou shouldest make thy nest as high as the eagle, I will bring thee down from thence, saith the Lord.
Jer. 49:16

They shall become as women.
Jer. 50:37

She that was great among the nations, and princess among the provinces, how is she become tributary!
Lam. 1:1

They that did feed delicately are desolate in the streets: they that were brought up in scarlet embrace dunghills.
Lam. 4:5

Those that be near, and those that be far from thee, shall mock thee.
Ezek. 22:5

I will deliver thee into the hand of them whom thou hatest.
Ezek. 23:28

Wherefore should they say among the people, Where is their God?
Joel 2:17
See also, e.g., Ps. 79:10

They shall lick the dust like a serpent, they shall move out of their holes like worms of the earth: they shall be afraid of the Lord our God.
Mic. 7:17

I will show the nations thy nakedness, and the kingdoms thy shame.
(thy: Nineveh)
Nah. 3:5

I will corrupt your seed, and spread dung upon your faces.
God to wayward priests
Mal. 2:3

[*See also* Contempt, Defeat, Outcast, Shame]

HUMILITY

Who am I, that I should go unto Pharaoh, and that I should bring forth the children of Israel out of Egypt?
Moses
Ex. 3:11

I am slow of speech, and of a slow tongue.
Moses
Ex. 4:10

I will not rule over you, neither shall my son rule over you: the Lord shall rule over you.
Gideon
Judg. 8:23

Who am I, O Lord God? and what is my house, that Thou hast brought me hitherto?
David
2 Sam. 7:18

Is this the manner of man, O Lord God?
2 Sam. 7:19

I am but a little child: I know not how to go out or come in.
Solomon to God
1 Kings 3:7

Am I God, to kill and to make alive?
2 Kings 5:7

Shall any teach God knowledge?
Job 21:22

He shall save the humble person.
Job 22:29

Serve the Lord with fear, and rejoice with trembling.
Ps. 2:11

The Lord is nigh unto them that are of a

broken heart; and saveth such as be of a contrite spirit.
Ps. 34:18

The meek shall inherit the earth.
Ps. 37:11
See also, e.g., Matt. 5:5

I am poor and sorrowful: let Thy salvation, O God, set me up on high.
Ps. 69:29

I had rather be a doorkeeper in the house of my God, than to dwell in the tents of wickedness.
Ps. 84:10

Not unto us, O Lord, not unto us, but unto Thy name give glory.
Ps. 115:1

The Lord preserveth the simple.
Ps. 116:6

Before honour is humility.
Prov. 15:33, Prov. 18:12

Better it is to be of an humble spirit with the lowly, than to divide the spoil with the proud.
Prov. 16:19

A man hath no preeminence above a beast: for all is vanity.
Eccl. 3:19

God is in heaven, and thou upon earth: therefore let thy words be few.
Eccl. 5:2

Let not the wise man glory in his wisdom, neither let the mighty man glory in his might, let not the rich man glory in his riches.
Jer. 9:23

We do not present our supplications before Thee for our righteousnesses, but for Thy great mercies.
Dan. 9:18

Walk humbly with thy God.
Mic. 6:8

Behold, thy King cometh unto thee: he is just, and having salvation; lowly, and riding upon an ass.
Zech. 9:9

[*See also* Arrogance, Audacity, Conceit, Equality, Gloating, Meekness, Modesty, Pride]

HUNGER

Behold, I am at the point to die: and what profit shall this birthright do to me?
Esau to Jacob
Gen. 25:32

They that were full have hired out themselves for bread.
1 Sam. 2:5

Men do not despise a thief, if he steal to satisfy his soul when he is hungry.
Prov. 6:30

If thine enemy be hungry, give him bread to eat; and if he be thirsty, give him water to drink.
Prov. 25:21
See also Rom. 12:20

Thou shalt eat, but not be satisfied.
Mic. 6:14

[*See also* Deprivation, Famine, Food, Thirst]

HUSBAND AND WIFE

See Marriage.

HYPOCRISY

How canst thou say, I love thee, when thine heart is not with me?
Delilah to Samson
Judg. 16:15

The triumphing of the wicked is short, and the joy of the hypocrite but for a moment.
Job 20:5

What is the hope of the hypocrite, though he hath gained, when God taketh away his soul?
Job 27:8

The workers of iniquity, which speak peace to their neighbours, but mischief is in their hearts.
Ps. 28:3

They bless with their mouth, but they curse inwardly.
Ps. 62:4

This people draw near Me with their

mouth, and with their lips do honour Me, but have removed their heart far from Me.
Isa. 29:13
See also Matt. 15:8

Their fear toward Me is taught by the precept of men.
Isa. 29:13

In the day of your fast ye find pleasure.
Isa. 58:3

One speaketh peaceably to his neighbour with his mouth, but in heart he layeth his wait.
Jer. 9:8

With their mouth they show much love, but their heart goeth after their covetousness.
Ezek. 33:31

[*See also* Deception, Lies, Rituals, Sincerity]

IDOLATRY

Thou shalt have no other gods before Me.
First Commandment
Ex. 20:3
See also Deut. 5:7

Thou shalt not make unto thee any graven image.
Second Commandment
Ex. 20:4
See also Deut. 5:8

He that sacrificeth unto any god, save unto the Lord only, he shall be utterly destroyed.
Ex. 22:20

Make no mention of the name of other gods.
Ex. 23:13

In the day when I visit I will visit their sin upon them.
God to Moses
Ex. 32:34

The Lord, whose name is Jealous, is a jealous God.
Ex. 34:14

All the curses that are written in this book shall lie upon him.
Deut. 29:20

Put away the gods which your fathers served on the other side of the flood.
Josh. 24:14

God forbid that we should forsake the Lord, to serve other gods.
Josh. 24:16

They would not hearken unto their judges, but they went a whoring after other gods.
Judg. 2:17
See also 1 Chron. 5:25

Ye have forsaken Me, and served other gods: wherefore I will deliver you no more.
Judg. 10:13

If the Lord be God, follow Him: but if Baal, then follow him.
1 Kings 18:21

But the high places were not taken away: the people still sacrificed and burnt incense.
2 Kings 12:3

They caused their sons and their daughters to pass through the fire.
2 Kings 17:17

As did their fathers, so do they unto this day.
2 Kings 17:41

My wrath shall be kindled against this place, and shall not be quenched.
2 Kings 22:17

The land was polluted with blood.
Ps. 106:38

They that make them are like unto them; so is every one that trusteth in them.
Ps. 115:8, Ps. 135:18

They worship the work of their own hands, that which their own fingers have made.
Isa. 2:8

They shall be greatly ashamed, that trust

in graven images, that say to the molten images, Ye are our gods.
Isa. 42:17

They have turned their back unto Me, and not their face.
Jer. 2:27

As ye have forsaken Me, and served strange gods in your land, so shall ye serve strangers in a land that is not your's.
Jer. 5:19

Go not after other gods to serve them.
Jer. 25:6, Jer. 35:15

They give gifts to all whores: but thou givest thy gifts to all thy lovers.
Ezek. 16:33

Woe unto him that saith to the wood, Awake; to the dumb stone, Arise.
Hab. 2:19

[*See also* Backsliding, False Gods, Godlessness, Monotheism, Worship]

IDOLS

Against all the gods of Egypt I will execute judgment: I am the Lord.
Ex. 12:12

Ye shall not make with Me gods of silver, neither shall ye make unto you gods of gold.
Ex. 20:23

Turn ye not unto idols, nor make to yourselves molten gods.
Lev. 19:4

The work of men's hands, wood and stone, which neither see, nor hear, nor eat, nor smell.
Deut. 4:28

Thou shalt not make thee any graven image.
Deut. 5:8

The graven images of their gods shall ye burn with fire.
Deut. 7:25

It is an abomination to the Lord.
E.g., Deut. 7:25

Ye shall throw down their altars.
Judg. 2:2

Peradventure he sleepeth, and must be awaked.
Elijah, about Baal
1 Kings 18:27

Ye shall not fear other gods.
2 Kings 17:37

They were no gods, but the work of men's hands, wood and stone.
2 Kings 19:18, Isa. 37:19

Their idols are silver and gold, the work of men's hands.
Ps. 115:4
See also Ps. 135:15

They have mouths, but they speak not: eyes have they, but they see not.
Ps. 115:5, Ps. 135:16
See also Rev. 9:20

They have ears, but they hear not: noses have they, but they smell not.
Ps. 115:6

Feet have they, but they walk not: neither speak they through their throat.
Ps. 115:7

The idols He shall utterly abolish.
Isa. 2:18

Thou shalt cast them away as a menstruous cloth.
Isa. 30:22

Ye are of nothing, and your work of nought: an abomination is he that chooseth you.
Isa. 41:24

Their works are nothing: their molten images are wind and confusion.
Isa. 41:29

Let them arise, if they can save thee in the time of thy trouble.
God to Jews
Jer. 2:28

They are vanity, and the work of errors: in the time of their visitation they shall perish.
Jer. 10:15, Jer. 51:18

Ye provoke Me unto wrath with the works of your hands.
Jer. 44:8
See also Jer. 25:6

Your altars shall be desolate, and your

images shall be broken: and I will cast down your slain men before your idols.
Ezek. 6:4

Pollute ye My holy name no more with your gifts, and with your idols.
Ezek. 20:39

The workman made it; therefore it is not God.
Hos. 8:6

What profiteth the graven image that the maker thereof hath graven it?
Hab. 2:18

They comfort in vain.
Zech. 10:2

[*See also* False Gods, Godlessness, Idolatry, Monotheism, Worship]

IGNORANCE

They were both naked, the man and his wife, and were not ashamed.
Gen. 2:25

If a soul sin, and commit any of these things which are forbidden to be done by the commandments of the Lord; though he wist it not, yet is he guilty.
Lev. 5:17

They are a nation void of counsel, neither is there any understanding in them.
Deut. 32:28

He multiplieth words without knowledge.
Job 35:16

Who is this that darkeneth counsel by words without knowledge?
Job 38:2

A brutish man knoweth not; neither doth a fool understand this.
Ps. 92:6

Ye fools, when will ye be wise?
Ps. 94:8

Fools die for want of wisdom.
Prov. 10:21

Folly is joy to him that is destitute of wisdom.
Prov. 15:21

My people are gone into captivity, because they have no knowledge.
Isa. 5:13

Who is blind as he that is perfect, and blind as the Lord's servant?
Isa. 42:19

Every man is brutish in his knowledge.
Jer. 10:14

The people that doth not understand shall fall.
Hos. 4:14

[*See also* Knowledge, Naivete, Understanding, Wisdom]

IMAGINATION

See Dreams, Future, Visions.

IMMINENCE

The time is come, the day draweth near.
Ezek. 7:12
See also Ezek. 7:7

The day of the Lord is near.
Ezek. 30:3

[*See also* Time]

IMMORALITY

Do not prostitute thy daughter, to cause her to be a whore; lest the land fall to whoredom, and the land become full of wickedness.
Lev. 19:29

How is the faithful city become an harlot!
Isa. 1:21

Thy silver is become dross, thy wine mixed with water.
Isa. 1:22

Thou hast polluted the land with thy whoredoms and with thy wickedness.
Jer. 3:2

As is the mother, so is her daughter.
Ezek. 16:44

[*See also* Decadence, Depravity, Lust, Prostitution, Sin]

IMMORTALITY

See Death, Eternal Life, Resurrection.

IMPARTIALITY

Neither shalt thou countenance a poor man in his cause.
Ex. 23:3

Thou shalt not wrest the judgment of thy poor in his cause.
Ex. 23:6

Thou shalt not respect the person of the poor, nor honour the person of the mighty.
Lev. 19:15

Ye shall not respect persons in judgment.
Deut. 1:17
See also Deut. 16:19

Ye shall hear the small as well as the great.
Deut. 1:17

Though it be in Jonathan my son, he shall surely die.
Saul
1 Sam. 14:39

[*See also* Equality, Fairness, Justice, Neutrality]

IMPATIENCE

How long will it be ere ye make an end of words?
Job 18:2

Lord, how long wilt Thou look on?
Ps. 35:17

How long shall the adversary reproach? shall the enemy blaspheme Thy name for ever?
Ps. 74:10

How long, Lord?
Ps. 79:5, Ps. 89:46

He that maketh haste to be rich shall not be innocent.
Prov. 28:20

O thou sword of the Lord, how long will it be ere thou be quiet?
Jer. 47:6

O Lord, how long shall I cry, and Thou wilt not hear!
Hab. 1:2

[*See also* Exasperation, Patience]

IMPENITENCE

And the children of Israel did evil again in the sight of the Lord.
E.g., Judg. 3:12

This is a rebellious people, lying children, children that will not hear the law of the Lord.
Isa. 30:9

They have made their faces harder than a rock.
Jer. 5:3

They hearkened not, nor inclined their ear to turn from their wickedness.
Jer. 44:5

Thou hast not remembered the days of thy youth, when thou wast naked and bare.
Ezek. 16:22

All this evil is come upon us: yet made we not our prayer before the Lord our God.
Dan. 9:13

They made their hearts as an adamant stone, lest they should hear the law.
Zech. 7:12

[*See also* Repentance, Stubbornness]

IMPOSSIBILITY

See God's Power, Possibility.

IMPRISONMENT

He bringeth out those which are bound with chains.
Ps. 68:6

Let the sighing of the prisoner come before Thee.
Ps. 79:11

The Lord looseth the prisoners.
Ps. 146:7

To proclaim liberty to the captives, and

the opening of the prison to them that are bound.
Isa. 61:1

They have cut off my life in the dungeon, and cast a stone upon me.
Lam. 3:53

The earth with her bars was about me for ever: yet hast Thou brought up my life from corruption.
Jonah 2:6

[*See also* Captivity, Persecution]

INCEST

The nakedness of thy father, or the nakedness of thy mother, shalt thou not uncover.
Lev. 18:7
See also Lev. 18:8–17

For their's is thine own nakedness.
Lev. 18:10

Cursed be he that lieth with his father's wife.
Deut. 27:20

Cursed be he that lieth with his sister.
Deut. 27:22

Do not thou this folly.
2 Sam. 13:12

Whither shall I cause my shame to go?
2 Sam. 13:13

INDECISION

Choose you this day whom ye will serve.
Josh. 24:15

How long halt ye between two opinions?
1 Kings 18:21

As a drunken man staggereth in his vomit.
Isa. 19:14

[*See also* Certainty, Decisions, Laziness, Neutrality]

INDEPENDENCE

Thou shalt lend unto many nations, but thou shalt not borrow.
Deut. 15:6
See also Deut. 28:12

Thou shalt reign over many nations, but they shall not reign over thee.
Deut. 15:6

Every one turned to his course, as the horse rusheth into the battle.
Jer. 8:6

[*See also* Freedom]

INDIVIDUAL, IMPORTANCE OF

What is man, that Thou art mindful of him? and the son of man, that Thou visitest him?
Ps. 8:4
See also Heb. 2:6

I will judge you every one after his ways.
Ezek. 33:20

[*See also* Mankind]

INEVITABILITY

See Certainty, Death, Mortality.

INFINITY

I will multiply thy seed as the stars of the heaven, and as the sand which is upon the sea shore.
God to Abraham
Gen. 22:17

They came as grasshoppers for multitude; for both they and their camels were without number.
Judg. 6:5

They that hate me without a cause are more than the hairs of mine head.
Ps. 69:4

He telleth the number of the stars; He calleth them all by their names.
Ps. 147:4

The number of the children of Israel shall be as the sand of the sea, which cannot be measured nor numbered.
Hos. 1:10

[*See also* Abundance]

Wherefore have ye rewarded evil for good?
Gen. 44:4

Hast thou taken us away to die in the wilderness?
Israelites to Moses
Ex. 14:11
See also Num. 21:5

It had been better for us to serve the Egyptians, than that we should die in the wilderness.
Ex. 14:12

Ye have wept in the ears of the Lord.
Num. 11:18

Would God that we had died in the land of Egypt!
Num. 14:2

Do ye thus requite the Lord, O foolish people and unwise? is not He thy father that hath bought thee? hath He not made thee, and established thee?
Deut. 32:6

Wherefore kick ye at My sacrifice and at Mine offering?
1 Sam. 2:29

Art thou come unto me to call my sin to remembrance?
1 Kings 17:18

Wilt thou condemn Him that is most just?
Job 34:17

They have rewarded me evil for good, and hatred for my love.
Ps. 109:5
See also 1 Sam. 25:21

Whoso rewardeth evil for good, evil shall not depart from his house.
Prov. 17:13

They were as fed horses in the morning: every one neighed after his neighbour's wife.
Jer. 5:8

I have loved you, saith the Lord. Yet ye say, Wherein hast Thou loved us?
Mal. 1:2

[*See also* Gratitude]

He sold his birthright unto Jacob.
(He: Esau)
Gen. 25:33

If a man die, and have no son, then ye shall cause his inheritance to pass unto his daughter.
Num. 27:8

Behold, I have set the land before you: go in and possess the land which the Lord sware unto your fathers.
Deut. 1:8

The Lord commanded Moses to give us an inheritance among our brethren.
(us: Zelophehad's daughters)
Josh. 17:4

The Lord is the portion of mine inheritance.
Ps. 16:5

He heapeth up riches, and knoweth not who shall gather them.
Ps. 39:6

A good man leaveth an inheritance to his children's children.
Prov. 13:22

House and riches are the inheritance of fathers: and a prudent wife is from the Lord.
Prov. 19:14

Who knoweth whether he shall be a wise man or a fool?
Eccl. 2:19

Our inheritance is turned to strangers, our houses to aliens.
Lam. 5:2

[*See also* Heritage, Reward]

INJUSTICE

Keep thee far from a false matter.
Ex. 23:7

He destroyeth the perfect and the wicked.
Job 9:22

The earth is given into the hand of the

wicked: He covereth the faces of the judges thereof.
Job 9:24

I cry aloud, but there is no judgment.
Job 19:7

Wherefore do the wicked live, become old, yea, are mighty in power?
Job 21:7

How oft is the candle of the wicked put out! and how oft cometh their destruction upon them!
Job 21:17

Far be it from God, that He should do wickedness.
Job 34:10

Lord, how long shall the wicked, how long shall the wicked triumph?
Ps. 94:3

We wait for light, but behold obscurity; for brightness, but we walk in darkness.
Isa. 59:9

They judge not the cause, the cause of the fatherless, yet they prosper.
Jer. 5:28

Wherefore doth the way of the wicked prosper? wherefore are all they happy that deal very treacherously?
Jeremiah to God
Jer. 12:1

Wherefore lookest Thou upon them that deal treacherously, and holdest Thy tongue when the wicked devoureth the man that is more righteous than he?
Hab. 1:13

[*See also* Corruption, Judgment, Justice, Lawlessness]

INNOCENCE

They were both naked, the man and his wife, and were not ashamed.
Gen. 2:25

Behold, his daughter came out to meet him with timbrels and with dances.
(his: Jephthah)
Judg. 11:34

Now shall I be more blameless than the

Philistines, though I do them a displeasure.
Judg. 15:3

I did but taste a little honey with the end of the rod.
1 Sam. 14:43

What have I done? what is mine iniquity?
David
1 Sam. 20:1

If there be in me iniquity, slay me thyself.
David to Jonathan
1 Sam. 20:8

Wherefore shall he be slain? what hath he done?
Jonathan to Saul, about David
1 Sam. 20:32

Wickedness proceedeth from the wicked: but mine hand shall not be upon thee.
1 Sam. 24:13

What evil is in mine hand?
1 Sam. 26:18

I and my kingdom are guiltless before the Lord.
2 Sam. 3:28

As a man falleth before wicked men, so fellest thou.
2 Sam. 3:34

They went in their simplicity, and they knew not any thing.
2 Sam. 15:11

As for these sheep, what have they done?
1 Chron. 21:17
See also 2 Sam. 24:17

If thou wert pure and upright; surely now He would awake for thee.
Job 8:6

God will not cast away a perfect man, neither will He help the evil doers.
Job 8:20

Make me to know my transgression and my sin.
Job to God
Job 13:23

My witness is in heaven, and my record is on high.
Job 16:19

Till I die I will not remove mine integrity from me.
Job 27:5

Let me be weighed in an even balance, that God may know mine integrity.
Job 31:6

Then let mine arm fall from my shoulder blade, and mine arm be broken from the bone.
Job 31:22

Oh that one would hear me!
Job 31:35

Let thistles grow instead of wheat, and cockle instead of barley.
Job 31:40

He was righteous in his own eyes.
(He: Job)
Job 32:1

False witnesses did rise up; they laid to my charge things that I knew not.
Ps. 35:11

A little child shall lead them.
Isa. 11:6

He is brought as a lamb to the slaughter.
Isa. 53:7
See also Jer. 11:19, Acts 8:32

Thou hast not remembered the days of thy youth, when thou wast naked and bare.
Ezek. 16:22

[*See also* Guilt, Naivete]

INNOVATION

There is no new thing under the sun.
Eccl. 1:9

That which hath been is now; and that which is to be hath already been.
Eccl. 3:15

That which hath been is named already.
Eccl. 6:10

INSANITY

See Madness.

INSINCERITY

See Hypocrisy, Sincerity.

INSPIRATION

Go, and I will be with thy mouth, and teach thee what thou shalt say.
God to Moses
Ex. 4:12

The word that God putteth in my mouth, that shall I speak.
Num. 22:38

The Spirit of the Lord came upon Gideon, and he blew a trumpet.
Judg. 6:34

The Spirit of the Lord will come upon thee.
Samuel to Saul
1 Sam. 10:6

The Spirit of the Lord spake by me, and His word was in my tongue.
2 Sam. 23:2

The hand of the Lord was upon me.
Ezek. 37:1

Your old men shall dream dreams, your young men shall see visions.
Joel 2:28
See also Acts 2:17

INSTABILITY

Unstable as water, thou shalt not excel.
Gen. 49:4

Your goodness is as a morning cloud, and as the early dew it goeth away.
Hos. 6:4

[*See also* Indecision]

INSTIGATION

And the serpent said unto the woman, Ye shall not surely die.
Gen. 3:4

Entice him, and see wherein his great strength lieth.
Philistines to Delilah
Judg. 16:5

Doth Job fear God for nought?
Satan to God
Job 1:9

Touch all that he hath, and he will curse Thee to Thy face.
Satan to God, about Job
Job 1:11

These six things doth the Lord hate: yea, seven are an abomination unto Him: A proud look, a lying tongue, and hands that shed innocent blood, An heart that deviseth wicked imaginations, feet that be swift in running to mischief, A false witness that speaketh lies, and he that soweth discord among brethren.
Prov. 6:16–19

[*See also* Provocation]

INSTINCT

The stork in the heaven knoweth her appointed times; and the turtle and the crane and the swallow observe the time of their coming; but My people know not the judgment of the Lord.
God to Jews
Jer. 8:7

INSTRUCTION

God exalteth by His power: who teacheth like Him?
Job 36:22

Make me to understand the way of Thy precepts: so shall I talk of Thy wondrous works.
Ps. 119:27

How sweet are Thy words unto my taste! yea, sweeter than honey to my mouth!
Ps. 119:103

He will teach us of His ways, and we will walk in His paths.
Isa. 2:3, Mic. 4:2

[*See also* Criticism, Education, Guidance, Heedfulness, Knowledge]

INSULTS

Am I a dog, that thou comest to me with staves?
Goliath to David
1 Sam. 17:43

Am I a dog's head?
2 Sam. 3:8

A fool's wrath is presently known: but a prudent man covereth shame.
Prov. 12:16

A brother offended is harder to be won than a strong city.
Prov. 18:19

Take no heed unto all words that are spoken; lest thou hear thy servant curse thee.
Eccl. 7:21

INTEGRITY

Though I should receive a thousand shekels of silver in mine hand, yet would I not put forth mine hand against the king's son.
2 Sam. 18:12

If thou wilt give me half thine house, I will not go in with thee, neither will I eat bread nor drink water in this place.
1 Kings 13:8

What the Lord saith unto me, that will I speak.
1 Kings 22:14
See also 2 Chron. 18:13

Dost thou still retain thine integrity? curse God, and die.
Job's wife to Job
Job 2:9

Till I die I will not remove mine integrity from me.
Job 27:5

My righteousness I hold fast, and will not

let it go: my heart shall not reproach me so long as I live.
Job 27:6

As for me, I will walk in mine integrity.
Ps. 26:11

The integrity of the upright shall guide them.
Prov. 11:3

They hate him that rebuketh in the gate, and they abhor him that speaketh uprightly.
Amos 5:10

[*See also* Character, Conscience, Corruption, Honesty, Righteousness]

INTELLIGENCE

See Education, Ignorance, Knowledge, Understanding.

INTENTIONS

They shall not deliver the slayer up into his hand; because he smote his neighbour unwittingly, and hated him not beforetime.
Josh. 20:5

Man looketh on the outward appearance, but the Lord looketh on the heart.
1 Sam. 16:7

Thou didst well in that it was in thine heart.
God to David
2 Chron. 6:8

[*See also* Motivation, Purpose]

INTERCESSION

Speak thou with us, and we will hear: but let not God speak with us, lest we die.
Israelites to Moses
Ex. 20:19

He stood between the dead and the living; and the plague was stayed.
(He: Aaron)
Num. 16:48

Enquire of the Lord for me, and for the people.
2 Kings 22:13

INTERMARRIAGE

They will turn away thy son from following Me, that they may serve other gods.
Deut. 7:4

Come not among these nations, these that remain among you.
Josh. 23:7

Is there never a woman among the daughters of thy brethren, or among all my people, that thou goest to take a wife of the uncircumcised Philistines?
(thou: Samson)
Judg. 14:3

Ye shall not go in to them, neither shall they come in unto you: for surely they will turn away your heart after their gods.
1 Kings 11:2

I rent my garment and my mantle, and plucked off the hair of my head and of my beard.
Ezra 9:3

Give not your daughters unto their sons, neither take their daughters unto your sons.
Ezra 9:12

Did not Solomon king of Israel sin by these things?
Neh. 13:26

INTOXICATION

See Drunkenness, Liquor, Pleasure.

ISRAEL

A land flowing with milk and honey.
E.g., Ex. 3:8

I am the Lord your God, which brought you forth out of the land of Egypt, to give you the land of Canaan, and to be your God.
E.g., Lev. 25:38

If the Lord delight in us, then He will bring us into this land.
Joshua and Caleb
Num. 14:8

I have given you the land to possess it.
God to Israelites
Num. 33:53

Behold, I have set the land before you: go in and possess the land which the Lord sware unto your fathers.
Deut. 1:8

It is a good land which the Lord our God doth give us.
Deut. 1:25

A land which the Lord thy God careth for: the eyes of the Lord thy God are always upon it.
Deut. 11:12

Every place whereon the soles of your feet shall tread shall be your's.
Deut. 11:24
See also Josh. 1:3

Behold the land of Canaan, which I give unto the children of Israel for a possession.
God to Moses
Deut. 32:49

Divide thou it by lot unto the Israelites for an inheritance.
Josh. 13:6

Ye shall possess their land, as the Lord your God hath promised unto you.
Josh. 23:5

I have given you a land for which ye did not labour.
Josh. 24:13

Unto thee will I give the land of Canaan, the lot of your inheritance.
1 Chron. 16:18, Ps. 105:11

I will ordain a place for My people Israel.
1 Chron. 17:9

They shall dwell in their place, and shall be moved no more.
1 Chron. 17:9

He will make her wilderness like Eden, and her desert like the garden of the Lord.
Isa. 51:3

Ye shall know that I am the Lord, when I shall bring you into the land of Israel.
Ezek. 20:42

[*See also* Chosen People, Jerusalem]

JEALOUSY

Give me children, or else I die.
Rachel to Jacob
Gen. 30:1

They hated him yet the more for his dreams, and for his words.
(They: Joseph's brothers)
Gen. 37:8

They have ascribed unto David ten thousands, and to me they have ascribed but thousands.
Saul
1 Sam. 18:8

What can he have more but the kingdom?
Saul about David
1 Sam. 18:8

Saul eyed David from that day and forward.
1 Sam. 18:9

Fret not thyself because of him who prospereth.
Ps. 37:7

Jealousy is the rage of a man.
Prov. 6:34

Let not thine heart envy sinners.
Prov. 23:17

Wrath is cruel, and anger is outrageous; but who is able to stand before envy?
Prov. 27:4

Better is the sight of the eyes than the wandering of the desire.
Eccl. 6:9

Jealousy is cruel as the grave: the coals thereof are coals of fire, which hath a most vehement flame.
Song 8:6

[*See also* Envy, Zeal]

JERUSALEM

The city of David, which is Zion.
1 Kings 8:1

Jerusalem, the city which I have chosen Me to put My name.
1 Kings 11:36
See also 2 Kings 21:4

Jerusalem, the city which the Lord did choose out of all the tribes of Israel, to put His name there.
1 Kings 14:21

I have chosen Jerusalem, that My name might be there.
2 Chron. 6:6
See also 1 Kings 8:29

In Jerusalem shall My name be for ever.
2 Chron. 33:4

Come, and let us build up the wall of Jerusalem, that we be no more a reproach.
Neh. 2:17

God is in the midst of her; she shall not be moved.
Ps. 46:5

The joy of the whole earth, is mount Zion.
Ps. 48:2

The city of the great King.
Ps. 48:2, Matt. 5:35

The Lord loveth the gates of Zion more than all the dwellings of Jacob.
Ps. 87:2

When the Lord shall build up Zion, He shall appear in His glory.
Ps. 102:16

They shall prosper that love thee.
Ps. 122:6

As the mountains are round about Jerusalem, so the Lord is round about His people.
Ps. 125:2

The Lord hath chosen Zion; He hath desired it for His habitation.
Ps. 132:13

This is My rest for ever: here will I dwell.
Ps. 132:14

By the rivers of Babylon, there we sat down, yea, we wept, when we remembered Zion.
Ps. 137:1

If I forget thee, O Jerusalem, let my right hand forget her cunning.
Ps. 137:5

If I do not remember thee, let my tongue cleave to the roof of my mouth.
Ps. 137:6

The city of righteousness, the faithful city.
Isa. 1:26

Zion shall be redeemed with judgment, and her converts with righteousness.
Isa. 1:27

Out of Zion shall go forth the law, and the word of the Lord from Jerusalem.
Isa. 2:3

The Lord hath founded Zion, and the poor of His people shall trust in it.
Isa. 14:32

The Lord shall comfort Zion: He will comfort all her waste places.
Isa. 51:3

In My wrath I smote thee, but in My favour have I had mercy on thee.
Isa. 60:10

The nation and kingdom that will not serve thee shall perish.
Isa. 60:12

The Lord shall be unto thee an everlasting light.
Isa. 60:19

For Zion's sake will I not hold My peace, and for Jerusalem's sake I will not rest.
Isa. 62:1

Keep not silence, And give Him no rest, till He establish, and till He make Jerusalem a praise in the earth.
Isa. 62:6–7

Rejoice ye with Jerusalem, and be glad with her, all ye that love her.
Isa. 66:10

How doth the city sit solitary, that was full of people! how is she become as a widow!
Lam. 1:1
See also Lam. 1:2–22

She that was great among the nations, and princess among the provinces, how is she become tributary!
Lam. 1:1

Among all her lovers she hath none to comfort her.
Lam. 1:2

Her friends have dealt treacherously with her, they are become her enemies.
Lam. 1:2

From the daughter of Zion all her beauty is departed: her princes are become like harts that find no pasture.
Lam. 1:6

All that honoured her despise her, because they have seen her nakedness.
Lam. 1:8

Is this the city that men call The perfection of beauty, The joy of the whole earth?
Lam. 2:15

The Lord dwelleth in Zion.
Joel 3:21

The law shall go forth of Zion, and the word of the Lord from Jerusalem.
Mic. 4:2

The Lord shall yet comfort Zion, and shall yet choose Jerusalem.
Zech. 1:17

[*See also* Israel]

JEWS

See Chosen People.

JOY

See Happiness, Laughter, Tears.

JUDGING

Thou shalt not respect the person of the poor, nor honour the person of the mighty.
Lev. 19:15

In righteousness shalt thou judge thy neighbour.
Lev. 19:15

Judge righteously between every man and his brother, and the stranger that is with him.
Deut. 1:16

Ye shall not be afraid of the face of man; for the judgment is God's.
Deut. 1:17

Thou shalt not respect persons, neither take a gift.
Deut. 16:19
See also Deut. 1:17

A gift doth blind the eyes of the wise, and pervert the words of the righteous.
Deut. 16:19
See also Ex. 23:8

Take heed what ye do: for ye judge not for man, but for the Lord.
2 Chron. 19:6

Let the fear of the Lord be upon you.
2 Chron. 19:7

[*See also* Fairness, Justice]

JUDGMENT

Shall not the Judge of all the earth do right?
Abraham to God
Gen. 18:25

The Lord shall judge His people.
E.g., Deut. 32:36

I will render vengeance to Mine enemies, and will reward them that hate Me.
Deut. 32:41

The Lord shall judge the ends of the earth.
1 Sam. 2:10

If one man sin against another, the judge shall judge him: but if a man sin against the Lord, who shall intreat for him?
1 Sam. 2:25

Let me be weighed in an even balance, that God may know mine integrity.
Job 31:6

Judgment is before Him; therefore trust thou in Him.
Job 35:14

God judgeth the righteous, and God is angry with the wicked every day.
Ps. 7:11

He that planted the ear, shall He not hear? He that formed the eye, shall He not see?
Ps. 94:9

He shall judge the world with righteousness, and the people with His truth.
Ps. 96:13

With righteousness shall He judge the world.
Ps. 98:9

If Thou, Lord, shouldest mark iniquities, O Lord, who shall stand?
Ps. 130:3

Enter not into judgment with Thy servant: for in Thy sight shall no man living be justified.
Ps. 143:2

God shall judge the righteous and the wicked.
Eccl. 3:17

God shall bring every work into judgment.
Eccl. 12:14

Howl ye; for the day of the Lord is at hand.
Isa. 13:6

By fire and by His sword will the Lord plead with all flesh: and the slain of the Lord shall be many.
Isa. 66:16

I have set My face against this city for evil, and not for good, saith the Lord.
(city: Jerusalem)
Jer. 21:10

And they shall know that I am the Lord.
Ezek. 6:10

I will judge thee according to thy ways, and will recompense thee for all thine abominations.
Ezek. 7:8

I will judge you every one after his ways.
Ezek. 33:20

I will destroy the fat and the strong; I will feed them with judgment.
Ezek. 34:16

Multitudes, multitudes in the valley of decision: for the day of the Lord is near.
Joel 3:14

The day of the Lord is near upon all the heathen.
Obad. 15

I will be a swift witness against the sorcerers, and against the adulterers, and against false swearers, and against those that oppress the hireling in his wages.
Mal. 3:5

[*See also* Criticism, Judgment Day, Misjudgment, Punishment, Responsibility, Retribution]

JUDGMENT DAY

Alas for the day! for the day of the Lord is at hand.
Joel 1:15

The day of the Lord cometh.
E.g., Joel 2:1

The day of the Lord is great and very terrible; and who can abide it?
Joel 2:11

Woe unto you that desire the day of the Lord!
Amos 5:18

Behold, the day cometh, that shall burn as an oven; and all the proud, yea, and all that do wickedly, shall be stubble.
Mal. 4:1

[*See also* Apocalypse, End Days]

JUSTICE

Whoso sheddeth man's blood, by man shall his blood be shed.
Gen. 9:6

One law shall be to him that is homeborn, and unto the stranger that sojourneth among you.
Ex. 12:49

Thou shalt give life for life, Eye for eye, tooth for tooth, hand for hand, foot for foot, Burning for burning, wound for wound, stripe for stripe.
Ex. 21:23–25
See also Lev. 24:20, Deut. 19:21

Thou shalt not wrest the judgment of thy poor in his cause.
Ex. 23:6

I will not justify the wicked.
God
Ex. 23:7

Ye shall have one manner of law, as well for the stranger, as for one of your own country.
Lev. 24:22
See also Num. 9:14

The murderer shall surely be put to death.
E.g., Num. 35:16
See also Ex. 21:12, Lev. 24:17

Ye shall hear the small as well as the great.
Deut. 1:17

At the mouth of two witnesses, or three witnesses, shall he that is worthy of death be put to death; but at the mouth of one witness he shall not be put to death.
Deut. 17:6

Justify the righteous, and condemn the wicked.
Deut. 25:1

As I have done, so God hath requited me.
Judg. 1:7

If he will show himself a worthy man, there shall not an hair of him fall to the earth.
1 Kings 1:52

Divide the living child in two, and give half to the one, and half to the other.
1 Kings 3:25

Give her the living child, and in no wise slay it: she is the mother thereof.
1 Kings 3:27

Hast thou found me, O mine enemy?
Ahab to Elijah
1 Kings 21:20

I will cause him to fall by the sword in his own land.
2 Kings 19:7, Isa. 37:7

Render unto every man according unto all his ways, whose heart Thou knowest.
2 Chron. 6:30

They hanged Haman on the gallows that he had prepared for Mordecai.
Esther 7:10

Unto God would I commit my cause.
Job 5:8

O that one might plead for a man with God, as a man pleadeth for his neighbour!
Job 16:21

The light of the wicked shall be put out, and the spark of his fire shall not shine.
Job 18:5

The triumphing of the wicked is short, and the joy of the hypocrite but for a moment.
Job 20:5

They are exalted for a little while, but are gone and brought low.
(they: the wicked)
Job 24:24

Oh that one would hear me!
Job 31:35

God will not do wickedly, neither will the Almighty pervert judgment.
Job 34:12

Let them be taken in the devices that they have imagined.
Ps. 10:2

Give them after the work of their hands; render to them their desert.
Ps. 28:4

Evil shall slay the wicked.
Ps. 34:21

I have been young, and now am old; yet have I not seen the righteous forsaken.
Ps. 37:25

Thou renderest to every man according to his work.
Ps. 62:12
See also, e.g., Matt. 16:27

Defend the poor and fatherless: do justice to the afflicted and needy.
Ps. 82:3

Justice and judgment are the habitation of Thy throne: mercy and truth shall go before Thy face.
Ps. 89:14

As he loved cursing, so let it come unto him: as he delighted not in blessing, so let it be far from him.
Ps. 109:17

The wicked shall fall by his own wickedness.
Prov. 11:5

To do justice and judgment is more acceptable to the Lord than sacrifice.
Prov. 21:3

Many seek the ruler's favour; but every man's judgment cometh from the Lord.
Prov. 29:26

Open thy mouth, judge righteously, and plead the cause of the poor and needy.
Prov. 31:9

He shall not fail nor be discouraged, till he have set judgment in the earth.
Isa. 42:4

I the Lord love judgment.
Isa. 61:8

To subvert a man in his cause, the Lord approveth not.
Lam. 3:36

O Lord, Thou hast seen my wrong: judge Thou my cause.
Lam. 3:59

According to their deserts will I judge them.
Ezek. 7:27

The Lord our God is righteous in all His works which He doeth.
Dan. 9:14

Ye have plowed wickedness, ye have reaped iniquity.
Hos. 10:13

Let judgment run down as waters, and righteousness as a mighty stream.
Amos 5:24

Thy reward shall return upon thine own head.
Obad. 15

Do justly.
Mic. 6:8

Though it tarry, wait for it; because it will surely come.
Hab. 2:3
See also Heb. 10:37

Execute true judgment, and show mercy and compassions every man to his brother.
Zech. 7:9

Oppress not the widow, nor the fatherless, the stranger, nor the poor.
Zech. 7:10

Execute the judgment of truth and peace in your gates.
Zech. 8:16

[*See also* Fairness, Guilt, Impartiality, Injustice, Innocence, Judging, Restitution, Judgment, Wickedness]

K

KINDNESS

Drink, and I will give thy camels drink also.
Rebekah
Gen. 24:14

The Lord deal kindly with you, as ye have dealt with the dead, and with me.
Naomi
Ruth 1:8

Let her glean even among the sheaves, and reproach her not.
Ruth 2:15

Thou hast showed more kindness in the latter end than at the beginning.
Ruth 3:10

Let them be of those that eat at thy table.
1 Kings 2:7

The merciful man doeth good to his own soul: but he that is cruel troubleth his own flesh.
Prov. 11:17

The tender mercies of the wicked are cruel.
Prov. 12:10

If thine enemy be hungry, give him bread to eat; and if he be thirsty, give him water to drink.
Prov. 25:21
See also Rom. 12:20

Even the sea monsters draw out the breast, they give suck to their young ones.
Lam. 4:3

Let none of you imagine evil against his brother in your heart.
Zech. 7:10
See also Zech. 8:17

[*See also* Altruism, Compassion, Generosity, Hospitality]

KINGS

See Monarchy.

KNOWLEDGE

Of every tree of the garden thou mayest freely eat: But of the tree of the knowledge of good and evil, thou shalt not eat.
> *Gen. 2:16–17*

Ye shall not eat of it, neither shall ye touch it, lest ye die.
> *(it: tree of knowledge)*
> *Gen. 3:3*

Your eyes shall be opened, and ye shall be as gods, knowing good and evil.
> *Gen. 3:5*

And the eyes of them both were opened, and they knew that they were naked.
> *Gen. 3:7*

Who told thee that thou wast naked?
> *Gen. 3:11*

The Lord God said, Behold, the man is become as one of us, to know good and evil.
> *Gen. 3:22*

The secret things belong unto the Lord our God: but those things which are revealed belong unto us and to our children for ever.
> *Deut. 29:29*

The Lord is a God of knowledge, and by Him actions are weighed.
> *1 Sam. 2:3*

Canst thou by searching find out God?
> *Job 11:7*

Shall any teach God knowledge?
> *Job 21:22*

Let us choose to us judgment: let us know among ourselves what is good.
> *Job 34:4*

Have the gates of death been opened unto thee? or hast thou seen the doors of the shadow of death?
> *God to Job*
> *Job 38:17*

I am a stranger in the earth: hide not Thy commandments from me.
> *Ps. 119:19*

I understand more than the ancients, because I keep Thy precepts.
> *Ps. 119:100*

A wise man will hear, and will increase learning.
> *Prov. 1:5*

The fear of the Lord is the beginning of knowledge.
> *Prov. 1:7*

Get wisdom, get understanding: forget it not.
> *Prov. 4:5*

Wise men lay up knowledge.
> *Prov. 10:14*

Through knowledge shall the just be delivered.
> *Prov. 11:9*

Knowledge is easy unto him that understandeth.
> *Prov. 14:6*

The heart of him that hath understanding seeketh knowledge.
> *Prov. 15:14*

The ear of the wise seeketh knowledge.
> *Prov. 18:15*

He that increaseth knowledge increaseth sorrow.
> *Eccl. 1:18*

Have ye not known? have ye not heard? hath it not been told you from the beginning?
> *Isa. 40:21*

Thy wisdom and thy knowledge, it hath perverted thee; and thou hast said in thine heart, I am, and none else beside me.
> *Isa. 47:10*

The stork in the heaven knoweth her appointed times; and the turtle and the crane and the swallow observe the time of their coming; but My people know not the judgment of the Lord.
> *God to Jews*
> *Jer. 8:7*

Because thou hast rejected knowledge, I will also reject thee.
God
Hos. 4:6

[*See also* Education, Experience, God's Knowledge, Ignorance, Understanding, Wisdom]

KNOWLEDGE OF GOD

And they shall know that I am the Lord their God, that brought them forth out of the land of Egypt.
Ex. 29:46

And ye shall know that I am the Lord.
1 Kings 20:28

Know thou the God of thy father.
1 Chron. 28:9

We know Him not, neither can the number of His years be searched out.
Job 36:26

The secret of the Lord is with them that fear Him.
Ps. 25:14

Be still, and know that I am God.
Ps. 46:10

The earth shall be full of the knowledge of the Lord, as the waters cover the sea.
Isa. 11:9

They shall all know Me, from the least of them unto the greatest.
Jer. 31:34
See also Heb. 8:11

Ye shall know that I am the Lord, when I set My face against them.
Ezek. 15:7

I will be known in the eyes of many nations, and they shall know that I am the Lord.
Ezek. 38:23

[*See also* Acknowledgment, Disobedience, Salvation, Testimony]

LABOR

See Business, Work.

LAMENT

How are the mighty fallen!
E.g., 2 Sam. 1:19

Tell it not in Gath, publish it not in the streets of Askelon.
2 Sam. 1:20

I have no son to keep my name in remembrance.
2 Sam. 18:18

How doth the city sit solitary, that was full of people! how is she become as a widow!
Lam. 1:1
See also Lam. 1:2–22

Alas for the day! for the day of the Lord is at hand.
Joel 1:15

Woe is me!
E.g., Mic. 7:1

[*See also* Anguish, Grief, Jerusalem, Mourning]

LANGUAGE

See Communication, Eloquence, Speech.

LAST JUDGMENT

See Apocalypse, Judgment Day.

LAUGHTER

Even in laughter the heart is sorrowful.
Prov. 14:13

I said of laughter, It is mad: and of mirth, What doeth it?
Eccl. 2:2

A time to weep, and a time to laugh.
Eccl. 3:4

Sorrow is better than laughter: for by the sadness of the countenance the heart is made better.
Eccl. 7:3

As the crackling of thorns under a pot, so is the laughter of the fool.
Eccl. 7:6

LAW

Ye shall have one manner of law, as well for the stranger, as for one of your own country.
Lev. 24:22
See also Ex. 12:49, Num. 9:14

[*See also* Commandments, Judging, Justice, Scripture]

LAWLESSNESS

The earth is given into the hand of the wicked: He covereth the faces of the judges thereof.
Job 9:24

If the foundations be destroyed, what can the righteous do?
Ps. 11:3

The wicked watcheth the righteous, and seeketh to slay him.
Ps. 37:32

Deliver me from the workers of iniquity, and save me from bloody men.
Ps. 59:2

When the wicked spring as the grass, and when all the workers of iniquity do flourish; it is that they shall be destroyed for ever.
Ps. 92:7

Rivers of waters run down mine eyes, because they keep not Thy law.
Ps. 119:136

A wise king scattereth the wicked.
Prov. 20:26

There shall be no reward to the evil man; the candle of the wicked shall be put out.
Prov. 24:20

Judgment is turned away backward, and justice standeth afar off.
Isa. 59:14

Truth is fallen in the street, and equity cannot enter.
Isa. 59:14

The law is no more.
Lam. 2:9

The land is full of bloody crimes, and the city is full of violence.
Ezek. 7:23

Wherefore lookest Thou upon them that deal treacherously, and holdest Thy tongue when the wicked devoureth the man that is more righteous than he?
Hab. 1:13

[*See also* Corruption, Crime, Injustice, Wickedness]

LAZINESS

He becometh poor that dealeth with a slack hand: but the hand of the diligent maketh rich.
Prov. 10:4

He that sleepeth in harvest is a son that causeth shame.
Prov. 10:5

As vinegar to the teeth, and as smoke to the eyes, so is the sluggard to them that send him.
Prov. 10:26

In all labour there is profit: but the talk of the lips tendeth only to penury.
Prov. 14:23

An idle soul shall suffer hunger.
Prov. 19:15

Love not sleep, lest thou come to poverty.
Prov. 20:13

The slothful man saith, There is a lion without, I shall be slain in the streets.
Prov. 22:13
See also Prov. 26:13

Drowsiness shall clothe a man with rags.
Prov. 23:21

The sluggard is wiser in his own conceit than seven men that can render a reason.
Prov. 26:16

The fool foldeth his hands together, and eateth his own flesh.
Eccl. 4:5

By much slothfulness the building decayeth.
Eccl. 10:18

He that observeth the wind shall not sow; and he that regardeth the clouds shall not reap.
Eccl. 11:4

Their strength is to sit still.
Isa. 30:7

[*See also* Diligence, Work]

LEADERSHIP

Can we find such a one as this is, a man in whom the Spirit of God is?
Pharaoh to Joseph
Gen. 41:38

The sceptre shall not depart from Judah, nor a lawgiver from between his feet, until Shiloh come.
Jacob to Judah
Gen. 49:10

Who made thee a prince and a judge over us?
(thee: Moses)
Ex. 2:14

The children of Israel have not hearkened unto me; how then shall Pharaoh hear me?
Moses to God
Ex. 6:12

What shall I do unto this people? they be almost ready to stone me.
Moses
Ex. 17:4

Thou wilt surely wear away, both thou, and this people that is with thee.
Jethro to Moses
Ex. 18:18

Show them the way wherein they must walk, and the work that they must do.
Ex. 18:20

Provide out of all the people able men, such as fear God, men of truth, hating covetousness.
Jethro to Moses
Ex. 18:21

Every great matter they shall bring unto thee, but every small matter they shall judge.
Ex. 18:22
See also Ex. 18:26

Wherefore have I not found favour in Thy sight, that Thou layest the burden of all this people upon me?
Moses to God
Num. 11:11

Have I conceived all this people? have I begotten them, that Thou shouldest say unto me, Carry them in thy bosom, as a nursing father beareth the sucking child?
Moses to God
Num. 11:12

The man whom the Lord doth choose, he shall be holy.
Num. 16:7

The cause that is too hard for you, bring it unto me, and I will hear it.
Moses
Deut. 1:17

Whithersoever thou sendest us, we will go.
Josh. 1:16

They feared him, as they feared Moses, all the days of his life.
Josh. 4:14

Follow after me: for the Lord hath delivered your enemies.
Judg. 3:28

The Spirit of the Lord came upon Gideon, and he blew a trumpet.
Judg. 6:34

They have not rejected thee, but they have rejected Me, that I should not reign over them.
God to Samuel
1 Sam. 8:7

Because thou hast rejected the word of the

Lord, He hath also rejected thee from being king.
Samuel to Saul
1 Sam. 15:23

Arise, anoint him; for this is he.
God to Samuel, about David
1 Sam. 16:12

Who am I, O Lord God? and what is my house, that Thou hast brought me hitherto?
David
2 Sam. 7:18

Give therefore Thy servant an understanding heart to judge Thy people, that I may discern between good and bad.
Solomon
1 Kings 3:9

Walk before Me, as David thy father walked, in integrity of heart, and in uprightness.
1 Kings 9:4

Happy are thy men, happy are these thy servants, which stand continually before thee.
Queen of Sheba to Solomon
1 Kings 10:8

Because the Lord loved Israel for ever, therefore made He thee king.
Queen of Sheba to Solomon
1 Kings 10:9

Elijah passed by him, and cast his mantle upon him.
1 Kings 19:19
See also 2 Kings 2:13

Let a double portion of thy spirit be upon me.
Elisha to Elijah
2 Kings 2:9

As thou hast said, so must we do.
Ezra 10:12

Where no counsel is, the people fall.
Prov. 11:14

Excellent speech becometh not a fool: much less do lying lips a prince.
Prov. 17:7

Where there is no vision, the people perish.
Prov. 29:18

Better is a poor and a wise child than an old and foolish king, who will no more be admonished.
Eccl. 4:13

Woe to thee, O land, when thy king is a child.
Eccl. 10:16

Thou hast clothing, be thou our ruler.
Isa. 3:6

A little child shall lead them.
Isa. 11:6

I will bring the blind by a way that they knew not; I will lead them in paths that they have not known.
God
Isa. 42:16

Woe be unto the pastors that destroy and scatter the sheep of My pasture!
Jer. 23:1

My people hath been lost sheep: their shepherds have caused them to go astray.
Jer. 50:6

Woe be to the shepherds of Israel that do feed themselves! should not the shepherds feed the flocks?
Ezek. 34:2

Smite the shepherd, and the sheep shall be scattered.
Zech. 13:7
See also Matt. 26:31, Mark 14:27

[*See also* Ambition, Authority, Corruption, Government, Models, Monarchy]

LENIENCY

See Compassion, Forgiveness, Punishment.

LIES

The Strength of Israel will not lie.
1 Sam. 15:29

Should thy lies make men hold their peace?
Job 11:3

Ye are forgers of lies, ye are all physicians of no value.
Job to his friends
Job 13:4

I said in my haste, All men are liars.
Ps. 116:11

These six things doth the Lord hate: yea, seven are an abomination unto Him: A proud look, a lying tongue, and hands that shed innocent blood, An heart that deviseth wicked imaginations, feet that be swift in running to mischief, A false witness that speaketh lies, and he that soweth discord among brethren.
Prov. 6:16–19

The wicked is snared by the transgression of his lips.
Prov. 12:13

A lying tongue is but for a moment.
Prov. 12:19

Lying lips are abomination to the Lord.
Prov. 12:22

A righteous man hateth lying.
Prov. 13:5

Excellent speech becometh not a fool: much less do lying lips a prince.
Prov. 17:7

Woe unto them that call evil good, and good evil; that put darkness for light, and light for darkness; that put bitter for sweet, and sweet for bitter!
Isa. 5:20

Their tongue is deceitful in their mouth.
Mic. 6:12

Thou speakest lies in the name of the Lord.
Zech. 13:3

[*See also* Deception, Dishonesty, Honesty, Hypocrisy, Perjury, Truth]

LIFE

The Lord God formed man of the dust of the ground, and breathed into his nostrils the breath of life.
Gen. 2:7

The life of all flesh is the blood thereof.
Lev. 17:14

Wherefore is light given to him that is in misery, and life unto the bitter in soul?
Job 3:20

What is mine end, that I should prolong my life?
Job 6:11

Wherefore then hast Thou brought me forth out of the womb? Oh that I had given up the ghost, and no eye had seen me!
Job 10:18

Man that is born of a woman is of few days, and full of trouble.
Job 14:1

The spirit of God hath made me, and the breath of the Almighty hath given me life.
Job 33:4

We spend our years as a tale that is told.
Ps. 90:9

The days of our years are threescore years and ten; and if by reason of strength they be fourscore years, yet is their strength labour and sorrow.
Ps. 90:10

Teach us to number our days, that we may apply our hearts unto wisdom.
Ps. 90:12

Give me understanding, and I shall live.
Ps. 119:144

Let my soul live, and it shall praise Thee.
Ps. 119:175

The fear of the Lord prolongeth days: but the years of the wicked shall be shortened.
Prov. 10:27

The fear of the Lord is a fountain of life.
Prov. 14:27

Vanity of vanities; all is vanity.
Eccl. 1:2
See also Eccl. 12:8

Therefore I hated life.
Eccl. 2:17

All his days are sorrows, and his travail grief; yea, his heart taketh not rest in the night.
Eccl. 2:23

A pleasant thing it is for the eyes to behold the sun.
Eccl. 11:7

Cursed be the day wherein I was born: let

not the day wherein my mother bare me be blessed.
Jer. 20:14

Wherefore came I forth out of the womb to see labour and sorrow?
Jer. 20:18

Ye shall live; and ye shall know that I am the Lord.
Ezek. 37:6

Seek the Lord, and ye shall live.
Amos 5:6
See also Amos 5:4

Seek good, and not evil, that ye may live.
Amos 5:14

[*See also* Age, Death, Mortality]

LIFE AND DEATH

I have set before you life and death, blessing and cursing: therefore choose life, that both thou and thy seed may live.
Deut. 30:19

There is no god with Me: I kill, and I make alive; I wound, and I heal: neither is there any that can deliver out of My hand.
Deut. 32:39

The Lord killeth, and maketh alive: He bringeth down to the grave, and bringeth up.
1 Sam. 2:6

Naked came I out of my mother's womb, and naked shall I return thither.
Job 1:21

Unto God the Lord belong the issues from death.
Ps. 68:20

According to the greatness of Thy power preserve Thou those that are appointed to die.
Ps. 79:11

Shall Thy lovingkindness be declared in the grave? or Thy faithfulness in destruction?
Ps. 88:11

Take me not away in the midst of my days.
Ps. 102:24

I shall not die, but live, and declare the works of the Lord.
Ps. 118:17

Man is like to vanity: his days are as a shadow that passeth away.
Ps. 144:4

He that keepeth the commandment keepeth his own soul; but he that despiseth His ways shall die.
Prov. 19:16

A time to be born, and a time to die.
Eccl. 3:2

I praised the dead which are already dead more than the living which are yet alive.
Eccl. 4:2

A good name is better than precious ointment; and the day of death than the day of one's birth.
Eccl. 7:1

Why shouldest thou die before thy time?
Eccl. 7:17

There is one event to the righteous, and to the wicked; to the good and to the clean, and to the unclean.
Eccl. 9:2

A living dog is better than a dead lion.
Eccl. 9:4

The living know that they shall die: but the dead know not any thing.
Eccl. 9:5

As the days of a tree are the days of My people, and Mine elect shall long enjoy the work of their hands.
Isa. 65:22

Behold, I set before you the way of life, and the way of death.
Jer. 21:8

Make you a new heart and a new spirit: for why will ye die?
Ezek. 18:31

[*See also* Death, Eternal Life, Life, Mortality]

And God said, Let there be light: and there was light.
    Gen. 1:3

Darkness which may be felt.
    Ex. 10:21

The people that walked in darkness have seen a great light.
    Isa. 9:2
    See also Matt. 4:16, Luke 1:79

[*See also* Enlightenment, Nature, Night, Spirituality]

LIQUOR

Wine that maketh glad the heart of man.
    Ps. 104:15

Wine is a mocker, strong drink is raging.
    Prov. 20:1

Look not thou upon the wine when it is red.
    Prov. 23:31

It biteth like a serpent, and stingeth like an adder.
    Prov. 23:32

Give strong drink unto him that is ready to perish, and wine unto those that be of heavy hearts.
    Prov. 31:6

Let him drink, and forget his poverty, and remember his misery no more.
    Prov. 31:7

Eat thy bread with joy, and drink thy wine with a merry heart.
    Eccl. 9:7

Whoredom and wine and new wine take away the heart.
    Hos. 4:11

[*See also* Drunkenness, Pleasure]

See Heedfulness.

LONELINESS

It is not good that the man should be alone; I will make him an help meet for him.
    Gen. 2:18

My kinsfolk have failed, and my familiar friends have forgotten me.
    Job 19:14

I am a brother to dragons, and a companion to owls.
    Job 30:29

How long wilt Thou forget me, O Lord? for ever? how long wilt Thou hide Thy face from me?
    Ps. 13:1

When my father and my mother forsake me, then the Lord will take me up.
    Ps. 27:10

I am forgotten as a dead man out of mind: I am like a broken vessel.
    Ps. 31:12

I looked for some to take pity, but there was none; and for comforters, but I found none.
    Ps. 69:20

Woe to him that is alone when he falleth; for he hath not another to help him up.
    Eccl. 4:10

Among all her lovers she hath none to comfort her.
    (her: Jerusalem)
    Lam. 1:2

They shall be desolate in the midst of the countries that are desolate.
    Ezek. 30:7

[*See also* Abandonment, Desolation, Fellowship, Friendship]

See Age, Mortality.

LOSS

The Lord gave, and the Lord hath taken away; blessed be the name of the Lord.
Job 1:21

A time to get, and a time to lose.
Eccl. 3:6

I will restore to you the years that the locust hath eaten.
Joel 2:25

[*See also* Acceptance, Profit, Reward]

LOVE

Jacob served seven years for Rachel; and they seemed unto him but a few days, for the love he had to her.
Gen. 29:20

Israel loved Joseph more than all his children, because he was the son of his old age.
Gen. 37:3

Now let me die, since I have seen thy face, because thou art yet alive.
Jacob to Joseph
Gen. 46:30

Thou shalt love thy neighbour as thyself.
E.g., Lev. 19:18, Matt. 19:19

The apple of His eye.
Deut. 32:10

How canst thou say, I love thee, when thine heart is not with me?
Delilah to Samson
Judg. 16:15

Am not I better to thee than ten sons?
(I: Hannah's husband)
1 Sam. 1:8

In their death they were not divided.
(they: Saul and Jonathan)
2 Sam. 1:23

Would God I had died for thee, O Absalom, my son, my son!
2 Sam. 18:33

O my Lord, give her the living child, and in no wise slay it.
1 Kings 3:26

Hatred stirreth up strifes: but love covereth all sins.
Prov. 10:12

Better is a dinner of herbs where love is, than a stalled ox and hatred therewith.
Prov. 15:17

A time to love, and a time to hate.
Eccl. 3:8

Let him kiss me with the kisses of his mouth: for thy love is better than wine.
Song 1:2

His banner over me was love.
Song 2:4

Stay me with flagons, comfort me with apples: for I am sick of love.
Song 2:5

I sought him, but I found him not.
Song 3:1, 2

In the broad ways I will seek him whom my soul loveth.
Song 3:2

How much better is thy love than wine! and the smell of thine ointments than all spices!
Song 4:10

Let my beloved come into his garden, and eat his pleasant fruits.
Song 4:16

I am my beloved's, and my beloved is mine.
Song 6:3

I am my beloved's, and his desire is toward me.
Song 7:10

Set me as a seal upon thine heart, as a seal upon thine arm.
Song 8:6

Love is strong as death.
Song 8:6

Many waters cannot quench love, neither can the floods drown it.
Song 8:7

She shall follow after her lovers, but she shall not overtake them.
Hos. 2:7

Your goodness is as a morning cloud, and as the early dew it goeth away.
Hos. 6:4

I have loved you, saith the Lord. Yet ye say, Wherein hast Thou loved us?
Mal. 1:2

Was not Esau Jacob's brother? saith the Lord: yet I loved Jacob.
Mal. 1:2
See also Rom. 9:13

[*See also* Brotherhood, Friendship, God's Love, God's Mercy, Hatred]

LOVE OF GOD

Thou shalt love the Lord thy God with all thine heart, and with all thy soul, and with all thy might.
Deut. 6:5
See also, e.g., Matt. 22:37

Love Him.
Deut. 10:12

Love the Lord thy God.
E.g., Deut. 19:9

Take good heed therefore unto yourselves, that ye love the Lord your God.
Josh. 23:11
See also Deut. 4:15

Let them that love Him be as the sun when he goeth forth in his might.
Judg. 5:31

As the hart panteth after the water brooks, so panteth my soul after Thee, O God.
Ps. 42:1

My soul thirsteth after Thee, as a thirsty land.
Ps. 143:6

[*See also* Reverence]

LOYALTY

Enviest thou for my sake?
Moses to Joshua
Num. 11:29

He will not forsake thee, neither destroy thee, nor forget the covenant of thy fathers which He sware unto them.
Deut. 4:31

I will not fail thee, nor forsake thee.
(I: God)
Josh. 1:5
See also Deut. 31:6, Heb. 13:5

He left nothing undone of all that the Lord commanded Moses.
Josh. 11:15

Intreat me not to leave thee.
Ruth 1:16

Whither thou goest, I will go; and where thou lodgest, I will lodge: thy people shall be my people, and thy God my God.
Ruth 1:16

Where thou diest, will I die, and there will I be buried.
Ruth 1:17

I will raise Me up a faithful priest.
1 Sam. 2:35

Who is so faithful among all thy servants as David?
1 Sam. 22:14

Blessed be ye of the Lord; for ye have compassion on me.
Saul
1 Sam. 23:21

In what place my lord the king shall be, whether in death or life, even there also will thy servant be.
2 Sam. 15:21

Hast not Thou made an hedge about him, and about his house?
Satan to God, of Job
Job 1:10

The Lord will not cast off His people, neither will He forsake His inheritance.
Ps. 94:14

A faithful man who can find?
Prov. 20:6

Thine own friend, and thy father's friend, forsake not.
Prov. 27:10

[*See also* Allegiance, Allies, Betrayal, Faithfulness]

See Chance.

LUST

Keep thee from the evil woman, from the flattery of the tongue of a strange woman.
Prov. 6:24

Lust not after her beauty in thine heart; neither let her take thee with her eyelids.
Prov. 6:25

Can a man take fire in his bosom, and his clothes not be burned?
Prov. 6:27

Can one go upon hot coals, and his feet not be burned?
Prov. 6:28

He goeth after her straightway, as an ox goeth to the slaughter.
Prov. 7:22

Give not thy strength unto women, nor thy ways to that which destroyeth kings.
Prov. 31:3

They were as fed horses in the morning: every one neighed after his neighbour's wife.
Jer. 5:8

[*See also* Adultery, Desire, Immorality, Prostitution]

MADNESS

Have I need of mad men, that ye have brought this fellow to play the mad man in my presence?
1 Sam. 21:15

Surely oppression maketh a wise man mad.
Eccl. 7:7

MAN AND WOMAN

One man among a thousand have I found; but a woman among all those have I not.
Eccl. 7:28

[*See also* Family, Mankind, Marriage, Women]

MANAGEMENT

See Business, Leadership.

MANKIND

Let them have dominion over the fish of the sea, and over the fowl of the air, and over the cattle, and over all the earth, and over every creeping thing that creepeth.
Gen. 1:26

God created man in His own image, in the image of God created He him; male and female created He them.
Gen. 1:27

Be fruitful, and multiply, and replenish the earth, and subdue it.
Gen. 1:28

The Lord God formed man of the dust of the ground, and breathed into his nostrils the breath of life.
Gen. 2:7

Dust thou art, and unto dust shalt thou return.
Gen. 3:19

God created man, in the likeness of God made He him.
Gen. 5:1

Male and female created He them; and blessed them.
Gen. 5:2

It repented the Lord that He had made man on the earth.
Gen. 6:6

There is no man that sinneth not.
1 Kings 8:46, 2 Chron. 6:36

All the people, both small and great.
2 Kings 23:2

Shall mortal man be more just than God? shall a man be more pure than his maker?
Job 4:17

Man is born unto trouble.
Job 5:7

What is man, that Thou shouldest magnify him? and that Thou shouldest set Thine heart upon him?
Job 7:17

Man that is born of a woman is of few days, and full of trouble.
Job 14:1

Can a man be profitable unto God, as he that is wise may be profitable unto himself?
Job 22:2

How can he be clean that is born of a woman?
Job 25:4

Yea, the stars are not pure in His sight. How much less man, that is a worm? and the son of man, which is a worm?
Job 25:5-6

God is greater than man.
Job 33:12

They all are the work of His hands.
Job 34:19

If thou sinnest, what doest thou against Him?
Job 35:6

Canst thou draw out leviathan with an hook? or his tongue with a cord which thou lettest down?
God to Job
Job 41:1

What is man, that Thou art mindful of him? and the son of man, that Thou visitest him?
Ps. 8:4
See also Heb. 2:6

Thou hast made him a little lower than the angels, and hast crowned him with glory and honour.
Ps. 8:5
See also Heb. 2:7

There is none that doeth good, no, not one.
Ps. 14:3, Ps. 53:3, Rom. 3:12

Every man at his best state is altogether vanity.
Ps. 39:5

Surely men of low degree are vanity, and men of high degree are a lie.
Ps. 62:9

He remembered that they were but flesh; a wind that passeth away, and cometh not again.
Ps. 78:39

They are like grass which groweth up. In the morning it flourisheth, and groweth up; in the evening it is cut down, and withereth.
Ps. 90:5-6

It is He that hath made us, and not we ourselves.
Ps. 100:3

As for man, his days are as grass: as a flower of the field, so he flourisheth.
Ps. 103:15

I will praise Thee; for I am fearfully and wonderfully made.
Ps. 139:14

Lord, what is man, that Thou takest knowledge of him! or the son of man, that Thou makest account of him!
Ps. 144:3

All his days are sorrows, and his travail grief; yea, his heart taketh not rest in the night.
Eccl. 2:23

A man hath no preeminence above a beast: for all is vanity.
Eccl. 3:19

All flesh is grass, and all the goodliness thereof is as the flower of the field.
Isa. 40:6
See also 1 Pet. 1:24

All nations before Him are as nothing.
Isa. 40:17

Who art thou, that thou shouldest be

afraid of a man that shall die, and of the son of man which shall be made as grass?
Isa. 51:12

We are the clay, and Thou our potter.
Isa. 64:8

We all are the work of Thy hand.
Isa. 64:8

[*See also* Human Nature, Man and Woman, Mortality]

MANNERS

See Courtesy.

MARRIAGE

And they shall be one flesh.
Gen. 2:24

Thy desire shall be to thy husband, and he shall rule over thee.
God to Eve
Gen. 3:16

Are there yet any more sons in my womb, that they may be your husbands?
Naomi to Ruth and Orpah
Ruth 1:11

Would ye tarry for them till they were grown?
Ruth 1:13

Rejoice with the wife of thy youth.
Prov. 5:18

A virtuous woman is a crown to her husband.
Prov. 12:4

Whoso findeth a wife findeth a good thing, and obtaineth favour of the Lord.
Prov. 18:22

House and riches are the inheritance of fathers: and a prudent wife is from the Lord.
Prov. 19:14

A faithful man who can find?
Prov. 20:6

It is better to dwell in a corner of the housetop, than with a brawling woman in a wide house.
Prov. 21:9
See also Prov. 25:24

It is better to dwell in the wilderness, than with a contentious and an angry woman.
Prov. 21:19

Who can find a virtuous woman? for her price is far above rubies.
Prov. 31:10

She looketh well to the ways of her household, and eateth not the bread of idleness.
(she: wife)
Prov. 31:27

Many daughters have done virtuously, but thou excellest them all.
Prov. 31:29

Let us be called by thy name, to take away our reproach.
Isa. 4:1

Let none deal treacherously against the wife of his youth.
Mal. 2:15

Take heed to your spirit, that ye deal not treacherously.
Mal. 2:16

[*See also* Adultery, Family, Nagging, Strife, Women]

MARTYRDOM

Let me die the death of the righteous, and let my last end be like his!
Num. 23:10

For Thy sake are we killed all the day long; we are counted as sheep for the slaughter.
Ps. 44:22

Precious in the sight of the Lord is the death of His saints.
Ps. 116:15

The Lord hath laid on him the iniquity of us all.
Isa. 53:6

[*See also* Persecution]

MATERIALISM

Man doth not live by bread only, but by every word that proceedeth out of the mouth of the Lord.
>
> *Deut. 8:3*
> *See also, e.g., Matt. 4:4*

[*See also* Greed, Spirituality, Wealth]

MATURITY

See Age, Experience, Growth.

MEDICINE

See Healing.

MEEKNESS

The meek shall eat and be satisfied: they shall praise the Lord that seek Him.
>
> *Ps. 22:26*

The meek will He guide in judgment: and the meek will He teach His way.
>
> *Ps. 25:9*

The meek shall inherit the earth.
>
> *Ps. 37:11*
> *See also, e.g., Matt. 5:5*

The Lord lifteth up the meek: He casteth the wicked down to the ground.
>
> *Ps. 147:6*

He is brought as a lamb to the slaughter.
>
> *Isa. 53:7*
> *See also Jer. 11:19, Acts 8:32*

Seek righteousness, seek meekness: it may be ye shall be hid in the day of the Lord's anger.
>
> *Zeph. 2:3*

[*See also* Humility]

MEMORIALS

See Burial, Remembrance.

MEMORY

See Remembrance.

MENSTRUATION

The custom of women is upon me.
>
> *Gen. 31:35*

MERCY

Let not our hand be upon him; for he is our brother and our flesh.
>
> *Judah to his brothers*
> *Gen. 37:27*

And God Almighty give you mercy before the man.
>
> *Jacob to his sons*
> *Gen. 43:14*

The Lord thy God is a merciful God.
>
> *Deut. 4:31*

Show us, we pray thee, the entrance into the city, and we will show thee mercy.
>
> *Judg. 1:24*

Some bade me kill thee: but mine eye spared thee.
>
> *David to Saul*
> *1 Sam. 24:10*

If a man find his enemy, will he let him go well away?
>
> *Saul to David*
> *1 Sam. 24:19*

Go up in peace to thine house.
>
> *1 Sam. 25:35*

Let him turn to his own house, and let him not see my face.
>
> *(him: Absalom)*
> *2 Sam. 14:24*

It is enough: stay now thine hand.
>
> *God to an angel*
> *2 Sam. 24:16, 1 Chron. 21:15*

In thy days I will not do it for David thy father's sake: but I will rend it out of the hand of thy son.
>
> *God to Solomon*
> *1 Kings 11:12*

Let me fall now into the hand of the Lord; for very great are His mercies: but let me not fall into the hand of man.
> *1 Chron. 21:13*
> *See also 2 Sam. 24:14*

God hast punished us less than our iniquities deserve.
> *Ezra 9:13*
> *See also Job 11:6*

Rebuke me not in Thine anger, neither chasten me in Thy hot displeasure.
> *Ps. 6:1*
> *See also Ps. 38:1*

Have mercy upon me, O Lord; for I am weak.
> *Ps. 6:2*

Be merciful unto me, O God: for man would swallow me up.
> *Ps. 56:1*

God be merciful unto us, and bless us; and cause His face to shine upon us.
> *Ps. 67:1*

If Thou, Lord, shouldest mark iniquities, O Lord, who shall stand?
> *Ps. 130:3*

Enter not into judgment with Thy servant: for in Thy sight shall no man living be justified.
> *Ps. 143:2*

O Lord, be gracious unto us; we have waited for Thee.
> *Isa. 33:2*

I am merciful, saith the Lord, and I will not keep anger for ever.
> *God to Jews*
> *Jer. 3:12*

Thy life I will give unto thee for a prey in all places whither thou goest.
> *Jer. 45:5*

Though He cause grief, yet will He have compassion.
> *Lam. 3:32*

Mine eye shall not spare thee, neither will I have pity: but I will recompense thy ways.
> *E.g., Ezek. 7:4*
> *See also Ezek. 9:5*

Not for your sakes do I this, saith the Lord God.
> *Ezek. 36:32*
> *See also Ezek. 36:22*

To the Lord our God belong mercies and forgivenesses, though we have rebelled against Him.
> *Dan. 9:9*

I am God, and not man.
> *Hos. 11:9*

God repented of the evil, that He had said that He would do unto them; and He did it not.
> *Jonah 3:10*

In wrath remember mercy.
> *Hab. 3:2*

I will spare them, as a man spareth his own son that serveth him.
> *God to Israelites*
> *Mal. 3:17*

[*See also* Compassion, Forgiveness, God's Mercy, Kindness, Suffering]

MERIT

See Favoritism, Justice, Reward, Success.

MESSENGERS

See News, Reliability.

MESSIANIC HOPES AND PROPHECIES

The sceptre shall not depart from Judah, nor a lawgiver from between his feet, until Shiloh come.
> *Jacob to Judah*
> *Gen. 49:10*

I shall see him, but not now: I shall behold him, but not nigh: there shall come a Star out of Jacob, and a Sceptre shall rise out of Israel.
> *Num. 24:17*

The Lord thy God will raise up unto thee a Prophet from the midst of thee, of thy brethren, like unto me; unto him ye shall hearken.
> *Moses*
> *Deut. 18:15*
> *See also Deut. 18:18*

Thou wilt not leave my soul in hell; neither wilt Thou suffer Thine Holy One to see corruption.
Ps. 16:10

I looked for some to take pity, but there was none; and for comforters, but I found none.
Ps. 69:20

A virgin shall conceive, and bear a son, and shall call his name Immanuel.
Isa. 7:14

Unto us a child is born, unto us a son is given.
Isa. 9:6

Of the increase of his government and peace there shall be no end.
Isa. 9:7

There shall come forth a rod out of the stem of Jesse, and a Branch shall grow out of his roots.
Isa. 11:1

The spirit of the Lord shall rest upon him, the spirit of wisdom and understanding, the spirit of counsel and might, the spirit of knowledge and of the fear of the Lord.
Isa. 11:2

He shall not judge after the sight of his eyes, neither reprove after the hearing of his ears.
Isa. 11:3

With righteousness shall he judge the poor.
Isa. 11:4

Prepare ye the way of the Lord, make straight in the desert a highway for our God.
Isa. 40:3
See also, e.g., Matt. 3:3

He shall not fail nor be discouraged, till he have set judgment in the earth.
Isa. 42:4

I will also give thee for a light to the Gentiles.
Isa. 49:6
See also Acts 13:47

He is despised and rejected of men; a man of sorrows, and acquainted with grief.
Isa. 53:3

He was despised, and we esteemed him not.
Isa. 53:3

He hath borne our griefs, and carried our sorrows: yet we did esteem him stricken, smitten of God, and afflicted.
Isa. 53:4

He was wounded for our transgressions, he was bruised for our iniquities.
Isa. 53:5

The Lord hath laid on him the iniquity of us all.
Isa. 53:6

He was oppressed, and he was afflicted, yet he opened not his mouth.
Isa. 53:7

He bare the sin of many, and made intercession for the transgressors.
Isa. 53:12

I will raise unto David a righteous Branch, and a King shall reign and prosper.
Jer. 23:5

Behold, thy King cometh unto thee: he is just, and having salvation; lowly, and riding upon an ass.
Zech. 9:9

I will send My messenger, and he shall prepare the way before Me.
Mal. 3:1

Who may abide the day of his coming? and who shall stand when he appeareth?
Mal. 3:2

Behold, I will send you Elijah the prophet before the coming of the great and dreadful day of the Lord.
Mal. 4:5

[*Note:* Quotations in this category reflect Christian beliefs and not Jewish ones.]

MINISTRY

Serve Him in sincerity and in truth.
Josh. 24:14

Blessed be he that cometh in the name of the Lord.
Ps. 118:26
See also, e.g., Matt. 21:9

Here am I; send me.
Isaiah to God
Isa. 6:8

Cursed be he that doeth the work of the Lord deceitfully.
Jer. 48:10

[*See also* Clergy, Evangelism, Preaching, Service to God, Underprivileged]

MIRACLES

Behold, the bush burned with fire, and the bush was not consumed.
Ex. 3:2

The children of Israel walked upon dry land in the midst of the sea; and the waters were a wall unto them on their right hand, and on their left.
Ex. 14:29

Speak ye unto the rock before their eyes; and it shall give forth his water.
God to Moses
Num. 20:8

He smote the rock twice: and the water came out abundantly.
(He: Moses)
Num. 20:11

Your eyes have seen what I have done in Egypt.
Josh. 24:7

Where be all His miracles which our fathers told us of?
Judg. 6:13

[*See also* God's Power, Healing, Wonders]

MISERY

See Anguish.

MISJUDGMENT

Call for Samson, that he may make us sport.
Judg. 16:25

Make us a king to judge us like all the nations.
1 Sam. 8:5

Nay; but we will have a king over us.
1 Sam. 8:19

Surely the bitterness of death is past.
Agag, king of the Amalekites
1 Sam. 15:32

Thou art but a youth, and he a man of war.
Saul to David about Goliath
1 Sam. 17:33

I will give thy flesh unto the fowls of the air, and to the beasts of the field.
Goliath to David
1 Sam. 17:44

The king of Israel is come out to seek a flea, as when one doth hunt a partridge in the mountains.
1 Sam. 26:20

Behold, I have played the fool, and have erred exceedingly.
1 Sam. 26:21

There is nothing among my treasures that I have not showed them.
2 Kings 20:15, Isa. 39:4

But he forsook the counsel which the old men gave him.
2 Chron. 10:8

In his disease he sought not to the Lord, but to the physicians.
2 Chron. 16:12

He hath borne our griefs, and carried our sorrows: yet we did esteem him stricken, smitten of God, and afflicted.
Isa. 53:4

[*See also* Rashness]

MISSION

Whom shall I send, and who will go for us? Then said I, Here am I; send me.
God to Isaiah, and response
Isa. 6:8

I will also give thee for a light to the Gentiles.
Isa. 49:6
See also Acts 13:47

To proclaim liberty to the captives, and
the opening of the prison to them that are
bound.
Isa. 61:1

Arise, go to Nineveh.
Jonah 1:2, Jonah 3:2

And ye shall know that the Lord of hosts
hath sent me.
Zech. 2:9

[*See also* Duty, Goals, Purpose]

MISSIONARIES

See Evangelism.

MOBS

Thou shalt not follow a multitude to do
evil.
Ex. 23:2

The multitude of many people, which
make a noise like the noise of the seas.
Isa. 17:12

[*See also* Public Opinion]

MOCKERY

Behold, this dreamer cometh.
(dreamer: Joseph)
Gen. 37:19

Thou seest the shadow of the mountains
as if they were men.
Judg. 9:36

Go and cry unto the gods which ye have
chosen; let them deliver you.
God to Israelites
Judg. 10:14

Call for Samson, that he may make us
sport.
Judg. 16:25

Peradventure he sleepeth, and must be
awaked.
Elijah, about Baal
1 Kings 18:27

Go up, thou bald head; go up, thou bald
head.
2 Kings 2:23

No doubt but ye are the people, and
wisdom shall die with you.
Job to his friends
Job 12:2

The just upright man is laughed to scorn.
Job 12:4

Art thou the first man that was born? or
wast thou made before the hills?
Job 15:7

After that I have spoken, mock on.
Job 21:3

Wherefore should the heathen say, Where
is now their God?
Ps. 115:2
See also Ps. 79:10

Scorners delight in their scorning, and
fools hate knowledge.
Prov. 1:22

He that is void of wisdom despiseth his
neighbour: but a man of understanding
holdeth his peace.
Prov. 11:12

Be ye not mockers.
Isa. 28:22

Let now the astrologers, the stargazers,
the monthly prognosticators, stand up,
and save thee from these things.
Isa. 47:13

Is this the city that men call The perfection of beauty, The joy of the whole earth?
Lam. 2:15

[*See also* Contempt, Scorn]

MODELS

Surely this great nation is a wise and
understanding people.
Deut. 4:6

There was not among the children of
Israel a goodlier person than he.
(he: Saul)
1 Sam. 9:2

Like unto him was there no king before
him, that turned to the Lord with all his
heart.
(him: Josiah)
2 Kings 23:25

And the Lord said unto Satan, Hast thou considered my servant Job?
Job 1:8

There is none like him in the earth, a perfect and an upright man, one that feareth God, and escheweth evil.
(him: Job)
Job 1:8, Job 2:3

Mark the perfect man, and behold the upright: for the end of that man is peace.
Ps. 37:37

[*See also* Leadership]

MODESTY

Few and evil have the days of the years of my life been.
Jacob to Pharaoh
Gen. 47:9

Seemeth it to you a light thing to be a king's son in law?
1 Sam. 18:23

Let another man praise thee, and not thine own mouth.
Prov. 27:2

[*See also* Conceit, Humility, Pride, Publicity]

MONARCHY

Make us a king to judge us like all the nations.
1 Sam. 8:5

He will take your fields, and your vineyards, and your oliveyards, even the best of them, and give them to his servants.
1 Sam. 8:14

Nay; but we will have a king over us.
1 Sam. 8:19

Hearken unto their voice, and make them a king.
God to Samuel
1 Sam. 8:22

Seemeth it to you a light thing to be a king's son in law?
1 Sam. 18:23

I will not put forth mine hand against my lord; for he is the Lord's anointed.
David to Saul
1 Sam. 24:10

Because the Lord loved Israel for ever, therefore made He thee king.
Queen of Sheba to Solomon
1 Kings 10:9

I exalted thee out of the dust, and made thee prince over My people Israel.
1 Kings 16:2

Like unto him was there no king before him, that turned to the Lord with all his heart.
(him: Josiah)
2 Kings 23:25

God save the king.
2 Chron. 23:11

Serve the Lord with fear, and rejoice with trembling.
Ps. 2:11

There is no king saved by the multitude of an host.
Ps. 33:16

It is He that giveth salvation unto kings.
Ps. 144:10

By me kings reign, and princes decree justice.
(me: wisdom)
Prov. 8:15

The wrath of a king is as messengers of death.
Prov. 16:14

The king's wrath is as the roaring of a lion; but his favour is as dew upon the grass.
Prov. 19:12

A wise king scattereth the wicked.
Prov. 20:26

Mercy and truth preserve the king.
Prov. 20:28

Fear thou the Lord and the king: and meddle not with them that are given to change.
Prov. 24:21

The honour of kings is to search out a matter.
Prov. 25:2

The heart of kings is unsearchable.
Prov. 25:3

Take away the wicked from before the king, and his throne shall be established in righteousness.
Prov. 25:5

The king that faithfully judgeth the poor, his throne shall be established for ever.
Prov. 29:14

Many seek the ruler's favour; but every man's judgment cometh from the Lord.
Prov. 29:26

Keep the king's commandment.
Eccl. 8:2

Where the word of a king is, there is power.
Eccl. 8:4

In mercy shall the throne be established: and he shall sit upon it in truth.
Isa. 16:5

[*See also* Assassination, Government, Leadership, Sovereignty]

MONEY

Money answereth all things.
Eccl. 10:19

[*See also* Borrowing, Materialism, Usury, Wealth]

MONOTHEISM

Hear, O Israel: The Lord our God is one Lord.
Deut. 6:4
See also, e.g., Mark 12:29

Rebel not against the Lord, nor rebel against us, in building you an altar beside the altar of the Lord.
Josh. 22:19

There is none beside Thee.
1 Sam. 2:2

There is none else.
1 Kings 8:60

How long halt ye between two opinions? if the Lord be God, follow Him: but if Baal, then follow him.
Elijah to Israelites
1 Kings 18:21

Thou art the God, even Thou alone.
2 Kings 19:15, Isa. 37:16

Be still, and know that I am God.
Ps. 46:10

I will be exalted among the heathen, I will be exalted in the earth.
Ps. 46:10

Know ye that the Lord He is God.
Ps. 100:3
See also 1 Kings 18:39

And ye shall know that I am the Lord.
E.g., Ezek. 25:5

Thou shalt know no god but Me: for there is no saviour beside Me.
Hos. 13:4

[*See also* False Gods, God's Uniqueness, Idolatry]

MORALITY

See Decadence, Depravity, Immorality, Righteousness.

MORTALITY

Dust thou art, and unto dust shalt thou return.
Gen. 3:19

We must needs die, and are as water spilt on the ground, which cannot be gathered up again.
2 Sam. 14:14

My days are swifter than a weaver's shuttle, and are spent without hope.
Job 7:6

Our days upon earth are a shadow.
Job 8:9
See also 1 Chron. 29:15

Remember, I beseech Thee, that Thou hast made me as the clay.
Job 10:9

Are not my days few? cease then, and let me alone, that I may take comfort a little.
Job 10:20

Man that is born of a woman is of few days, and full of trouble.
Job 14:1

He cometh forth like a flower, and is cut down.
Job 14:2

What is man, that Thou art mindful of him? and the son of man, that Thou visitest him?
Ps. 8:4
See also Heb. 2:6

None can keep alive his own soul.
Ps. 22:29

Lord, make me to know mine end, and the measure of my days.
Ps. 39:4

Mine age is as nothing before Thee.
Ps. 39:5

Wise men die, likewise the fool and the brutish person perish, and leave their wealth to others.
Ps. 49:10

He remembered that they were but flesh; a wind that passeth away, and cometh not again.
Ps. 78:39

Remember how short my time is: wherefore hast Thou made all men in vain?
Ps. 89:47

What man is he that liveth, and shall not see death?
Ps. 89:48

They are like grass which groweth up. In the morning it flourisheth, and groweth up; in the evening it is cut down, and withereth.
Ps. 90:5-6

My days are like a shadow that declineth; and I am withered like grass.
Ps. 102:11

But Thou, O Lord, shalt endure for ever.
Ps. 102:12
See also, e.g., Ps. 9:7

He knoweth our frame; He remembereth that we are dust.
Ps. 103:14

As for man, his days are as grass: as a flower of the field, so he flourisheth.
Ps. 103:15

Man is like to vanity: his days are as a shadow that passeth away.
Ps. 144:4

His breath goeth forth, he returneth to his earth; in that very day his thoughts perish.
Ps. 146:4

One generation passeth away, and another generation cometh: but the earth abideth for ever.
Eccl. 1:4

All are of the dust, and all turn to dust again.
Eccl. 3:20

It is better to go to the house of mourning, than to go to the house of feasting: for that is the end of all men; and the living will lay it to his heart.
Eccl. 7:2

There is no man that hath power over the spirit to retain the spirit.
Eccl. 8:8

All flesh is grass, and all the goodliness thereof is as the flower of the field.
Isa. 40:6
See also 1 Pet. 1:24

The grass withereth, the flower fadeth: but the word of our God shall stand for ever.
Isa. 40:8
See also 1 Pet. 1:24-25

Thou shalt be a man, and no God, in the hand of him that slayeth thee.
Ezek. 28:9
See also Ezek. 28:2

Your fathers, where are they? and the prophets, do they live for ever?
Zech. 1:5

[*See also* Age, Death, Frailty, Life, Life and Death, Mankind]

MOTHERHOOD

See Birth, Child-Rearing, Childlessness, Children, Fertility, Parents.

MOTIVATION

Every way of a man is right in his own eyes: but the Lord pondereth the hearts.
Prov. 21:2

I do not this for your sakes, O house of Israel, but for Mine holy name's sake, which ye have profaned.
Ezek. 36:22
See also Ezek. 36:32

Will a lion roar in the forest, when he hath no prey?
Amos 3:4

[*See also* Behavior, Intentions, Self-Interest]

MOURNING

Rend your clothes, and gird you with sackcloth, and mourn.
2 Sam. 3:31

Now he is dead, wherefore should I fast? can I bring him back again?
David, about his son
2 Sam. 12:23

I rent my garment and my mantle, and plucked off the hair of my head and of my beard.
Ezra 9:3

A time to weep, and a time to laugh; a time to mourn, and a time to dance.
Eccl. 3:4

The heart of the wise is in the house of mourning; but the heart of fools is in the house of mirth.
Eccl. 7:4

On all their heads shall be baldness, and every beard cut off.
Isa. 15:2

Gird you with sackcloth, lament and howl: for the fierce anger of the Lord is not turned back.
Jer. 4:8

Gird thee with sackcloth, and wallow thyself in ashes: make thee mourning, as for an only son.
Jer. 6:26

[*See also* Anguish, Death, Grief, Lament, Sorrow]

MURDER

Whoso sheddeth man's blood, by man shall his blood be shed.
Gen. 9:6

Let not our hand be upon him; for he is our brother and our flesh.
Judah to his brothers
Gen. 37:27

Thou shalt not kill.
Sixth Commandment
Ex. 20:13, Deut. 5:17
See also, e.g., Matt. 19:18

The murderer shall surely be put to death.
E.g., Num. 35:16
See also Ex. 21:12, Lev. 24:17

Ye shall take no satisfaction for the life of a murderer, which is guilty of death: but he shall be surely put to death.
Num. 35:31

The land cannot be cleansed of the blood that is shed therein, but by the blood of him that shed it.
Num. 35:33

Thine eye shall not pity him.
Deut. 19:13

Cursed be he that taketh reward to slay an innocent person.
Deut. 27:25

They shall not deliver the slayer up into his hand; because he smote his neighbour unwittingly, and hated him not beforetime.
Josh. 20:5

Wherefore then wilt thou sin against innocent blood?
> *Jonathan to King Saul*
> *1 Sam. 19:5*

As a man falleth before wicked men, so fellest thou.
> *2 Sam. 3:34*

Thou art a wise man, and knowest what thou oughtest to do unto him.
> *1 Kings 2:9*

The land was polluted with blood.
> *Ps. 106:38*

These six things doth the Lord hate: yea, seven are an abomination unto Him: A proud look, a lying tongue, and hands that shed innocent blood, An heart that deviseth wicked imaginations, feet that be swift in running to mischief, A false witness that speaketh lies, and he that soweth discord among brethren.
> *Prov. 6:16–19*

They hunt every man his brother with a net.
> *Mic. 7:2*

[*See also* Assassination, Capital Punishment, Death, Violence]

MUSIC

Praise the Lord with harp: sing unto Him with the psaltery and an instrument of ten strings.
> *Ps. 33:2*

Praise Him with the sound of the trumpet: praise Him with the psaltery and harp.
> *Ps. 150:3*

Praise Him with the timbrel and dance: praise Him with stringed instruments and organs.
> *Ps. 150:4*

Praise Him upon the loud cymbals: praise Him upon the high sounding cymbals.
> *Ps. 150:5*

[*See also* Song]

MYSTERY

The way of an eagle in the air; the way of a serpent upon a rock; the way of a ship in the midst of the sea; and the way of a man with a maid.
> *Prov. 30:19*

Watchman, what of the night?
> *Isa. 21:11*

There is a God in heaven that revealeth secrets.
> *Dan. 2:28*

Mene, Mene, Tekel, Upharsin.
> *Dan. 5:25*

[*See also* Riddles, Secrecy, Wonders]

N

NAGGING

Thou dost but hate me, and lovest me not.
> *Samson's wife*
> *Judg. 14:16*

His soul was vexed unto death.
> *(His: Samson)*
> *Judg. 16:16*

If I be shaven, then my strength will go from me.
> *Judg. 16:17*

It is better to dwell in a corner of the housetop, than with a brawling woman in a wide house.
> *Prov. 21:9*
> *See also Prov. 25:24*

It is better to dwell in the wilderness, than with a contentious and an angry woman.
> *Prov. 21:19*

A continual dropping in a very rainy day and a contentious woman are alike.
> *Prov. 27:15*

[*See also* Strife]

NAIVETE

Behold the fire and the wood: but where is the lamb for a burnt offering?
Isaac to Abraham
Gen. 22:7

Wherefore have ye beguiled us?
Josh. 9:22

Who is this uncircumcised Philistine, that he should defy the armies of the living God?
David, about Goliath
1 Sam. 17:26

What is my sin before thy father, that he seeketh my life?
David to Jonathan
1 Sam. 20:1

There is nothing among my treasures that I have not showed them.
2 Kings 20:15, Isa. 39:4

Wherefore doeth the Lord our God all these things unto us?
Jer. 5:19

[*See also* Innocence]

NAKEDNESS

They were both naked, the man and his wife, and were not ashamed.
Gen. 2:25

And the eyes of them both were opened, and they knew that they were naked.
Gen. 3:7

I was afraid, because I was naked.
Adam
Gen. 3:10

For their's is thine own nakedness.
Lev. 18:10

Naked came I out of my mother's womb, and naked shall I return thither.
Job 1:21

Thy nakedness shall be uncovered, yea, thy shame shall be seen.
Isa. 47:3

NAMES

Whatsoever Adam called every living creature, that was the name thereof.
Gen. 2:19

As his name is, so is he.
1 Sam. 25:25

That which hath been is named already.
Eccl. 6:10

[*See also* Reputation]

NATURE

And God made two great lights; the greater light to rule the day, and the lesser light to rule the night.
Gen. 1:16

Ye shall not pollute the land wherein ye are.
Num. 35:33

Defile not therefore the land which ye shall inhabit.
Num. 35:34

The tree of the field is man's life.
Deut. 20:19

Can the rush grow up without mire? can the flag grow without water?
Job 8:11

Speak to the earth, and it shall teach thee: and the fishes of the sea shall declare unto thee.
Job 12:8

Stand still, and consider the wondrous works of God.
Job 37:14

The trees of the Lord are full of sap.
Ps. 104:16

How manifold are Thy works! in wisdom hast Thou made them all.
Ps. 104:24

The earth is full of Thy riches.
Ps. 104:24

He commandeth, and raiseth the stormy wind, which lifteth up the waves thereof.
Ps. 107:25

The works of the Lord are great.
Ps. 111:2

The mountains skipped like rams, and the little hills like lambs.
Ps. 114:4

All are Thy servants.
Ps. 119:91

Let them praise the name of the Lord: for He commanded, and they were created.
Ps. 148:5

The sun also ariseth.
Eccl. 1:5

To every thing there is a season, and a time to every purpose under the heaven.
Eccl. 3:1

A time to be born, and a time to die; a time to plant, and a time to pluck up that which is planted.
Eccl. 3:2

A pleasant thing it is for the eyes to behold the sun.
Eccl. 11:7

The grass withereth, the flower fadeth: but the word of our God shall stand for ever.
Isa. 40:8
See also 1 Pet. 1:24–25

For the mountains will I take up a weeping and wailing, and for the habitations of the wilderness a lamentation.
Jer. 9:10

The Lord hath His way in the whirlwind and in the storm, and the clouds are the dust of His feet.
Nah. 1:3

[*See also* Creation, Cultivation, Earth, Heaven and Earth, Instinct, Night and Day, Oceans, Rain, Seasons]

NEGOTIATION

Wilt Thou also destroy the righteous with the wicked?
Abraham to God
Gen. 18:23

Peradventure there shall lack five of the fifty righteous: wilt Thou destroy all the city for lack of five?
Gen. 18:28

Our life for your's, if ye utter not this our business.
Josh. 2:14

It is naught, it is naught, saith the buyer: but when he is gone his way, then he boasteth.
Prov. 20:14

Come now, and let us reason together, saith the Lord.
Isa. 1:18

If ye think good, give me my price; and if not, forbear.
Zech. 11:12

[*See also* Compromise]

NEIGHBORS

Thou shalt not covet thy neighbour's house, thou shalt not covet thy neighbour's wife, nor his manservant, nor his maidservant, nor his ox, nor his ass, nor any thing that is thy neighbour's.
Ex. 20:17
See also Deut. 5:21

Thou shalt love thy neighbour as thyself.
E.g., Lev. 19:18, Matt. 19:19

He that is void of wisdom despiseth his neighbour: but a man of understanding holdeth his peace.
Prov. 11:12

Let none of you imagine evil in your hearts against his neighbour.
Zech. 8:17
See also Zech. 7:10

[*See also* Brotherhood]

NEUTRALITY

Curse ye bitterly the inhabitants thereof; because they came not to the help of the Lord.
Judg. 5:23

[*See also* Choice, Impartiality]

It is no good report that I hear.
1 Sam. 2:24

Tell it not in Gath, publish it not in the streets of Askelon.
2 Sam. 1:20

I am sent to thee with heavy tidings.
1 Kings 14:6

He shall hear a rumour, and shall return to his own land.
(He: Sennacherib)
2 Kings 19:7
See also Isa. 37:7

As cold waters to a thirsty soul, so is good news from a far country.
Prov. 25:25

He that sendeth a message by the hand of a fool cutteth off the feet.
Prov. 26:6

How beautiful upon the mountains are the feet of him that bringeth good tidings, that publisheth peace.
Isa. 52:7
See also Nah. 1:15, Rom. 10:15

Publish, and set up a standard; publish, and conceal not.
Jer. 50:2

NIGHT

A thick darkness in all the land of Egypt three days.
Ex. 10:22

Desire not the night, when people are cut off in their place.
Job 36:20

Watchman, what of the night?
Isa. 21:11

I clothe the heavens with blackness, and I make sackcloth their covering.
Isa. 50:3

NIGHT AND DAY

And God called the light Day, and the darkness He called Night. And the evening and the morning were the first day.
Gen. 1:5

The day is Thine, the night also is Thine: Thou hast prepared the light and the sun.
Ps. 74:16

The morning cometh, and also the night.
Isa. 21:12

[*See also* Light and Darkness, Nature]

NOISE

The multitude of many people, which make a noise like the noise of the seas.
Isa. 17:12

A rushing like the rushing of mighty waters!
Isa. 17:12

The suburbs shall shake at the sound of the cry of thy pilots.
Ezek. 27:28

NOVELTY

See Innovation.

OATHS

Swear unto me by the Lord.
Josh. 2:12

As the Lord thy God liveth.
1 Kings 18:10

So let the gods do to me, and more.
Jezebel to Elijah
1 Kings 19:2
See also 1 Sam. 14:44

Thus saith the Lord God; As I live.
E.g., Ezek. 33:27

[*See also* Promises]

Of every tree of the garden thou mayest freely eat: But of the tree of the knowledge of good and evil, thou shalt not eat.
> *Gen. 2:16–17*

Walk before Me, and be thou perfect.
> *God to Abram*
> *Gen. 17:1*

In thy seed shall all the nations of the earth be blessed; because thou hast obeyed My voice.
> *God to Abraham*
> *Gen. 22:18*

Upon me be thy curse, my son: only obey my voice.
> *Rebekah to Jacob*
> *Gen. 27:13*

If ye will obey My voice indeed, and keep My covenant, then ye shall be a peculiar treasure unto Me above all people: for all the earth is Mine.
> *Ex. 19:5*

All that the Lord hath spoken we will do.
> *Ex. 19:8*
> *See also Ex. 24:3*

Keep My statutes, and do them: I am the Lord which sanctify you.
> *Lev. 20:8*

If ye walk in My statutes, and keep My commandments, and do them; Then I will give you rain in due season, and the land shall yield her increase, and the trees of the field shall yield their fruit.
> *Lev. 26:3–4*

If Balak would give me his house full of silver and gold, I cannot go beyond the word of the Lord my God, to do less or more.
> *Num. 22:18*
> *See also Num. 24:13*

The word that God putteth in my mouth, that shall I speak.
> *Num. 22:38*

Must I not take heed to speak that which the Lord hath put in my mouth?
> *Num. 23:12*

All that the Lord speaketh, that I must do.
> *Num. 23:26*

Take heed to thyself, and keep thy soul diligently, lest thou forget the things which thine eyes have seen.
> *Deut. 4:9*

O that there were such an heart in them, that they would fear Me, and keep all My commandments always.
> *Deut. 5:29*

Ye shall not turn aside to the right hand or to the left.
> *Deut. 5:32*
> *See also Josh. 23:6*

Thou shalt keep the commandments of the Lord thy God, to walk in His ways, and to fear Him.
> *Deut. 8:6*

Serve the Lord thy God with all thy heart and with all thy soul.
> *Deut. 10:12*
> *See also, e.g., Josh. 22:5*

Circumcise therefore the foreskin of your heart, and be no more stiffnecked.
> *Deut. 10:16*

Serve Him with all your heart and with all your soul.
> *Deut. 11:13*

Behold, I set before you this day a blessing and a curse; A blessing, if ye obey the commandments of the Lord your God, which I command you this day: And a curse, if ye will not obey.
> *Deut. 11:26–28*

What thing soever I command you, observe to do it: thou shalt not add thereto, nor diminish from it.
> *Deut. 12:32*

The Lord shall make thee the head, and not the tail; and thou shalt be above only, and thou shalt not be beneath.
> *Deut. 28:13*

This book of the law shall not depart out of thy mouth.
> *Josh. 1:8*

All that thou commandest us we will do, and whithersoever thou sendest us, we will go.
> *Israelites to Joshua*
> *Josh. 1:16*

According to the commandment of the Lord shall ye do.
Josh. 8:8

He left nothing undone of all that the Lord commanded Moses.
Josh. 11:15

Walk in all His ways.
E.g., Josh. 22:5
See also Deut. 19:9

Keep His commandments.
E.g., Josh. 22:5

The Lord our God will we serve, and His voice will we obey.
Josh. 24:24

Do to me according to that which hath proceeded out of thy mouth.
Judg. 11:36

All that thou sayest unto me I will do.
Ruth 3:5

Fear the Lord, and serve Him, and obey His voice.
1 Sam. 12:14

Fear the Lord, and serve Him in truth with all your heart.
1 Sam. 12:24

Hearken thou unto the voice of the words of the Lord.
Samuel to Saul
1 Sam. 15:1

Hath the Lord as great delight in burnt offerings and sacrifices, as in obeying the voice of the Lord?
1 Sam. 15:22

To obey is better than sacrifice, and to hearken than the fat of rams.
1 Sam. 15:22

Keep the charge of the Lord thy God, to walk in His ways.
1 Kings 2:3

Let your heart therefore be perfect with the Lord our God.
1 Kings 8:61

Walk before Me, as David thy father

walked, in integrity of heart, and in uprightness.
1 Kings 9:4

He did that which was right in the sight of the Lord.
2 Kings 14:3

Keep His commandments and His testimonies and His statutes.
2 Kings 23:3

Set your heart and your soul to seek the Lord your God.
1 Chron. 22:19

Know thou the God of thy father.
1 Chron. 28:9

Walk after the Lord.
2 Chron. 34:31

Let it be done according to the law.
Ezra 10:3

As thou hast said, so must we do.
Ezra 10:12

Lay up His words in thine heart.
Job 22:22

All the paths of the Lord are mercy and truth unto such as keep His covenant.
Ps. 25:10

When Thou saidst, Seek ye My face; my heart said unto Thee, Thy face, Lord, will I seek.
Ps. 27:8

Teach me, O Lord, the way of Thy statutes; and I shall keep it unto the end.
Ps. 119:33

Give me understanding, and I shall keep Thy law.
Ps. 119:34
See also Ps. 119:73

Blessed is every one that feareth the Lord; that walketh in His ways.
Ps. 128:1

Teach me to do Thy will.
Ps. 143:10

The way of the Lord is strength to the upright.
Prov. 10:29

Whoso despiseth the word shall be de-

stroyed: but he that feareth the commandment shall be rewarded.
Prov. 13:13

Whoso keepeth the law is a wise son.
Prov. 28:7

He that keepeth the law, happy is he.
Prov. 29:18

Keep the king's commandment.
Eccl. 8:2

Fear God, and keep His commandments:
for this is the whole duty of man.
Eccl. 12:13

If ye be willing and obedient, ye shall eat
the good of the land.
Isa. 1:19

O that thou hadst hearkened to My commandments! then had thy peace been as a
river, and thy righteousness as the waves
of the sea.
Isa. 48:18

Obey My voice, and I will be your God,
and ye shall be My people.
Jer. 7:23

Amend your ways and your doings, and
obey the voice of the Lord your God.
Jer. 26:13

Obey, I beseech thee, the voice of the
Lord.
Jer. 38:20

I am the Lord your God; walk in My
statutes, and keep My judgments.
Ezek. 20:19

The lion hath roared, who will not fear?
the Lord God hath spoken, who can but
prophesy?
Amos 3:8

[*See also* Acceptance, Authority, Backsliding, Commandments, Disobedience,
Law, Rebellion, Reward, Sin]

OBSTACLES

The way of the wicked is as darkness: they
know not at what they stumble.
Prov. 4:19

Every valley shall be exalted, and every
mountain and hill shall be made low.
Isa. 40:4
See also Luke 3:5

The crooked shall be made straight, and
the rough places plain.
Isa. 40:4
See also Luke 3:5

I will break in pieces the gates of brass,
and cut in sunder the bars of iron.
Isa. 45:2

Prepare the way, take up the stumblingblock out of the way of My people.
Isa. 57:14

I will lay stumblingblocks before this people, and the fathers and the sons together
shall fall upon them.
Jer. 6:21

I will hedge up thy way with thorns, and
make a wall, that she shall not find her
paths.
Hos. 2:6

OCEANS

The gathering together of the waters
called He Seas.
Gen. 1:10

He maketh the deep to boil like a pot.
Job 41:31

The voice of the Lord is upon the waters.
Ps. 29:3

They that go down to the sea in ships, that
do business in great waters; These see the
works of the Lord, and His wonders in the
deep.
Ps. 107:23–24

All the rivers run into the sea; yet the sea
is not full.
Eccl. 1:7

OLD AGE

See Age.

OMENS

Shall the shadow go forward ten degrees,
or go back?
2 Kings 20:9

Let the shadow return backward ten degrees.
2 Kings 20:10

He delivereth and rescueth, and He worketh signs and wonders in heaven and in earth.
Dan. 6:27

[*See also* Astrology]

OMNIPOTENCE

See God's Power.

OMNISCIENCE

See God's Knowledge.

OPPORTUNISM

Why are ye come unto me now when ye are in distress?
Jephthah to his stepbrothers
Judg. 11:7

Let us build with you: for we seek your God, as ye do.
Ezra 4:2

Wealth maketh many friends; but the poor is separated from his neighbour.
Prov. 19:4

Every man is a friend to him that giveth gifts.
Prov. 19:6

OPPORTUNITY

The Lord thy God hath set the land before thee: go up and possess it.
Deut. 1:21

Seek ye the Lord while He may be found, call ye upon Him while He is near.
Isa. 55:6

I called you, but ye answered not.
God
Jer. 7:13

OPPRESSION

Ye shall no more give the people straw to make brick.
Ex. 5:7

Fulfil your works, your daily tasks, as when there was straw.
Ex. 5:13

My father chastised you with whips, but I will chastise you with scorpions.
2 Chron. 10:11, 14
See also 1 Kings 12:11

Let not the proud oppress me.
Ps. 119:122

Deliver me from the oppression of man.
Ps. 119:134

The Lord looseth the prisoners.
Ps. 146:7

He that oppresseth the poor reproacheth his Maker.
Prov. 14:31

Rob not the poor, because he is poor: neither oppress the afflicted in the gate.
Prov. 22:22

Relieve the oppressed.
Isa. 1:17

He looked for judgment, but behold oppression; for righteousness, but behold a cry.
Isa. 5:7

They shall cry unto the Lord because of the oppressors, and He shall send them a saviour.
Isa. 19:20

Our necks are under persecution: we labour, and have no rest.
Lam. 5:5

I will make thy grave; for thou art vile.
(thy: Nineveh)
Nah. 1:14

[*See also* Cruelty, Persecution, Tyrants]

See Hope.

See Preaching, Speech.

See Widows and Orphans.

Though thou deckest thee with ornaments of gold, though thou rentest thy face with painting, in vain shalt thou make thyself fair.
> *Jer. 4:30*

[*See also* Boasting, Humility, Modesty]

The Lord God sent him forth from the garden of Eden, to till the ground from whence he was taken. So He drove out the man.
> *Gen. 3:23–24*

A fugitive and a vagabond shalt thou be in the earth.
> *Gen. 4:12*

And Cain went out from the presence of the Lord, and dwelt in the land of Nod, on the east of Eden.
> *Gen. 4:16*

His hand will be against every man, and every man's hand against him.
> *(him: Ishmael)*
> *Gen. 16:12*

I am a brother to dragons, and a companion to owls.
> *Job 30:29*

I am a worm, and no man; a reproach of men, and despised of the people.
> *Ps. 22:6*

I am become a stranger unto my brethren, and an alien unto my mother's children.
> *Ps. 69:8*

The stone which the builders refused is become the head stone of the corner.
> *Ps. 118:22*
> *See also, e.g., Mark 12:10*

I am small and despised: yet do not I forget Thy precepts.
> *Ps. 119:141*

He is despised and rejected of men; a man of sorrows, and acquainted with grief.
> *Isa. 53:3*

[*See also* Estrangement, Exile, Rejection]

See Idolatry.

See Anguish, Birth, Healing, Suffering.

The garden of Eden.
> *Gen. 3:23*

[*See also* Heaven, Heaven and Earth]

Shall a child be born unto him that is an hundred years old? and shall Sarah, that is ninety years old, bear?
> *Gen. 17:17*

I am Joseph; doth my father yet live?
> *Gen. 45:3*

Honour thy father and thy mother.
> *Fifth Commandment*
> *Ex. 20:12*
> *See also, e.g., Matt. 19:19*

He that smiteth his father, or his mother, shall be surely put to death.
> *Ex. 21:15*

He that curseth his father, or his mother, shall surely be put to death.
> *Ex. 21:17*
> *See also, e.g., Lev. 20:9, Matt. 15:4*

Ye shall fear every man his mother, and his father.
> *Lev. 19:3*

Honour thy father and thy mother, as the Lord thy God hath commanded thee; that thy days may be prolonged.
> *Deut. 5:16*
> *See also Ex. 20:12, Eph. 6:2–3*

Would God I had died for thee, O Absalom, my son, my son!
> *2 Sam. 18:33*

Ask on, my mother: for I will not say thee nay.
> *1 Kings 2:20*

O my Lord, give her the living child, and in no wise slay it.
> *1 Kings 3:26*

When my father and my mother forsake me, then the Lord will take me up.
> *Ps. 27:10*

Receive my sayings; and the years of thy life shall be many.
> *(thy: children)*
> *Prov. 4:10*

Attend to my words; incline thine ear unto my sayings.
> *(thine: children)*
> *Prov. 4:20*

A wise son maketh a glad father: but a foolish man despiseth his mother.
> *Prov. 15:20*

He that begetteth a fool doeth it to his sorrow.
> *Prov. 17:21*

Hearken unto thy father that begat thee, and despise not thy mother when she is old.
> *Prov. 23:22*

Her children arise up, and call her blessed.
> *Prov. 31:28*

Can a woman forget her sucking child, that she should not have compassion on the son of her womb?
> *Isa. 49:15*

They may forget, yet will I not forget thee.
> *God, about parents*
> *Isa. 49:15*

A son honoureth his father, and a servant his master: if then I be a father, where is Mine honour?
> *Mal. 1:6*

[*See also* Age, Children, Family, Marriage]

PASSION

See Desire, Love, Lust.

PASSWORD

Say now Shibboleth.
> *Judg. 12:6*

PATIENCE

How long shall I bear with this evil congregation, which murmur against Me?
> *Num. 14:27*

Their foot shall slide in due time.
> *Deut. 32:35*

Let not Thine anger be hot against me, and I will speak but this once.
> *Judg. 6:39*

Would ye tarry for them till they were grown?
> *Ruth 1:13*

His day shall come to die.
> *1 Sam. 26:10*

After that I have spoken, mock on.
> *Job 21:3*

I gave ear to your reasons, whilst ye searched out what to say.
> *Job 32:11*

Wait on the Lord.
> *Ps. 27:14*

Our soul waiteth for the Lord: He is our help and our shield.
Ps. 33:20

I wait for the Lord, my soul doth wait.
Ps. 130:5

My soul waiteth for the Lord more than they that watch for the morning.
Ps. 130:6

He that is slow to wrath is of great understanding.
Prov. 14:29

A soft answer turneth away wrath.
Prov. 15:1

He that is slow to anger is better than the mighty.
Prov. 16:32

The patient in spirit is better than the proud in spirit.
Eccl. 7:8

This is our God; we have waited for Him, and He will save us: this is the Lord.
Isa. 25:9

Blessed are all they that wait for Him.
Isa. 30:18

Shall a nation be born at once?
Isa. 66:8

It is good that a man should both hope and quietly wait for the salvation of the Lord.
Lam. 3:26

It is good for a man that he bear the yoke in his youth.
Lam. 3:27

Blessed is he that waiteth.
Dan. 12:12

Though it tarry, wait for it; because it will surely come.
Hab. 2:3
See also Heb. 10:37

Wait ye upon Me, saith the Lord, until the day that I rise up to the prey.
Zeph. 3:8

[*See also* Anger, Exasperation, Fortitude, Impatience, Restraint, Temper]

If thou wilt take the left hand, then I will go to the right; or if thou depart to the right hand, then I will go to the left.
Gen. 13:9

Go in peace.
E.g., Ex. 4:18

And the land rested from war.
Josh. 11:23

How long shall it be then, ere thou bid the people return from following their brethren?
2 Sam. 2:26

Is it not good, if peace and truth be in my days?
2 Kings 20:19

Ye shall not go up, nor fight against your brethren.
2 Chron. 11:4, 1 Kings 12:24

He maketh peace in His high places.
Job 25:2

Seek peace, and pursue it.
Ps. 34:14

Behold, how good and how pleasant it is for brethren to dwell together in unity!
Ps. 133:1

To the counsellors of peace is joy.
Prov. 12:20

When a man's ways please the Lord, he maketh even his enemies to be at peace with him.
Prov. 16:7

It is an honour for a man to cease from strife.
Prov. 20:3

They shall beat their swords into plowshares, and their spears into pruninghooks: nation shall not lift up sword against nation, neither shall they learn war any more.
Isa. 2:4
See also Mic. 4:3

The wolf also shall dwell with the lamb, and the leopard shall lie down with the

kid; and the calf and the young lion and the fatling together.
Isa. 11:6

A little child shall lead them.
Isa. 11:6

The earth shall be full of the knowledge of the Lord, as the waters cover the sea.
Isa. 11:9

How beautiful upon the mountains are the feet of him that bringeth good tidings, that publisheth peace.
Isa. 52:7
See also Nah. 1:15, Rom. 10:15

The wolf and the lamb shall feed together, and the lion shall eat straw like the bullock.
Isa. 65:25

We looked for peace, but no good came; and for a time of health, and behold trouble!
Jer. 8:15

They shall sit every man under his vine and under his fig tree; and none shall make them afraid.
Mic. 4:4

Love the truth and peace.
Zech. 8:19

[*See also* Brotherhood, Serenity, War, War and Peace]

PERFECTION

He is the Rock, His work is perfect.
Deut. 32:4

And the Lord said unto Satan, Hast thou considered my servant Job?
Job 1:8

There is none like him in the earth, a perfect and an upright man, one that feareth God, and escheweth evil.
(him: Job)
Job 1:8, Job 2:3

As for God, His way is perfect.
Ps. 18:30, 2 Sam. 22:31

Every man at his best state is altogether vanity.
Ps. 39:5

That which is crooked cannot be made

straight: and that which is wanting cannot be numbered.
Eccl. 1:15

There is not a just man upon earth, that doeth good, and sinneth not.
Eccl. 7:20

I am the rose of Sharon, and the lily of the valleys.
Song 2:1

The crooked shall be made straight, and the rough places plain.
Isa. 40:4
See also Luke 3:5

[*See also* Models]

PERJURY

Thou shalt not bear false witness.
Ninth Commandment
Ex. 20:16
See also, e.g., Deut. 5:20,
  Matt. 19:18

Do unto him, as he had thought to have done unto his brother.
Deut. 19:19

A false witness will utter lies.
Prov. 14:5

Every one that sweareth shall be cut off.
Zech. 5:3

Love no false oath.
Zech. 8:17

[*See also* Dishonesty, Honesty, Lies]

PERMANENCE

It is a covenant of salt for ever before the Lord.
Num. 18:19

Oh that my words were now written! oh that they were printed in a book!
Job 19:23

The counsel of the Lord standeth for ever.
Ps. 33:11

Riches are not for ever.
Prov. 27:24

One generation passeth away, and another

generation cometh: but the earth abideth for ever.
Eccl. 1:4

That which now is in the days to come shall all be forgotten.
Eccl. 2:16

Whatsoever God doeth, it shall be for ever.
Eccl. 3:14

Write it before them in a table, and note it in a book, that it may be for the time to come for ever and ever.
Isa. 30:8

The grass withereth, the flower fadeth: but the word of our God shall stand for ever.
Isa. 40:8
See also 1 Pet. 1:24–25

Written with a pen of iron, and with the point of a diamond: it is graven upon the table of their heart.
Jer. 17:1

I am the Lord, I change not.
Mal. 3:6

[*See also* Ephemera, Eternal Life, Eternity, Mortality]

PERSECUTION

I have not sinned against thee; yet thou huntest my soul to take it.
David to Saul
1 Sam. 24:11

I, even I only, am left; and they seek my life, to take it away.
1 Kings 19:10, 14
See also Rom. 11:3

Think not with thyself that thou shalt escape in the king's house, more than all the Jews.
Mordecai to Esther
Esther 4:13

How can I endure to see the evil that shall come unto my people?
Esther 8:6

Behold, He findeth occasions against me, He counteth me for His enemy.
Job 33:10

The wicked in his pride doth persecute the poor.
Ps. 10:2

The assembly of the wicked have inclosed me: they pierced my hands and my feet.
Ps. 22:16

Deliver me not over unto the will of mine enemies: for false witnesses are risen up against me.
Ps. 27:12

The wicked watcheth the righteous, and seeketh to slay him.
Ps. 37:32

The plowers plowed upon my back: they made long their furrows.
Ps. 129:3

I hid not my face from shame and spitting.
Isa. 50:6

They hunt our steps, that we cannot go in our streets: our end is near, our days are fulfilled.
Lam. 4:18

Our persecutors are swifter than the eagles of the heaven: they pursued us upon the mountains, they laid wait for us in the wilderness.
Lam. 4:19

[*See also* Martyrdom, Suffering]

PERSEVERANCE

O God, strengthen my hands.
Neh. 6:9

The Lord gave Job twice as much as he had before.
Job 42:10

We went through fire and through water.
Ps. 66:12

Harder than flint have I made thy forehead.
Ezek. 3:9

Blessed is he that waiteth.
Dan. 12:12

[*See also* Determination, Diligence, Effort, Fortitude, Strength]

PERSPECTIVE

Behold, I am at the point to die: and what profit shall this birthright do to me?
Esau to Jacob
Gen. 25:32

O that they were wise, that they understood this, that they would consider their latter end!
Deut. 32:29

Is not the gleaning of the grapes of Ephraim better than the vintage of Abiezer?
Judg. 8:2

After whom dost thou pursue? after a dead dog, after a flea.
David to Saul
1 Sam. 24:14

How long have I to live, that I should go up with the king unto Jerusalem?
2 Sam. 19:34

Shall we receive good at the hand of God, and shall we not receive evil?
Job 2:10

Our days upon earth are a shadow.
Job 8:9
See also 1 Chron. 29:15

Mine age is as nothing before Thee.
Ps. 39:5

A thousand years in Thy sight are but as yesterday when it is past.
Ps. 90:4

Better is a dinner of herbs where love is, than a stalled ox and hatred therewith.
Prov. 15:17

What hath the wise more than the fool?
Eccl. 6:8

It is better to go to the house of mourning, than to go to the house of feasting: for that is the end of all men; and the living will lay it to his heart.
Eccl. 7:2

In the day of prosperity be joyful, but in the day of adversity consider.
Eccl. 7:14

The nations are as a drop of a bucket, and are counted as the small dust of the balance.
Isa. 40:15

They that be slain with the sword are better than they that be slain with hunger.
Lam. 4:9

PERSUASION

Stand still, that I may reason with you before the Lord.
1 Sam. 12:7

How forcible are right words!
Job 6:25

Produce your cause, saith the Lord; bring forth your strong reasons.
Isa. 41:21

[*See also* Eloquence, Proof]

PESSIMISM

See Despair, Hope.

PHILANTHROPY

See Charity, Generosity.

PITY

See Compassion, Mercy.

PLAGUE

The waters that were in the river were turned to blood.
Ex. 7:20

The frogs came up, and covered the land.
Ex. 8:6

All the dust of the land became lice.
Ex. 8:17

This is the finger of God.
Ex. 8:19

There came a grievous swarm of flies into the house of Pharaoh, and into his servants' houses, and into all the land.
Ex. 8:24

All the cattle of Egypt died: but of the

cattle of the children of Israel died not one.
Ex. 9:6

A boil breaking forth with blains upon man, and upon beast.
Ex. 9:10

I will stretch out My hand, that I may smite thee and thy people with pestilence.
Ex. 9:15

The hail shall come down upon them, and they shall die.
Ex. 9:19

There was hail, and fire mingled with the hail, very grievous.
Ex. 9:24

And when it was morning, the east wind brought the locusts.
Ex. 10:13

A thick darkness in all the land of Egypt three days.
Ex. 10:22

I will pass through the land of Egypt this night, and will smite all the firstborn in the land of Egypt, both man and beast.
Ex. 12:12

The sword is without, and the pestilence and the famine within.
Ezek. 7:15

[*See also* Healing]

PLANNING

Consider of it, take advice, and speak your minds.
Judg. 19:30

The Lord bringeth the counsel of the heathen to nought.
Ps. 33:10

The counsel of the Lord standeth for ever.
Ps. 33:11

Ponder the path of thy feet.
Prov. 4:26

There is a way which seemeth right unto a man, but the end thereof are the ways of death.
Prov. 14:12, Prov. 16:25

A man's heart deviseth his way: but the Lord directeth his steps.
Prov. 16:9

Where there is no vision, the people perish.
Prov. 29:18

The ants are a people not strong, yet they prepare their meat in the summer.
Prov. 30:25

A time to plant, and a time to pluck up.
Eccl. 3:2

Better is the end of a thing than the beginning thereof.
Eccl. 7:8

Thy counsels of old are faithfulness and truth.
Isa. 25:1

They shall also build houses, but not inhabit them; and they shall plant vineyards, but not drink the wine thereof.
Zeph. 1:13
See also Amos 5:11

[*See also* Building, Cooperation, Readiness, Scheming]

PLEAS

Hast thou not reserved a blessing for me?
Esau to Isaac
Gen. 27:36

Do Thou unto us whatsoever seemeth good unto Thee; deliver us only, we pray Thee, this day.
Judg. 10:15

Hear, O our God; for we are despised.
Neh. 4:4

Are not my days few? cease then, and let me alone, that I may take comfort a little.
Job 10:20

Oh that one would hear me!
Job 31:35

Lord, be Thou my helper.
Ps. 30:10

Hide not Thy face from Thy servant; for I am in trouble.
Ps. 69:17
See also Ps. 102:2

Keep not Thou silence, O God: hold not Thy peace.
Ps. 83:1

They cry unto the Lord in their trouble, and He saveth them out of their distresses.
Ps. 107:19

Help me, O Lord my God: O save me according to Thy mercy.
Ps. 109:26

Do not abhor us, for Thy name's sake, do not disgrace the throne of Thy glory.
Jer. 14:21

Heal me, O Lord, and I shall be healed; save me, and I shall be saved.
Jer. 17:14

Be not a terror unto me: Thou art my hope in the day of evil.
Jer. 17:17

Remember, O Lord, what is come upon us: consider, and behold our reproach.
Lam. 5:1

[*See also* Prayer]

PLEASURE

Can that which is unsavoury be eaten without salt?
Job 6:6

Is there any taste in the white of an egg?
Job 6:6

Stolen waters are sweet, and bread eaten in secret is pleasant.
Prov. 9:17

He that loveth pleasure shall be a poor man.
Prov. 21:17

He that loveth wine and oil shall not be rich.
Prov. 21:17

I said of laughter, It is mad: and of mirth, What doeth it?
Eccl. 2:2

Every man should eat and drink, and enjoy the good of all his labour, it is the gift of God.
Eccl. 3:13
See also *Eccl. 5:18*

A man hath no better thing under the sun, than to eat, and to drink, and to be merry.
Eccl. 8:15

Eat thy bread with joy, and drink thy wine with a merry heart.
Eccl. 9:7

Let us eat and drink; for to morrow we shall die.
Isa. 22:13, 1 Cor. 15:32

[*See also* Happiness, Laughter]

POPULATION

See Covenant, Fertility, Growth.

POSSIBILITY

Is any thing too hard for the Lord?
Gen. 18:14

If Balak would give me his house full of silver and gold, I cannot go beyond the word of the Lord my God, to do less or more.
Num. 22:18
See also *Num. 24:13*

Shall the shadow go forward ten degrees, or go back?
2 Kings 20:9

Who can make that straight, which He hath made crooked?
Eccl. 7:13

I am the Lord, the God of all flesh: is there any thing too hard for Me?
Jer. 32:27

It is a rare thing that the king requireth.
Dan. 2:11

[*See also* Ability, God's Power, Skepticism]

POSTERITY

I will make thy seed as the dust of the earth: so that if a man can number the dust of the earth, then shall thy seed also be numbered.
God to Abram
Gen. 13:16
See also *Gen. 28:14*

A nation and a company of nations shall be of thee, and kings shall come out of thy loins.

Gen. 35:11

Who shall declare his generation?

Isa. 53:8

[*See also* Heritage]

POTENTIAL

A little cloud out of the sea, like a man's hand.

1 Kings 18:44

POVERTY

The poor shall never cease out of the land.

Deut. 15:11

He raiseth up the poor out of the dust, and lifteth up the beggar from the dunghill.

1 Sam. 2:8
See also Ps. 113:7

Naked came I out of my mother's womb, and naked shall I return thither.

Job 1:21

He saveth the poor from the sword, from their mouth, and from the hand of the mighty.

(He: God)
Job 5:15

The poor hath hope.

Job 5:16

The needy shall not always be forgotten: the expectation of the poor shall not perish for ever.

Ps. 9:18

The wicked in his pride doth persecute the poor.

Ps. 10:2

Who is like unto Thee, which deliverest the poor from him that is too strong for him?

Ps. 35:10

A little that a righteous man hath is better than the riches of many wicked.

Ps. 37:16

I am poor and needy; yet the Lord thinketh upon me.

Ps. 40:17

Blessed is he that considereth the poor: the Lord will deliver him in time of trouble.

Ps. 41:1

The Lord heareth the poor, and despiseth not His prisoners.

Ps. 69:33

I am poor and needy: make haste unto me, O God.

Ps. 70:5

Yet a little sleep, a little slumber, a little folding of the hands to sleep: So shall thy poverty come.

Prov. 6:10–11

The destruction of the poor is their poverty.

Prov. 10:15

The poor is hated even of his own neighbour: but the rich hath many friends.

Prov. 14:20

He that oppresseth the poor reproacheth his Maker.

Prov. 14:31

He that honoureth Him hath mercy on the poor.

Prov. 14:31

Better it is to be of an humble spirit with the lowly, than to divide the spoil with the proud.

Prov. 16:19

Whoso mocketh the poor reproacheth his Maker.

Prov. 17:5

He that hath pity upon the poor lendeth unto the Lord; and that which he hath given will He pay him again.

Prov. 19:17

Whoso stoppeth his ears at the cry of the poor, he also shall cry himself, but shall not be heard.

Prov. 21:13

Drowsiness shall clothe a man with rags.

Prov. 23:21

The righteous considereth the cause of the

poor: but the wicked regardeth not to know it.
Prov. 29:7

The king that faithfully judgeth the poor, his throne shall be established for ever.
Prov. 29:14

The poor man's wisdom is despised, and his words are not heard.
Eccl. 9:16

[*See also* Charity, Underprivileged, Wealth]

POWER

How shall I curse, whom God hath not cursed? or how shall I defy, whom the Lord hath not defied?
Balaam to Balak
Num. 23:8

He will take your fields, and your vineyards, and your oliveyards, even the best of them, and give them to his servants.
(He: a king)
1 Sam. 8:14

Am I God, to kill and to make alive?
2 Kings 5:7

Canst thou bind the sweet influences of Pleiades, or loose the bands of Orion?
God to Job
Job 38:31

Canst thou draw out leviathan with an hook? or his tongue with a cord which thou lettest down?
God to Job
Job 41:1

Power belongeth unto God.
Ps. 62:11

The king's wrath is as the roaring of a lion; but his favour is as dew upon the grass.
Prov. 19:12

Where the word of a king is, there is power.
Eccl. 8:4

He shall open, and none shall shut; and he shall shut, and none shall open.
Isa. 22:22

A little one shall become a thousand, and a small one a strong nation.
Isa. 60:22

[*See also* Authority, God's Power, Strength]

PRAISE

Saul hath slain his thousands, and David his ten thousands.
E.g., 1 Sam. 18:7

Because the Lord loved Israel for ever, therefore made He thee king.
Queen of Sheba to Solomon
1 Kings 10:9

A man shall be commended according to his wisdom.
Prov. 12:8

[*See also* Flattery]

PRAISE OF GOD

I will sing unto the Lord, for He hath triumphed gloriously: the horse and his rider hath He thrown into the sea.
Ex. 15:1
See also Ex. 15:21

I will publish the name of the Lord: ascribe ye greatness unto our God.
Deut. 32:3

Give, I pray thee, glory to the Lord God.
Josh. 7:19

Bless ye the Lord.
Judg. 5:9

Speak, ye that ride on white asses, ye that sit in judgment, and walk by the way.
Judg. 5:10

The pillars of the earth are the Lord's, and He hath set the world upon them.
1 Sam. 2:8

Exalted be the God of the rock of my salvation.
2 Sam. 22:47

I will give thanks unto Thee, O Lord, among the heathen, and I will sing praises unto Thy name.
2 Sam. 22:50
See also Ps. 18:49

Blessed be the Lord God of Israel for ever and ever.
1 Chron. 16:36

Praise the Lord; for His mercy endureth for ever.
E.g., 2 Chron. 20:21

Stand up and bless the Lord your God for ever and ever.
Neh. 9:5

Blessed be Thy glorious name, which is exalted above all blessing and praise.
Neh. 9:5

In death there is no remembrance of Thee: in the grave who shall give Thee thanks?
Ps. 6:5

Give unto the Lord, O ye mighty, give unto the Lord glory and strength.
Ps. 29:1

Many, O Lord my God, are Thy wonderful works.
Ps. 40:5

I will be exalted among the heathen, I will be exalted in the earth.
Ps. 46:10

God is the King of all the earth: sing ye praises with understanding.
Ps. 47:7

O Lord, open Thou my lips; and my mouth shall show forth Thy praise.
Ps. 51:15

Blessed be God.
E.g., Ps. 68:35

I will praise the name of God with a song, and will magnify Him with thanksgiving.
Ps. 69:30

Let the heaven and earth praise Him, the seas, and every thing that moveth therein.
Ps. 69:34

Shall Thy lovingkindness be declared in the grave? or Thy faithfulness in destruction?
Ps. 88:11

Give unto the Lord the glory due unto His name.
Ps. 96:8, 1 Chron. 16:29

Make a joyful noise unto the Lord.
Ps. 100:1

All that is within me, bless His holy name.
Ps. 103:1

Praise ye the Lord.
E.g., Ps. 104:35

Make known His deeds among the people.
Ps. 105:1, 1 Chron. 16:8

Oh that men would praise the Lord for His goodness, and for His wonderful works to the children of men!
E.g., Ps. 107:8

From the rising of the sun unto the going down of the same the Lord's name is to be praised.
Ps. 113:3

Not unto us, O Lord, not unto us, but unto Thy name give glory.
Ps. 115:1

The dead praise not the Lord.
Ps. 115:17

Praise the Lord, all ye nations: praise Him, all ye people.
Ps. 117:1
See also Rom. 15:11

Praise ye the name of the Lord; praise Him, O ye servants of the Lord.
Ps. 135:1

Ye that fear the Lord, bless the Lord.
Ps. 135:20

I will bless Thy name for ever and ever.
Ps. 145:1

While I live will I praise the Lord.
Ps. 146:2

It is good to sing praises unto our God.
Ps. 147:1

Praise ye the Lord from the heavens: praise Him in the heights.
Ps. 148:1

Let every thing that hath breath praise the Lord.
Ps. 150:6

Praise the Lord, call upon His name,

declare His doings among the people, make mention that His name is exalted.
Isa. 12:4

I will exalt Thee, I will praise Thy name; for Thou hast done wonderful things.
Isa. 25:1

Publish ye, praise ye, and say, O Lord, save Thy people.
Jer. 31:7

[*See also* Gratitude, Song, Testimony]

PRAYER

Remember me, I pray Thee, and strengthen me, I pray Thee, only this once, O God.
Samson
Judg. 16:28

For this child I prayed; and the Lord hath given me my petition.
Hannah
1 Sam 1:27

God forbid that I should sin against the Lord in ceasing to pray for you.
Samuel to Israelites
1 Sam. 12:23

In my distress I called upon the Lord.
2 Sam. 22:7, Ps. 18:6

He did hear my voice out of His temple, and my cry did enter into His ears.
2 Sam. 22:7

Hear Thou in heaven Thy dwelling place: and when Thou hearest, forgive.
1 Kings 8:30
See also, e.g., 1 Kings 8:39

Hearken unto them in all that they call for unto Thee.
1 Kings 8:52

Let these my words, wherewith I have made supplication before the Lord, be nigh unto the Lord our God day and night.
1 Kings 8:59

Lift up thy prayer for the remnant that are left.
2 Kings 19:4
See also Isa. 37:4

Remember now how I have walked before Thee in truth and with a perfect heart.
2 Kings 20:3
See also Isa. 38:3

I have heard thy prayer, I have seen thy tears: behold, I will heal thee.
2 Kings 20:5

Keep me from evil, that it may not grieve me!
1 Chron. 4:10

Turn not away the face of thine anointed.
2 Chron. 6:42

The good Lord pardon every one That prepareth his heart to seek God.
2 Chron. 30:18–19

Let Thine ear now be attentive, and Thine eyes open.
Neh. 1:6

Think upon me, my God, for good.
Neh. 5:19
See also Neh. 12:31

I cry unto Thee, and Thou dost not hear me: I stand up, and Thou regardest me not.
Job 30:20

He heareth the cry of the afflicted.
Job 34:28

The Lord will hear when I call unto Him.
Ps. 4:3

He forgetteth not the cry of the humble.
Ps. 9:12

Why standest Thou afar off, O Lord? why hidest Thou Thyself in times of trouble?
Ps. 10:1

Let the words of my mouth, and the meditation of my heart, be acceptable in Thy sight, O Lord, my strength, and my redeemer.
Ps. 19:14

I cry in the daytime, but Thou hearest not; and in the night season, and am not silent.
Ps. 22:2

Be not far from me; for trouble is near; for there is none to help.
Ps. 22:11

Unto Thee, O Lord, do I lift up my soul.
Ps. 25:1

Blessed be the Lord, because He hath heard the voice of my supplications.
Ps. 28:6

I sought the Lord, and He heard me, and delivered me from all my fears.
Ps. 34:4

The righteous cry, and the Lord heareth.
Ps. 34:17

O Lord: keep not silence: O Lord, be not far from me.
Ps. 35:22

Forsake me not, O Lord: O my God, be not far from me.
Ps. 38:21
See also Ps. 71:12

Deliver me from the deceitful and unjust man.
Ps. 43:1

Call upon Me in the day of trouble: I will deliver thee, and thou shalt glorify Me.
Ps. 50:15

As for me, I will call upon God; and the Lord shall save me.
Ps. 55:16

He shall deliver the needy when he crieth; the poor also, and him that hath no helper.
Ps. 72:12

In the day of my trouble I will call upon Thee.
Ps. 86:7

He shall call upon Me, and I will answer him: I will be with him in trouble.
Ps. 91:15

Hear my prayer, O Lord, and let my cry come unto Thee.
Ps. 102:1

Because He hath inclined His ear unto me, therefore will I call upon Him as long as I live.
Ps. 116:2

In my distress I cried unto the Lord, and He heard me.
Ps. 120:1

Out of the depths have I cried unto Thee, O Lord.
Ps. 130:1

Grant not, O Lord, the desires of the wicked.
Ps. 140:8

The Lord is nigh unto all them that call upon Him, to all that call upon Him in truth.
Ps. 145:18

The sacrifice of the wicked is an abomination to the Lord: but the prayer of the upright is His delight.
Prov. 15:8

The Lord is far from the wicked: but He heareth the prayer of the righteous.
Prov. 15:29

God is in heaven, and thou upon earth: therefore let thy words be few.
Eccl. 5:2

When ye spread forth your hands, I will hide Mine eyes from you.
Isa. 1:15

O Lord, be gracious unto us; we have waited for Thee.
Isa. 33:2

Incline Thine ear, O Lord, and hear; open Thine eyes, O Lord, and see.
Isa. 37:17
See also 2 Kings 19:16

Seek ye the Lord while He may be found, call ye upon Him while He is near.
Isa. 55:6

Your sins have hid His face from you, that He will not hear.
Isa. 59:2

Ye shall seek Me, and find Me, when ye shall search for Me with all your heart.
Jer. 29:13

Call unto Me, and I will answer thee.
Jer. 33:3

Pour out thine heart like water before the face of the Lord.
Lam. 2:19

I called upon Thy name, O Lord, out of the low dungeon.
Lam. 3:55

Thou hast heard my voice: hide not Thine ear.
Lam. 3:56

Though they cry in Mine ears with a loud voice, yet will I not hear them.
Ezek. 8:18

O my God, incline Thine ear, and hear; open Thine eyes, and behold our desolations.
Dan. 9:18

We do not present our supplications before Thee for our righteousnesses, but for Thy great mercies.
Dan. 9:18

O Lord, hear; O Lord, forgive; O Lord, hearken and do.
Dan. 9:19

Defer not, for Thine own sake, O my God: for Thy city and Thy people are called by Thy name.
Dan. 9:19

Whosoever shall call on the name of the Lord shall be delivered.
Joel 2:32
See also, e.g., Acts 2:21

Out of the belly of hell cried I, and Thou heardest my voice.
Jonah 2:2

O Lord, how long shall I cry, and Thou wilt not hear!
Hab. 1:2

As He cried, and they would not hear; so they cried, and I would not hear, saith the Lord of hosts.
Zech. 7:13

They shall call on My name, and I will hear them.
Zech. 13:9

[*See also* Assistance, Pleas, Worship, and the Appendix at p. 273]

PREACHING

Hear, O Israel: The Lord our God is one Lord.
Deut. 6:4
See also, e.g., Mark 12:29

The Lord gave the word: great was the company of those that published it.
Ps. 68:11

Give ye ear, and hear my voice; hearken, and hear my speech.
Isa. 28:23

Blessed are ye that sow beside all waters.
Isa. 32:20

Let the earth hear, and all that is therein; the world, and all things that come forth of it.
Isa. 34:1

Lift up thy voice with strength; lift it up, be not afraid.
Isa. 40:9

Lift up thy voice like a trumpet, and show My people their transgression.
Isa. 58:1

Preach good tidings unto the meek.
Isa. 61:1
See also Luke 4:18

Thou shalt go to all that I shall send thee, and whatsoever I command thee thou shalt speak.
Jer. 1:7

Hear ye the word of the Lord.
Jer. 21:11

O earth, earth, earth, hear the word of the Lord.
Jer. 22:29

Thou shalt say unto them, Thus saith the Lord God.
E.g., Ezek. 2:4

If thou warn the wicked, and he turn not from his wickedness, nor from his wicked way, he shall die in his iniquity; but thou hast delivered thy soul.
Ezek. 3:19, 21

Thus saith the Lord God; He that heareth, let him hear; and he that forbeareth, let him forbear.
Ezek. 3:27

Cause Jerusalem to know her abominations.
Ezek. 16:2

[*See also* Evangelism, God's Word, Ministry, Speech, Testimony]

PREDICTIONS

See Future, Prophecy.

PREJUDICE

See Brotherhood, Equality.

PREPAREDNESS

See Readiness, Vigilance.

PRIDE

How are the mighty fallen!
E.g., 2 Sam. 1:19

Pride compasseth them about as a chain; violence covereth them as a garment.
(them: the wicked)
Ps. 73:6

When pride cometh, then cometh shame.
Prov. 11:2

Pride goeth before destruction, and an haughty spirit before a fall.
Prov. 16:18

A man's pride shall bring him low.
Prov. 29:23

The patient in spirit is better than the proud in spirit.
Eccl. 7:8

Let him that glorieth glory in this, that he understandeth and knoweth Me, that I am the Lord.
Jer. 9:24
See also, e.g., 1 Cor. 1:31

Be not proud.
Jer. 13:15

Those that walk in pride He is able to abase.
Dan. 4:37

Though thou set thy nest among the stars, thence will I bring thee down, saith the Lord.
Obad. 4

[*See also* Arrogance, Boasting, Conceit, Confidence, Humility]

PRIESTHOOD

All the firstborn are Mine.
Num. 3:13

The priesthood of the Lord is their inheritance.
Josh. 18:7

I have lent him to the Lord.
Hannah, of her child
1 Sam. 1:28

As long as he liveth he shall be lent to the Lord.
1 Sam. 1:28

They shall go in, for they are holy.
2 Chron. 23:6

I am their inheritance.
Ezek. 44:28

He is the messenger of the Lord of hosts.
Mal. 2:7

[*See also* Clergy, Ministry]

PRINCIPLES

See Integrity.

PRIORITIES

See Goals, Values.

PRISON

See Imprisonment.

PROCRASTINATION

If we tarry till the morning light, some mischief will come upon us.
2 Kings 7:9

He that observeth the wind shall not sow; and he that regardeth the clouds shall not reap.
Eccl. 11:4

Seek ye the Lord while He may be found, call ye upon Him while He is near.
Isa. 55:6

[*See also* Laziness]

See Blasphemy.

Shall I drink the blood of these men that have put their lives in jeopardy?
> *David*
> *1 Chron. 11:19*

Treasures of wickedness profit nothing.
> *Prov. 10:2*

In all labour there is profit.
> *Prov. 14:23*

What hath man of all his labour, and of the vexation of his heart, wherein he hath laboured under the sun?
> *Eccl. 2:22*

What profit hath he that worketh in that wherein he laboureth?
> *Eccl. 3:9*

By thy great wisdom and by thy traffick hast thou increased thy riches.
> *Ezek. 28:5*

Ye have sown much, and bring in little; ye eat, but ye have not enough; ye drink, but ye are not filled.
> *Hag. 1:6*

[*See also* Loss, Reward, Values, Wealth]

See Success.

Is the Lord's hand waxed short?
> *Num. 11:23*

Hath He said, and shall He not do it? or hath He spoken, and shall He not make it good?
> *Num. 23:19*

When thou shalt vow a vow unto the Lord thy God, thou shalt not slack to pay it.
> *Deut. 23:21*

If thou shalt forbear to vow, it shall be no sin in thee.
> *Deut. 23:22*

All are come to pass unto you, and not one thing hath failed thereof.
> *Joshua to Israelites*
> *Josh. 23:14*

The Lord be witness between us, if we do not so according to thy words.
> *Judg. 11:10*

I have opened my mouth unto the Lord, and I cannot go back.
> *Judg. 11:35*

When I begin, I will also make an end.
> *God to Samuel*
> *1 Sam. 3:12*

When thou vowest a vow unto God, defer not to pay it.
> *Eccl. 5:4*

Better is it that thou shouldest not vow, than that thou shouldest vow and not pay.
> *Eccl. 5:5*

Shall I bring to the birth, and not cause to bring forth?
> *Isa. 66:9*

I will do it; I will not go back, neither will I spare, neither will I repent.
> *Ezek. 24:14*

[*See also* Covenant, Oaths]

Hear now, ye rebels; must we fetch you water out of this rock?
> *Num. 20:10*

The God that answereth by fire, let Him be God.
> *1 Kings 18:24*

Hear me, O Lord, hear me, that this people may know that Thou art the Lord God, and that Thou hast turned their heart back again.
> *1 Kings 18:37*

And ye shall know that I am the Lord.
> *1 Kings 20:28*

Thou shalt see it with thine eyes, but shalt not eat thereof.
2 Kings 7:2

I will not ask, neither will I tempt the Lord.
Isa. 7:12

[*See also* Doubt, Testimony]

PROPERTY

The land shall not be sold for ever: for the land is Mine; for ye are strangers and sojourners with Me.
Lev. 25:23

Cursed be he that removeth his neighbour's landmark.
Deut. 27:17
See also Deut. 19:14

The world is Mine, and the fulness thereof.
Ps. 50:12
See also Ex. 19:5

Remove not the ancient landmark, which thy fathers have set.
Prov. 22:28
See also Prov. 23:10

[*See also* Materialism, Wealth]

PROPHECY

Would God that all the Lord's people were prophets, and that the Lord would put His spirit upon them!
Moses to Joshua
Num. 11:29

When a prophet speaketh in the name of the Lord, if the thing follow not, nor come to pass, that is the thing which the Lord hath not spoken.
Deut. 18:22

I hate him; for he doth not prophesy good concerning me, but evil.
1 Kings 22:8

Speak that which is good.
1 Kings 22:13

Hear ye the word of the Lord.
E.g., 2 Kings 7:1

Good is the word of the Lord which thou hast spoken.
2 Kings 20:19, Isa. 39:8

Believe in the Lord your God, so shall ye be established; believe His prophets, so shall ye prosper.
2 Chron. 20:20

I have set thee for a tower and a fortress among My people.
God to Jeremiah
Jer. 6:27

I am the Lord: I will speak, and the word that I shall speak shall come to pass.
Ezek. 12:25

This is the day whereof I have spoken.
Ezek. 39:8

The day of the Lord cometh.
E.g., Joel 2:1

Write the vision, and make it plain.
Hab. 2:2

And ye shall know that the Lord of hosts hath sent me.
Zech. 2:9

[*See also* False Prophets, Messianic Hopes and Prophecies, Scripture]

PROSELYTIZATION

See Evangelism.

PROSPERITY

If ye walk in My statutes, and keep My commandments, and do them; Then I will give you rain in due season, and the land shall yield her increase, and the trees of the field shall yield their fruit.
Lev. 26:3–4

The Lord make His face shine upon thee, and be gracious unto thee.
Num. 6:25

The Lord maketh poor, and maketh rich: He bringeth low, and lifteth up.
1 Sam. 2:7

Give rain upon Thy land, which Thou hast given to Thy people.
1 Kings 8:36

The Lord was with him; and he prospered whithersoever he went forth.
2 Kings 18:7

Acquaint now thyself with Him, and be at peace: thereby good shall come unto thee.
Job 22:21

If they obey and serve Him, they shall spend their days in prosperity, and their years in pleasures.
Job 36:11

The righteous shall flourish like the palm tree: he shall grow like a cedar in Lebanon.
Ps. 92:12

In the day of prosperity be joyful, but in the day of adversity consider.
Eccl. 7:14

The parched ground shall become a pool, and the thirsty land springs of water.
Isa. 35:7

All thy children shall be taught of the Lord; and great shall be the peace of thy children.
Isa. 54:13

In the peace thereof shall ye have peace.
Jer. 29:7

Like as I have brought all this great evil upon this people, so will I bring upon them all the good that I have promised.
Jer. 32:42

The plowman shall overtake the reaper, and the treader of grapes him that soweth seed.
Amos 9:13

The streets of the city shall be full of boys and girls playing in the streets.
Zech. 8:5

Corn shall make the young men cheerful, and new wine the maids.
Zech. 9:17

[*See also* Abundance, Adversity, Reward, Success, Wealth]

PROSTITUTION

Do not prostitute thy daughter, to cause her to be a whore; lest the land fall to whoredom, and the land become full of wickedness.
Lev. 19:29

Thou shalt not bring the hire of a whore, or the price of a dog, into the house of the Lord.
Deut. 23:18

The lips of a strange woman drop as an honeycomb, and her mouth is smoother than oil.
Prov. 5:3

Keep thee from the evil woman, from the flattery of the tongue of a strange woman.
Prov. 6:24

By means of a whorish woman a man is brought to a piece of bread.
Prov. 6:26

Her house is the way to hell.
Prov. 7:27

A whore is a deep ditch; and a strange woman is a narrow pit.
Prov. 23:27

They give gifts to all whores: but thou givest thy gifts to all thy lovers.
Ezek. 16:33

Whoredom and wine and new wine take away the heart.
Hos. 4:11

[*See also* Adultery, Immorality, Lust, Sin]

PROTECTION

See Deliverance, God's Protection, Safety, Vigilance.

PROVOCATION

Now shall I be more blameless than the Philistines, though I do them a displeasure.
Judg. 15:3

They provoked Him to jealousy with their sins.
1 Kings 14:22

Provoke Me not to anger with the works of your hands; and I will do you no hurt.
Jer. 25:6
See also *Jer. 44:8*

[See also God's Anger, Instigation]

PRUDENCE

He that is surety for a stranger shall smart for it.
Prov. 11:15

He that keepeth his mouth keepeth his life: but he that openeth wide his lips shall have destruction.
Prov. 13:3

The wisdom of the prudent is to understand his way.
Prov. 14:8

Whoso keepeth his mouth and his tongue keepeth his soul from troubles.
Prov. 21:23

A prudent man forseeth the evil, and hideth himself: but the simple pass on, and are punished.
Prov. 22:3

A fool uttereth all his mind: but a wise man keepeth it in till afterwards.
Prov. 29:11

A time to keep silence, and a time to speak.
Eccl. 3:7

Be not rash with thy mouth.
Eccl. 5:2

Be not over much wicked, neither be thou foolish: why shouldest thou die before thy time?
Eccl. 7:17

Yielding pacifieth great offences.
Eccl. 10:4

A bird of the air shall carry the voice, and that which hath wings shall tell the matter.
Eccl. 10:20

The prudent shall keep silence in that time; for it is an evil time.
Amos 5:13

Keep the doors of thy mouth from her that lieth in thy bosom.
Mic. 7:5

[See also Rashness, Warning]

PUBLIC OPINION

Ye shall not be afraid of the face of man; for the judgment is God's.
Deut. 1:17

Hearken unto their voice, and make them a king.
God to Samuel
1 Sam. 8:22

I feared the people, and obeyed their voice.
Saul to Samuel
1 Sam. 15:24

No doubt but ye are the people, and wisdom shall die with you.
Job to his friends
Job 12:2

Hath he not sent me to the men that sit upon the wall?
Isa. 36:12
See also 2 Kings 18:27

[See also Mobs]

PUBLICITY

His fame was noised throughout all the country.
Josh. 6:27

For men to search their own glory is not glory.
Prov. 25:27

PUNISHMENT

Upon thy belly shalt thou go, and dust shalt thou eat all the days of thy life.
God to serpent
Gen. 3:14

In sorrow thou shalt bring forth children.
God to Eve
Gen. 3:16

In the sweat of thy face shalt thou eat bread, till thou return unto the ground.
Gen. 3:19

A fugitive and a vagabond shalt thou be in the earth.
Gen. 4:12

My punishment is greater than I can bear.
Cain to God
Gen. 4:13

He that curseth his father, or his mother, shall surely be put to death.
Ex. 21:17
See also, e.g., Lev. 20:9, Matt. 15:4

Thou shalt give life for life, Eye for eye, tooth for tooth, hand for hand, foot for foot, Burning for burning, wound for wound, stripe for stripe.
Ex. 21:23–25
See also Lev. 24:20, Deut. 19:21

Whosoever hath sinned against Me, him will I blot out of My book.
Ex. 32:33

In the day when I visit I will visit their sin upon them.
God to Moses
Ex. 32:34

His blood shall be upon him.
Lev. 20:9

He that killeth a beast, he shall restore it: and he that killeth a man, he shall be put to death.
Lev. 24:21

Ye shall sow your seed in vain, for your enemies shall eat it.
Lev. 26:16

They that hate you shall reign over you; and ye shall flee when none pursueth you.
Lev. 26:17

If her father had but spit in her face, should she not be ashamed seven days?
Num. 12:14

Surely they shall not see the land which I sware unto their fathers, neither shall any of them that provoked Me.
Num. 14:23

Your carcases shall fall in this wilderness.
God to Israelites
Num. 14:29

Because ye are turned away from the Lord, therefore the Lord will not be with you.
Num. 14:43

Shall one man sin, and wilt Thou be wroth with all the congregation?
Num. 16:22

He made them wander in the wilderness forty years, until all the generation, that had done evil in the sight of the Lord, was consumed.
Num. 32:13

The land cannot be cleansed of the blood that is shed therein, but by the blood of him that shed it.
Num. 35:33

But I must die in this land, I must not go over Jordan.
Moses
Deut. 4:22

The Lord shall scatter you among the nations, and ye shall be left few in number among the heathen.
Moses to Israelites
Deut. 4:27

I the Lord thy God am a jealous God, visiting the iniquity of the fathers upon the children unto the third and fourth generation of them that hate Me, And showing mercy unto thousands of them that love Me and keep My commandments.
Deut. 5:9–10

He will not be slack to him that hateth Him, He will repay him to his face.
Deut. 7:10

Cursed shalt thou be in the city, and cursed shalt thou be in the field.
Deut. 28:16

Thou shalt become an astonishment, a proverb, and a byword, among all nations.
Deut. 28:37
See also 1 Kings 9:7

Ye shall be left few in number, whereas ye were as the stars of heaven for multitude.
Deut. 28:62

Thou shalt fear day and night, and shalt have none assurance of thy life.
Deut. 28:66

The sword without, and terror within, shall destroy both the young man and the

virgin, the suckling also with the man of gray hairs.
Deut. 32:25

Their foot shall slide in due time.
Deut. 32:35

The day of their calamity is at hand, and the things that shall come upon them make haste.
Deut. 32:35

Thou shalt see the land before thee; but thou shalt not go thither.
God to Moses
Deut. 32:52

The children of Israel walked forty years in the wilderness.
Josh. 5:6
See also Num. 14:33

He that is taken with the accursed thing shall be burnt with fire, he and all that he hath.
Josh. 7:15

Let them be hewers of wood and drawers of water.
Josh. 9:21

As I have done, so God hath requited me.
Judg. 1:7

The Lord hath testified against me.
Ruth 1:21

It is the Lord: let Him do what seemeth Him good.
1 Sam. 3:18
See also 2 Sam. 15:26

The Lord will not hear you in that day.
1 Sam. 8:18

Thy kingdom shall not continue.
Samuel to Saul
1 Sam. 13:14

Though it be in Jonathan my son, he shall surely die.
Saul
1 Sam. 14:39

His day shall come to die.
1 Sam. 26:10

As the Lord liveth, ye are worthy to die.
1 Sam. 26:16
See also 1 Sam. 26:10

The Lord shall reward the doer of evil according to his wickedness.
2 Sam. 3:39

I will not put thee to death with the sword.
1 Kings 2:8

And they shall answer, Because they forsook the Lord their God.
1 Kings 9:9

In thy days I will not do it for David thy father's sake: but I will rend it out of the hand of thy son.
God to Solomon
1 Kings 11:12

Thy carcase shall not come unto the sepulchre of thy fathers.
1 Kings 13:22

Get thee to thine own house: and when thy feet enter into the city, the child shall die.
1 Kings 14:12

Because he humbleth himself before Me, I will not bring the evil in his days: but in his son's days will I bring the evil.
1 Kings 21:29

There came forth two she bears out of the wood, and tare forty and two children.
2 Kings 2:24

Thou shalt not build an house unto My name, because thou hast shed much blood upon the earth.
God to David
1 Chron. 22:8

The fathers shall not die for the children, neither shall the children die for the fathers, but every man shall die for his own sin.
2 Chron. 25:4
See also, e.g., Deut. 24:16

His power and His wrath is against all them that forsake Him.
Ezra 8:22

God hast punished us less than our iniquities deserve.
Ezra 9:13
See also Job 11:6

He taketh the wise in their own craftiness.
Job 5:13

He destroyeth the perfect and the wicked.
Job 9:22

The eyes of the wicked shall fail, and they shall not escape.
    Job 11:20

God distributeth sorrows in His anger.
    Job 21:17

He shall drink of the wrath of the Almighty.
    Job 21:20

Drought and heat consume the snow waters: so doth the grave those which have sinned.
    Job 24:19

Then let mine arm fall from my shoulder blade, and mine arm be broken from the bone.
    Job 31:22

Let thistles grow instead of wheat, and cockle instead of barley.
    Job 31:40

The Lord knoweth the way of the righteous: but the way of the ungodly shall perish.
    Ps. 1:6

Break Thou the arm of the wicked and the evil man.
    Ps. 10:15

Evil shall slay the wicked.
    Ps. 34:21

As wax melteth before the fire, so let the wicked perish at the presence of God.
    Ps. 68:2

When the wicked spring as the grass, and when all the workers of iniquity do flourish; it is that they shall be destroyed for ever.
    Ps. 92:7

Let the sinners be consumed out of the earth, and let the wicked be no more.
    Ps. 104:35

Let his days be few; and let another take his office.
    (his: the wicked)
    Ps. 109:8

It is time for Thee, Lord, to work: for they have made void Thy law.
    Ps. 119:126

The Lord preserveth all them that love Him: but all the wicked will He destroy.
    Ps. 145:20

The curse of the Lord is in the house of the wicked: but He blesseth the habitation of the just.
    Prov. 3:33

The lamp of the wicked shall be put out.
    Prov. 13:9

A reproof entereth more into a wise man than an hundred stripes into a fool.
    Prov. 17:10

When the scorner is punished, the simple is made wise.
    Prov. 21:11

Woe unto the wicked! it shall be ill with him: for the reward of his hands shall be given him.
    Isa. 3:11

The mean man shall be brought down, and the mighty man shall be humbled.
    Isa. 5:15

Lord, how long?
    Isa. 6:11

What will ye do in the day of visitation, and in the desolation which shall come from far?
    Isa. 10:3

Her time is near to come, and her days shall not be prolonged.
    (Her: Babylon)
    Isa. 13:22

Fear, and the pit, and the snare, are upon thee, O inhabitant of the earth.
    Isa. 24:17

The wisdom of their wise men shall perish, and the understanding of their prudent men shall be hid.
    Isa. 29:14
    See also 1 Cor. 1:19

Thou shalt not know from whence it riseth.
    Isa. 47:11

With his stripes we are healed.
    Isa. 53:5

According to their deeds, accordingly He will repay.
    Isa. 59:18

As ye have forsaken Me, and served strange gods in your land, so shall ye serve strangers in a land that is not your's.
Jer. 5:19

They have sown wheat, but shall reap thorns: they have put themselves to pain, but shall not profit.
Jer. 12:13

Such as are for death, to death; and such as are for the sword, to the sword.
Jer. 15:2

He will give them that are wicked to the sword, saith the Lord.
Jer. 25:31

Their dead bodies shall be for meat unto the fowls of the heaven, and to the beasts of the earth.
Jer. 34:20

Behold, I will set My face against you for evil.
Jer. 44:11

He that fleeth from the fear shall fall into the pit; and he that getteth up out of the pit shall be taken in the snare.
Jer. 48:44
See also Isa. 24:18

They whose judgment was not to drink of the cup have assuredly drunken.
Jer. 49:12

I will make thee small among the heathen, and despised among men.
Jer. 49:15

He that is far off shall die of the pestilence; and he that is near shall fall by the sword; and he that remaineth and is besieged shall die by the famine.
Ezek. 6:12

The time is come, the day draweth near.
Ezek. 7:12
See also Ezek. 7:7

They shall go out from one fire, and another fire shall devour them.
Ezek. 15:7

Shall he escape that doeth such things?
Ezek. 17:15

I will execute great vengeance upon them with furious rebukes.
Ezek. 25:17

I will pour out My wrath upon them like water.
Hos. 5:10

They consider not in their hearts that I remember all their wickedness.
Hos. 7:2

Thorns shall be in their tabernacles.
Hos. 9:6

Give them, O Lord: what wilt Thou give? give them a miscarrying womb and dry breasts.
Hos. 9:14

I will set Mine eyes upon them for evil, and not for good.
Amos 9:4

Thy reward shall return upon thine own head.
Obad. 15

Thou shalt sow, but thou shalt not reap.
Mic. 6:15

The Lord is slow to anger, and great in power, and will not at all acquit the wicked.
Nah. 1:3

They shall also build houses, but not inhabit them; and they shall plant vineyards, but not drink the wine thereof.
Zeph. 1:13
See also Amos 5:11

[*See also* Capital Punishment, Desolation, Discipline, Forgiveness, God's Anger, Judgment, Plague, Retribution, Revenge, Reward, Sin]

PURITY

Neither will I be with you any more, except ye destroy the accursed from among you.
God to Joshua
Josh. 7:12

Sanctify yourselves against to morrow.
Josh. 7:13
See also Josh. 3:5

Thou canst not stand before thine enemies, until ye take away the accursed thing from among you.
Josh. 7:13

Who can bring a clean thing out of an unclean? not one.
Job 14:4

Yea, the stars are not pure in His sight. How much less man, that is a worm? and the son of man, which is a worm?
Job 25:5-6

Who shall ascend into the hill of the Lord? or who shall stand in His holy place? He that hath clean hands, and a pure heart; who hath not lifted up his soul unto vanity, nor sworn deceitfully.
Ps. 24:3-4

Wash me, and I shall be whiter than snow.
Ps. 51:7

Be ye clean, that bear the vessels of the Lord.
Isa. 52:11

Thou art of purer eyes than to behold evil.
Habakkuk to God
Hab. 1:13

[*See also* Contamination, Corruption, Evil]

PURPOSE

God did send me before you to preserve life.
Joseph to his brothers
Gen. 45:5

The Lord hath made all things for Himself: yea, even the wicked for the day of evil.
Prov. 16:4

I will give them one heart, and one way, that they may fear Me for ever.
Jer. 32:39

[*See also* Duty, Goals, Intentions, Mission]

QUALITY

The excellency of dignity.
Gen. 49:3

None were of silver.
1 Kings 10:21

Thy silver is become dross, thy wine mixed with water.
Isa. 1:22

Reprobate silver shall men call them, because the Lord hath rejected them.
Jer. 6:30

[*See also* Perfection, Purity, Value]

QUANTITY

The Lord did not set His love upon you, nor choose you, because ye were more in number than any people; for ye were the fewest of all people: But because the Lord loved you.
Deut. 7:7-8

There is no restraint to the Lord to save by many or by few.
Jonathan
1 Sam. 14:6

As the sand that is by the sea for multitude.
2 Sam. 17:11
See also, e.g., Judg. 7:12

[*See also* Abundance, Infinity, Size]

QUESTIONING

See Authority, Skepticism.

QUOTATIONS

Every one that useth proverbs shall use this proverb against thee.
Ezek. 16:44

[*See also* Speech]

RAIN

A little cloud out of the sea, like a man's hand.
> *1 Kings 18:44*

Hath the rain a father? or who hath begotten the drops of dew?
> *Job 38:28*

He watereth the hills from His chambers.
> *Ps. 104:13*

A continual dropping in a very rainy day and a contentious woman are alike.
> *Prov. 27:15*

If the clouds be full of rain, they empty themselves upon the earth.
> *Eccl. 11:3*

He causeth the vapours to ascend from the ends of the earth: He maketh lightnings with rain, and bringeth forth the wind out of His treasures.
> *Jer. 51:16*
> *See also Ps. 135:7*

RAINBOW

I do set My bow in the cloud, and it shall be for a token of a covenant between Me and the earth.
> *God to Noah*
> *Gen. 9:13*

RASHNESS

Whatsoever cometh forth of the doors of my house to meet me, when I return in peace from the children of Ammon, shall surely be the Lord's.
> *Judg. 11:31*

I have opened my mouth unto the Lord, and I cannot go back.
> *Judg. 11:35*

Uzza put forth his hand to hold the ark; for the oxen stumbled. And the anger of the Lord was kindled against Uzza, and He smote him.
> *1 Chron. 13:9–10*
> *See also 2 Sam. 6:6–7*

Set a watch, O Lord, before my mouth; keep the door of my lips.
> *Ps. 141:3*

He that is hasty of spirit exalteth folly.
> *Prov. 14:29*

He that hasteth with his feet sinneth.
> *Prov. 19:2*

Seest thou a man that is hasty in his words? there is more hope of a fool than of him.
> *Prov. 29:20*

Let not thine heart be hasty to utter any thing before God.
> *Eccl. 5:2*

Every one turned to his course, as the horse rusheth into the battle.
> *Jer. 8:6*

[*See also* Misjudgment, Prudence]

READINESS

Sanctify yourselves against to morrow.
> *Josh. 7:13*
> *See also Josh. 3:5*

Is not the Lord gone out before thee?
> *Judg. 4:14*

Speak, Lord; for Thy servant heareth.
> *1 Sam. 3:9*

Set thine house in order; for thou shalt die, and not live.
> *2 Kings 20:1, Isa. 38:1*

Every man hath his sword upon his thigh because of fear in the night.
> *Song 3:8*

Prepare ye the way of the Lord, make straight in the desert a highway for our God.
> *Isa. 40:3*
> *See also, e.g., Matt. 3:3*

Every valley shall be exalted, and every mountain and hill shall be made low.
> *Isa. 40:4*
> *See also Luke 3:5*

They have blown the trumpet, even to

make all ready; but none goeth to the battle.
Ezek. 7:14

Be thou prepared.
Ezek. 38:7

Prepare to meet thy God, O Israel.
Amos 4:12

I will send My messenger, and he shall prepare the way before Me.
Mal. 3:1

[*See also* Vigilance]

REBELLION

Thou hast overthrown them that rose up against Thee: Thou sentest forth Thy wrath, which consumed them as stubble.
Ex. 15:7

Your murmurings are not against us, but against the Lord.
Moses to Israelites
Ex. 16:8

Wherefore do ye tempt the Lord?
Moses
Ex. 17:2

Hath the Lord indeed spoken only by Moses?
Num. 12:2

Rebel not ye against the Lord, neither fear ye the people of the land.
Num. 14:9

How long shall I bear with this evil congregation, which murmur against Me?
Num. 14:27

Ye have been rebellious against the Lord from the day that I knew you.
Deut. 9:24

They are a perverse and crooked generation.
Deut. 32:5

God forbid that we should rebel against the Lord.
Josh. 22:29

They turned quickly out of the way which their fathers walked in.
Judg. 2:17

Rebellion is as the sin of witchcraft.
Samuel to Saul
1 Sam. 15:23

I will raise up evil against thee out of thine own house.
God to David
2 Sam. 12:11

All Israel stoned him with stones.
1 Kings 12:18

Fight ye not against the Lord God of your fathers; for ye shall not prosper.
2 Chron. 13:12

Why dost thou strive against Him? for He giveth not account of any of His matters.
Job 33:13

He addeth rebellion unto his sin.
Job 34:37

Fear thou the Lord and the king: and meddle not with them that are given to change.
Prov. 24:21

Keep the king's commandment.
Eccl. 8:2

Woe unto him that striveth with his Maker!
Isa. 45:9

Be not thou rebellious like that rebellious house.
Ezek. 2:8

Woe unto them! for they have fled from Me: destruction unto them! because they have transgressed against Me.
Hos. 7:13

[*See also* Disobedience, Godlessness, Government, Strife]

RECIPROCITY

Thou shalt give life for life, Eye for eye, tooth for tooth, hand for hand, foot for foot, Burning for burning, wound for wound, stripe for stripe.
Ex. 21:23–25
See also Lev. 24:20, Deut. 19:21

Blessed is he that blesseth thee, and cursed is he that curseth thee.
Num. 24:9

Do unto him, as he had thought to have done unto his brother.
Deut. 19:19

As they did unto me, so have I done unto them.
Samson
Judg. 15:11

Them that honour Me I will honour, and they that despise Me shall be lightly esteemed.
1 Sam. 2:30

As thy sword hath made women childless, so shall thy mother be childless among women.
Samuel to Amalekite king
1 Sam. 15:33

The Lord is with you, while ye be with Him.
2 Chron. 15:2

Because ye have forsaken the Lord, He hath also forsaken you.
2 Chron. 24:20
See also 2 Chron. 15:2

He that watereth shall be watered also himself.
Prov. 11:25

They shall be My people, and I will be their God.
E.g., Jer. 24:7

Take vengeance upon her; as she hath done, do unto her.
Jer. 50:15

Because they trespassed against Me, therefore hid I My face from them.
Ezek. 39:23

Turn ye unto Me, saith the Lord of hosts, and I will turn unto you.
Zech. 1:3

[*See also* Consequences, Retribution]

REDEMPTION

Redeem us for Thy mercies' sake.
Ps. 44:26

Zion shall be redeemed with judgment, and her converts with righteousness.
Isa. 1:27

Fear not: for I have redeemed thee, I have called thee by thy name; thou art Mine.
Isa. 43:1

The redeemed of the Lord shall return, and come with singing unto Zion.
Isa. 51:11

With his stripes we are healed.
Isa. 53:5

Ye shall know that I am the Lord, when I shall bring you into the land of Israel.
Ezek. 20:42

I will seek that which was lost, and bring again that which was driven away, and will bind up that which was broken, and will strengthen that which was sick.
Ezek. 34:16

[*See also* Salvation]

REFUGE

See Safety, Sanctuary.

REGRET

It repented the Lord that He had made man on the earth.
Gen. 6:6

It repenteth Me that I have set up Saul to be king.
1 Sam. 15:11

Wherefore then hast Thou brought me forth out of the womb? Oh that I had given up the ghost, and no eye had seen me!
Job 10:18

O that thou hadst hearkened to My commandments! then had thy peace been as a river, and thy righteousness as the waves of the sea.
Isa. 48:18

Cursed be the day wherein I was born: let not the day wherein my mother bare me be blessed.
Jer. 20:14

Thou shalt remember thy ways, and be ashamed.
Ezek. 16:61

Ye shall lothe yourselves in your own sight for all your evils that ye have committed.
Ezek. 20:43

REHABILITATION

See Renewal.

REJECTION

I will not return with thee: for thou hast rejected the word of the Lord.
1 Sam. 15:26

The Spirit of the Lord departed from Saul.
1 Sam. 16:14

Israel shall be a proverb and a byword among all people.
1 Kings 9:7
See also Deut. 28:37

If thou forsake Him, He will cast thee off for ever.
1 Chron. 28:9

I cry unto Thee, and Thou dost not hear me: I stand up, and Thou regardest me not.
Job 30:20

Thou art the God of my strength: why dost Thou cast me off?
Ps. 43:2

Turn not away the face of Thine anointed.
Ps. 132:10

They have turned their back unto Me, and not their face.
Jer. 2:27

Reprobate silver shall men call them, because the Lord hath rejected them.
Jer. 6:30

I called you, but ye answered not.
God
Jer. 7:13

Though they shall cry unto Me, I will not hearken unto them.
Jer. 11:11

I spake unto thee in thy prosperity; but thou saidst, I will not hear.
Jer. 22:21

They have turned unto Me the back, and not the face.
Jer. 32:33

From the daughter of Zion all her beauty is departed: her princes are become like harts that find no pasture.
Lam. 1:6

Thus saith the Lord God; Behold, I, even I, am against thee.
Ezek. 5:8

Ye are not My people, and I will not be your God.
Hos. 1:9

[*See also* Abandonment, God's Anger]

RELIABILITY

It is better to trust in the Lord than to put confidence in man.
Ps. 118:8

It is better to trust in the Lord than to put confidence in princes.
Ps. 118:9

As vinegar to the teeth, and as smoke to the eyes, so is the sluggard to them that send him.
Prov. 10:26

A wicked messenger falleth into mischief: but a faithful ambassador is health.
Prov. 13:17

He that sendeth a message by the hand of a fool cutteth off the feet.
Prov. 26:6

The mountains shall depart, and the hills be removed; but My kindness shall not depart from thee.
Isa. 54:10

RELIANCE

If the Lord do not help thee, whence shall I help thee?
2 Kings 6:27

Let not him that is deceived trust in vanity: for vanity shall be his recompence.
Job 15:31

Some trust in chariots, and some in horses: but we will remember the name of the Lord our God.
Ps. 20:7

The Lord is my shepherd; I shall not want.
Ps. 23:1

Unto Thee, O Lord, do I lift up my soul.
Ps. 25:1

The Lord is my light and my salvation; whom shall I fear? the Lord is the strength of my life; of whom shall I be afraid?
Ps. 27:1

In Thee, O Lord, do I put my trust; let me never be ashamed.
Ps. 31:1

There is no king saved by the multitude of an host.
Ps. 33:16

Our soul waiteth for the Lord: He is our help and our shield.
Ps. 33:20

Blessed is that man that maketh the Lord his trust.
Ps. 40:4
See also, e.g., Ps. 34:8

Surely men of low degree are vanity, and men of high degree are a lie.
Ps. 62:9

Ye that fear the Lord, trust in the Lord: He is their help and their shield.
Ps. 115:11

In Thee is my trust; leave not my soul destitute.
Ps. 141:8

Put not your trust in princes, nor in the son of man.
Ps. 146:3

Confidence in an unfaithful man in time of trouble is like a broken tooth, and a foot out of joint.
Prov. 25:19

Trust ye not in lying words.
Jer. 7:4

The way of man is not in himself: it is not in man that walketh to direct his steps.
Jer. 10:23

Cursed be the man that trusteth in man, and maketh flesh his arm, and whose heart departeth from the Lord.
Jer. 17:5

Let me see Thy vengeance on them: for unto Thee have I opened my cause.
Jeremiah to God
Jer. 20:12
See also Jer. 11:20

But thou didst trust in thine own beauty.
Ezek. 16:15

[*See also* God's Protection, God's Support, Trust]

REMEMBRANCE

Remember this day, in which ye came out from Egypt, out of the house of bondage.
Ex. 13:3

Take heed to thyself, and keep thy soul diligently, lest thou forget the things which thine eyes have seen.
Deut. 4:9

Forget not the Lord thy God.
Deut. 8:11
See also Deut. 6:12

What mean ye by these stones?
Josh. 4:6

Behold, this stone shall be a witness unto us.
Josh. 24:27

They shall not say, This is Jezebel.
2 Kings 9:37

Their memorial is perished with them.
Ps. 9:6

If I forget thee, O Jerusalem, let my right hand forget her cunning.
Ps. 137:5

There is no remembrance of the wise more than of the fool for ever.
Eccl. 2:16

That which now is in the days to come shall all be forgotten.
Eccl. 2:16

Remember ye not the former things, neither consider the things of old.
Isa. 43:18

They may forget, yet will I not forget thee.
God, about parents
Isa. 49:15

They shall not take of thee a stone for a corner, nor a stone for foundations; but thou shalt be desolate for ever, saith the Lord.
Jer. 51:26

Wherefore dost Thou forget us for ever, and forsake us so long time?
Lam. 5:20

They consider not in their hearts that I remember all their wickedness.
Hos. 7:2

[*See also* Abandonment, Fame, History]

RENEWAL

Be fruitful, and multiply, and replenish the earth.
God to Noah, after the flood
Gen. 9:1

He restoreth my soul.
Ps. 23:3

A time to break down, and a time to build up.
Eccl. 3:3

They that wait upon the Lord shall renew their strength.
Isa. 40:31

Awake, awake; put on thy strength, O Zion; put on thy beautiful garments, O Jerusalem.
Isa. 52:1

I create new heavens and a new earth: and the former shall not be remembered, nor come into mind.
Isa. 65:17

Come, and let us join ourselves to the Lord.
Jer. 50:5

Turn Thou us unto Thee, O Lord, and we shall be turned; renew our days as of old.
Lam. 5:21

I will take the stony heart out of their flesh, and will give them an heart of flesh.
Ezek. 11:19
See also Ezek. 36:26

REPENTANCE

I have sinned this time: the Lord is righteous, and I and my people are wicked.
Pharaoh
Ex. 9:27

Forgive, I pray thee, my sin only this once.
Pharaoh to Moses
Ex. 10:17

It is the blood that maketh an atonement for the soul.
Lev. 17:11

Make confession unto Him.
Josh. 7:19

Do Thou unto us whatsoever seemeth good unto Thee; deliver us only, we pray Thee, this day.
Judg. 10:15

He is not a man, that He should repent.
1 Sam. 15:29

Turn ye from your evil ways, and keep My commandments and My statutes.
2 Kings 17:13

Turn again unto the Lord.
2 Chron. 30:9

The Lord your God is gracious and merciful, and will not turn away His face from you, if ye return unto Him.
2 Chron. 30:9

Make confession unto the Lord God of your fathers, and do His pleasure.
Ezra 10:11

To depart from evil is understanding.
Job 28:28

I abhor myself, and repent in dust and ashes.
Job 42:6

When He slew them, then they sought Him.
Ps. 78:34

Fear the Lord, and depart from evil.
Prov. 3:7
See also Ps. 34:14, Ps. 37:27

By the fear of the Lord men depart from evil.
Prov. 16:6

Put away the evil of your doings from before Mine eyes.
Isa. 1:16

Cease to do evil.
Isa. 1:16

Turn ye unto Him from whom the children of Israel have deeply revolted.
Isa. 31:6

Let him return unto the Lord, and He will have mercy upon him.
Isa. 55:7

Is not this the fast that I have chosen? to loose the bands of wickedness, to undo the heavy burdens, and to let the oppressed go free.
Isa. 58:6

Turn thou unto Me.
Jer. 3:7
See also Jer. 4:1

Break up your fallow ground, and sow not among thorns.
Jer. 4:3

Take away the foreskins of your heart.
Jer. 4:4

Wash thine heart from wickedness, that thou mayest be saved.
Jer. 4:14

Can the Ethiopian change his skin, or the leopard his spots? then may ye also do good, that are accustomed to do evil.
Jer. 13:23

I am weary with repenting.
God to Jeremiah
Jer. 15:6

Return ye now every one from his evil way.
Jer. 18:11

Amend your ways and your doings, and obey the voice of the Lord your God.
Jer. 26:13

Return ye now every man from his evil way, and amend your doings.
Jer. 35:15

Let us search and try our ways, and turn again to the Lord.
Lam. 3:40

If the wicked will turn from all his sins that he hath committed, and keep all My statutes, and do that which is lawful and right, he shall surely live.
Ezek. 18:21
See also Ezek. 33:19

Repent, and turn yourselves from all your transgressions; so iniquity shall not be your ruin.
Ezek. 18:30

Make you a new heart and a new spirit: for why will ye die?
Ezek. 18:31

Turn yourselves, and live ye.
Ezek. 18:32

He that taketh warning shall deliver his soul.
Ezek. 33:5

Turn ye, turn ye from your evil ways; for why will ye die?
Ezek. 33:11
See also Jonah 3:8

Come, and let us return unto the Lord.
Hos. 6:1

It is time to seek the Lord.
Hos. 10:12

Rend your heart, and not your garments, and turn unto the Lord.
Joel 2:13

Seek the Lord, and ye shall live.
Amos 5:6
See also Amos 5:4

Turn ye unto Me, saith the Lord of hosts, and I will turn unto you.
Zech. 1:3

Turn ye now from your evil ways, and from your evil doings.
Zech. 1:4

Return unto Me, and I will return unto you, saith the Lord of hosts.
Mal. 3:7

[*See also* Forgiveness, Punishment, Sin]

See Reliability, Spokesmen.

REPUTATION

Thou knowest the people, that they are set on mischief.
Aaron to Moses
Ex. 32:22

How are the mighty fallen!
E.g., 2 Sam. 1:19

The half was not told me.
Queen of Sheba to Solomon
1 Kings 10:7

I believed not their words, until I came, and mine eyes had seen it.
Queen of Sheba to Solomon
2 Chron. 9:6
See also 1 Kings 10:7

Behold, the one half of the greatness of thy wisdom was not told me.
2 Chron. 9:6
See also 1 Kings 10:7

The wise shall inherit glory: but shame shall be the promotion of fools.
Prov. 3:35

The memory of the just is blessed: but the name of the wicked shall rot.
Prov. 10:7

A good name is rather to be chosen than great riches.
Prov. 22:1

There is no remembrance of the wise more than of the fool for ever.
Eccl. 2:16

A good name is better than precious ointment.
Eccl. 7:1

[*See also* Achievement, Fame, Shame]

See Assistance, Danger, Deliverance.

RESPECT

The excellency of dignity.
Gen. 49:3

Thou shalt not revile the gods, nor curse the ruler of thy people.
Ex. 22:28
See also Acts 23:5

Honour the face of the old man.
Lev. 19:32

They feared him, as they feared Moses, all the days of his life.
Josh. 4:14

Loose thy shoe from off thy foot; for the place whereon thou standest is holy.
Josh. 5:15
See also Ex. 3:5

Them that honour Me I will honour, and they that despise Me shall be lightly esteemed.
1 Sam. 2:30

I will not put forth mine hand against my lord; for he is the Lord's anointed.
David to Saul
1 Sam. 24:10

Ask on, my mother: for I will not say thee nay.
1 Kings 2:20

The Lord your God ye shall fear.
2 Kings 17:39

Let him alone; let no man move his bones.
2 Kings 23:18

Before honour is humility.
Prov. 15:33, Prov. 18:12

Despise not thy mother when she is old.
Prov. 23:22

As snow in summer, and as rain in harvest, so honour is not seemly for a fool.
Prov. 26:1

Her children arise up, and call her blessed.
Prov. 31:28

My people shall know My name.
Isa. 52:6

A son honoureth his father, and a servant his master: if then I be a father, where is Mine honour?
Mal. 1:6

[*See also* Homage]

RESPONSIBILITY

Am I my brother's keeper?
Cain
Gen. 4:9

Upon me be thy curse, my son: only obey my voice.
Rebekah to Jacob
Gen. 27:13

If thou meet thine enemy's ox or his ass going astray, thou shalt surely bring it back to him again.
Ex. 23:4

Wherefore have I not found favour in Thy sight, that Thou layest the burden of all this people upon me?
Moses to God
Num. 11:11

Have I conceived all this people? have I begotten them, that Thou shouldest say unto me, Carry them in thy bosom, as a nursing father beareth the sucking child?
Moses to God
Num. 11:12

Shall your brethren go to war, and shall ye sit here?
Num. 32:6

The cause that is too hard for you, bring it unto me, and I will hear it.
Moses
Deut. 1:17

Upon me, my lord, upon me let this iniquity be.
1 Sam. 25:24

Lo, I have sinned, and I have done wick-

edly: but these sheep, what have they done?
David to God
2 Sam. 24:17
See also 1 Chron. 21:17

If the Lord do not help thee, whence shall I help thee?
2 Kings 6:27

Every man shall be put to death for his own sin.
E.g., 2 Kings 14:6

The fathers shall not die for the children, neither shall the children die for the fathers, but every man shall die for his own sin.
2 Chron. 25:4
See also, e.g., Deut. 24:16

Gird up now thy loins like a man.
Job 38:3

He was wounded for our transgressions, he was bruised for our iniquities.
Isa. 53:5

Hast thou not procured this unto thyself, in that thou hast forsaken the Lord thy God?
God to Jews
Jer. 2:17

Every one shall die for his own iniquity: every man that eateth the sour grape, his teeth shall be set on edge.
Jer. 31:30

Cursed be he that keepeth back his sword from blood.
Jer. 48:10

The soul that sinneth, it shall die.
Ezek. 18:4, 20

His blood shall be upon him.
E.g., Ezek. 18:13

I have set thee a watchman unto the house of Israel.
Ezek. 33:7

O Israel, thou hast destroyed thyself; but in Me is thine help.
Hos. 13:9

[*See also* Blame, Duty, Guilt]

When ye go, ye shall not go empty.
God to Moses
Ex. 3:21

If the thief be found, let him pay double.
Ex. 22:7

Whom the judges shall condemn, he shall pay double unto his neighbour.
Ex. 22:9

He shall make amends for the harm that he hath done.
Lev. 5:16

He shall restore that which he took violently away.
Lev. 6:4

He that killeth a beast shall make it good; beast for beast.
Lev. 24:18
See also Lev. 24:21

[*See also* Justice, Restoration, Retribution, Revenge]

RESTORATION

The desert shall rejoice, and blossom as the rose.
Isa. 35:1

The eyes of the blind shall be opened, and the ears of the deaf shall be unstopped.
Isa. 35:5

Then shall the lame man leap as an hart, and the tongue of the dumb sing.
Isa. 35:6

Again I will build thee, and thou shalt be built, O virgin of Israel.
Jer. 31:4

This land that was desolate is become like the garden of Eden.
Ezek. 36:35

I will restore to you the years that the locust hath eaten.
Joel 2:25

The plowman shall overtake the reaper, and the treader of grapes him that soweth seed.
Amos 9:13

The streets of the city shall be full of boys and girls playing in the streets.
Zech. 8:5

[*See also* Redemption, Renewal]

RESTRAINT

Let not the anger of my lord wax hot.
Aaron to Moses
Ex. 32:22

How shall I curse, whom God hath not cursed? or how shall I defy, whom the Lord hath not defied?
Balaam to Balak
Num. 23:8

I will not put forth mine hand against my lord; for he is the Lord's anointed.
David to Saul
1 Sam. 24:10

The Lord judge between me and thee, and the Lord avenge me of thee: but mine hand shall not be upon thee.
David to Saul
1 Sam. 24:12

When the Lord had delivered me into thine hand, thou killedst me not.
Saul to David
1 Sam. 24:18

Blessed be thy advice, and blessed be thou, which hast kept me this day from coming to shed blood.
1 Sam. 25:33

Return every man to his house; for this thing is from Me.
1 Kings 12:24
See also 2 Chron. 11:4

Ye shall not go up, nor fight against your brethren.
2 Chron. 11:4, 1 Kings 12:24

He that is void of wisdom despiseth his neighbour: but a man of understanding holdeth his peace.
Prov. 11:12

A fool's wrath is presently known: but a prudent man covereth shame.
Prov. 12:16

He that is slow to anger appeaseth strife.
Prov. 15:18

It is an honour for a man to cease from strife.
Prov. 20:3

Whoso keepeth his mouth and his tongue keepeth his soul from troubles.
Prov. 21:23

I will not ask, neither will I tempt the Lord.
Isa. 7:12

[See also Anger, Forgiveness, Patience, Prudence, Revenge, Temper, Temptation]

RESURRECTION

If a man die, shall he live again?
Job 14:14

Though after my skin worms destroy this body, yet in my flesh shall I see God.
Job 19:26

He will swallow up death in victory.
Isa. 25:8

Awake and sing, ye that dwell in dust.
Isa. 26:19

Son of man, can these bones live?
Ezek. 37:3

O ye dry bones, hear the word of the Lord.
Ezek. 37:4

Many of them that sleep in the dust of the earth shall awake, some to everlasting life, and some to shame and everlasting contempt.
Dan. 12:2

[See also Eternal Life]

RETRIBUTION

Whoso sheddeth man's blood, by man shall his blood be shed.
Gen. 9:6

Eye for eye, tooth for tooth, hand for hand, foot for foot.
Ex. 21:24
See also Matt. 5:38

The land cannot be cleansed of the blood that is shed therein, but by the blood of him that shed it.
Num. 35:33

Why hast thou troubled us? the Lord shall trouble thee this day.
Joshua to Achan
Josh. 7:25

He is an holy God; He is a jealous God; He will not forgive your transgressions nor your sins.
Josh. 24:19

Whithersoever they went out, the hand of the Lord was against them for evil.
Judg. 2:15

The dead which he slew at his death were more than they which he slew in his life.
(he: Samson)
Judg. 16:30

As thy sword hath made women childless, so shall thy mother be childless among women.
Samuel to Amalekite king
1 Sam. 15:33

He shall lie with thy wives in the sight of this sun.
(He: David's neighbor)
2 Sam. 12:11

The Lord shall return thy wickedness upon thine own head.
1 Kings 2:44

In the place where dogs licked the blood of Naboth shall dogs lick thy blood, even thine.
(thy: Ahab)
1 Kings 21:19

I will bring evil upon thee, and will take away thy posterity.
1 Kings 21:21

I will cause him to fall by the sword in his own land.
2 Kings 19:7, Isa. 37:7

Whosoever heareth of it, both his ears shall tingle.
2 Kings 21:12
See also 1 Sam. 3:11

I will wipe Jerusalem as a man wipeth a dish, wiping it, and turning it upside down.
2 Kings 21:13

I will forsake the remnant of Mine inheritance, and deliver them into the hand of their enemies.
2 Kings 21:14

Behold, I will bring evil upon this place, and upon the inhabitants thereof.
2 Kings 22:16

The sword of the Lord.
E.g., 1 Chron. 21:12

They hanged Haman on the gallows that he had prepared for Mordecai.
Esther 7:10

Give them after the work of their hands; render to them their desert.
Ps. 28:4

Let them be blotted out of the book of the living, and not be written with the righteous.
Ps. 69:28

Let his children be fatherless, and his wife a widow.
Ps. 109:9

As he loved cursing, so let it come unto him: as he delighted not in blessing, so let it be far from him.
Ps. 109:17

Let the wicked fall into their own nets.
Ps. 141:10

He that diggeth a pit shall fall into it.
Eccl. 10:8

Thy men shall fall by the sword, and thy mighty in the war.
Isa. 3:25

The sword of the Lord is filled with blood, it is made fat with fatness.
Isa. 34:6

The moth shall eat them up like a garment, and the worm shall eat them like wool.
Isa. 51:8

I will not keep silence, but will recompense.
Isa. 65:6

He shall come up as clouds, and his chariots shall be as a whirlwind.
Jer. 4:13

Mine eye shall not spare thee, neither will

I have pity: but I will recompense thy ways.
E.g., Ezek. 7:4
See also Ezek. 9:5

Ye shall know that I am the Lord, when I set My face against them.
Ezek. 15:7

I will destroy the fat and the strong; I will feed them with judgment.
Ezek. 34:16

Their blood shall be poured out as dust, and their flesh as the dung.
Zeph. 1:17

As He cried, and they would not hear; so they cried, and I would not hear, saith the Lord of hosts.
Zech. 7:13

[*See also* Forgiveness, God's Anger, Judgment, Punishment, Revenge]

REVELATION

Stand thou still a while, that I may show thee the word of God.
Samuel to Saul
1 Sam. 9:27

REVENGE

The voice of thy brother's blood crieth unto Me from the ground.
Gen. 4:10

Should he deal with our sister as with an harlot?
Gen. 34:31

Against all the gods of Egypt I will execute judgment: I am the Lord.
Ex. 12:12

Thou shalt give life for life, Eye for eye, tooth for tooth, hand for hand, foot for foot, Burning for burning, wound for wound, stripe for stripe.
Ex. 21:23–25
See also Lev. 24:20, Deut. 19:21

I would make the remembrance of them to cease from among men.
Deut. 32:26

To Me belongeth vengeance, and recompense.
Deut. 32:35

I will render vengeance to Mine enemies, and will reward them that hate Me.
Deut. 32:41

I will make Mine arrows drunk with blood, and My sword shall devour flesh.
Deut. 32:42

As the Lord liveth, if ye had saved them alive, I would not slay you.
Judg. 8:19

Now shall I be more blameless than the Philistines, though I do them a displeasure.
Judg. 15:3

As they did unto me, so have I done unto them.
Samson
Judg. 15:11

Remember me, I pray Thee, and strengthen me, I pray Thee, only this once, O God.
Samson
Judg. 16:28

Slay both man and woman, infant and suckling, ox and sheep, camel and ass.
Samuel to Saul
1 Sam. 15:3

I will deliver thine enemy into thine hand, that thou mayest do to him as it shall seem good unto thee.
God to David
1 Sam. 24:4

Shall the sword devour for ever?
2 Sam. 2:26

Let not his hoar head go down to the grave in peace.
1 Kings 2:6

Hold him not guiltless.
1 Kings 2:9

Thou art a wise man, and knowest what thou oughtest to do unto him.
1 Kings 2:9

The dogs shall eat Jezebel by the wall of Jezreel.
1 Kings 21:23

There came forth two she bears out of the wood, and tare forty and two children.
2 Kings 2:24

Turn their reproach upon their own head.
Neh. 4:4

Let not their sin be blotted out from before Thee.
Neh. 4:5

Destroy Thou them, O God; let them fall by their own counsels.
Ps. 5:10

It is God that avengeth me.
Ps. 18:47, 2 Sam. 22:48

The righteous shall rejoice when he seeth the vengeance: he shall wash his feet in the blood of the wicked.
Ps. 58:10

Keep not Thou silence, O God: hold not Thy peace.
Ps. 83:1

God, to whom vengeance belongeth.
Ps. 94:1

Let his days be few; and let another take his office.
(his: the wicked)
Ps. 109:8

Let mine adversaries be clothed with shame, and let them cover themselves with their own confusion.
Ps. 109:29

Let the high praises of God be in their mouth, and a twoedged sword in their hand; To execute vengeance upon the heathen.
Ps. 149:6–7

Say not, I will do so to him as he hath done to me.
Prov. 24:29

I will ease Me of Mine adversaries, and avenge Me of Mine enemies.
Isa. 1:24

They shall take them captives, whose captives they were.
Isa. 14:2

Awake, awake, put on strength, O arm of the Lord; awake, as in the ancient days, in the generations of old.
Isa. 51:9

Shall not My soul be avenged on such a nation as this?
Jer. 5:9

Pour out Thy fury upon the heathen that know Thee not, and upon the families that call not on Thy name.
Jer. 10:25

Let me see Thy vengeance on them: for unto Thee have I revealed my cause.
Jer. 11:20
See also Jer. 20:12

They that spoil thee shall be a spoil, and all that prey upon thee will I give for a prey.
Jer. 30:16

The sword shall devour, and it shall be satiate and made drunk with their blood.
Jer. 46:10

O thou sword of the Lord, how long will it be ere thou be quiet?
Jer. 47:6

All ye that bend the bow, shoot at her, spare no arrows: for she hath sinned against the Lord.
(her: Babylon)
Jer. 50:14

Take vengeance upon her; as she hath done, do unto her.
Jer. 50:15

According to all that she hath done, do unto her: for she hath been proud against the Lord, against the Holy One of Israel.
Jer. 50:29

He shall come up like a lion from the swelling of Jordan unto the habitation of the strong.
Jer. 50:44
See also Jer. 49:19

Do unto them, as Thou hast done unto me.
Lam. 1:22

I have no pleasure in the death of the wicked.
Ezek. 33:11

As thou hast done, it shall be done unto thee.
Obad. 15

God is jealous, and the Lord revengeth.
Nah. 1:2

The Lord will take vengeance on His adversaries.
Nah. 1:2

[*See also* Enemies, Forgiveness, Punishment, Restraint, Retribution]

REVERENCE

Put off thy shoes from off thy feet, for the place whereon thou standest is holy ground.
Ex. 3:5
See also Josh. 5:15

Thou shalt fear the Lord thy God; Him shalt thou serve, and to Him shalt thou cleave, and swear by His name.
Deut. 10:20
See also Deut. 6:13

Fear the Lord, and serve Him, and obey His voice.
1 Sam. 12:14

As the heaven is high above the earth, so great is His mercy toward them that fear Him.
Ps. 103:11

The Lord taketh pleasure in them that fear Him, in those that hope in His mercy.
Ps. 147:11

Their fear toward Me is taught by the precept of men.
Isa. 29:13

The Lord is in His holy temple: let all the earth keep silence before Him.
Hab. 2:20

[*See also* Awe, Fear of God]

REVERSAL

The elder shall serve the younger.
Gen. 25:23, Rom. 9:12

They that were full have hired out themselves for bread.
1 Sam. 2:5

How are the mighty fallen!
E.g., 2 Sam. 1:19

The victory that day was turned into mourning.
2 Sam. 19:2

They shall become a prey and a spoil to all their enemies.
2 Kings 21:14

The stone which the builders refused is become the head stone of the corner.
Ps. 118:22
See also, e.g., Mark 12:10

The mean man shall be brought down, and the mighty man shall be humbled.
Isa. 5:15

A little one shall become a thousand, and a small one a strong nation.
Isa. 60:22

She that was great among the nations, and princess among the provinces, how is she become tributary!
Lam. 1:1

The crown is fallen from our head: woe unto us, that we have sinned!
Lam. 5:16

Exalt him that is low, and abase him that is high.
Ezek. 21:26

REVOLUTION

See Rebellion, Strife.

REWARD

If thou doest well, shalt thou not be accepted?
God to Cain
Gen. 4:7

In thy seed shall all the nations of the earth be blessed; because thou hast obeyed My voice.
God to Abraham
Gen. 22:18

If ye will obey My voice indeed, and keep My covenant, then ye shall be a peculiar treasure unto Me above all people: for all the earth is Mine.
Ex. 19:5

If ye walk in My statutes, and keep My commandments, and do them; Then I will give you rain in due season, and the land shall yield her increase, and the trees of the field shall yield their fruit.
Lev. 26:3–4

I will walk among you, and will be your God, and ye shall be My people.
Lev. 26:12
See also 2 Cor. 6:16

I the Lord thy God am a jealous God, visiting the iniquity of the fathers upon the children unto the third and fourth generation of them that hate Me, And showing mercy unto thousands of them that love Me and keep My commandments.
Deut. 5:9–10

Blessed shalt thou be in the city, and blessed shalt thou be in the field.
Deut. 28:3

The Lord shall make thee the head, and not the tail; and thou shalt be above only, and thou shalt not be beneath.
Deut. 28:13

I will build him a sure house; and he shall walk before Mine anointed for ever.
1 Sam. 2:35

The Lord render to every man his righteousness and his faithfulness.
1 Sam. 26:23

Ask what I shall give thee.
God to Solomon
1 Kings 3:5, 2 Chron. 1:7

I have also given thee that which thou hast not asked, both riches, and honour.
God to Solomon
1 Kings 3:13

Thou shalt be gathered into thy grave in peace.
2 Kings 22:20

Your work shall be rewarded.
2 Chron. 15:7

The Lord is able to give thee much more.
2 Chron. 25:9

Remember me, O my God, for good.
Neh. 13:31
See also Neh. 5:19

What shall be done unto the man whom the king delighteth to honour?
Esther 6:6

What is the hope of the hypocrite, though

he hath gained, when God taketh away his soul?
Job 27:8

The Lord gave Job twice as much as he had before.
Job 42:10

The Lord preserveth the faithful, and plentifully rewardeth the proud doer.
Ps. 31:23

Many sorrows shall be to the wicked: but he that trusteth in the Lord, mercy shall compass him about.
Ps. 32:10

Those that wait upon the Lord, they shall inherit the earth.
Ps. 37:9

The meek shall inherit the earth.
Ps. 37:11
See also, e.g., Matt. 5:5

The righteous shall inherit the land.
Ps. 37:29

Verily there is a reward for the righteous.
Ps. 58:11

No good thing will He withhold from them that walk uprightly.
Ps. 84:11

Thou shalt eat the labour of thine hands.
Ps. 128:2

The Lord lifteth up the meek: He casteth the wicked down to the ground.
Ps. 147:6

Withhold not good from them to whom it is due, when it is in the power of thine hand to do it.
Prov. 3:27

He that troubleth his own house shall inherit the wind.
Prov. 11:29

The fruit of the righteous is a tree of life.
Prov. 11:30

He that tilleth his land shall have plenty of bread.
Prov. 28:19

Many seek the ruler's favour; but every man's judgment cometh from the Lord.
Prov. 29:26

God giveth to a man that is good in His sight wisdom, and knowledge, and joy.
Eccl. 2:26

Every man should eat and drink, and enjoy the good of all his labour, it is the gift of God.
Eccl. 3:13
See also Eccl. 5:18

Cast thy bread upon the waters: for thou shalt find it after many days.
Eccl. 11:1

Sow ye, and reap.
Isa. 37:30, 2 Kings 19:29

He that putteth his trust in Me shall possess the land, and shall inherit My holy mountain.
Isa. 57:13

As the days of a tree are the days of My people, and Mine elect shall long enjoy the work of their hands.
Isa. 65:22

The hand of the Lord shall be known toward His servants, and His indignation toward His enemies.
Isa. 66:14

Refrain thy voice from weeping, and thine eyes from tears: for thy work shall be rewarded, saith the Lord.
Jer. 31:16

They have sown the wind, and they shall reap the whirlwind.
Hos. 8:7

Sow to yourselves in righteousness, reap in mercy.
Hos. 10:12

What profiteth the graven image that the maker thereof hath graven it?
Hab. 2:18

[*See also* Blessing, Eternal Life, Profit, Punishment, Success, Victory, Wealth]

RIDDLES

Out of the eater came forth meat, and out of the strong came forth sweetness.
Judg. 14:14

What is sweeter than honey? and what is
stronger than a lion?
Judg. 14:18

RIGHTEOUSNESS

Can we find such a one as this is, a man in
whom the Spirit of God is?
Pharaoh to Joseph
Gen. 41:38

In righteousness shalt thou judge thy
neighbour.
Lev. 19:15

All that do unrighteously, are an abomination unto the Lord thy God.
Deut. 25:16

Thou art more righteous than I: for thou
hast rewarded me good, whereas I have
rewarded thee evil.
Saul to David
1 Sam. 24:17

He did that which was right in the sight of
the Lord.
2 Kings 14:3

One that feared God, and eschewed evil.
(one: Job)
Job 1:1

Shall mortal man be more just than God?
shall a man be more pure than his maker?
Job 4:17

How should man be just with God?
Job 9:2

Is it any pleasure to the Almighty, that
thou art righteous?
Job 22:3

I was eyes to the blind, and feet was I to
the lame.
Job 29:15

With kings are they on the throne.
(they: the righteous)
Job 36:7

His delight is in the law of the Lord; and
in His law doth he meditate day and night.
Ps. 1:2

There is none that doeth good, no, not
one.
Ps. 14:3, Ps. 53:3, Rom. 3:12

He leadeth me in the paths of righteousness for His name's sake.
Ps. 23:3

Shout for joy, all ye that are upright in
heart.
Ps. 32:11

The eyes of the Lord are upon the righteous, and His ears are open unto their
cry.
Ps. 34:15

The steps of a good man are ordered by
the Lord: and He delighteth in his way.
Ps. 37:23

I have been young, and now am old; yet
have I not seen the righteous forsaken.
Ps. 37:25

The righteous shall inherit the land.
Ps. 37:29

Mark the perfect man, and behold the
upright: for the end of that man is peace.
Ps. 37:37

The salvation of the righteous is of the
Lord: He is their strength in the time of
trouble.
Ps. 37:39

Verily there is a reward for the righteous.
Ps. 58:11

No good thing will He withhold from
them that walk uprightly.
Ps. 84:11

The righteous shall flourish like the palm
tree: he shall grow like a cedar in Lebanon.
Ps. 92:12

Righteousness and judgment are the habitation of His throne.
Ps. 97:2

Light is sown for the righteous, and gladness for the upright in heart.
Ps. 97:11

With righteousness shall He judge the
world.
Ps. 98:9

Precious in the sight of the Lord is the
death of His saints.
Ps. 116:15

I have done judgment and justice: leave
me not to mine oppressors.
Ps. 119:121

The Lord is righteous in all His ways, and holy in all His works.
Ps. 145:17

The Lord loveth the righteous.
Ps. 146:8

The path of the just is as the shining light, that shineth more and more unto the perfect day.
Prov. 4:18

Righteousness delivereth from death.
Prov. 10:2, Prov. 11:4

The labour of the righteous tendeth to life: the fruit of the wicked to sin.
Prov. 10:16

The lips of the righteous feed many.
Prov. 10:21

The mouth of the just bringeth forth wisdom.
Prov. 10:31

When it goeth well with the righteous, the city rejoiceth.
Prov. 11:10

To him that soweth righteousness shall be a sure reward.
Prov. 11:18

The desire of the righteous is only good: but the expectation of the wicked is wrath.
Prov. 11:23

The fruit of the righteous is a tree of life.
Prov. 11:30

The thoughts of the righteous are right: but the counsels of the wicked are deceit.
Prov. 12:5

In the house of the righteous is much treasure: but in the revenues of the wicked is trouble.
Prov. 15:6

To do justice and judgment is more acceptable to the Lord than sacrifice.
Prov. 21:3

God giveth to a man that is good in His sight wisdom, and knowledge, and joy.
Eccl. 2:26

One man among a thousand have I found; but a woman among all those have I not.
Eccl. 7:28

God that is holy shall be sanctified in righteousness.
Isa. 5:16

The way of the just is uprightness.
Isa. 26:7

The work of righteousness shall be peace.
Isa. 32:17

Bread shall be given him; his waters shall be sure.
(him: the righteous)
Isa. 33:16

In righteousness shalt thou be established.
Isa. 54:14

Though these three men, Noah, Daniel, and Job, were in it, they should deliver but their own souls by their righteousness.
Ezek. 14:14

He is just, he shall surely live, saith the Lord God.
Ezek. 18:9

The righteousness of the righteous shall not deliver him in the day of his transgression.
Ezek. 33:12

O Lord, righteousness belongeth unto Thee.
Dan. 9:7

Sow to yourselves in righteousness, reap in mercy.
Hos. 10:12

Do justly.
Mic. 6:8

The just shall live by his faith.
Hab. 2:4
See also, e.g., Rom. 1:17

[*See also* Evil, Goodness, Integrity, Justice, Self-Righteousness, Sin, Virtue, Wickedness]

RISK

Is not this the blood of the men that went in jeopardy of their lives?
2 Sam. 23:17

With the jeopardy of their lives they brought it.
1 Chron. 11:19

RITUALS

Hath the Lord as great delight in burnt offerings and sacrifices, as in obeying the voice of the Lord?
1 Sam. 15:22

To do justice and judgment is more acceptable to the Lord than sacrifice.
Prov. 21:3

To what purpose is the multitude of your sacrifices unto Me?
Isa. 1:11

Bring no more vain oblations.
Isa. 1:13

I desired mercy, and not sacrifice; and the knowledge of God more than burnt offerings.
Hos. 6:6
See also Matt. 9:13

[*See also* Circumcision, Sacrifices]

ROBBERY

Thou shalt not steal.
Eighth Commandment
Ex. 20:15
See also Lev. 19:11, Deut. 5:19,
Matt. 19:18

If the thief be found, let him pay double.
Ex. 22:7

Rob not the poor, because he is poor: neither oppress the afflicted in the gate.
Prov. 22:22

[*See also* Crime, Criminals]

ROMANCE

The way of an eagle in the air; the way of a serpent upon a rock; the way of a ship in the midst of the sea; and the way of a man with a maid.
Prov. 30:19

Let him kiss me with the kisses of his mouth: for thy love is better than wine.
Song 1:2

Rise up, my love, my fair one, and come away.
Song 2:10

I am my beloved's, and his desire is toward me.
Song 7:10

Set me as a seal upon thine heart, as a seal upon thine arm.
Song 8:6

[*See also* Love]

SABBATH

And God blessed the seventh day, and sanctified it: because that in it He had rested from all His work which God created and made.
Gen. 2:3

Remember the sabbath day, to keep it holy.
Fourth Commandment
Ex. 20:8

Six days shalt thou labour, and do all thy work: But the seventh day is the sabbath of the Lord thy God: in it thou shalt not do any work.
Ex. 20:9–10
See also Ex. 35:2, Deut. 5:13–14

Six days thou shalt do thy work, and on the seventh day thou shalt rest.
Ex. 23:12
See also Ex. 34:21, Ex. 35:2

My sabbaths ye shall keep: for it is a sign between Me and you throughout your generations.
Ex. 31:13

Every one that defileth it shall surely be put to death.
Ex. 31:14

In six days the Lord made heaven and

earth, and on the seventh day He rested, and was refreshed.
Ex. 31:17

Keep the sabbath day to sanctify it.
Deut. 5:12

Hallow My sabbaths; and they shall be a sign between Me and you, that ye may know that I am the Lord your God.
Ezek. 20:20

SACRIFICE

See Martyrdom.

SACRIFICES

Behold the fire and the wood: but where is the lamb for a burnt offering?
Isaac to Abraham
Gen. 22:7

He that sacrificeth unto any god, save unto the Lord only, he shall be utterly destroyed.
Ex. 22:20

If thou wilt offer a burnt offering, thou must offer it unto the Lord.
Judg. 13:16

To obey is better than sacrifice, and to hearken than the fat of rams.
1 Sam. 15:22

I desired mercy, and not sacrifice; and the knowledge of God more than burnt offerings.
Hos. 6:6
See also Matt. 9:13

[*See also* Rituals]

SACRILEGE

Thou shalt not bring the hire of a whore, or the price of a dog, into the house of the Lord.
Deut. 23:18

Why wilt thou swallow up the inheritance of the Lord?
2 Sam. 20:19

Let her not be slain in the house of the Lord.
2 Kings 11:15
See also 2 Chron. 23:14

Uzza put forth his hand to hold the ark; for the oxen stumbled. And the anger of the Lord was kindled against Uzza, and He smote him.
1 Chron. 13:9–10
See also 2 Sam. 6:6–7

I will curse your blessings.
God to wayward priests
Mal. 2:2

[*See also* Holiness]

SAFETY

The beloved of the Lord shall dwell in safety by Him.
Deut. 33:12

The eternal God is thy refuge.
Deut. 33:27

There shall not one hair of thy son fall to the earth.
2 Sam. 14:11

Thou hast enlarged my steps under me; so that my feet did not slip.
2 Sam. 22:37

The Lord also will be a refuge for the oppressed, a refuge in times of trouble.
Ps. 9:9

Deliver me not over unto the will of mine enemies: for false witnesses are risen up against me.
Ps. 27:12

God is our refuge and strength, a very present help in trouble.
Ps. 46:1

In the shadow of Thy wings will I make my refuge.
Ps. 57:1

Lead me to the rock that is higher than I.
Ps. 61:2

My God is the rock of my refuge.
Ps. 94:22

The Lord is on my side; I will not fear.
Ps. 118:6
See also Heb. 13:6

Hold Thou me up, and I shall be safe.
Ps. 119:117

The Lord shall preserve thee from all evil:
He shall preserve thy soul.
   Ps. 121:7

Set up the standard toward Zion.
   Jer. 4:6

They shall dwell with confidence, when I
have executed judgments upon all those
that despise them.
   Ezek. 28:26

The ways of the Lord are right, and the
just shall walk in them: but the transgressors shall fall therein.
   Hos. 14:9

Seek righteousness, seek meekness: it may
be ye shall be hid in the day of the Lord's
anger.
   Zeph. 2:3

[*See also* God's Protection, God's Support, Peace, Sanctuary, Security]

SALUTATIONS

The Lord be with you.
   Ruth 2:4

The Lord bless thee.
   Ruth 2:4

[*See also* Blessings]

SALVATION

I have waited for Thy salvation, O Lord.
   Jacob
   Gen. 49:18

The Lord is my strength and song, and He
is become my salvation.
   Ex. 15:2

He is my shield, and the horn of my
salvation, my high tower, and my refuge.
   David
   2 Sam. 22:3

Salvation belongeth unto the Lord.
   Ps. 3:8

Save me for Thy mercies' sake.
   E.g., Ps. 6:4

He that walketh uprightly, and worketh

righteousness, and speaketh the truth in
his heart.
   Ps. 15:2

The salvation of the righteous is of the
Lord: He is their strength in the time of
trouble.
   Ps. 37:39

My soul waiteth upon God: from Him
cometh my salvation.
   Ps. 62:1

In God is my salvation and my glory.
   Ps. 62:7

Cause Thy face to shine; and we shall be
saved.
   Ps. 80:3, 7, 19

Salvation is far from the wicked: for they
seek not Thy statutes.
   Ps. 119:155

They that dwell in the land of the shadow
of death, upon them hath the light shined.
   Isa. 9:2

To whom will ye flee for help? and where
will ye leave your glory?
   Isa. 10:3

God is my salvation; I will trust, and not
be afraid.
   Isa. 12:2

With joy shall ye draw water out of the
wells of salvation.
   Isa. 12:3

My salvation shall be for ever, and My
righteousness shall not be abolished.
   Isa. 51:6

In vain is salvation hoped for from the
hills, and from the multitude of mountains.
   Jer. 3:23

Heal me, O Lord, and I shall be healed;
save me, and I shall be saved.
   Jer. 17:14

Flee out of the midst of Babylon, and
deliver every man his soul.
   Jer. 51:6

It is good that a man should both hope
and quietly wait for the salvation of the
Lord.
   Lam. 3:26

If thou warn the wicked, and he turn not

from his wickedness, nor from his wicked way, he shall die in his iniquity; but thou hast delivered thy soul.
Ezek. 3:19, 21

Salvation is of the Lord.
Jonah 2:9

I will rejoice in the Lord, I will joy in the God of my salvation.
Hab. 3:18

The Lord thy God in the midst of thee is mighty; He will save, He will rejoice over thee with joy.
Zeph. 3:17

Unto you that fear My name shall the Sun of righteousness arise with healing in his wings.
Mal. 4:2

[*See also* Deliverance, Eternal Life, Redemption]

SANCTUARY

And they shall be your refuge from the avenger of blood.
(they: cities of refuge)
Josh. 20:3

They shall not deliver the slayer up into his hand; because he smote his neighbour unwittingly, and hated him not beforetime.
Josh. 20:5

Let her not be slain in the house of the Lord.
2 Kings 11:15
See also 2 Chron. 23:14

SARCASM

See Mockery.

SATISFACTION

And God saw the light, that it was good.
Gen. 1:4

And God saw every thing that He had made, and, behold, it was very good.
Gen. 1:31

Glory of this, and tarry at home.
2 Kings 14:10

A good man shall be satisfied from himself.
Prov. 14:14

Hell and destruction are never full; so the eyes of man are never satisfied.
Prov. 27:20

The horseleach hath two daughters, crying, Give, give.
Prov. 30:15

There are three things that are never satisfied, yea, four things say not, It is enough: The grave; and the barren womb; the earth that is not filled with water; and the fire that saith not, It is enough.
Prov. 30:15–16

There is nothing better, than that a man should rejoice in his own works.
Eccl. 3:22

All the labour of man is for his mouth, and yet the appetite is not filled.
Eccl. 6:7

Better is the sight of the eyes than the wandering of the desire.
Eccl. 6:9

[*See also* Complaints, Contentment, Greed, Happiness, Serenity]

SCAPEGOAT

One lot for the Lord, and the other lot for the scapegoat.
Lev. 16:8

Let him go for a scapegoat into the wilderness.
Lev. 16:10

The goat shall bear upon him all their iniquities.
Lev. 16:22

[*See also* Blame]

Let the wicked fall into their own nets.
Ps. 141:10

The way of the wicked He turneth upside down.
Ps. 146:9

The wicked shall fall by his own wickedness.
Prov. 11:5

Whoso diggeth a pit shall fall therein.
Prov. 26:27

Let none of you imagine evil in your hearts against his neighbour.
Zech. 8:17
See also Zech. 7:10

[*See also* Instigation, Strategy, Traps]

SCORN

The daughter of Zion hath despised thee, and laughed thee to scorn; the daughter of Jerusalem hath shaken her head at thee.
2 Kings 19:21, Isa. 37:22

Hear, O our God; for we are despised.
Neh. 4:4

When thou mockest, shall no man make thee ashamed?
Job 11:3

Young children despised me; I arose, and they spake against me.
Job 19:18

He addeth rebellion unto his sin.
Job 34:37

Wherefore should the heathen say, Where is their God?
Ps. 79:10
See also, e.g., Ps. 115:2

The stone which the builders refused is become the head stone of the corner.
Ps. 118:22
See also, e.g., Mark 12:10

I am small and despised: yet do not I forget Thy precepts.
Ps. 119:141

All that honoured her despise her, because they have seen her nakedness.
Lam. 1:8

Nineveh is laid waste: who will bemoan her?
Nah. 3:7

Ye have wearied the Lord with your words.
Mal. 2:17

[*See also* Contempt, Criticism, Mockery]

SCRIPTURE

Ye shall not add unto the word which I command you, neither shall ye diminish ought from it.
Deut. 4:2

Man doth not live by bread only, but by every word that proceedeth out of the mouth of the Lord.
Deut. 8:3
See also, e.g., Matt. 4:4

This book of the law shall not depart out of thy mouth.
Josh. 1:8

Thou shalt meditate therein day and night.
Josh. 1:8

Observe to do according to all that is written therein.
Josh. 1:8

Turn not aside therefrom to the right hand or to the left.
Josh. 23:6

Great is the wrath of the Lord that is kindled against us, because our fathers have not hearkened unto the words of this book.
2 Kings 22:13

His delight is in the law of the Lord; and in His law doth he meditate day and night.
Ps. 1:2

The Lord gave the word: great was the company of those that published it.
Ps. 68:11

How sweet are Thy words unto my taste! yea, sweeter than honey to my mouth!
Ps. 119:103

Thy word is a lamp unto my feet, and a light unto my path.
Ps. 119:105

Thy word is true from the beginning.
Ps. 119:160

Add thou not unto His words.
Prov. 30:6

Seek ye out of the book of the Lord, and read.
Isa. 34:16

Hear ye the word of the Lord.
Jer. 21:11

The law shall go forth of Zion, and the word of the Lord from Jerusalem.
Mic. 4:2

[*See also* Commandments, God's Word, Prophecy]

SEARCHING

Thou shalt find Him, if thou seek Him with all thy heart and with all thy soul.
Deut. 4:29

If thou seek Him, He will be found of thee.
1 Chron. 28:9
See also 2 Chron. 15:2

Canst thou by searching find out God?
Job 11:7

When Thou saidst, Seek ye My face; my heart said unto Thee, Thy face, Lord, will I seek.
Ps. 27:8

In the broad ways I will seek him whom my soul loveth.
Song 3:2

Seek ye the Lord while He may be found, call ye upon Him while He is near.
Isa. 55:6

I am sought of them that asked not for Me; I am found of them that sought Me not.
Isa. 65:1
See also Rom. 10:20

Ye shall seek Me, and find Me, when ye shall search for Me with all your heart.
Jer. 29:13

It is time to seek the Lord.
Hos. 10:12

Seek good, and not evil, that ye may live.
Amos 5:14

[*See also* Devotion]

SEAS

See Oceans.

SEASONS

While the earth remaineth, seedtime and harvest, and cold and heat, and summer and winter, and day and night shall not cease.
Gen. 8:22

By the breath of God frost is given.
Job 37:10

Who can stand before His cold?
Ps. 147:17

To every thing there is a season, and a time to every purpose under the heaven.
Eccl. 3:1

Lo, the winter is past, the rain is over and gone.
Song 2:11

The flowers appear on the earth; the time of the singing of birds is come, and the voice of the turtle is heard in our land.
Song 2:12

The harvest is past, the summer is ended, and we are not saved.
Jer. 8:20

[*See also* Nature and the Appendix at p. 274]

SECRECY

Be sure your sin will find you out.
Num. 32:23

The secret things belong unto the Lord our God: but those things which are re-

vealed belong unto us and to our children for ever.
Deut. 29:29

Our life for your's, if ye utter not this our business.
Josh. 2:14

If thou utter this our business, then we will be quit of thine oath.
Josh. 2:20

Behold, I have not told it my father nor my mother, and shall I tell it thee?
Samson to his wife
Judg. 14:16

Entice him, and see wherein his great strength lieth.
Philistines to Delilah
Judg. 16:5

The Lord searcheth all hearts.
1 Chron. 28:9

No thought can be withholden from Thee.
Job 42:2

Pour out your heart before Him: God is a refuge for us.
Ps. 62:8

My sins are not hid from Thee.
Ps. 69:5

He that teacheth man knowledge, shall not He know?
Ps. 94:10

A talebearer revealeth secrets: but he that is of a faithful spirit concealeth the matter.
Prov. 11:13

The eyes of the Lord are in every place, beholding the evil and the good.
Prov. 15:3

Discover not a secret to another.
Prov. 25:9

A bird of the air shall carry the voice, and that which hath wings shall tell the matter.
Eccl. 10:20

Woe unto them that seek deep to hide their counsel from the Lord.
Isa. 29:15

Speak, I pray thee, unto thy servants in the Syrian language.
Isa. 36:11
See also 2 Kings 18:26

Can any hide himself in secret places that I shall not see him? saith the Lord. Do not I fill heaven and earth?
Jer. 23:24

Let no man know of these words, and thou shalt not die.
Jer. 38:24

Shut thou up the vision; for it shall be for many days.
Dan. 8:26

[*See also* Exposure, God's Knowledge, Mystery]

SECURITY

Against any of the children of Israel shall not a dog move his tongue.
Ex. 11:7

As thy days, so shall thy strength be.
Deut. 33:25

They were a wall unto us both by night and day, all the while we were with them keeping the sheep.
1 Sam. 25:16

The Lord is our defence.
Ps. 89:18

They that trust in the Lord shall be as mount Zion, which cannot be removed.
Ps. 125:1

Except the Lord keep the city, the watchman waketh but in vain.
Ps. 127:1

As arrows are in the hand of a mighty man; so are children of the youth.
Ps. 127:4

Whoso putteth his trust in the Lord shall be safe.
Prov. 29:25

Bread shall be given him; his waters shall be sure.
(him: the righteous)
Isa. 33:16

[*See also* God's Protection, God's Support, Safety]

SEDUCTION

See Temptation.

SELF-AWARENESS

Let us search and try our ways, and turn again to the Lord.
Lam. 3:40

SELF-CONFIDENCE

See Confidence.

SELF-CONTROL

Take ye therefore good heed unto yourselves.
Deut. 4:15

Set a watch, O Lord, before my mouth; keep the door of my lips.
Ps. 141:3

He that hath no rule over his own spirit is like a city that is broken down.
Prov. 25:28

[*See also* Anger, Temper, Temptation]

SELF-DECEPTION

Knowest thou not yet that Egypt is destroyed?
Pharaoh's servants to Pharaoh
Ex. 10:7

There is a way which seemeth right unto a man, but the end thereof are the ways of death.
Prov. 14:12, Prov. 16:25

We have made lies our refuge, and under falsehood have we hid ourselves.
Isa. 28:15

They are drunken, but not with wine; they stagger, but not with strong drink.
Isa. 29:9

Deceive not yourselves.
Jer. 37:9

Thy terribleness hath deceived thee, and the pride of thine heart.
Jer. 49:16

[*See also* Deception, Misjudgment]

SELF-DENIAL

As thou livest, and as thy soul liveth, I will not do this thing.
Uriah to David
2 Sam. 11:11

Be it far from me, O Lord, that I should do this.
2 Sam. 23:17

[*See also* Denial, Self-Control, Temptation]

SELF-HATRED

I abhor myself, and repent in dust and ashes.
Job 42:6

Whoso is partner with a thief hateth his own soul.
Prov. 29:24

Ye shall lothe yourselves in your own sight for all your evils that ye have committed.
Ezek. 20:43

SELF-INCRIMINATION

The man that hath done this thing shall surely die.
David to Nathan
2 Sam. 12:5

Thine own lips testify against thee.
Job 15:6
See also 2 Sam. 1:16

[*See also* Guilt]

SELF-INTEREST

Doth Job fear God for nought?
Satan to God
Job 1:9

Hast not Thou made an hedge about him, and about his house?
Satan to God, of Job
Job 1:10

Skin for skin, yea, all that a man hath will he give for his life.
Satan to God
Job 2:4

I wrought for My name's sake, that it should not be polluted before the heathen.
Ezek. 20:9, 14

[*See also* Motivation, Selfishness, Selflessness]

SELF-PITY

Kill me, I pray thee, out of hand, if I have found favour in Thy sight; and let me not see my wretchedness.
Moses to God
Num. 11:15

I have no son to keep my name in remembrance.
2 Sam. 18:18

I should have been as though I had not been; I should have been carried from the womb to the grave.
Job 10:19

The just upright man is laughed to scorn.
Job 12:4

My kinsfolk have failed, and my familiar friends have forgotten me.
Job 19:14

Mark me, and be astonished.
Job 21:5

I am a brother to dragons, and a companion to owls.
Job 30:29

What man is like Job, who drinketh up scorning like water?
Job 34:7

I am a worm, and no man; a reproach of men, and despised of the people.
Ps. 22:6

Woe is me now! for the Lord hath added grief to my sorrow.
Jer. 45:3

[*See also* Depression, Despair]

SELF-RIGHTEOUSNESS

He was righteous in his own eyes.
(He: Job)
Job 32:1

Wilt thou condemn Me, that thou mayest be righteous?
Job 40:8

All the ways of a man are clean in his own eyes; but the Lord weigheth the spirits.
Prov. 16:2

Be not righteous over much; neither make thyself over wise.
Eccl. 7:16

I am holier than thou.
Isa. 65:5

[*See also* Conceit]

SELF-SUFFICIENCY

See Cooperation.

SELFISHNESS

Let it be neither mine nor thine, but divide it.
1 Kings 3:26

Is it not good, if peace and truth be in my days?
2 Kings 20:19

He that withholdeth corn, the people shall curse him: but blessing shall be upon the head of him that selleth it.
Prov. 11:26

Whoso stoppeth his ears at the cry of the poor, he also shall cry himself, but shall not be heard.
Prov. 21:13

They judge not the cause, the cause of the fatherless, yet they prosper.
Jer. 5:28

[*See also* Altruism, Greed, Poverty, Underprivileged]

SELFLESSNESS

Would God that all the Lord's people were prophets, and that the Lord would put His spirit upon them!
Moses to Joshua
Num. 11:29

Thou shalt be king over Israel, and I shall be next unto thee.
Jonathan to David
1 Sam. 23:17

Shall I drink the blood of these men that have put their lives in jeopardy?
David
1 Chron. 11:19

[*See also* Altruism, Charity, Generosity, Self-Interest, Selfishness]

SEPARATION

The Lord do so to me, and more also, if ought but death part thee and me.
Ruth 1:17

In their death they were not divided.
(they: Saul and Jonathan)
2 Sam. 1:23

SERENITY

Now let me die, since I have seen thy face, because thou art yet alive.
Jacob to Joseph
Gen. 46:30

The Lord bless thee, and keep thee: The Lord make His face shine upon thee, and be gracious unto thee: The Lord lift up His countenance upon thee, and give thee peace.
Num. 6:24–26

How goodly are thy tents, O Jacob, and thy tabernacles, O Israel!
Num. 24:5

The Lord is my shepherd; I shall not want.
Ps. 23:1

Great peace have they which love Thy law.
Ps. 119:165

Better is a dry morsel, and quietness therewith, than an house full of sacrifices with strife.
Prov. 17:1

There is no peace, saith the Lord, unto the wicked.
Isa. 48:22
See also Ps. 57:21

[*See also* Contentment, Peace, Satisfaction]

SERVANTS

See Employees, Freedom, Slavery, Work.

SERVICE

See Altruism, Charity, Ministry.

SERVICE TO GOD

Serve the Lord thy God with all thy heart and with all thy soul.
Deut. 10:12
See also, e.g., Josh. 22:5

Serve ye the Lord.
Josh. 24:14

Deliver us out of the hand of our enemies, and we will serve Thee.
1 Sam. 12:10

Let it be known this day that Thou art God in Israel, and that I am Thy servant.
Elijah
1 Kings 18:36

Serve Him with a perfect heart and with a willing mind.
1 Chron. 28:9

Minister unto Him.
2 Chron. 29:11

Serve the Lord your God, that the fierceness of His wrath may turn away from you.
2 Chron. 30:8

Make a joyful noise unto the Lord.
Ps. 100:1

Serve the Lord with gladness: come before His presence with singing.
Ps. 100:2

[*See also* Devotion, Ministry]

SEVERITY

My punishment is greater than I can bear.
> *Cain to God*
> *Gen. 4:13*

My little finger shall be thicker than my father's loins.
> *1 Kings 12:10, 2 Chron. 10:10*

Thou hast broken the yokes of wood; but thou shalt make for them yokes of iron.
> *Jer. 28:13*

[*See also* Cruelty, Oppression]

SEX

See Adultery, Homosexuality, Immorality, Incest, Lust, Prostitution.

SHAME

If her father had but spit in her face, should she not be ashamed seven days?
> *Num. 12:14*

Thou shalt become an astonishment, a proverb, and a byword, among all nations.
> *Deut. 28:37*
> *See also 1 Kings 9:7*

Why abodest thou among the sheepfolds, to hear the bleatings of the flocks?
> *Judg. 5:16*

Tell it not in Gath, publish it not in the streets of Askelon.
> *2 Sam. 1:20*

Tarry at Jericho until your beards be grown.
> *2 Sam. 10:5, 1 Chron. 19:5*

Thy carcase shall not come unto the sepulchre of thy fathers.
> *1 Kings 13:22*

The dogs shall eat Jezebel.
> *2 Kings 9:10*

There shall be none to bury her.
> *(her: Jezebel)*
> *2 Kings 9:10*

Our iniquities are increased over our head, and our trespass is grown up unto the heavens.
> *Ezra 9:6*

Let me not be ashamed, let not mine enemies triumph over me.
> *Ps. 25:2*

Wherefore should the heathen say, Where is their God?
> *Ps. 79:10*
> *See also, e.g., Ps. 115:2*

When pride cometh, then cometh shame.
> *Prov. 11:2*

Thou shalt heap coals of fire upon his head.
> *Prov. 25:22*
> *See also Rom. 12:20*

They declare their sin as Sodom, they hide it not.
> *Isa. 3:9*

Thou hadst a whore's forehead, thou refusedst to be ashamed.
> *Jer. 3:3*

All that forsake Thee shall be ashamed.
> *Jer. 17:13*

Remember, O Lord, what is come upon us: consider, and behold our reproach.
> *Lam. 5:1*

The crown is fallen from our head: woe unto us, that we have sinned!
> *Lam. 5:16*

Thou shalt remember thy ways, and be ashamed.
> *Ezek. 16:61*

The unjust knoweth no shame.
> *Zeph. 3:5*

[*See also* Humiliation, Nakedness]

SHAMELESSNESS

See Audacity.

SHARING

What goodness the Lord shall do unto us, the same will we do unto thee.
> *Num. 10:32*

Divide the spoil of your enemies with your brethren.
Joshua
Josh. 22:8

[*See also* Charity, Cooperation, Generosity, Selfishness, Underprivileged]

SIBLINGS

Am I my brother's keeper?
Cain
Gen. 4:9

The voice of thy brother's blood crieth unto Me from the ground.
Gen. 4:10

The elder shall serve the younger.
Gen. 25:23, Rom. 9:12

He sold his birthright unto Jacob.
(He: Esau)
Gen. 25:33

The voice is Jacob's voice, but the hands are the hands of Esau.
Isaac
Gen. 27:22

They hated him yet the more for his dreams, and for his words.
(They: Joseph's brothers)
Gen. 37:8

Behold, this dreamer cometh.
(dreamer: Joseph)
Gen. 37:19

Let not our hand be upon him; for he is our brother and our flesh.
Judah to his brothers
Gen. 37:27

His younger brother shall be greater than he.
Gen. 48:19

A friend loveth at all times, and a brother is born for adversity.
Prov. 17:17

A brother offended is harder to be won than a strong city.
Prov. 18:19

Was not Esau Jacob's brother? saith the Lord: yet I loved Jacob.
Mal. 1:2
See also Rom. 9:13

SICKNESS

See Healing.

SIGHT

Thou seest the shadow of the mountains as if they were men.
Judg. 9:36

Lord, I pray Thee, open his eyes, that he may see.
2 Kings 6:17

Hast Thou eyes of flesh? or seest Thou as man seest?
Job 10:4

Better is the sight of the eyes than the wandering of the desire.
Eccl. 6:9

Mine eye affecteth mine heart.
Lam. 3:51

[*See also* Blindness]

SILENCE

As people being ashamed steal away when they flee in battle.
2 Sam. 19:3

If I hold my tongue, I shall give up the ghost.
Job 13:19

Hold thy peace, and I shall teach thee wisdom.
Job 33:33

He that refraineth his lips is wise.
Prov. 10:19

Even a fool, when he holdeth his peace, is counted wise.
Prov. 17:28

A time to keep silence, and a time to speak.
Eccl. 3:7

He was oppressed, and he was afflicted, yet he opened not his mouth.
Isa. 53:7

The prudent shall keep silence in that time; for it is an evil time.
Amos 5:13

[*See also* Speech, Verbosity]

SIN

She took of the fruit thereof, and did eat.
(She: Eve)
Gen. 3:6

Who told thee that thou wast naked?
Gen. 3:11

If thou doest not well, sin lieth at the door.
Gen. 4:7

Be sure your sin will find you out.
Num. 32:23

And the children of Israel did evil again in the sight of the Lord.
E.g., Judg. 3:12

It is no good report that I hear.
1 Sam. 2:24

If one man sin against another, the judge shall judge him: but if a man sin against the Lord, who shall intreat for him?
1 Sam. 2:25

We have sinned, because we have forsaken the Lord.
1 Sam. 12:10

Though it be in Jonathan my son, he shall surely die.
Saul
1 Sam. 14:39

There is no man that sinneth not.
1 Kings 8:46, 2 Chron. 6:36

He walked in all the sins of his father.
E.g., 1 Kings 15:3

Every man shall be put to death for his own sin.
E.g., 2 Kings 14:6

They have done that which was evil in My sight, and have provoked Me to anger, since the day their fathers came forth out of Egypt.
2 Kings 21:15

He did that which was evil in the sight of the Lord his God.
E.g., 2 Chron. 36:12

If iniquity be in thine hand, put it far away.
Job 11:14

Who can bring a clean thing out of an unclean? not one.
Job 14:4

How can he be clean that is born of a woman?
Job 25:4

If thou sinnest, what doest thou against Him?
Job 35:6

There is none that doeth good, no, not one.
Ps. 14:3, Ps. 53:3, Rom. 3:12

Remember not the sins of my youth.
Ps. 25:7

They are more than the hairs of mine head.
Ps. 40:12

In sin did my mother conceive me.
Ps. 51:5

If Thou, Lord, shouldest mark iniquities, O Lord, who shall stand?
Ps. 130:3

Stolen waters are sweet, and bread eaten in secret is pleasant.
Prov. 9:17

The labour of the righteous tendeth to life: the fruit of the wicked to sin.
Prov. 10:16

Fools make a mock at sin.
Prov. 14:9

Righteousness exalteth a nation: but sin is a reproach to any people.
Prov. 14:34

Suffer not thy mouth to cause thy flesh to sin.
Eccl. 5:6

There is not a just man upon earth, that doeth good, and sinneth not.
Eccl. 7:20

He was wounded for our transgressions, he was bruised for our iniquities.
Isa. 53:5

All we like sheep have gone astray.
Isa. 53:6

The Lord hath laid on him the iniquity of us all.
Isa. 53:6

Your sins have hid His face from you, that He will not hear.
Isa. 59:2

Our sins testify against us.
Isa. 59:12

O Lord, why hast Thou made us to err from Thy ways, and hardened our heart from Thy fear?
Isa. 63:17

Though thou wash thee with nitre, and take thee much soap, yet thine iniquity is marked before Me.
Jer. 2:22

The soul that sinneth, it shall die.
Ezek. 18:4, 20

The son shall not bear the iniquity of the father, neither shall the father bear the iniquity of the son.
Ezek. 18:20
See also, e.g., Deut. 24:16

The righteousness of the righteous shall not deliver him in the day of his transgression.
Ezek. 33:12

Because they trespassed against Me, therefore hid I My face from them.
Ezek. 39:23

[*See also* Adultery, Behavior, Confession, Decadence, Depravity, Disobedience, Evil, Forgiveness, Godlessness, Immorality, Prostitution, Punishment, Repentance, Righteousness, Sinners, Wickedness]

SINCERITY

Thou shalt find Him, if thou seek Him with all thy heart and with all thy soul.
Deut. 4:29

What hast thou to do with peace? turn thee behind me.
2 Kings 9:18, 19

If thou seek Him, He will be found of thee.
1 Chron. 28:9
See also 2 Chron. 15:2

With flattering lips and with a double heart do they speak.
Ps. 12:2

Bring no more vain oblations.
Isa. 1:13

Ye shall seek Me, and find Me, when ye shall search for Me with all your heart.
Jer. 29:13

I desired mercy, and not sacrifice; and the knowledge of God more than burnt offerings.
Hos. 6:6
See also Matt. 9:13

Rend your heart, and not your garments, and turn unto the Lord.
Joel 2:13

[*See also* Devotion, Hypocrisy, Rituals]

SINNERS

Whosoever hath sinned against Me, him will I blot out of My book.
Ex. 32:33

They are a perverse and crooked generation.
Deut. 32:5

The light of the wicked shall be put out, and the spark of his fire shall not shine.
Job 18:5

Drought and heat consume the snow waters: so doth the grave those which have sinned.
Job 24:19

The Lord knoweth the way of the righteous: but the way of the ungodly shall perish.
Ps. 1:6

Blessed is he whose transgression is forgiven.
Ps. 32:1

Let the sinners be consumed out of the earth, and let the wicked be no more.
Ps. 104:35

Let me not eat of their dainties.
Ps. 141:4

The way of transgressors is hard.
Prov. 13:15

Evil pursueth sinners.
Prov. 13:21

Let not thine heart envy sinners.
Prov. 23:17

To the sinner He giveth travail, to gather and to heap up.
Eccl. 2:26

Though a sinner do evil an hundred times, and his days be prolonged, yet surely I know that it shall be well with them that fear God.
Eccl. 8:12

Woe unto them that draw iniquity with cords of vanity, and sin as it were with a cart rope.
Isa. 5:18

He shall destroy the sinners.
Isa. 13:9

I will not pity, nor spare, nor have mercy, but destroy them.
Jer. 13:14

He that fleeth of them shall not flee away, and he that escapeth of them shall not be delivered.
Amos 9:1

Though they dig into hell, thence shall Mine hand take them; though they climb up to heaven, thence will I bring them down.
Amos 9:2

Their blood shall be poured out as dust, and their flesh as the dung.
Zeph. 1:17

[*See also* Sin, Wicked People]

SIZE

There were giants in the earth in those days.
Gen. 6:4

We were in our own sight as grasshoppers.
Num. 13:33

The ants are a people not strong, yet they prepare their meat in the summer.
Prov. 30:25

[*See also* Abundance, Growth, Quantity]

SKEPTICISM

Shall a child be born unto him that is an hundred years old? and shall Sarah, that is ninety years old, bear?
Gen. 17:17

Hear now, ye rebels; must we fetch you water out of this rock?
Num. 20:10

The God that answereth by fire, let Him be God.
1 Kings 18:24

Nay, my lord, thou man of God, do not lie unto thine handmaid.
2 Kings 4:16

If the prophet had bid thee do some great thing, wouldest thou not have done it?
2 Kings 5:13

If the Lord would make windows in heaven, might this thing be?
2 Kings 7:2
See also 2 Kings 7:19

Thou shalt see it with thine eyes, but shalt not eat thereof.
2 Kings 7:2

I believed not their words, until I came, and mine eyes had seen it.
Queen of Sheba to Solomon
2 Chron. 9:6
See also 1 Kings 10:7

I will work a work in your days, which ye will not believe, though it be told you.
Hab. 1:5
See also Acts 13:41

[*See also* Belief, Doubt, Faith, Possibility]

See Ability, Chance.

SLANDER

Thy tongue deviseth mischiefs; like a sharp razor, working deceitfully.
Ps. 52:2

Swords are in their lips.
Ps. 59:7

Deliver my soul, O Lord, from lying lips, and from a deceitful tongue.
Ps. 120:2

They have sharpened their tongues like a serpent; adders' poison is under their lips.
Ps. 140:3
See also Rom. 3:13

He that hideth hatred with lying lips, and he that uttereth a slander, is a fool.
Prov. 10:18

An hypocrite with his mouth destroyeth his neighbour.
Prov. 11:9

[*See also* Gossip, Lies, Speech]

SLAVERY

I am the Lord thy God, which have brought thee out of the land of Egypt, out of the house of bondage.
Ex. 20:2
See also, e.g., Ex. 29:46, Deut. 5:6

Remember that thou wast a bondman in the land of Egypt, and the Lord thy God redeemed thee.
Deut. 15:15
See also Deut. 5:15, Deut. 24:22

Thou shalt not deliver unto his master the servant which is escaped from his master unto thee.
Deut. 23:15

Will ye even sell your brethren?
Neh. 5:8

[*See also* Captivity, Freedom]

All the night make I my bed to swim; I water my couch with my tears.
Ps. 6:6

He that keepeth Israel shall neither slumber nor sleep.
Ps. 121:4

I will not give sleep to mine eyes, or slumber to mine eyelids, Until I find out a place for the Lord.
Ps. 132:4–5

Yet a little sleep, a little slumber, a little folding of the hands to sleep: So shall thy poverty come.
Prov. 6:10–11

Love not sleep, lest thou come to poverty.
Prov. 20:13

Drowsiness shall clothe a man with rags.
Prov. 23:21

The sleep of a labouring man is sweet.
Eccl. 5:12

The abundance of the rich will not suffer him to sleep.
Eccl. 5:12

SLOTH

See Laziness.

SNAKES

Now the serpent was more subtil than any beast of the field.
Gen. 3:1

Thou art cursed above all cattle, and above every beast of the field.
Gen. 3:14

Upon thy belly shalt thou go, and dust shalt thou eat all the days of thy life.
God to serpent
Gen. 3:14

[*See also* Temptation]

See Conceit.

Sodom and Gomorrah.
Gen. 18:20, Gen. 19:28

Whosoever lieth with a beast shall surely be put to death.
Ex. 22:19

Cursed be he that lieth with any manner of beast.
Deut. 27:21

[*See also* Homosexuality]

See Peace, War, War and Peace, Weapons.

Hear, O ye kings; give ear, O ye princes; I, even I, will sing unto the Lord.
Judg. 5:3

Awake, awake, utter a song.
Judg. 5:12

With my song will I praise Him.
Ps. 28:7

Shout unto God with the voice of triumph.
Ps. 47:1

Make a joyful noise unto God, all ye lands: Sing forth the honour of His name.
Ps. 66:1–2

Sing unto God, ye kingdoms of the earth; O sing praises unto the Lord.
Ps. 68:32

O come, let us sing unto the Lord: let us make a joyful noise to the rock of our salvation.
Ps. 95:1

Sing unto the Lord, all the earth.
Ps. 96:1, 1 Chron. 16:23

Make a joyful noise unto the Lord, all the earth: make a loud noise, and rejoice, and sing praise.
Ps. 98:4
See also Ps. 100:1

Make a joyful noise unto the Lord.
Ps. 100:1

Serve the Lord with gladness: come before His presence with singing.
Ps. 100:2

I will sing unto the Lord as long as I live: I will sing praise to my God while I have my being.
Ps. 104:33

Sing unto Him, sing psalms unto Him: talk ye of all His wondrous works.
Ps. 105:2, 1 Chron. 16:9

Sing praises unto His name; for it is pleasant.
Ps. 135:3

How shall we sing the Lord's song in a strange land?
Ps. 137:4

Sing unto the Lord with thanksgiving.
Ps. 147:7

Let them praise His name in the dance: let them sing praises unto Him with the timbrel and harp.
Ps. 149:3
See also Ps. 150:4

Sing unto the Lord; for He hath done excellent things.
Isa. 12:5

Make sweet melody, sing many songs, that thou mayest be remembered.
Isa. 23:16

Sing unto the Lord a new song, and His praise from the end of the earth.
Isa. 42:10

Sing unto the Lord, praise ye the Lord.
Jer. 20:13

[*See also* Music, Praise of God]

I am this day weak, though anointed king.
2 Sam. 3:39

This day is a day of trouble, and of rebuke, and blasphemy.
2 Kings 19:3, Isa. 37:3

It came to pass, when I heard these words, that I sat down and wept.
Neh. 1:4

By the rivers of Babylon, there we sat down, yea, we wept, when we remembered Zion.
Ps. 137:1

He healeth the broken in heart, and bindeth up their wounds.
Ps. 147:3

Even in laughter the heart is sorrowful.
Prov. 14:13

By sorrow of the heart the spirit is broken.
Prov. 15:13

He that increaseth knowledge increaseth sorrow.
Eccl. 1:18

A time to weep, and a time to laugh; a time to mourn, and a time to dance.
Eccl. 3:4

Sorrow is better than laughter: for by the sadness of the countenance the heart is made better.
Eccl. 7:3

The new wine mourneth, the vine languisheth, all the merry hearted do sigh.
Isa. 24:7

They shall not drink wine with a song.
Isa. 24:9

He is despised and rejected of men; a man of sorrows, and acquainted with grief.
Isa. 53:3

More are the children of the desolate than the children of the married wife, saith the Lord.
Isa. 54:1

For the mountains will I take up a weeping and wailing, and for the habitations of the wilderness a lamentation.
Jer. 9:10

Wherefore came I forth out of the womb to see labour and sorrow?
Jer. 20:18

Mine eye affecteth mine heart.
Lam. 3:51

[*See also* Anguish, Grief, Mourning, Tears]

SOUL

Thou wilt not leave my soul in hell; neither wilt Thou suffer Thine Holy One to see corruption.
Ps. 16:10

None can keep alive his own soul.
Ps. 22:29

He restoreth my soul.
Ps. 23:3

He satisfieth the longing soul, and filleth the hungry soul with goodness.
Ps. 107:9

He that winneth souls is wise.
Prov. 11:30

A true witness delivereth souls.
Prov. 14:25

He that keepeth the commandment keepeth his own soul; but he that despiseth His ways shall die.
Prov. 19:16

Behold, all souls are Mine.
Ezek. 18:4

SOVEREIGNTY

The Lord shall reign for ever and ever.
E.g., Ex. 15:18

Thine is the kingdom, O Lord, and Thou art exalted as head above all.
1 Chron. 29:11

Why dost thou strive against Him? for He giveth not account of any of His matters.
Job 33:13

The kingdom is the Lord's.
Ps. 22:28

The earth is the Lord's, and the fulness thereof.
Ps. 24:1, 1 Cor. 10:26

God is the King of all the earth: sing ye praises with understanding.
Ps. 47:7

Justice and judgment are the habitation of

Thy throne: mercy and truth shall go before Thy face.
Ps. 89:14

The Lord reigneth; let the earth rejoice.
Ps. 97:1

Righteousness and judgment are the habitation of His throne.
Ps. 97:2

Thou, O Lord, remainest for ever; Thy throne from generation to generation.
Lam. 5:19

The kingdom shall be the Lord's.
Obad. 21

[*See also* Authority, God's Power, Monarchy]

SPEECH

Who hath made man's mouth? or who maketh the dumb, or deaf, or the seeing, or the blind? have not I the Lord?
Ex. 4:11

He shall be to thee instead of a mouth, and thou shalt be to him instead of God.
God to Moses, about Aaron
Ex. 4:16

The word that God putteth in my mouth, that shall I speak.
Num. 22:38

Give ear, O ye heavens, and I will speak; and hear, O earth, the words of my mouth.
Deut. 32:1

Say now Shibboleth.
Judg. 12:6

What the Lord saith unto me, that will I speak.
1 Kings 22:14
See also 2 Chron. 18:13

How forcible are right words!
Job 6:25

Thy mouth uttereth thine iniquity.
Job 15:5

Thou choosest the tongue of the crafty.
Job 15:5

Who is this that darkeneth counsel by words without knowledge?
Job 38:2

Keep thy tongue from evil, and thy lips from speaking guile.
Ps. 34:13
See also 1 Pet. 3:10

My tongue is the pen of a ready writer.
Ps. 45:1

O Lord, open Thou my lips; and my mouth shall show forth Thy praise.
Ps. 51:15

Set a watch, O Lord, before my mouth; keep the door of my lips.
Ps. 141:3

In the multitude of words there wanteth not sin.
Prov. 10:19

The tongue of the just is as choice silver: the heart of the wicked is little worth.
Prov. 10:20

In all labour there is profit: but the talk of the lips tendeth only to penury.
Prov. 14:23

A soft answer turneth away wrath.
Prov. 15:1

A word spoken in due season, how good is it!
Prov. 15:23

Pleasant words are as an honeycomb, sweet to the soul, and health to the bones.
Prov. 16:24

He that hath a perverse tongue falleth into mischief.
Prov. 17:20

A fool's mouth is his destruction, and his lips are the snare of his soul.
Prov. 18:7

Be not rash with thy mouth.
Eccl. 5:2

Suffer not thy mouth to cause thy flesh to sin.
Eccl. 5:6

[*See also* Advice, Candor, Communication, Eloquence, Gossip, Lies, Persuasion, Preaching, Quotations, Silence, Slander, Verbosity]

Come down unto me, tarry not.
Gen. 45:9

They were swifter than eagles, they were stronger than lions.
2 Sam. 1:23

He did fly upon the wings of the wind.
Ps. 18:10

The race is not to the swift, nor the battle to the strong, neither yet bread to the wise, nor yet riches to men of understanding, nor yet favour to men of skill; but time and chance happeneth to them all.
Eccl. 9:11

He shall come up as clouds, and his chariots shall be as a whirlwind.
Jer. 4:13

Our persecutors are swifter than the eagles of the heaven.
Lam. 4:19

The flight shall perish from the swift.
Amos 2:14

He that is swift of foot shall not deliver himself: neither shall he that rideth the horse.
Amos 2:15

They shall fly as the eagle that hasteth to eat.
Hab. 1:8

[*See also* Urgency]

SPIES

Ye are spies; to see the nakedness of the land ye are come.
Joseph to his brothers
Gen. 42:9

[*See also* Betrayal, Treachery]

See Inspiration.

SPIRITUALISM

Regard not them that have familiar spirits, neither seek after wizards, to be defiled by them.
Lev. 19:31

All that do these things are an abomination unto the Lord.
Deut. 18:12

Bring me up Samuel.
1 Sam. 28:11

Why hast thou disquieted me, to bring me up?
Samuel to Saul
1 Sam. 28:15

SPIRITUALITY

Man doth not live by bread only, but by every word that proceedeth out of the mouth of the Lord.
Deut. 8:3
See also, e.g., Matt. 4:4

In Thy light shall we see light.
Ps. 36:9

Create in me a clean heart, O God; and renew a right spirit within me.
Ps. 51:10

There is that maketh himself rich, yet hath nothing: there is that maketh himself poor, yet hath great riches.
Prov. 13:7

Eat ye that which is good, and let your soul delight itself in fatness.
Isa. 55:2

[*See also* God's Presence, Light and Darkness, Materialism]

SPOILS OF WAR

There shall cleave nought of the cursed thing to thine hand.
Deut. 13:17

Keep yourselves from the accursed thing, lest ye make yourselves accursed.
Josh. 6:18

Divide the spoil of your enemies with your brethren.
Joshua
Josh. 22:8

Whomsoever the Lord our God shall drive out from before us, them will we possess.
Judg. 11:24

SPOKESMEN

He shall be to thee instead of a mouth, and thou shalt be to him instead of God.
God to Moses, about Aaron
Ex. 4:16

[*See also* Intercession, Reliability]

SPORTSMANSHIP

See Competition.

STAMINA

See Fortitude.

STATUS

The Lord maketh poor, and maketh rich: He bringeth low, and lifteth up.
1 Sam. 2:7

I had rather be a doorkeeper in the house of my God, than to dwell in the tents of wickedness.
Ps. 84:10

Thou hast lifted me up, and cast me down.
Ps. 102:10

I will make thee small among the heathen, and despised among men.
Jer. 49:15

[*See also* Appearance, Authority]

STOICISM

See Acceptance.

STRANGERS

See Foreigners, Hospitality.

STRATEGY

Let us go down, and there confound their language, that they may not understand one another's speech.
Gen. 11:7

Turn in, my lord, turn in to me; fear not.
Jael to Sisera
Judg. 4:18

Take an heifer with thee, and say, I am come to sacrifice to the Lord.
God to Samuel
1 Sam. 16:2

I will be a lying spirit in the mouth of all his prophets.
1 Kings 22:22

Ahab served Baal a little; but Jehu shall serve him much.
2 Kings 10:18

[*See also* Planning, Scheming, Traps]

STRENGTH

The Lord is my strength and song, and He is become my salvation.
Ex. 15:2

Thy right hand, O Lord, is become glorious in power: Thy right hand, O Lord, hath dashed in pieces the enemy.
Ex. 15:6

He lay down as a lion, and as a great lion: who shall stir him up?
Num. 24:9

No man hath been able to stand before you unto this day.
Joshua to Israelites
Josh. 23:9

One man of you shall chase a thousand:

for the Lord your God, He it is that fighteth for you.
Josh. 23:10

As the man is, so is his strength.
Judg. 8:21

Out of the eater came forth meat, and out of the strong came forth sweetness.
Judg. 14:14

What is sweeter than honey? and what is stronger than a lion?
Judg. 14:18

With the jawbone of an ass, heaps upon heaps, with the jaw of an ass have I slain a thousand men.
Samson
Judg. 15:16

If I be shaven, then my strength will go from me.
Judg. 16:17

By strength shall no man prevail.
1 Sam. 2:9

They were swifter than eagles, they were stronger than lions.
2 Sam. 1:23

He lift up his spear against eight hundred, whom he slew at one time.
2 Sam. 23:8

Be thou strong therefore, and show thyself a man.
David to Solomon
1 Kings 2:2

With him is an arm of flesh; but with us is the Lord our God.
2 Chron. 32:8

The joy of the Lord is your strength.
Neh. 8:10

Will He esteem thy riches? no, not gold, nor all the forces of strength.
Job 36:19

Hast thou an arm like God?
God to Job
Job 40:9

He esteemeth iron as straw, and brass as rotten wood.
Job 41:27

The Lord is my strength and my shield.
Ps. 28:7

There is no king saved by the multitude of an host.
Ps. 33:16

A mighty man is not delivered by much strength.
Ps. 33:16

I will not trust in my bow, neither shall my sword save me.
Ps. 44:6

The Lord is my strength and song, and is become my salvation.
Ps. 118:14

Blessed be the Lord my strength, which teacheth my hands to war, and my fingers to fight.
Ps. 144:1

The way of the Lord is strength to the upright.
Prov. 10:29

A wise man is strong.
Prov. 24:5

Wisdom strengtheneth the wise more than ten mighty men which are in the city.
Eccl. 7:19

The race is not to the swift, nor the battle to the strong, neither yet bread to the wise, nor yet riches to men of understanding, nor yet favour to men of skill; but time and chance happeneth to them all.
Eccl. 9:11

Wisdom is better than strength.
Eccl. 9:16

The Lord Jehovah is my strength and my song; He also is become my salvation.
Isa. 12:2

Trust ye in the Lord for ever: for in the Lord Jehovah is everlasting strength.
Isa. 26:4

In quietness and in confidence shall be your strength.
Isa. 30:15

He shall come up like a lion from the swelling of Jordan unto the habitation of the strong.
Jer. 50:44
See also Jer. 49:19

Wisdom and might are His.
Dan. 2:20

The people that do know their God shall be strong.
Dan. 11:32

The Lord God is my strength.
Hab. 3:19
See also Isa. 49:5

Not by might, nor by power, but by My spirit, saith the Lord of hosts.
Zech. 4:6

[*See also* Fortitude, Frailty, Weakness]

STRIFE

Knowest thou not that it will be bitterness in the latter end?
2 Sam. 2:26

He that troubleth his own house shall inherit the wind.
Prov. 11:29

Better is a dinner of herbs where love is, than a stalled ox and hatred therewith.
Prov. 15:17

Better is a dry morsel, and quietness therewith, than an house full of sacrifices with strife.
Prov. 17:1

The beginning of strife is as when one letteth out water: therefore leave off contention.
Prov. 17:14

Every fool will be meddling.
Prov. 20:3

Cast out the scorner, and contention shall go out; yea, strife and reproach shall cease.
Prov. 22:10

Where no wood is, there the fire goeth out: so where there is no talebearer, the strife ceaseth.
Prov. 26:20

[*See also* Arguments, Nagging, Trouble, Unity, War, War and Peace]

STUBBORNNESS

I will harden his heart, that he shall not let the people go.
Ex. 4:21

I know not the Lord, neither will I let Israel go.
Pharaoh
Ex. 5:2

How long wilt thou refuse to humble thyself before Me? let My people go.
God to Pharaoh
Ex. 10:3

Thou art a stiffnecked people.
E.g., Ex. 33:3

Circumcise therefore the foreskin of your heart, and be no more stiffnecked.
Deut. 10:16

They ceased not from their own doings, nor from their stubborn way.
Judg. 2:19

Stubbornness is as iniquity and idolatry.
1 Sam. 15:23

They would not hear, but hardened their necks.
2 Kings 17:14

They have done that which was evil in My sight, and have provoked Me to anger, since the day their fathers came forth out of Egypt.
2 Kings 21:15

Be ye not stiffnecked, as your fathers were.
2 Chron. 30:8

If ye will hear His voice, Harden not your heart.
Ps. 95:7–8
See also, e.g., Heb. 3:15

If ye refuse and rebel, ye shall be devoured with the sword: for the mouth of the Lord hath spoken it.
Isa. 1:20

Hear ye indeed, but understand not; and see ye indeed, but perceive not.
Isa. 6:9
See also, e.g., Matt. 13:14

Hear, ye deaf; and look, ye blind, that ye may see.
Isa. 42:18

Who is blind, but My servant? or deaf, as My messenger that I sent?
Isa. 42:19

Who is blind as he that is perfect, and blind as the Lord's servant?
Isa. 42:19

Thou art obstinate, and thy neck is an iron sinew, and thy brow brass.
Isa. 48:4

Take away the foreskins of your heart.
Jer. 4:4

They are brass and iron; they are all corrupters.
Jer. 6:28

I will take the stony heart out of their flesh, and will give them an heart of flesh.
Ezek. 11:19
See also Ezek. 36:26

[*See also* Impenitence]

SUBMISSION

See Acceptance, Authority.

SUCCESS

The Lord shall make thee the head, and not the tail; and thou shalt be above only, and thou shalt not be beneath.
Deut. 28:13

I exalted thee out of the dust, and made thee prince over My people Israel.
1 Kings 16:2

Believe in the Lord your God, so shall ye be established; believe His prophets, so shall ye prosper.
2 Chron. 20:20

God hath power to help, and to cast down.
2 Chron. 25:8

As long as he sought the Lord, God made him to prosper.
2 Chron. 26:5

The God of heaven, He will prosper us.
Neh. 2:20

What is the hope of the hypocrite, though he hath gained, when God taketh away his soul?
Job 27:8

He shall be like a tree planted by the rivers of water, that bringeth forth his fruit in his season.
Ps. 1:3

The righteous shall inherit the land.
Ps. 37:29

Promotion cometh neither from the east, nor from the west, nor from the south. But God is the judge: He putteth down one, and setteth up another.
Ps. 75:6–7

They go from strength to strength.
Ps. 84:7

The stone which the builders refused is become the head stone of the corner.
Ps. 118:22
See also, e.g., Mark 12:10

This is the Lord's doing; it is marvellous in our eyes.
Ps. 118:23
See also, e.g., Matt. 21:42

He becometh poor that dealeth with a slack hand: but the hand of the diligent maketh rich.
Prov. 10:4

Commit thy works unto the Lord, and thy thoughts shall be established.
Prov. 16:3

The race is not to the swift, nor the battle to the strong, neither yet bread to the wise, nor yet riches to men of understanding, nor yet favour to men of skill; but time and chance happeneth to them all.
Eccl. 9:11

If ye will not believe, surely ye shall not be established.
Isa. 7:9

Being planted, shall it prosper?
Ezek. 17:10

Not by might, nor by power, but by My spirit, saith the Lord of hosts.
Zech. 4:6

[*See also* Achievement, Ambition, Defeat, Failure, Prosperity, Reward, Victory, Wealth]

SUFFERING

Lord, wherefore hast Thou so evil entreated this people?
Moses
Ex. 5:22

He breaketh me with a tempest, and multiplieth my wounds without cause.
Job 9:17

Are not my days few? cease then, and let me alone, that I may take comfort a little.
Job 10:20

The wicked man travaileth with pain all his days.
Job 15:20

He delivereth the poor in his affliction.
Job 36:15

For Thy sake are we killed all the day long; we are counted as sheep for the slaughter.
Ps. 44:22

Thou feedest them with the bread of tears.
Ps. 80:5

Thou hast lifted me up, and cast me down.
Ps. 102:10

I praised the dead which are already dead more than the living which are yet alive.
Eccl. 4:2

I have chosen thee in the furnace of affliction.
Isa. 48:10

He was wounded for our transgressions, he was bruised for our iniquities.
Isa. 53:5

He was oppressed, and he was afflicted, yet he opened not his mouth.
Isa. 53:7

He bare the sin of many, and made intercession for the transgressors.
Isa. 53:12

My sighs are many, and my heart is faint.
Lam. 1:22

Though He cause grief, yet will He have compassion.
Lam. 3:32

Remember, O Lord, what is come upon us: consider, and behold our reproach.
Lam. 5:1

Shall there be evil in a city, and the Lord hath not done it?
Amos 3:6

[*See also* Anguish, Compassion, Grief, Mercy, Persecution, Torment]

SUPERSTITION

Be not dismayed at the signs of heaven; for the heathen are dismayed at them.
Jer. 10:2

[*See also* Idols, Omens]

SUPPORT

See God's Support.

SURVIVAL

Of every living thing of all flesh, two of every sort shalt thou bring into the ark, to keep them alive with thee.
Gen. 6:19

The more they afflicted them, the more they multiplied and grew.
(them: Hebrews in Egypt)
Ex. 1:12

The remnant that is escaped of the house of Judah shall yet again take root downward, and bear fruit upward.
2 Kings 19:30
See also Isa. 37:31

Out of Jerusalem shall go forth a remnant.
2 Kings 19:31, Isa. 37:32

Skin for skin, yea, all that a man hath will he give for his life.
Satan to God
Job 2:4

I am escaped with the skin of my teeth.
Job 19:20

The Lord blessed the latter end of Job more than his beginning.
Job 42:12

Unless the Lord had been my help, my soul had almost dwelt in silence.
Ps. 94:17

Except the Lord of hosts had left unto us a very small remnant, we should have been as Sodom.
Isa. 1:9
See also Rom. 9:29

We are left but a few of many.
Jer. 42:2

Can thine heart endure, or can thine hands be strong, in the days that I shall deal with thee?
Ezek. 22:14

[Life and Death, Perseverance]

SUSTENANCE
See Food.

SWEARING
See Blasphemy, Oaths, Promises.

SYMBOLISM
See Omens.

SYMPATHY
Miserable comforters are ye all.
Job to his friends
Job 16:2

Though they shall cry unto Me, I will not hearken unto them.
Jer. 11:11

Is it nothing to you, all ye that pass by?
Lam. 1:12

[*See also* Comfort, Compassion]

T

TACT
A soft answer turneth away wrath.
Prov. 15:1

Pleasant words are as an honeycomb,

sweet to the soul, and health to the bones.
Prov. 16:24

A soft tongue breaketh the bone.
Prov. 25:15

[*See also* Prudence, Restraint]

TAINT
See Contamination.

TASTE
See Discernment, Flavor.

TEACHING
Show them the way wherein they must walk, and the work that they must do.
Ex. 18:20

My speech shall distil as the dew, as the small rain upon the tender herb, and as the showers upon the grass.
Deut. 32:2

[*See also* Child-Rearing, Education, Guidance, Instruction]

TEARS
All the night make I my bed to swim; I water my couch with my tears.
Ps. 6:6

Weeping may endure for a night, but joy cometh in the morning.
Ps. 30:5

Rivers of waters run down mine eyes, because they keep not Thy law.
Ps. 119:136

They that sow in tears shall reap in joy.
Ps. 126:5

He that goeth forth and weepeth, bearing precious seed, shall doubtless come again with rejoicing, bringing his sheaves with him.
Ps. 126:6

A time to weep, and a time to laugh.
Eccl. 3:4

Oh that my head were waters, and mine

eyes a fountain of tears, that I might weep day and night.
Jer. 9:1

Refrain thy voice from weeping, and thine eyes from tears: for thy work shall be rewarded, saith the Lord.
Jer. 31:16

Mine eye runneth down with water, because the comforter that should relieve my soul is far from me.
Lam. 1:16

[*See also* Grief, Sorrow]

TEMPER

Let not the anger of my lord wax hot.
Aaron to Moses
Ex. 32:22

Cease from anger, and forsake wrath.
Ps. 37:8

A fool's wrath is presently known: but a prudent man covereth shame.
Prov. 12:16

He that is soon angry dealeth foolishly.
Prov. 14:17

For a small moment have I forsaken thee; but with great mercies will I gather thee.
Isa. 54:7

[*See also* Anger, Patience, Restraint]

TEMPERANCE

See Behavior, Excess.

TEMPTATION

And the serpent said unto the woman, Ye shall not surely die.
Gen. 3:4

Your eyes shall be opened, and ye shall be as gods, knowing good and evil.
Gen. 3:5

She took of the fruit thereof, and did eat.
(She: Eve)
Gen. 3:6

The serpent beguiled me, and I did eat.
Eve
Gen. 3:13

If thou doest not well, sin lieth at the door.
Gen. 4:7

Look not behind thee.
Angel to Lot and his wife
Gen. 19:17

His wife looked back from behind him, and she became a pillar of salt.
Gen. 19:26

Ye shall not tempt the Lord your God.
Deut. 6:16

Take heed to yourselves, that your heart be not deceived.
Deut. 11:16

Tell me, I pray thee, wherein thy great strength lieth.
Delilah
Judg. 16:6

And the Lord said unto Satan, Hast thou considered my servant Job?
Job 1:8

Dost thou still retain thine integrity? curse God, and die.
Job's wife to Job
Job 2:9

As for me, I will walk in mine integrity.
Ps. 26:11

If sinners entice thee, consent thou not.
Prov. 1:10

Discretion shall preserve thee, understanding shall keep thee.
Prov. 2:11

Enter not into the path of the wicked, and go not in the way of evil men.
Prov. 4:14

The lips of a strange woman drop as an honeycomb, and her mouth is smoother than oil.
Prov. 5:3

Keep thee from the evil woman, from the flattery of the tongue of a strange woman.
Prov. 6:24

Lust not after her beauty in thine heart; neither let her take thee with her eyelids.
Prov. 6:25

Can a man take fire in his bosom, and his clothes not be burned?
Prov. 6:27

As a bird hasteth to the snare, and knoweth not that it is for his life.
Prov. 7:23

Let not thine heart decline to her ways, go not astray in her paths.
Prov. 7:25

She hath cast down many wounded: yea, many strong men have been slain by her.
Prov. 7:26

Look not thou upon the wine when it is red.
Prov. 23:31

Woe unto him that giveth his neighbour drink.
Hab. 2:15

[*See also* Restraint, Self-Control, Self-Denial]

TEN COMMANDMENTS, THE

And he was there with the Lord forty days and forty nights.
(he: Moses)
Ex. 34:28

Two tables of stone written with the finger of God.
Deut. 9:10

[*See also* Commandments and the Appendix at p. 272]

TERROR

The sword without, and terror within, shall destroy both the young man and the virgin, the suckling also with the man of gray hairs.
Deut. 32:25

The ears of every one that heareth it shall tingle.
1 Sam. 3:11
See also 2 Kings 21:12

Let not Thy dread make me afraid.
Job 13:21

The terrors of the shadow of death.
Job 24:17

Pangs and sorrows shall take hold of them; they shall be in pain as a woman that travaileth.
Isa. 13:8

Howl, O gate; cry, O city; thou, whole Palestina, art dissolved.
Isa. 14:31

They shall clothe themselves with trembling.
Ezek. 26:16

The suburbs shall shake at the sound of the cry of thy pilots.
Ezek. 27:28

I have caused My terror in the land of the living.
Ezek. 32:32

[*See also* Destruction, Fear, Violence]

TESTIMONY

Speak ye unto the rock before their eyes; and it shall give forth his water.
God to Moses
Num. 20:8

Your eyes have seen what I have done in Egypt.
Josh. 24:7

Ye are witnesses against yourselves that ye have chosen you the Lord, to serve Him.
Josh. 24:22

Behold, this stone shall be a witness unto us.
Josh. 24:27

Stand still, that I may reason with you before the Lord.
1 Sam. 12:7

Let it be known this day that Thou art God in Israel, and that I am Thy servant.
Elijah
1 Kings 18:36

Let the shadow return backward ten degrees.
2 Kings 20:10

Declare His glory among the heathen; His marvellous works among all nations.
1 Chron. 16:24
See also Ps. 96:3

Make known His deeds among the people.
Ps. 105:1, 1 Chron. 16:8

In all thy ways acknowledge Him.
Prov. 3:6

Praise the Lord, call upon His name, declare His doings among the people, make mention that His name is exalted.
Isa. 12:4

Lift up thy voice with strength; lift it up, be not afraid.
Isa. 40:9

Ye are My witnesses, saith the Lord.
Isa. 43:10, 12

[*See also* Evangelism, Praise of God]

TESTING

Through them I may prove Israel, whether they will keep the way of the Lord to walk therein.
Judg. 2:22

Thou art weighed in the balances, and art found wanting.
Dan. 5:27

[*See also* Competition]

THANKSGIVING

See Gratitude.

THIRST

Oh that one would give me drink of the water of the well of Bethlehem.
2 Sam. 23:15, 1 Chron. 11:17

In my thirst they gave me vinegar to drink.
Ps. 69:21

The tongue of the sucking child cleaveth to the roof of his mouth for thirst.
Lam. 4:4

[*See also* Deprivation, Famine, Hunger]

THOUGHTS

Thou, even Thou only, knowest the hearts of all the children of men.
1 Kings 8:39

The Lord knoweth the thoughts of man, that they are vanity.
Ps. 94:11
See also 1 Cor. 3:20

There is not a word in my tongue, but, lo, O Lord, Thou knowest it altogether.
Ps. 139:4

The thoughts of the wicked are an abomination to the Lord.
Prov. 15:26

My thoughts are not your thoughts, neither are your ways My ways, saith the Lord.
Isa. 55:8

How long shall thy vain thoughts lodge within thee?
Jer. 4:14

I know the things that come into your mind, every one of them.
Ezek. 11:5

[*See also* Secrecy]

THREAT

Intendest thou to kill me, as thou killedst the Egyptian?
Ex. 2:14

Neither will I be with you any more, except ye destroy the accursed from among you.
God to Joshua
Josh. 7:12

Show us, we pray thee, the entrance into the city, and we will show thee mercy.
Judg. 1:24

The ears of every one that heareth it shall tingle.
1 Sam. 3:11
See also 2 Kings 21:12

So let the gods do to me, and more.
Jezebel to Elijah
1 Kings 19:2
See also 1 Sam. 14:44

In the place where dogs licked the blood of Naboth shall dogs lick thy blood, even thine.
(thy: Ahab)
1 Kings 21:19

My father chastised you with whips, but I will chastise you with scorpions.
2 Chron. 10:11, 14
See also 1 Kings 12:11

I have not said in vain that I would do this evil unto them.
Ezek. 6:10

TIME

And God called the light Day, and the darkness He called Night. And the evening and the morning were the first day.
Gen. 1:5

Jacob served seven years for Rachel; and they seemed unto him but a few days, for the love he had to her.
Gen. 29:20

The sun stood still, and the moon stayed, until the people had avenged themselves upon their enemies.
Josh. 10:13

The sun stood still in the midst of heaven, and hasted not to go down about a whole day.
Josh. 10:13

Shall the shadow go forward ten degrees, or go back?
2 Kings 20:9

Our days upon earth are a shadow.
Job 8:9
See also 1 Chron. 29:15

Waters wear the stones.
Job 14:19

A thousand years in Thy sight are but as yesterday when it is past.
Ps. 90:4

One generation passeth away, and another generation cometh: but the earth abideth for ever.
Eccl. 1:4

That which now is in the days to come shall all be forgotten.
Eccl. 2:16

To every thing there is a season, and a time to every purpose under the heaven.
Eccl. 3:1

A time to be born, and a time to die; a time to plant, and a time to pluck up that which is planted.
Eccl. 3:2

A time to kill, and a time to heal; a time to break down, and a time to build up.
Eccl. 3:3

That which hath been is now; and that which is to be hath already been.
Eccl. 3:15

The race is not to the swift, nor the battle to the strong, neither yet bread to the wise, nor yet riches to men of understanding, nor yet favour to men of skill; but time and chance happeneth to them all.
Eccl. 9:11

Lord, how long?
Isa. 6:11

Remember ye not the former things, neither consider the things of old.
Isa. 43:18

I will restore to you the years that the locust hath eaten.
Joel 2:25

[*See also* Imminence, Procrastination and the Appendix at p. 274]

TIMIDITY

The children of Israel have not hearkened unto me; how then shall Pharaoh hear me?
Moses to God
Ex. 6:12

If thou wilt go with me, then I will go.
Barak to Deborah
Judg. 4:8

[*See also* Confidence, Cowardice, Fear]

TITHE

Of all that Thou shalt give me I will surely give the tenth unto Thee.
Gen. 28:22

The tithe of the land, whether of the seed of the land, or of the fruit of the tree, is the Lord's.
Lev. 27:30

Honour the Lord with thy substance, and with the firstfruits of all thine increase.
Prov. 3:9

[*See also* Charity]

TOLERANCE

Love ye therefore the stranger: for ye were strangers in the land of Egypt.
Deut. 10:19

Thou shalt not muzzle the ox when he treadeth out the corn.
Deut. 25:4
See also 1 Cor. 9:9

Shouldest thou help the ungodly, and love them that hate the Lord?
2 Chron. 19:2

For all this His anger is not turned away, but His hand is stretched out still.
E.g., Isa. 5:25, Isa. 9:17

Thou art of purer eyes than to behold evil.
Habakkuk to God
Hab. 1:13

[*See also* Equality, Forgiveness]

TORMENT

In the morning thou shalt say, Would God it were even! and at even thou shalt say, Would God it were morning!
Deut. 28:67

Let not his hoar head go down to the grave in peace.
1 Kings 2:6

How long will ye vex my soul, and break me in pieces with words?
Job 19:2

[*See also* Anguish, Grief, Suffering]

TRADITION

He did evil in the sight of the Lord, and walked in the way of his father.
E.g., 1 Kings 15:26

As did their fathers, so do they unto this day.
2 Kings 17:41

Remove not the ancient landmark, which thy fathers have set.
Prov. 22:28
See also Prov. 23:10

Ask for the old paths, where is the good way, and walk therein, and ye shall find rest for your souls.
Jer. 6:16

[*See also* Heritage, Inheritance, Rituals]

TRAITORS

See Betrayal, Loyalty, Treachery.

TRANSVESTITES

The woman shall not wear that which pertaineth unto a man, neither shall a man put on a woman's garment: for all that do so are abomination unto the Lord thy God.
Deut. 22:5

[*See also* Homosexuality]

TRAPS

Say now Shibboleth.
Judg. 12:6

As a bird hasteth to the snare, and knoweth not that it is for his life.
Prov. 7:23

I will spread My net upon him, and he shall be taken in My snare.
Ezek. 17:20

[*See also* Strategy]

TREACHERY

Let not mine hand be upon him, but let the hand of the Philistines be upon him.
Saul about David
1 Sam. 18:17

The words of his mouth were smoother than butter, but war was in his heart.
Ps. 55:21

His words were softer than oil, yet were they drawn swords.
Ps. 55:21

One speaketh peaceably to his neighbour with his mouth, but in heart he layeth his wait.
Jer. 9:8

[*See also* Betrayal, Loyalty]

TRIBULATION

See Suffering.

TROUBLE

Evil will befall you in the latter days.
Deut. 31:29

Let Him deliver me out of all tribulation.
1 Sam. 26:24

Man is born unto trouble.
Job 5:7

The Lord also will be a refuge for the oppressed, a refuge in times of trouble.
Ps. 9:9

Many are the afflictions of the righteous: but the Lord delivereth him out of them all.
Ps. 34:19

Give us help from trouble: for vain is the help of man.
Ps. 60:11

In the day of my trouble I will call upon Thee.
Ps. 86:7

My soul is full of troubles: and my life draweth nigh unto the grave.
Ps. 88:3

The days of our years are threescore years and ten; and if by reason of strength they be fourscore years, yet is their strength labour and sorrow.
Ps. 90:10

Hide not Thy face from me in the day when I am in trouble.
Ps. 102:2
See also Ps. 69:17

I was brought low, and He helped me.
Ps. 116:6

He that seeketh mischief, it shall come unto him.
Prov. 11:27

A prudent man forseeth the evil, and hideth himself: but the simple pass on, and are punished.
Prov. 22:3

If thou faint in the day of adversity, thy strength is small.
Prov. 24:10

All his days are sorrows, and his travail grief; yea, his heart taketh not rest in the night.
Eccl. 2:23

We looked for peace, but no good came; and for a time of health, and behold trouble!
Jer. 8:15

All mine enemies have heard of my trouble; they are glad that Thou hast done it.
Lam. 1:21

The Lord is good, a strong hold in the day of trouble.
Nah. 1:7

[*See also* Anguish, Assistance, Danger, Escape, God's Protection, God's Support, Safety]

Let Him do to me as seemeth good unto Him.
> *2 Sam. 15:26*

Our eyes are upon Thee.
> *2 Chron. 20:12*

Blessed are all they that put their trust in Him.
> *Ps. 2:12*

Let all those that put their trust in Thee rejoice: let them ever shout for joy.
> *Ps. 5:11*

The Lord is my rock, and my fortress, and my deliverer; my God, my strength, in whom I will trust.
> *Ps. 18:2*

Some trust in chariots, and some in horses: but we will remember the name of the Lord our God.
> *Ps. 20:7*

Into Thine hand I commit my spirit.
> *Ps. 31:5*

Commit thy way unto the Lord; trust also in Him.
> *Ps. 37:5*

Blessed is that man that maketh the Lord his trust.
> *Ps. 40:4*
> *See also, e.g., Ps. 34:8*

As for me, I will call upon God; and the Lord shall save me.
> *Ps. 55:16*

In God I have put my trust; I will not fear what flesh can do unto me.
> *Ps. 56:4*
> *See also Ps. 56:11*

In Thee, O Lord, do I put my trust.
> *Ps. 71:1*
> *See also, e.g., 1 Sam. 22:3*

Trust thou in the Lord.
> *Ps. 115:9*

Hold Thou me up, and I shall be safe.
> *Ps. 119:117*

Trust in the Lord with all thine heart.
> *Prov. 3:5*

Whoso trusteth in the Lord, happy is he.
> *Prov. 16:20*

Trust ye in the Lord for ever: for in the Lord Jehovah is everlasting strength.
> *Isa. 26:4*

He that putteth his trust in Me shall possess the land, and shall inherit My holy mountain.
> *Isa. 57:13*

Blessed is the man that trusteth in the Lord, and whose hope the Lord is.
> *Jer. 17:7*

I will look unto the Lord; I will wait for the God of my salvation.
> *Mic. 7:7*

He knoweth them that trust in Him.
> *Nah. 1:7*

[*See also* Betrayal, Faith, God's Protection, God's Support, Reliability, Reliance, Safety]

TRUTH

What the Lord saith unto me, that will I speak.
> *1 Kings 22:14*
> *See also 2 Chron. 18:13*

The ear trieth words, as the mouth tasteth meat.
> *Job 34:3*

His truth endureth to all generations.
> *Ps. 100:5*

The works of His hands are verity and

judgment; all His commandments are sure.
Ps. 111:7

The truth of the Lord endureth for ever.
Ps. 117:2

Thy law is the truth.
Ps. 119:142

Thy word is true from the beginning.
Ps. 119:160

Every way of a man is right in his own eyes: but the Lord pondereth the hearts.
Prov. 21:2

Buy the truth, and sell it not.
Prov. 23:23

Thy counsels of old are faithfulness and truth.
Isa. 25:1

Truth is fallen in the street, and equity cannot enter.
Isa. 59:14

Truth is perished, and is cut off from their mouth.
Jer. 7:28

The law shall go forth of Zion, and the word of the Lord from Jerusalem.
Mic. 4:2

Love the truth and peace.
Zech. 8:19

[*See also* Candor, Credibility, Dishonesty, Honesty, Lies]

TYRANTS

This is the day in which the Lord hath delivered Sisera into thine hand.
Deborah to Barak
Judg. 4:14

My little finger shall be thicker than my father's loins.
1 Kings 12:10, 2 Chron. 10:10

Give me thy vineyard, that I may have it for a garden of herbs.
Ahab to Naboth
1 Kings 21:2

Princes have persecuted me without a cause: but my heart standeth in awe of Thy word.
Ps. 119:161

Envy thou not the oppressor, and choose none of his ways.
Prov. 3:31

Woe unto them that decree unrighteous decrees.
Isa. 10:1

Thy pomp is brought down to the grave, and the noise of thy viols.
Isa. 14:11

The worm is spread under thee, and the worms cover thee.
Isa. 14:11

How art thou fallen from heaven, O Lucifer, son of the morning!
Isa. 14:12

They that spoil thee shall be a spoil, and all that prey upon thee will I give for a prey.
Jer. 30:16

The prince shall not take of the people's inheritance by oppression.
Ezek. 46:18

He shall come to his end, and none shall help him.
Dan. 11:45

As thou hast done, it shall be done unto thee.
Obad. 15

[*See also* Oppression]

U

UNCERTAINTY

See Decisions, Doubt.

UNDERPRIVILEGED

Thou shalt open thine hand wide unto thy brother, to thy poor, and to thy needy, in thy land.
Deut. 15:11

Remember that thou wast a bondman in the land of Egypt.

Deut. 24:22

See also Deut. 5:15

He heareth the cry of the afflicted.

Job 34:28

He forgetteth not the cry of the humble.

Ps. 9:12

O God, lift up Thine hand: forget not the humble.

Ps. 10:12

He shall deliver the needy when he crieth; the poor also, and him that hath no helper.

Ps. 72:12

Precious shall their blood be in His sight.

Ps. 72:14

Defend the poor and fatherless: do justice to the afflicted and needy.

Ps. 82:3

Though the Lord be high, yet hath He respect unto the lowly.

Ps. 138:6

The Lord upholdeth all that fall, and raiseth up all those that be bowed down.

Ps. 145:14

Rob not the poor, because he is poor: neither oppress the afflicted in the gate.

Prov. 22:22

Open thy mouth, judge righteously, and plead the cause of the poor and needy.

Prov. 31:9

Relieve the oppressed, judge the fatherless, plead for the widow.

Isa. 1:17

I the God of Israel will not forsake them.

Isa. 41:17

[*See also* Charity, Poverty, Wealth, Widows and Orphans]

The thunder of His power who can understand?

Job 26:14

Man knoweth not the price thereof.

Job 28:13

To depart from evil is understanding.

Job 28:28

The ear trieth words, as the mouth tasteth meat.

Job 34:3

Great things doeth He, which we cannot comprehend.

Job 37:5

Be ye not as the horse, or as the mule, which have no understanding.

Ps. 32:9

Teach me, O Lord, the way of Thy statutes; and I shall keep it unto the end.

Ps. 119:33

Give me understanding, and I shall keep Thy law.

Ps. 119:34

See also Ps. 119:73

Give me understanding, and I shall live.

Ps. 119:144

Wisdom is the principal thing; therefore get wisdom: and with all thy getting get understanding.

Prov. 4:7

O ye simple, understand wisdom: and, ye fools, be ye of an understanding heart.

Prov. 8:5

In the lips of him that hath understanding wisdom is found.

Prov. 10:13

A man of understanding hath wisdom.

Prov. 10:23

The wisdom of the prudent is to understand his way.

Prov. 14:8

He that is slow to wrath is of great understanding.

Prov. 14:29

Understanding is a wellspring of life unto

him that hath it: but the instruction of
fools is folly.
Prov. 16:22

Hear ye indeed, but understand not; and
see ye indeed, but perceive not.
Isa. 6:9
See also, e.g., Matt. 13:14

In the latter days ye shall consider it.
Jer. 30:24

[*See also* Clarity, Compassion, Education,
Folly, Ignorance, Knowledge, Wisdom]

UNITY

The whole earth was of one language, and
of one speech.
Gen. 11:1

Now nothing will be restrained from
them, which they have imagined to do.
Gen. 11:6

Behold, how good and how pleasant it is
for brethren to dwell together in unity!
Ps. 133:1

A threefold cord is not quickly broken.
Eccl. 4:12

[*See also* Cooperation]

UNIVERSE

See Earth, Heaven and Earth, Nature.

URGENCY

Thou art my help and my deliverer; O
Lord, make no tarrying.
Ps. 70:5
See also Ps. 40:17

[*See also* Speed]

USURY

Thou shalt not give him thy money upon
usury, nor lend him thy victuals for increase.
Lev. 25:37

Thou shalt not lend upon usury to thy

brother; usury of money, usury of victuals, usury of any thing that is lent upon
usury.
Deut. 23:19

Unto a stranger thou mayest lend upon
usury; but unto thy brother thou shalt not
lend upon usury.
Deut. 23:20

[*See also* Borrowing]

VALUE

Take away the dross from the silver, and
there shall come forth a vessel for the
finer.
Prov. 25:4

They shall be as the stones of a crown,
lifted up as an ensign upon His land.
Zech. 9:16

[*See also* Quality]

VALUES

Behold, I am at the point to die: and what
profit shall this birthright do to me?
Esau to Jacob
Gen. 25:32

He that killeth a beast, he shall restore it:
and he that killeth a man, he shall be put
to death.
Lev. 24:21

Man looketh on the outward appearance,
but the Lord looketh on the heart.
1 Sam. 16:7

I dwell in an house of cedar, but the ark of
God dwelleth within curtains.
David
2 Sam. 7:2

Thou lovest thine enemies, and hatest thy
friends.
2 Sam. 19:6

If the foundations be destroyed, what can the righteous do?
Ps. 11:3

Teach us to number our days, that we may apply our hearts unto wisdom.
Ps. 90:12

The law of Thy mouth is better unto me than thousands of gold and silver.
Ps. 119:72

Wisdom is the principal thing; therefore get wisdom: and with all thy getting get understanding.
Prov. 4:7

Where no oxen are, the crib is clean: but much increase is by the strength of the ox.
Prov. 14:4

In the house of the righteous is much treasure: but in the revenues of the wicked is trouble.
Prov. 15:6

Labour not to be rich.
Prov. 23:4

Wherefore do ye spend money for that which is not bread?
Isa. 55:2

Eat ye that which is good, and let your soul delight itself in fatness.
Isa. 55:2

Let him that glorieth glory in this, that he understandeth and knoweth Me, that I am the Lord.
Jer. 9:24
See also, e.g., 1 Cor. 1:31

[*See also* Goals, Materialism, Spirituality]

VANITY

See Arrogance, Conceit, Futility.

VENGEANCE

See Revenge.

VERBOSITY

Should a wise man utter vain knowledge, and fill his belly with the east wind?
Job 15:2

How long will it be ere ye make an end of words?
Job 18:2

He multiplieth words without knowledge.
Job 35:16

He that hath knowledge spareth his words.
Prov. 17:27

A fool uttereth all his mind: but a wise man keepeth it in till afterwards.
Prov. 29:11

A fool's voice is known by multitude of words.
Eccl. 5:3

[*See also* Eloquence, Silence, Speech]

VICTIMS

See Innocence, Martyrdom, Persecution.

VICTORY

Let us flee from the face of Israel; for the Lord fighteth for them.
Ex. 14:25

I will sing unto the Lord, for He hath triumphed gloriously: the horse and his rider hath He thrown into the sea.
Ex. 15:1
See also Ex. 15:21

Thy right hand, O Lord, is become glorious in power: Thy right hand, O Lord, hath dashed in pieces the enemy.
Ex. 15:6

Thou hast overthrown them that rose up against Thee: Thou sentest forth Thy wrath, which consumed them as stubble.
Ex. 15:7

Ye shall chase your enemies, and they shall fall before you by the sword.
Lev. 26:7

Ye shall be saved from your enemies.
Num. 10:9

Not for thy righteousness, or for the uprightness of thine heart, dost thou go to possess their land: but for the wickedness

of these nations the Lord thy God doth drive them out.
Deut. 9:5

Every place whereon the soles of your feet shall tread shall be your's.
Deut. 11:24
See also Josh. 1:3

Shout; for the Lord hath given you the city.
Joshua, at Jericho
Josh. 6:16

Fear them not: for I have delivered them into thine hand.
God to Joshua
Josh. 10:8

The Lord fought for Israel.
Josh. 10:14

No man hath been able to stand before you unto this day.
Joshua to Israelites
Josh. 23:9

The Lord your God, He it is that fighteth for you.
Josh. 23:10
See also Josh. 23:3

The Lord shall sell Sisera into the hand of a woman.
Judg. 4:9

With the jawbone of an ass, heaps upon heaps, with the jaw of an ass have I slain a thousand men.
Samson
Judg. 15:16

Go up; for to morrow I will deliver them into thine hand.
God to Israelites
Judg. 20:28

My mouth is enlarged over mine enemies; because I rejoice in Thy salvation.
1 Sam. 2:1

David prevailed over the Philistine with a sling and with a stone.
1 Sam. 17:50

The victory that day was turned into mourning.
2 Sam. 19:2

I beat them as small as the dust of the earth, I did stamp them as the mire of the street.
2 Sam. 22:43

The God that answereth by fire, let Him be God.
1 Kings 18:24

Have the gods of the nations delivered them which my fathers have destroyed?
Sennacherib to Hezekiah
2 Kings 19:12, Isa. 37:12

When they arose early in the morning, behold, they were all dead corpses.
2 Kings 19:35, Isa. 37:36

I know that Thou favourest me, because mine enemy doth not triumph over me.
Ps. 41:11

His enemies shall lick the dust.
Ps. 72:9

Sit thou at My right hand, until I make thine enemies thy footstool.
Ps. 110:1
See also, e.g., Matt. 22:44

This is the day which the Lord hath made; we will rejoice and be glad in it.
Ps. 118:24

It is He that giveth salvation unto kings.
Ps. 144:10

The horse is prepared against the day of battle: but safety is of the Lord.
Prov. 21:31

He shall cry, yea, roar; He shall prevail against His enemies.
Isa. 42:13

A little one shall become a thousand, and a small one a strong nation.
Isa. 60:22

He shall array himself with the land of Egypt, as a shepherd putteth on his garment.
Jer. 43:12

Their mighty ones are beaten down, and are fled apace, and look not back.
Jer. 46:5

Let not the swift flee away, nor the mighty man escape.
Jer. 46:6

The kingdom shall be the Lord's.
Obad. 21

Thine hand shall be lifted up upon thine

adversaries, and all thine enemies shall be cut off.
Mic. 5:9

[*See also* Confidence, Defeat, Reward, Success]

VIEWPOINT

See Perspective.

VIGILANCE

He that keepeth Israel shall neither slumber nor sleep.
Ps. 121:4

Except the Lord keep the city, the watchman waketh but in vain.
Ps. 127:1

Go, set a watchman, let him declare what he seeth.
Isa. 21:6

Awake, awake, stand up, O Jerusalem.
Isa. 51:17

[*See also* Deception, Readiness]

VINDICATION

Why are ye come unto me now when ye are in distress?
Jephthah to his stepbrothers
Judg. 11:7

The stone which the builders refused is become the head stone of the corner.
Ps. 118:22
See also, e.g., Mark 12:10

Where are now your prophets which prophesied unto you, saying, The king of Babylon shall not come?
Jer. 37:19

They shall lick the dust like a serpent, they shall move out of their holes like worms of

the earth: they shall be afraid of the Lord our God.
Mic. 7:17

VIOLENCE

He that smiteth his father, or his mother, shall be surely put to death.
Ex. 21:15

He smote them hip and thigh.
Judg. 15:8

The sword shall never depart from thine house.
(thine: David)
2 Sam. 12:10

Thou shalt not build an house unto My name, because thou hast shed much blood upon the earth.
God to David
1 Chron. 22:8

The Lord trieth the righteous: but the wicked and him that loveth violence His soul hateth.
Ps. 11:5

Evil shall hunt the violent man to overthrow him.
Ps. 140:11

Envy thou not the oppressor, and choose none of his ways.
Prov. 3:31

The land is full of bloody crimes, and the city is full of violence.
Ezek. 7:23

Woe to the bloody city! it is all full of lies and robbery.
(it: Nineveh)
Nah. 3:1

Woe to him that buildeth a town with blood.
Hab. 2:12

[*See also* Desolation, Destruction, Murder, Terror, War]

VIRTUE

A virtuous woman is a crown to her husband.
Prov. 12:4

Who can find a virtuous woman? for her price is far above rubies.
Prov. 31:10

Many daughters have done virtuously, but thou excellest them all.
Prov. 31:29

[*See also* Goodness, Honesty, Integrity, Kindness, Righteousness]

VISION

See Sight.

VISIONS

The word of the Lord was precious in those days.
1 Sam. 3:1

O ye dry bones, hear the word of the Lord.
Ezek. 37:4

Your old men shall dream dreams, your young men shall see visions.
Joel 2:28
See also Acts 2:17

[*See also* Dreams, Future]

VITALITY

The life of all flesh is the blood thereof.
Lev. 17:14

The trees of the Lord are full of sap.
Ps. 104:16

Whatsoever thy hand findeth to do, do it with thy might.
Eccl. 9:10

[*See also* Fortitude]

VOLUNTEERS

Let no man's heart fail because of him; thy servant will go and fight with this Philistine.
David, about Goliath
1 Sam. 17:32

Who is there among you of all His people?

The Lord his God be with him, and let him go up.
2 Chron. 36:23, Ezra 1:3

Whom shall I send, and who will go for us? Then said I, Here am I; send me.
God to Isaiah, and response
Isa. 6:8

WAGES

Because thou art my brother, shouldest thou therefore serve me for nought? tell me, what shall thy wages be?
Laban to Jacob
Gen. 29:15

Did not I serve with thee for Rachel?
Jacob to Laban
Gen. 29:25

Let them deliver it into the hand of the doers of the work.
2 Kings 22:5

The recompence of a man's hands shall be rendered unto him.
Prov. 12:14

[*See also* Employees]

WAR

Ye shall be saved from your enemies.
Num. 10:9

Go not up, for the Lord is not among you.
Num. 14:42
See also Deut. 1:42

Because ye are turned away from the Lord, therefore the Lord will not be with you.
Num. 14:43

Shall your brethren go to war, and shall ye sit here?
Num. 32:6

Dread not, neither be afraid of them. The Lord your God which goeth before you, He shall fight for you.
Deut. 1:29–30

As a consuming fire He shall destroy

them, and He shall bring them down before thy face.
Deut. 9:3

All that thou commandest us we will do, and whithersoever thou sendest us, we will go.
Israelites to Joshua
Josh. 1:16

Joshua drew not his hand back, wherewith he stretched out the spear.
Josh. 8:26

Stay ye not, but pursue after your enemies.
Josh. 10:19

Whosoever is fearful and afraid, let him return and depart early.
Gideon to his soldiers
Judg. 7:3

The Lord saveth not with sword and spear: for the battle is the Lord's.
David to Goliath
1 Sam. 17:47

Shall the sword devour for ever?
2 Sam. 2:26

The sword devoureth one as well as another.
David, about Bathsheba's husband
2 Sam. 11:25

The wood devoured more people that day than the sword.
2 Sam. 18:8

Let not him that girdeth on his harness boast himself as he that putteth it off.
1 Kings 20:11

This day is a day of trouble, and of rebuke, and blasphemy.
2 Kings 19:3, Isa. 37:3

The battle is not your's, but God's.
2 Chron. 20:15

With him is an arm of flesh; but with us is the Lord our God.
2 Chron. 32:8

Forbear thee from meddling with God, who is with me, that He destroy thee not.
2 Chron. 35:21

Blessed be the Lord my strength, which

teacheth my hands to war, and my fingers to fight.
Ps. 144:1

Let the high praises of God be in their mouth, and a twoedged sword in their hand; To execute vengeance upon the heathen.
Ps. 149:6-7

By wise counsel thou shalt make thy war.
Prov. 24:6

Nation shall not lift up sword against nation, neither shall they learn war any more.
Isa. 2:4

They shall have no pity on the fruit of the womb; their eye shall not spare children.
Isa. 13:18

They shall fight every one against his brother, and every one against his neighbour; city against city, and kingdom against kingdom.
Isa. 19:2

Go not forth into the field, nor walk by the way; for the sword of the enemy and fear is on every side.
Jer. 6:25

Let not the swift flee away, nor the mighty man escape.
Jer. 46:6

The sword shall devour, and it shall be satiate and made drunk with their blood.
Jer. 46:10

They have blown the trumpet, even to make all ready; but none goeth to the battle.
Ezek. 7:14

He that is in the field shall die with the sword; and he that is in the city, famine and pestilence shall devour him.
Ezek. 7:15

By the swords of the mighty will I cause thy multitude to fall.
Ezek. 32:12

Beat your plowshares into swords, and your pruninghooks into spears: let the weak say, I am strong.
Joel 3:10

[*See also* Battle Calls, Conquest, Defeat,

God's Protection, Peace, Spoils of War, Violence, Weapons]

WAR AND PEACE

Go not up, neither fight; for I am not among you.
Deut. 1:42

When thou comest nigh unto a city to fight against it, then proclaim peace unto it.
Deut. 20:10

Thou doest me wrong to war against me.
Judg. 11:27

What hast thou to do with peace? turn thee behind me.
2 Kings 9:18, 19

Why shouldest thou meddle to thy hurt?
2 Kings 14:10

The words of his mouth were smoother than butter, but war was in his heart.
Ps. 55:21

Scatter Thou the people that delight in war.
Ps. 68:30

I am for peace: but when I speak, they are for war.
Ps. 120:7

Except the Lord keep the city, the watchman waketh but in vain.
Ps. 127:1

With good advice make war.
Prov. 20:18

A time to kill, and a time to heal; a time to break down, and a time to build up.
Eccl. 3:3

A time to love, and a time to hate; a time of war, and a time of peace.
Eccl. 3:8

Wisdom is better than weapons of war.
Eccl. 9:18

They shall beat their swords into plowshares, and their spears into pruninghooks: nation shall not lift up sword against nation, neither shall they learn war any more.
Isa. 2:4
See also Mic. 4:3

Saying, Peace, peace; when there is no peace.
Jer. 6:14, Jer. 8:11

O thou sword of the Lord, how long will it be ere thou be quiet?
Jer. 47:6

They shall seek peace, and there shall be none.
Ezek. 7:25

They have seduced My people, saying, Peace; and there was no peace.
Ezek. 13:10

[*See also* Peace, War]

WARNING

The Lord set a mark upon Cain.
Gen. 4:15

Look not behind thee.
Angel to Lot and his wife
Gen. 19:17

Go not up, for the Lord is not among you.
Num. 14:42
See also Deut. 1:42

Beware lest thou forget the Lord.
Deut. 6:12
See also Deut. 8:11

Ye shall not tempt the Lord your God.
Deut. 6:16

Evil will befall you in the latter days.
Deut. 31:29

The Lord will not hear you in that day.
1 Sam. 8:18

If ye shall still do wickedly, ye shall be consumed.
1 Sam. 12:25

If thou save not thy life to night, to morrow thou shalt be slain.
Michal to David
1 Sam. 19:11

A little cloud out of the sea, like a man's hand.
1 Kings 18:44

Why shouldest thou meddle to thy hurt?
2 Kings 14:10

Turn ye from your evil ways, and keep My commandments and My statutes.
2 Kings 17:13

Fight ye not against the Lord God of your fathers; for ye shall not prosper.
2 Chron. 13:12

Forbear thee from meddling with God, who is with me, that He destroy thee not.
2 Chron. 35:21

Let the earth hear, and all that is therein; the world, and all things that come forth of it.
Isa. 34:1

Let not your prophets and your diviners, that be in the midst of you, deceive you.
Jer. 29:8

I have spoken unto them, but they have not heard; and I have called unto them, but they have not answered.
Jer. 35:17

Deceive not yourselves.
Jer. 37:9

Be not thou rebellious like that rebellious house.
Ezek. 2:8

The time is come, the day of trouble is near.
Ezek. 7:7
See also Ezek. 7:12

Hear ye the word of the Lord.
E.g., Ezek. 13:2

He that taketh warning shall deliver his soul.
Ezek. 33:5

Mene, Mene, Tekel, Upharsin.
Dan. 5:25

The day of the Lord cometh.
E.g., Joel 2:1

Prepare to meet thy God, O Israel.
Amos 4:12

[See also Heedfulness, Prudence, Vigilance]

WATER

Unstable as water, thou shalt not excel.
Gen. 49:4

Can the rush grow up without mire? can the flag grow without water?
Job 8:11

Waters wear the stones.
Job 14:19

He maketh me to lie down in green pastures: He leadeth me beside the still waters. He restoreth my soul.
Ps. 23:2–3

Stolen waters are sweet, and bread eaten in secret is pleasant.
Prov. 9:17

He that watereth shall be watered also himself.
Prov. 11:25

Cast thy bread upon the waters: for thou shalt find it after many days.
Eccl. 11:1

Many waters cannot quench love, neither can the floods drown it.
Song 8:7

Blessed are ye that sow beside all waters.
Isa. 32:20

I will make the wilderness a pool of water, and the dry land springs of water.
Isa. 41:18

Every one that thirsteth, come ye to the waters, and he that hath no money; come ye, buy, and eat.
Isa. 55:1

[*See also* Oceans, Thirst]

WEAKNESS

The children are come to the birth, and there is not strength to bring forth.
2 Kings 19:3, Isa. 37:3

My days are like a shadow that declineth; and I am withered like grass.
Ps. 102:11

He giveth power to the faint; and to them that have no might He increaseth strength.
Isa. 40:29

They shall become as women.
Jer. 50:37

All hands shall be feeble, and all knees shall be weak as water.
Ezek. 7:17

Thy strong holds shall be like fig trees with the firstripe figs: if they be shaken, they shall even fall into the mouth of the eater.
Nah. 3:12

[*See also* Fortitude, Strength]

WEALTH

Thou shalt remember the Lord thy God: for it is He that giveth thee power to get wealth.
Deut. 8:18

The Lord maketh poor, and maketh rich: He bringeth low, and lifteth up.
1 Sam. 2:7

I have also given thee that which thou hast not asked, both riches, and honour.
God to Solomon
1 Kings 3:13

None were of silver.
1 Kings 10:21

All that is in the heaven and in the earth is Thine.
1 Chron. 29:11

Riches and honour come of Thee.
1 Chron. 29:12

All things come of Thee.
1 Chron. 29:14

King Solomon passed all the kings of the earth in riches and wisdom.
2 Chron. 9:22

Will He esteem thy riches? no, not gold, nor all the forces of strength.
Job 36:19

A little that a righteous man hath is better than the riches of many wicked.
Ps. 37:16

He heapeth up riches, and knoweth not who shall gather them.
Ps. 39:6

Wise men die, likewise the fool and the brutish person perish, and leave their wealth to others.
Ps. 49:10

Be not thou afraid when one is made rich,

when the glory of his house is increased; For when he dieth he shall carry nothing away.
Ps. 49:16–17

If riches increase, set not your heart upon them.
Ps. 62:10

I was envious at the foolish, when I saw the prosperity of the wicked.
Ps. 73:3

Riches profit not in the day of wrath.
Prov. 11:4

He that trusteth in his riches shall fall.
Prov. 11:28

There is that maketh himself rich, yet hath nothing: there is that maketh himself poor, yet hath great riches.
Prov. 13:7

He that gathereth by labour shall increase.
Prov. 13:11

Better is little with the fear of the Lord than great treasure and trouble therewith.
Prov. 15:16

How much better is it to get wisdom than gold!
Prov. 16:16

Better is a dry morsel, and quietness therewith, than an house full of sacrifices with strife.
Prov. 17:1

Wealth maketh many friends; but the poor is separated from his neighbour.
Prov. 19:4

Riches certainly make themselves wings; they fly away as an eagle toward heaven.
Prov. 23:5

Riches are not for ever.
Prov. 27:24

Give me neither poverty nor riches; feed me with food convenient for me.
Prov. 30:8

The abundance of the rich will not suffer him to sleep.
Eccl. 5:12

As he came forth of his mother's womb,

naked shall he return to go as he came, and shall take nothing of his labour.
Eccl. 5:15

It is the stumblingblock of their iniquity.
Ezek. 7:19

Ye have built houses of hewn stone, but ye shall not dwell in them; ye have planted pleasant vineyards, but ye shall not drink wine of them.
Amos 5:11
See also Zeph. 1:13

Neither their silver nor their gold shall be able to deliver them in the day of the Lord's wrath.
Zeph. 1:18
See also Ezek. 7:19

The silver is Mine, and the gold is Mine, saith the Lord of hosts.
Hag. 2:8

[*See also* Greed, Materialism, Money, Poverty, Profit, Prosperity, Sharing, Underprivileged, Values]

WEAPONS

Thou comest to me with a sword, and with a spear, and with a shield: but I come to thee in the name of the Lord of hosts.
David to Goliath
1 Sam. 17:45

The Lord saveth not with sword and spear: for the battle is the Lord's.
David to Goliath
1 Sam. 17:47
See also 2 Chron. 20:15

David prevailed over the Philistine with a sling and with a stone.
1 Sam. 17:50

How are the mighty fallen, and the weapons of war perished!
2 Sam. 1:27

I will not trust in my bow, neither shall my sword save me.
Ps. 44:6

They shall beat their swords into plowshares, and their spears into pruninghooks: nation shall not lift up sword against nation, neither shall they learn war any more.
Isa. 2:4
See also Mic. 4:3

Their arrows shall be as of a mighty expert man; none shall return in vain.
Jer. 50:9

Beat your plowshares into swords, and your pruninghooks into spears: let the weak say, I am strong.
Joel 3:10

[*See also* War, War and Peace]

WICKED PEOPLE

The wicked man travaileth with pain all his days.
Job 15:20

His remembrance shall perish from the earth, and he shall have no name in the street.
Job 18:17

His bones are full of the sin of his youth.
Job 20:11

They are as stubble before the wind, and as chaff that the storm carrieth away.
Job 21:18

The worm shall feed sweetly on him; he shall be no more remembered.
Job 24:20

They are exalted for a little while, but are gone and brought low.
Job 24:24

If his children be multiplied, it is for the sword.
Job 27:14

Let them be taken in the devices that they have imagined.
Ps. 10:2

Break Thou the arm of the wicked and the evil man.
Ps. 10:15

They shall soon be cut down like the grass, and wither as the green herb.
Ps. 37:2

The wicked borroweth, and payeth not again.
Ps. 37:21

They say, Who shall see them?
Ps. 64:5

As wax melteth before the fire, so let the wicked perish at the presence of God.
Ps. 68:2

Pride compasseth them about as a chain; violence covereth them as a garment.
Ps. 73:6

Let his days be few; and let another take his office.
Ps. 109:8

As he loved cursing, so let it come unto him: as he delighted not in blessing, so let it be far from him.
Ps. 109:17

Salvation is far from the wicked: for they seek not Thy statutes.
Ps. 119:155

Grant not, O Lord, the desires of the wicked.
Ps. 140:8

Let me not eat of their dainties.
Ps. 141:4

The Lord preserveth all them that love Him: but all the wicked will He destroy.
Ps. 145:20

The wicked shall be cut off from the earth.
Prov. 2:22

They sleep not, except they have done mischief.
Prov. 4:16

When the wicked perish, there is shouting.
Prov. 11:10

The tender mercies of the wicked are cruel.
Prov. 12:10

A wicked man is loathsome, and cometh to shame.
Prov. 13:5

Let him return unto the Lord, and He will have mercy upon him.
Isa. 55:7

The wicked are like the troubled sea,

when it cannot rest, whose waters cast up mire and dirt.
Isa. 57:20

As a cage is full of birds, so are their houses full of deceit.
Jer. 5:27

Prophesy against them, prophesy, O son of man.
Ezek. 11:4

[*See also* Evil, Punishment, Sinners, Wickedness]

WICKEDNESS

Thou shalt not follow a multitude to do evil.
Ex. 23:2

Not for thy righteousness, or for the uprightness of thine heart, dost thou go to possess their land: but for the wickedness of these nations the Lord thy God doth drive them out.
Deut. 9:5

Count not thine handmaid for a daughter of Belial.
1 Sam. 1:16

The children of Belial.
E.g., 1 Sam. 10:27

If ye shall still do wickedly, ye shall be consumed.
1 Sam. 12:25

He walked in all the sins of his father.
E.g., 1 Kings 15:3

He disappointeth the devices of the crafty, so that their hands cannot perform their enterprise.
(He: God)
Job 5:12

They that hate thee shall be clothed with shame; and the dwelling place of the wicked shall come to nought.
Job 8:22

There is no darkness, nor shadow of death, where the workers of iniquity may hide themselves.
Job 34:22

The way of the ungodly shall perish.
Ps. 1:6

The wicked shall be turned into hell, and all the nations that forget God.
Ps. 9:17

The wicked in his pride doth persecute the poor.
Ps. 10:2

The Lord trieth the righteous: but the wicked and him that loveth violence His soul hateth.
Ps. 11:5

Many sorrows shall be to the wicked: but he that trusteth in the Lord, mercy shall compass him about.
Ps. 32:10

Deliver me from the deceitful and unjust man.
Ps. 43:1

The wicked are estranged from the womb: they go astray as soon as they be born, speaking lies.
Ps. 58:3

Deliver me from the workers of iniquity, and save me from bloody men.
Ps. 59:2

The workers of iniquity shall be scattered.
Ps. 92:9

Ye fools, when will ye be wise?
Ps. 94:8

The way of the wicked is as darkness: they know not at what they stumble.
Prov. 4:19

The wicked shall fall by his own wickedness.
Prov. 11:5

The wicked shall not be unpunished.
Prov. 11:21

The way of the wicked is an abomination unto the Lord.
Prov. 15:9

The seed of evildoers shall never be renowned.
Isa. 14:20

There is no peace, saith the Lord, unto the wicked.
Isa. 48:22
See also Ps. 57:21

Thou hast polluted the land with thy whoredoms and with thy wickedness.
Jer. 3:2

He will give them that are wicked to the sword, saith the Lord.
Jer. 25:31

The whirlwind of the Lord goeth forth with fury, a continuing whirlwind: it shall fall with pain upon the head of the wicked.
Jer. 30:23

If thou warn the wicked, and he turn not from his wickedness, nor from his wicked way, he shall die in his iniquity; but thou hast delivered thy soul.
Ezek. 3:19, 21

I have no pleasure in the death of the wicked.
Ezek. 33:11

If the wicked turn from his wickedness, and do that which is lawful and right, he shall live.
Ezek. 33:19
See also Ezek. 18:21

[*See also* Corruption, Decadence, Depravity, Evil, Good and Evil, Immorality, Justice, Lawlessness, Punishment, Righteousness, Sin, Sinners]

WIDOWS AND ORPHANS

If thou afflict them in any wise, and they cry at all unto Me, I will surely hear their cry.
Ex. 22:23

A father of the fatherless, and a judge of the widows, is God in His holy habitation.
Ps. 68:5

Defend the poor and fatherless: do justice to the afflicted and needy.
Ps. 82:3

Plead for the widow.
Isa. 1:17

Leave thy fatherless children, I will preserve them alive; and let thy widows trust in Me.
Jer. 49:11

In Thee the fatherless findeth mercy.
Hos. 14:3
See also Ps. 10:14

Oppress not the widow, nor the fatherless, the stranger, nor the poor.
Zech. 7:10

[*See also* Compassion, Underprivileged]

WILL POWER

See Temptation.

WINE

See Drunkenness, Liquor, Pleasure.

WISDOM

In the hearts of all that are wise hearted I have put wisdom.
Ex. 31:6

Give therefore Thy servant an understanding heart to judge Thy people, that I may discern between good and bad.
Solomon
1 Kings 3:9

Divide the living child in two, and give half to the one, and half to the other.
1 Kings 3:25

Give her the living child, and in no wise slay it: she is the mother thereof.
1 Kings 3:27

The wisdom of God was in him.
(him: Solomon)
1 Kings 3:28

Give me now wisdom and knowledge.
Solomon to God
2 Chron. 1:10

Behold, the one half of the greatness of thy wisdom was not told me.
2 Chron. 9:6
See also 1 Kings 10:7

King Solomon passed all the kings of the earth in riches and wisdom.
2 Chron. 9:22

No doubt but ye are the people, and wisdom shall die with you.
Job to his friends
Job 12:2

It cannot be gotten for gold, neither shall silver be weighed for the price thereof.
Job 28:15

The price of wisdom is above rubies.
Job 28:18

God understandeth the way thereof.
Job 28:23

Days should speak, and multitude of years should teach wisdom.
Job 32:7

Great men are not always wise: neither do the aged understand judgment.
Job 32:9

Hold thy peace, and I shall teach thee wisdom.
Job 33:33

Teach us to number our days, that we may apply our hearts unto wisdom.
Ps. 90:12

Whoso is wise, and will observe these things, even they shall understand the lovingkindness of the Lord.
Ps. 107:43

The fear of the Lord is the beginning of wisdom.
Ps. 111:10, Prov. 9:10
See also Job 28:28

Wisdom crieth without; she uttereth her voice in the streets.
Prov. 1:20

The Lord giveth wisdom: out of His mouth cometh knowledge and understanding.
Prov. 2:6

Discretion shall preserve thee, understanding shall keep thee.
Prov. 2:11

Happy is the man that findeth wisdom, and the man that getteth understanding.
Prov. 3:13

All the things thou canst desire are not to be compared unto her.
Prov. 3:15

Length of days is in her right hand; and in her left hand riches and honour.
Prov. 3:16

Her ways are ways of pleasantness, and all her paths are peace.
Prov. 3:17

She is a tree of life to them that lay hold upon her.
Prov. 3:18

Forsake her not, and she shall preserve thee: love her, and she shall keep thee.
Prov. 4:6

Wisdom is the principal thing; therefore get wisdom: and with all thy getting get understanding.
Prov. 4:7

She shall bring thee to honour, when thou dost embrace her.
Prov. 4:8

Say unto wisdom, Thou art my sister; and call understanding thy kinswoman.
Prov. 7:4

Wisdom is better than rubies.
Prov. 8:11

By me kings reign, and princes decree justice. By me princes rule, and nobles, even all the judges of the earth.
(me: wisdom)
Prov. 8:15–16

I love them that love me.
Prov. 8:17

Those that seek me early shall find me.
Prov. 8:17

Whoso findeth me findeth life, and shall obtain favour of the Lord.
Prov. 8:35

He that sinneth against me wrongeth his own soul.
Prov. 8:36

All they that hate me love death.
Prov. 8:36

Wisdom hath builded her house, she hath hewn out her seven pillars.
Prov. 9:1

A wise son maketh a glad father: but a foolish son is the heaviness of his mother.
Prov. 10:1

The mouth of the just bringeth forth wisdom.
Prov. 10:31

A man shall be commended according to his wisdom.
Prov. 12:8

How much better is it to get wisdom than gold!
Prov. 16:16

Even a fool, when he holdeth his peace, is counted wise.
Prov. 17:28

Through wisdom is an house builded; and by understanding it is established.
Prov. 24:3

A wise man is strong.
Prov. 24:5

My son, eat thou honey, because it is good; and the honeycomb, which is sweet to thy taste: So shall the knowledge of wisdom be unto thy soul.
Prov. 24:13–14

The sluggard is wiser in his own conceit than seven men that can render a reason.
Prov. 26:16

In much wisdom is much grief.
Eccl. 1:18

Wisdom excelleth folly, as far as light excelleth darkness.
Eccl. 2:13

The wise man's eyes are in his head; but the fool walketh in darkness.
Eccl. 2:14

How dieth the wise man? as the fool.
Eccl. 2:16

Better is a poor and a wise child than an old and foolish king, who will no more be admonished.
Eccl. 4:13

What hath the wise more than the fool?
Eccl. 6:8

The heart of the wise is in the house of mourning; but the heart of fools is in the house of mirth.
Eccl. 7:4

Wisdom is good with an inheritance.
Eccl. 7:11

Wisdom giveth life to them that have it.
Eccl. 7:12

Wisdom strengtheneth the wise more than ten mighty men which are in the city.
Eccl. 7:19

I said, I will be wise; but it was far from me.
Eccl. 7:23

A man's wisdom maketh his face to shine.
Eccl. 8:1

A wise man's heart discerneth both time and judgment.
Eccl. 8:5

Wisdom is better than strength.
Eccl. 9:16

Wisdom is better than weapons of war.
Eccl. 9:18

The words of the wise are as goads.
Eccl. 12:11

The wisdom of their wise men shall perish, and the understanding of their prudent men shall be hid.
Isa. 29:14
See also 1 Cor. 1:19

They are wise to do evil, but to do good they have no knowledge.
Jer. 4:22

Is counsel perished from the prudent? is their wisdom vanished?
Jer. 49:7

By thy great wisdom and by thy traffick hast thou increased thy riches.
Ezek. 28:5

Wisdom and might are His.
Dan. 2:20

He giveth wisdom unto the wise, and knowledge to them that know understanding.
Dan. 2:21

[*See also* Education, Experience, Folly, Fools, Ignorance, Knowledge, Understanding]

WITCHCRAFT

Thou shalt not suffer a witch to live.
Ex. 22:18

Regard not them that have familiar spir-

its, neither seek after wizards, to be defiled by them.
Lev. 19:31

All that do these things are an abomination unto the Lord.
Deut. 18:12

I will be a swift witness against the sorcerers.
Mal. 3:5

WITNESS

See Perjury, Testimony.

WOMEN

It is not good that the man should be alone; I will make him an help meet for him.
Gen. 2:18

The rib, which the Lord God had taken from man, made He a woman.
Gen. 2:22

This is now bone of my bones, and flesh of my flesh.
Adam, about Eve
Gen. 2:23

She shall be called Woman, because she was taken out of man.
Gen. 2:23

Thy desire shall be to thy husband, and he shall rule over thee.
God to Eve
Gen. 3:16

Why should the name of our father be done away from among his family, because he hath no son?
Num. 27:4

If a man die, and have no son, then ye shall cause his inheritance to pass unto his daughter.
Num. 27:8

The Lord commanded Moses to give us an inheritance among our brethren.
(us: Zelophehad's daughters)
Josh. 17:4

The Lord shall sell Sisera into the hand of a woman.
Judg. 4:9

The lips of a strange woman drop as an

honeycomb, and her mouth is smoother than oil.
Prov. 5:3

Every wise woman buildeth her house: but the foolish plucketh it down with her hands.
Prov. 14:1

Give not thy strength unto women, nor thy ways to that which destroyeth kings.
Prov. 31:3

Who can find a virtuous woman? for her price is far above rubies.
Prov. 31:10

Favour is deceitful, and beauty is vain: but a woman that feareth the Lord, she shall be praised.
Prov. 31:30

As is the mother, so is her daughter.
Ezek. 16:44

Keep the doors of thy mouth from her that lieth in thy bosom.
Mic. 7:5

[*See also* Beauty, Man and Woman, Mankind, Marriage, Nagging]

WONDERS

What hath God wrought!
Num. 23:23

We have seen this day that God doth talk with man, and he liveth.
Deut. 5:24

The sun stood still, and the moon stayed, until the people had avenged themselves upon their enemies.
Josh. 10:13

And there was no day like that before it or after it.
Josh. 10:14

Many, O Lord my God, are Thy wonderful works.
Ps. 40:5

This is the Lord's doing; it is marvellous in our eyes.
Ps. 118:23
See also, e.g., Matt. 21:42

The way of an eagle in the air; the way of a serpent upon a rock; the way of a ship in the midst of the sea; and the way of a man with a maid.
Prov. 30:19

I will work a work in your days, which ye will not believe, though it be told you.
Hab. 1:5
See also Acts 13:41

[*See also* Awe, Miracles, Mystery, Nature]

WORK

In the sweat of thy face shalt thou eat bread, till thou return unto the ground.
Gen. 3:19

The Lord God sent him forth from the garden of Eden, to till the ground from whence he was taken. So He drove out the man.
Gen. 3:23–24

Because thou art my brother, shouldest thou therefore serve me for nought? tell me, what shall thy wages be?
Laban to Jacob
Gen. 29:15

Six days shalt thou labour, and do all thy work: But the seventh day is the sabbath of the Lord thy God: in it thou shalt not do any work.
Ex. 20:9–10
See also Ex. 35:2, Deut. 5:13–14

Six days thou shalt do thy work, and on the seventh day thou shalt rest.
Ex. 23:12
See also Ex. 34:21, Ex. 35:2

Thou shalt rejoice before the Lord thy God in all that thou puttest thine hands unto.
Deut. 12:18

Let them be hewers of wood and drawers of water.
Josh. 9:21

Go to the ant, thou sluggard; consider her ways, and be wise.
Prov. 6:6

He becometh poor that dealeth with a

slack hand: but the hand of the diligent maketh rich.
Prov. 10:4

He that gathereth by labour shall increase.
Prov. 13:11

In all labour there is profit: but the talk of the lips tendeth only to penury.
Prov. 14:23

Commit thy works unto the Lord, and thy thoughts shall be established.
Prov. 16:3

Seest thou a man diligent in his business? he shall stand before kings.
Prov. 22:29

What profit hath a man of all his labour which he taketh under the sun?
Eccl. 1:3

What hath man of all his labour, and of the vexation of his heart, wherein he hath laboured under the sun?
Eccl. 2:22

What profit hath he that worketh in that wherein he laboureth?
Eccl. 3:9

Every man should eat and drink, and enjoy the good of all his labour, it is the gift of God.
Eccl. 3:13
See also Eccl. 5:18

The sleep of a labouring man is sweet.
Eccl. 5:12

Whatsoever thy hand findeth to do, do it with thy might.
Eccl. 9:10

[*See also* Business, Cooperation, Diligence, Effort, Employees, Laziness]

WORRY

Why tarry the wheels of his chariots?
Judg. 5:28

Cast thy burden upon the Lord, and He shall sustain thee.
Ps. 55:22

Pour out your heart before Him: God is a refuge for us.
Ps. 62:8

Better is an handful with quietness, than

both the hands full with travail and vexation of spirit.
Eccl. 4:6

The abundance of the rich will not suffer him to sleep.
Eccl. 5:12

The misery of man is great upon him.
Eccl. 8:6

WORSHIP

He is my God, and I will prepare Him an habitation; my father's God, and I will exalt Him.
Ex. 15:2

Ye shall serve the Lord your God.
Ex. 23:25

Let them make Me a sanctuary; that I may dwell among them.
Ex. 25:8

Thou shalt love the Lord thy God with all thine heart, and with all thy soul, and with all thy might.
Deut. 6:5
See also, e.g., Matt. 22:37

Serve Him with all your heart and with all your soul.
Deut. 11:13

Offer not thy burnt offerings in every place that thou seest.
Deut. 12:13

Turn ye not aside: for then should ye go after vain things, which cannot profit nor deliver.
1 Sam. 12:21

I have surely built Thee an house to dwell in, a settled place for Thee to abide in for ever.
Solomon to God
1 Kings 8:13

Him shall ye fear, and Him shall ye worship, and to Him shall ye do sacrifice.
2 Kings 17:36

The glory of the Lord had filled the house of God.
2 Chron. 5:14

Who shall ascend into the hill of the Lord? or who shall stand in His holy place? He that hath clean hands, and a

pure heart; who hath not lifted up his soul unto vanity, nor sworn deceitfully.
Ps. 24:3–4

When Thou saidst, Seek ye My face; my heart said unto Thee, Thy face, Lord, will I seek.
Ps. 27:8

Give unto the Lord, O ye mighty, give unto the Lord glory and strength.
Ps. 29:1

Come, let us worship and bow down: let us kneel before the Lord our maker.
Ps. 95:6

Give unto the Lord the glory due unto His name.
Ps. 96:8, 1 Chron. 16:29

Worship the Lord in the beauty of holiness.
Ps. 96:9, 1 Chron. 16:29

Seek the Lord, and His strength: seek His face evermore.
Ps. 105:4
See also 1 Chron. 16:11

Keep thy foot when thou goest to the house of God, and be more ready to hear, than to give the sacrifice of fools.
Eccl. 5:1

Come ye, and let us go up to the mountain of the Lord.
Isa. 2:3

With my soul have I desired Thee in the night; yea, with my spirit within me will I seek Thee early.
Isa. 26:9

This people draw near Me with their mouth, and with their lips do honour Me, but have removed their heart far from Me.
Isa. 29:13
See also Matt. 15:8

Unto Me every knee shall bow, every tongue shall swear.
Isa. 45:23
See also Rom. 14:11

Come, and let us go up to the mountain of the Lord, and to the house of the God of Jacob.
Mic. 4:2

[*See also* Churches, Devotion, False

Gods, God's Temple, Godlessness, Idolatry, Idols, Prayer, Rituals]

WRATH

See Anger.

Y

YOUTH

The flower of their age.
1 Sam. 2:33

His bones are full of the sin of his youth.
Job 20:11

Remember not the sins of my youth.
Ps. 25:7

The young lions roar after their prey, and seek their meat from God.
Ps. 104:21

I am a stranger in the earth: hide not Thy commandments from me.
Ps. 119:19

The glory of young men is their strength: and the beauty of old men is the grey head.
Prov. 20:29

Woe to thee, O land, when thy king is a child.
Eccl. 10:16

Rejoice, O young man, in thy youth.
Eccl. 11:9

Let thy heart cheer thee in the days of thy youth.
Eccl. 11:9

Childhood and youth are vanity.
Eccl. 11:10

Remember now thy Creator in the days of thy youth.
Eccl. 12:1

Say not, I am a child: for thou shalt go to all that I shall send thee, and whatsoever I command thee thou shalt speak.
God to Jeremiah
Jer. 1:7

It is good for a man that he bear the yoke in his youth.
Lam. 3:27

Your old men shall dream dreams, your young men shall see visions.
Joel 2:28
See also Acts 2:17

[*See also* Age, Children, Experience]

ZEAL

I the Lord thy God am a jealous God.
E.g., Ex. 20:5

The Lord, whose name is Jealous, is a jealous God.
Ex. 34:14

The Lord thy God is a consuming fire, even a jealous God.
Deut. 4:24
See also Heb. 12:29

I have been very jealous for the Lord God of hosts.
1 Kings 19:10

Come with me, and see my zeal for the Lord.
2 Kings 10:16

God is jealous, and the Lord revengeth.
Nah. 1:2

[*See also* Devotion, Enthusiasm]

APPENDIX

Contents

The Ten Commandments

I am the Lord thy God, which have brought thee out of the land of Egypt, out of the house of bondage.

Thou shalt have no other gods before Me.

Thou shalt not make unto thee any graven image, or any likeness of any thing that is in heaven above, or that is in the earth beneath, or that is in the water under the earth:

Thou shalt not bow down thyself to them, nor serve them: for I the Lord thy God am a jealous God, visiting the iniquity of the fathers upon the children unto the third and fourth generation of them that hate Me;

And showing mercy unto thousands of them that love Me, and keep My commandments.

Thou shalt not take the name of the Lord thy God in vain; for the Lord will not hold him guiltless that taketh His name in vain.

Remember the sabbath day, to keep it holy.

Six days shalt thou labour, and do all thy work:

But the seventh day is the sabbath of the Lord thy God: in it thou shalt not do any work, thou, nor thy son, nor thy daughter, thy manservant, nor thy maidservant, nor thy cattle, nor thy stranger that is within thy gates:

For in six days the Lord made heaven and earth, the sea, and all that in them is, and rested the seventh day: wherefore the Lord blessed the sabbath day, and hallowed it.

Honour thy father and thy mother: that thy days may be long upon the land which the Lord thy God giveth thee.

Thou shalt not kill.

Thou shalt not commit adultery.

Thou shalt not steal.

Thou shalt not bear false witness against thy neighbour.

Thou shalt not covet thy neighbour's house, thou shalt not covet thy neighbour's wife, nor his manservant, nor his maidservant, nor his ox, nor his ass, nor any thing that is thy neighbour's.

Ex. 20:2–17
See also Deut. 5:6–21

Psalm 23

The Lord is my shepherd; I shall not want.

He maketh me to lie down in green pastures: He leadeth me beside the still waters.

He restoreth my soul: He leadeth me in the paths of righteousness for His name's sake.

Yea, though I walk through the valley of the shadow of death, I will fear no evil: for Thou art with me; Thy rod and Thy staff they comfort me.

Thou preparest a table before me in the presence of mine enemies: Thou anointest my head with oil; my cup runneth over.

Surely goodness and mercy shall follow me all the days of my life: and I will dwell in the house of the Lord for ever.

"To Every Thing There Is a Season . . ."

To every thing there is a season, and a time to every purpose under the heaven:

A time to be born, and a time to die; a time to plant, and a time to pluck up that which is planted;

A time to kill, and a time to heal; a time to break down, and a time to build up;

A time to weep, and a time to laugh; a time to mourn, and a time to dance;

A time to cast away stones, and a time to gather stones together; a time to embrace, and a time to refrain from embracing;

A time to get, and a time to lose; a time to keep, and a time to cast away;

A time to rend, and a time to sew; a time to keep silence, and a time to speak;

A time to love, and a time to hate; a time of war, and a time of peace.

Eccl. 3:1–8

KEY-WORD INDEX

Explanation

This Index gives the key words in every quotation in the book (except for "God" and "Lord," which appear too often to make it practical), together with a few adjacent words to provide the context. It serves two purposes.

If you remember certain words from a quotation but cannot remember the entire quotation or its citation, you can look up the word here and locate the page number on which that quotation first appears (it may be placed in other categories as well).

The Index also serves as a supplement to the categories in the book itself. For example, although there is no category titled "heart" in the main section, readers seeking quotations about that word can easily find them with this Key-Word Index.

A

abase
  a. him that is high, 212
  He is able to a., 188
abhor
  a. him that speaketh, 48
  a. myself, and repent, 203
  a. us, for Thy name's, 99
  soul shall a. you, 119
abide
  a. day of his coming, 15
  place for Thee to a., 33
  terrible; and who can a.,
    141
abideth
  earth a. for ever, 68
Abiezer
  vintage of A., 179
able
  a. men, such as fear, 113
  a. to build Him an house,
    33
  a. to deliver us, 50
  a. to overcome, 39
  a. to stand, 102
  a. to stand before, 236
  a. to stand before envy, 9
  He is a. to abase, 188
  Lord is a. to give, 212
  not a. to go up, 45
abode
  know thy a., 100
abodest
  why a. thou among, 67
abolish
  idols He shall a., 129
abolished
  righteousness not be a.,
    218
abomination
  a. is he that chooseth, 129
  a. to the Lord, 25
  a. to the Lord, 129
  a. unto the Lord, 235
  a. unto the Lord, 25
  false balance is a., 25
  it is a., 123
  lying lips are a., 149
  seven are an a., 12
  way of the wicked is a.,
    262
  wicked are an a., 77
  wicked is an a., 29
abominations
  all thine a., 141
  know her a., 187
above
  a. a beast, 127
  a. the heights, 14
  in heaven a., 104
  in heaven a., 109
  Lord is a. all gods, 100
  shalt be a. only, 170

Abraham
  A. gave up the ghost, 50
  God of A., 96
abroad
  a. the sword bereaveth, 52
Absalom
  A. O A., 116
  even with A., 36
  O A. my son, 116
absent
  a. one from another, 2
abundance
  a. of the rich, 231
  a. with increase, 115
abundant
  a. in goodness, 110
acceptable
  a. in Thy sight, 185
  judgment is more a., 142
accepted
  shalt thou not be a., 3
accomplished
  desire a., 3
according
  a. to all that she hath, 12
  a. to the greatness, 101
  a. to thy words, 6
  a. unto all his ways, 90
account
  He giveth not a. of, 38
accursed
  a. thing from among, 43
  a. thing, lest, 41
  destroy the a., 196
  make yourselves a., 41
accustomed
  a. to do evil, 28
acknowledge
  a. My might, 4
  a. thine iniquity, 39
  all thy ways a. Him, 3
acquaint
  a. now thyself with Him, 2
acquit
  not at all a. the wicked,
    196
actions
  Him a. are weighed, 54
Adam
  whatsoever A. called, 167
add
  a. thou not His, 221
  a. unto the word, 220
  a. unto thy days, 37
  shalt not a., 35
adder
  stingeth like an a., 151
adders'
  a. poison is under, 119
addeth
  a. rebellion unto, 199
admonished
  who will no more be a.,
    5

adulterer
  a. and the adulteress, 4
adulterers
  against the a., 4
adulteress
  adulterer and the a., 4
adultery
  a. with a woman, 4
  not commit a., 4
adversaries
  a. be clothed with shame,
    72
  ease Me of Mine a., 210
  lifted up upon thine a.,
    254
  us, or our a., 7
  vengeance on His a., 211
adversary
  a. had written a book, 3
  a. unto thine a., 7
  how long shall the a., 21
adversity
  brother is born for a., 93
  day of a., 92
  in the day of a., 179
advice
  blessed be thy a., 5
  good a. make war, 5
  take a. and speak, 5
afar
  heard even a. off, 27
  justice standeth a., 146
  not a God a. off, 104
  why standest Thou a., 13
afflict
  if thou a. them, 262
afflicted
  a. yet he opened not, 159
  cry of the a., 185
  justice to the a., 142
  more they a. them, 4
  oppress the a., 173
  smitten of God, and a.,
    21
affliction
  furnace of a., 101
  poor in his a., 55
afflictions
  a. of the righteous, 247
affrighted
  fear, and is not a., 44
afraid
  a. because I was naked, 78
  a. for the terror, 86
  a. nor dismayed, 70
  a. of a man, 86
  a. of the face, 140
  a. of the Lord, 126
  a. of the words, 70
  a. of thee, 32
  a. of their faces, 70
  a. of their revilings, 48
  a. of their words, 44
  a. of them, 70

a. when one is made rich, 73
be not a., 70
be not a., 71
be not a., 44
be not a., 86
dread make me a., 86
fearful and a., 86
none shall make them a., 177
trust, and not be a., 81
up, be not a., 40
whom hast thou been a., 111
whom shall I be a., 44
after
before it or a., 266
again
a. I will build, 32
a. take root, 240
bring him back a., 51
cannot be gathered up a., 163
turn a. unto the Lord, 203
against
I, even I, am a. thee, 72
Lord gone out a. me, 9
age
a. is as nothing, 164
died in a good old a., 50
even to your old a., 6
flower of their a., 268
good old a., 51
good old a., 6
son of his old a., 85
thine old a., 114
time of old a., 6
aged
a. understand judgment, 6
agreed
except they be a., 43
agreement
hell are we at a., 12
Ahab
A. served Baal, 53
none like unto A., 76
air
bird of the a., 192
eagle in the a., 166
fowl of the a., 9
fowls of the a., 23
alas
a. for the day, 141
alien
a. unto my mother's, 75
aliens
houses to a., 40
alike
all things come a., 52
alive
a. this day, 32
art yet a., 50
keep a. his own soul, 164
keep them a., 10

kill and to make a., 119
kill, and I make a., 102
killeth and maketh a., 102
living which are yet a., 150
preserve them a., 262
saved them a., 210
all
a. are of the dust, 74
a. are the work, 74
a. are Thy servants, 168
a. go unto one place, 52
a. is vanity, 49
a. is vanity, 59
a. is vanity and, 49
a. that a man hath, 224
a. that he hath is, 28
a. that is in heaven, 120
a. that is within me, 184
a. that thou sayest, 171
a. the congregation, 41
a. the labour of man, 8
a. the people, 66
a. the rivers run, 26
a. the ways of a man, 224
a. them for good, 105
a. them that forsake, 16
a. things come alike, 52
a. things come of Thee, 259
a. things have I seen, 6
a. those that put, 118
beast: for a. is vanity, 127
chance happeneth to a., 235
earth is for a., 43
exalted as head above a., 233
excellest them a., 156
for a. this His anger, 246
hast Thou made them a., 167
iniquity of us a., 156
touch a. that he hath, 28
Almighty
A. give you mercy, 22
A. hath dealt, 9
A. pervert judgment, 76
arrows of the A., 9
breath of the A., 149
I am God A., 110
pleasure to the A., 11
that the A. would answer, 3
what is the A., 14
wrath of the A., 98
alone
a. that I may speak, 26
God, even Thou a., 163
how can one be warm a., 24
let him a., 205
let him a., 2
let me a., 164
that man should be a., 151

Thou, art Lord a., 109
trodden winepress a., 7
woe to him that is a., 43
aloud
I cry a., 58
singing, and cry a., 159
altar
a. beside the altar, 163
a. of the Lord, 163
cast down his a., 83
altars
a. shall be desolate, 61
throw down their a., 129
always
mindful a. of His covenant, 82
am
a. as thou art, 7
I A. that I A., 96
I a. the Lord, 96
ambassador
faithful a., 70
amends
make a. for the harm, 207
amiss
have done a., 39
Ammon
children of A., 198
among
God is a. you, 104
Lord a. us, or not, 66
Lord is not a. you, 255
ancient
a. days, 107
a. is wisdom, 6
a. landmark, 190
of a. times, 95
ancients
understand more than a., 79
angel
a. of God, 11
a. of the Lord, 72
a. spake unto me, 53
God hath sent His a., 56
angels
lower than the a., 155
anger
a. be hot, 98
a. endureth but a moment, 98
a. is outrageous, 9
a. of my Lord, 207
a. of the Lord, 98
a. resteth in, 9
away from His fierce a., 91
cease from a., 8
day of the Lord's a., 61
day of the Lord's a., 157
draw out Thine a., 98
execute vengeance in a., 98
fierce a. of the Lord, 165
fierceness of His a., 98
for all this His a., 246

for all this His a., 98
keep His a. for ever, 91
Mine a. was kindled, 21
not in Thine a., 29
provoke Me not to a., 191
provoked Me to a., 77
retaineth not His a., 91
secret pacifieth a., 9
slow to a., 36
slow to a., 37
slow to a., 111
slow to a., 37
slow to a., 196
slow to a. appeaseth, 8
slow to a. is, 9
sorrows in His a., 195
will not keep a., 91
angry
 a. dealeth foolishly, 242
 a. man stirreth, 9
 a. with the wicked, 140
 a. with us for ever, 98
 friendship with a. man, 9
 than with an a. woman,
  156
 wilt Thou be a., 91
anguish
 a. her that bringeth, 20
 a. is come upon, 9
 a. of my spirit, 26
 trouble and a., 34
anoint
 arise, a. him, 148
anointed
 against the Lord's a., 12
 face of thine a., 185
 face of Thine a., 201
 Lord's a., 162
 though a. king, 232
 touch not Mine a., 32
 walk before Mine a., 212
anointest
 a. my head with oil, 22
another
 feignest to be a., 53
 for he hath not a., 43
 one as well as a., 49
answer
 a. a fool, 90
 a. not a fool, 90
 a. turneth away wrath, 8
 a. you, I will declare, 26
 Almighty would a., 3
 and they shall a., 194
 any that will a., 13
 called, ye did not a., 65
 I will a. him, 186
 I will a. thee, 186
 right hand, and a. me, 55
 timber shall a., 3
 what shall I a., 42
answered
 called you, but ye a., 173
 have not a., 65

He a. them not, 54
Lord a. him not, 1
nor any that a., 83
answereth
 God a. me no more, 1
 God that a. by fire, 189
 money a. all things, 49
 rich a. roughly, 44
ant
 go to the a., 62
ants
 a. are a people, 62
anything
 is a. too hard for, 103
appear
 a. in His glory, 139
appearance
 outward a., 137
appeareth
 stand when he a., 15
appeaseth
 anger a. strife, 8
appetite
 a. is not filled, 8
 man given to a., 96
apple
 a. of his eye, 32
 a. of the eye, 106
apples
 comfort me with a., 152
 like a. of gold, 69
appoint
 who will a. Me the time,
  15
appointed
 a. times, 65
 a. to die, 36
 at the time a., 10
approach
 causest to a., 118
approveth
 cause, the Lord a. not, 20
arise
 a. and let us flee, 74
 a. go to Nineveh, 161
 a. with healing, 15
 His light a., 104
 let them a. if they, 129
 to the dumb stone, a., 129
 when I fall, I shall a., 23
ariseth
 sun also a., 42
ark
 a. of God, 125
 a. of God dwelleth, 33
 bring into the a., 10
 hand to hold the a., 198
arm
 a. be broken, 135
 a. fall from my shoulder,
  135
 a. like God, 237
 a. of flesh, 237
 a. of the Lord, 107

a. of the wicked, 195
flesh his a., 202
seal upon thine a., 152
with an outstretched a., 55
armies
 defy the a. of God, 14
army
 a. of heaven, 103
array
 a. himself with the land,
  253
arrogancy
 a. come out, 11
 a. of the proud, 12
arrow
 a. shall go forth, 107
 a. that flieth, 86
 shoot an a., 54
arrows
 a. drunk with blood,
  210
 a. of the Almighty, 9
 a. shall be as of a, 3
 as a. are in the hand, 222
 spare no a., 211
ascend
 a. above the heights, 14
 a. into the hill, 122
 if I a. up into heaven, 74
ashamed
 a. seven days, 193
 forsake Thee shall be a., 16
 let me not be a., 72
 let me not be a., 81
 man make thee a., 220
 never be a., 202
 not a. that wait for Me, 63
 people being a., 45
 prophets shall be a., 84
 refusedst to be a., 226
 shall be greatly a., 129
 ways, and be a., 201
 were not a., 130
ashes
 remembrances like a., 5
 repent in dust and a., 203
 wallow thyself in a., 165
aside
 turn not a., 220
ask
 a. of me, seeing, 12
 a. on, my mother, 175
 a. what I shall give, 95
 generations: a. thy father,
  79
 I will not a., 190
 young children a., 85
asked
 a. not for Me, 42
 He a. water, 53
 which thou hast not a., 212
Askelon
 not in the streets of A.,
  116

ass
a. his master's crib, 15
bridle for the a., 64
jawbone of an a., 237
riding upon an a., 127
wild a. bray, 37
assembly
a. of the saints, 87
a. of the wicked, 178
asses
ride on white a., 183
astonished
mark me, and be a., 224
astonishment
a. and an hissing, 54
become an a., 193
drink water with a., 85
astray
a. as soon as born, 17
a. in her paths, 4
a. like a lost sheep, 42
caused them to go a.
16
sheep have gone a., 16
astrologers
let now the a., 14
atonement
a. for the soul, 23
attend
a. to my words, 117
attentive
ear now be a., 185
attire
bride her a. yet My, 16
authority
righteous are in a., 114
avenge
a. Me of Mine enemies,
210
the Lord a., 207
avenged
people had a. themselves,
107
soul be a., 112
avenger
a. of blood, 219
avengeth
God that a. me, 210
avenging
a. of Israel, 114
avoid
a. it, pass not by it, 77
awake
a. a. put on strength, 107
a. a. stand up, 254
a. a. utter, 232
a. and sing, 125
a. as in the ancient, 107
a. put on thy strength, 203
of the earth shall a., 71
saith to the wood, a., 129
surely now He would a., 21
awaked
sleeps, and must be a., 129

awaketh
drinketh; but he a., 63
eateth; but he a., 63
away
a. from the Lord, 41
a. when they flee, 45
anger not turned a., 98
Lord hath taken a., 2
not cast thee a., 101
not taken a., 128
that which was driven a.,
120
turn a. your heart, 137
awe
heart standeth in a., 4

B

Baal
Ahab served B., 53
but if B. then follow, 31
Babel
B. because the Lord, 36
babes
mouth of b., 31
Babylon
B. shall become heaps, 54
flee out of B., 75
king of B., 3
king of B. shall not, 5
palace of king of B., 125
rivers of B., 123
back
and look not b., 253
b. from the sword, 44
can I bring him b., 51
degrees, or go b., 172
drew not his hand b., 60
I will not go b. neither, 61
keep nothing b., 26
plowed upon my b., 9
rod for the fool's b., 64
rod is for the b., 63
turned their b., 129
turned unto Me the b., 16
who shall turn it b., 98
wife looked b., 41
backs
Israel turneth their b., 45
backsliding
b. daughter, 16
backward
shadow return b., 173
bad
between good and b., 63
Balak
B. would give me, 170
balance
false b. is, 25
small dust of the b., 114
weighed in an even b., 39
balances
b. of deceit, 25
weighed in the b., 244

ye shall have just b., 25
bald
go up, thou b. head, 161
baldness
heads shall be b., 165
balm
b. in Gilead, 34
bands
b. of Orion, 183
b. of wickedness, 85
banner
b. over me was love, 152
bare
naked and b., 79
barley
cockle instead of b., 135
handfuls of b., 84
barren
b. and bearest not, 87
b. woman to keep house,
88
grave; and the b. womb, 52
sing, O b., 159
bars
cut in sunder the b., 172
earth with her b., 56
battle
b. is not your's, 7
b. is the Lord's, 39
b. to the strong, 28
day of b., 253
flee in b., 45
forefront of the b., 19
Lord mighty in b., 103
none goeth to the b., 199
rusheth into the b., 132
bay
green b. tree, 77
beam
b. out of the timber, 3
bear
b. a son, 87
b. his sin, 21
b. no tidings, 36
b. robbed of her whelps,
50
b. robbed of her whelps, 8
b. the yoke, 176
b. with this evil, 175
downward, and b. fruit,
240
goat shall b. upon, 219
greater than I can b., 193
ninety years old, b., 87
paw of the b., 39
wounded spirit who can b.,
57
beard
b. cut off, 165
head and of my b., 9
beards
b. be grown, 226
bearest
barren, and b. not, 87

bearing
  b. precious seed, 48
bears
  roar all like b., 9
  two she b., 194
beast
  b. for b., 207
  blains upon b., 180
  both man and b., 88
  every b. of the field, 231
  killeth a b., 207
  killeth a b., 193
  lieth with a b., 232
  life of his b., 10
  manner of b., 232
  preeminence above a b.,
    127
  subtil than any b., 231
beasts
  b. of the earth, 196
  b. of the field, 23
  of men befalleth b., 52
beat
  b. him with the rod, 30
  b. their swords, 176
  b. them as small, 10
  b. your plowshares, 256
beaten
  mighty ones are b. down,
    253
beatest
  b. him with the rod, 30
beautiful
  b. garments, 203
  b. upon the mountains, 169
beauty
  b. is departed, 140
  b. is vain, 17
  b. of holiness, 268
  b. of old men, 79
  lust not after her b., 4
  perfection of b., 140
  trust in thine own b., 17
because
  b. the Lord loved Israel,
    148
  b. the Lord loved you, 32
  b. ye have forsaken, 75
bed
  b. in the darkness, 58
  make I my b. to swim, 231
  make my b. in hell, 74
  slumberings upon the b.,
    67
beds
  evil upon their b., 47
been
  hath already b., 135
  that which hath b., 135
  that which hath b. is, 135
Beersheba
  even to B., 66
befall
  evil will b., 247

befallen
  all this b. us, 66
befalleth
  b. the sons of men, 52
  of men b. beasts, 52
before
  b. I formed thee, 20
  b. the sun, 125
  b. thou camest out, 20
  day like that b., 266
  do b. all Israel, 125
  gone out b. thee, 39
  stand b. this holy Lord,
    102
  walk b. Me, as David, 124
begetteth
  he that b. a fool, 175
beggar
  lifteth up the b., 55
begin
  when I b., 17
beginning
  b. of knowledge, 87
  b. of my strength, 88
  b. of strife is, 238
  b. of wisdom, 87
  in the b. God created, 17
  more than his b., 55
  than at the b., 143
  than the b., 71
  told you from the b., 100
  true from the b., 221
begotten
  b. the drops of dew, 198
  have I b. them, 147
beguiled
  serpent b. me, 20
  wherefore have ye b., 53
behind
  look not b., 242
  turn thee b., 229
being
  while I have my b., 232
Belial
  children of B., 261
  daughter of B., 261
  sons of B., 76
believe
  b. His prophets, 81
  b. in the Lord, 81
  ere they b. Me, 80
  if ye will not b., 19
  not b. though it be told,
    230
believed
  b. not their words, 205
believeth
  b. shall not make haste, 19
belly
  b. of hell, 187
  b. shall swell, 4
  came out of the b., 58
  fill his b. with wind, 252
  formed thee in the b., 20

upon thy b. shalt, 48
belong
  b. the issues from death,
    55
  b. unto the Lord, 144
  b. unto us, 144
beloved
  b. come into his garden,
    152
  b. is mine, 35
  b. of the Lord, 217
  given the dearly b., 1
  I am my b.'s and his, 35
  I am my b.'s and my, 35
  voice of my b., 67
bemoan
  waste: who will b. her, 57
bend
  b. their tongues, 64
  ye that b. the bow, 211
beneath
  in earth b., 104
  not be b., 170
bereaved
  b. of my children, 30
bereaveth
  sword b., 52
beseech
  b. Thee, o Lord, 42
  obey, I b., 172
  remember, I b. Thee, 92
beseiged
  remaineth and is b., 10
beside
  any God b., 99
  b. Me is no saviour, 109
  b. Me there is no God, 109
  none else b. me, 38
best
  b. of them is as a brier, 43
  even the b. of, 162
  every man at his b., 92
Bethlehem
  well of B., 244
better
  b. for me to die, 59
  b. is a dinner of herbs, 152
  b. is a dry morsel, 225
  b. is a little with, 64
  b. is a neighbour, 13
  b. is a poor, 5
  b. is an handful, 8
  b. is it to get wisdom, 259
  b. is little with, 41
  b. is the end, 71
  b. is the poor, 29
  b. is the sight of, 57
  b. is thy love, 152
  b. than a liar, 64
  b. than laughter, 146
  b. than strength, 237
  b. than the mighty, 9
  b. than the proud, 176
  b. than the vintage, 179

b. than weapons, 257
b. thing under the sun, 49
b. to be of an humble, 127
b. to dwell in a corner, 156
b. to dwell in the, 156
b. to go to the house, 52
b. to hear the rebuke, 48
b. to thee than ten, 30
b. to trust, 114
b. to trust in the, 201
good name is b. than, 205
heart is made b., 146
living dog is b., 125
love is b., 152
lovingkindness is b., 100
obey b. than sacrifice, 171
open rebuke is b., 26
there is nothing b., 3
two are b. than one, 42
between
b. me and thee, 207
Lord be witness b., 6
beware
b. lest thou forget, 82
bid
if prophet had b., 5
bidden
Lord hath b. him, 2
bind
b. the sweet influences, 183
b. them about thy neck, 28
b. up that which was, 120
smitten, and He will b.,
103
bindeth
b. up their wounds, 233
cry not when He b., 3
sore, and b. up, 102
bird
b. hasteth to the snare, 243
b. of the air, 192
birds
cage is full of b., 47
singing of b., 221
birth
come to the b., 258
shall I bring to the b., 189
than day of one's b., 3
birthright
profit shall this b., 57
sold his b., 133
bitter
b. for sweet, 149
b. in soul, 9
b. thing is sweet, 57
clusters are b., 20
evil thing and b., 16
sweet for b., 149
bitterly
curse ye b., 67
dealt very b., 9
bitterness
b. in the latter, 20
b. of death, 160

b. of my soul, 26
b. to her that bare, 31
filled me with b., 20
knoweth his own b., 9
black
b. but comely, 17
blackness
heavens with b., 169
blade
fall from my shoulder b.,
135
blameless
b. than the Philistines, 134
blaspheme
shall the enemy b., 21
blasphemed
every day is b., 21
blasphemy
of rebuke, and b., 58
bleating
meaneth then this b., 53
bleatings
b. of the flocks, 67
blemish
no b. in him, 17
bless
b. His holy name, 184
b. the Lord, 18
b. them that b. thee, 105
b. Thy name for ever, 184
b. with their mouth, 127
b. ye the Lord, 183
except thou b. me, 22
fear the Lord, b. the, 184
Lord b. thee, 107
Lord b. thee, 22
merciful unto us, and b.,
22
will b. thee, 34
blessed
and b. them, 46
and call her b., 175
b. are all, 248
b. are they that wait, 81
b. are ye that sow, 69
b. be God, 97
b. be he that b. thee, 22
b. be he that cometh, 159
b. be the Lord, 184
b. be the Lord, 115
b. be the Lord, 97
b. be the Lord, 237
b. be the Lord, 114
b. be the name, 97
b. be the name, 2
b. be the name of, 22
b. be thou, which, 5
b. be thy advice, 5
b. be Thy glorious, 184
b. be ye, 36
b. is every one that, 87
b. is he that blesseth, 32
b. is he that considereth,
29

b. is he that waiteth, 176
b. is he whose transgres-
sion, 91
b. is man that feareth, 87
b. is man that walketh, 36
b. is that man that, 118
b. is that trusteth, 119
b. is the man whom, 118
b. is the man whose, 81
b. is the nation, 101
b. shalt thou be, 22
b. the latter end, 55
earth be b., 22
earth be b., 32
families be b., 85
God b. the seventh day,
216
mother bare me be b., 20
of the just is b., 205
blesseth
blessed is he that b., 32
He b. the habitation, 22
blessing
b. and a curse, 22
b. and cursing, 150
b. be upon the head of, 25
b. if ye obey, 22
b. of the Lord, 29
delighted not in b., 142
exalted above all b., 184
hast thou but one b., 9
reserved a b., 9
blessings
I will curse your b., 49
blew
b. a trumpet, 17
blind
b. but My servant, 239
b. to wander, 23
bring the b. by a way, 73
eyes of the b., 23
eyes of the b., 23
eyes to the b., 7
gift doth b., 24
look, ye b., 238
perfect, and b., 130
stumblingblock before b.,
118
who is b., 130
who maketh the b., 46
blood
arrows drunk with b., 210
avenger of b., 219
b. be upon thy head, 117
b. of him that shed, 165
b. of Naboth, 27
b. of these men, 189
b. shall be poured, 209
b. shall be upon him, 118
b. shall be upon him, 21
b. shall pursue, 49
b. that is shed, 165
b. that maketh an atone-
ment, 23

brother's b. crieth, 79
buildeth a town with b.,
114
drunk with their b., 27
filled with b., 209
flesh is the b. thereof, 23
from coming to shed b., 5
hands are full of b., 117
innocent b., 21
innocent b., 166
is not this the b., 44
keepeth sword from b., 62
polluted with b., 128
precious shall their b. be,
250
prepare thee unto b., 49
shall dogs lick thy b., 27
shall his b. be shed, 141
shed innocent b., 12
shed much b. upon, 194
sheddeth man's b., 141
wash his feet in the b.,
210
waters turned to b., 179
bloody
full of b. crimes, 146
save me from b. men, 146
woe to the b. city, 47
blossom
b. as the rose, 207
blot
b. out of My book, 193
blotted
b. out of the book, 72
sin be b. out, 210
blow
b. the trumpet, 17
b. the trumpet, 107
blown
b. the trumpet, 199
boast
b. not thyself of to, 23
harness b. himself, 23
boasteth
way, then he b., 25
bodies
dead b., 196
body
worms destroy this b., 51
boil
b. breaking forth, 180
b. like a pot, 103
bondage
house of b., 92
bondman
b. in Egypt, 36
b. in Egypt, 250
bone
b. of my bones, 265
be broken from the b., 135
break a b., 129
tongue breaketh the b., 11
bones
b. are full of the sin, 260

bone of my b., 265
can these b. live, 208
dry bones, hear the word,
208
health to the b., 234
keepeth all his b., 247
move his b., 205
spirit drieth the b., 57
book
adversary had written b., 3
b. of the law, 170
blot out of My b., 193
blotted out of the b., 72
note it in a b., 122
printed in a b., 23
seek ye out of the b., 221
words of this b., 65
written in this b., 128
books
of making many b., 24
born
astray as soon as b., 17
b. for adversity, 93
b. in the land, 74
b. unto trouble, 155
clean that is b., 155
cursed be day I was b., 20
first man that was b.?, 6
man b. of a woman, 149
nation be b., 176
shall a child b., 87
time to be b., 17
unto us a child is b., 159
wherein I was b., 58
borrow
shalt not b., 24
borrower
b. is servant, 24
so with the b., 24
borroweth
wicked b. and payeth, 24
bosom
b. of fools, 9
carry them in thy b., 147
fire in his b., 4
lieth in thy b., 20
bought
father that hath b., 133
bound
b. with chains, 92
to them that are b., 56
bow
b. for lies, 64
bend the b., 211
knee shall b., 7
My b. in the cloud, 44
trust in my b., 237
worship and b. down,
268
bowed
all those that be b., 108
where he b., 12
bowl
b. be broken, 63

boys
b. and girls playing, 191
branch
B. shall grow, 159
righteous B., 159
brass
b. and iron, 239
b. as rotten wood, 237
brow b., 239
flesh of b., 58
gates of b., 172
brawling
b. woman in a wide house,
156
bray
b. a fool in a mortar, 90
wild ass b., 37
bread
b. eaten in secret, 65
b. of idleness, 156
b. of tears, 116
b. shall be given, 215
b. to the hungry, 37
b. to the wise, 28
brought to a piece of b.,
191
by b. only, 157
cast thy b., 8
eat b. by weight, 85
eat thy b. with joy, 89
every one a loaf of b., 27
for which is not b., 252
give him b., 72
hired for b., 127
morsel of b., 125
neither will I eat b., 41
not a famine of b., 85
pieces of b., 84
plenty of b., 62
shalt thou eat b., 192
young children ask b., 85
breadth
perceived b. of the earth,
12
break
b. a bone, 129
b. me in pieces, 78
b. not Thy covenant, 45
b. Thou the arm, 195
built will I b., 60
I will b. in pieces, 172
time to b. down, 120
breaketh
b. me with a tempest, 240
no man b. it, 85
soft tongue b., 11
breast
draw out the b., 30
breasts
b. are like two young, 17
b. to clusters of grapes, 23
womb and dry b., 49
breath
b. goeth forth, 8

b. is corrupt, 51
b. of God, 221
b. of life, 45
b. of the Almighty, 149
every thing that hath b., 184
takest away their b., 10
breathed
b. into his nostrils, 45
brethren
b. go to war, 206
b. to dwell together, 24
daughters of thy b., 137
enemies with your b., 227
fight against your b., 176
fight for your b., 17
following their b., 176
inheritance among our b., 74
of thy b., 158
sell your b., 115
soweth discord among b., 12
stranger unto my b., 75
bribery
tabernacles of b., 24
bricks
b. are fallen down, 12
straw to make b., 173
bride
b. her attire, yet My, 16
bridle
b. for the ass, 64
b. in thy lips, 125
brier
best of them is as a b., 43
brightness
b. but we walk in, 63
reason of thy b., 38
bring
b. forth your reasons, 11
b. me up Samuel, 235
can I b. him back, 51
bringeth
b. down to grave, 102
b. low, and lifteth, 102
broad
b. ways I will seek, 57
broken
b. and a contrite heart, 42
b. spirit drieth the, 57
b. the yokes, 26
bind that which was b., 120
city that is b., 223
cord is not quickly b., 43
golden bowl be b., 63
healeth the b. in heart, 233
images shall be b., 61
like a b. tooth, 20
like a b. vessel, 59
mine arm be b., 135
of a b. heart, 116
one of them is b., 247

spirit is b., 233
brooks
after the water b., 153
brother
a b. offended is, 91
b. and our flesh, 157
b. is born for adversity, 93
b. to dragons, 58
because thou art my b., 25
closer than a b., 93
every man against his b., 20
every man to his b., 37
every one against his b., 28
evil against his b., 24
from thy poor b., 29
hand of my b., 86
hunt every man his b., 166
man and his b., 140
my b.'s keeper, 24
not Esau Jacob's b., 153
than a b. far off, 13
unto his b., 177
unto thy b., 90
usury to thy b., 251
voice of thy b.'s blood, 79
wide unto thy b., 29
younger b. shall be, 88
brought
b. me forth of the womb, 58
b. me home again, 50
b. you forth out, 137
gone and b. low, 142
lives they b. it, 44
brow
b. brass, 239
bruised
b. for our iniquities, 159
brutish
b. in his knowledge, 130
b. man knoweth not, 130
b. person perish, 164
hateth reproof is b., 47
bucket
drop of a b., 114
buckler
He is a b., 105
shield and b., 106
build
again I will b., 32
b. but I will throw down, 95
b. him a sure house, 212
b. Him an house, 33
b. houses, but not, 94
b. Me an house, 108
b. up the wall, 139
b. up Zion, 139
b. with hewn stones, 12
except the Lord b., 3
house which I b., 99
labour in vain that b., 3
let us b. with you, 53

not b. an house unto, 194
that ye b. unto Me, 33
time to b. up, 120
builded
wisdom b. her house, 264
wisdom is an house b., 3
builders
stone which the b., 174
buildeth
b. a town with blood, 114
b. her house, 123
riseth up and b., 48
woe unto him that b., 43
building
b. you an altar, 163
the b. decayeth, 25
built
b. houses of hewn stone, 63
b. O virgin of Israel, 32
b. Thee an house, 33
house which I have b., 33
that which I have b., 60
bullock
chastised, as a b., 64
eat straw like the b., 24
burden
b. upon the Lord, 108
layest the b., 147
burdens
undo the heavy b., 85
buried
b. in a good age, 6
there will I be b., 50
burn
b. as an oven, 141
b. that none can quench, 98
fire shall b., 5
gods shall ye b., 129
jealousy b. like fire, 91
burned
bush b. with fire, 104
clothes not be b., 4
feet not be b., 4
thou shalt not be b., 34
burneth
wickedness b. as the, 77
burning
b. fiery furnace, 50
b. for b., 141
burnt
b. with fire, 194
more than b. offerings, 216
still sacrificed and b., 128
bury
b. me not, 25
none to b. her, 226
bush
b. burned with fire, 104
b. was not consumed, 104
business
b. in great waters, 172
diligent in his b., 2

■ 284 ■

utter not this our b., 168
utter this our b., 6
butter
b. and honey, 63
smoother than b., 69
buy
b. the truth, 249
come ye, b. and eat, 57
buyer
as with the b., 24
let not the b. rejoice, 66
naught, saith the b., 25
byword
b. among all people, 201
proverb, and a b., 193

C

cage
c. is full, 47
Cain
C. went out, 174
set a mark upon C., 105
slayeth C. vengeance, 105
calamity
c. is at hand, 194
c. of his father, 31
day of my c., 71
calf
c. and the young lion, 10
call
all them that c., 13
c. for Samson, 160
c. me Mara, 9
c. my sin, 29
c. not on Thy name, 112
c. now, if there be, 13
c. on My name and I, 13
c. on the Lord, 55
c. unto Me and I will, 186
c. upon Him in truth, 13
c. upon His name, 115
c. upon His name, 76
c. upon Me in the day, 13
c. ye on the name, 27
c. ye upon Him while, 173
hear when I c., 185
I will c. upon God, 13
in all that they c., 185
shall c. upon Me, 186
therefore will I c. upon, 186
trouble I will c., 186
whosoever shall c. on, 13
called
c. by name of Lord, 32
c. thee by thy name, 101
c. unto them but, 65
c. upon Thy name, 59
c. ye did not answer, 65
c. you, but ye answered, 173
in my distress I c., 185
Thy people are c. by, 91

calm
sea may be c., 21
came
c. I out of my mother's, 2
lo, it c. to little, 63
wherefore came I forth, 59
camel
sheep, c. and ass, 10
camels
c. drink also, 143
c. were without number, 132
c. were without number, 2
Canaan
give the land of C., 45
land of C., 137
land of C. which, 138
candle
c. of the wicked, 134
c. of the wicked, 146
cankerworm
c. hath left, 61
hath the c. eaten, 61
cannot
c. go back, 189
captives
c. whose c. they were, 92
liberty to the c., 56
captivity
are for c. to c., 60
gone into c., 79
turn back your c., 84
carcase
c. of Jezebel, 25
c. shall not come unto, 194
carcases
c. shall fall, 50
care
by weight, and with c., 85
careth
God c. for, 138
carried
c. from the womb, 224
carry
c. them in thy bosom, 147
dieth he shall c., 73
cart
sin with a c. rope, 230
cast
c. a stone, 59
c. away a perfect man, 1
c. his mantle, 148
c. me down, 236
c. me not off, 6
c. out the scorner, 238
c. thee off for ever, 16
c. them away, 129
c. thy bread, 8
c. thy burden upon, 108
dost Thou c. me off, 108
not c. off His people, 153
time to c. away, 53
to c. down, 102

caterpillar
hath the c. eaten, 61
cattle
and over the c., 9
c. of Egypt died, 180
cursed above all c., 231
grow for the c., 48
cause
c. His face to shine, 22
c. My fury to rest, 98
c. of the fatherless, 134
c. of the poor, 183
c. of the poor, 143
c. that is too hard, 147
c. them to know, 103
c. Thy face to shine, 100
c. thy flesh to sin, 228
c. was of God, 102
c. which I knew not, 7
debate thy c. with, 11
hate me without a c., 72
judge not the c., 134
judge Thou my c., 143
man in his c., 20
neighbour without c., 124
not c. to bring forth, 189
opened my c., 72
persecuted me without c., 4
poor in his c., 131
poor man in his c., 131
produce your c., 11
revealed my c., 211
strive not without c., 11
to God commit my c., 13
wounds without c., 240
caused
c. them to go astray, 16
causeth
c. the grass to grow, 48
c. the vapours, 198
cease
and reproach shall c., 238
c. from anger, 8
c. from strife, 11
c. from troubling, 51
c. to do evil, 204
night shall not c., 221
of the proud to c., 12
poor shall never c., 182
remembrance to c., 10
ceased
c. not from their own, 238
ceasing
c. to pray, 185
cedar
c. in Lebanon, 116
house of c., 33
celebrate
death cannot c., 52
chafed
c. in their minds, 8
chaff
as c. that is driven, 73

■ 285 ■

c. before the wind, 72
c. that the storm, 260
c. to the wheat, 14
chain
compasseth them as a c., 188
chains
bound with c., 92
Chaldees
servants of the C., 2
chambers
c. by wrong, 43
hills from His c., 198
chance
c. happeneth to them all, 235
change
am the Lord, I c. not, 97
c. his skin, 28
that are given to c., 162
charge
c. of the Lord, 171
laid to my c., 135
chariot
c. of fire, 96
chariots
c. be as a whirlwind, 209
some trust in c., 202
wheels of his c., 50
chase
angel of the Lord c., 72
c. a thousand, 237
c. your enemies, 71
one c. a thousand, 1
shall c. them, 45
chasten
c. thy son while, 30
neither c. me in Thy hot, 29
chasteneth
c. his son, 63
God c. thee, 63
loveth him c., 30
chastening
despise not the c., 29
chastise
c. you with scorpions, 173
chastised
c. as a bullock, 64
c. you with whips, 173
cheer
c. thee in the days, 268
cheereth
c. God and man, 8
cheerful
heart maketh a c., 119
young men c., 191
cheese
curdled me like c., 46
chide
will not always c., 91
chief
father made him the c., 85

child
beareth the sucking c., 147
begetteth a wise c., 31
but a little c., 126
c. be born, 87
c. in two, 38
c. left to himself, 30
c. shall lead them, 31
city, the c. shall die, 49
correction from the c., 30
even a c. is known by, 28
for this c. I prayed, 20
forth her first c., 20
give her the living c., 36
give her the living c., 142
heart of a c., 30
king is a c., 148
poor and a wise c. than, 5
say not, I am a c., 67
sucking c., 37
tongue of the sucking c., 244
train up a c., 30
travail with c., 30
unto us a c. is born, 159
childhood
c. and youth are, 268
childless
c. among women, 200
made women c., 200
children
alien unto my mother's c., 75
bereaved of my c., 30
c. are an heritage, 31
c. are come to the birth, 258
c. arise up, and call, 175
c. ask bread, 85
c. be fatherless, 49
c. be multiplied, 260
c. despised me, 220
c. die for the fathers, 194
c. for ever, 144
c. of Belial, 261
c. of the desolate, 31
c. of the Lord, 31
c. of the married, 31
c. shall be taught, 69
c. that will not hear, 65
c.'s c. are the crown, 114
c.'s teeth are set, 21
die for the c., 194
diligently unto thy c., 34
eye shall not spare c., 10
eyes of his c., 19
father pitieth his c., 36
give me c., 30
given to the c., 120
hearts of all the c., 100
inheritance to c.'s c., 114
iniquity upon the c., 193
joyful mother of c., 88
leave thy fatherless c., 262

lying c., 65
peace of thy c., 69
resembled the c., 17
so are c. of the youth, 222
sorrow bring forth c., 20
tare forty and two c., 194
than all his c., 30
the c. of Ammon, 198
woe to the rebellious c., 16
wonderful works to c., 184
children of Israel
against c. shall not a dog, 105
among the c. a goodlier, 161
c. did evil, 131
c. did evil again, 16
c. died not one, 180
c. for a possession, 138
c. have not hearkened, 147
c. out of Egypt, 126
c. remembered, 16
c. walked, 74
c. walked forty years, 78
from the day that the c., 56
number of the c., 33
chimney
smoke out of the c., 73
choose
c. life, that, 31
c. none of his ways, 249
c. out of all the tribes, 139
c. thee one, 31
c. to us judgment, 53
c. you this day, 31
evil, and c. the good, 63
Lord doth c., 147
nor c. you because, 32
shall yet c. Jerusalem, 56
choosest
c. the tongue, 234
man whom Thou c., 118
chooseth
abomination is he that c., 129
chosen
c. Jacob unto Himself, 32
c. Me to put My name, 139
c. than great riches, 205
c. thee in the furnace, 101
c. you the Lord, 31
fast that I have c., 85
God hath c. thee, 32
have c. Jerusalem, 139
Lord hath c. Zion, 139
servant; I have c., 101
which ye have c., 83
circumcise
c. the flesh, 33
c. the foreskin, 33
c. yourselves to the, 7
cistern
out of thine own c., 4

cities
  like c. not inhabited, 57
city
  c. against c., 28
  c. and Thy people, 91
  c. become an harlot, 130
  c. famine and pestilence,
    61
  c. is full of violence, 146
  c. of David, 138
  c. of Jericho, 48
  c. of righteousness, 139
  c. of the great King, 139
  c. rejoiceth, 119
  c. sit solitary, 54
  c. that is broken, 223
  c. which I have chosen,
    139
  come into this c., 54
  comest nigh unto a c., 257
  cry, O c., 66
  cursed in the c., 193
  defend this c., 105
  destroy all the c., 38
  entrance into the c., 157
  evil in a c. and the, 61
  face against this c., 113
  faithful c., 139
  feet enter into the c., 49
  given you the c., 17
  in the c. and blessed, 22
  is this the c. that, 140
  Jerusalem, the c., 139
  make thee a desolate c., 57
  streets of the c., 191
  the Lord keep the c., 222
  woe to the bloody c., 47
  won than a strong c., 91
  words upon this c., 66
clay
  c. is in the potter's, 60
  made me as the c., 92
  shall c. say to him, 14
  we are the c., 46
clean
  be ye c. that bear, 197
  c. and to the unclean, 150
  c. hands, and a pure, 124
  c. in his own eyes, 224
  c. thing out, 43
  create in me a c. heart,
    235
  crib is c., 69
  how can he be c., 155
cleansed
  c. of the blood, 165
clear
  c. as the sun, 17
cleave
  c. nought of the cursed,
    115
  c. to the roof, 7
  c. unto the Lord, 82
  Him shalt thou c., 7

cleaveth
  c. to the roof, 244
climb
  c. up to heaven, 75
closer
  c. than a brother, 93
cloth
  menstruous c., 129
clothe
  c. the heavens, 169
  c. themselves with, 243
  drowsiness shall c., 147
clothed
  c. with shame, 72
  c. with shame, 72
clothes
  c. not be burned, 4
  c. waxed not old, 108
  rend your c., 165
clothing
  c. be thou our ruler, 148
cloud
  be as the morning c., 73
  c. out of the sea, 182
  is as a morning c., 113
  My bow in the c., 44
  pillar of a c., 105
clouds
  c. are the dust of His, 104
  c. be full of rain, 198
  heights of the c., 14
  regardeth the c., 147
  shall come up as c., 209
  truth unto the c., 100
clusters
  c. are bitter, 20
coals
  c. thereof c. of fire, 138
  go upon hot c., 4
  heap c. of fire upon, 226
coat
  c. of many colours, 85
cockatrice
  shall come forth a c., 66
cockle
  c. instead of barley, 135
cold
  as c. waters to a, 169
  c. and heat, 221
  stand before His c., 103
colours
  coat of many c., 85
come
  c. again with rejoicing, 48
  c. alike to all, 52
  c. and let us join, 19
  c. before His presence, 184
  c. down unto me, 235
  c. forth a rod, 159
  c. not among, 111
  c. now, and let us, 36
  c. on me what will, 26
  c. to pass, 189
  c. unto me now, 173

  c. ye to the waters, 57
  c. ye, buy, and eat, 57
  days to c., 178
  evil to c., 52
  for the time to c., 122
  him c. unto me, 7
  how to go out or c., 126
  it will surely c., 143
  let my cry c., 186
  neither shall it c. to, 70
  not c. into this city, 54
  remember what is c., 181
  shall not c. nigh, 50
  time is c., 66
  time is c., 130
comely
  black, but c., 17
  good and c. for one, 89
comest
  c. to me with a sword, 80
cometh
  another generation c., 68
  behold, the day c., 141
  behold, thy King c., 127
  c. in the name of the, 159
  c. not again, 91
  c. out of the north, 60
  day of the Lord c., 141
  help c. from the Lord, 13
  joy c. in the morning, 118
  morning c., 42
  whatsoever c. forth, 198
  whence c. my help, 13
comfort
  c. all her waste, 139
  c. in vain, 130
  c. me with apples, 152
  c. thine heart, 125
  c. ye My people, 34
  Lord shall c. Zion, 139
  Lord shall yet c. Zion, 56
  none to c., 2
  so will I c., 34
  staff they c. me, 34
  that I may take c., 164
comforted
  I will be c., 98
  that thou hast c. me, 114
comforter
  c. that should relieve, 34
comforters
  c. but I found none, 34
  miserable c., 34
comforteth
  am He that c., 34
  mother c., 34
coming
  before the c. of the, 159
  c. in, and thy rage, 100
  day of his c., 15
  meet thee at thy c., 52
  time of their c., 65
command
  soever I c. you, 35

whatsoever I c. thee, 187
word which I c., 220
commanded
c. and it stood fast, 46
c. and they were created, 168
God hath c., 18
Lord c. Moses, 153
Lord c. Moses, 74
whatsoever is c., 109
commandest
all that thou c., 170
commandeth
He c. and raiseth the, 168
commandment
according to the c., 171
c. is a lamp, 117
c. of the Lord, 4
feareth the c., 172
he that keepeth the c., 35
keep the king's c., 163
commandments
all His c. are sure, 111
c. are my delights, 34
c. of the Lord, 34
fear God, and keep His c., 67
hearkened to My c., 172
hide not Thy c., 144
keep all My c., 87
keep His c., 171
keep His c., 35
keep My c., 65
keep My c., 170
keep My c., 18
keep the c., 34
love Me and keep My c., 193
may learn Thy c., 35
commended
man shall be c., 183
commit
c. thy works unto, 239
to God c. my cause, 13
committed
evils that ye have c., 201
companion
c. of fools, 36
c. of riotous men, 36
c. to owls, 58
company
c. of nations, 22
compare
will ye c. unto Him, 109
compared
not to be c. unto her, 263
compass
mercy shall c. him, 81
compasseth
pride c. them about, 188
compassion
c. on the son, 37
for ye have c., 36
full of c., 37

God full of c., 101
yet will He have c., 158
compassions
show mercy and c., 37
complain
c. in the bitterness, 26
complaint
is my c. to man, 37
comprehend
which we cannot c., 100
comtempt
some to everlasting c., 71
conceal
publish, and c., 169
concealeth
faithful spirit c., 93
prudent man c., 23
conceit
wise in his own c., 90
wise in his own c., 38
wiser in his own c., 38
conceive
sin did my mother c., 20
thou shalt c., 87
virgin shall c., 159
conceived
c. all this people, 147
condemn
c. Him that is most just, 38
c. the wicked, 142
judges shall c., 207
wilt thou c. Me, 224
condemneth
thine own mouth c., 117
confession
c. unto the Lord, 203
make c. unto Him, 203
confidence
c. in an unfaithful, 20
dwell with c., 218
quietness and in c., 81
than put c. in man, 201
than put c. in princes, 114
confident
fool rageth, and is c., 77
confirm
c. the feeble knees, 70
confound
c. the language, 36
c. their language, 36
confusion
wind and c., 129
with their own c., 72
congregation
all the c., 41
evil c., 175
consent
c. thou not, 36
consider
c. and behold, 181
c. her ways, 62
c. not in their hearts, 47
c. the things of old, 203

c. the wondrous, 167
c. the years, 79
c. their latter end, 58
c. your ways, 19
latter days ye shall c., 251
people doth not c., 15
considereth
c. the poor, 29
consume
c. the tabernacles, 24
drought and heat c., 51
famine shall c., 85
consumed
c. them as stubble, 199
let sinners be c., 195
prophets be c., 84
the Lord shall be c., 16
ye shall be c., 257
consumeth
fire that c., 4
consuming
as a c. fire, 60
contain
heavens cannot c., 33
heavens cannot c. Him, 33
contend
c. with horses, 37
content
c. and dwelt, 41
contention
c. shall go out, 238
leave off c., 238
continual
c. dropping in a, 166
merry heart hath a c., 119
continually
seek His face c., 107
continue
kingdom shall not c., 194
continued
name shall be c., 84
contrite
be of a c. spirit, 116
broken and a c. heart, 42
convenient
c. for thee to go, 93
feed me with food c., 41
converts
c. with righteousness, 139
cord
c. be loosed, 63
threefold c. is not, 43
tongue with a c., 155
cords
c. of vanity, 230
corn
c. shall make the young, 191
treadeth out the c., 70
withholdeth c., 25
corner
dwell in a c., 156
head stone of the c., 174
stone for a c., 10

cornerstone
  laid the c., 46
corpses
  were all dead c., 27
correct
  c. me, but with judgment, 117
correcteth
  Lord loveth He c., 29
  man whom God c., 29
correction
  c. is grievous, 16
  rod of c., 30
  weary of His c., 29
  withhold not c., 30
corrupt
  breath is c., 51
  c. your seed, 126
corrupted
  c. thy wisdom, 38
corrupters
  iron; they are all c., 239
corruption
  c. Thou art my father, 51
  Holy One to see c., 75
  up my life from c., 56
couch
  my c. with my tears, 231
counsel
  c. of the heathen, 93
  c. of the Lord, 177
  c. of the ungodly, 36
  darkeneth c. by words, 130
  forsook the c., 5
  hear c. and receive, 5
  hearkeneth unto c., 5
  hide their c. from, 64
  is c. perished, 5
  nation void of c., 32
  spirit of c., 159
  that take c. but not, 16
  where no c. is, 117
  wise c. make war, 256
counsellor
  be called Wonderful, C., 159
counsellors
  multitude of c., 5
  to the c. of peace, 176
counsels
  c. of old, 83
  c. of the wicked, 5
  fall by their own c., 72
  multitude of thy c., 5
count
  c. all my steps, 100
  c. not thine handmaid, 261
  c. the dust, 2
counted
  c. as sheep, 50
  c. as the small dust, 114
  fool is c. wise, 90
countenance
  c. of his friend, 28

c. sad, seeing, 56
lift up His c., 22
maketh a cheerful c., 119
sadness of the c., 146
show of their c., 118
counteth
  c. me for His enemy, 178
countries
  disperse thee in the c., 79
  midst of the c., 57
  remember Me in far c., 79
country
  news from a far c., 169
  nor see his native c., 79
  throughout all the c., 84
courage
  be of good c., 44
  be of good c., 39
  be of good c., 70
  strong and of a good c., 70
  strong, and of good c., 39
courageous
  be strong and c., 70
  c. among the mighty, 54
course
  turned to his c., 132
courses
  stars in their c., 12
covenant
  break not Thy c., 45
  c. is with thee, 44
  c. of salt, 44
  c. of thy fathers, 1
  c. that I have made, 45
  c. with death, 12
  c. with our fathers, 32
  keep My c., 170
  mindful always of His c., 82
  mindful of His c., 45
  such as keep His c., 110
  token of a c., 44
  token of the c., 33
  words of this c., 45
cover
  worms shall c., 51
covereth
  c. the faces of judges, 134
covering
  destruction hath no c., 103
  sackcloth their c., 169
covet
  c. thy neighbor's wife, 4
  not c. thy neighbor's, 73
covetousness
  given to c., 43
  goeth after their c., 128
  truth, hating c., 113
crackling
  c. of thorns, 146
craftiness
  in their own c., 47
crafty
  devices of the c., 102

tongue of the c., 234
crane
  turtle and the c., 65
create
  c. in me a clean heart, 235
  c. new heavens, 46
  peace, and c. evil, 112
created
  c. He him, 45
  c. He them, 46
  c. He them, 45
  c. him for My glory, 46
  c. it not in vain, 46
  c. the waster, 60
  commanded and were c., 168
  God c. man, 45
  God c. man, 154
  God c. the heaven, 17
  hath not one God c., 25
  work which God c., 216
creator
  remember now thy C., 97
creature
  c. that was the name, 167
creeping
  over every c. thing, 9
crib
  ass his master's c., 15
  c. is clean, 69
cried
  belly of hell c. I, 187
  c. and I would not hear, 187
  c. but there was none, 54
  c. to Me, 55
  c. unto the Lord, 186
  depths have I c., 59
  He c. and they would, 187
crieth
  brother's blood c., 79
  c. out against me, 20
  needy when he c., 186
  voice of him that c., 44
  wisdom c. without, 263
crimes
  full of bloody c., 146
crooked
  c. generation, 199
  c. shall be made straight, 172
  c. things straight, 73
  that which is c., 3
  which He hath made c., 3
crown
  c. is fallen, 212
  c. of his head, 17
  c. of old men, 114
  c. to her husband, 156
  head is a c. of glory, 6
  stones of a c., 102
crowned
  c. him with glory, 155

D. his ten thousands, 84
D. prevailed over, 253
D. thy father's sake, 157
hand of D., 81
Nathan said to D, 3
raise unto D., 159
Saul eyed D., 138
servants as D., 153
soul of D., 93
sure mercies of D., 22
unto him, curse D., 94
David's
servant D. sake, 105
day
alas for the d., 141
alive this d., 32
all the d. long, 87
before them by d., 105
call upon me in d. of, 13
called the light d., 169
choose you this d., 31
cursed be the d., 20
d. and night, 221
d. cometh that shall burn,
141
d. draweth near, 130
d. his thoughts perish, 8
d. I am going, 50
d. in which the Lord, 249
d. is a d. of trouble, 58
d. is holy, 122
d. is Thine, 169
d. of adversity, 92
d. of adversity consider,
179
d. of battle, 253
d. of death than the, 3
d. of his coming, 15
d. of his transgression, 16
d. of my calamity, 71
d. of my death, 6
d. of my trouble I will, 186
d. of the Lord, 66
d. of the Lord at hand, 60
d. of the Lord cometh, 141
d. of the Lord is, 141
d. of the Lord is great, 141
d. of the Lord is near, 112
d. of the Lord's anger, 61
d. of their calamity, 194
d. of trouble, 66
d. of trouble, 107
d. of visitation, 195
d. of wrath, 259
d. of your fast, 85
d. shall come to die, 175
d. that God doth talk,
104
d. that I knew you, 65
d. that I rise, 176
d. that Moses sent, 91
d. the Lord hath made, 27
d. their fathers came, 77
d. thou shalt bear, 36

d. when I am in trouble,
247
d. when I visit, 128
d. wherein my mother, 20
deliver them in the d., 98
deliver us only this d., 180
desire the d. of the, 141
do they unto this d., 128
done unto this d., 82
down while it was yet d.,
116
dreadful d. of the Lord,
159
Egypt unto this d., 56
even unto this d., 39
every d. is blasphemed, 21
fear d. and night, 49
hear you in that d., 194
hid in the d., 157
hope in d. of evil, 125
in d. of prosperity, 179
kept me this d., 5
killed all the d., 156
knowest not what a d., 23
known this d., 99
let the d. perish, 58
light to rule the d., 14
meditate d. and night, 214
meditate d. and night, 220
more people that d., 256
more unto the perfect d.,
215
naked in that d., 54
nigh unto the Lord d., 185
night shineth as the d., 74
no d. like that, 266
of decision: for the d., 141
remember the sabbath d.,
216
remember this d., 92
seventh d. He rested, 46
seventh d. is the sabbath,
216
seventh d. thou shalt rest,
216
smite thee by d., 106
stand at the latter d., 81
strong this d. as, 91
than d. of one's birth, 3
the first d., 169
the seventh d., 216
this d. weak, 232
this d. will the Lord, 39
this is the d. whereof, 190
trouble thee this d., 47
very rainy d. and a, 166
victory that d., 116
wall night and d., 222
weep d. and night, 242
wicked for d. of evil, 46
with the wicked every d.,
140
days
a work in your d., 230

add unto thy d., 37
ancient d., 107
are not my d. few, 164
ashamed seven d., 193
d. are a shadow, 164
d. are as a shadow, 150
d. are as grass, 155
d. are extinct, 51
d. are fulfilled, 66
d. are like a shadow, 56
d. are sorrows, 59
d. are swifter, 58
d. as of old, 203
d. be prolonged, 112
d. may be prolonged, 175
d. not be prolonged, 60
d. of a tree, 101
d. of darkness, 52
d. of his life, 147
d. of Methuselah, 6
d. of my life, 22
d. of My people, 101
d. of my vanity, 6
d. of old, 79
d. of our years are, 149
d. of the years, 162
d. of thy life, 48
d. of thy youth, 97
d. of thy youth, 79
d. should speak, 79
d. so shall thy strength, 22
d. that I shall deal, 241
d. to come, 178
earth in those d., 230
evil in his d., 42
fear prolongeth d., 87
few d. and full, 149
find it after many d., 8
forty d. and forty nights,
89
full of d., 51
have forgotten Me d., 16
in his son's d. will I, 42
in six d. the Lord, 46
in six d. the Lord, 46
in the latter d., 247
in the latter d. ye, 251
in thy d. I will not, 157
length of d. is in, 263
length of d. understanding,
6
length of thy d., 97
let his d. be few, 195
measure of my d., 164
midst of his d., 64
midst of my d., 150
number our d., 149
pain all his d., 240
precious in those d., 255
seemed but a few d., 152
shall be for many d., 95
six d. shalt thou labour,
216
six d. thou shalt do, 216

spend d. in prosperity, 191
truth be in my d., 176
with the Lord forty d., 243
daytime
cry in the d., 59
dead
better than a d., 125
d. and the living, 137
d. bodies shall be for, 196
d. dog, 78
d. know not any thing, 150
d. man out of mind, 59
d. praise not the Lord, 52
d. which are already d.,
150
d. which he slew, 3
dealt with the d., 22
fell down d., 12
I praised the d., 150
king's son is d., 36
now he is d., 2
were all d. corpses, 27
deaf
curse the d., 118
d. as My messenger, 239
ears of the d., 23
hear, ye d., 238
maketh dumb, or d., 46
deal
d. gently for my sake, 36
d. very treacherously, 134
Lord d. kindly with, 22
neither d. falsely, 18
dealeth
every one d. falsely, 43
dealt
d. very bitterly, 9
dearly
given the d. beloved, 1
death
adulterer put to d., 4
as the shadow of d., 47
be put to d., 26
beast be put to d., 232
belong the issues from d.,
55
between me and d., 50
bitterness of d., 160
covenant with d., 12
curseth be put to d., 175
d. cannot celebrate, 52
d. for his own sin, 117
d. of His saints, 156
d. of the righteous, 50
d. part thee and me, 93
d. shall feed, 51
d. there is no remem-
brance, 51
d. they were not divided,
50
d. with the sword, 51
day of d. than the, 3
day of my d., 6
delivereth from d., 52

doors of shadow of d., 12
gates of d., 12
good, and d. and evil, 18
guide even unto d., 75
guilty of d., 26
hate me love d., 264
home there is as d., 52
in d. or life, 153
killeth be put to d., 26
life and d. blessing, 150
love is strong as d., 152
messengers of d., 9
murderer put to d., 142
no pleasure in the d., 52
nor shadow of d., 47
O d., I will be thy, 52
of the shadow of d., 243
pleasure in the d. of, 52
pursueth it to his own d.,
47
put to d., 216
put to d., 193
put to d., 26
put to d., 123
shadow of d., 39
shadow of d., 218
shadow of d., 51
shall not see d., 51
sleep of d., 13
slew at his d., 3
such as are for d. to d.,
196
surely be put to d., 26
surely put me to d., 5
swallow up d., 52
vexed unto d., 166
way of d., 150
ways of d., 180
worthy of d., 26
debate
d. thy cause with, 11
decayeth
building d., 25
deceit
balances of d., 25
d. is in the heart, 64
d. shall not dwell, 64
houses full of d., 47
wicked are d., 5
deceitful
deliver me from the d.,
106
favour is d., 17
from a d. tongue, 231
heart is d., 77
kisses of enemy are d., 48
tongue is d., 149
deceitfully
sharp razor, working d., 42
vanity, nor sworn d., 122
work of the Lord d., 68
deceive
d. not with thy lips, 124
d. not yourselves, 223

diviners d. you, 53
whom thou trustest d., 21
deceived
heart be not d., 83
let not him that is d., 202
of thine heart hath d., 38
terribleness hath d., 38
deceiver
cursed be the d., 53
decision
valley of d., 141
deckest
d. thee with ornaments, 17
declare
answer you, I will d., 26
d. His doings, 76
d. his generation, 122
d. His glory, 76
d. His righteousness, 99
d. if thou knowest, 12
d. it in the isles, 76
d. My glory among, 76
d. the works of the Lord,
61
d. their sin, 226
d. unto us the riddle, 19
d. what he seeth, 254
if I d. it unto, 5
declared
be d. in the grave, 150
decline
d. to her ways, 4
decree
d. unrighteous d.s, 114
princes d. justice, 162
deed
d. dwell with men, 109
no such d. done, 56
deeds
according to their d., 195
make known his d., 76
deep
d. to boil, 103
face of the d., 28
when d. sleep falleth, 67
wonders in the d., 172
defence
God is my d., 106
He is my d., 39
Lord is our d., 222
defend
d. the poor, 142
d. this city, 105
defer
d. not to pay, 189
d. not, for Thine own, 91
deferred
hope d., 125
defied
Lord hath not d., 48
defile
d. not the land, 47
d. yourselves with their,
112

defiled
    d. by them, 235
defileth
    every one that d. it, 216
defy
    d. the armies, 14
    how shall I d., 48
degree
    men of high d., 28
    men of low d., 28
degrees
    forward ten d., 172
    return backward ten d.,
        173
delicately
    they that did feed d., 126
delight
    commandments are my d.,
        34
    d. himself with God, 21
    d. in burnt offerings, 171
    d. is in the law, 214
    d. to do honour, 38
    just weight is His d., 25
    law is my d., 35
    Lord d. in us, 40
    people that d. in war, 257
    scorners d. in their, 89
    soul d., 235
    upright is His d., 29
delighted
    d. not in blessing, 142
delighteth
    d. to honour, 123
    He d. in his way, 18
    He d. in mercy, 91
deliver
    am with thee to d., 70
    bear, He will d., 39
    cannot profit nor d., 267
    continually, He will d., 40
    d. but their own souls, 61
    d. every man his soul, 75
    d. him in time of trouble,
        29
    d. his soul, 75
    d. it into the hand, 255
    d. me because of mine, 55
    d. me from mine enemies,
        72
    d. me from the deceitful,
        106
    d. me from the oppression,
        173
    d. me from the workers,
        146
    d. me in Thy righteous-
        ness, 55
    d. me not over, 178
    d. me out of, 247
    d. me, I pray, 86
    d. my soul, 231
    d. out of My hand, 102
    d. the needy, 186

d. the slayer, 137
d. thee into mine hand, 39
d. thee into the hand, 54
d. them in the day, 98
d. them into, 70
d. them into the hand, 1
d. them into thine hand,
    107
d. thine enemy, 107
d. us from the burning, 50
d. us from the heathen, 55
d. us only, 180
d. us out, 225
d. you no more, 77
d. you out of my hands, 21
d. you out of the hand, 55
I will d. thee, 13
let them d. you, 83
not d. him in the day, 16
of foot shall not d., 75
shall the mighty d., 40
upright shall d., 55
will surely d. thee, 107
delivered
    d. by much strength, 237
    d. me from all my fears, 55
    d. me out of the paw, 39
    d. me to the ungodly, 4
    d. Sisera into, 249
    d. the land, 40
    d. them into thine hand,
        72
    d. them into thine hand,
        253
    d. you out, 55
    gods of the nations d., 11
    Lord d. me into, 114
    shall be d., 13
    shall not be d., 75
    thou hast d. thy soul, 187
deliverer
    fortress, and my d., 106
    help and my d., 108
    tower, and my d., 107
deliverest
    d. the poor from, 100
delivereth
    d. and rescueth, 56
    d. from death, 52
    d. him out of them all, 247
    d. the poor, 55
    true witness d. souls, 124
depart
    d. away from him, 101
    d. from evil, 76
    d. from evil, 77
    d. from evil, 18
    d. from evil, 87
    d. from Judah, 147
    d. out of thy mouth, 170
    d. to the right, 31
    evil shall not d., 112
    foolishness d., 90
    kindness shall not d., 100

mountains shall d., 100
old, he will not d., 30
return and d., 86
sword shall never d., 49
departed
    beauty is d., 140
    glory d. from Israel, 125
    God is d., 1
    Lord d. from Saul, 201
    Lord is d., 12
departeth
    d. from evil, 77
    whose heart d., 202
depths
    out of the d., 59
derision
    have me in d., 6
desert
    d. like the garden, 138
    d. shall rejoice, 207
    render to them their d.,
        142
    straight in the d., 159
deserts
    according to their d., 143
deserve
    than our iniquities d., 158
desire
    all things thou canst d.,
        263
    d. accomplished, 3
    d. is toward me, 35
    d. is, that the Almighty, 3
    d. not the night, 169
    d. of the righteous, 79
    d. of the wicked, 8
    d. shall be to thy husband,
        14
    d. to return, 79
    upon earth that I d., 13
    wandering of the d., 57
    when the d. cometh, 125
    woe unto you that d., 141
desired
    d. it for His habitation,
        139
    d. mercy and not, 216
    more to be d., 35
    soul have I d., 62
desires
    d. of the wicked, 186
desireth
    His soul d., 103
    what thy soul d., 93
desolate
    altars shall be d., 61
    children of the d., 31
    countries that are d., 57
    d. for ever, 10
    d. in the streets, 126
    I will make thee d., 57
    land that was d., 207
    make thee a d. city, 57
    shall be d. in the midst, 57

desolation
  d. which shall come, 195
desolations
  behold our d., 187
despise
  d. not the chastening, 29
  d. not thy mother, 6
  do not d. a thief, 47
  fools d. wisdom, 68
  he will d. the wisdom, 5
  honoured her d., 43
  they that d. Me, 200
  Thou wilt not d., 42
  upon all those that d., 218
despised
  and d. among men, 196
  children d. me, 220
  d. and rejected, 159
  d. and we esteemed not,
    126
  d. of the people, 174
  d. the commandment, 4
  daughter of Zion hath d.,
    220
  for we are d., 180
  heart shall be d., 56
  I am small and d., 82
  wisdom is d., 5
despiseth
  d. his neighbour, 161
  d. his own soul, 64
  d. His ways shall, 35
  d. not His prisoners, 182
  d. the word, 172
  fool d., 31
  foolish man d., 31
  that d. his neighbour, 119
destitute
  d. of wisdom, 89
  leave not my soul d., 124
destroy
  d. both the young, 60
  d. the accursed, 196
  d. the righteous, 60
  d. the sinners, 230
  d. Thou them, 72
  d. ye utterly, 10
  flood to d. the earth, 44
  have mercy, but d., 60
  I will d. the fat, 141
  neither d. thee, 1
  pastors that d., 148
  shall d. them, 60
  that He d. thee not, 108
  therefore I will not d., 90
  Thou d. all the city, 38
  waster to d., 60
  wicked will He d., 195
  worms d. this body, 51
destroyed
  be utterly d., 123
  Egypt is d., 26
  fathers have d., 11
  fools shall be d., 36

foundations be d., 146
Israel, thou hast d., 108
shall be d. for ever, 146
word shall be d., 172
destroyeth
  d. his neighbour, 231
  d. his own soul, 4
  d. the perfect, 51
  gift d. the heart, 24
  one sinner d., 43
  that which d. kings, 154
destruction
  cometh their d., 134
  consumeth to d., 4
  d. cometh, 60
  d. hath no covering, 103
  d. of the poor, 182
  d. of the princes, 114
  d. to workers of iniquity,
    60
  d. unto them, 16
  faithfulness in d., 150
  fool's mouth is his d., 90
  grave, I will be thy d., 52
  hell and d. are never, 121
  lips shall have d., 192
  pride goeth before d., 80
devices
  d. of the crafty, 102
  d. they have imagined, 142
devise
  d. not evil against, 20
  woe to them that d., 47
deviseth
  d. his way, 18
  d. wicked imaginations, 12
  tongue d. mischiefs, 20
devoted
  every d. thing, 122
devour
  and pestilence shall d., 61
  another fire shall d., 75
  sword d. forever, 210
  sword shall d., 27
  sword shall d. flesh, 210
devoured
  d. with the sword, 238
  earth shall be d., 61
  wood d., 256
devoureth
  sword d. one, 49
  wicked d. the man, 134
dew
  and as the early d., 113
  as the early d., 73
  d. falleth, 40
  distil as the d., 69
  distil as the d., 66
  drops of d., 198
  favour is as d., 9
diamond
  point of a d., 178
did
  as they d. unto me, 200

thou d. well in that, 137
die
  appointed to d., 36
  better for me to d., 59
  cause him to d., 26
  cause me to d., 53
  city, the child shall d., 49
  curse God, and d., 28
  d. and not live, 51
  d. and return, 10
  d. by the famine, 10
  d. for his own iniquity,
    206
  d. for his own sin, 194
  d. for the fathers, 194
  d. for thirst, 58
  d. for want of wisdom, 130
  d. in the wilderness, 58
  d. in the wilderness, 86
  d. in this land, 2
  d. of the pestilence, 10
  d. the death, 50
  d. with the Philistines, 50
  d. with the sword, 61
  despiseth His ways shall
    d., 35
  diest, will I d., 50
  else I d., 30
  fathers shall not d., 194
  for why will ye d., 150
  for why will ye d., 52
  hateth reproof shall d., 47
  he shall even d. thereby, 16
  I shall not d., 61
  if a man d., 133
  if a man d., 51
  know that they shall d.,
    150
  lest we d., 15
  lest ye d., 144
  let me d., 50
  man that shall d., 86
  must needs d., 163
  point to d., 57
  rod, he shall not d., 30
  shall come to d., 175
  shall not surely d., 136
  shall surely d., 15
  shall surely d., 131
  shall surely d., 223
  shalt not d., 222
  shalt not d., 34
  shalt surely d., 80
  sinneth, it shall d., 206
  smiteth so that he d., 26
  thou shalt d. because, 121
  till I d. I will not, 135
  time to d., 17
  to morrow we shall d., 27
  why shouldest thou d., 150
  wicked shall d. in his, 187
  wisdom shall d., 161
  wise men d., 164
  worthy to d., 67

died
  cattle of Egypt d., 180
  d. in a good old, 50
  d. in a good old age, 51
  why d. I not, 58
  would God I had d., 116
  would God we had d., 58
diest
  where thou d., 50
dieth
  d. he shall carry, 73
  death of him that d., 52
  how d. the wise man, 52
  man d. and wasteth, 51
difference
  teach My people the d., 33
dig
  though they d. into hell, 75
diggeth
  d. a pit shall fall, 77
  whoso d. a pit, 220
dignity
  excellency of d., 28
diligent
  d. in his business, 2
  d. maketh rich, 146
diligently
  let it be d. done, 109
  teach them d., 34
dim
  gold become d., 9
diminish
  d. ought from it, 220
  nor d. from, 35
dinner
  better is d. of herbs, 152
direct
  Lord d. his steps, 18
  man to d. his steps, 202
dirt
  cast up mire and d., 261
disappointeth
  He d. the devices, 102
discern
  d. between good and bad, 63
  d. between the righteous, 113
discerneth
  wise man's heart d., 63
discord
  soweth d. among brethren, 12
discouraged
  fail nor be d., 143
  neither be d., 70
discover
  d. not a secret, 20
discretion
  d. shall preserve, 242
  fair woman without d., 17
  heavens by His d., 46
disdained
  fathers I would have d., 6

disease
  d. he sought not, 89
disgrace
  d. the throne, 99
dish
  man wipeth a d., 60
dismayed
  afraid nor d., 70
  be not d., 125
  d. at their looks, 86
  d. by reason, 70
  dread not, nor be d., 39
  heathen are d., 14
  neither be d., 70
  neither be thou d., 86
  not d. at the signs, 14
disperse
  d. thee in the countries, 79
displeased
  David d. the Lord, 76
displeasure
  do them a d., 134
  hot d., 29
disposing
  d. thereof is of the, 28
disquieted
  why hast thou d. me, 235
dissolved
  whole Palestina, art d., 66
distil
  d. as the dew, 69
  d. as the dew, 66
distress
  d. I cried unto the Lord, 186
  in my d. I called, 185
  out of their d., 55
  when ye are in d., 173
distributeth
  d. sorrows in His anger, 195
ditch
  whore is a deep d., 191
divers
  bag d. weights, 25
  d. measures, 25
  d. weights and, 25
divide
  d. the living child, 38
  d. the spoil, 227
  d. the spoil, 127
  d. thou it by lot, 138
  nor thine, but d. it, 224
divided
  d. the sea, 97
  were not d., 50
diviners
  d. nor to your dreamers, 5
  prophets and your d., 53
do
  as she hath done, d., 200
  courage, and d. it, 70
  d. all that is in, 70
  d. it for thee, 93

  d. it with thy might, 69
  d. not thou this folly, 132
  d. so to him as he hath, 210
  d. that which is right, 18
  d. them, that ye, 34
  d. to him as, 107
  d. to me according, 2
  d. unto him, as, 177
  d. unto thee, 114
  d. unto them, 211
  d. unto us, 114
  d. what seemeth good, 53
  d. what seemeth Him good, 2
  d. with them what seemeth, 38
  God d. so and more, 80
  let Him d. to me, 248
  Lord d. so to me, 93
  Lord, and d. good, 18
  not d. this, 69
  observe to d. it, 35
  shall He not d. it, 82
  speaketh, that I must d., 170
  spoken we will d., 170
  that will I d. for, 73
  what thou oughtest to d., 166
  will I d. for you, 114
  will ye d. in the day of, 195
doctrine
  d. shall drop, 66
doer
  rewardeth the proud d., 82
doers
  hand of the d., 255
doeth
  desireth, that He d., 103
  none that d. good, 43
  whatsoever God d., 178
  when God d. this, 50
  wherefore d. the Lord, 167
dog
  am I a d., 41
  am I a d.'s head, 136
  as a d. returneth to his, 90
  dead d., 78
  living d. is better, 125
  not a d. move his tongue, 105
  price of a d., 29
  servant a d., 28
dogs
  d. licked the blood, 27
  d. of my flock, 6
  d. shall eat Jezebel, 27
  d. shall eat Jezebel, 226
doing
  this is the Lord's d., 239
doings
  d. among the people, 76

evil of your d., 204
from your evil d., 77
known by his d., 28
their own d. nor, 238
dominion
    d. over the fish, 9
done
    all that she hath d., 12
    as I have d., 142
    as thou hast d., 211
    as Thou hast d. unto, 211
    d. according to the law, 35
    d. excellent things, 232
    d. unto his brother, 177
    d. very foolishly, 42
    d. wonderful things, 185
    daughters have d., 156
    hast d. right, 42
    have d. perversely, 39
    have d. wickedly, 42
    how I have d. it, 95
    it shall be d. unto, 211
    no such deed d., 56
    not have d. it, 5
    seen what I have d., 160
    sheep, what have they d., 206
    spake, and it was d., 46
    to him as he hath d., 210
    what hath he d., 134
    what have I d., 134
    what I have d., 4
    what shall be d., 123
    wherefore hast thou d., 94
door
    d. of my lips, 198
    sin lieth at the d., 80
doorkeeper
    rather be a d., 127
doors
    d. of my house, 198
    d. of shadow of death, 12
    d. to the traveller, 125
    keep the d. of thy mouth, 20
double
    d. heart do they speak, 64
    d. portion of thy spirit, 122
doubt
    no d. but ye are the, 161
dove
    wings, like a d., 74
doves
    sore like d., 9
down
    bring d. like lambs, 60
    bring them d., 11
    but I will throw d., 95
    cast d. his altar, 83
    cast me d., 236
    d. to the grave, 126
    d. to the grave, 102
    d. to the grave, 51
    evening it is cut d., 155

going d. of the same, 184
I will bring thee d., 75
let us go d., 36
maketh me to lie d., 34
man shall be brought d., 126
putteth d. one, 239
sat d. and wept, 233
those that be bowed d., 108
to cast d., 102
when thou liest d., 34
will I bring thee d., 188
will I bring them d., 75
dragons
    brother to d., 58
    dwellingplace for d., 54
draw
    d. out Thine anger, 98
    d. thy sword, 125
drawers
    d. of water, 194
draweth
    d. nigh unto the grave, 6
    day d. near, 130
dread
    d. make me afraid, 86
    d. not, neither, 70
    d. not, nor be dismayed, 39
    let Him be your d., 86
dreadful
    d. day of the Lord, 159
dream
    let him tell a d., 67
    old men shall d., 67
    prophet that hath a d., 67
    show me the d., 67
dreamer
    d. of dreams, 83
    this d. cometh, 161
dreamers
    diviners, nor to your d., 5
dreameth
    hungry man d., 63
    thirsty man d., 63
dreams
    dreamer of d., 83
    hated him for his d., 66
    old men shall dream d., 67
    prophets, nor by d., 1
    scarest me with d., 66
drieth
    broken spirit d., 57
drink
    camels d. also, 143
    d. and enjoy the, 89
    d. and I will give, 143
    d. but ye are not, 69
    d. of the water, 244
    d. of the wrath, 98
    d. the blood, 189
    d. the sweet, 27
    d. thy wine, 89

d. water by measure, 85
d. water in this place, 41
d. waters out of thine, 4
d. wine with a song, 233
eat, and to d., 49
give him water to d., 72
give strong d., 151
giveth his neighbour d., 67
let him d. and forget, 59
let us eat and d., 27
man should eat and d., 181
may follow strong d., 67
not d. wine of them, 63
not to d. of the cup, 196
not with strong d., 67
strong d. is raging, 151
vinegar to d., 48
vineyards, but not d., 94
wine nor strong d., 58
drinketh
    d. but he awaketh, 63
    d. up my spirit, 9
    d. up scorning, 224
drive
    d. out from before, 40
drop
    d. as an honeycomb, 4
    d. as the rain, 66
    d. of a bucket, 114
dropping
    continual d. in a, 166
drops
    begotten the d. of dew, 198
dross
    silver is become d., 130
    take away the d., 251
drought
    d. and heat consume, 51
drown
    neither can floods d., 152
drowsiness
    d. shall clothe, 147
drunk
    arrows d. with blood, 210
    d. neither wine nor, 58
    d. with their blood, 27
drunkard
    d. and the glutton, 67
drunken
    d. but not with wine, 67
    d. man staggereth, 67
    d. with wormwood, 20
    have assuredly d., 196
    long wilt thou be d., 3
dry
    better is a d. morsel, 225
    d. bones, hear the word, 208
    d. land springs, 258
    walked upon d. land, 74
    womb and d. breasts, 49
due
    glory d. unto His name, 115

glory d. unto His name, 184
good to whom it is d., 115
slide in d. time, 175
spoken in d. season, 5

dumb
maketh the d., 46
to the d. stone, Arise, 129
tongue of the d., 120

dung
d. upon the face, 25
d. upon your faces, 126
flesh as the d., 209

dungeon
life in the d., 59
out of the low d., 59

dunghill
beggar from the d., 55
needy out of the d., 37

dunghills
in scarlet embrace d., 126

dust
alike in the d., 51
all are of the d., 74
all turn to d., 74
clouds are the d. of His, 104
d. of Jacob, 2
d. of the balance, 114
d. of the earth, 2
d. of the earth, 30
d. of the land, 179
d. shalt thou eat, 48
d. thou art, 23
dwell in d., 125
formed man of the d., 45
hide thee in the d., 74
lick the d., 126
lick the d., 126
number the d., 2
out of the d., 55
out of the d., 102
poor out of the d., 37
poured out as d., 209
remembereth we are d., 37
repent in d., 203
return to their d., 10
sleep in the d. of, 71
small as the d., 10
unto d. shalt thou, 23

duty
whole d. of man, 67

dwell
but ye shall not d. in, 63
d. in a corner, 156
d. in an house of cedar, 33
d. in dust, 125
d. in house of the Lord, 22
d. in safety, 217
d. in the land, 218
d. in the tents, 127
d. in the wilderness, 156
d. in their place, 32
d. together in unity, 24

d. with confidence, 218
d. with the lamb, 10
deceit shall not d., 64
here will I d., 139
house to d. in, 33
I may d. among them, 33
I will d. in the midst, 105
they that d. therein, 68
will God d. with men, 109

dwellest
d. in the midst of, 36

dwelleth
Lord d. in Zion, 140

dwelling
d. place of the wicked, 72
heaven Thy d. place, 90

dwellingplace
d. for dragons, 54

dwellings
more than all the d., 139

dwelt
d. in silence, 13
d. on the other side, 41

E

eagle
fly as the e., 235
fly away as an e., 73
high as the e., 75
way of an e., 166

eagles
swifter than e., 44
swifter than the e., 235
with wings as e., 19

ear
because He inclined His e., 186
e. filled with hearing, 8
e. now be attentive, 185
e. of the wise, 144
e. to your reasons, 175
e. trieth words, 248
give e. O ye heavens, 234
give e. O ye princes, 232
give ye e., 187
He that planted the e., 104
hide not Thine e., 186
incline Thine e., 55
incline thine e., 117
incline Thine e., 13
incline Thine e., 187
nor inclined their e., 121

early
and as the e. dew it, 113
cloud, and as the e. dew, 73
return and depart e., 86
rise up e., 67
seek me e., 264
will I seek Thee e., 62

ears
cry did enter into His e., 185

cry in Mine e., 91
e. but they hear not, 129
e. of a fool, 5
e. of every one, 243
e. of the deaf, 23
e. of the Lord, 37
e. shall tingle, 208
hearing of his e., 80
His e. are open, 106
openeth the e. of men, 67
opening the e., 111
sheep in mine e., 53
up into Mine e., 11
whoso stoppeth his e., 29

earth
and in the e. is Thine, 120
beasts of the e., 196
before Him, all the e., 87
between Me and the e., 44
blood upon the e., 194
breadth of the e., 12
called the dry land e., 68
consumed out of the e., 195
cut off from the e., 261
days upon e., 164
dust of the e., 71
dust of the e., 2
dust of the e., 30
dust of the e., 10
dust of the e., 2
e. abideth for ever, 68
e. also is Thine, 120
e. beneath, 109
e. e. e. hear the word, 59
e. full of the goodness, 68
e. given to the wicked, 134
e. hath He given, 120
e. is full of His, 99
e. is full of Thy riches, 167
e. is Mine, 68
e. is My footstool, 104
e. is the Lord's, 68
e. is the Lord's, 233
e. keep silence before, 109
e. make a loud noise, 27
e. shall be devoured, 61
e. shall be filled, 99
e. shall be full, 82
e. that is not filled, 52
e. was of one language, 251
e. was without form, 28
e. with her bars, 56
empty themselves upon e., 198
end of the e., 232
ends of the e., 198
ends of the e., 140
exalted in the e., 99
face of the e., 68
face of the e., 85
fall to the e., 217
families of the e., 22
families of the e., 85

fill heaven and e., 74
flood to destroy the e., 44
flowers appear on the e., 221
forsaken the e., 78
foundations of the e., 14
giants in the e., 230
hangeth the e. upon, 46
He hath made the e., 46
hear, O e. the words, 234
heaven and e. praise, 184
heaven and the e., 17
heaven or in e., 99
heaven, and thou upon e., 127
high above all the e., 77
high above the e., 101
in e. beneath, 104
inhabitant of the e., 59
inhabitants of the e., 103
inherit the e., 81
joy of the whole e., 139
joy of the whole e., 140
Judge of all the e., 101
judges of the e., 114
judgment in the e., 143
judgments in all the e., 104
just man on e., 177
King of all the e., 184
kingdoms of the e., 55
kingdoms of the e., 232
kings of the e., 259
latter day upon the e., 81
let the e. be glad, 27
let the e. hear, 187
let the e. rejoice, 103
like Me in all the e., 109
like worms of the e., 126
made heaven and e., 13
made heaven and e., 46
made heaven and e., 46
made man on the e., 46
made the e. by His, 46
meek of the e., 62
meek shall inherit the e., 127
men on the e., 109
nations of the e., 32
new e. and the former, 46
none like him in the e., 162
none upon e. I desire, 13
or on e. beneath, 109
over all the e., 9
people of the e., 84
people of the e., 101
perish from the e., 84
perished out of the e., 112
pillars of the e., 68
praise in the e., 139
profit of the e., 43
rain was upon the e., 89
replenish the e., 14
replenish the e., 30

returneth to his e., 8
sing all the e., 232
speak to the e., 102
stranger in the e., 144
thou be in the e., 48
throughout the whole e., 104
way of all the e., 50
way of all the e., 51
while the e. remaineth, 221
whole e. rejoiceth, 57
worketh wonders in e., 56
east
belly with the e. wind, 252
e. wind brought, 180
from the e. nor, 239
on the e. of Eden, 174
easy
knowledge is e., 144
eat
bread to e., 72
come ye, buy, and e., 57
comely for one to e., 89
dogs shall e., 27
dogs shall e. Jezebel, 226
dust shalt thou e., 48
e. and be satisfied, 157
e. at thy table, 114
e. bread by weight, 85
e. bread nor drink, 41
e. but not be satisfied, 49
e. but ye have not, 69
e. his pleasant fruits, 152
e. of their dainties, 230
e. that thou mayest have, 89
e. the fat, 2
e. the fat, 27
e. the good of the land, 172
e. the labour of, 69
e. the sons, 28
e. them like wool, 60
e. thou honey, 89
e. thy bread with joy, 89
e. ye that which is good, 235
enemies shall e. it, 94
evil, thou shalt not e., 112
fruit thereof, and did e., 64
hasteth to e., 235
hear, nor e., 129
honey shall he e., 63
let us e. and drink, 27
lion shall e. straw, 24
man should e. and drink, 181
mayest freely e. but, 112
me, and I did e., 20
moth shall e., 60
poor of thy people may e., 48
shall not e. of it, 144
shalt not e. thereof, 190

shalt thou e. bread, 192
sighing before I e., 9
sons shall e. fathers, 28
sun, than to e., 49
tree, and I did e., 20
eaten
bread e. in secret, 65
e. sour grapes, 21
e. without salt, 88
hath the cankerworm e., 61
hath the caterpillar e., 61
that the locust hath e., 91
eater
into the mouth of the e., 107
out of the e., 213
eateth
e. but he awaketh, 63
e. his own flesh, 147
e. not the bread, 156
e. the sour grape, 206
she e. and wipeth, 4
Eden
east of E., 174
from the garden of E., 174
garden of E., 174
like the garden of E., 207
wilderness like E., 138
edge
teeth are set on e., 21
teeth set on e., 206
egg
white of an e., 88
Egypt
a thick darkness in E., 169
bondman in E., 36
bondman in E., 250
bury me not in E., 25
came forth out of E., 77
came out from E., 92
cattle of E. died, 180
died in the land of E., 58
E. as a shepherd, 253
E. is destroyed, 26
firstborn in E., 88
forth out of E., 55
gods of E., 129
Israel out of E., 126
out of the land of E., 55
out of the land of E., 11
out of the land of E., 137
strangers in E., 90
strangers in E., 24
through E. this night, 88
up out of E., 56
Egyptian
killedst the E., 244
Egyptians
serve the E., 86
elder
e. shall serve, 88
elders
e. and they will tell thee, 79

elect
  e. shall long enjoy, 101
Elijah
  doest thou here, E., 67
  E. passed by him, 148
  E. the prophet, 159
else
  there is none e., 109
  there is none e., 163
embrace
  when thou dost e., 264
emptied
  land shall be utterly e., 57
empty
  full of rain, they e., 198
  home again e., 50
  not go e., 92
  over the e. place, 46
  soul is e., 63
enchanters
  dreamers, nor to your e., 5
end
  better is the e., 71
  blessed the latter e., 55
  come to his e. and, 249
  consider their latter e., 58
  e. is near, 66
  e. of all nations, 102
  e. of that man is peace, 162
  e. of the earth, 232
  e. shall be the vision, 71
  e. thereof are the ways, 180
  in the latter e., 143
  in the latter e., 20
  is the e. of all men, 52
  keep it unto the e., 35
  last e. be like his, 50
  make an e., 17
  make an e. of words, 131
  not make a full e., 102
  peace shall be no e., 159
  there is no e., 24
  time appointed the e., 10
  to know mine e., 164
  what is mine e., 58
  wise in thy latter e., 5
  years shall have no e., 75
ended
  summer is e., 59
  words of Job are e., 71
ends
  e. of the earth, 198
  e. of the earth, 140
endure
  can thine heart e., 241
  his name shall e., 84
  Lord shall e. for ever, 97
  Lord shalt e. for ever, 75
  Thou shalt e., 120
  weeping may e., 118
endureth
  anger e. but a moment, 98
  e. to all generations, 248

mercy e. for ever, 113
mercy e. for ever, 101
mercy e. for ever, 184
truth of the Lord e., 249
enemies
  avenge Me of Mine e., 210
  avenged upon their e., 107
  backs before their e., 45
  because of mine e., 55
  become her e., 20
  chase your e., 71
  deliver me from mine e., 72
  delivered your e., 147
  do to all your e., 54
  e. have heard, 96
  e. shall be cut off, 254
  e. shall lick, 126
  e. thy footstool, 106
  e. wrongfully rejoice, 72
  enlarged over mine e., 253
  even e. to be at peace, 18
  find out all Thine e., 72
  hand of all your e., 55
  hand of her e., 1
  hand of our e., 225
  hand of their e., 1
  indignation toward His e., 213
  let not mine e., 72
  lovest thine e., 93
  presence of mine e., 22
  prevail against His e., 103
  pursue after your e., 256
  saved from mine e., 55
  saved from your e., 252
  souls of thine e., 71
  spoil of your e., 227
  spoil to all their e., 126
  stand before thine e., 43
  subdue all thine e., 71
  vengeance to Mine e., 140
  will of mine e., 178
  wrath for His e., 98
  your e. shall eat it, 94
enemy
  become thine e., 12
  counteth me for His e., 178
  dashed in pieces the e., 236
  deliver thine e., 107
  e. doth not triumph, 100
  e. unto thine e., 7
  found me, O mine e., 142
  holdest me for Thine e., 1
  if thine e. be hungry, 72
  kisses of an e., 48
  man find his e., 71
  meet thine e.'s ox, 123
  not an e. that, 20
  rejoice not mine e., 23
  shall the e. blaspheme, 21
  sword of the e., 50

when thine e. falleth, 72
enjoy
  e. the good, 89
  e. the good of all his, 181
  e. the work of their, 101
enlarged
  e. my steps, 217
enough
  eat, but ye have not e., 69
  it is e., 157
  not e. for us, 40
  say not, it is e., 52
enquire
  e. of the Lord, 117
enquired
  Saul e. of the Lord, 1
  will not be e. of by, 14
ensign
  lifted up as an e., 102
enter
  e. into His ears, 185
  e. into the city, 49
  e. not into judgment, 141
  e. not into the path, 18
enterprise
  perform their e., 102
entice
  e. him, and see, 136
  e. thy husband, 19
  if sinners e., 36
entrance
  e. into the city, 157
enviest
  e. thou for my sake, 73
envious
  e. at the foolish, 73
envy
  able to stand before e., 9
  e. not the oppressor, 249
  e. slayeth the silly, 8
  heart e. sinners, 138
Ephraim
  grapes of E., 179
equal
  not My way e., 80
  shall I be e., 83
equity
  e. cannot enter, 146
err
  Thou made us to e., 229
errand
  secret e. unto, 53
erred
  e. exceedingly, 42
erreth
  refuseth reproof e., 47
errors
  work of e., 129
Esau
  E. thy firstborn, 53
  hands of E., 53
  not E. Jacob's brother, 153
escape
  cause me to e., 55

e. in the king's house, 178
nor mighty man e., 253
shall he e. that doeth, 75
wicked shall not e., 195
escaped
e. from his master, 231
e. of the house, 240
e. with the skin, 74
none e. nor remained, 61
escapeth
that e. shall not be, 75
establish
e. and till He make, 139
established
e. the world, 46
e. the world, 46
he hath e., 46
shall the throne be e., 163
shalt thou be e., 215
so shall ye be e., 81
thoughts shall be e., 239
throne shall be e., 163
throne shall be e., 163
ye shall not be e., 19
esteem
He e. thy riches, 237
esteemed
be lightly e., 200
despised, and we e., 126
esteemeth
e. iron as straw, 237
estranged
e. from the womb, 17
eternal
e. God is thy refuge, 217
Ethiopian
E. change his skin, 28
eunuchs
e. in the palace, 125
even
e. I only, am left, 58
e. I, am the Lord, 109
e. thou shalt say, 246
I. e. I, am He, 34
in an e. balance, 39
would God it were e., 246
evening
e. it is cut down, 155
e. withhold not thine, 62
the e. and the morning,
169
event
e. to the righteous, 150
ever
See "Forever"
everlasting
awake, some to e. life, 71
e. king, 97
e. strength, 237
mercy is e., 101
mercy is e., 111
mighty God, the e., 159
some to e. contempt, 71
unto thee an e. light, 117

evermore
time forth and for e., 97
every
e. man his righteousness,
212
e. one That prepareth, 91
e. purpose under, 168
Thou canst do e. thing,
103
to e. thing there is a, 168
everyone
e. against his brother, 28
e. against his neighbour,
28
evil
accustomed to do e., 28
against them for e., 54
all this great e. upon, 103
and from your e. doings,
77
cease to do e., 204
concerning me, but e., 5
death and e., 18
depart from e., 76
depart from e., 77
depart from e., 18
depart from e., 87
departeth from e., 77
did e. in the sight, 246
do e. in His sight, 4
done e. in the sight, 78
done that which was e., 77
e. again in the sight, 131
e. against his brother, 24
e. against thee, 199
e. against thy neighbour,
20
e. and not for good, 113
e. and the good, 104
e. came unto, 9
e. congregation, 175
e. entreated this people, 66
e. from his youth, 76
e. in the sight, 65
e. in your hearts, 77
e. is come upon us, yet,
131
e. is in mine hand, 134
e. pursueth sinners, 77
e. shall hunt, 254
e. shall not depart, 112
e. shall slay the wicked,
142
e. thing and bitter, 16
e. upon their beds, 47
e. upon this place, 209
e. we will obey, 3
e. will befall, 247
eyes than to behold e., 197
eyes upon them for e., 196
face against you for e., 196
feareth God, and
escheweth e., 162
few and e., 162

forseeth the e., 192
from his e. way, 204
from the e. to come, 52
God repented of the e., 91
God, and eschewed e., 214
good, and not e., 31
hate the e., 19
he that pursueth e., 47
heart full of e., 77
help the e. doers, 1
hope in day of e., 125
I will bring e., 10
I will fear no e., 39
I would do this e., 46
is to hate e., 77
Israel did e. again, 16
it is an e. time, 192
keep me from e., 76
keep thee from e. woman,
154
know good and e., 112
know to refuse the e., 63
knowing good and e., 72
knowledge of good and e.,
112
love the Lord, hate e., 77
man from his e., 204
multitude to do e., 36
not bring e. in his days, 42
not receive e., 2
peace, and create e., 112
preserve thee from all e.,
218
proceedeth not e., 113
punish the world for e., 77
put away the e., 204
put the e. away, 76
repent Me of the e., 91
repentest Thee of the e.,
37
reward doer of e., 194
reward to the e., 146
rewarded e. for good, 3
rewarded me e. for good,
112
rewarded thee e., 42
rewardeth e. for good, 112
see all the e., 36
shall there be e. in a, 61
that call e. good, 112
the e. that shall come, 9
them that imagine e., 64
though sinner do e., 112
tongue from e., 77
turn from your e. ways, 77
turn ye from your e., 52
turn ye from your e., 18
upon this city for e., 66
watch over them for e., 98
way of e. men, 18
wicked and the e., 195
wicked for day of e., 46
will I bring the e., 42
wise to do e., 112

f. of the judges, 134
spread dung upon your f., 126

fade
f. as a leaf, 92

fadeth
flower f., 109

fail
children shall f., 19
eyes of wicked shall f., 195
f. nor be discouraged, 143
f. with looking, 59
He will not f. thee, 107
man's heart f., 43
not f. thee nor, 1

failed
kinsfolk have f., 151
might hath f., 45
not f. one word, 45
one thing hath f., 189

faileth
their tongue f., 85
when my strength f., 6

faint
behold, he is f., 63
heart is f., 240
if thou f. in the day, 92
power to the f., 108

fainted
when my soul f., 44

fainthearted
fear not, neither be f., 70

fair
f. as the moon, 17
f. one, and come, 216
so is a f. woman, 17
that they were f., 17
vain make thyself f., 17

faith
live by his f. by his, 82

faithful
f. ambassador, 70
f. are the wounds of a, 48
f. city, 139
f. city become an harlot, 130
f. man who can find, 153
f. spirit concealeth, 93
preserveth the f., 82
up a f. priest, 33
who is so f., 153

faithfully
f. judgeth the poor, 163
speak My word f., 67

faithfulness
f. and truth, 83
f. in destruction, 150
righteousness and his f., 212

fall
diggeth a pit shall f., 220
diggeth a pit shall f., 77
f. by the sword, 142
f. by the sword, 209

f. by the sword, 10
f. by their own counsels, 72
f. from my shoulder, 135
f. into the hand, 58
f. into the mouth of, 107
f. into the pit, 66
f. into the pit, 75
f. into their own nets, 209
f. to the earth, 217
f. with pain, 98
hair f. to the earth, 142
let me f. into the hand, 158
let me not f. into, 48
not understand shall f., 130
people f., 117
pride before a f., 80
proud shall f., 12
riches shall f., 80
sons together shall f., 172
spirit before a f., 80
thousand shall f., 50
thy multitude to f., 256
transgressors shall f., 19
upholdeth all that f., 108
when I f. I shall arise, 23
wicked shall f. by, 142

fallen
bricks are f., 12
crown is f., 212
f. in the street, 146
f. unto me in pleasant, 122
how art thou f., 54
Judah is f., 21
mighty f., 145
mighty f. and, 54

falleth
alone when he f., 43
dew f. on the ground, 40
f. before wicked, 134
tongue f. into mischief, 64

fallow
break up your f. ground, 204

false
against f. swearers, 4
f. balance is, 25
f. witness that speaketh, 12
f. witness will utter, 28
f. witnesses are risen, 178
f. witnesses did rise up, 135
far from a f. matter, 123
love no f. oath, 177
not bear f. witness, 177

falsehood
f. have we hid, 64

falsely
every one dealeth f., 43
neither deal f., 18
prophesy f. in My name, 84

fame
f. was noised, 84

families
all f. of the earth, 22
f. of the earth, 85
f. that call not on Thy, 112

family
among his f., 121

famine
and the f. within, 50
are for the f. to the f., 60
by sword and f., 84
die by the f., 10
f. shall consume, 85
f. shall devour him, 61
f. was over all, 85
not a f. of bread, 85
send a f. in the land, 85

far
and those that be f., 126
be not f. from, 9
be not f. from me, 13
comforter is f. from me, 34
f. be it from God, 76
f. from me, 265
f. from me, O Lord, 223
f. from the wicked, 218
f. from the wicked, 108
f. from Thee shall perish, 16
f. off shall die, 10
God be not f. from, 1
good news from a f., 169
hear, ye that are f., 4
keep thee f., 123
let it be f. from him, 142
Lord be not f. from, 13
put it f. away, 18
remember Me in f., 79
than a brother f., 13
they are gone f. from Me, 75

fashioneth
say to him that f., 14

fast
day of your f., 85
f. that I have chosen, 85
righteousness I hold f., 40
when they f., 85
wherefore should I f., 2

fasting
humbled my soul with f., 85

fat
art waxen f., 53
destroy the f., 141
eat the f., 27
f. of rams, 171
f. of the land, 2
it is made f., 209

father
ask thy f., 79
bosom, as a nursing f., 147
calamity of his f., 31

corruption Thou art my f.,
51
curseth his f., 175
David thy f. walked, 124
David thy f.'s sake, 157
doth my f. yet live, 174
everlasting F., 159
f. and my mother forsake,
1
f. bear the iniquity of, 229
f. chastised you with
whips, 173
f. had but spit, 193
f. made him the chief, 85
f. of a fool, 90
f. of many nations, 44
f. of the fatherless, 262
f. pitieth his children, 36
f. that hath bought, 133
f. where is Mine honour,
175
f.'s instruction, 31
God of thy f., 145
God of thy f., 96
grief to his f., 31
have we not all one f., 25
heareth his f.'s, 47
hearken unto thy f., 175
honour thy f., 174
honour thy f., 175
iniquity of the f., 229
Jacob said unto his f., 53
lieth with his f.'s, 132
maketh a glad f., 31
maketh a glad f., 31
mother, and his f., 175
my f.'s God, 108
nakedness of thy f., 132
name of our f., 121
not told it my f., 222
one blessing, my f., 9
rain a f., 198
shameth his f., 36
sin before thy f., 167
sins of his f., 31
son honoureth his f., 175
that smiteth his f., 26
thicker than my f.'s, 226
Thou art my f., 97
Thou art our F., 97
thy f.'s friend, 93
way of his f., 246
will be his f., 107
fatherless
cause of the f., 134
children be f., 49
f. findeth mercy, 262
father of the f., 262
judge the f., 37
leave thy f. children, 262
poor and f., 142
widow, nor the f., 37
fathers
as did their f., 128

as He was with our f., 22
covenant of thy f., 1
covenant with our f., 32
die for the f., 194
f. and sons together, 172
f. found in Me, 75
f. have destroyed, 11
f. have eaten sour, 21
f. have not hearkened, 65
f. shall eat the sons, 28
f. shall not die, 194
f. told us of, 66
f. where are they, 165
God of his f., 16
God of your f., 94
God of your f., 203
gods which your f., 128
inheritance of f., 133
iniquity of the f., 193
Lord sware unto your f.,
133
me in derision, whose f., 6
sepulchre of thy f., 194
since the day their f., 77
sinned with our f., 39
sinned, we and our f., 39
sons shall eat their f., 28
statutes of your f., 112
stiffnecked, as your f., 238
sware unto their f., 193
way which their f., 16
which thy f. have set, 190
wickedness of your f., 122
fatness
art covered with f., 53
delight itself in f., 235
made fat with f., 209
favorest
know that Thou f., 100
favour
f. is as dew, 9
f. is deceitful, 17
f. of the Lord, 264
f. of the Lord, 156
f. to men of skill, 235
find f. in thy sight, 114
found f., 224
good man showeth f., 95
king's f., 8
My f. have I had mercy, 37
not found f., 147
seek the ruler's f., 143
fear
be strong, f. not, 70
better is little with f., 41
by the f. of the Lord, 87
delivered me from my f.,
55
f. and the pit, 59
f. before Him, 87
f. day and night, 49
f. every man his mother,
175
f. God for nought, 136

f. God, and keep, 67
f. in the night, 86
f. is on every side, 50
f. no evil, 39
f. not, 70
f. not neither be, 70
f. not to be servants, 2
f. not, but let your, 44
f. not, for I, 34
f. not, neither, 70
f. not: for I have, 101
f. not: for they that, 107
f. of God, 114
f. of the Lord, 140
f. of the Lord, 87
f. of the Lord, 87
f. of the Lord, 87
f. of the Lord all the, 87
f. of the Lord is, 87
f. of the Lord is, 87
f. of the Lord is to, 77
f. other gods, 129
f. the Lord, 18
f. the Lord, 87
f. the Lord, 38
f. the Lord, 171
f. the Lord, 62
f. the Lord, bless, 184
f. them not, 253
f. them not, neither, 86
f. thou not, 125
f. thou the Lord and, 162
f. toward Me is taught, 128
f. what flesh can do, 86
f. ye not, 34
f. ye not, 70
f. ye not Me, 15
f. ye not the reproach, 48
f. ye the people, 70
fleeth from the f., 75
for f. of the Lord, 74
God ye shall f., 205
heart from Thy f., 229
Him shall ye f., 97
I will not f., 39
let Him be your f., 86
meat unto them that f., 89
mocketh at f., 44
noise of the f., 66
not f. them, 71
of the f. of the Lord, 159
pitieth them that f., 36
pleasure in them that f.,
211
roared, who will not f., 172
serve the Lord with f., 126
such as f. God, 113
that they may f. Me, 197
they would f. Me, 87
to f. Him, 34
to me; f. not, 12
toward them that f. Him,
101
unto thee; f. not, 34

unto you that f. My, 15
upon them that f. Him,
106
well with them that f., 112
whom shall I f., 86
with them that f. Him, 87
ye that f. the Lord, 87
feared
as they f. Moses, 147
f. above all gods, 87
f. God, and eschewed, 214
f. him, as, 147
f. that thou hast lied, 111
f. the people, 78
God greatly to be f., 87
feareth
but a woman that f., 17
f. an oath, 74
f. the commandment, 172
f. the Lord, 87
one that f. God, 162
that f. the Lord, 87
wise man f., 77
fearful
f. and afraid, 86
f. in praises, 15
fearfully
f. and wonderfully made,
46
feast
hath a continual f., 119
feasting
house of f., 52
fed
as f. horses, 133
feeble
confirm the f. knees, 70
hands shall be f., 259
feed
death shall f., 51
f. among the lilies, 17
f. me with food, 41
f. My flock, 107
f. the flocks, 43
f. them with judgment, 141
lamb shall f., 24
righteous f. many, 5
shepherds that do f., 43
they that did f., 126
worm shall f. sweetly, 51
feedest
f. them with the bread, 116
feet
between his f., 147
dust of His f., 104
f. did not slip, 217
f. have they but, 129
f. in the blood, 210
f. not be burned, 4
f. of him that bringeth, 169
f. shall tread, 138
f. swelled, 108
f. that be swift, 12
f. was I to the lame, 7

fool cutteth off the f., 169
hasteth with his f., 198
lamp unto my f., 73
net for his f., 88
path of thy f., 180
pierced my f., 178
shoes off thy f., 122
when thy f. enter, 49
feignest
why f. thou thyself, 53
fell
f. down dead, 12
felt
darkness which may be f.,
151
female
male and f. created He, 46
male and f. created He, 45
few
are not my days f., 164
f. and evil, 162
left but a f. of many, 241
left f. in number, 78
left f. in number, 193
let his days be f., 195
let thy words be f., 127
save by many or by f., 39
seemed but a f. days, 152
woman is of f. days, 149
fewest
f. of all people, 32
field
as flower of the f., 155
beast of the f., 231
beast of the f., 231
beasts of the f., 23
blessed in the f., 22
cursed in the f., 193
face of the f., 25
flower of the f., 155
forth into the f., 50
in the f. shall die, 61
served by the f., 43
smell of a f., 30
tree of the f., 167
trees of the f., 170
fields
take your f., 162
fierce
away from His f. anger, 91
fierceness
f. of His wrath, 91
in the f. of His anger, 98
fiery
burning f. furnace, 50
f. flying serpent, 66
fig
and under his f. tree, 177
holds shall be like f., 107
fight
a city to f. against it, 257
against whom ye f., 54
f. against your brethren,
176

f. every one against, 28
f. for you, 70
f. for you, 71
f. for your brethren, 17
f. with this Philistine, 43
f. ye not against, 94
fingers to f., 237
God shall f. for us, 39
Lord shall f. for you, 7
may f. together, 27
neither f., 107
they shall f. against, 72
fighteth
f. for you, 107
Lord f. for them, 105
figs
with the firstripe f., 107
fill
do not I f. heaven and, 74
filled
appetite is not f., 8
drink, but ye are not f., 69
earth that is not f., 52
f. me with bitterness, 20
f. the house of God, 267
f. with the glory, 99
filleth
f. the hungry soul, 57
find
by searching f. out God,
11
f. a virtuous woman, 156
f. favour in thy sight, 114
f. it after many days, 8
f. out all Thine enemies,
72
f. rest for your souls, 246
f. such a one as this, 147
f. those that hate, 72
seek me early shall f., 264
seek Me, and f., 62
shall not f. her paths, 172
shall not f. it, 95
shalt f. Him, 19
them that f. knowledge, 33
until I f. a place for, 33
findeth
f. occasions against, 178
fatherless f. mercy, 262
man that f. wisdom, 119
whatsoever thy hand f., 69
whoso f. a wife f., 156
whoso f. me f. life, 264
fine
than much f. gold, 35
finer
vessel for the f., 251
finger
f. of God, 179
f. of God, 243
f. shall be thicker, 226
fingers
f. have made, 128
f. to fight, 237

fire
  another f. shall devour, 75
  answereth by f., 189
  burn with f., 129
  burned with f., 104
  burneth as the f., 77
  burnt with f., 194
  can a man take f. in, 4
  chariot of f., 96
  coals of f., 138
  consuming f., 110
  consuming f., 60
  f. and by His sword, 141
  f. and the wood, 167
  f. goeth out, 113
  f. mingled with the hail, 180
  f. of my jealousy, 61
  f. shall burn, 5
  f. shall consume, 24
  f. that consumeth, 4
  f. that saith not, 52
  fury come like f., 98
  heap coals of f., 226
  in a pillar of f., 105
  jealousy burn like f., 91
  melteth before the f., 195
  midst of the f., 15
  out from one f., 75
  pass through the f., 128
  poured out like f., 98
  spark of his f., 142
  walkest through the f., 34
  went through f., 50
  words in thy mouth f., 69
firmament
  called the f. heaven, 120
  f. sheweth His handywork, 99
first
  f. child, 20
  f. man that was born, 6
  I am He; I am the f., 109
  I am the f., 109
  the f. day, 169
firstborn
  Esau thy f., 53
  f. are Mine, 88
  f. of thy sons, 40
  Israel My f., 32
  my f. my might, 88
  smite all the f., 88
  unto Me all the f., 40
  was not the f., yet, 85
firstfruits
  f. of all thine increase, 246
fish
  dominion over the f., 9
fishes
  f. of the sea, 102
five
  lack f. of the fifty, 38
flag
  f. grow without water, 116

flagons
  stay me with f., 152
flame
  hath a most vehement f., 138
flattereth
  a man that f., 88
  f. with his lips, 88
flattering
  f. mouth worketh, 5
  with f. lips, 64
flattery
  f. of the tongue, 154
  f. to his friends, 19
flea
  dead dog, after a f., 78
  seek a f., 78
fled
  f. apace, and look not, 253
  men of war f., 54
  they have f. from Me, 16
flee
  f. away naked, 54
  f. before Thee, 71
  f. from the face, 105
  f. in battle, 45
  f. out of the midst, 75
  f. when none pursueth, 86
  let not the swift f., 253
  let us f., 74
  look upon thee shall f., 57
  man as I f., 44
  one thousand shall f., 86
  shall not f. away, 75
  to whom will ye f., 74
  wicked f. when no, 40
fleeth
  f. of them shall not, 75
  that f. from the fear, 75
  who f. from the noise, 66
flesh
  all f. is grass, 155
  arm of f., 237
  brother and our f., 157
  cause thy f. to sin, 228
  eateth his own f., 147
  eyes of f., 78
  f. as the dung, 209
  f. of brass, 58
  f. of my f., 265
  f. of your foreskin, 33
  f. shall I see God, 51
  fear what f. can do, 86
  give thy f. unto fowls, 23
  God of all f., 103
  good piece of f., 27
  hair of my f., 86
  heart of f., 203
  heart out of their f., 203
  life of all f., 23
  living thing of all f., 10
  maketh f. his arm, 202
  plead with all f., 141
  shall be one f., 156

sword shall devour f., 210
  that they were but f., 91
  troubleth his own f., 48
  weariness of the f., 68
flies
  swarm of f., 179
flieth
  arrow that f., 86
flight
  f. shall perish from the, 235
  go by f., 93
  ten thousand to f., 1
flint
  harder than f., 178
flock
  dogs of my f., 6
  f. was scattered, 68
  shepherd doth his f., 33
  ye My f. the f., 102
flocks
  bleatings of the f., 67
  shepherds feed the f., 43
flood
  f. to destroy the earth, 44
  other side of the f., 128
floods
  neither can the f., 152
floor
  out of the f., 73
flourish
  of iniquity do f., 146
  righteous shall f., 116
flourisheth
  field, so he f., 155
  morning it f., 155
flower
  a f. and is cut down, 164
  f. fadeth, 109
  f. of the field, 155
  f. of their age, 268
  goodliness as f. of field, 155
flowers
  f. appear on the earth, 221
flowing
  land f. with milk, 137
fly
  f. as the eagle, 235
  f. away as an eagle, 73
  f. away, and be at rest, 74
  f. upon the wings, 235
flying
  fiery f. serpent, 66
folding
  f. of the hands, 182
follow
  but if Baal, then f., 31
  f. after her lovers but, 94
  f. after me, 147
  f. me all the days, 22
  f. their own spirit, 84
  God, f. Him, 31

not f. a multitude, 36
thing f. not, 83
following
  f. the Lord, 61
  f. their brethren, 176
  from f. Me, 137
folly
  do not thou this f., 132
  f. is joy to him that, 89
  fool according to his f., 90
  fool in his f., 50
  fool returneth to his f., 90
  fools is f., 89
  instruction of fools is f., 251
  spirit exalteth f., 89
  wisdom excelleth f., 89
food
  feed me with f., 41
fool
  a f. according to his, 90
  begetteth a f., 175
  bray a f. in a mortar, 90
  by the hand of a f., 169
  die, likewise the f., 164
  doth a f. understand, 130
  ears of a f., 5
  even a f. when he, 90
  f. despiseth father's, 31
  f. foldeth his hands, 147
  f. hath said, 14
  f. in his folly, 50
  f. rageth, and is, 77
  f. returneth to his folly, 90
  f. uttereth all his mind, 192
  f. walketh in darkness, 90
  f. will be meddling, 90
  f.'s mouth is his, 90
  f.'s voice is known by, 90
  f.'s wrath, 136
  father of a f., 90
  laughter of the f., 146
  more hope of a f., 38
  more hope of a f., 198
  own heart is a f., 38
  played the f., 42
  rod for the f.'s back, 64
  seemly for a f., 90
  slander, is a f., 26
  speech becometh not a f., 69
  stripes into a f., 48
  way of a f., 5
  wise man or a f., 133
  wise man? as the f., 52
  wise more than of the f., 202
  wise more than the f., 179
foolish
  envious at the f., 73
  f. man despiseth, 31
  f. man reproacheth, 47
  f. people and unwise, 133

f. plucketh it down, 123
f. son is a grief, 31
f. son is the calamity, 31
f. son is the heaviness, 31
forsake the f. and, 36
neither be thou f., 18
people is f., 89
than an old and f. king, 5
woe unto the f., 84
wrath killeth the f., 8
foolishly
  angry dealeth f., 242
  done very f., 42
foolishness
  f. is bound, 30
  f. of fools, 89
  f. of man perverteth, 8
  fools proclaimeth f., 23
  will not his f. depart, 90
fools
  bosom of f., 9
  companion of f., 36
  f. despise wisdom, 68
  f. die for want, 130
  f. hate knowledge, 89
  f. make a mock, 228
  f. when will ye be wise, 130
  foolishness of f., 89
  heart of f., 23
  heart of f., 90
  instruction of f. is, 251
  no pleasure in f., 90
  promotion of f., 96
  sacrifice of f., 268
  song of f., 48
  ye f. be ye of an, 250
foot
  broken tooth, and a f., 20
  f. for f., 208
  f. shall slide, 175
  keep thy f. when thou, 268
  my f. slippeth, 108
  shoe off thy f., 205
  sole of his f., 17
  swift of f. shall not, 75
  withdraw thy f., 125
footmen
  run with the f., 37
footstool
  earth is My f., 104
  enemies thy f., 106
for
  or f. our adversaries, 7
forbear
  f. thee from meddling, 108
  f. to vow, 189
  forbeareth, let him f., 121
  price; and if not, f., 168
forbeareth
  f. let him forebear, 121
forbid
  f. that I should sin, 185
  f. that we forsake, 82

f. that we should rebel, 199
forbidden
  f. to be done, 34
force
  not strengthen his f., 40
forces
  f. of strength, 237
forcible
  f. are right words, 124
forefront
  f. of the battle, 19
forehead
  have I made thy f., 178
  whore's f., 226
foreskin
  f. of your heart, 33
  flesh of your f., 33
foreskins
  f. of your heart, 204
forest
  lion in the f., 20
  lion roar in the f., 165
forever
  angry with us f., 98
  before Mine anointed f., 212
  blaspheme Thy name f., 21
  bless Thy name f., 184
  blessed be God f., 22
  cast thee off f., 16
  counsel of the Lord f., 177
  desolate f., 10
  do they live f., 165
  earth abideth f., 68
  forget us f., 2
  God doeth, it shall be f., 178
  God f. and ever, 75
  God f. and ever, 18
  God of Israel f., 184
  hide Thyself f., 1
  house of the Lord f., 22
  keep His anger f., 91
  Lord endureth f., 249
  Lord shall endure f., 97
  Lord shalt endure f., 75
  may fear Me f., 197
  mercy endureth f., 184
  mercy endureth f., 113
  mercy endureth f., 101
  my portion f., 92
  name be f., 139
  name shall endure f., 84
  not His anger f., 91
  not keep anger f., 91
  not perish f., 124
  O Lord? f. how long, 1
  reign f. and ever, 75
  remainest f., 75
  riches are not f., 177
  salvation shall be f., 218
  shall be destroyed f., 146
  shall stand f., 109
  stablish his throne f., 108

sword devour f., 210
thanks unto Thee f., 115
this is My rest f., 139
throne be established f., 163
to abide in f., 33
trust ye in the Lord f., 237
wilt Thou be angry f., 91
word of God stand f., 109
forgers
  f. of lies, 34
forget
  covenant ye shall not f., 45
  drink and f. his poverty, 59
  f. her cunning, 1
  f. her ornaments, 16
  f. her sucking child, 37
  f. not the humble, 106
  f. not the Lord, 202
  f. the covenant, 1
  f. the Lord, 82
  f. the things, 18
  f. thee, O Jerusalem, 1
  f. Thy precepts, 82
  how long wilt Thou f., 1
  nations that f. God, 111
  they may f., 83
  Thou f. us for ever, 2
  understanding: f. it not, 144
  yet will I not f., 83
forgettest
  f. the Lord thy maker, 83
forgetteth
  f. not the cry, 185
forgive
  f. I pray thee, 203
  f. O Lord, hearken, 91
  f. your transgressions, 110
  when Thou hearest, f., 90
  will f. their iniquity, 91
forgiven
  transgression is f., 91
forgiveness
  belong mercies and f., 111
forgotten
  always be f., 124
  f. as a dead man, 59
  f. the wickedness, 122
  familiar friends have f., 151
  My people have f. Me, 16
  to come shall all be f., 178
  why hast Thou f., 1
form
  without f. and void, 28
formed
  f. it to be inhabited, 46
  f. man of the dust, 45
  f. thee in the belly, 20
  glory, I have f., 46
  He that f. the eye, 104
  times that I have f. it, 95

former
  f. shall not be, 46
  remember not the f., 203
forsake
  all that f. Thee, 16
  all them that f., 16
  anger, and f. wrath, 8
  f. her not, 264
  f. Him, He will cast, 16
  f. His inheritance, 153
  f. His people, 1
  f. me not when my strength, 6
  f. me not, O Lord, 1
  f. my sweetness, 8
  f. the foolish and, 36
  f. the Lord, 15
  f. the remnant, 1
  f. their own mercy, 83
  f. us so long time, 2
  fail nor f. thee, 1
  father and my mother f., 1
  father's friend, f., 93
  forbid that we should f., 82
  God, f. me not, 6
  He will f. you, 1
  if ye f. Him, 1
  Israel will not f., 85
  leave us, nor f., 1
  mercy and truth f., 28
  nor f. thee, 107
  not f. thee, 1
  that f. the Lord, 16
  will not f., 250
forsaken
  as ye have f. Me, 79
  because ye have f., 75
  f. Mine house, 1
  f. the Lord, 21
  hast f. the Lord, 16
  have f. Me, 77
  have not f. Him, 82
  He hath also f., 75
  Lord hath f. the earth, 78
  moment have I f., 1
  seen the righteous f., 1
  we have f. the Lord, 228
  why hast Thou f., 1
  Ye have f. Me, 1
forsaketh
  f. not His saints, 82
  to him that f. the way, 16
forseeth
  f. the evil, 192
forsook
  because they f. the Lord, 194
  f. the counsel, 5
  f. the Lord, 16
fortress
  f. among My people, 190
  goodness, and my f., 107
  refuge and my f., 108
  rock, and my f., 106

forty
  f. days and f. nights, 89
  f. days and f. nights, 243
  f. years, 78
  walked f. years, 78
forward
  shadow go f., 172
fought
  f. for Israel, 107
  f. from heaven, 12
  stars f. against Sisera, 12
found
  comforters, but I f. none, 34
  f. him not, 59
  f. in the way, 6
  f. of them that sought, 42
  f. out my riddle, 19
  good things f. in, 90
  hast thou f. me, 142
  have your fathers f., 75
  He will be f., 61
  He will be f., 62
  iniquity was not f., 124
  never be f., 10
  thousand have I f. but, 154
  while He may be f., 173
  wisdom is f., 250
foundations
  f. be destroyed, 146
  f. of the earth, 14
  let the f., 25
  stone for f., 10
founded
  Lord hath f. Zion, 139
fountain
  eyes a f., 242
  f. of life, 87
  f. of living waters, 97
four
  f. things say not, 52
fowl
  f. of the air, 9
fowls
  flesh unto the f., 23
  meat unto the f., 196
foxes
  the f. the little f., 60
frame
  knoweth our f., 37
free
  f. from his master, 51
  let the oppressed go f., 85
fret
  f. not thyself, 138
friend
  countenance of his f., 28
  every man is a f. to, 93
  f. loveth at all times, 93
  f. sticketh closer, 93
  kindness to thy f., 7
  thine own f. and, 93
  thy father's f. forsake, 93
  wounds of a f., 48

friends
f. dealt treacherously, 20
f. have forgotten me, 151
f. scorn me, 81
flattery to his f., 19
hatest thy f., 93
have pity upon me my f., 36
rich hath many f., 93
separateth chief f., 113
separateth very f., 116
wealth maketh many f., 93
friendship
f. with an angry man, 9
frogs
f. came up, 179
frost
God f. is given, 221
fruit
downward, and bear f., 240
f. of righteousness, 43
f. of the righteous, 213
f. of the tree, 246
f. of the wicked, 41
f. of the womb, 31
f. of the womb, 10
f. shall be a fiery, 66
forth his f., 239
my good f., 8
took of the f. thereof, 64
yield their f., 170
fruitful
be f. and multiply, 30
f. and multiply, 30
fruits
eat his pleasant f., 152
gather in the f., 48
fugitive
f. and a vagabond, 48
fulfil
f. your works, 173
fulfilled
our days are f., 66
full
destruction are never f., 121
earth shall be f., 82
f. of blood, 117
f. of bloody crimes, 146
f. of lies and, 47
f. of sap, 167
f. of the goodness, 68
f. of Thy riches, 167
f. of trouble, 149
f. of violence, 146
f. with travail, 8
God f. of compassion, 101
house f. of sacrifices, 225
quiver f. of them, 31
sea is not f., 26
they that were f., 127
was f. of people, 54
went out f., 50

fulness
and the f. thereof, 233
f. thereof, 103
f. thereof; the world, 68
roar, and the f., 27
furious
f. rebukes, 98
furnace
burning fiery f., 50
f. of affliction, 101
furrows
long their f., 9
fury
f. to rest, 98
f. upon the heathen, 98
goeth forth with f., 98
His f. is poured, 98
lest my f. come forth, 98
pour out Thy f., 112

G

gained
though he hath g., 127
gall
grapes of g., 20
turned judgment into g., 43
gallows
hanged Haman on the g., 142
garden
become like the g. of, 207
beloved come into his g., 152
from the g. of Eden, 174
g. of Eden, 174
g. of herbs, 73
g. of the Lord, 138
soul as a watered g., 119
tree of the g., 112
garment
covereth them as a g., 188
eat them like a g., 60
man put on a woman's g., 246
putteth on his g., 253
rent my g., 9
garments
beautiful g., 203
heart, and not your g., 204
gate
afflicted in the g., 173
howl, O g., 66
judgment in the g., 19
rebuketh in the g., 48
gates
g. of brass, 172
g. of death, 12
loveth the g. of Zion, 139
peace in your g., 143
Gath
tell it not in G., 116

gather
g. him, and keep, 33
g. in the fruits, 48
knoweth not who shall g., 133
mercies will I g., 1
gathered
cannot be g. again, 163
g. into thy grave, 51
he that g. little, 80
he that g. much, 80
gathereth
he that g. by labour, 259
gathering
g. together of the waters, 68
gave
Lord g. Job twice, 178
Lord g. the word, 187
return unto God who g., 52
the Lord g., 2
gavest
g. thou the goodly, 12
generation
another g. cometh, 68
arose another g., 111
crooked g., 199
declare his g., 122
fourth g., 193
g. passeth away, 68
g. that set not their, 65
rebellious g., 65
throne from g. to g., 75
until all the g., 78
generations
anger to all g., 98
in the g. of old, 107
throughout your g., 216
truth endureth to all g., 248
years of many g., 79
Gentiles
glory among the G., 76
light to the G., 117
gently
g. for my sake, 36
ghost
Abraham gave up the g., 50
give up the g., 58
give up the g., 2
given up the g., 58
giveth up the g., 51
giants
g. in the earth, 230
Gideon
came upon G., 17
Lord, and of G., 17
gift
g. destroyeth the heart, 24
g. doth blind, 24
g. in secret, 9

labour, it is the g. of, 181
take a g., 24
gifts
g. to all thy lovers, 129
g. to all whores, 129
no more with your g., 21
that giveth g., 93
Gilead
balm in G, 34
gird
g. thee with sackcloth, 165
g. up now thy loins, 206
g. you with sackcloth, 165
g. you with sackcloth, 165
girded
like a virgin g. with, 54
girdeth
that g. on his harness, 23
girls
boys and g. playing, 191
give
daughters, crying, g. g.,
115
g. as he is able, 29
g. for his life, 224
g. forth his water, 80
g. him bread, 72
g. I pray, 183
g. me a man, 27
g. me drink, 244
g. me half thine house, 41
g. me my price, 168
g. me neither poverty, 41
g. me now wisdom, 96
g. me thy vineyard, 73
g. not thy strength, 154
g. not your daughters, 137
g. rain upon Thy land, 190
g. strong drink, 151
g. thanks unto the Lord,
115
g. thanks unto Thee, 115
g. thanks unto Thee, 183
g. the land of Canaan, 45
g. the sacrifice, 268
g. Thee thanks, 51
g. them a miscarrying, 49
g. them after the work, 142
g. them one heart, 197
g. them to his servants,
162
g. therefore Thy servant,
63
g. thy flesh unto, 23
g. unto Me, 40
g. unto the children, 138
g. unto the Lord, 184
g. unto the Lord, 115
g. unto the Lord, 184
g. up the ghost, 58
g. up the ghost, 2
g. us an inheritance, 74
glory will I not g., 99
God doth g. us, 138

Lord is able to g., 212
may g. thanks, 55
what I shall g., 95
what wilt Thou g., 49
given
bread shall be g., 215
g. me life, 149
g. me my petition, 20
g. meat unto, 89
g. rest unto His people,
114
g. thee that which, 212
g. up the ghost, 58
g. you a land, 138
g. you the city, 17
g. you the land, 138
that which he hath g., 8
wherefore is light g., 9
giveth
friend to him that g., 93
g. his neighbour drink, 67
g. unto the poor, 29
God g. to a man, 22
He g. thee power, 259
showeth mercy and g., 24
to the sinner He g., 116
glad
g. in the Lord, 118
g. that Thou hast done, 96
heart be g. when he, 72
Jerusalem, and be g., 139
let the earth be g., 27
maketh a g. father, 31
maketh a g. father, 31
rejoice and be g., 27
wine that maketh g., 151
gladness
g. for the upright, 118
serve the Lord with g., 184
glean
g. even among the sheaves,
95
gleaning
g. of the grapes, 179
glorified
I will be g., 33
glorify
and thou shalt g. Me, 13
glorious
become g. in power, 236
blessed be Thy g., 184
g. in holiness, 15
glory
appear in His g., 139
created him for My g., 46
crowned him with g., 155
declare His g., 76
declare my g. among, 76
declareth g. of God, 99
full of His g., 99
g. among the heathen, 99
g. due unto His name, 115
g. due unto His name, 184
g. in his might, 23

g. in his riches, 23
g. in his wisdom, 23
g. is departed, 125
g. of the Lord, 267
g. of the Lord, 99
g. of this, and, 219
g. of young men is, 79
g. to the Lord, 183
g. ye in His holy name,
118
great is the g., 99
He is the King of g., 110
head is a crown of g., 6
leave your g., 74
let him that g. in, 81
Lord g. and strength, 184
my g. and the lifter, 34
My g. into shame, 78
My g. will I not give, 99
own g. is not g., 23
people see His g., 99
power, and the g., 99
salvation and my g., 96
sanctified by My g., 41
search their own g., 23
this King of g., 103
throne of Thy g., 99
unto Thy name give g., 96
when g. is increased, 73
wise shall inherit g., 96
glutton
g. shall come to poverty,
67
go
all g. unto one place, 52
cannot g. back, 189
g. and cry, 83
g. in peace, 22
g. not forth, 50
g. not in the way, 18
g. not up, 255
g. not up, 107
g. out or come in, 126
g. out with haste, 93
g. over this Jordan, 62
g. the way of all, 51
g. to all that I shall, 187
g. up in peace, 157
g. up to the mountain, 123
g. up to the mountain, 62
g. up; for I will deliver,
107
g. whence I shall not, 51
g. your way, 27
I shall g. to him, 51
I will g. forth, 84
let her not g., 68
let him g. up, 255
let Israel g., 11
let Israel g., 111
Let My people g., 92
Let My people g., 11
Lord g. before you, 93
nor g. by flight, 93

not g. empty, 92
not g. in to them, 137
not g. thither, 63
not g. up, nor fight, 176
not let the people g., 48
not let thee g., 22
then I will g., 246
to g. as he came, 94
way he should g., 30
who will g. for us, 160
wilt g. with me, 246
goads
wise are as g., 117
goat
g. shall bear upon, 219
goats
and I punished the g., 21
rams with he g., 60
goblet
like a round g., 17
god
if he be a g., 83
know no g. but Me, 163
no g. with Me, 102
sacrificeth unto any g., 123
gods
after their g., 137
all the g. are idols, 83
be as g. knowing, 72
cry unto the g., 83
exalted far above all g., 77
fear other g., 129
fear other g., 45
feared above all g., 87
g. are g. of the hills, 54
g. of Egypt, 129
g. of gold, 129
g. of silver, 129
g. shall be a snare, 71
g. which your fathers, 128
God above all g., 99
God of g., 110
greater than all g., 99
have the g. delivered, 11
images, Ye are our g., 129
let the g. do to me, 169
Lord is above all g., 100
molten g., 129
name of other g., 128
name of your g., 27
no g. but the work of, 129
not revile the g., 113
O Lord, among the g., 15
other g. before Me, 128
other g. to serve, 16
serve other g., 137
serve other g., 82
serve strange g., 15
served other g., 77
served strange g., 79
their g. shall ye burn, 129
whoring after other g., 83
worship Him, all ye g.,
123

goest
whither thou g., 61
whithersoever thou g., 104
whithersoever thou g., 35
goeth
g. down to the grave, 51
g. forth and weepeth, 48
Lord g. before you, 70
sore for him that g., 79
going
g. out, and thy coming,
100
goings
pondereth all his g., 100
seeth all his g., 100
gold
as a jewel of g. in, 17
g. become dim, 9
g. is Mine, 260
gods of g., 129
gotten for g., 263
idols are silver and g., 129
knowledge rather than g.,
68
like apples of g., 69
more desired than g., 35
not g. nor all the, 237
ornaments of g., 17
silver and g., 170
silver nor their g., 98
sockets of fine g., 23
than thousands of g., 252
wisdom than g., 259
golden
g. bowl be broken, 63
Gomorrah
Sodom and G., 53
good
a g. old age, 6
as is the g. so, 74
as seemeth g. unto Him,
248
be of g. courage, 44
be of g. courage, 39
be of g. courage, 70
bringeth g. tidings, 169
destroyeth much g., 43
discern between g. and, 63
do not My words do g., 34
do what seemeth g., 53
do with me as seem g., 26
due season, how g., 5
earth, that doeth g., 177
eat that which is g., 235
evil and the g., 104
evil, and choose the g., 63
evil, and not for g., 113
evil, and not for g., 66
evil, and not for g., 98
evil, and not for g., 196
findeth a g. thing, 156
for g. that seek Him, 105
for He is g., 113
g. advice make war, 5

g. and comely for one, 89
g. and convenient, 93
g. and to the clean, 150
g. at the hand, 2
g. for a man that, 176
g. heed unto, 223
g. in His sight, 81
g. in my sight, 11
g. in the sight of, 18
g. is the word, 109
g. land, 138
g. Lord pardon, 91
g. man is perished, 112
g. man leaveth, 114
g. man shall be satisfied,
219
g. man showeth favour, 95
g. name is better, 205
g. name is to be chosen,
205
g. of all his labour, 181
g. of all his labour, 89
g. of the land, 172
g. old age, 51
g. piece of flesh, 27
g. reward for their, 42
g. shall come, 2
g. that a man should, 176
g. that I have promised,
103
g. thing to give thanks, 115
g. things found in, 90
g. to sing praises, 184
g. unto them that wait, 7
g. way, and walk, 246
God, for g., 22
honey, because it is g., 89
how g. and how pleasant,
24
if ye think g. give, 168
is it not g., 176
it shall seem g. unto, 107
it was very g., 11
know g. and evil, 112
know what is g., 53
knowing g. and evil, 72
knowledge of g. and evil,
112
life and g. and death, 18
light that it was g., 11
looked for g., 9
Lord is g., 113
Lord is g. a strong, 107
Lord, and do g., 18
love the g., 19
make it g., 82
merciful man doeth g., 48
merry heart doeth g., 57
my g. fruit, 8
no g. report, 169
no g. thing will He, 213
none that doeth g., 43
not g. that the man, 151
not prophesy g., 5

of g. courage, 39
peace, but no g., 79
preach g. tidings, 187
proceedeth not evil and g.,
 113
remember for g., 212
rewarded evil for g., 3
rewarded me evil for g.,
 112
rewarded me g., 42
rewardeth evil for g., 112
righteous is only g., 79
seek g. and not evil, 31
so is g. news from a far,
 169
speak that which is g., 5
steps of a g. man, 18
strong and of a g., 70
teach them the g., 68
that call evil g., 112
then may ye also do g., 28
thing is not g., 67
to a man that is g., 22
to do g. they have no, 112
what seemeth g., 38
what seemeth Him g., 2
whatsoever seemeth g., 180
whether it be g. or, 3
wisdom is g. with an, 264
withhold not g. from, 115
goodlier
 g. person than, 161
goodliness
 g. as the flower, 155
goodly
 g. are thy tents, 17
 g. heritage, 122
 g. wings unto, 12
goodness
 abundant in g., 110
 for Thy g.' sake, 91
 full of g. of Lord, 68
 g. and mercy shall follow,
  22
 g. and my fortress, 107
 g. is as a morning cloud,
  113
 g. the Lord shall do, 114
 hungry soul with g., 57
 Lord for His g., 184
government
 increase of his g., 159
grace
 g. in Thy sight, 116
gracious
 be g. unto us, 158
 g. and full of, 37
 g. God, and merciful, 37
 g. unto thee, 190
 God g., 101
 God is g., 101
 God, merciful and g., 110
 He is g. and merciful, 111
 merciful and g., 36

grape
 eateth the sour g., 206
grapes
 bring forth g., 63
 brought forth wild g., 63
 clusters of g., 23
 g. are g. of gall, 20
 g. of Ephraim, 179
 have eaten sour g., 21
 treader of g., 191
 vines have tender g., 60
grass
 all flesh is g., 155
 bray when he hath g., 37
 causeth g. to grow, 48
 cut down like the g., 260
 days are as g, 155
 dew upon the g., 9
 g. withereth, 109
 like g. which groweth, 155
 shall be made as g., 86
 showers upon the g., 69
 wicked spring as the g.,
  146
 withered like g., 56
grasshoppers
 g. for multitude, 132
 sight as g., 86
grave
 be declared in the g., 150
 brought down to the g.,
  126
 cruel as the g., 138
 down to the g., 102
 down to the g., 210
 draweth nigh unto the g., 6
 g. cannot praise, 52
 g. is mine house, 58
 gathered into thy g., 51
 I will make thy g., 61
 in the g. who shall, 51
 it is enough: the g., 52
 laid in the g., 51
 O g., I will be thy, 52
 so doth the g. those, 51
 to the g. shall come up, 51
 womb to the g., 224
graven
 any g. image, 128
 g. image, 129
 g. images, 129
 g. images, 129
 g. upon the table, 178
 maker thereof hath g., 130
 profiteth the g. image, 130
graves
 g. are ready, 51
gray
 man of g. hairs, 60
 old men is the g. head, 79
grayheaded
 old and g., 6
great
 and of g. mercy, 37

as a g. lion, 32
as well as the g., 131
both small and g., 66
brought all this g. evil, 103
by thy g. wisdom, 62
city of the g. King, 139
day of the Lord is g., 141
every g. matter, 147
exceeding g. reward, 105
g. a God as our, 100
g. and dreadful day, 159
g. are His mercies, 158
g. in power, 196
g. is His mercy, 101
g. is our God, 99
g. is our Lord, 100
g. is the Lord, 100
g. is the wrath, 65
g. men not always wise, 6
g. mercies, 1
g. name's sake, 1
g. nation, 32
g. offences, 192
g. revenues, 64
g. shall be the peace, 69
g. strength lieth, 136
g. things doeth He, 100
g. things for thyself, 8
g. treasure and trouble, 41
g. was the company, 187
God is g., 99
house I build is g., 99
is of g. understanding, 176
Lord g. and terrible, 17
make thee a g. nation, 31
mercy is g., 100
misery of man is g., 267
name shall be g. among, 76
seen a g. light, 73
small and g. are there, 51
thee do some g. thing, 5
Thou art g. O Lord, 99
two g. lights, 14
was g. among the, 40
works of the Lord are g.,
 168
greater
 brother be g., 88
 g. light to rule, 14
 g. than all gods, 99
 God g. than man, 115
 punishment is g., 193
greatest
 even unto the g., 43
 least of them to the g., 4
greatly
 g. to be praised, 100
 God g. to be feared, 87
greatness
 ascribe ye g. unto, 76
 g. and the power, 99
 g. of Thy mercy, 101
 g. of Thy power, 36
 g. of thy wisdom, 205

green
g. bay tree, 77
g. pastures, 34
wither as the g. herb, 260
grew
multiplied and g., 4
grief
acquainted with g., 159
and his travail g., 59
g. to his father, 31
g. to my sorrow, 224
though He cause g., 158
wisdom is much g., 264
griefs
borne our g., 21
grieve
that it may not g., 76
grievous
correction is g., 16
ground
dew falleth on the g., 40
down to the g., 157
dust of the g., 45
fallow g., 204
parched g., 191
return unto the g., 192
spilt on the g., 163
standest is holy g., 122
to till the g., 174
unto Me from the g., 79
grow
g. instead of wheat, 135
g. like a cedar, 116
g. out of his roots, 159
g. up without mire, 116
g. without water, 116
grass to g., 48
groweth
flourisheth, and g. up, 155
like grass which g., 155
grown
art g. thick, 53
beards be g., 226
g. up unto the heavens, 226
till they were g., 156
guide
g. even unto death, 75
meek will He g., 117
upright shall g. them, 137
guile
lips from speaking g., 77
guiltless
anointed, and be g., 12
g. before the Lord, 134
hold him not g., 210
not hold him g., 21
guilty
g. of death, 26
yet is he g., 34

H

habitation
desired it for His h., 139

h. of His throne, 214
h. of the just, 22
h. of the strong, 211
h. of Thy throne, 142
holy h., 262
prepare Him an h., 108
habitations
h. of the wilderness, 168
hail
fire mingled with the h., 180
h. shall come down, 180
there was h., 180
treasures of the h., 79
hair
at an h. breadth, 3
h. of my flesh, 86
h. of thy son, 217
not an h. of him fall, 142
plucked off the h., 9
hairs
h. of mine head, 2
h. of mine head, 72
hoar h., 6
man of gray h., 60
half
give h. to the one, 38
h. of the greatness, 205
h. thine house, 41
h. was not told, 88
hallow
h. My sabbaths, 217
halt
h. ye between, 27
Haman
hanged H. on the gallows, 142
hand
am I a God at h., 104
by the h. of a fool, 169
calamity is at h., 194
day of the Lord at h., 60
day of the Lord is at h., 141
dealeth with a slack h., 146
deceit are in his h., 25
deliver out of My h., 102
deliver thee into the h., 54
deliver thee to mine h., 39
deliver them to thine h., 107
delivered them to thine h., 72
drew not his h., 60
evil is in mine h., 134
fall into the h. of man, 48
for it is nigh at h., 15
h. be upon him, 157
h. for h., 208
h. I commit my spirit, 108
h. is stretched out, 246
h. is stretched out, 98
h. is stretched out, 98
h. of a mighty man, 222

h. of a woman, 253
h. of all your enemies, 55
h. of David, 81
h. of God, 2
h. of God hath touched, 36
h. of her enemies, 1
h. of him that slayeth, 12
h. of Joab, 42
h. of my brother, 86
h. of our enemies, 225
h. of our God, 105
h. of the diligent, 146
h. of the doers of, 255
h. of the Lord, 158
h. of the Lord, 54
h. of the Lord, 9
h. of the Lord shall be, 213
h. of the Lord was, 135
h. of the mighty, 106
h. of the Philistines, 21
h. of the uncircumcised, 58
h. of the wicked, 134
h. of their enemies, 1
h. of this Philistine, 39
h. riches and honour, 263
h. shall be lifted, 254
h. shall find out all, 72
h. shall not be upon, 207
h. waxed short, 46
h. will be against, 71
h. with the wicked, 36
I am in your h., 26
iniquity be in thine h., 18
into thine h., 253
is in her right h., 263
know Mine h., 103
land into his h., 40
let not mine h., 21
lift up Thine h., 106
lifted up his h., 65
like a man's h., 182
man's h. against him, 71
mine h. shall not be, 47
Mine h. take them, 75
not put forth mine h., 162
open thine h. wide, 29
out of h., 224
out of their h., 55
potter's h., 60
power of thine h., 115
put forth mine h., 136
put not forth thine h., 28
rend it out of the h., 157
right h. forget, 1
right h. shall find, 72
right h. shall save, 106
save with Thy right h., 55
sheep of His h., 101
shut thine h., 29
Sisera into thine h., 249
sit thou at My right h., 106
slack not thy h., 7
slayer up into his h., 137
so are ye in Mine h., 60

stay now thine h., 157
stretch forth his h., 12
stretch out My h., 180
Thine h. is power, 102
thousand at thy right h.,
50
thy h. findeth to do, do, 69
Thy right h. O Lord, 236
twoedged sword in h., 210
Uzza put forth his h., 198
with the right h., 108
withhold not thine h., 62
work of Thy h., 46
handful
better is an h., 8
handfuls
h. of barley, 84
handmaid
count not thine h., 261
lie unto thine h., 88
remember thine h., 114
hands
can thine h. be strong, 241
deliver you out of my h.,
21
down with her h., 123
fear not but let your h., 44
folding of the h., 182
fool foldeth his h., 147
h. are full of blood, 117
h. are the h., 53
h. be weak, 69
h. cannot perform, 102
h. full with travail, 8
h. make whole, 102
h. of the wicked, 4
h. shall be feeble, 259
h. that shed innocent, 12
h. to war, 237
he that hath clean h., 124
labour of thine h., 69
pierced my h., 178
puttest thine h. unto, 266
recompence of a man's h.,
255
reward of his h., 195
spread forth your h., 1
strengthen my h., 92
strengthen ye the weak h.,
70
the h. of Esau, 53
with works of your h., 191
with works of your h., 98
work of His h., 74
work of men's h., 129
work of men's h., 129
work of men's h., 129
work of the h., 17
work of their h., 142
work of their h., 101
work of their own h., 128
works of His h. are, 111
handywork
sheweth His h., 99

hanged
h. Haman on the gallows,
142
he that is h., 50
hangeth
h. the earth, 46
Hannah
Elkanah knew H., 88
happy
h. are thy men, 148
h. are thy servants, 148
h. is he that hath, 81
h. is that people, 112
h. is the man, 29
h. is the man that, 31
h. is the man that, 119
law, h. is he, 35
mercy on the poor, h., 37
trusteth in the Lord, h.,
119
wherefore are they h., 134
hard
any thing too h., 103
h. for the Lord, 80
too h. for you, 147
transgressors is h., 230
harden
h. his heart, 48
h. not your heart, 19
h. thine heart, 29
hardened
h. our heart, 229
h. their necks, 238
harder
h. than a rock, 131
h. than flint, 178
h. to be won, 91
harlot
city become an h., 130
played the h., 16
sister as with an h., 209
harm
amends for the h., 207
do My prophets no h., 32
done thee no h., 11
harness
girdeth on his h., 23
harp
praise the Lord with h.,
166
psaltery and h., 166
with the timbrel and h., 49
hart
as the h. panteth, 153
leap as an h., 120
harts
princes are like h., 140
harvest
h. is past, 59
rain in h., 90
seedtime and h., 221
sleepeth in h., 146
haste
go out with h., 93

h. to be rich, 8
h. unto me, O God, 13
make h. to help, 13
said in my h., 149
shall not make h., 19
upon them make h., 194
hasteth
eagle that h., 235
h. to the snare, 243
h. with his feet, 198
hasty
h. of spirit, 89
heart be h. to utter, 198
man that is h., 198
hate
dost but h. me, 53
find out those that h., 72
h. him that rebuketh, 48
h. me without a cause, 72
h. the evil, 19
h. thee shall be clothed, 72
I h. him; for he doth, 5
is to h. evil, 77
lest he h. thee, 47
love the Lord, h. evil, 77
love them that h., 7
reward them that h., 140
that h. Me, 193
that h. me love death, 264
them that h. Thee, 71
they that h. you, 193
things doth the Lord h., 12
time to h., 119
weary of thee, and so h.,
125
hated
and h. him not, 137
h. him yet the more, 66
hatred wherewith he h.,
119
poor is h., 93
therefore have I h., 20
therefore I h. life, 57
hatest
h. thy friends, 93
of them whom thou h., 54
hateth
h. his own soul, 47
h. his son, 30
h. reproof is brutish, 47
h. reproof shall die, 47
righteous man h., 149
that h. Him, 83
violence His soul h., 254
hating
truth, h. covetousness, 113
hatred
h. for my love, 112
h. stirreth strifes, 11
h. wherewith he hated, 119
hideth h., 26
stalled ox and h., 152
haughtiness
lay low the h., 12

haughty
  eyes are upon the h., 11
  h. spirit before a fall, 80
head
  anointest my h., 22
  art exalted as h., 233
  blood upon thy h., 117
  crown of his h., 17
  dog's h., 136
  eyes are in his h., 90
  fallen from our h., 212
  fire upon his h., 226
  go up, thou bald h., 161
  h. and not the tail, 170
  h. of him that selleth, 25
  h. of the wicked, 98
  h. stone of the corner, 174
  h. were waters, 242
  hair of my h., 9
  hairs of mine h., 2
  hairs of mine h., 72
  hoar h. go down, 210
  hoary h. is a crown, 6
  increased over our h., 226
  lifter up of mine h., 34
  old men is the grey h., 79
  return upon his own h., 41
  return upon thine own h.,
    143
  upon their own h., 210
  upon thine own h., 208
heads
  h. shall be baldness, 165
heal
  behold, I will h., 185
  h. me, O Lord, 120
  time to h., 120
  torn, and He will h., 103
  wound, and I h., 102
healed
  his stripes we are h., 120
  I shall be h., 120
healeth
  h. the broken in heart,
    233
healing
  h. in his wings, 15
health
  faithful ambassador is h.,
    70
  h. to the bones, 234
  time of h., 79
heap
  h. coals of fire, 226
heapeth
  h. up riches, 133
heaps
  ass, h. upon h., 237
  Babylon shall become h.,
    54
hear
  and they would not h., 187
  cried and I would not h.,
    187

cry, and Thou wilt not h.,
    131
  dost not h. me, 58
  ears, but they h. not, 129
  h. a rumour, 55
  h. any more the voice, 6
  h. counsel, and receive, 5
  h. instruction, and be, 5
  h. me, O Lord, h. me, 189
  h. my prayer, 186
  h. my speech, 187
  h. my voice, 187
  h. now, ye rebels, 189
  h. O earth, 234
  h. O Israel, 163
  h. O Lord, forgive, 91
  h. O our God, 180
  h. O ye kings, 232
  h. open Thine eyes, 13
  h. the bleatings, 67
  h. the rebuke, 48
  h. the small, 131
  h. the song of fools, 48
  h. the word of the, 76
  h. the word of the, 208
  h. the word of the, 121
  h. the word of the Lord, 59
  h. their cry, 262
  h. Thou in heaven, 90
  h. thy servant curse, 48
  h. thy words but, 65
  h. ye deaf, 238
  h. ye indeed, 238
  h. ye that are far, 4
  h. ye the word, 187
  h. ye the word, 258
  h. ye the word, 190
  h. you in that day, 194
  He did h. my voice, 185
  heareth, let him h., 121
  I the Lord will h., 85
  I will h. it, 147
  I will not h., 121
  if ye will h. His voice, 19
  lest they should h., 65
  let the earth h., 187
  Lord will h. when, 185
  more ready to h. than, 268
  name, and I will h., 13
  neither see, nor h., 129
  not h. the law, 65
  not h. their cry, 85
  one would h. me, 135
  people h. the voice, 15
  report that I h., 169
  shall He not h., 104
  shall Pharoah h. me, 147
  spake, ye did not h., 65
  that He will not h., 186
  Thine ear, and h., 187
  we will h., 15
  wise man will h., 121
  would not h., 238
  yet will I not h., 91

heard
  but they have not h., 65
  h. even afar off, 27
  h. me, and delivered, 55
  h. my voice: hide not, 186
  h. the secret, 38
  h. these words, 233
  h. thy prayer, 185
  h. thy prayer, 37
  hast h. and live?, 15
  have ye not h., 100
  He h. me, 186
  He hath h. the voice, 115
  not h. long ago, 95
  shall not be h., 29
  such as they have not h.,
    98
  words are not h., 5
  words which thou hast h.,
    70
hearest
  Thou h. not, 59
  when Thou h. forgive, 90
heareth
  but he h. not, 111
  cry, and the Lord h., 186
  every one that h., 243
  h. the prayer of the, 108
  He h. the cry, 185
  Lord h. the poor, 182
  scorner h. not rebuke, 47
  that h. let him hear, 121
  Thy servant h., 120
  whosoever h. of it, 208
  wise son h., 47
hearing
  famine of h. the words, 85
  filled with h., 8
  h. of his ears, 80
hearken
  forgive; O Lord, h., 91
  h. and hear my speech,
    187
  h. not to your prophets, 5
  h. than fat of rams, 171
  h. thou unto the voice, 171
  h. unto the words, 83
  h. unto their judges, 83
  h. unto their voice, 2
  h. unto them, 185
  h. unto thy father, 175
  him ye shall h., 158
  not h. unto them, 201
hearkened
  h. not, nor inclined, 121
  h. to My commandments,
    172
  h. unto the words, 65
heart
  according to thy h., 7
  all that is in thine h., 70
  all thine h., 153
  all thy h., 19
  all thy h., 28

all thy h., 35
all your h., 170
bound in the h., 30
broken and a contrite h., 42
brother in your h., 24
but in h. he layeth, 128
can thine h. endure, 241
comfort thine h., 125
create in me a clean h., 235
deceit is in the h., 64
destroyeth the h., 24
eye affecteth mine h., 227
fool said in his h., 14
foreskin of your h., 33
foreskins of your h., 204
give them one h., 197
glad the h. of man, 151
h. be not deceived, 83
h. be perfect, 171
h. cheer thee, 268
h. decline to her ways, 4
h. deviseth his way, 18
h. envy sinners, 138
h. full of evil, 77
h. goeth after, 128
h. hath continual feast, 119
h. is deceitful, 77
h. is faint, 240
h. is made better, 146
h. is not with, 127
h. is privy, 40
h. is sorrowful, 145
h. knoweth his own, 9
h. of flesh, 203
h. of fools, 23
h. of fools, 90
h. of him that hath, 144
h. of kings, 163
h. of the righteous, 64
h. of the wicked, 124
h. of the wise, 69
h. of the wise, 90
h. rejoiceth, 118
h. said unto Thee, 81
h. shall not reproach, 40
h. standeth in awe, 4
h. taketh not rest, 59
h. that deviseth, 12
h. waketh, 67
h. was not perfect, 16
hands, and a pure h., 124
harden his h., 48
harden not your h., 19
harden thine h., 29
hardened our h., 229
healeth the broken in h., 233
her beauty in thine h., 4
high look and a proud h., 12
hypocrites in h. heap, 3

imagination of man's h., 76
in integrity of h., 124
lay it to his h., 52
let h. of them rejoice, 118
let not thine h. be glad, 72
looketh on the h., 137
madness is in their h., 77
make you a new h., 150
maketh the h. sick, 125
meditation of my h., 185
merry h. doeth good, 57
merry h. maketh, 119
mine eyes and mine h., 104
no man's h. fail, 43
not thine h. be hasty, 198
of a broken h., 116
perverse h., 56
pour out thine h., 186
pour out your h., 81
prepareth his h., 91
pride of thine h., 38
pride of thine h. hath, 38
removed their h., 128
rend your h., 204
said in thine h., 38
seal upon thine h., 152
set not their h. aright, 65
set not your h., 259
set Thine h. upon him, 155
set your h. and soul, 62
sorrow of the h., 233
stony h., 203
strength of my h., 92
strengthen your h., 39
such an h. in them, 87
table of their h., 178
take away the h., 151
trusteth in his own h., 38
truth in his h., 218
turn away your h., 137
turned their h. back, 189
understanding h., 250
understanding h., 63
upright in h., 118
upright in h., 118
uprightness of thine h., 253
vexation of his h., 49
vision of their own h., 84
war was in his h., 69
was in thine h., 137
wash thine h., 204
whose h. departeth from, 202
whose h. Thou knowest, 90
wine with a merry h., 89
wise man's h., 63
with a double h., 64
with a perfect h., 82
with a perfect h., 62
with all his h., 161
with all thine h., 248

with all your h., 62
with all your h., 62
with all your h., 83
word hid in mine h., 35
word in thy h., 35
words in thine h., 35
hearted
  merry h. do sigh, 233
  that are wise h., 263
hearts
  apply our h. unto, 149
  consider not in their h., 47
  evil in your h., 77
  h. as an adamant stone, 65
  h. of all that are wise, 263
  h. of all the children, 100
  h. of the people, 45
  Lord pondereth the h., 165
  Lord searcheth all h., 100
  mischief is in their h., 53
  prepare your h., 61
  that be of heavy h., 151
heat
  cold and h., 221
  drought and h. consume, 51
  then they have h., 24
heathen
  among the h., 78
  among the h., 183
  counsel of the h., 93
  deliver us from the h., 55
  exalted among the h., 99
  fury upon the h., 112
  fury upon the h., 98
  glory among the h., 76
  glory among the h., 99
  great among the h., 76
  h. are dismayed, 14
  h. shall see My judgment, 99
  near upon all the h., 112
  polluted before the h., 99
  say among the h., 76
  scatter thee among the h., 79
  small among the h., 196
  vengeance upon the h., 210
  way of the h., 18
  wherefore should the h., 220
  wherefore should the h., 1
heaven
  army of h., 103
  as an eagle toward h., 73
  by the God of h., 109
  called the firmament h., 120
  climb up to h., 75
  do not I fill h. and, 74
  eagles of the h., 235
  fallen from h., 54
  fought from h., 12
  fowls of the h., 196

God created the h., 17
God in h. above, 109
God in h. above, 104
God in h. that revealeth,
67
God is in h., 127
God of h., 239
h. and earth praise, 184
h. and in the earth, 120
h. even the heavens, 120
h. is high above, 101
h. is My throne, 104
h. of h. cannot contain, 33
h. of h. cannot contain, 33
h. or in earth, 99
hear Thou in h., 90
height of h., 99
if I ascend up into h., 74
in h. above, 109
made h. and earth, 13
made h. and earth, 46
made h. and earth, 46
purpose under the h., 168
seeing the h., 33
signs of h., 14
stars of h., 193
stars of the h., 44
still in the midst of h., 102
stork in the h., 65
under the h. is Mine, 103
whom have I in h., 81
windows in h., 230
witness is in h., 108
wonders in h. and in, 56
heavens
  clothe the h., 169
  create new h., 46
  from the h. praise, 184
  give ear, o ye h., 234
  God is in the h., 103
  great unto the h., 100
  grown up unto the h., 226
  h. are Thine, 120
  h. declare His, 99
  h. declare the glory, 99
  let the h. rejoice, 27
  Lord made the h., 83
  stretched out the h., 46
  the h. are the Lord's, 120
  were the h. made, 46
heaviness
  foolish son is the h., 31
heavy
  h. burdens, 85
  with h. tidings, 169
hedge
  h. up thy way, 172
  made an h. about him, 105
  sharper than a thorn h., 43
heed
  good h. therefore, 18
  good h. unto, 223
  h. to thyself, 18
  h. to your spirit, 156

h. to yourselves, 83
h. unto all words, 48
h. what ye do, 140
heifer
  plowed with my h., 19
  take an h., 236
height
  h. of heaven, 99
heights
  h. of the clouds, 14
  praise Him in the h., 184
hell
  belly of h., 187
  deliver his soul from h., 30
  dig into h., 75
  h. and destruction are, 121
  h. are we at agreement, 12
  h. from beneath, 52
  h. hath enlarged, 52
  H. is naked, 103
  house is the way to h., 4
  make my bed in h., 74
  soul in h., 75
  wicked turned into h., 111
help
  God of Jacob for his h., 81
  h. and my deliverer, 108
  h. and our shield, 176
  h. and their shield, 87
  h. cometh from the Lord,
    13
  h. from trouble, 106
  h. is in the name of, 7
  h. me, O Lord, 13
  h. the evil, 1
  h. the ungodly, 7
  I will h. saith, 108
  I will h. thee, 108
  if the Lord do not h., 13
  in Me is thine h., 13
  Lord had been my h., 13
  make haste to h., 13
  make him an h. meet, 151
  none shall h., 249
  none to h., 9
  not another to h. him, 43
  not to h. of the Lord, 67
  power to h., 102
  present h. in trouble, 92
  vain is the h. of man, 13
  whence cometh my h., 13
  whence shall I h., 13
  will ye flee for h., 74
helped
  low, and He h., 13
helper
  be Thou my h., 13
  him that hath no h., 186
helpers
  peace be to thine h., 22
helpeth
  for thy God h., 22
hemlock
  righteousness into h., 43

herb
  h. for the service, 48
  rain upon the tender h., 69
  wither as the green h., 260
herbs
  better is dinner of h., 152
  garden of h., 73
here
  doest thou h. Elijah, 67
  h. a little, there, 68
  h. am I, 160
heritage
  children are an h., 31
  give not Thine h. to, 91
  goodly h., 122
  h. is unto Me as lion, 20
  left Mine h., 1
hewers
  h. of wood, 194
hewn
  built houses of h., 63
  h. out her seven pillars,
    264
  will build with h., 12
hid
  falsehood have we h., 64
  h. His face, 186
  h. I My face from them,
    200
  h. in the day, 157
  h. not my face, 178
  prudent men shall be h.,
    195
  sins are not h., 39
  word h. in mine heart, 35
hide
  h. himself in secret, 74
  h. me under the shadow,
    106
  h. Mine eyes, 1
  h. not Thine ear, 186
  h. not Thy command-
    ments, 144
  h. not Thy face, 13
  h. not Thy face, 247
  h. thee in the dust, 74
  h. their counsel from, 64
  h. Thyself for ever, 1
  how long wilt Thou h., 1
  of iniquity may h., 47
  Sodom, they h. it not, 226
hidest
  h. Thou Thy face, 1
  why h. Thou Thyself, 13
hideth
  evil, and h., 192
  h. hatred, 26
  h. His face, 104
  h. not from Thee, 74
  he that h. his eyes, 29
high
  abase him that is h., 212
  h. above all the earth, 77
  h. above the earth, 101

h. as the eagle, 75
h. places were not taken, 128
like the most H., 14
Lord on h. is, 103
men of h. degree, 28
Most H., 110
mouth of the most H., 113
my h. tower, and my, 107
peace in His h. places, 176
record is on h., 108
set me up on h., 127
that hath an h. look, 12
though the Lord be h., 37
higher
  rock that is h., 217
highway
  desert a h., 159
hill
  ascend into the h., 122
  h. is not enough, 40
  h. shall be made low, 172
hills
  eyes unto the h., 13
  gods of the h., 54
  h. be removed, 100
  hoped for from the h., 95
  little h. like lambs, 15
  made before the h., 6
  watereth the h., 198
himself
  only upon h., 28
hinder
  who can h. Him, 102
hip
  smote them h. and thigh, 254
hire
  h. of a whore, 29
hired
  h. out themselves, 127
  oppress an h. servant, 25
hireling
  oppress the h. in wages, 265
hissing
  astonishment, and an h., 54
hoar
  h. hairs, 6
  h. head go down, 210
hoary
  h. head is a crown, 6
hold
  h. him not guiltless, 210
  not h. My peace, 139
holdest
  wherefore h. Thy tongue, 134
holes
  move out of their h., 126
holier
  h. than thou, 224

holiness
  beauty of h., 268
  glorious in h., 15
  h. unto the Lord, 122
holy
  against the H. one, 12
  an h. God, 110
  be ye h., 18
  between the h. and, 33
  bless His h. name, 184
  but for Mine h. name's, 99
  day is h. unto, 122
  for they are h., 188
  glory ye in His h. name, 118
  God that is h., 215
  h. h. h. is the Lord, 122
  h. habitation, 262
  h. in all His works, 111
  h. mountain, 213
  h. people, 32
  h. unto the Lord, 122
  h. unto the Lord, 33
  is in His h. temple, 109
  none h. as the Lord, 122
  pollute ye My h., 21
  sabbath, keep it h., 216
  saith the H. One, 83
  shall be h., 147
  stand before this h., 102
  stand in His h. place, 122
  standest is h., 205
  standest is h. ground, 122
  suffer Thine H. One, 75
  thanks to Thy h. name, 55
  ye shall be h., 122
  your God am h., 122
home
  h. again empty, 50
  h. there is as death, 52
  tarry at h., 219
homeborn
  him that is h., 74
honey
  butter and h., 63
  eat thou h. because, 89
  milk and h., 137
  sweeter also than h., 35
  sweeter than h., 136
  sweeter than h., 214
  taste a little h., 78
honeycomb
  drop as an h., 4
  h. which is sweet, 89
  honey and the h., 35
  words are as an h., 234
honour
  before h. is humility, 127
  bring thee to h., 264
  crowned him with h., 155
  delight to do h., 38
  delighteth to h., 123
  for thine h., 96
  full of h., 51

h. come of Thee, 84
h. for a man to cease, 11
h. is not seemly, 90
h. of kings is, 163
h. person of the mighty, 85
h. the face, 6
h. the Lord with, 246
h. thy father, 174
h. thy father, 175
I will h., 200
king's h., 114
left hand riches and h., 263
riches, and h., 212
sing forth the h., 232
that h. Me, 200
where is Mine h., 175
with their lips do h., 128
honoured
  that h. her despise her, 43
honoureth
  a son h. his father, 175
  h. Him hath mercy, 37
hook
  h. in thy nose, 125
  leviathan with a h., 155
hope
  ashamed of my h., 81
  h. and quietly wait, 176
  h. deferred, 125
  h. for Thy truth, 52
  h. hath He removed, 58
  h. in His mercy, 211
  h. in the day of evil, 125
  h. in the Lord, 39
  h. is in the Lord, 81
  h. of the hypocrite, 127
  h. shall perish, 83
  h. the Lord is, 119
  His word do I h., 109
  more h. of a fool, 198
  more h. of a fool than, 38
  poor hath h., 124
  prisoners of h., 125
  spent without h., 58
  Thou art my h., 124
  where is now my h., 58
  while there is h., 30
hoped
  in vain is salvation h., 95
horn
  h. of my salvation, 105
hornet
  sent the h., 12
horse
  as the h. rusheth, 132
  be not as the h., 10
  h. and his rider, 183
  h. is prepared against, 253
  he that rideth the h., 75
  whip for the h., 64
horseleach
  h. hath two daughters, 115

horses
  as fed h., 133
  contend with h., 37
  my h. as thy h., 7
  some in h., 202
host
  destroy ye her h., 10
  multitude of an h., 162
hosts
  except the Lord of h., 241
  God of h., 269
  h. is His name, 110
  h. is His name, 56
  holy, is the Lord of h., 122
  King, the Lord of h., 15
  Lord God of h., 12
  Lord of h., 110
  Lord of h. hath sent, 161
  Lord of h. is His name, 97
  messenger of Lord of h.,
    188
  name of the Lord of h., 80
  saith the Lord of h., 260
  saith the Lord of h., 238
  saith the Lord of h., 76
hot
  anger be h., 98
  anger of my Lord wax h.,
    207
  go upon h. coals, 4
  h. displeasure, 29
house
  barren woman to keep h.,
    88
  build him a sure h., 212
  build Him an h., 33
  build Me an h., 108
  buildeth her h., 123
  built Thee an h., 33
  called a h. of prayer, 33
  come into thine h., 87
  depart from thine h., 49
  doors of my h., 198
  dwell in the h., 22
  dwell within my h., 64
  escape in the king's h., 178
  every man to his h., 207
  evil depart from his h.,
    112
  forsaken Mine h., 1
  from thy neighbour's h.,
    125
  glory of his h., 73
  goest to the h. of God,
    268
  grave is mine h., 58
  h. by unrighteousness, 43
  h. full of sacrifices, 225
  h. full of silver, 170
  h. is the way to hell, 4
  h. of bondage, 92
  h. of cedar, 33
  h. of God, 267
  h. of Israel, 60

h. of Judah, 240
h. of mirth, 90
h. of mourning, 90
h. of mourning than to, 52
h. of my pilgrimage, 34
h. of Pharoah, 179
h. of the God, 109
h. of the God of Jacob, 62
h. of the Lord, 29
h. of the Lord, 108
h. of the righteous, 215
h. of the wicked, 22
h. unto My name, 194
h. which I build, 99
h. which I have built, 33
half thine h., 41
hedge about his h., 105
is the h. of Israel, 32
like that rebellious h., 199
Lord build the h., 3
me and my h. we, 31
midst of a rebellious h., 36
Mine h. shall be called, 33
not covet thy neighbor's h.,
  73
out of thine own h., 199
peace to thine h., 157
poor to thy h., 37
rebellious h., 86
sakes, O h. of Israel, 99
set thine h. in order, 51
sittest in thine h., 34
than to h. of feasting, 52
to thine own h., 49
troubleth his own h., 85
turn to his own h., 78
watchman unto the h., 206
what is my h., 126
where is the h., 33
wisdom builded her h.,
  264
wisdom is an h. builded, 3
woman in a wide h., 156
household
  ways of her h., 156
houses
  build h. but not, 94
  h. and riches are the, 133
  h. full of deceit, 47
  h. of hewn stone, 63
  h. to aliens, 40
housetops
  corner of the h. than, 156
how
  h. are the mighty, 145
  h. are the mighty, 54
  h. long halt ye, 27
  h. long shall, 176
  h. long wilt thou mourn,
    115
  h. to go out, 126
howl
  h. O gate, 66
  h. ye; for the day, 60

I will wail and h., 116
  lament and h., 165
humble
  better of an h. spirit, 127
  cry of the h., 185
  forget not the h., 106
  refuse to h. thyself, 11
  save the h. person, 126
humbled
  h. my soul with fasting,
    85
  h. themselves; therefore,
    90
  mighty man shall be h.,
    126
humbleth
  because he h. himself, 42
humbly
  walk h. with thy God, 127
humility
  before honour is h., 127
hundred
  against eight h., 237
  do evil an h. times, 112
  h. stripes into a fool, 48
hunger
  idle soul shall suffer h.,
    146
  slain with h., 52
hungry
  bread to the h., 37
  enemy be h., 72
  h. man dreameth, 63
  h. soul with goodness, 57
  steal when he is h., 47
  to the h. soul every, 57
hunt
  evil shall h., 254
  h. a partridge, 78
  h. every man his brother,
    166
  h. our steps, 66
huntest
  h. my soul, 178
hurt
  meddle to thy h., 257
  people, but the h., 26
  turn and do you h., 15
  will do you no h., 191
husband
  crown to her h., 156
  desire shall be to thy h.,
    14
  entice thy h., 19
  lament for the h., 54
husbands
  may be your h., 9
hypocrite
  h. with his mouth, 231
  h.'s hope shall perish, 83
  hope of the h., 127
  joy of the h., 76
hypocrites
  h. in heart heap, 3

I

idle
  i. soul shall suffer, 146
idleness
  bread of i., 156
idolatry
  iniquity and i., 238
idols
  defile yourselves with i.,
    112
  gifts, and with your i., 21
  gods of the people are i.,
    83
  i. are silver and gold, 129
  i. He shall abolish, 129
  slain men before your i.,
    61
  turn ye not unto i., 129
if
  i. the Lord be with us, 66
  i. ye seek Him, 62
ill
  shall be i. with him, 195
image
  any graven i., 128
  graven i., 129
  in the i. of God, 45
  man in His own i., 45
  profiteth the graven i., 130
images
  graven i., 129
  graven i., 129
  i. shall be broken, 61
  molten i., 129
  say to molten i., 129
imagination
  i. of man's heart, 76
imaginations
  deviseth wicked i., 12
imagine
  i. evil against, 24
  i. evil in your hearts, 77
  them that i. evil, 64
imagined
  devices they have i., 142
  they have i. to do, 8
Immanuel
  shall call his name I., 159
incense
  sacrificed and burnt i., 128
incline
  i. Thine ear, 55
  i. thine ear, 117
  i. Thine ear, 13
inclined
  because He i. His ear, 186
  hearkened not, nor i., 121
increase
  firstfruits of thine i., 246
  i. is by the strength, 69
  i. of his government, 159
  if riches i. set not, 259
  labour shall i., 259

land shall yield her i., 170
loveth abundance with i.,
  115
thy victuals for i., 251
will i. learning, 121
increased
  glory of his house is i., 73
  not i. the joy, 116
  our iniquities are i., 226
  traffick hast thou i., 62
increaseth
  against Thee i., 111
  i. knowledge i. sorrow, 49
  i. strength, 108
  woe to him that i., 47
indignation
  i. toward His enemies, 213
  stand before His i., 98
infant
  woman, i. and suckling, 10
infinite
  understanding is i., 100
influences
  i. of Pleiades, 183
inhabit
  houses, but not i., 94
  which ye shall i., 47
inhabitant
  hissing, without an i., 54
  i. of the earth, 59
inhabitants
  curse ye bitterly the i., 67
  i. of the earth, 103
  i. of the land, 15
  unto all the i., 92
  upon the i., 209
inhabited
  cities that are not i., 57
  formed it to be i., 46
inherit
  i. My holy mountain, 213
  i. the earth, 81
  i. the wind, 85
  meek shall i., 127
  righteous shall i., 213
  wise shall i. glory, 96
inheritance
  forsake His i., 153
  I am their i., 188
  i. among our brethren, 74
  i. is turned to, 40
  i. of fathers, 133
  i. to pass, 133
  Israelites for an i., 138
  leaveth an i., 114
  Lord is their i., 33
  Lord is their i., 188
  lot of your i., 45
  portion of mine i., 133
  remnant of Mine i., 1
  swallow up the i., 60
  take of the people's i., 249
  to be Thine i., 101
  wisdom good with i., 264

iniquities
  all their i., 219
  bruised for our i., 159
  i. are increased over, 226
  i. by showing mercy, 19
  less than our i., 158
  pine away for your i., 116
  shouldest mark i., 141
iniquity
  acknowledge thine i., 39
  be in me i., 134
  committeth i., 16
  devise i. and work evil, 47
  die for his own i., 206
  draw i. with cords, 230
  father bear the i. of, 229
  forgive their i., 91
  from the workers of i., 146
  i. be in thine hand, 18
  i. do flourish, 146
  i. have your fathers, 75
  i. is marked before, 118
  i. not be your ruin, 204
  i. of the father, 229
  i. of the fathers, 193
  i. was not found, 124
  laid on him the i., 156
  mine i., 134
  of i. shall be scattered, 262
  reaped i., 143
  shall die in his i., 187
  stubbornness is as i., 238
  stumblingblock of i., 260
  take away the i., 42
  truth and without i., 110
  upon me let this i., 206
  uttereth thine i., 117
  we have committed i., 39
  wicked for their i., 77
  workers of i., 53
  workers of i., 60
  workers of i. may hide, 47
innocent
  i. blood, 166
  lay not upon us i., 21
  rich shall not be i., 8
  shed i. blood, 12
  slay an i. person, 12
instead
  i. of a mouth, 234
  i. of eyes, 79
  i. of God, 234
instruction
  counsel, and receive i., 5
  despise wisdom and i., 68
  despiseth father's i., 31
  he that refuseth i., 64
  heareth his father's i., 47
  i. and be wise, 5
  i. of fools is, 251
  i. to a wise man, 5
  my i. and not silver, 68
  sealeth their i., 67
  whoso loveth i., 47

instrument
  i. of ten strings, 166
instruments
  stringed i., 166
integrity
  i. of heart, 124
  i. of the upright, 137
  know mine i., 39
  remove mine i., 135
  retain thine i., 28
  walk in mine i., 137
  walketh in his i., 124
intendest
  i. thou to kill, 244
intercession
  i. for the transgressors, 159
  now make i., 14
interpretation
  dream, and the i., 67
interpretations
  i. belong to God, 66
intreat
  i. me not, 61
  who shall i. for him, 140
intreaties
  poor useth i., 44
iron
  brass and i., 239
  i. as straw, 237
  i. sharpeneth i., 28
  i. sinew, 239
  pen of i., 178
  sunder the bars of i., 172
  yokes of i., 26
Isaac
  God of I., 96
isles
  declare it in the i., 76
Israel
  avenging of I., 114
  but I. doth not know, 15
  departed from I., 125
  do before all I., 125
  face of I., 105
  fought for I., 107
  fourth part of I., 2
  God of I., 110
  He that keepeth I., 32
  He that scattered I., 33
  he that troubleth I., 21
  hear, O I., 163
  Holy One of I., 12
  house of I., 60
  house of I., 206
  I. for His treasure, 32
  I. have deeply revolted,
    204
  I. is My son, 32
  I. loved Joseph, 30
  I. shall be a proverb, 201
  I. stoned him, 199
  I. thou hast destroyed, 108
  I. turneth their backs, 45
  I. will not forsake, 250

I. will not forsake, 85
into the land of I., 138
is the house of I., 32
king over I., 225
let I. go, 11
let I. go, 111
Lord loved I., 148
may prove I., 244
meet thy God, O I., 199
My people I., 45
prince over My people I.,
  102
sakes, O house of I., 99
shepherds of I., 43
Solomon king of I., 137
Strength of I., 148
tabernacles, O I., 17
Thou art God in I., 99
tribes of I., 139
unto His people I., 114
virgin of I., 32
See also "Children of
  Israel"
Israelites
  I. for an inheritance, 138
issues
  belong the i. from death, 55
ivory
  tower of i., 23

J

Jacob
  birthright unto J., 133
  dust of J., 2
  dwellings of J., 139
  God of J., 96
  God of J. for his help, 81
  house of the God of J., 62
  J. said unto his father, 53
  J. served seven years, 152
  Lord hath chosen J., 32
  not Esau J.'s brother, 153
  Star out of J., 158
  tents, O J., 17
  voice is J.'s, 53
  yet I loved J., 153
jaw
  j. of an ass, 237
jawbone
  j. of an ass, 237
jealous
  a j. God, 110
  am a j. God, 193
  God is j., 211
  is a j. God, 110
  j. for the Lord, 269
  j. God, 110
  j. God, 110
  whose name is J., 110
jealousy
  fire of My j., 61
  j. burn like fire, 91
  j. is cruel, 138

j. is the rage, 138
provoked Him to j., 98
Jehovah
  J. is everlasting strength,
    237
  J. is my strength, 237
  name alone is J., 110
Jehu
  J. shall serve, 53
jeopardy
  j. of their lives, 44
  j. of their lives, 44
  lives in j., 189
Jericho
  city of J., 48
  tarry at J., 226
Jerusalem
  cause J. to know, 187
  daughters of J., 17
  forget thee, O J., 1
  garments, O J., 203
  have chosen J., 139
  J. a praise in the, 139
  J. is ruined, 21
  J. shall My name, 139
  J. the city, 139
  J. the city which the Lord,
    139
  J.'s sake I will not, 139
  joy of J., 27
  king unto J., 179
  out of J., 240
  rejoice ye with J., 139
  round about J., 101
  shall yet choose J., 56
  stand up, O J., 254
  wall of J., 139
  wipe J. as a man wipeth,
    60
  word of the Lord from J.,
    35
  word of the Lord from J.,
    140
Jesse
  out of the stem of J., 159
jewel
  as a j. of gold in, 17
jewels
  thighs are like j., 17
Jews
  more than all the J., 178
Jezebel
  carcase of J., 25
  dogs shall eat J., 27
  dogs shall eat J., 226
  not say, this is J., 25
Jezreel
  wall of J., 27
Joab
  hand of J., 42
Job
  considered my servant J.,
    162
  J. fear God, 136

J. twice as much, 178
latter end of J., 55
man is like J., 224
men, Noah, Daniel, and J., 61
words of J. are ended, 71
join
come, and let us j., 19
joint
foot out of j., 20
joints
j. of thy thighs, 17
Jonathan
J. loved him, 93
shalt surely die, J., 80
soul of J., 93
though it be in J., 131
Jordan
not go over J., 2
other side J., 41
over this J., 62
swelling of J., 211
Joseph
I am J., 174
Israel loved J., 30
Joshua
J. drew not his hand, 60
journey
j. that thou takest, 96
joy
eat thy bread with j., 89
folly is j. to him that, 89
fool hath no j., 90
j. cometh in the morning, 118
j. in the God, 119
j. of Jerusalem, 27
j. of the hypocrite, 76
j. of the Lord, 237
j. of the whole earth, 139
j. of the whole earth, 140
j. shall ye draw, 218
knowledge, and j., 22
not increased the j., 116
over thee with j., 219
peace is j., 176
reap in j., 48
shout for j., 118
shout for j., 118
songs and everlasting j., 92
wise child shall have j., 31
joyful
j. mother of children, 88
j. noise to the rock, 232
j. noise unto God, 232
make a j. noise, 184
prosperity be j., 179
Judah
depart from J., 147
house of J., 240
J. is fallen, 21
judge
deserts will I j., 143
God is the j., 239

he shall not j., 80
j. His people, 140
j. not for man, 140
j. not the cause, 134
J. of all, 101
j. of the widows, 262
j. righteously, 143
j. righteously, 140
j. shall j. him, 140
j. the fatherless, 37
j. the world, 140
j. the world, 141
j. thee according, 141
j. Thou my cause, 143
j. thy neighbor, 140
j. Thy people, 63
j. you every one, 132
king to j., 73
Lord is our j., 97
Lord shall j., 140
matter they shall j., 147
prince and a j., 147
righteousness shall he j., 159
shall j. the righteous, 141
the Lord j. between, 207
judges
faces of the j., 134
hearken unto their j., 83
j. of the earth, 114
j. shall condemn, 207
judgeth
j. the poor, 163
j. the righteous, 140
judgment
aged understand j., 6
Almighty pervert j., 76
bring every work into j., 54
choose to us j., 53
correct me, but with j., 117
enter not into j., 141
establish j. in the gate, 19
execute true j., 19
feed them with j., 141
God of j., 111
guide in j., 117
have done j. and justice, 1
I will execute j., 129
j. in the earth, 143
j. into gall, 43
j. is before Him, 140
j. is God's, 140
j. is turned away, 146
j. is with the Lord, 81
j. of truth, 143
j. run down as waters, 143
j. that I have executed, 99
j. was not to drink, 196
justice and j., 142
keep mercy and j., 82
keep ye j., 18
looked for j., 63
Lord love j., 143
Lord loveth j., 82

man's j. cometh from, 143
not wrest the j., 131
people know not the j., 65
persons in j., 131
redeemed with j., 139
righteousness and j., 214
sit in j., 183
there is no j., 58
time and j., 63
to do justice and j., 142
unrighteousness in j., 25
verity and j., 111
judgments
executed j. upon, 218
His j. are in all, 104
keep My j., 172
observe their j., 112
just
habitation of the j., 22
Him that is most j., 38
j. and having salvation, 127
j. and right is He, 110
j. be delivered, 55
j. he shall surely live, 215
j. man walketh in, 124
j. shall live by his, 82
j. shall walk, 19
j. upright man, 161
j. weight, 25
j. with God, 39
memory of the j., 205
mortal man be more j., 18
mouth of the j., 215
must be j. ruling, 114
not a j. man on earth, 177
path of the j., 215
shall have j. balances, 25
teach a j. man, 5
tongue of the j., 124
way of the j., 215
justice
done judgment and j., 1
j. and judgment, 142
j. standeth afar, 146
j. to the afflicted, 142
judgment, and do j., 18
princes decree j., 162
to do j. and judgment, 142
justified
no man living be j., 141
justify
j. the righteous, 142
not j. the wicked, 76
justly
do j., 143

K

keep
bless thee and k. thee, 107
except the Lord k., 222
k. all My statutes, 204
k. her; she is thy life, 68

k. no god but Me, 163
k. not at what they, 172
k. not how to go, 126
k. not the day, 6
k. not the judgment, 65
k. not the Lord, 111
k. that I am God, 145
k. that I am the Lord, 141
k. that I am the Lord, 145
k. that I am the Lord, 138
k. that I am the Lord, 15
k. that I am the Lord, 11
k. that I am the Lord, 145
k. that My name, 103
k. that they shall die, 150
k. that Thou art Lord, 55
k. that Thou art Lord, 189
k. that Thou canst do, 103
k. the number, 27
k. thou the God, 145
k. thou, that we k., 11
k. thy abode, 100
k. to refuse the evil, 63
k. whether ye love, 83
k. ye that the Lord, 110
let no man k. of these, 222
live; and ye shall k., 150
make me to k. mine end, 164
may k. Thee, 116
not k. from whence, 195
people shall k. My name, 206
people that do k. their, 82
shall not He k., 100
that ye may k. that I, 217
to k. my transgression, 134
wicked regardeth not to k., 183
wicked: who can k. it, 77
knowest
if thou k. it all, 12
k. all the wickedness, 40
k. not what a day may, 23
k. the hearts, 100
k. the people, 76
k. thou not, 20
k. thou not yet, 26
k. what thou oughtest, 166
Thou k. it altogether, 100
whose heart Thou k., 90
knoweth
brutish man k. not, 130
k. her appointed times, 65
k. his own bitterness, 9
k. not it is his life, 243
k. not the price, 250
k. not who shall gather, 133
k. our frame, 37
k. them that trust, 13
Lord k. the thoughts of, 94

ox k. his owner, 15
understandeth and k. Me, 81
unjust k. no shame, 226
who k. whether he shall, 133
knowing
k. good and evil, 72
knowledge
because have no k., 79
beginning of k., 87
brutish in his k., 130
do good they have no k., 112
fools hate k., 89
full of the k., 82
give me now k., 96
God of k., 54
he that increaseth k., 49
He that teacheth man k., 100
k. is easy, 144
k. it hath perverted, 38
k. of God more than, 216
k. rather than gold, 68
k. spareth his words, 252
lips should keep k., 33
loveth k., 47
man concealeth k., 23
of His mouth cometh k., 263
right that find k., 33
so shall k. of wisdom, 264
spirit of k., 159
takest k. of him, 155
teach God k., 126
thou hast rejected k., 145
through k. shall the just, 55
tree of k., 112
understanding seeketh k., 144
utter vain k., 252
wisdom, and k., 22
wise men lay up k., 144
wise seeketh k., 144
wise, and k. to them, 97
words without k., 130
words without k., 130
known
child is k. by, 28
fool's voice is k. by, 90
have not k. Me, 89
have ye not k., 100
k. in the eyes of, 145
k. toward His servants, 213
let it be k. this day, 99
make k. His deeds, 76
mighty power to be k., 55
paths they have not k., 73
people I have not k., 15
wrath is presently k., 136

L

labour
good of all his l., 181
good of all his l., 89
he that gathereth by l., 259
l. and have no rest, 173
l. in vain that build, 3
l. not to be rich, 8
l. of man is for, 8
l. of the righteous, 41
l. of thine hands, 69
l. there is profit, 189
man of all his l., 94
man of all his l., 49
nothing of his l., 94
reward for their l., 42
six days shalt thou l., 216
strength l. and sorrow, 149
why l. I in vain, 58
womb to see l. and, 59
ye did not l., 138
laboured
l. for the wind, 49
l. under the sun, 49
laboureth
in that wherein he l., 189
labouring
sleep of a l. man, 231
lack
little had no l., 80
to the poor shall not l., 29
laid
be strongly l., 25
l. on him the iniquity, 156
lamb
dwell with the l., 10
l. for a burnt offering, 167
l. to the slaughter, 52
wolf and l. shall, 24
lambs
l. to the slaughter, 60
little hills like l., 15
lame
feet was I to the l., 7
l. man leap, 120
lament
l. and howl, 165
l. like a virgin, 54
lamentation
neighbour l., 116
wilderness a l., 168
lamp
commandment is a l., 117
l. of the wicked, 195
l. unto my feet, 73
Thou art my l., 81
land
a strange l., 90
all the l., 92
all the l. is before, 93
as a thirsty l., 153
born in the l., 74
bring into this l., 40

l. but a few of many, 241
l. hand riches, 263
l. Mine heritage, 1
or to the l., 170
remnant that are l., 185
right hand or to the l., 35
take the l. hand, 31
therefore have I also l., 1
legs
l. are as pillars, 23
lend
l. him thy victuals, 251
l. unto many nations, 24
l. upon usury, 90
not l. upon usury, 251
lender
as with the l., 24
servant to the l., 24
lendeth
l. unto the Lord, 8
showeth favour, and l., 95
length
l. of days is in, 263
l. of days understanding, 6
lent
l. him to the Lord, 188
leopard
l. his spots, 28
l. shall lie down, 10
less
do l. or more, 170
hast punished us l., 158
how much l. man, 155
much l. this house, 33
leviathan
draw out l., 155
liar
better than a l., 64
liars
all men are l., 149
liberty
l. to the captives, 56
proclaim l., 92
lice
land became l., 179
lick
l. the dust, 126
l. the dust, 126
shall dogs l., 27
licked
l. the blood, 27
lie
cause them to l. down, 107
high degree are a l., 28
if two l. together, 24
Israel will not l., 148
l. down in green, 34
l. down in the dust, 51
l. down with the kid, 10
l. one to another, 18
l. unto thine handmaid, 88
l. with thy wives, 125
not l. with mankind, 123
that He should l., 110

lied
l. and not remembered
Me, 111
lies
be born, speaking l., 17
bow for l., 64
forgers of l., 34
full of l. and, 47
l. our refuge, 64
l. shall perish, 64
should thy l. make men, 37
speakest l. in the name, 84
telleth l. shall not, 64
will utter l., 28
with l. ye have made, 64
witness that speaketh l., 12
liest
l. thou thus upon, 70
lieth
from her that l. in thy, 20
l. with a beast, 232
l. with any beast, 232
l. with his father's, 132
l. with his sister, 132
life
all the days of my l., 22
Almighty given me l., 149
and my l. is preserved, 15
assurance of thy l., 49
better than l., 100
breath of l., 45
choose l. that, 31
cut off my l., 59
days of his l., 147
days of thy l., 48
desire tree of l., 125
findeth me findeth l., 264
for she is thy l., 68
fountain of l., 87
give for his l., 224
give l. for l., 141
He is thy l., 97
in death or l., 153
it is your l., 35
keepeth his l., 192
l. and death,, 150
l. and good, 18
l. draweth nigh, 6
l. I will give thee, 75
l. is yet whole, 9
l. of a murderer, 26
l. of all flesh, 23
l. of his beast, 10
l. unto the bitter, 9
my l. from corruption, 56
our l. for your's, 168
prolong my l., 58
restorer of thy l., 114
righteous tendeth to l., 41
save not thy l., 257
seek my l., 58
seeketh my l., 167
seeketh my l. seeketh, 50
seeketh thy l., 50

she is a tree of l., 264
slew in his l., 3
snare for my l., 53
some to everlasting l., 71
strength of my l., 44
that it is for his l., 243
therefore I hated l., 57
thy l. shall be many, 5
to preserve l., 197
tree is man's l., 167
tree of l., 213
way of l., 150
weary of my l., 56
wellspring of l., 251
wisdom giveth l., 264
years of my l., 162
lift
l. up his spear, 237
l. up mine eyes, 13
l. up my soul, 185
l. up Thine hand, 106
l. up thy prayer, 185
l. up thy voice, 40
l. up thy voice, 29
lifted
l. me up, 236
l. up his soul, 122
lifteth
l. the needy, 37
l. up the beggar, 55
l. up the meek, 157
light
and there was l., 45
called the l. day, 169
darkness for l. and l., 149
everlasting l., 117
fire, to give them l., 105
God saw the l., 11
greater l. to rule, 14
have seen a great l., 73
His l. arise, 104
is as the shining l., 215
l. excelleth darkness, 89
l. is sown, 118
l. of the wicked, 142
l. thing to be, 162
l. to the Gentiles, 117
l. unto my path, 73
l. upon him, 40
law is l., 117
lesser l. to rule, 14
let there be l., 45
Lord is my l., 86
Lord shall be a l., 82
make darkness l., 73
rebel against the l., 47
send out Thy l., 117
Thou prepared the l., 169
Thy l. shall we see l., 96
till the morning l., 188
upon them hath the l.,
218
wait for l., 63
waited for l., 9

locusts
brought the l., 180
lodge
l. in the street, 125
l. not in the street, 50
lodgest, I will l., 61
vain thoughts l., 77
lodgest
where thou l., 61
loins
gird up now thy l., 206
kings out of thy l., 22
than my father's l., 226
long
forsake us so l., 2
heard l. ago, 95
how l. Lord, 55
how l. refuse ye, 65
how l. shall this man, 26
how l. shall thy vain, 77
how l. will it be, 131
how l. will it be, 80
how l. will it be ere, 131
how l. will ye turn, 78
how l. will ye vex, 78
how l. wilt thou go, 16
how l. wilt Thou look, 131
how l. wilt thou refuse, 11
l. as he liveth, 188
l. as he sought, 239
l. as I live, 40
l. as I live, 186
l. have I to live, 179
l. shall I cry, 131
l. shall the adversary, 21
l. shall the wicked, 43
l. their furrows, 9
l. will this people, 77
l. wilt Thou forget, 1
l. wilt Thou hide, 1
Lord, how l., 195
sing as l. as I live, 232
longing
satisfieth the l. soul, 57
longsuffering
God l. and, 101
look
all they that l. upon, 57
and l. not back, 253
high l. and a proud, 12
how long wilt Thou l., 131
I will l. unto the Lord, 82
l. not behind, 242
l. ye blind, 238
proud l., 12
looked
l. for good, 9
l. for judgment, 63
l. for much and lo, 63
l. for peace but, 79
l. for some to take pity, 34
l. upon My people, 101
wife l. back, 41

lookest
wherefore l. Thou upon, 134
looketh
l. on the heart, 137
l. on the outward, 137
l. well to the ways, 156
looking
fail with l., 59
looks
dismayed at their l., 86
loose
l. the bands, 85
l. the bands of, 183
loosed
silver cord be l., 63
looseth
l. the prisoners, 131
lord
all my l.'s servants, 74
lords
Lord of l., 110
lose
time to l., 3
lost
astray like a l. sheep, 42
people hath been l., 16
seek that which was l., 120
lot
divide thou it by l., 138
l. for the scapegoat, 219
l. is cast, 28
l. of your inheritance, 45
one l. for the Lord, 219
lothe
l. yourselves in your, 201
loud
l. cymbals, 166
make a l. noise, 27
with a l. voice, 91
love
all ye that l. her, 139
banner over me was l., 152
better is thy l., 152
better than secret l., 26
dinner of herbs where l., 152
few days, for the l., 152
greater than the l., 119
hatred for my l., 112
His l. upon you, 32
l. among the daughters, 17
l. covereth all, 11
l. her, and she shall, 264
l. Him, 153
l. him as thyself, 90
l. is better than wine, 152
l. is strong as death, 152
l. mercy, 37
l. no false oath, 177
l. not sleep, 146
l. the good, 19
l. the Lord, 153
l. the Lord, 153

l. the Lord, 18
l. the Lord, hate evil, 77
l. the truth, 177
l. them that hate, 7
l. them that l. me, 264
l. thy neighbor, 24
l. to me was wonderful, 93
l. ye the stranger, 24
let them that l., 96
Lord l. judgment, 143
mouth they show much l., 128
passing the l. of women, 93
preserveth all that l., 195
prosper that l. thee, 139
rise up, my l., 216
say I l. thee, 127
sick of l., 152
that l. Me, 193
they which l. Thy law, 35
time to l., 119
waters cannot quench l., 152
whether l. the Lord, 83
wise man, and he will l., 47
loved
as he l. cursing, 142
as he l. his own soul, 93
because the Lord l. you, 32
he l. him, 93
I have l. you saith, 133
Israel l. Joseph, 30
Jonathan l. him as his, 93
l. are turned against, 20
Lord l. Israel, 148
wherein hast Thou l., 133
yet I l. Jacob, 153
lovers
among all her l. she, 2
follow after her l. but, 94
gifts to all thy l., 129
harlot with many l., 16
lovest
l. me not, 53
l. thine enemies, 93
loveth
he that l. pleasure, 181
him that l. violence, 254
l. abundance, 115
l. at all times, 93
l. him chasteneth, 30
l. knowledge, 47
l. silver, 115
l. the gates of Zion, 139
l. to oppress, 25
l. wine and oil, 181
Lord l. judgment, 82
Lord l. the righteous, 100
scorner l. not one, 47
whom my soul l., 57
whom the Lord l. He, 29
whoso l. instruction, 47

lovingkindness
l. is better than life, 100
shall Thy l. be declared, 150
understand the l. of, 100

low
bringeth l. and lifteth, 102
exalt him that is l., 212
gone and brought l., 142
I was brought l., 13
lay l. the haughtiness, 12
men of l. degree, 28
mountain and hill made l., 172
pride shall bring him l., 188

lower
l. than the angels, 155

lowly
humble spirit with l., 127
l. and riding upon an, 127
respect unto the l., 37

Lucifer
L. son of the morning, 54

lucre
turned aside after l., 43

lust
l. not after her beauty, 4

lying
from l. lips, 231
hatred with l. lips, 26
l. children, 65
l. lips a prince, 69
l. lips are abomination, 149
l. spirit in the mouth, 236
l. tongue is but for, 149
man hateth l., 149
observe l. vanities, 83
proud look, a l. tongue, 12
trust not in l. words, 64

M

mad
laughter, it is m., 146
maketh a wise man m., 154
need of m. men, 77
play the m. man, 77

made
hath He not m. thee, 133
He m. me not, 56
m. all things for Himself, 46
work say of him that m., 56

madness
m. is in their heart, 77

magnify
m. Him with thanksgiving, 115
Thou shouldest m. him, 155

maid
as with the m., 84
m. forget her ornaments, 16
way of a man with a m., 4

maids
new wine the m. cheerful, 191

maidservant
nor his m., 73

majesty
victory, and the m., 99

make
kill and to m. alive, 119

maker
before the Lord our m., 268
forgettest thy m., 83
graven image that the m., 130
more pure than his m., 18
reproacheth his M., 173
reproacheth his M., 21
striveth with his M., 121
the m. of them all, 74

maketh
m. me to lie down, 34
m. sore, and bindeth, 102

male
m. and female created, 45
m. and female created He, 46

males
m. shall be the Lord's, 30

man
against every m., 71
and he a m. of war, 10
and the son of m. that, 132
angry m. stirreth, 9
art a wise m., 166
art thou the first m., 6
as a drunken m., 67
as a m. falleth, 134
as the m. is, 28
be done unto the m., 123
blains upon m., 180
blessed is m. that walketh, 36
blessed is that m. that, 118
brutish m. knoweth not, 130
by m. shall his blood, 141
can a m. take fire in, 4
cast away a perfect m., 1
cheereth God and m., 8
clothe a m. with rage, 147
come not near any m., 107
cursed be the m., 45
cursed be the m., 202
cursed be the m., 48
dead m. out of mind, 59
deceitful and unjust m., 106
deliver every m. his, 75

destroy both young m., 60
dieth the wise m., 52
duty of m., 67
end of that m. is peace, 162
every m. at his best, 92
every m. be put to death, 117
every m. is a friend to, 93
every m. is brutish, 130
every m. shall die, 194
every m. shall give, 29
every m. the truth, 124
every m. to his brother, 37
every way of a m., 165
eyes of m. are never, 8
eyes upon ways of m., 100
face of m., 140
face of the old m., 6
faithful m. who can find, 153
fall into the hand of m., 48
fear every m. his mother, 175
field is m.'s life, 167
firstborn, both m. and, 88
foolish m. despiseth, 31
foolish m. reproacheth, 47
friendship with angry m., 9
from m. made He a woman, 45
give me a m., 27
glad the heart of m., 151
God created m., 45
God created m., 154
God doth talk with m., 104
God formed m., 45
God greater than m., 115
God is not a m., 110
good for a m. that, 176
good m. is perished, 112
good m. leaveth, 114
hand of a mighty m., 222
happy is the m. that, 31
happy is the m. that, 119
He drove out the m., 174
He had made m., 46
He that teacheth m., 100
herb for service of m., 48
how long shall this m., 26
how much less m., 155
hungry m. dreameth, 63
hunt every m. his, 166
hunt the violent m., 254
I am God, and not m., 158
if a m. die, 133
if a m. die, 51
if m. can number, 2
is my complaint to m., 37
judge not for m., 140
just m. walketh in, 124
killeth a m., 26
killeth a m., 193

vain is the help of m., 13
way of a m. with a, 166
way of m. is not in, 202
ways of a m., 224
ways of m. are before, 100
what can m. do unto, 39
what hath m. of all his, 49
what is m., 132
what is m., 155
what is m., 155
what m. is he that, 51
whelps meet a m., 50
when m.'s ways please, 18
when no m. pursueth, 40
wicked and the evil m.,
  195
wicked devoureth the m.,
  134
wicked m. is loathsome,
  261
wicked m. travaileth, 240
will a m. rob God, 29
wise m. feareth, 77
wise m. is strong, 237
wise m. keepeth it in, 192
wise m. or a fool, 133
wise m. than an hundred,
  48
wise m. will hear, 121
wise m.'s eyes are in, 90
wise m.'s heart, 63
worm, and no m., 174
worthy m., 142
manifold
  how m. are Thy works,
  167
mankind
  not lie with m., 123
manner
  this the m. of man, 126
manservant
  nor his m., 73
mantle
  Elijah cast his m., 148
  rent my m., 9
many
  left but a few of m., 241
  life shall be m., 5
  m. are the afflictions, 247
  m. O Lord my God, 184
  m. seek the ruler's, 143
  of making m. books, 24
  save by m. or by few, 39
Mara
  call me M., 9
marble
  pillars of m., 23
mark
  m. me, and be astonished,
  224
  m. the perfect man, 162
  set a m. upon Cain, 105
  upon whom is the m.,
  107

marked
  iniquity is m., 118
married
  children of the m., 31
marvelous
  m. in our eyes, 239
  m. works among nations,
  76
master
  ass his m.'s crib, 15
  deliver unto his m., 231
  escaped from his m., 231
  free from his m., 51
  servant honoureth his m.,
  175
  so with his m., 84
matter
  every great m., 147
  far from a false m., 123
  repeateth a m., 116
matters
  account of His m., 38
mean
  m. man shall be brought,
  126
  m. ye by these stones, 202
meaneth
  m. then this bleating, 53
measure
  drink water by m., 85
  in weight, or in m., 25
  m. of my days, 164
  mouth without m., 52
measured
  not be m. nor numbered,
  33
measures
  divers m., 25
meat
  bodies shall be for m., 196
  came forth m., 213
  m. in the summer, 62
  m. unto them that fear, 89
  mouth tasteth m., 248
  prey, and seek their m., 6
  shall be m. for you, 10
meddle
  m. not with him that, 88
  m. not with them, 162
  m. to thy hurt, 257
meddling
  fool will be m., 90
  forbear thee from m., 108
medicine
  good like a m., 57
medicines
  in vain use many m., 66
meditate
  m. day and night, 214
  m. therein day, 220
meditation
  m. of my heart, 185
meek
  good tidings to m., 187

lifteth up the m., 157
m. of the earth, 62
m. shall eat, 157
m. shall inherit, 127
m. will He guide, 117
m. will He teach, 117
meekness
  seek m., 157
meet
  daughter came out to m.,
  134
  moved for thee to m., 52
  my house to m. me, 198
  prepare to m. thy God,
  199
  rich and poor m., 74
  robbed of her whelps m.,
  50
melody
  make sweet m., 84
melted
  hearts of the people m., 45
melteth
  m. before the fire, 195
memorial
  m. is perished with, 10
memory
  m. of the just, 205
men
  able m. such as fear, 113
  all m. are liars, 149
  as if they were m., 86
  beauty of old m. is, 79
  befalleth the sons of m., 52
  before wicked m., 134
  blood of the m., 44
  blood of these m., 189
  cast down your slain m.,
  61
  cease from among m., 10
  children of m., 120
  children of m., 100
  city that m. call, 140
  companion of riotous m.,
  36
  counsel which the old m.,
  5
  crown of old m., 114
  despised among m., 196
  favour to m. of skill, 235
  for m. to search, 23
  for you to weary m., 78
  glory of young m. is, 79
  happy are thy m., 148
  is the end of all m., 52
  let the m. go, 26
  m. are not always wise, 6
  m. depart from evil, 87
  m. do not despise a, 47
  m. have been slain by, 4
  m. hold their peace, 37
  m. is full of evil, 77
  m. of high degree, 28
  m. of low degree, 28

m. of truth, 113
m. of understanding, 235
m. of war fled, 54
m. on the earth, 109
m. say not of me, 125
m. shall fall, 209
m. shall see visions, 67
made all m. in vain, 164
need of mad m., 77
none upright among m., 112
of My pasture, are m., 102
oh that m. would praise, 184
old m. shall dream, 67
openeth the ears of m., 67
play the m., 44
precept of m., 128
prudent m. shall be hid, 195
quit yourselves like m., 43
rejected of m., 159
reproach of m., 174
reproach of m., 48
ruleth over m., 114
save me from bloody m., 146
saw the daughters of m., 17
sent me to the m., 192
silver shall m. call, 197
slain a thousand m., 237
sleep falleth upon m., 67
sons of m. how long, 78
spare not her young m., 10
ten mighty m., 237
than seven m. that can, 38
though these three m., 61
voice of singing m., 6
walketh with wise m., 36
way of evil m., 18
wisdom of their wise m., 195
wise m. die, 164
wise m. turn away wrath, 9
work of m.'s hands, 129
work of m.'s hands, 129
work of m.'s hands, 129
young m. cheerful, 191
Mene
M. M. Tekel, Upharsin, 166
menstruous
m. cloth, 129
merchant
he is a m., 25
mercies
but for Thy great m., 127
great are His m., 158
redeem us for Thy m.', 200
save me for Thy m., 218
save me for Thy m.', 13
sure m. of David, 22
tender m. come unto, 37

tender m. of the wicked, 48
to the Lord belong m., 111
with great m. will I, 1
merciful
be m. unto us, 22
God, m. and gracious, 110
gracious and m., 101
gracious God, and m., 37
He is gracious and m., 111
I am m. saith the Lord, 91
Lord is m., 36
m. God, 110
m. man doeth good, 48
m. Thou wilt show, 110
m. unto me, O God, 158
show Thyself m., 110
mercy
according to Thy m., 91
according to Thy m., 13
anger, and of great m., 37
cruel, and have no m., 40
fatherless findeth m., 262
forsake their own m., 83
great is His m., 101
greatness of Thy m., 101
have m. upon, 92
He delighteth in m., 91
He will have m., 204
hope in His m., 211
I had m. on thee, 37
keep m. and judgment, 82
let not m. and truth, 28
love m., 37
m. and not sacrifice, 216
m. and truth preserve, 162
m. before the man, 22
m. endureth for ever, 113
m. endureth for ever, 101
m. endureth for ever, 184
m. is everlasting, 101
m. is everlasting, 111
m. O Lord, held me up, 108
m. on the poor, 37
m. on the poor, 37
m. shall follow me, 22
m. shall not depart, 101
m. shall the throne, 163
m. to the poor, 19
paths of the Lord are m., 110
plenteous in m., 101
plenteous in m., 36
reap in m., 19
righteous showeth m., 24
show m. and compassions, 37
show thee m., 157
showing m. unto thousands, 193
spare, nor have m., 60
throne: m. and truth, 142
Thy m. is great, 100

with Lord there is m., 101
wrath remember m., 9
merry
drink, and to be m., 49
m. heart doeth good, 57
m. heart hath continual, 119
m. heart maketh, 119
m. hearted do sigh, 233
wine with a m., 89
message
a m. by the hand of, 169
m. from God, 12
messenger
deaf, as My m., 239
king is as m. of death, 9
m. of the Lord of hosts, 188
send My m. and he, 159
wicked m., 70
Methuselah
days of M., 6
midst
dwell in the m. of thee, 105
God is in the m., 139
m. of his days, 64
m. of my days, 150
might
acknowledge My m., 4
all thy m., 153
do it with thy m., 69
goeth forth in his m., 96
m. hath failed, 45
man glory in his m., 23
Mine hand and My m., 103
my firstborn, my m., 88
not by m. nor by, 238
power and m., 102
spirit of counsel and m., 159
that have no m., 108
wisdom and m. are His, 237
mightier
m. than the noise, 103
mighty
better than the m., 9
Counsellor, the m., 159
hand of a m. man, 222
hand of the m., 106
Lord m. in battle, 103
Lord strong and m., 103
m. expert man, 3
m. fallen, 145
m. fallen, 54
m. God, 104
m. in power, 134
m. in the war, 209
m. man glory, 23
m. man is not delivered, 237

m. man shall be humbled,
126
m. ones are beaten down,
253
m. power to be known, 55
m. shall flee away, 54
m. waves of the sea, 103
midst of thee is m., 219
more than ten m., 237
neither shall the m., 40
nor m. man escape, 253
person of the m., 85
righteousness as a m., 143
rushing of m. waters, 169
swords of the m., 256
with a m. hand, 55
ye m. give unto the Lord,
184

milk
gave him m., 53
m. and honey, 137
poured me out as m., 46

mind
come into your m., 100
dead man out of m., 59
fool uttereth all his m.,
192
nor come into m., 46
with a willing m., 62

mindful
art m. of him, 132
ever m. of His covenant,
45
m. always of His covenant,
82

minds
chafed in their m., 8
speak your m., 5

mine
all souls are M., 97

minister
m. unto Him, 225

miracles
where be all His m., 66

mire
m. of the street, 10
rush grow up without m.,
116
waters cast up m., 261

mirth
house of m., 90
m. what doeth it, 146

miscarrying
give them a m., 49

mischief
except they have done m.,
261
falleth into m., 70
in running to m., 12
m. is in their hearts, 53
m. shall return, 41
m. will come upon, 188
seeketh m., 247
set on m., 76

tongue deviseth m., 20
tongue falleth into m., 64

miserable
m. comforters, 34

misery
m. of man is great, 267
remember his m., 59
that is in m., 9

miss
hair breadth, and not m., 3

mistress
so with her m., 84

mock
do ye so m. Him, 53
far from thee, shall m.,
126
fools make a m., 228
I have spoken, m. on, 161

mocker
wine is a m., 151

mockers
be ye not m., 161

mockest
when thou m., 220

mocketh
m. at fear, 44
man m. another, 53
whoso m. the poor, 21

molten
m. gods, 129
m. images, 129
say to m. images, 129

moment
anger endureth but a m.,
98
for a small m., 1
hypocrite but for a m., 76
tongue is but for a m., 149

money
he that hath no m., 57
m. answereth all, 49
m. upon usury, 251
spend m. for that which,
252
time to receive m., 115
usury of m., 251

monsters
sea m. draw out, 30

moon
fair as the m., 17
m. stayed, until, 107
nor the m. by night, 106

Mordecai
prepared for M., 142

more
be moved no m., 32
deliver you no m., 77
devoured m. people, 256
do so and m., 80
give thee much m., 212
gods do to me, and m.,
169
hear any m. the voice, 6
m. are the children, 31

m. in number, 32
m. just than God, 18
m. pure than his maker, 18
m. sons in my womb, 9
m. than all the Jews, 178
m. than his beginning, 55
m. than ten mighty, 237
m. than the hairs, 2
m. they afflicted, 4
m. they multiplied, 4
m. to be desired are, 35
no m. a reproach, 139
were m. than, 3
what can he have m., 8
wise m. than the fool, 179
with us are m., 107

morning
be as the m. cloud, 73
early in the m., 27
early in the m., 67
fed horses in the m., 133
goodness as a m. cloud,
113
joy cometh in the m., 118
m. cometh, 42
m. is to them, 47
m. it flourisheth, 155
m. sow thy seed, 62
m. thou shalt say, 246
m. were the first day, 169
son of the m., 54
tarry till the m., 188
watch for the m., 124
when it was m., 180
would God it were m., 246

morsel
better is a dry m., 225
m. of bread, 125

mortal
m. man be more just, 18

mortar
fool in a m., 90

Moses
as He was with M., 22
as I was with M., 7
as they feared M., 147
day that M. sent, 91
Lord commanded M., 153
Lord commanded M., 74
M. lifted up, 65
remember the law of M.,
35
spoken only by M., 73

most
be like the m. High, 14

moth
m. shall eat, 60

mother
alien unto my m.'s chil-
dren, 75
as is the m., 122
ask on, my m., 175
be a joyful m., 88
bringeth his m. shame, 30

curseth his m., 175
day my m. bare me, 20
despise not thy m., 6
despiseth his m., 31
father and my m. forsake, 1
father and thy m., 175
father nor my m., 222
fear every man his m., 175
forth of his m.'s womb, 52
heaviness of his m., 31
honour thy m., 174
m. be childless, 200
m. comforteth, 34
nakedness of thy m., 132
out of my m.'s womb, 2
she is the m., 142
sin did my m. conceive, 20
that smiteth his m., 26
worm, Thou art my m., 51
mount
earth, is m. Zion, 139
m. up with wings, 19
shall be as m. Zion, 19
mountain
holy m., 213
m. of the Lord, 123
m. shall be made low, 172
the m. of the Lord, 62
mountains
as the m. are round, 101
beautiful upon the m., 169
for m. will I take up, 168
m. shall depart, 100
m. skipped like rams, 15
multitude of m., 95
partridge in the m., 78
pursued us upon the m., 72
shadow of the m., 86
mourn
m. not, nor weep, 122
m. one toward another, 116
m. sore like doves, 9
nor the seller m., 66
rule, the people m., 114
time to m., 119
wilt thou m. for Saul, 115
with sackcloth, and m., 165
mourneth
new wine m., 233
mourning
house of m., 90
house of m. than to, 52
m. as for an only son, 165
victory turned into m., 116
mouth
a watch before my m., 198
bless with their m., 127
cut off from their m., 249
deceitful in their m., 149

depart out of thy m., 170
doors of thy m., 20
fall into the m. of, 107
flattering m. worketh, 5
fool's m. is his, 90
God be in their m., 210
he that keepeth his m., 192
hear the words of my m., 234
honey to my m., 136
hypocrite with his m., 231
I will be with thy m., 69
instead of a m., 234
kisses of his m., 152
law of Thy m., 252
Lord hath put in my m., 123
m. and yet the appetite, 8
m. but in heart, 128
m. is enlarged, 253
m. is smoother than oil, 4
m. like a sharp sword, 48
m. of all his prophets, 236
m. of one witness, 26
m. of the just, 215
m. of the Lord, 238
m. of the Lord, 157
m. of the most High, 113
m. of two witnesses, 26
m. shall show forth, 184
m. tasteth meat, 248
m. they show much love, 128
made man's m., 46
near Me with their m., 128
not out of the m. of, 84
not thine own m., 162
open thy m., 143
opened her m., 52
opened my m., 189
opened not his m., 159
or opened the m., 40
out of His m. cometh, 263
out of m. of babes, 31
out of your m., 11
proceeded out of thy m., 2
putteth in my m., 135
rash with thy m., 192
roof of his m., 244
roof of my m., 7
suffer not thy m., 228
sword, from their m., 106
teacheth his m., 69
thine own m. condemneth, 117
thy m. uttereth thine, 117
truth was in his m., 124
where is now thy m., 23
whoso keepeth his m., 192
wipeth her m. and saith, 4
word in thy m., 35
words in thy m. fire, 69
words of his m., 69
words of my m., 185

mouths
m. but they speak not, 129
shut the lions' m., 56
move
m. his bones, 205
m. out of their holes, 126
moved
be m. no more, 32
I shall not be m., 39
m. for thee to meet, 52
shall not be m., 139
moveth
and every thing that m., 184
moving
m. thing that liveth, 10
much
gathered m. had nothing, 80
looked for m. and lo, 63
m. wisdom is m. grief, 264
ye have sown m. and, 69
mule
be ye not as m., 10
multiplied
children be m., 260
m. and grew, 4
m. the nation, 116
multiplieth
m. my wounds, 240
m. words without, 130
multiply
fruitful and m., 30
fruitful and m., 30
m. thy seed, 44
m. thy seed, 34
multitude
by the sea side for m., 2
cause thy m. to fall, 256
grasshoppers for m., 132
heaven for m., 193
king saved by the m., 162
m. of counsellors, 5
m. of many people, 161
m. of mountains, 95
m. of people, 114
m. of thy counsels, 5
m. of words, 234
m. of years, 79
m. of your sacrifices, 216
not follow a m., 36
reason of this great m., 70
sea for m., 197
voice is known by m., 90
wrath is upon all the m., 66
multitudes
m. m. in the valley of, 141
murderer
life of a m., 26
m. shall surely be, 142
murmur
m. against Me, 175

murmurings
m. are not against, 199
must
so m. we do, 148
muzzle
m. the ox, 70

N

Naboth
blood of N., 27
naked
afraid because I was n., 78
flee away n., 54
go stripped and n., 116
Hell is n., 103
knew that they were n.,
144
n. and bare, 79
n. came I out, 2
n. shall he return, 52
n. shall I return, 2
that thou wast n., 117
were both n., 130
nakedness
n. of thy father, 132
n. of thy mother, 132
n. shall be uncovered, 126
nations thy n., 126
see the n. of the land, 3
seen her n., 43
thine own n., 132
name
abhor us, for Thy n.'s, 99
as his n. is, 28
bless His holy n., 184
bless Thy n., 184
blessed be the n. of, 22
call his n. Immanuel, 159
call not on Thy n., 112
call on My n. and I, 13
call on the n. of the, 13
call upon His n., 115
call upon His n., 76
called by thy n., 59
called by Thy n., 91
called thee by thy n., 101
called upon Thy n., 59
chosen Me to put My n.,
139
come to thee in the n., 80
cometh in n. of Lord, 159
enemy blaspheme Thy n.,
21
falsely in My n., 84
for His n.'s sake, 214
for Mine holy n.'s sake, 99
glory due unto His n., 115
glory due unto His n., 184
glory ye in His holy n., 118
good n. is better, 205
good n. is to be chosen,
205
great n.'s sake, 1

help is in the n. of, 7
His n. shall be called, 159
honour of His n., 232
hosts is His n., 97
hosts is His n., 110
hosts is His n., 56
house unto My n., 194
I will make you a n., 84
Jerusalem, that My n., 139
lies in the n. of, 84
Lord is His n., 103
Lord is His n., 110
may praise Thy n., 55
My n. shall be great, 76
n. alone is Jehovah, 110
n. be forever, 139
n. in remembrance, 145
n. in the dance, 49
n. in vain, 21
n. is blasphemed, 21
n. is exalted, 76
n. is The Lord, 103
n. is to be praised, 184
n. of God in vain, 21
n. of God with a song, 115
n. of other gods, 128
n. of our father, 121
n. of the Lord, 97
n. of the Lord, 184
n. of the Lord, 107
n. of the Lord, 83
n. of the Lord, 32
n. of the Lord, 27
n. of the Lord, 2
n. of the wicked, 205
n. of your gods, 27
n. shall be continued, 84
n. shall endure for ever, 84
no n. in the street, 84
people shall know My n.,
206
pollute ye My holy n., 21
praise the n. of the, 168
praise Thy n., 185
publish n. of the Lord, 76
put His n. there, 139
remember the n. of the
Lord, 202
saved for His n.'s sake, 55
sing praises unto His n.,
232
sing praises unto Thy n.,
183
swear by His n., 7
thanks to Thy holy n., 55
that fear My n., 15
that is My n., 99
Thy glorious n., 184
true in the n. of, 5
unto Thy n. give glory, 96
was the n. thereof, 167
whose n. is Jealous, 110
wrought for My n.'s sake,
99

named
which hath been is n., 135
names
them all by their n., 120
Nathan
N. said to David, 3
nation
a great n., 31
avenged on such a n., 112
blessed is the n., 101
exalteth a n., 114
great n., 32
lift up sword against n.,
256
multiplied the n., 116
n. and a company of n., 22
n. shall not lift, 256
n. that obeyeth not, 65
n. that will not serve, 139
n. void of counsel, 32
shall a n. be born, 176
small one a strong n., 116
nations
among all n., 193
among these n., 111
eyes of many n., 145
father of many n., 44
full end of all n., 102
gods of the n. delivered, 11
great among the n., 40
lend unto many n., 24
like all the n., 73
n. and declare it, 76
n. are as a drop, 114
n. before Him are as, 114
n. of the earth, 32
n. that forget God, 111
n. thy nakedness, 126
prepare the n., 17
reign over many n., 132
scatter among the n., 78
sight of the n., 34
the Lord, all ye n., 184
trumpet among the n., 17
wickedness of these n., 253
works among all n., 76
native
nor see his n. country, 79
naught
n. saith the buyer, 25
navel
n. is like a round, 17
nay
not say thee n., 175
near
come not n., 107
day draweth n., 130
day of the Lord is n., 66
day of the Lord is n., 141
day of trouble is n., 66
end is n., 66
n. to come, 60
n. upon all the heathen,
112

neighbour that is n., 13
that is n. shall fall, 10
this people draw n., 128
those that be n. and, 126
trouble is n., 9
while He is n., 173
ye that are n., 4
neck
bind them about thy n., 28
n. is an iron, 239
n. is as a tower, 23
necks
hardened their n., 238
n. are under persecution,
173
need
n. of mad men, 77
needs
must n. die, 163
needy
afflicted and n., 142
cause of the poor and n.,
143
deliver the n., 186
I am poor and n., 13
lifteth the n., 37
n. shall not always, 124
poor and n., 25
poor and n. yet, 182
to thy n., 29
when the poor and n., 85
neighbour
better is a n. that is, 13
cause with thy n., 11
covet thy n.'s wife, 4
despiseth his n., 161
despiseth his n., 119
destroyeth his n., 231
double unto his n., 207
even of his own n., 93
every one against his n., 28
evil against thy n., 20
flattereth his n., 88
from thy n.'s house, 125
giveth his n. drink, 67
hearts against his n., 77
judge thy n., 140
love thy n., 24
n.'s landmark, 190
neighed after his n.'s, 133
not covet thy n.'s, 73
peace to their n., 53
peaceably to his n., 128
pleadeth for his n., 58
separated from his n., 93
smote his n., 137
teach every one her n., 116
truth to his n., 124
witness against thy n., 124
neighed
n. after his neighbour's,
133
neither
n. mine nor thine, 224

nest
n. among the stars, 188
n. as high as the, 75
net
brother with a n., 166
fall into their own n., 209
n. for his feet, 88
spread My n., 247
never
destruction are n. full, 121
evildoers shall n., 31
eyes of man are n., 8
n. a woman among, 137
n. be ashamed, 202
n. be found again, 10
that are n. satisfied, 52
new
heart and a n. spirit, 150
make you a n. heart, 150
n. earth, 46
n. heavens and, 46
n. thing under the sun, 135
n. wine mourneth, 233
n. wine the maids, 191
wine and n. wine, 151
news
so is good n., 169
next
n. unto thee, 225
nigh
but not n., 158
come n. Me, 122
for it is n. at hand, 15
Lord is n. unto, 116
Lord is n. unto all, 13
n. unto the grave, 6
n. unto the Lord, 185
n. unto thee, 35
shall not come n., 50
night
all the n. make I, 231
by n. in a pillar, 105
cometh, and also the n., 42
darkness He called n., 169
day and n., 220
desire not the n., 169
desired Thee in the n., 62
Egypt this n., 88
endure for a n., 118
fear day and n., 49
fear in the n., 86
fled by n., 54
in the n. season, 59
meditate day and n., 214
might weep day and n.,
242
n. also is Thine, 169
n. shall not cease, 221
n. shineth as the day, 74
n. to be much observed, 92
nor the moon by n., 106
not rest in the n., 59
rule the n., 14
terror by n., 86

unto the Lord day and n.,
185
wall n. and day, 222
what of the n., 166
nights
forty days and forty n., 89
forty days and forty n.,
243
nine
n. hundred sixty and n., 6
Nineveh
arise, go to N., 161
N. is laid waste, 57
nitre
wash thee with n., 118
no
n. man that sinneth not,
155
Noah
three men, N., Daniel, 61
nobles
princes rule, and n., 114
Nod
dwelt in the land of N.,
174
noise
fleeth from the n., 66
joyful n. unto God, 232
make a joyful n., 232
make a joyful n., 184
make a loud n., 27
n. of many waters, 103
n. of thy viols, 126
noised
fame was n., 84
none
comforters, but I found n.,
34
n. beside Thee, 163
n. can keep alive, 164
n. else beside me, 38
n. escaped, 61
n. goeth to the battle, 199
n. holy as the Lord, 122
n. like him in the earth,
162
n. like Me, 109
n. like Me, 109
n. like Thee, 99
n. like unto Ahab, 76
n. shall help, 249
n. shall open, 15
n. shall return, 3
n. shall shut, 15
n. that doeth good, 43
n. that moved, 40
n. to comfort, 2
n. to help, 9
n. to save them, 54
n. upon earth I desire, 13
n. upright among men, 112
n. were of silver, 197
people there was n., 7
pity, but there was n., 34

shall be n. to bury, 226
there is n. else, 109
there is n. else, 163
there shall be n., 61
north
cometh out of the n., 60
stretcheth out the n., 46
nose
hook in thy n., 125
n. is as the tower, 23
noses
n. have they but, 129
nostrils
n. the breath of life, 45
note
n. it in a book, 122
nothing
age is as n., 164
and have seen n., 84
before Him are as n., 114
carry n. away, 73
had n. over, 80
hangeth earth upon n., 46
is it n. to you, all, 241
keep n. back, 26
left n. undone, 153
n. among my treasures,
160
n. but which is true, 5
n. will be restrained, 8
profiteth a man n., 21
rich, yet hath n., 235
shall be as n., 72
take n. of his labour, 94
there is n. better than, 3
whom n. is prepared, 29
wickedness profit n., 47
works are n., 129
ye are of n., 129
nought
counsel of heathen to n.,
93
fear God for n., 136
serve me for n., 25
wicked shall come to n., 72
work of n., 129
nourisher
n. of thine old age, 114
now
come unto me n., 173
hath been is n., 135
that which n. is, 178
number
camels were without n.,
132
camels were without n., 2
days without n., 16
left few in n., 78
left few in n., 193
man can n. the dust, 2
more in n., 32
n. of His years, 145
n. of the children, 33
n. of the fourth, 2

n. of the people, 27
n. of the stars, 120
n. ye the people, 27
teach us to n., 149
numbered
not be measured nor n.,
33
seed also be n., 2
wanting cannot be n., 3
nursing
bosom, as a n. father, 147

O

oath
feareth an o., 74
love no false o., 177
quit of thine o., 6
obedient
willing and o., 172
obey
evil, we will o., 3
if they o. and serve, 191
if ye o. My voice, 170
o. better than sacrifice, 171
o. His voice, 11
o. His voice, 171
o. I beseech, 172
o. my voice, 101
o. my voice, 20
o. the commandments, 22
o. the voice, 172
voice will we o., 171
obeyed
not o. His voice, 79
o. My voice, 32
o. not His voice, 65
o. their voice, 78
obeyeth
o. not the voice, 65
o. not the words, 45
obeying
o. the voice of the Lord,
171
oblations
bring no more vain o., 216
obscurity
behold o., 63
observe
crane and the swallow o.,
65
o. lying vanities, 83
o. their judgments, 112
o. to do according, 220
o. to do it, 35
wise, and will o., 100
observed
night to be much o., 92
observest
but thou o. not, 111
observeth
he that o. the wind, 147
obstinate
o. and thy neck, 239

occasions
findeth o. against, 178
offences
pacifieth great o., 192
offended
a brother o. is, 91
offer
o. a burnt offering, 114
o. it unto the Lord, 114
o. not thy burnt, 267
o. thee three things, 31
offering
at Mine o., 43
lamb for a burnt o., 167
offer a burnt o., 114
offerings
delight in burnt o., 171
God more than burnt o.,
216
offer not thy burnt o., 267
tithes and o., 29
office
another take his o., 195
oft
how o. is the candle, 134
o. cometh their destruc-
tion, 134
oil
anointest my head with o.,
22
loveth wine and o., 181
mouth smoother than o., 4
softer than o., 69
ointment
better than precious o.,
205
smell of thine o., 152
old
beauty of o. men, 79
clothes waxed not o., 108
counsel which the o. men,
5
counsels of o., 83
crown of o. men, 114
days as of o., 203
days of o., 79
died in a good o., 50
even to your o. age, 6
face of the o. man, 6
good o. age, 51
good o. age, 6
hundred years o., 87
I am o., 6
in the generations of o.,
107
mother when she is o., 6
nourisher of o. age, 114
o. and foolish king, 5
o. and stricken, 6
o. men shall dream, 67
o. paths, 246
son of his o. age, 85
things of o., 203
time of o. age, 6

when he is o., 30
when I am o. and, 6
wicked live, become o., 134
young, and now am o., 1
oliveyards
vineyards, and your o., 162
once
only this o., 185
sin only this o., 203
speak but this o., 98
one
all go unto o. place, 52
but o. blessing, my father, 9
can o. be warm alone, 24
choose thee o., 31
doeth good, no, not o., 43
flee at the rebuke of o., 86
God is o. Lord, 163
hath not o. God created, 25
have o. ordinance, 74
have we not all o., 25
not failed o. word, 45
not o. hair, 217
o. as well as, 49
o. become a thousand, 116
o. chase a thousand, 1
o. event to righteous, 150
o. generation passeth, 68
o. half of the greatness, 205
o. heart, and o. way, 197
o. law shall be to him, 74
o. lot for the Lord, 219
o. man among a thousand, 154
o. man shall chase, 237
o. man sin, 41
o. man sin, 140
o. manner of law, 142
o. sinner destroyeth, 43
o. thing hath failed, 189
pardon every o., 91
shall be o. flesh, 156
slew at o. time, 237
two are better than o., 42
only
even Thou o. knowest, 100
o. this once, 185
open
he shall o. and none, 15
His ears are o., 106
none shall o., 15
o. his eyes, 72
o. rebuke is better, 26
o. Thine eyes, 13
o. Thine eyes, 187
o. Thou my lips, 184
o. thy mouth, 143
opened
blind shall be o., 23
but I o. my doors, 125
eyes shall be o., 72

gates of death been o., 12
have I o. my cause, 72
o. her mouth, 52
o. my mouth, 189
o. not his mouth, 159
or o. the mouth, 40
were o. and they knew, 144
openeth
o. the ears of men, 67
o. the eyes of the blind, 23
o. wide his lips, 192
opening
o. of the prison, 56
o. the ears, 111
opinions
between two o., 27
oppress
let not the proud o., 12
loveth to o., 25
o. an hired servant, 25
o. not the widow, 37
o. the afflicted, 173
stranger, nor o. him, 90
that o. the hireling, 4
oppressed
I am o., 59
let the o. go free, 85
o. and he was afflicted, 159
refuge for the o., 217
relieve the o., 173
oppresseth
that o. the poor, 173
oppression
but behold o., 63
inheritance by o., 249
o. maketh a wise man mad, 154
o. of man, 173
oppressors
because of the o., 56
envy thou not the o., 249
leave me not to mine o., 1
ordain
o. a place, 45
order
set thine house in o., 51
ordered
steps of good man are o., 18
ordinance
have one o., 74
kept His o., 21
organs
praise Him with o., 166
Orion
loose the bands of O., 183
ornaments
deckest thee with o., 17
forget her o., 16
ought
o. but death part, 93
oughtest
what thou o. to do, 166

ourselves
not we o., 46
out
Lord gone o. before, 39
o. of the eater, 213
o. of your mouth, 11
outrageous
anger is o., 9
outstretched
with an o. arm, 55
outward
looketh on the o., 137
oven
burn as an o., 141
overcome
able to o., 39
overflow
shall not o. thee, 34
overtake
but she shall not o., 94
plowman shall o., 191
overthrow
violent man to o., 254
overthrown
o. them that rose up, 199
owls
companion to o., 58
owner
ox knoweth his o., 15
ox
as an o. goeth to the, 4
muzzle the o., 70
nor his o., 73
o. knoweth his owner, 15
slay o. and sheep, 10
stalled o. and hatred, 152
strength of the o., 69
thine enemy's o., 123
oxen
for the o. stumbled, 198
where no o. are, 69

P

pacifieth
gift in secret p., 9
p. great offences, 192
pain
fall with p., 98
in p. as a woman, 243
p. all his days, 240
put themselves to p., 94
painting
thy face with p., 17
pair
p. of shoes, 43
palace
eunuchs in the p., 125
Palestina
whole P. art dissolved, 66
palm
flourish like the p., 116
like to a p., 23

pangs
p. and sorrows, 243
panteth
p. after the water, 153
p. my soul after Thee, 153
parched
p. ground shall, 191
pardon
God ready to p., 101
good Lord p., 91
p. them whom I reserve, 91
part
ought but death p., 93
partner
p. with a thief, 47
partridge
hunt a p., 78
pass
all ye that p. by, 241
bring it to p., 27
come to p., 190
come to p., 189
p. not by it, 77
p. through the land, 88
p. through the waters, 34
shall it come to p., 70
so shall it come to p., 94
turn from it, and p., 77
passed
Elijah p. by him, 148
passeth
one generation p., 68
wind that p. away, 91
past
death is p., 160
harvest is p., 59
winter is p., 221
yesterday when it is p., 179
pastors
p. that destroy, 148
pasture
flock of My p., 102
harts that find no p., 140
people of His p., 101
sheep of My p., 148
pastures
green p., 34
path
light unto my p., 73
p. of the just, 215
p. of the wicked, 18
p. of thy feet, 180
paths
astray in her p., 4
her p. are peace, 264
lead them in p., 73
not find her p., 172
old p., 246
p. of righteousness, 214
p. of the Lord, 110
teach me Thy p., 117
walk in His p., 18

patient
p. in spirit, 176
paw
p. of the lion, 39
pay
defer not to p., 189
let him p. double, 207
not slack to p., 189
shall p. double unto, 207
vow and not p., 24
will He p. him again, 8
payeth
wicked borroweth, and p., 24
peace
be at p. thereby good, 2
counsellors of p., 176
end of that man is p., 162
even enemies to be at p., 18
Father, the Prince of P., 159
go in p., 22
go up in p., 157
grave in p., 210
great p. have they, 35
her paths are p., 264
hold not Thy p., 13
hold thy p., 121
hold your p., 7
holdeth his p., 90
holdeth his p., 161
I am for p., 257
in the p. thereof, 191
iniquity, which speak p., 53
into thy grave in p., 51
looked for p. but, 79
Lord give thee p., 22
love the truth and p., 177
men hold their p., 37
no p. unto the world, 74
not hold My p., 139
p. and create evil, 112
p. and there was no p., 257
p. and truth be, 176
p. be to thine helpers, 22
p. be unto thee, 22
p. be unto thee, 34
p. been as a river, 172
p. in His high places, 176
p. in your gates, 143
p. of thy children, 69
p. there shall be no end, 159
proclaim p., 257
return at all in p., 66
return in p., 198
righteousness shall be p., 215
saying P. and there was, 257
saying, p. p., 53
seek p. and pursue, 176

shall seek p. and, 61
that publisheth p., 169
thereof shall ye have p., 191
thou to do with p., 229
time of p., 257
when there is no p., 53
peaceably
one speaketh p., 128
peacocks
wings unto the p., 12
peculiar
p. treasure unto Me, 32
peeped
opened the mouth or p., 40
pen
p. of iron, 178
tongue is the p., 234
penury
tendeth only to p., 146
people
against the p., 45
all the p., 66
among all my p., 137
ants are a p., 62
art a stiffnecked p., 238
as with the p., 84
authority, the p. rejoice, 114
be My p., 32
bid the p. return, 176
burden of all this p., 147
byword among all p., 201
cast off His p., 153
city and Thy p., 91
comfort ye My p., 34
conceived all this p., 147
days of My p., 101
despised of the p., 174
devoured more p., 256
do unto this p., 58
doings among the p., 76
evil entreated this p., 66
evil upon this p., 103
fear ye the p., 70
feared the p., 78
fewest of all p., 32
fire, and this p. wood, 69
foolish p. and unwise, 133
forsake His p., 1
fortress among My p., 190
full of p., 54
give the p. straw, 173
given rest unto His p., 114
given to Thy p., 190
happy is that p., 112
hearts of the p., 45
His deeds among the p., 76
holy p., 32
in the multitude of p., 114
it is My p., 4
judge His p., 140
knowest the p., 76

Let My p. go, 92
Let My p. go, 11
looked upon My p., 101
make you His p., 32
Me above all p., 32
me, and for the p., 117
men for our p., 44
multitude of many p., 161
my p. are wicked, 117
my p. as thy p., 42
my p. as thy p., 7
no counsel is, p. fall, 117
no doubt ye are the p., 161
not let the p. go, 48
not take of the p.'s, 249
number of the p., 27
number ye the p., 27
of all His p., 255
of all the p. able men, 113
of the p. there was, 7
p. are cut off, 169
p. being ashamed, 45
p. doth not consider, 15
p. draw near Me, 128
p. hath been lost, 16
p. have forgotten Me, 16
p. hear the voice, 15
p. I have not known, 15
p. into captivity, 79
p. is foolish, 89
p. know not the judgment,
  65
p. of His pasture, 101
p. of the earth, 101
p. provoke Me, 77
p. see His glory, 99
p. shall curse, 25
p. shall know My name,
  206
p. still sacrificed, 128
p. that delight in war, 257
p. that do know their, 82
p. that is with thee, 78
p. that walked in, 73
p. their transgression, 29
p. were prophets, 190
p. with His truth, 140
place for My p., 45
pleasure in His p., 101
pollute Me among My p.,
  84
poor of His p., 139
poor of thy p., 48
portion is His p., 32
praise among all p., 84
praise Him, all ye p., 184
prayer for all p., 33
prince over My p., 102
rebellious p., 65
reproach to any p., 114
round about His p., 101
rule, the p. mourn, 114
ruler of thy p., 113
save Thy p., 185

say among the p., 126
seduced My p., 257
shall be My p., 7
shall be My p. and I, 45
shall be My p. and I, 62
sow them among the p., 79
spare Thy p., 91
special p. unto Himself, 32
teach My p. the, 33
that this p. may know, 189
the p. that doth not, 130
thy p. shall be my p., 42
thy p. with pestilence, 180
to judge Thy p., 63
to Me for a p., 32
understanding p., 32
vision, the p. perish, 117
want of p., 114
welfare of this p., 26
ye are not My p., 201
ye shall be My p., 101
ye shall be My p., 7
perceive
  see ye indeed, but p., 238
perceived
  p. the breadth of, 12
perfect
  be thou p., 38
  blind as he that is p., 130
  cast away a p. man, 1
  destroyeth the p., 51
  heart was not p., 16
  His way is p., 97
  let your heart be p., 171
  maketh my way p., 92
  mark the p. man, 162
  more unto the p. day, 215
  p. and an upright man,
    162
  p. heart and with, 62
  p. with the Lord, 39
  with a p. heart, 82
  work is p., 97
perfection
  p. of beauty, 140
perform
  hands cannot p., 102
  p. His word, 102
perish
  brutish person p., 164
  day his thoughts p., 8
  desire shall p., 8
  far from Thee shall p., 16
  flight shall p. from, 235
  hypocrite's hope shall p.,
    83
  let the day p., 58
  let the wicked p., 195
  lies shall p., 64
  not p. for ever, 124
  not serve thee shall p., 139
  ready to p., 151
  remembrance shall p., 84
  they shall p., 120

ungodly shall p., 111
vision, the people p., 117
visitation they shall p., 129
when the wicked p., 52
wise men shall p., 195
perished
  good man is p., 112
  is counsel p. from, 5
  memorial is p., 10
  truth is p., 249
  weapons of war p., 54
perpetual
  sleep a p. sleep, 52
perpetually
  shall be there p., 104
persecute
  p. the poor, 178
persecuted
  princes have p., 4
persecution
  necks are under p., 173
persecutors
  p. are swifter, 235
person
  brutish p. perish, 164
  goodlier p. than, 161
  p. of the mighty, 85
  p. of the poor, 85
  save the humble p., 126
  slay an innocent p., 12
persons
  not respect p., 24
  p. in judgment, 131
perverse
  p. and crooked, 199
  p. heart, 56
  p. in his ways, 29
  p. tongue falleth, 64
perversely
  have done p., 39
pervert
  Almighty p. judgment,
    76
perverted
  knowledge, it hath p., 38
perverteth
  man p. his way, 8
pestilence
  die of the p., 10
  p. and the famine, 50
  p. shall devour him, 61
  thy people with p., 180
pestle
  wheat with a p., 90
petition
  given me my p., 20
Pharoah
  He showeth unto P., 66
  house of P., 179
  I should go unto P., 126
  shall P. hear me, 147
Philistine
  fight with this P., 43
  hand of this P., 39

pollute
  p. Me among My people, 84
  p. the land, 46
  p. ye My holy name, 21
polluted
  p. before the heathen, 99
  p. the land with thy, 130
  p. with blood, 128
pomp
  p. is brought down, 126
ponder
  p. the path of thy feet, 180
pondereth
  He p. all his goings, 100
pool
  ground shall become a p., 191
  wilderness a p., 258
poor
  at the cry of the p., 29
  because he is p., 173
  better is a p. and, 5
  better is the p., 29
  cause of the p., 183
  cause of the p., 143
  considereth the p., 29
  countenance a p. man, 131
  crieth; the p. also, 186
  defend the p., 142
  deliverest the p., 100
  delivereth the p., 55
  destruction of the p., 182
  expectation of the p., 124
  friends; but the p., 93
  giveth unto the p., 29
  he becometh p. that, 146
  I am p. and needy, 182
  I am p. and needy, 13
  judge the p., 159
  judgeth the p., 163
  Lord heareth the p., 182
  maketh himself p., 235
  maketh p. and maketh rich, 102
  mercy on the p., 37
  mercy on the p., 37
  mercy to the p., 19
  mocketh the p., 21
  p. and needy, 25
  p. and sorrowful, 127
  p. brother, 29
  p. for a pair of shoes, 43
  p. from the sword, 106
  p. hath hope, 124
  p. is hated, 93
  p. man is better, 64
  p. man's wisdom, 5
  p. of His people, 139
  p. of thy people, 48
  p. out of the dust, 37
  p. out of the dust, 55
  p. shall never cease, 182
  p. that are cast out, 37

p. useth intreaties, 44
persecute the p., 178
person of the p., 85
pity upon the p., 8
pleasure shall be a p., 181
rich and p. meet, 74
rob not the p., 173
stranger, nor the p., 37
that oppresseth the p., 173
the judgment of thy p., 131
to thy p., 29
when the p. and needy, 85
portion
  double p. of thy spirit, 122
  my p. for ever, 92
  p. is His people, 32
  p. of mine inheritance, 133
portions
  send p. unto them, 29
possess
  go up and p., 96
  p. the land, 213
  p. the land, 133
  p. their land, 253
  the land to p. it, 138
  them will we p., 40
possessed
  land to be p., 6
possession
  also taken p., 29
  Israel for a p., 138
posterity
  take away thy p., 10
pot
  boil like a p., 103
  thorns under a p., 146
potter
  clay, and Thou our p., 46
  p.'s hand, 60
pour
  p. out my wrath, 98
  p. out thine heart, 186
  p. out Thy fury, 112
  p. out your heart, 81
poured
  blood shall be p., 209
  p. me out as milk, 46
  p. out like fire, 98
  p. out like the waters, 9
  p. out my soul, 58
poverty
  forget his p., 59
  glutton shall come to p., 67
  lest thou come to p., 146
  p. nor riches, 41
  poor is their p., 182
  so shall thy p. come, 182
power
  become glorious in p., 236
  earth by His p., 46
  exalteth by His p., 136
  great in p., 196
  greatness of Thy p., 36

greatness, and the p., 99
hath is in thy p., 28
king is, there is p., 15
made the earth by His p., 46
mighty in p., 134
no man that hath p., 52
nor by might, nor by p., 238
of great p., 100
p. and His wrath, 16
p. belongeth unto God, 183
p. of thine hand, 115
p. to be known, 55
p. to get wealth, 259
p. to help, 102
p. to the faint, 108
p. to weep, 115
strength and p., 92
Thine hand is p., 102
thunder of His p., 103
praise
  above all blessing and p., 184
  dead p. not the Lord, 52
  grave cannot p., 52
  hath breath p. the Lord, 184
  He is thy p., 97
  heaven and earth p., 184
  His p. from the end, 232
  Jerusalem a p., 139
  let another man p., 162
  live will I p., 184
  oh that men would p., 184
  p. among all people, 84
  p. Him, O ye servants, 184
  p. Him in the heights, 184
  p. Him upon the high, 166
  p. Him upon the loud, 166
  p. Him with stringed, 166
  p. Him with the psaltery, 166
  p. Him with the sound, 166
  p. Him with the timbrel, 166
  p. Him, all ye people, 184
  p. His name in the dance, 49
  p. the Lord, 184
  p. the Lord that, 157
  p. the Lord with harp, 166
  p. the Lord, all ye, 184
  p. the Lord, call, 76
  p. the name of God, 115
  p. the name of the Lord, 168
  p. Thee; for I am, 46
  p. Thy name, 185
  p. ye the Lord, 184
  p. ye the Lord, 232

p. ye the Lord, 114
p. ye the Lord from, 184
p. ye the name of the, 184
p. ye, and say, 185
prison, that I may p., 55
rejoice, and sing p., 27
show forth Thy p., 184
sing p. to my God, 232
song will I p., 232
soul shall p. Thee, 149
praised
greatly to be p., 100
I p. the dead, 150
name is to be p., 184
she shall be p., 17
worthy to be p., 55
praises
fearful in p., 15
good to sing p., 184
let the high p., 210
let them sing p., 49
p. unto His name, 232
sing p., 183
sing p. unto the Lord, 232
sing ye p. with, 184
pray
ceasing to p., 185
forgive, I p. thee, 203
I p. thee, glory, 183
if we p. unto Him, 14
kill me, I p., 224
prayed
for this child I p., 20
prayer
hear my p., 186
heard thy p., 37
heart thy p., 185
house of p., 33
let p. become sin, 72
lift up thy p., 185
p. of the righteous, 108
p. of the upright, 29
yet made we not our p., 131
preach
p. good tidings, 187
preacher
saith the p., 59
precept
p. must be upon p., 68
taught by the p. of men, 128
precepts
because I keep Thy p., 79
forget Thy p., 82
way of Thy p., 136
precious
bearing p. seed, 48
better than p. ointment, 205
p. in the sight of, 156
p. shall their blood, 250
word p. in those days, 255

preeminence
p. above a beast, 127
prepare
p. Him an habitation, 108
p. the nations against, 17
p. the way, 172
p. the way before Me, 159
p. thee unto blood, 49
p. to meet thy God, 199
p. ye the way, 159
p. your hearts, 61
yet they p. their meat, 62
prepared
be thou p., 199
gallows that he had p., 142
horse is p., 253
nothing is p., 29
Thou p. the light, 169
preparest
p. a table before, 22
prepareth
p. his heart, 91
presence
come before His p., 184
p. of mine enemies, 22
p. of the Lord, 174
tremble at My p., 15
wicked perish at the p., 195
present
p. help in trouble, 92
preserve
discretion shall p., 242
greatness of Thy power p., 36
p. the king, 162
p. thee from all evil, 218
p. thee: love her, 264
p. them alive, 262
p. thy soul, 218
to p. life, 197
wise shall p., 69
preserveth
Lord p. the faithful, 82
p. all them that love, 195
p. the simple, 108
prevail
p. against His enemies, 103
p. against Thee, 107
shall no man p., 237
they shall not p., 72
prevented
p. me in the day, 71
prey
hold of the p., 6
p. and a spoil, 126
p. in all places, 75
rise up to the p., 176
roar after their p., 6
spoil, and all that p., 211
when he hath no p., 165
will I give for a p., 211

price
give me my p., 168
knoweth not the p., 250
p. is far above rubies, 156
p. of a dog, 29
p. of wisdom, 263
weighed for the p., 263
pride
man's p. shall bring, 188
p. before a fall, 80
p. before destruction, 80
p. compasseth them about, 188
p. of thine heart, 38
p. of thine heart hath, 38
those that walk in p., 188
when p. cometh, 188
wicked in his p., 178
priest
a faithful p., 33
even unto the p., 43
p.'s lips should keep, 33
so with the p., 84
priesthood
p. of the Lord, 188
seek ye the p., 8
prince
Father, the P. of Peace, 159
lying lips a p., 69
p. over My people, 102
p. shall not take, 249
who made thee a p., 147
princes
and p. decree justice, 162
destruction of the p., 114
give ear, O ye p., 232
p. are become like harts, 140
p. have persecuted, 4
p. rule, and nobles, 114
than confidence in p., 114
trust in p., 202
princess
p. among the provinces, 40
principal
wisdom is the p., 250
printed
p. in a book, 23
prison
opening of the p., 56
soul out of p., 55
prisoner
sighing of the p., 131
prisoners
despiseth not His p., 182
looseth the p., 131
p. of hope, 125
privy
heart is p., 40
proceeded
p. out of thy mouth, 2
proceedeth
p. not evil and good, 113

proclaim
　p. liberty, 92
　p. liberty, 56
　p. peace unto it, 257
profane
　holy and p., 33
profaned
　sake, which ye have p., 99
profit
　cannot p. nor deliver, 267
　labour there is p., 189
　p. of the earth, 43
　p. shall this birthright, 57
　pain, but shall not p., 94
　riches p. not, 259
　what p. hath a man, 94
　what p. hath he that, 189
　what p. hath he that, 49
　what p. is it, 21
　what p. should we have, 14
　wickedness p. nothing, 47
profitable
　p. unto God, 155
　wise may be p., 155
profiteth
　p. a man nothing, 21
　what p. the graven image,
　　130
prognosticators
　monthly p., 14
prolong
　p. my life, 58
prolonged
　days be p., 112
　days may be p., 175
　days shall not be p., 60
promise
　of all His good p., 45
promised
　as God hath p., 40
　good that I have p., 103
promoted
　p. over the trees, 8
promotion
　p. cometh neither from,
　　239
　p. of fools, 96
prophesied
　prophets which p., 5
　to them, yet they p., 84
prophesy
　not p. good, 5
　p. against them, p., 29
　p. falsely in My name, 84
　spoken, who can but p.,
　　172
prophet
　Elijah the p., 159
　if the p. had bid, 5
　p. also as thou art, 53
　p. even unto the priest, 43
　P. from the midst, 158
　p. that hath a dream, 67
　when a p. speaketh, 83

words of that p., 83
prophets
　believe His p., 81
　do My p. no harm, 32
　hearken not to your p., 5
　I am against the p., 84
　if they be p., 14
　let not your p., 53
　mouth of all his p., 236
　neither by p., 1
　not sent these p. yet, 84
　p. be consumed, 84
　p. do they live forever, 165
　p. shall be ashamed, 84
　people were p., 190
　where are now your p., 5
　woe unto the foolish p.,
　　84
prosper
　fatherless, yet they p., 134
　He will p. us, 239
　made him to p., 239
　p. in all that ye do, 35
　p. that love thee, 139
　p. whithersoever thou, 35
　planted, shall it p., 116
　reign and p., 159
　shall not p., 94
　so shall ye p., 81
　way of the wicked p., 134
prospered
　p. whithersoever he went,
　　191
prospereth
　because of him who p.,
　　138
prosperity
　day of p. be joyful, 179
　days in p., 191
　p. of the wicked, 73
　spake in thy p., 121
prostitute
　p. thy daughter, 31
proud
　arrogancy of the p., 12
　be not p., 188
　high look and a p. heart,
　　12
　let not the p. oppress, 12
　O thou most p., 12
　oven; and all the p., 141
　p. against the Lord, 12
　p. look, a lying tongue, 12
　p. shall stumble, 12
　rewardeth the p. doer, 82
　spoil with the p., 127
　than p. in spirit, 176
prove
　through them I may p.,
　　244
proverb
　Israel shall be a p., 201
　p. and a byword, 193
　shall use this p., 197

proverbs
　every one that useth p.,
　　197
proveth
　God p. you, 83
provide
　p. out of all people, 113
provinces
　princess among the p., 40
provoke
　p. Me not to anger, 191
　p. Me unto wrath, 98
　people p. Me, 77
provoked
　p. Him to jealousy, 98
　p. Me to anger, 77
　them that p. Me, 193
prudent
　p. man concealeth, 23
　p. man covereth, 136
　p. man forseeth, 192
　p. men shall be hid, 195
　p. shall keep silence, 192
　p. wife is from the Lord,
　　133
　perished from the p., 5
　wisdom of the p., 192
pruninghooks
　p. into spears, 256
　spears into p., 176
psalms
　sing p. unto Him, 232
psaltery
　praise Him with the p.,
　　166
　sing with the p., 166
publish
　p. and conceal, 169
　p. and set up a, 169
　p. it not, 116
　p. the name of the Lord,
　　76
　p. ye, praise ye, 185
published
　company of those that p.,
　　187
publisheth
　p. peace, 169
punish
　p. the world, 77
punished
　and I p. the goats, 21
　p. us less than, 158
　pass on, and are p., 192
　when scorner is p., 68
punishment
　my p. is greater, 193
pure
　hands, and a p. heart, 124
　if thou wert p. and, 21
　man be more p., 18
　stars are not p., 155
purer
　p. eyes than to behold, 197

purpose
  p. is the multitude, 216
  p. under the heaven, 168
purposed
  as I have p., 94
pursue
  after whom dost thou p., 78
  blood shall p., 49
  p. after your enemies, 256
  seek peace, and p., 176
pursued
  p. us upon the mountains, 72
pursueth
  flee when no man p., 40
  none p. you, 86
put
  as he that p. it off, 23

Q

quench
  burn that none can q., 98
  waters cannot q., 152
quenched
  wrath shall not be q., 128
quickly
  come up to us q., 7
  cord is not q., 43
quiet
  ere thou be q., 131
quietness
  handful with q., 8
  morsel, and q., 225
  q. and in confidence, 81
quit
  q. of thine oath, 6
quiver
  q. full of them, 31

R

race
  r. is not to the swift, 28
Rachel
  like R. and like Leah, 87
  serve with thee for R., 6
  seven years for R., 152
rage
  jealousy is the r., 138
  r. against Me, 100
  r. against Me, 11
rageth
  but the fool r., 77
raging
  strong drink is r., 151
rags
  clothe a man with r., 147
rain
  clouds be full of r., 198
  drop as the r., 66
  lightnings with r., 198
  r. a father, 198

r. in due season, 170
r. in harvest, 90
r. is over, 221
r. upon Thy land, 190
r. was upon the earth, 89
small r. upon, 69
rainy
  very r. day and a, 166
raise
  none shall r. him up, 12
  r. Me up, 33
  r. unto David, 159
raiseth
  all that fall, and r., 108
  He r. up the poor, 37
  r. the stormy wind, 168
  r. up the poor, 55
rams
  fat of r., 171
  r. with he goats, 60
  skipped like r., 15
ran
  prophets, yet they r., 84
ransomed
  r. of the Lord, 92
rare
  it is a r. thing that, 181
rash
  r. with thy mouth, 192
rather
  r. be a doorkeeper, 127
razor
  like a sharp r., 20
read
  book of the Lord, and r., 221
ready
  God r. to pardon, 101
  graves are r., 51
  more r. to hear, 268
  pen of a r. writer, 234
  r. to perish, 151
  r. to stone me, 58
  to make all r., 199
reap
  but thou shalt not r., 69
  clouds shall not r., 147
  r. in joy, 48
  r. in mercy, 19
  r. the whirlwind, 69
  r. thorns, 94
  sow ye, and r., 69
reaped
  r. iniquity, 143
reaper
  overtake the r., 191
reason
  by r. of thy brightness, 38
  dismayed by r., 70
  if by r. of strength, 149
  let us r. together, 36
  men that can render a r., 38
  r. with you, 179

reasons
  ear to your r., 175
  strong r., 11
rebel
  if ye refuse and r., 238
  r. against the light, 47
  r. against the Lord, 199
  r. against us, 163
  r. not against, 163
  r. not ye against, 70
rebelled
  though we have r., 111
rebellest
  r. against me, 11
rebellion
  r. is as the sin, 199
  r. unto his sin, 199
  taught rebellion, 121
rebellious
  midst of a r., 36
  r. against the Lord, 65
  r. children, 16
  r. generation, 65
  r. like that r. house, 199
  r. people, 65
  they be a r. house, 86
rebels
  hear now, ye r., 189
rebuke
  flee at the r., 86
  of r. and blasphemy, 58
  r. a wise man, 47
  r. is better, 26
  r. me not, 29
  r. of the wise, 48
  scorner heareth not r., 47
rebukes
  furious r., 98
rebuketh
  hate him that r., 48
receive
  counsel, and r., 5
  not r. evil, 2
  r. a thousand shekels, 136
  r. good at the hand, 2
  r. my instruction, 68
  r. my sayings, 5
  time to r. money, 115
recompence
  r. of a man's hands, 255
recompense
  r. thee for all, 141
  r. thy ways, 158
  silence, but will r., 209
  vengeance, and r., 210
record
  r. is on high, 108
red
  wine when it is r., 151
redeem
  r. us for Thy mercies', 200
redeemed
  for I have r., 101
  God r. thee, 36

r. of the Lord shall, 101
Zion shall be r., 139
redeemer
  my strength, and my r., 185
  R. is strong, 56
  r. liveth, 81
  thy Saviour and thy R., 97
refrain
  r. thy voice, 213
refraineth
  r. his lips, 227
refuge
  eternal God is thy r., 217
  God is a r., 81
  God is our r., 92
  lies our r., 64
  r. and my fortress, 108
  r. for the oppressed, 217
  r. from the avenger, 219
  r. in times of trouble, 217
  rock of my r., 217
  tower, and my r., 105
  will I make my r., 217
refuse
  be wise, and r. it not, 5
  if ye r. and rebel, 238
  r. the evil, 63
  r. to humble thyself, 11
  r. ye to keep, 65
refused
  stone which builders r., 174
refuseth
  he that r. instruction, 64
  r. reproof erreth, 47
regardest
  Thou r. me not, 58
reign
  by me kings r., 162
  Lord shall r. for ever, 75
  not r. over, 147
  r. and prosper, 159
  r. over many nations, 132
  r. over thee, 132
  r. over you, 193
reigneth
  that the Lord r., 76
  the Lord r., 103
reject
  knowledge, I will also r., 145
rejected
  because thou hast r., 145
  because thou r. the word, 41
  have r. Me, 147
  Lord hath r., 197
  not r. thee, 147
  r. of men, 159
  r. the word, 201
  r. thee from being king, 41
  seeing I have r., 115

rejoice
  authority, the people r., 114
  desert shall r., 207
  enemies wrongfully r., 72
  heart of them r., 118
  let not the buyer r., 66
  let the earth r., 103
  let the heavens r., 27
  make a loud noise, and r., 27
  man should r. in his own, 3
  r. and be glad, 27
  r. before the Lord, 266
  r. in the Lord, 119
  r. in Thy salvation, 253
  r. not against me, 23
  r. not when thine enemy, 72
  r. O young man, 268
  r. over thee with joy, 219
  r. with the wife of, 156
  r. with trembling, 126
  r. ye with Jerusalem, 139
  righteous shall r., 210
  trust in Thee r., 118
rejoiceth
  city r., 119
  heart r., 118
  whole earth r., 57
rejoicing
  come again with r., 48
relieve
  r. my soul is far, 34
  r. the oppressed, 173
rely
  r. on the Lord, 72
remained
  none escaped nor r., 61
remainest
  r. for ever, 75
remaineth
  r. and is besieged, 10
  spirit r. among, 34
remember
  if I do not r., 7
  mercy r. Thou me, 91
  r. all their wickedness, 47
  r. break not, 45
  r. his misery, 59
  r. how short my time, 164
  r. I beseech Thee, 92
  r. Me in far countries, 79
  r. me, I pray, 185
  r. me, O my God, 212
  r. not the sins, 91
  r. now how I have walked, 82
  r. now thy Creator, 97
  r. that thou wast, 36
  r. that thou wast, 250
  r. the days of darkness, 52
  r. the days of old, 79

r. the Lord, 259
r. the Lord, 17
r. the name of the Lord, 202
r. their sin no more, 91
r. thine handmaid, 114
r. this day, 92
r. thy ways and be, 201
r. what is come, 181
r. ye not the former, 203
r. ye the law of, 35
wrath r. mercy, 9
remembered
  be no more r., 51
  former shall not be r., 46
  hast not r. Me, 111
  Lord r. her, 88
  not r. the days of thy, 79
  r. not the Lord, 16
  r. they were but flesh, 91
  thou mayest be r., 84
  wept, when we r., 123
  within me I r. the, 44
remembereth
  r. that we are dust, 37
remembrance
  death there is no r., 51
  name in r., 145
  no r. of the wise, 202
  r. of them to cease, 10
  r. shall perish, 84
  sin to r., 29
remembrances
  r. are like unto ashes, 5
remnant
  Jerusalem go forth a r., 240
  r. of Mine inheritance, 1
  r. that are left, 185
  r. that is escaped, 240
  very small r., 241
remove
  r. mine integrity, 135
  r. not the ancient, 190
removed
  cannot be r., 19
  hills be r., 100
  hope hath He r., 58
  r. their heart, 128
rend
  r. your clothes, 165
  r. your heart, 204
  time to r., 60
render
  r. to every man, 212
  r. to them their desert, 142
  r. unto every man, 90
renderest
  r. to every man, 142
renew
  r. a right spirit, 235
  r. our days as of, 203
  r. their strength, 203

renowned
  shall never be r., 31
rent
  r. my garment, 9
repay
  accordingly He will r., 195
  r. him to his face, 83
repeateth
  he that r. a matter, 116
repent
  God will turn and r., 91
  r. and turn, 204
  r. in dust, 203
  r. Me of the evil, 91
  spare, neither will I r., 61
  that He should r., 110
  that He should r., 27
repented
  God r. of the evil, 91
  r. the Lord, 46
repentest
  r. Thee of the evil, 37
repenteth
  r. Me that I, 200
repenting
  weary with r., 78
replenish
  r. the earth, 14
  r. the earth, 30
report
  no good r., 169
reproach
  be no more a r., 139
  behold our r., 181
  heart shall not r., 40
  heritage to r., 91
  r. her not, 95
  r. of men, 48
  r. of men, and despised,
    174
  r. shall not be wiped, 4
  shall the adversary r., 21
  sin is a r., 114
  strife and r. cease, 238
  take away our r., 59
  turn their r., 210
reproached
  enemy that r., 20
reproacheth
  foolish man r., 47
  r. his Maker, 173
  r. his Maker, 21
reprobate
  r. silver, 197
reproof
  hateth r. shall die, 47
  r. entereth more, 48
  r. is brutish, 47
  refuseth r. erreth, 47
reprove
  loveth not one that r., 47
  r. after the hearing, 80
  r. kings for their sakes, 32
  r. not a scorner, 47

require
  God r. of thee, 28
  what doth the Lord r., 19
  whatsoever thou shalt r.,
    114
requite
  r. the Lord, 133
requited
  God hath r., 142
rescueth
  delivereth and r., 56
resembled
  r. the children, 17
reserve
  pardon them whom I r., 91
  r. a blessing, 9
  r. wrath for His enemies,
    98
respect
  not r. persons, 24
  not r. the person, 85
  r. persons in judgment,
    131
  r. unto the lowly, 37
rest
  fly away, and be at r., 74
  give Him no r., 139
  given r. unto His people,
    114
  heart taketh not r., 59
  labour, and have no r., 173
  let it r., 48
  My r. for ever, 139
  r. for your souls, 246
  r. upon him, 159
  sake I will not r., 139
  sea, when it cannot r., 261
  thou shalt r., 216
  weary be at r., 51
rested
  r. from all His work, 216
  r. from war, 176
  seventh day He r., 46
restore
  he shall r. it, 193
  r. that which he took, 207
  r. to you the years, 91
restorer
  r. of thy life, 114
restoreth
  r. my soul, 203
restrained
  nothing will be r., 8
restraint
  no r. to the Lord, 39
retain
  r. thine integrity, 28
retaineth
  r. not His anger, 91
return
  come, and let us r., 204
  desire to r., 79
  dust shalt thou r., 23
  let the shadow r., 173

mischief shall r., 41
naked shall he r., 52
naked shall I r. hither, 2
none shall r., 3
not r. with thee, 201
r. and come to Zion, 92
r. and come with, 101
r. and depart, 86
r. at all in peace, 66
r. every man, 207
r. from following, 176
r. no more, nor see, 79
r. thy wickedness, 208
r. to his earth, 8
r. to his own land, 55
r. to their dust, 10
r. unto Him, 101
r. unto Me and I will r.,
    204
r. unto the ground, 192
r. unto the Lord, 204
r. ye now every man, 204
r. ye now every one, 204
reward shall r. upon, 143
same shall he r., 54
shall not r. to me, 51
shall they not r., 79
spirit shall r., 52
thither they r., 42
when I r., 198
whence I shall not r., 51
yet r. again to Me, 16
revealed
  r. my cause, 211
  things which are r., 144
revealeth
  heaven that r. secrets, 67
revengeth
  jealous, and the Lord r.,
    211
revenues
  r. of the wicked, 215
  r. without right, 64
revile
  not r. the gods, 113
revive
  Thou wilt r. me, 50
revolted
  deeply r., 204
reward
  exceeding great r., 105
  fruit of womb is His r., 31
  r. for the righteous, 213
  r. for their labour, 42
  r. of his hands, 195
  r. shall return upon, 143
  r. the doer of evil, 194
  r. them that hate, 140
  r. to the evil man, 146
  shall be a sure r., 215
  taketh r. to slay, 12
rewarded
  commandment shall be r.,
    172

r. evil for good, 3
r. me evil for good, 112
r. me good, 42
r. thee evil, 42
work shall be r., 212
work shall be r., 213
rewardeth
r. evil for good, 112
r. the proud doer, 82
rib
r. taken from man, 45
rich
abundance of the r., 231
diligent maketh r., 146
haste to be r., 8
labour not to be r., 8
not the r. man glory, 23
poor, and maketh r., 102
r. and poor meet, 74
r. answereth roughly, 44
r. hath many friends, 93
r. yet hath nothing, 235
shall not be r., 181
ways, though he be r., 29
when one is made r., 73
riches
better than the r. of, 73
both r. and honour, 212
chosen than great r., 205
full of days, r., 51
full of Thy r., 167
glory in his r., 23
He esteem thy r., 237
heapeth up r., 133
houses and r. are the, 133
if r. increase, set not, 259
in r. and wisdom, 259
increased thy r., 62
left hand r., 263
nor yet r. to men of, 235
poverty nor r., 41
r. and not by right, 64
r. are not for ever, 177
r. come of Thee, 84
r. make themselves wings,
73
r. profit not, 259
trusteth in his r., 80
yet hath great r., 235
riddle
declare unto us the r., 19
found out my r., 19
ride
r. on white asses, 183
rider
r. hath He thrown, 183
rideth
neither shall he that r., 75
riding
r. upon an ass, 127
right
days is in her r., 263
depart to the r., 31
do that which is r., 18

do that which is r., 204
earth do r., 101
forcible are r. words, 124
go to the r., 31
hand or the left, 170
hast done r., 42
just and r. is He, 110
r. hand forget, 1
r. hand of righteousness,
108
r. hand or to the left, 35
r. hand shall find, 72
r. hand shall save, 106
r. in his own eyes, 5
r. in his own eyes, 165
r. in the sight of, 171
r. to them that find, 33
renew a r. spirit, 235
revenues without r., 64
riches, and not by r., 64
righteous are r., 5
save with Thy r. hand, 55
sit thou at My r. hand, 106
thousand at thy r. hand, 50
Thy r. hand, O Lord, 236
to the r. hand, 220
turned not to the r., 61
way which seemeth r., 180
ways of the Lord are r., 19
righteous
afflictions of the r., 247
art more r., 42
death of the r., 50
desire of the r., 79
destroy the r., 60
discern between the r., 113
five of the fifty r., 38
fruit of the r., 213
God shall judge the r., 141
heart of the r., 64
house of the r., 215
judgeth the r., 140
justify the r., 142
let the r. smite, 3
light is sown for the r., 118
lips of the r., 5
little that r. man hath, 73
Lord are upon the r., 106
Lord is r., 110
loveth the r., 100
man that is more r., 134
one event to the r., 150
pervert the words of r., 24
prayer of the r., 108
r. are in authority, 114
r. Branch, 159
r. considereth the cause,
183
r. cry, 186
r. in all His ways, 111
r. in all His works, 97
r. in his own eyes, 135
r. is taken away, 52
r. man hateth lying, 149

r. man regardeth, 10
r. over much, 38
r. runneth into it, 107
r. shall flourish, 116
r. shall inherit, 213
r. shall rejoice, 210
r. showeth mercy, 24
r. tendeth to life, 41
reward for the r., 213
righteousness of the r., 16
salvation of the r., 214
seen the r. forsaken, 1
sold the r. for silver, 43
that thou art r., 11
that thou mayest be r., 224
the Lord is r., 117
thoughts of the r., 5
trieth the r., 254
way of the r., 100
well with the r., 119
what can the r. do, 146
when the r. turneth, 16
wicked watcheth the r., 50
written with the r., 72
righteously
judge r., 143
judge r. between, 140
righteousness
before Thee for our r., 127
break off thy sins by r., 19
city of r., 139
converts with r., 139
deliver me in Thy r., 55
established in r., 163
found in the way of r., 6
fruit of r., 43
hand of My r., 108
heavens declare His r., 99
in r. shalt thou be, 215
judge the world with r.,
140
little with r., 64
not for thy r., 253
own souls by their r., 61
paths of r., 214
r. and judgment, 214
r. as a mighty stream, 143
r. as the waves, 172
r. belongeth unto Thee,
215
r. but behold a cry, 63
r. delivereth, 52
r. exalteth a nation, 114
r. I hold fast, 40
r. not be abolished, 218
r. of the righteous, 16
r. of the upright, 55
r. shall be sure reward, 215
r. shall He judge, 141
r. shalt thou judge, 140
r. that he hath done, 91
sanctified in r., 215
seek r., 157
showeth forth r., 124

sow in r. reap in mercy, 19
Sun of r., 15
to every man his r., 212
turneth from his r., 16
with r. shall he judge, 159
work of r., 215
worketh r., 218
riotous
companion of r. men, 36
rise
day that I r., 176
false witnesses did r., 135
r. up against Thee, 111
r. up early, 67
risen
false witnesses are r., 178
risest
down and when thou r. up,
34
riseth
from whence it r., 195
rising
from r. of the sun, 184
river
peace been as a r., 172
r. were turned to blood,
179
rivers
all the r. run, 26
by the r. of Babylon, 123
place from whence the r.,
42
r. of water, 239
r. of waters run down, 65
through the r., 34
roar
let the sea r., 27
r. all like bears, 9
r. and lay hold of, 6
r. He shall prevail, 103
r. like the sea, 40
r. like young lions, 6
will a lion r., 165
young lions r., 6
roared
lion hath r. who, 172
waves r., 97
roaring
wrath is as the r., 9
roarings
r. are poured out, 9
rob
r. not the poor, 173
will a man r. God, 29
robbed
bear r. of her whelps, 8
r. of her whelps, 50
wherein have we r. Thee,
29
yet ye have r. Me, 29
robbery
full of lies and r., 47
rock
enter into the r., 74

except their R. had sold, 1
God my r. why hast Thou,
1
harder than a r., 131
He is the R., 97
He only is my r., 39
Lord is my r., 106
out of this r., 189
r. of my refuge, 217
r. of my salvation, 97
r. of my salvation, 183
r. of our salvation, 232
r. that is higher, 217
serpent upon a r., 166
smote the r., 65
smote the r. twice, 160
speak unto the r., 80
rod
beat him with the r., 30
beatest him with the r., 30
come forth a r., 159
r. and Thy staff, 34
r. for the fool's back, 64
r. he smote, 65
r. is for the back, 63
r. of correction, 30
spareth his r., 30
roes
like two young r., 17
roof
cleaveth to the r., 244
r. of my mouth, 7
root
out of the serpent's r., 66
take r. downward, 240
roots
out of his r., 159
rope
sin with a cart r., 230
rose
blossom as the r., 207
r. of Sharon, 17
rot
thigh shall r., 4
wicked shall r., 205
rotten
brass as r. wood, 237
rough
r. places plain, 172
roughly
rich answereth r., 44
round
mountains are r., 101
navel is like a r., 17
r. about His people, 101
rubies
price is far above r., 156
wisdom is above r., 263
wisdom is better than r.,
264
ruin
mouth worketh r., 5
shall not be your r.,
204

ruined
Jerusalem is r., 21
rule
by me princes r., 114
light to r. the day, 14
light to r. the night, 14
Lord shall r., 113
r. over his own spirit, 223
r. over you, 113
shall r. over thee, 14
son r. over, 113
when wicked beareth r.,
114
ruler
clothing, be thou our r.,
148
curse the r., 113
many seek the r.'s, 143
ruleth
r. over men, 114
ruling
r. in the fear, 114
rumour
hear a r., 55
run
judgment r. down as, 143
r. and not be weary, 19
r. to and fro, 104
r. to and fro to seek, 95
r. with the footmen, 37
runneth
cup r. over, 2
r. down with water, 34
righteous r. into it, 107
running
r. to mischief, 12
r. waters out of thine, 4
rush
r. grow up without mire,
116
rusheth
r. into the battle, 132
rushing
r. like the r., 169

S

sabbath
keep the s., 217
remember the s. day, 216
seventh day is the s., 216
sabbaths
hallow My s., 217
s. ye shall keep, 216
sackcloth
gird thee with s., 165
gird you with s., 165
gird you with s., 165
s. their covering, 169
virgin girded with s., 54
sacrifice
Him shall ye do s., 97
kick ye at My s., 43
mercy, and not s., 216

more acceptable than s., 142
obey better than s., 171
s. of fools, 268
s. of the wicked, 29
s. to the Lord, 236
sacrificed
  s. and burnt, 128
sacrifices
  burnt offerings and s., 171
  house full of s., 225
  multitude of your s., 216
sacrificeth
  s. unto any god, 123
sad
  countenance s. seeing, 56
  heart of righteous s., 64
sadness
  s. of the countenance, 146
safe
  and I shall be s., 217
  in the Lord shall be s., 81
  into it, and is s., 107
safety
  counsellors there is s., 5
  dwell in s., 217
  s. is of the Lord, 253
said
  as thou hast s., 148
  hath He s. and not, 82
saints
  assembly of the s., 87
  death of His s., 156
  forsaketh not His s., 82
saith
  s. the Lord, 15
  s. the Lord, 109
  what the Lord s., 136
  ye say, the Lord s., 53
sake
  for His name's s., 214
  for Mine holy name's s., 99
  for Mine own s., 105
  for my s., 73
  for Thy goodness' s., 91
  for Thy mercies' s., 218
  for Thy name's s., 99
  for Thy s. are we killed, 156
  gently for my s., 36
  great name's s., 1
  Jerusalem's s., 139
  me for Thy mercies' s., 13
  My servant David's s., 105
  not, for Thine own s., 91
  redeem for Thy mercies' s., 200
  saved for His name's s., 55
  wrought for My name's s., 99
  Zion's s. will I not, 139
sakes
  do not this for your s., 99

kings for their s., 32
not for your s., 158
salt
  covenant of s., 44
  eaten without s., 88
  pillar of s., 41
salvation
  become my s., 237
  cometh my s., 218
  God is my s., 96
  God is my s., 81
  God of my s., 82
  God of my s., 119
  He is become my s., 218
  He only is my s., 39
  horn of my s., 105
  is become my s., 237
  just, and having s., 127
  my light and my s., 86
  rejoice in Thy s., 253
  rock of my s., 97
  rock of my s., 183
  rock of our s., 232
  s. belongeth unto, 218
  s. is far from wicked, 218
  s. is of the Lord, 219
  s. of the Lord, 70
  s. of the righteous, 214
  s. shall be for ever, 218
  s. unto kings, 162
  sorrowful: let Thy s., 127
  vain is s. hoped, 95
  wait for the s., 176
  waited for Thy s., 218
  wells of s., 218
same
  s. shall he return, 54
  Thou art the s., 75
Samson
  call for S., 160
  Philistines upon thee, S., 49
  Philistines upon thee, S., 19
  S. said, let me die, 50
Samuel
  bring me up S., 235
sanctified
  out of the womb I s., 20
  s. in righteousness, 215
  s. in them, 122
  seventh day, and s. it, 216
  tabernacle shall be s., 41
sanctify
  Lord which s. you, 170
  s. unto Me, 40
  s. yourselves, 196
  to s. it, 217
sanctuary
  make Me a s., 33
sand
  as the s. of the sea, 33
  s. by the sea side, 2
  s. that is by the sea, 197

s. which is upon the sea, 44
sap
  full of s., 167
Sarah
  S. that is ninety, 87
sat
  s. down and wept, 233
  there we s. down, 123
Satan
  Lord said unto S., 162
satiate
  s. and made drunk, 27
satisfaction
  take no s., 26
satisfied
  eat and be s., 157
  eat, but not be s., 49
  eye is not s., 8
  eyes of man are never s., 8
  good man shall be s., 219
  not be s. with silver, 115
  that are never s., 52
satisfieth
  s. the longing soul, 57
satisfy
  steal to s. his soul, 47
Saul
  departed from S., 201
  mourn for S., 115
  S. enquired, 1
  S. eyed David, 138
  S. hath slain, 84
  S. to be king, 200
save
  ear unto me, and s., 55
  God s. the king, 162
  He will s., 176
  He will s. us, 97
  healed; s. me and, 120
  I am with you to s., 71
  if they can s. thee, 129
  is God, s. the Lord, 109
  Lord shall s., 13
  mighty; He will s., 219
  none to s. them, 54
  quickly, and s., 7
  right hand shall s., 106
  s. by many or by few, 39
  s. it , for Mine own, 105
  s. me according to, 13
  s. me for Thy mercies', 218
  s. me for Thy mercies', 13
  s. me from bloody men, 146
  s. me, O God, 13
  s. not thy life, 257
  s. the humble person, 126
  s. Thou us out, 55
  s. Thy people, 185
  s. with Thy right hand, 55
  shall my sword s., 237
  stand up, and s., 14

saved
and we shall be s., 100
ended, and we are not s.,
59
s. by the multitude, 162
s. from mine enemies, 55
s. from your enemies, 252
s. them alive, 210
s. them for His name's, 55
save me, and I be s., 120
that thou mayest be s., 204
saveth
He s. them out, 55
Lord s. not with sword, 80
s. such of a contrite, 116
s. the poor, 106
saviour
beside Me there is no s.,
109
Lord am thy S., 97
send them a s., 56
there is no s. beside, 163
saw
God s. every thing, 11
say
canst thou s. I love, 127
none can s. unto Him, 103
not s. thee nay, 175
s. among the heathen, 76
s. not, I am a child, 67
s. not, I will do, 210
s. now Shibboleth, 175
s. unto Him, What doest,
102
s. unto wisdom, 264
searched out what to s.,
175
shall the work s., 56
should the heathen s., 220
what thou shalt s., 69
what ye shall s., 73
wherefore should they s.,
126
who shall then s., 94
sayest
all that thou s., 171
sayings
ear unto my s., 117
receive my s., 5
scapegoat
lot for the s., 219
s. into the wilderness, 219
scarest
s. me with dreams, 66
scarlet
brought up in s., 126
sins be as s., 91
scatter
s. the sheep, 148
s. thee among the heathen,
79
s. Thou the people, 257
s. you among the nations,
78

scattered
flock was s., 68
He that s. Israel, 33
iniquity shall be s., 262
sheep shall be s., 148
whither I have s. you, 102
sceptre
s. shall not depart, 147
S. shall rise, 158
scorn
friends s. me, 81
laughed thee to s., 220
laughed to s., 161
scorner
cast out the s., 238
reprove not a s., 47
s. heareth not rebuke, 47
s. loveth not one, 47
when s. is punished, 68
scorners
s. delight in their, 89
scornful
seat of the s., 36
scorning
delight in their s., 89
drinketh up s., 224
scorpions
chastise you with s., 173
sea
am I a s. or a whale, 78
as the sand of the s., 33
cloud out of the s., 182
divided the s., 97
dry land in the s., 74
earth, the s. and, 46
fish of the s., 9
fishes of the s., 102
go down to the s., 172
let the s. roar, 27
midst of the s., 166
mighty waves of the s., 103
roareth like the s., 40
run into the s., 26
s. is not full, 26
s. may be calm, 21
s. monsters draw out, 30
sand by the s. side, 2
sand that is by the s., 197
thrown into the s., 183
troubled s., 261
waters cover the s., 82
waves of the s., 172
sea shore
upon the s., 44
seal
s. upon thine arm, 152
set me as a s., 152
sealeth
s. their instruction, 67
search
earth, and none did s., 68
s. and try our ways, 204
s. for Me, 62
s. out a matter, 163

s. their own glory, 23
searched
His years be s. out, 145
knew not I s. out, 7
s. out what to say, 175
searcheth
Lord s. all hearts, 100
searching
canst thou by s., 11
seas
earth praise Him, the s.,
184
waters called He s., 68
season
fruit in his s., 239
in the night s., 59
rain in due s., 170
spoken in due s., 5
there is a s., 168
seat
sitteth in the s., 36
secret
better than s. love, 26
bread eaten in s., 65
discover not a s., 20
gift in s., 9
hide himself in s., 74
s. errand unto thee, 53
s. of God, 38
s. of the Lord, 87
s. things belong, 144
secretly
didst it s., 125
secrets
talebearer revealeth s., 113
that revealeth s., 67
seduced
s. My people, 257
see
blind, that ye may s., 238
but they s. not, 129
come, let us s., 28
let him not s., 78
my flesh shall I s. God, 51
neither s. nor hear, 129
no man s. Me, 104
not He s. my ways, 100
not s. my wretchedness,
224
not s. the land, 193
open Thine eyes and s., 13
places that I not s., 74
s. all the evil, 36
s. eye to eye, 6
s. His glory, 99
s. my zeal, 269
s. now that I, 109
s. the land before, 63
s. Thy vengeance, 211
s. wherein his great, 136
s. ye indeed but, 238
say, who shall s., 47
shall He not s., 104
shall s. him, but, 158

that he may s., 72
the heathen shall s. My, 99
seed
  bearing precious s., 48
  corrupt your s., 126
  him that soweth s., 191
  multiply thy s., 34
  s. also be numbered, 2
  s. as the dust, 2
  s. may live, 31
  s. of evildoers, 31
  s. of the land, 246
  s. shall all the families, 85
  s. shall all the nations, 32
  s. shall be as dust, 30
  seed as the s., 44
  sow thy s., 62
  sow your s., 94
seedtime
  s. and harvest, 221
seeing
  deaf, or the s., 46
  s. many things, 111
  satisfied with s., 8
seek
  broad ways I will s., 57
  for good that s. Him, 105
  if thou s. Him, 61
  if ye s. Him, 62
  Lord that s. Him, 157
  many s. the ruler's, 143
  needy s. water, 85
  none did search or s., 68
  rejoice that s. the Lord,
    118
  run to and fro to s., 95
  s. a flea, 78
  s. deep to hide, 64
  s. good, and not evil, 31
  s. Him with all, 19
  s. His face continually, 107
  s. His face evermore, 62
  s. me early shall find, 264
  s. Me, and find, 62
  s. meekness, 157
  s. my life, 58
  s. peace, and pursue, 176
  s. righteousness, 157
  s. that which was lost, 120
  s. the Lord, 62
  s. the Lord and ye, 150
  s. their meat, 6
  s. thou great things, 8
  s. Thy servant, 42
  s. ye My face, 81
  s. ye the Lord, 62
  s. ye the Lord while, 173
  s. ye the priesthood, 8
  s. you out of the book, 221
  shall s. peace, and, 61
  soul to s. the Lord, 62
  they s. not Thy statutes,
    218
  Thy face, Lord, will I s., 81

thyself? s. them not, 8
time to s. the Lord, 204
we s. your God, 53
will I s. Thee early, 62
seeketh
  s. mischief, 247
  s. my life, 167
  s. my life s. thy, 50
  s. not the welfare, 26
  s. to slay him, 50
  soul that s. Him, 7
  understanding s. knowl-
    edge, 144
  wise s. knowledge, 144
seemeth
  do what s. good, 53
  s. good unto Thee, 180
  what s. good unto, 38
  what s. Him good, 2
seen
  all things have I s., 6
  and have s. nothing, 84
  deed done nor s., 56
  eyes have s., 18
  hast thou s. the doors, 12
  have s. God, 15
  no eye had s. me, 58
  s. a great light, 73
  s. God face to face, 15
  s. her nakedness, 43
  s. my wrong, 143
  s. the King, 15
  s. the righteous, 1
  s. this day that, 104
  s. thy face, 50
  s. thy tears, 185
  s. thy tears, 37
  s. what I have done, 160
  until mine eyes had s., 205
seest
  s. the shadow, 86
  s. Thou as man s., 78
seeth
  declare what he s., 254
  He s. all his goings, 100
  Lord s. not as man, 10
  Lord s. us not, 78
  not as man s., 10
  s. the vengeance, 210
sell
  s. himself to work, 76
  s. Sisera into the hand, 253
  s. your brethren, 115
  truth, and s. it not, 249
seller
  nor the s. mourn, 66
  so with the s., 24
selleth
  head of him that s., 25
send
  here am I; s. me, 160
  s. me before you, 197
  s. portions unto them, 29
  s. you Elijah, 159

that I shall s. thee, 187
whom shall I s., 160
will s. My messenger, 159
sendest
  whithersoever thou s., 147
sent
  I am s. to thee, 169
  Lord of hosts hath s., 161
  name: I have not s., 84
  s. me hither but God, 59
separate
  s. them from among, 101
separated
  poor is s. from his, 93
separateth
  s. chief friends, 113
  s. very friends, 116
sepulchre
  s. of thy fathers, 194
serpent
  biteth like a s., 151
  dust like a s., 126
  fiery flying s., 66
  out of the s.'s root, 66
  s. beguiled me, 20
  s. said unto the woman,
    136
  s. was more subtil, 231
  tongues like a s., 119
  way of a s., 166
servant
  as with the s., 84
  blind as the Lord's s., 130
  blind, but My s., 239
  borrower is s., 24
  considered my s. Job, 162
  face from Thy s., 13
  hear thy s. curse, 48
  I am Thy s., 99
  iniquity of Thy s., 42
  is thy s. a dog, 28
  judgment with Thy s., 141
  law of Moses My s., 35
  oppress an hired s., 25
  s. an understanding, 63
  s. David's sake, 105
  s. honoureth his master,
    175
  s. I have chosen, 101
  s. is free, 51
  s. which is escaped, 231
  s. will go and fight, 43
  seek Thy s., 42
  there also will thy s. be,
    153
  Thy s. heareth, 120
  toward a wise s., 8
servants
  all are Thy s., 168
  give them to his s., 162
  hand from thy s., 7
  happy are these thy s., 148
  into his s.' houses, 179
  known toward His s., 213

not all my lord's s., 74
s. of the Chaldees, 2
s. of the Lord, 184
speak unto thy s., 222
serve
elder shall s., 88
God whom we s., 50
God will we s., 171
Him shalt thou s., 7
if they obey and s., 191
it is vain to s. God, 21
Jehu shall s., 53
kingdom that will not s.,
139
Lord, to s. Him, 31
other gods to s., 16
s. Him, 170
s. Him in sincerity, 123
s. Him in truth, 62
s. Him only, 61
s. Him with a perfect, 225
s. Him, and obey, 171
s. Lord with gladness, 184
s. me for nought?, 25
s. other gods, 137
s. other gods, 82
s. strange gods, 15
s. strangers, 79
s. the Egyptians, 86
s. the king of Babylon, 3
s. the Lord, 91
s. the Lord, 267
s. the Lord, 28
s. the Lord, 61
s. the Lord, 31
s. the Lord with fear, 126
s. with thee for Rachel, 6
s. ye the Lord, 225
shall s. me, 15
that we should s. Him, 14
whom ye will s., 31
will s. Thee, 225
served
Jacob s. seven years, 152
king himself is s., 43
s. Baal a little, 53
s. on the other side, 128
s. other gods, 77
s. strange gods, 79
servest
God whom thou s., 40
serveth
and him that s. Him not,
113
between him that s., 113
own son that s., 158
service
herb for the s. of man, 48
set
s. before you the way, 150
s. My face against, 196
seven
hewn out her s. pillars, 264
s. are an abomination, 12

than s. men that can, 38
sevenfold
taken on him s., 105
seventh
blessed the s. day, 216
s. day He rested, 46
s. day is the sabbath, 216
s. day thou shalt rest, 216
s. year let it rest, 48
sew
time to s., 60
shadow
as the s. of death, 47
darkness and the s., 51
darkness nor s. of death,
47
days are as a s., 150
days are like a s., 56
days upon earth are a s.,
164
doors of the s. of death, 12
of the s. of death, 243
s. go forward, 172
s. of death, 39
s. of death, 218
s. of the mountains, 86
s. of Thy wings, 106
s. of Thy wings, 217
s. return backward, 173
shake
s. at the sound, 61
shaken
if they be s., 107
shame
awake, some to s., 71
bringeth his mother s., 30
cause my s. to go, 132
clothed with s., 72
clothed with s., 72
cometh to s., 261
him that causeth s., 8
kingdoms thy s., 126
man covereth s., 136
my face from s., 178
pride, then cometh s., 188
s. shall be seen, 126
s. shall be the promotion,
96
son that causeth s., 146
unjust knoweth no s., 226
shameth
s. his father, 36
Sharon
rose of S., 17
sharp
like a s. razor, 20
mouth like a s. sword, 48
s. as a twoedged sword,
50
sharpened
s. their tongues, 119
sharpeneth
iron s. iron, 28
s. the countenance, 28

sharper
s. than a thorn, 43
shaven
s. then my strength, 166
sheaves
bringing his s., 48
even among the s., 95
shed
blood be s., 141
blood of him that s., 165
blood that is s., 165
from coming to s. blood, 5
s. innocent blood, 12
sheddeth
s. man's blood, 141
sheep
as for these s., 134
astray like a lost s., 42
bleating of the s., 53
hath been lost s., 16
keeping the s., 222
like s. they are laid, 51
s. for the slaughter, 50
s. have gone astray, 16
s. of His hand, 101
s. of My pasture, 148
s. shall be scattered, 148
s. what have they done,
206
slay ox and s., 10
sheepfolds
among the s., 67
shekels
s. of silver, 136
shepherd
as a s. doth his flock, 33
as a s. putteth, 253
Lord is my s., 106
smite the s. and the, 148
who is that s. that, 15
shepherds
kindled against the s., 21
lost sheep: their s., 16
s. feed the flocks, 43
woe be to the s., 43
Shibboleth
say now S., 175
shield
art a s. for me, 34
comest with a s., 80
deliverer; my s., 107
He is my s., 105
help and our s., 176
help and their s., 87
I am thy s., 105
s. and buckler, 106
s. unto them that put, 107
strength and my s., 106
Shiloh
until S. come, 147
shine
face to s., 22
face to s., 100
face to s., 265

fire shall not s., 142
s. upon thee, 190
shined
hath the light s., 218
shineth
night s. as the day, 74
s. more and more, 215
shining
just is as the s., 215
ship
way of a s., 166
ships
down to the sea in s., 172
shoe
loose thy s., 205
shoes
poor for a pair of s., 43
put off thy s., 122
shoot
s. an arrow, 54
s. at her, 211
short
hand waxed s., 46
s. my time is, 164
wicked is s., 76
shortened
wicked shall be s., 87
shoulder
arm fall from my s., 135
shout
ever s. for joy, 118
s. for joy, 118
s. for the Lord, 17
s. unto God, 118
shouting
perish, there is s., 52
show
father, and he will s., 79
s. me now Thy way, 116
s. thee the word, 209
s. them the way, 147
s. thyself a man, 28
s. us, we pray, 157
showed
signs which I have s., 80
treasures that I have not s.,
160
showers
s. upon the grass, 69
shut
Lord had s. them up, 1
none shall s., 15
s. the lions' mouths, 56
s. thine hand, 29
s. thou up the vision, 95
s. up her womb, 30
shuttle
weaver's s., 58
sick
maketh the heart s., 125
s. of love, 152
seeing thou art not s., 56
strengthen that was s.,
120

side
fear is on every s., 50
Lord is on my s., 39
on the Lord's s., 7
s. of the flood, 128
sides
thorns in your s., 71
sigh
merry hearted do s., 233
sighing
s. cometh before, 9
s. of the prisoner, 131
sighs
s. are many, 240
sight
acceptable in Thy s., 185
better is the s. of, 57
blood be in His s., 250
evil in His s., 4
evil in My s., 77
favour in Thy s., 147
favour in thy s., 114
good in His s., 81
good in His s., 22
good in my s., 11
grace in Thy s., 116
in the s. of the Lord, 78
in Thy s., 224
in your own s., 201
precious in the s. of, 156
pure in His s., 155
s. as grasshoppers, 86
s. of his eyes, 80
s. of the Lord, 65
s. of the Lord, 18
s. of the Lord, 131
s. of the Lord, 16
s. of the Lord, 246
s. of the Lord, 76
s. of the Lord, 171
s. of the nations, 34
s. of this sun, 125
tarry in my s., 64
thousand years in Thy s.,
179
Thy s. shall no man, 141
sign
s. between Me and you,
217
s. between Me and you,
216
signs
s. of heaven, 14
s. which I have showed, 80
worketh s. and wonders,
56
silence
dwelt in s., 13
keep not s., 139
keep not Thou s., 13
keep s. before Him, 109
Lord keep not s., 13
prudent shall keep s., 192
time to keep s., 26

will not keep s., 209
silent
am not s., 59
silly
envy slayeth the s., 8
silver
dross from the s., 251
gods of s., 129
gold in pictures of s., 69
idols are s. and gold, 129
instruction and not s., 68
loveth s., 115
neither their s. nor, 98
none were of s., 197
reprobate s., 197
righteous for s., 43
s. and gold, 170
s. be weighed, 263
s. cord be loosed, 63
s. is become dross, 130
s. is Mine, 260
satisfied with s., 115
shekels of s., 136
thousands of gold and s.,
252
tongue is as choice s., 124
simple
but the s. pass on, 192
making wise the s., 35
preserveth the s., 108
s. is made wise, 68
s. understand wisdom, 250
simplicity
went in their s., 134
sin
bare the s. of many, 159
bear his s., 21
cause thy flesh to s., 228
death for his own s., 117
declare their s., 226
did not Solomon s. by, 137
die for his own s., 194
fools mock at s., 228
forbid that I should s., 185
fruit of the wicked to s., 41
if a soul s., 34
in s. did my mother, 20
make me to know my s.,
134
my s. only this once, 203
no s. in thee, 189
not s. against Thee, 35
one man s., 41
one man s., 140
prayer become s., 72
rebellion unto his s., 199
remember their s., 91
s. against innocent, 166
s. against the Lord, 140
s. be blotted out, 210
s. is a reproach, 114
s. is ever before me, 39
s. lieth at the door, 80
s. of his youth, 260

s. of witchcraft, 199
s. to remembrance, 29
s. upon them, 128
s. will find you, 221
vanity, and s., 230
wanteth not s., 234
what is my s., 167
sincerity
  s. and in truth, 123
sinew
  iron s., 239
sing
  awake and s., 125
  good to s. praises, 184
  how shall we s., 79
  rejoice, and s., 27
  s. forth the honour, 232
  s. many songs, 84
  s. O barren, 159
  s. praise to my God, 232
  s. praises, 183
  s. praises to His name, 232
  s. praises unto Him, 49
  s. praises unto the Lord, 232
  s. psalms unto Him, 232
  s. unto God, ye kingdoms, 232
  s. unto Him, 232
  s. unto Him with the, 166
  s. unto the Lord, 232
  s. unto the Lord, 232
  s. unto the Lord, 232
  s. unto the Lord, 232
  s. unto the Lord, 232
  s. unto the Lord, 183
  s. unto the Lord, 232
  s. unto the Lord as long, 232
  s. with thanksgiving, 232
  s. ye praises, 184
  tongue of the dumb s., 120
singing
  before His presence s., 184
  break forth into s., 159
  s. men and women, 6
  time of the s., 221
  with s. unto Zion, 101
sinned
  arrows: for she hath s., 211
  grave those which s., 51
  I have, 42
  I have s., 206
  not s. against thee, 178
  s. against Me, 193
  s. against the Lord, 39
  s. against the Lord, 79
  s. against the Lord, 39
  s. this time, 117
  s. with our fathers, 39
  that we have s., 212
  we have s., 39
  we have s., 39
  we have s. because, 228

we have s. we have done, 39
sinner
  good, so is the s., 74
  s. destroyeth much good, 43
  though s. do evil, 112
  to the s. He giveth, 116
sinners
  destroy the s., 230
  evil pursueth s., 77
  heart envy s., 138
  if s. entice thee, 36
  let s. be consumed, 195
  way of s., 36
sinnest
  if thou s. what doest, 155
sinneth
  good, and s. not, 177
  hasteth with his feet s., 198
  his neighbour s., 119
  no man that s. not, 155
  s. against me wrongeth, 264
  soul that s. shall die, 206
sins
  break off thy s., 19
  jealousy with their s., 98
  love covereth all s., 11
  not forgive your s., 110
  s. are not hid, 39
  s. be as scarlet, 91
  s. have hid His face, 186
  s. of his father, 31
  s. of my youth, 91
  s. testify against us, 118
  turn from all his s., 204
Sisera
  delivered S. into, 249
  sell S. into the hand, 253
  stars fought against S., 12
sister
  lieth with his s., 132
  mother, and my s., 51
  our s. as an harlot, 209
  wisdom, thou art my s., 264
sit
  I s. in darkness, 82
  s. every man under, 177
  s. in judgment, 183
  s. thou at My right hand, 106
  s. upon it in truth, 163
  s. upon the wall, 192
  strength is to s., 147
sittest
  s. in thine house, 34
sitteth
  sinners, nor s., 36
six
  in s. days the Lord, 46
  in s. days the Lord, 46

s. days shalt thou labour, 216
s. days thou shalt do, 216
s. things doth the Lord, 12
s. years thou shalt sow, 48
skill
  favour to men of s., 235
skin
  change his s., 28
  s. for s., 224
  s. of my teeth, 74
  s. worms destroy, 51
skipped
  mountains s. like rams, 15
slack
  dealeth with a s. hand, 146
  s. not thy hand, 7
  s. to him that hateth, 83
  s. to pay, 189
slain
  not be s. in the house, 108
  s. a thousand men, 237
  s. his thousands, 84
  s. in the streets, 78
  s. men before your idols, 61
  s. of the Lord shall be, 141
  s. with hunger, 52
  s. with the sword, 52
  shall he be s., 134
  shalt be s., 257
  strong men have been s., 4
slander
  uttereth a s., 26
slaughter
  lamb to the s., 52
  lambs to the s., 60
  ox goeth to the s., 4
  sheep for the s., 50
slay
  evil shall s. the wicked, 142
  in no wise s. it, 36
  in no wise s. it, 142
  not s. you, 210
  s. an innocent person, 12
  s. both man and woman, 10
  s. me thyself, 134
  s. me, yet will I trust, 81
  seeketh to s. him, 50
  sword, and s. me, 125
slayer
  deliver the s., 137
slayeth
  before him that s. thee, 12
  envy s. the silly, 8
  hand of him that s., 12
  s. Cain, vengeance, 105
sleep
  love not s., 146
  neither slumber nor s., 32
  not give s. to mine, 33
  not suffer him to s., 231

of the hands to s., 182
s. a perpetual s., 52
s. but my heart, 67
s. falleth upon men, 67
s. in the dust, 71
s. of a labouring man, 231
s. the s. of death, 13
they s. not, except, 261
yet a little s., 182
sleepeth
  s. and must be awaked, 129
  s. in harvest, 146
slew
  dead which he s., 3
  s. at one time, 237
  s. in his life, 3
  when He s. them, 87
  woman s. him, 125
slide
  s. in due time, 175
sling
  could s. stones, 3
  s. and with a stone, 253
  s. out, 71
slippery
  way be dark and s., 49
slippeth
  my foot s., 108
slothful
  s. man saith, 78
slothfulness
  s. the building decayeth, 25
slow
  Lord is s. to anger, 196
  merciful, s. to anger, 111
  of a s. tongue, 69
  s. of speech, 69
  s. to anger, 36
  s. to anger, 37
  s. to anger, 8
  s. to anger, 9
  s. to anger, 37
  s. to wrath, 176
sluggard
  go to the ant, thou s., 62
  s. is wiser, 38
  s. to them that send, 146
slumber
  keepeth thee will not s., 106
  neither s. nor sleep, 32
  s. to mine eyelids, 33
  sleep, a little s., 182
slumberings
  s. upon the bed, 67
small
  both s. and great, 66
  every s. matter, 147
  for a s. moment, 1
  hear the s., 131
  I am s. and despised, 82
  is it a s. thing for you, 78
  left unto us a very s., 241

s. among the heathen, 196
s. and great are there, 51
s. as the dust, 10
s. dust of the balance, 114
s. one a strong nation, 116
s. rain upon, 69
strength is s., 92
smell
  but they s. not, 129
  eat, nor s., 129
  s. of a field, 30
  s. of my son, 30
  s. of thine ointments, 152
smite
  I may s. thee, 180
  let the righteous s., 3
  Lord shall s., 27
  s. all the firstborn, 88
  s. the shepherd and the, 148
  s. thee by day, 106
smiteth
  s. his father, 26
  that s. a man, 26
smitten
  s. and He will bind, 103
  s. five or six times, 73
  stricken, s. of God, 21
smoke
  s. out of the chimney, 73
  s. to the eyes, 146
smoother
  mouth is s., 4
  s. than butter, 69
smote
  in My wrath I s., 37
  s. his neighbour, 137
  s. them hip and thigh, 254
  Uzza, and he s. him, 98
snare
  bird hasteth to the s., 243
  gods shall be a s., 71
  pit, and the s., 59
  s. for my life, 53
  s. of his soul, 90
  s. unto us, 26
  taken in My s., 247
  taken in the s., 66
  taken in the s., 75
snared
  s. by the transgression, 149
snout
  gold in a swine's s., 17
snow
  consume the s. waters, 51
  s. in summer, 90
  treasures of the s., 79
  white as s., 91
  whiter than s., 197
soap
  take thee much s., 118
sockets
  s. of fine gold, 23

Sodom
  S. and Gomorrah, 53
  should have been as S., 241
  sin as S., 226
soft
  s. answer turneth away, 8
  s. tongue breaketh, 11
softer
  s. than oil, 69
sojourners
  s. with Me, 190
sold
  except their Rock had s., 1
  land shall not be s., 190
  s. his birthright, 133
  s. the righteous for, 43
sole
  s. of his foot, 17
soles
  s. of your feet, 138
solitary
  city sit s., 54
Solomon
  did not S. king of, 137
  King S. passed all, 259
son
  Absalom, my s. my s., 116
  Absalom, my s. my s., 116
  against the king's s., 136
  and bear a s., 159
  and the s. of man that, 132
  as for an only s., 165
  bear a s., 87
  because he hath no s., 121
  but in his s.'s days, 42
  chasten thy s. while, 30
  chasteneth his s., 63
  foolish s. heaviness of, 31
  foolish s. is a grief, 31
  foolish s. is calamity, 31
  hair of thy s., 217
  hand of thy s., 157
  hateth his s., 30
  have no s., 133
  is a wise s., 172
  Israel is My s., 32
  Jonathan my s., 131
  king's s. is dead, 36
  neither the s. of man, 110
  no s. to keep my name, 145
  O my s. Absalom, 116
  or the s. of man, 155
  s. eat thou honey, 264
  s. heareth his father's, 47
  s. honoureth his father, 175
  s. maketh a glad, 31
  s. of her womb, 37
  s. of his old age, 85
  s. of the morning, 54
  s. rule over, 113
  s. shall not bear, 229

sow
blessed are ye that s., 69
s. but shalt not reap, 69
s. in tears, 48
s. not among thorns, 204
s. them among the people, 79
s. thy seed, 62
s. to yourselves in, 19
s. ye, and reap, 69
s. your seed, 94
shalt s. the land, 48
wind shall not s., 147
soweth
him that s. seed, 191
s. discord among brethren, 12
to him that s., 215
sown
light is s., 118
s. the wind, 69
s. wheat but, 94
ye have s. much and, 69
spake
s. ye did not hear, 65
they s. against me, 220
spare
back, neither will I s., 61
eye shall not s., 10
eye shall not s., 158
let not your eye s., 61
s. me according, 101
s. no arrows, 211
s. them, as a man s., 158
s. Thy people, 91
s. ye not her young, 10
spared
mine eye s., 157
spareth
s. his rod, 30
spark
s. of his fire, 142
speak
alone, that I may s., 26
command thou shalt s., 187
days should s., 79
double heart do they s., 64
from me to s. unto, 11
heavens, and I will s., 234
heed to s. that which, 123
I s. they are for war, 257
I will s. and the word, 190
let not God s., 15
mouths, but they s. not, 129
neither s. they through, 129
s. a vision, 84
s. but this once, 98
s. I pray, 222
s. in the anguish, 26
s. Lord; for Thy, 120
s. My word faithfully, 67

s. not in the ears of a, 5
s. that which is good, 5
s. thou with us, 15
s. to the earth, 102
s. ye that ride, 183
s. ye the truth, 124
s. ye unto the rock, 80
s. your minds, 5
shall I s., 135
that will I s., 136
time to s., 26
word that I shall s., 190
speakest
s. lies in the name of, 84
speaketh
abhor him that s., 48
all the Lord s., 170
false witness that s., 12
one s. peaceably, 128
s. lies shall perish, 64
s. the truth, 218
s. truth, 124
when a prophet s., 83
speaking
be born, s. lies, 17
God s., 15
lips from s. guile, 77
spear
comest with a s., 80
lift up his s., 237
stretched out the s., 60
sword and s., 80
spears
pruninghooks into s., 256
s. into pruninghooks, 176
special
s. people unto Himself, 32
speech
excellent s. becometh, 69
hear my s., 187
of one s., 251
s. shall distil, 69
s. shall distil, 66
slow of s., 69
understand one another's s., 36
spend
s. our years, 149
wherefore do ye s., 252
spent
s. without hope, 58
spices
ointments than all s., 152
spies
ye are s., 3
spilt
as water s., 163
spirit
a wounded s. who, 57
and vexation of s., 8
anguish of my s., 26
be of a contrite s., 116
better of an humble s., 127
commit my s., 108

drinketh up my s., 9
faithful s. concealeth, 93
follow their own s., 84
hasty of s., 89
heart and a new s., 150
heed to your s., 156
His s. upon them, 190
lying s. in the mouth, 236
My s. remaineth among, 34
patient in s., 176
portion of thy s., 122
power over the s., 52
power, but by My s., 238
renew a right s., 235
rule over his own s., 223
s. before a fall, 80
s. drieth the bones, 57
s. is broken, 233
s. of counsel, 159
S. of God, 104
s. of God hath made, 149
S. of God is, 147
S. of the Lord, 17
S. of the Lord, 135
S. of the Lord, 201
S. of the Lord, 135
s. of the Lord shall, 159
S. of the Lord upon me, 104
s. of wisdom, 159
s. shall return unto, 52
s. to retain the s., 52
s. was not stedfast, 65
than proud in s., 176
the s. of knowledge, 159
vexation of s., 49
which way went the S., 11
with my s. within, 62
woman of a sorrowful s., 30
spirits
have familiar s., 235
Lord weigheth the s., 224
spit
s. in her face, 193
spitting
from shame and s., 178
spoil
s. of your enemies, 227
s. the vines, 60
s. thee shall be a s., 211
s. to all their enemies, 126
s. with the proud, 127
spoiled
emptied, and utterly s., 57
spoken
albeit I have not s., 53
day whereof I have s., 190
for I have s., 15
for the Lord hath s., 57
hath He s., 82
I have s. it, 27
I have s. mock on, 161

I the Lord have s., 27
Lord hath not s., 83
Lord hath not s., 66
Lord hath s. who can but, 172
of the Lord hath s., 238
ran: I have not s., 84
s. in due season, 5
s. only by Moses, 73
s. unto them but they, 65
that the Lord hath s., 170
which thou hast s., 109
word fitly s., 69
words that are s., 48
sport
  may make us s., 160
spots
  leopard his s., 28
spread
  s. dung upon your faces, 126
  s. forth your hands, 1
  s. My net, 247
spreading
  s. himself like a green, 77
spring
  s. as the grass, 146
springs
  s. of water, 258
staff
  rod and Thy s., 34
stagger
  s. but not with drink, 67
staggereth
  drunken man s., 67
stalled
  s. ox and hatred, 152
stamp
  s. them as the mire, 10
stand
  able to s. before, 102
  able to s. before envy, 9
  awake, s. up, 254
  it shall not s., 70
  not hear me, I s. up, 58
  s. at the latter day, 81
  s. before kings, 2
  s. before thee, 40
  s. before thine enemies, 43
  s. before you, 236
  s. in His holy place, 122
  s. still, and consider, 167
  s. still, and see, 70
  s. still, that, 179
  s. thou still, 209
  s. up and bless, 18
  s. up, and save, 14
  shepherd that will s., 15
  so shall it s., 94
  who can s. before His, 103
  who can s. before His, 98
  who shall s., 141
  who shall s. when, 15

standard
  s. toward Zion, 218
  set up a s., 169
  set ye up a s., 17
standest
  place whereon thou s., 205
  s. is holy ground, 122
  why s. Thou afar, 13
standeth
  counsel of the Lord s., 177
  heart s. in awe, 4
  s. in way of sinners, 36
star
  S. out of Jacob, 158
stargazers
  astrologers, the s., 14
stars
  nest among the s., 188
  number of the s., 120
  s. are not pure, 155
  s. in their courses, 12
  s. of heaven, 193
  s. of the heaven, 44
state
  man at his best s., 92
stature
  s. is like to a palm, 23
statutes
  commandments and My s., 18
  keep all My s., 204
  keep my s., 170
  s. have been my songs, 34
  s. of your fathers, 112
  seek not Thy s., 218
  testimonies and His s., 171
  walk in My s., 172
  walk in My s., 170
  way of Thy s., 35
staves
  comest to me with s., 41
stay
  Lord was my s., 71
  none can s. His hand, 103
  s. me with flagons, 152
  s. now thine hand, 157
steal
  ashamed s. away, 45
  s. to satisfy his soul, 47
  shall not s., 18
  shalt not s., 46
stem
  rod out of the s., 159
step
  s. between me and death, 50
steps
  count all my s., 100
  direct his s., 202
  directeth his s., 18
  enlarged my s., 217
  hunt our s., 66
  s. of a good man, 18

stiffnecked
  art a s. people, 238
  be no more s., 33
  be ye not s., 238
still
  be s. and know, 145
  beside the s. waters, 34
  stand s. that, 179
  stand thou s., 209
  strength is to sit s., 147
stingeth
  s. like an adder, 151
stir
  s. him up, 32
stolen
  s. waters are sweet, 65
stone
  cast a s., 59
  hands, wood and s., 129
  head s. of the corner, 174
  hearts as an adamant s., 65
  houses of hewn s., 63
  not take of thee a s., 10
  ready to s. me, 58
  s. for foundations, 10
  s. shall be a witness, 202
  s. shall cry, 3
  s. which the builders, 174
  sling and with a s., 253
  tables of s., 243
  to the dumb s. Arise, 129
  wood and s., 129
stoned
  s. him with stones, 199
stones
  build with hewn s., 12
  by these s., 202
  could sling s., 3
  s. of a crown, 102
  strength of s., 58
  waters wear the s., 61
stony
  s. heart, 203
stood
  s. between the dead, 137
stoppeth
  s. his ears, 29
stork
  s. in the heaven, 65
storm
  chaff that the s., 260
  whirlwind and in the s., 104
stormy
  raiseth the s. wind, 168
straight
  cannot be made s., 3
  crooked shall be made s., 172
  crooked things s., 73
  make s. in the desert, 159
  who can make that s., 3
straightway
  goeth after her s., 4

strange
lips of a s. woman, 4
s. woman is a narrow, 191
serve s. gods, 15
served s. gods, 79
song in a s. land, 79
stranger in a s. land, 90
tongue of a s. woman, 154
stranger
both for the s., 74
law for the s., 142
love ye the s., 24
neither vex a s., 90
s. did not lodge, 125
s. in a strange, 90
s. in the earth, 144
s. nor the poor, 37
s. that is with him, 140
s. that sojourneth, 74
s. thou mayest lend, 90
s. unto my brethren, 75
surety for a s., 24
strangers
for ye were s., 24
inheritance turned to s., 40
s. in the land of Egypt, 90
shall ye serve s., 79
ye are s., 190
straw
as when there was s., 173
iron as s., 237
lion shall eat s., 24
s. to make brick, 173
stream
as a mighty s., 143
street
fallen in the s., 146
lodge in the s., 125
lodge not in the s., 50
mire of the s., 10
no name in the s., 84
streets
cannot go in our s., 66
desolate in the s., 126
playing in the s., 191
s. of Askelon, 116
s. of the city shall, 191
slain in the s., 78
voice in the s., 263
strength
as my s. was then, 92
awake, put on s., 107
beginning of my s., 88
confidence shall be s., 81
delivered by much s., 237
everlasting s., 237
forces of s., 237
from s. to s., 92
give not thy s., 154
glory and s., 184
God is my s., 238
God is my s., 92
God of my s., 108
God, my s., 106

great s. lieth, 136
great s. lieth, 19
have s. when thou goest,
89
if by reason of s., 149
increaseth s., 108
Jehovah is my s., 237
Lord is my s., 106
Lord is my s., 237
Lord is my s. and song,
218
Lord is s. of my life, 44
Lord is your s., 237
man whose s., 81
my s. which teacheth, 237
not when my s. faileth, 6
put on thy s., 203
refuge and s., 92
renew their s., 203
s. and my redeemer, 185
s. in time of trouble, 214
s. is small, 92
s. is to sit still, 147
s. labour and sorrow, 149
S. of Israel, 148
s. of my heart, 92
s. of the ox, 69
s. shall no man prevail,
237
s. the s. of stones, 58
s. to bring forth, 258
s. to the upright, 171
s. will go from, 166
seek His s., 62
so is his s., 28
so is my s. now, 92
so shall thy s., 22
voice with s., 40
wisdom is better than s.,
237
young men is their s., 79
strengthen
I will s. thee, 108
s. me, I pray, 185
s. my hands, 92
s. that which was sick, 120
s. ye the weak hands, 70
s. your heart, 39
strong shall not s., 40
strengtheneth
wisdom s., 237
stretch
s. forth his hand, 12
s. out My hand, 180
stretched
hand is s., 246
hand is s. out still, 98
His hand is s., 98
s. out the heavens, 46
s. out the spear, 60
stretcheth
s. out the north, 46
stricken
esteem him s., 21

strife
anger appeaseth s., 8
beginning of s. is, 238
cease from s., 11
man stirreth up s., 9
of sacrifices with s., 225
s. and reproach cease, 238
talebearer, the s., 113
strifes
hatred stirreth s., 11
stringed
s. instruments, 166
strings
instrument of ten s., 166
stripe
s. for s., 141
stripes
his s. we are healed, 120
s. into a fool, 48
stripped
go s. and naked, 116
strive
s. against Him, 38
s. not with a man, 11
striveth
s. with his Maker, 121
strong
ants a people not s., 62
as s. this day, 91
battle to the s., 28
be s. and courageous, 70
be s. and quit, 43
be s. fear not, 70
be thou s., 28
destroy the fat and s., 141
follow s. drink, 67
from him that is too s.,
100
habitation of the s., 211
hands be s., 241
know God shall be s., 82
let your hands be s., 44
Lord is a s. tower, 107
Lord s. and mighty, 103
love is s., 152
out of the s., 213
Redeemer is s., 56
s. and of a good, 70
s. and of good courage, 39
s. drink is raging, 151
s. hold in the day of, 107
s. holds shall be like, 107
s. men have been slain, 4
s. reasons, 11
s. shall not strengthen, 40
small one a s. nation, 116
stagger, but not with s., 67
weak say, I am s., 256
wine nor s. drink, 58
wise man is s., 237
won than a s. city, 91
stronger
s. than a lion, 214
s. than lions, 44

s. than we, 45
they were s., 54
strongly
  foundations be s., 25
stubble
  consumed them as s., 199
  do wickedly, shall be s., 141
  s. before the wind, 260
  shall be as s., 5
stubborn
  s. and rebellious, 65
  their s. way, 238
stubbornness
  s. is as iniquity, 238
study
  s. is a weariness, 68
stumble
  know not at what they s., 172
  proud shall s., 12
stumbled
  ark; for the oxen s., 98
stumbleth
  glad when he s., 72
stumblingblock
  s. before the people, 172
  s. of their iniquity, 260
  take up the s., 172
subdue
  earth, and s. it, 14
  s. all thine enemies, 71
substance
  honour with thy s., 246
suburbs
  s. shall shake, 61
subvert
  s. a man in his cause, 20
suck
  s. to their young, 30
sucking
  beareth the s. child, 147
  s. child, 37
  tongue of the s., 244
suckling
  infant and s. ox, 10
  virgin, the s. also, 60
sucklings
  mouth of babes and s., 31
suffer
  proud heart will not I s., 12
  s. Thine Holy One, 75
  soul shall s. hunger, 146
suffered
  s. no man to do, 106
summer
  meat in the s., 62
  s. and winter, 221
  s. is ended, 59
  snow in s., 90
sun
  as long as the s., 84
  be as the s., 96

before the s., 125
behold the s., 149
better thing under s., 49
clear as the s., 17
from rising of the s., 184
laboured under the s., 49
light and the s., 169
new thing under the s., 135
s. also ariseth, 42
s. is gone down, 116
S. of righteousness, 15
s. shall not smite, 106
s. stood still, 107
s. stood still, 102
sight of this s., 125
taketh under the s., 94
supplication
  s. before the Lord, 185
supplications
  present our s., 127
  voice of my s., 115
sure
  s. mercies of David, 22
surely
  s. deliver thee, 107
  s. put me to death, 5
  shall s. be the Lord's, 198
  shall s. die, 15
  uprightly walketh s., 28
surety
  s. for a stranger, 24
sustain
  He shall s. thee, 108
swallow
  crane and the s., 65
  man would s. me up, 158
  s. up death, 52
  s. up the inheritance, 60
sware
  s. unto their fathers, 193
  s. unto them, 1
  s. unto your fathers, 133
swear
  s. by His name, 7
  s. unto me, 7
  tongue shall s., 7
swearers
  against false s., 4
sweareth
  every one that s., 177
  he that s. as he, 74
sweat
  s. of thy face, 192
sweet
  bitter for s. and s., 149
  bitter thing is s., 57
  drink the s., 27
  how s. are Thy words, 136
  labouring man is s., 231
  s. influences of Pleiades, 183
  s. melody, sing many, 84
  s. to the soul, 3
  s. to the soul, 234

s. to thy taste, 89
stolen waters are s., 65
sweeter
  s. also than honey, 35
  s. than honey, 136
  s. than honey, 214
sweetly
  worm shall feed s., 51
sweetness
  came forth s., 213
  forsake my s., 8
swelled
  feet s., 108
swelling
  lion from the s., 211
swift
  feet that be s., 12
  he that is s. of foot, 75
  let not s. flee away, 253
  perish from the s., 235
  race is not to the s., 28
  s. witness against, 265
swifter
  persecutors are s., 235
  s. than a weaver's, 58
  s. than eagles, 44
swim
  make I my bed to s., 231
swine
  gold in a s.'s snout, 17
sword
  are for the s. to the s., 196
  back from the s., 44
  by His s. will the Lord, 141
  by s. and famine, 84
  comest to me with a s., 80
  death with the s., 51
  devoured with the s., 238
  die with the s., 61
  draw thy s., 125
  every man hath his s., 86
  fall by the s., 142
  fall by the s., 209
  fall by the s., 71
  it is for the s., 260
  keepeth s. from blood, 62
  lift up s. against, 256
  mouth like a sharp s., 48
  near shall fall by s., 10
  no s. in the hand, 81
  poor from the s., 106
  s. bereaveth, 52
  s. devour forever, 210
  s. devoureth one, 49
  s. hath made women, 200
  s. in their hand, 210
  s. is without, 50
  s. of the enemy, 50
  s. of the Lord, 209
  s. of the Lord, 17
  s. of the Lord is, 209
  s. of the Lord, how long, 131

s. shall devour, 27
s. shall devour flesh, 210
s. shall never depart, 49
s. without, and terror, 60
saveth not with s., 80
shall my s. save, 237
sharp as a twoedged s., 50
slain with the s., 52
than the s., 256
wicked to the s., 196
swords
beat their s., 176
plowshares into s., 256
s. are in their lips, 231
s. of the mighty, 256
were they drawn s., 69
sworn
nor s. deceitfully, 122
Syrian
S. language, 222

T

tabernacle
t. shall be sanctified, 41
tabernacles
t. of bribery, 24
thorns in their t., 196
thy t. O Israel, 17
table
before them in a t., 122
eat at thy t., 114
graven upon the t., 178
preparest a t. before, 22
tables
t. of stone, 243
tail
head, and not the t., 170
take
t. me not away, 150
taken
Lord hath t., 2
not t. away, 128
t. in the devices, 142
taketh
t. away, who can hinder, 102
tale
t. that is told, 149
talebearer
t. among thy people, 113
t. revealeth secrets, 113
where there is no t., 113
words of a t., 113
talk
t. of the lips, 146
t. of Thy wondrous, 136
t. with man, 104
t. ye of all, 232
tarry
if we t. till, 188
lies shall not t., 64
t. at home, 219
t. at Jericho, 226

t. for them till, 156
t. not, 235
though it t., 143
why t. the wheels, 50
tarrying
Lord make no t., 108
tasks
your daily t., 173
taste
but t. a little honey, 78
sweet to thy t., 89
t. in the white, 88
words unto my t., 136
tasteth
mouth t. meat, 248
taught
fear toward Me is t., 128
t. of the Lord, 69
t. rebellion, 121
teach
earth, and it shall t., 102
meek will He t., 117
t. a just man, 5
t. God knowledge, 126
t. me Thy paths, 117
t. me Thy way, 18
t. me to do Thy will, 171
t. me, O Lord, the way, 35
t. My people the, 33
t. thee what thou say, 69
t. thee wisdom, 121
t. them diligently, 34
t. them the good, 68
t. us of His ways, 18
t. us to number, 149
t. your daughters, 116
years should t. wisdom, 79
teacheth
He that t. man, 100
heart t. his mouth, 69
t. my hands to war, 237
who t. like Him, 136
tears
bread of t., 116
eye poureth out t., 81
fountain of t., 242
seen thy t., 185
seen thy t., 37
sow in t., 48
thine eyes from t., 213
water my couch with t., 231
teeth
children's t. are set, 21
skin of my t., 74
t. shall be set on, 206
vinegar to the t., 146
Tekel
Mene, Mene, T. Upharsin, 166
tell
elders, and they will t., 79
shall I t. it thee, 222
t. it not, 116

t. me nothing, 5
t. me, I pray, 19
who can t. if God, 91
tempest
breaketh me with a t., 240
temple
is in His holy t., 109
voice out of His t., 185
tempt
do ye t. the Lord, 14
neither will I t., 190
t. the Lord, 18
ten
better than t. sons, 30
instrument of t. strings, 166
tender
t. mercies come unto, 37
t. mercies of the wicked, 48
upon the t. herb, 69
vines have t., 60
tenth
t. unto Thee, 246
tents
goodly are thy t., 17
t. of wickedness, 127
terrible
great and very t., 141
haughtiness of the t., 12
Lord great and t., 17
mighty God and t., 104
terribleness
t. hath deceived, 38
terrifiest
t. me through visions, 66
terror
be not a t., 125
caused my t., 243
t. by night, 86
t. of the shadow, 243
t. within, shall destroy, 60
testified
Lord hath t. against, 194
testify
lips t. against, 117
sins t., 118
t. against any person, 26
testimonies
commandments and His t., 171
testimony
t. of the Lord, 35
thanks
give t. unto the Lord, 115
give t. unto the Lord, 113
give t. unto Thee, 115
give t. unto Thee, 183
give Thee t., 51
t. to Thy holy name, 55
t. unto the Lord, 115
thanksgiving
magnify Him with t., 115
sing with t., 232

thick
art grown t., 53
thicker
finger shall be t., 226
thief
do not despise a t., 47
partner with a t., 47
t. be found, 207
thigh
smote them hip and t., 254
sword upon his t., 86
t. shall rot, 4
thighs
joints of thy t., 17
think
if ye t. good, give, 168
t. not with thyself, 178
t. upon me, 22
thinketh
yet the Lord t. upon, 182
thirst
die for t., 58
faileth for t., 85
nor a t. for water but, 85
t. they gave me vinegar, 48
tongue cleaveth for t., 244
thirsteth
every one that t., 57
soul t. after Thee, 153
soul t. for Thee, 62
thirsty
as a t. land, 153
t. give him water, 72
t. land springs, 191
t. man dreameth, 63
waters to a t. soul, 169
thistles
t. grow instead of wheat,
135
thorn
sharper than a t., 43
thorns
lily among t., 17
reap t., 94
sow not among t., 204
t. in their tabernacles, 196
t. in your sides, 71
t. under a pot, 146
up thy way with t., 172
thought
surely as I have t., 94
t. can be withholden, 222
thoughts
day his t. perish, 8
knoweth the t. of man, 94
My t. are not your t., 18
t. of the righteous, 5
t. of the wicked, 77
t. shall be established, 239
vain t., 77
thousand
chase a t., 1
chase a t., 237
one man among a t., 154

one shall become a t., 116
slain a t. men, 237
t. at thy right hand, 50
t. shall fall, 50
t. shall flee at, 86
t. shekels, 136
t. years in Thy sight, 179
two put ten t., 1
thousands
David his ten t., 84
mercy unto t., 193
slain his t., 84
than t. of gold and, 252
unto David ten t., 138
three
offer thee t. things, 31
t. things that are never, 52
threefold
t. cord is not quickly, 43
throat
knife to thy t., 96
speak through their t., 129
throne
disgrace the t., 99
habitation of His t., 214
habitation of Thy t., 142
heaven is My t., 104
kings are they on the t.,
214
mercy shall the t., 163
stablish his t., 108
t. from generation, 75
t. shall be established, 163
t. shall be established, 163
through
t. them I may prove, 244
thunder
t. of His power, 103
thyself
neighbor as t., 24
tidings
bear no t., 36
good t., 169
preach good t., 187
with heavy t., 169
till
to t. the ground, 174
tilleth
t. his land, 62
timber
beam out of the t., 3
timbrel
praise Him with the t., 166
with t. and dances, 134
with the t. and harp, 49
time
appoint Me the t., 15
deliver in t. of trouble, 29
die before thy t., 150
discerneth both time, 63
forsake us so long t., 2
from this t. forth, 97
in due t., 175
it is an evil t., 192

short my t. is, 164
silence in that t., 192
sinned this t., 117
slew at one t., 237
strength in t. of, 214
t. and chance happeneth,
235
t. appointed the end, 10
t. for Thee Lord to work,
111
t. is come, 66
t. is come, 130
t. is near to come, 60
t. of health, 79
t. of old age, 6
t. of peace, 257
t. of the end, 71
t. of the singing, 221
t. of their coming, 65
t. of their visitation, 129
t. of thy trouble, 129
t. of trouble, 20
t. of war, 257
t. to be born, 17
t. to break down, 120
t. to build up, 120
t. to cast away, 53
t. to come for ever, 122
t. to dance, 119
t. to die, 17
t. to every purpose, 168
t. to get, 3
t. to hate, 119
t. to heal, 120
t. to keep, 53
t. to keep silence, 26
t. to kill, 120
t. to laugh, 146
t. to lose, 3
t. to love, 119
t. to mourn, 119
t. to plant, 17
t. to pluck, 17
t. to receive money, 115
t. to rend, 60
t. to seek the Lord, 204
t. to sew, 60
t. to speak, 26
t. to weep, 146
times
do evil an hundred t., 112
in t. of trouble, 13
knoweth her appointed t.,
65
loveth at all t., 93
of ancient t., 95
smitten five or six t., 73
t. of trouble, 217
trust in Him at all t., 81
tingle
ears shall t., 208
heareth it shall t., 243
tithe
t. of the land, 246

tithes
t. and offerings, 29
together
can two walk t., 43
dwell t. in unity, 24
let us reason t., 36
lion and the fatling t., 10
shall feed t., 24
token
t. of a covenant, 44
t. of the covenant, 33
told
believe, though it be t., 230
fathers t. us of, 66
half was not t., 88
not t. it my father, 222
t. you from beginning, 100
tale that is t., 149
tomorrow
against t., 196
boast not thyself of t., 23
t. I will deliver, 70
t. shalt thou, 50
t. thou shalt be slain, 257
t. we shall die, 27
tongue
a soft t. breaketh, 11
dog move his t., 105
flattery of the t., 154
from a deceitful t., 231
His word was in my t., 135
hold my t., 2
lying t. is but for, 149
not a word in my t., 100
of a slow t., 69
perverse t. falleth, 64
proud look, a lying t., 12
t. and their doings, 21
t. cleave to the roof, 7
t. deviseth mischiefs, 20
t. faileth, 85
t. from evil, 77
t. is deceitful, 149
t. is the pen, 234
t. keepeth his soul, 192
t. of the crafty, 234
t. of the dumb, 120
t. of the just, 124
t. of the sucking, 244
t. shall swear, 7
t. with a cord, 155
wherefore holdest Thy t., 134
tongues
bend their t., 64
sharpened their t., 119
use their t. and say, 84
tonight
save not thy life t., 257
tooth
like a broken t., 20
t. for t., 208
tore
t. forty and two, 194

torn
t. and He will heal, 103
touch
neither shall ye t. it, 144
t. all that he hath, 28
t. not Mine anointed, 32
touched
hand of God hath t., 36
tower
high t. and my deliverer, 107
Lord is a strong t., 107
my high t., 105
neck is as a t., 23
nose is as the t., 23
t. and a fortress, 190
town
buildeth a t. with blood, 114
traffick
t. hast thou increased, 62
train
t. up a child, 30
transgressed
all have t. against Me, 14
because they have t., 16
t. against the Lord, 39
transgression
day of his t., 16
make me to know my t., 134
people their t., 29
t. of his lips, 149
whose t. is forgiven, 91
transgressions
all your t. so iniquity, 204
forgive your t., 110
wounded for our t., 159
transgressors
intercession for the t., 159
t. shall fall, 19
way of t., 230
travail
hands full with t., 8
sinner He giveth t., 116
sorrows, and his t., 59
t. with child, 30
travaileth
wicked man t., 240
woman that t., 243
traveller
doors to the t., 125
treacherously
deal not t., 156
deal very t., 134
friends dealt t. with, 20
t. against the wife, 156
upon them that deal t., 134
why do we deal t., 20
tread
feet shall t., 138
treader
t. of grapes, 191

treadeth
t. out the corn, 70
treasure
Israel for His t., 32
peculiar t. unto Me, 32
righteous is much t., 215
t. and trouble, 41
treasures
nothing among my t., 160
t. of the hail, 79
t. of the snow, 79
t. of wickedness, 47
wind out of His t., 198
tree
days of a t., 101
desire t. of life, 125
every t. of the garden, 112
fruit of the t., 246
gave me of the t., 20
green bay t., 77
hope removed like a t., 58
like the palm t., 116
like to a palm t., 23
of the t. of knowledge, 112
she is a t. of life, 264
sit under his fig t., 177
t. of life, 213
t. of the field, 167
t. planted by the rivers, 239
trees
promoted over the t., 8
t. of the field, 170
t. of the Lord, 167
t. with the firstripe, 107
tremble
inhabitants of the land t., 15
will ye not t., 15
trembling
clothe themselves with t., 243
rejoice with t., 126
trespass
t. is grown, 226
trespassed
because they t. against, 200
tribes
t. of Israel, 139
tribulation
out of all t., 247
tributary
is she become t., 40
trieth
ear t. words, 248
t. the righteous, 254
triumph
enemy doth not t., 100
let not mine enemies t., 72
shall the wicked t., 43
voice of t., 118
triumphed
He hath t. gloriously, 183

triumphing
t. of the wicked, 76
trodden
t. the winepress, 7
trouble
be with him in t., 186
born unto t., 155
call in day of t., 13
day of my t. I will call, 186
day of t., 58
day of t., 107
day of t. is near, 66
day when I am in t., 247
deliver in time of t., 29
for I am in t., 13
full of t., 149
great treasure and t., 41
health, and behold t., 79
heard of my t., 96
help from t., 106
Lord in their t., 55
present help in t., 92
refuge in times of t., 217
revenues of wicked is t.,
215
strength in time of t., 214
t. and anguish, 34
t. is near, 9
t. thee this day, 47
time of t., 20
time of thy t., 129
times of t., 13
walk in midst of t., 50
troubled
t. sea, 261
why hast thou t., 47
troubles
soul from t., 192
soul full of t., 6
troubleth
he that t. Israel, 21
t. his own flesh, 48
t. his own house, 85
troubling
cease from t., 51
true
execute t. judgment, 19
Lord is the t. God, 97
t. from the beginning, 221
t. witness delivereth, 124
that which is t., 5
truly
t. as I live, 99
trumpet
blew a t., 17
blow the t., 17
blow the t., 107
blown the t., 199
sound of the t., 166
voice like a t., 29
trust
all that t. in Him, 105
better to t. in the Lord,
201

God I have put my t., 86
He in whom I t., 107
His people shall t., 139
in Him will I t., 108
in Thee is my t., 124
in whom I will t., 106
knoweth them that t., 13
let thy widows t., 262
Lord do I put my t., 202
Lord do I put my t., 39
Lord put I my t., 106
maketh the Lord his t., 118
put their t. in Him, 107
putteth his t. in Me, 213
slay me, yet will I t., 81
some t. in chariots, 202
t. also in Him, 248
t. and not be afraid, 81
t. from my youth, 124
t. in graven images, 129
t. in Him, 81
t. in my bow, 237
t. in princes, 202
t. in the Lord, 18
t. in the Lord, 87
t. in the Lord than, 114
t. in the Lord with, 248
t. in Thee rejoice, 118
t. in thine own beauty, 17
t. in vanity, 202
t. thou in Him, 140
t. thou in the Lord, 248
t. ye in the Lord, 237
t. ye not in lying, 64
that t. in the Lord, 19
their t. in Him, 248
whom dost thou t., 11
whoso putteth his t., 81
trustest
God in whom thou t., 21
trusteth
every one that t., 128
t. in his own heart, 38
t. in his riches, 80
t. in the Lord, 119
t. in the Lord, 119
that t. in man, 202
that t. in the Lord, 81
truth
before Thee in t., 82
buy the t., 249
call upon Him in t., 13
cannot hope for Thy t., 52
faithfulness and t., 83
goodness and t., 110
he that speaketh t., 124
judgment of t., 143
law is the t., 35
law of t. was in, 124
love the t. and peace, 177
men of t., 113
paths are mercy and t., 110
peace and t. be, 176
people with His t., 140

plenteous in mercy and t.,
101
serve Him in t., 62
sincerity and in t., 123
sit upon it in t., 163
speaketh the t., 218
t. and without iniquity,
110
t. endureth to all, 248
t. forsake thee, 28
t. is fallen, 146
t. is perished, 249
t. of the Lord endureth,
249
t. preserve the king, 162
t. shall be thy shield, 106
t. to his neighbour, 124
t. unto the clouds, 100
throne: mercy and t., 142
Thy light and Thy t., 117
walk in Thy t., 18
try
t. our ways, 204
tumult
t. is come up, 11
t. of those that rise, 111
turn
and I will t. unto you, 200
God will t. and repent, 91
how long will ye t., 78
if the wicked will t., 204
not your garments, and t.,
204
repent, and t., 204
t. again to the Lord, 204
t. again unto the Lord,
203
t. and do you hurt, 15
t. aside to the right, 170
t. away from His fierce, 91
t. away from you, 91
t. away His face, 101
t. away thy son, 137
t. away your heart, 137
t. back your captivity, 84
t. from it, 77
t. in to me, 32
t. not aside, 220
t. not aside, 61
t. not away the face, 185
t. not away the face, 201
t. not from it, 35
t. thee back, 125
t. thee behind, 229
t. their reproach, 210
t. thou to thy God, 82
t. thou unto Me, 204
t. Thou us unto Thee, 203
t. ye from your evil, 52
t. ye from your evil, 18
t. ye not aside, 267
t. ye now from, 77
t. ye unto Him, 204
t. ye unto Me, 200

t. yourselves, and live, 204
who shall t. it back, 98
turned
anger is not t. back, 165
loved are t. against, 20
t. aside after lucre, 43
t. away from the Lord, 41
t. not to the right, 61
t. quickly out, 16
t. their back unto Me, 129
t. their heart back, 189
t. to his course, 132
t. to the Lord, 161
t. unto Me the back, 16
we shall be t., 203
turneth
t. back from the sword, 44
t. upside down, 220
turning
wiping it, and t., 60
turtle
times; and the t., 65
voice of the t., 221
twice
t. as much, 178
twins
young roes that are t., 17
two
between t. opinions, 27
can t. walk together, 43
if t. lie together, 24
t. are better than one, 42
t. of every sort, 10
t. tables of stone, 243
twoedged
sharp as a t. sword, 50
t. sword in their hand, 210

U

uncircumcised
hand of the u., 58
the u. Philistines, 137
u. Philistine, 14
unclean
clean out of an u., 43
clean, and to the u., 150
uncover
shalt thou not u., 132
uncovered
nakedness shall be u., 126
understand
aged u. judgment, 6
doth a fool u., 130
hear ye indeed, but u., 238
His power who can u., 103
make me to u., 136
not u. one another's, 36
people that doth not u.,
130
simple, u. wisdom, 250
u. his way, 192
u. more than ancients, 79
u. the lovingkindness, 100

understandest
u. thou, which is not, 11
understandeth
easy unto him that u., 144
God u. the way, 263
plain to him that u., 33
u. and knoweth Me, 81
understanding
any u. in them, 32
be ye of u. heart, 250
depart from evil is u., 76
get u. forget, 144
getting get u., 250
give me u., 171
give me u., 35
give me u., 149
is of great u., 176
knowledge and u., 263
length of days u., 6
man of u., 250
man of u. holdeth, 161
man that getteth u., 119
men of u., 235
mule, which have no u., 10
sing ye praises with u., 184
to them that know u., 97
u. heart, 63
u. is a wellspring, 251
u. is infinite, 100
u. it is established, 3
u. of their prudent, 195
u. people, 32
u. seeketh knowledge, 144
u. shall keep thee, 242
u. thy kinswoman, 264
u. wisdom is found, 250
void of u., 63
wisdom and u., 159
with a woman lacketh u., 4
your wisdom and u., 34
understood
wise, that they u., 58
undone
for I am u., 86
left nothing u., 153
unequal
are not your ways u., 80
unfaithful
confidence in an u., 20
ungodly
counsel of the u., 36
delivered me to the u., 4
help the u., 7
way of the u., 111
unity
dwell together in u., 24
unjust
deceitful and u. man, 106
u. knoweth no shame, 226
unpunished
wicked shall not be u., 262
unrighteous
be an u. witness, 36
decree u. decrees, 114

unrighteously
all that do u. are, 25
unrighteousness
house by u., 43
no u. in judgment, 25
unsavoury
u. be eaten, 88
unsearchable
kings is u., 163
unstable
u. as water, 28
unwise
foolish people and u., 133
unwittingly
smote his neighbour u.,
137
up
down one, and setteth u.,
239
get thee u., 70
grave, and bringeth u., 102
hold Thou me u., 217
Lord held me u., 108
low, and lifteth u., 102
raise Me u., 33
u. no more, 51
u. to the mountain, 123
Upharsin
Mene, Mene, Tekel, U.,
166
uphold
u. thee with the right, 108
upholdeth
u. all that fall, 108
upright
behold the u., 162
gladness for the u., 118
integrity of the u., 137
just u. man, 161
none u. among men, 112
perfect and an u. man, 162
prayer of the u., 29
pure and u., 21
righteousness of the u., 55
strength to the u., 171
u. in heart, 118
u. is sharper, 43
u. man Thou wilt show,
110
wilt show Thyself u., 110
uprightly
he that walketh u., 28
him that speaketh u., 48
him that walketh u., 34
that walk u., 213
that walketh u., 218
uprightness
integrity, and in u., 124
walketh in his u., 29
way of the just is u., 215
upside
turneth u. down, 220
upward
fail with looking u., 59

Uriah
  U. in the forefront, 19
usury
  as with taker of u., 60
  giver of u., 60
  lend upon u., 90
  thy money upon u., 251
  u. of money, 251
  u. of victuals, 251
  u. to thy brother, 251
utter
  u. a song, 232
  u. not this, 168
  u. this our business, 6
Uzza
  kindled against U., 98
  U. put forth his hand, 198

V

vagabond
  fugitive and a v., 48
vain
  beauty is v., 17
  bring no more v., 216
  comfort in v., 130
  created it not in v., 46
  go after v. things, 267
  His name in v., 21
  in v. is salvation, 95
  labour I in v., 58
  labour in v. that, 3
  made all men in v., 164
  name of God in v., 21
  none shall return in v., 3
  not said in v., 46
  sow your seed in v., 94
  utter v. knowledge, 252
  v. is the help of man, 13
  v. make thyself fair, 17
  v. shalt thou use, 66
  v. thing for you, 35
  v. thoughts, 77
  v. to serve God, 21
  watchman waketh in v.,
    222
valley
  lily of the v., 17
  multitudes in the v. of,
    141
  v. of the shadow, 39
  v. shall be exalted, 172
value
  physicians of no v., 34
vanished
  wisdom v., 5
vanities
  observe lying v., 83
  vanity of v., 49
vanity
  all is v., 49
  all is v., 49
  all is v., 59
  all that cometh is v., 59

are v. and the work, 129
beast: for all is v., 127
cords of v., 230
days of my v., 6
low degree are v., 28
man is like v., 150
state is altogether v., 92
that they are v., 94
this also is v., 59
trust in v., 202
up his soul into v., 122
v. of v., 59
v. of vanities, 49
v. shall be recompence,
  202
youth are v., 268
vapours
  causeth v. to ascend, 198
vehement
  a most v. flame, 138
vengeance
  execute great v., 98
  execute v. in anger, 98
  God will come with v., 70
  Me belongeth v., 210
  see Thy v., 211
  see Thy v. on them, 72
  seeth the v., 210
  slayeth Cain, v., 105
  take v., 200
  to whom v. belongeth, 210
  v. on His adversaries, 211
  v. to Mine enemies, 140
  v. upon the heathen, 210
verity
  of His hands are v., 111
vessel
  I am like a broken v., 59
  v. for the finer, 251
vessels
  bear the v., 197
vex
  neither v. a stranger, 90
  v. my soul, 78
vexation
  and v. of spirit, 8
  v. of his heart, 49
  vanity and v., 49
vexed
  v. unto death, 166
victory
  glory, and the v., 99
  swallow up death in v., 52
  v. that day turned, 116
victuals
  lend him thy v., 251
vile
  behold, I am v., 42
  for thou art v., 61
  so v. a thing, 38
vine
  every man under his v.,
    177
  v. languisheth, 233

vinegar
  thirst they gave me v., 48
  v. to the teeth, 146
vines
  spoil the v., 60
  v. have tender grapes, 60
vineyard
  give me thy v., 73
  v. of the Lord, 32
vineyards
  fields, and your v., 162
  plant v. but not, 94
  planted pleasant v. but, 63
vintage
  v. of Abiezer, 179
violence
  city is full of v., 146
  him that loveth v., 254
  v. covereth them, 188
violent
  hunt the v. man, 254
violently
  took v. away, 207
viols
  noise of thy v., 126
virgin
  lament like a v., 54
  v. of Israel, 32
  v. shall conceive, 159
  young man and the v., 60
virtuous
  find a v. woman, 156
  v. woman is a crown, 156
virtuously
  daughters have done v.,
    156
vision
  ashamed of his v., 84
  end shall be the v., 71
  shut thou up the v., 95
  v. of their own heart, 84
  where there is no v., 117
  write the v. and, 33
visions
  terrifiest me through v., 66
  young men shall see v., 67
visit
  day when I v., 128
  v. their sin, 128
visitation
  day of v., 195
  time of their v., 129
visitest
  that Thou v. him, 132
voice
  carry the v., 192
  fool's v. is known by, 90
  He did hear my v., 185
  hear my v., 187
  heard my v. hide, 186
  heardest my v., 187
  hearken thou unto the v.,
    171
  hearken unto their v., 2

w. as snow, 91
w. of an egg, 88
whiter
w. than snow, 197
whither
w. thou goest, 61
who
say, w. shall see, 47
w. am I, O Lord, 126
w. is God, 109
w. is like Me, 15
w. is on the Lord's, 7
w. is so faithful, 153
w. is that God, 21
w. is the Lord, 11
w. is there among, 255
w. will appoint, 15
where and w. is He, 58
whole
His hands make w., 102
joy of the w. earth, 139
life is yet w., 9
under the w. heaven, 103
w. duty of man, 67
w. earth is full, 99
w. earth rejoiceth, 57
whomsoever
w. the Lord, 40
whore
hire of a w., 29
to be a w., 31
w. is a deep ditch, 191
w.'s forehead, 226
whoredom
land fall to w., 31
land with thy w., 130
w. and wine, 151
whores
gifts to all w., 129
whoring
hast gone a w., 16
w. after other gods, 83
whorish
by means of a w., 191
why
Lord be with us, w., 66
w. are ye come, 173
wicked
angry with the w., 140
arm of the w., 195
blood of the w., 210
candle of the w., 134
candle of the w., 146
casteth the w., 157
condemn the w., 142
counsels of the w., 5
death of the w., 52
desire of the w., 8
desires of the w., 186
desperately w., 77
deviseth w. imaginations,
12
dwelling place of the w., 72
evil shall slay the w., 142

expectation of the w., 79
eyes of the w., 195
falleth before w., 134
far from the w., 108
from his w. way, 187
fruit of the w., 41
give them that are w., 196
hand of the w., 134
hand with the w., 36
hands of the w., 4
head of the w., 98
heart of the w., 124
how long shall the w., 43
if I be w. why then, 58
if I be w. woe, 2
if the w. turn from, 262
if the w. will turn, 204
in the house of the w., 22
lamp of the w., 195
let the w. fall, 209
light of the w., 142
mercies of the w., 48
my people are w., 117
name of the w., 205
no peace unto the w., 74
not acquit the w., 196
not justify the w., 76
not over much w., 18
path of the w., 18
perfect and the w., 51
proceedeth from the w., 47
prosperity of the w., 73
revenues of the w., 215
riches of many w., 73
righteous and the w., 141
righteous and the w., 113
righteous with the w., 60
righteous, and to the w.,
150
sacrifice of the w., 29
salvation far from w., 218
scattereth the w., 146
so let the w. perish, 195
sorrows be to the w., 81
take away the w., 163
thoughts of the w., 77
triumphing of the w., 76
w. and him that loveth,
254
w. are estranged, 17
w. are like the troubled,
261
w. be no more, 195
w. borroweth, and payeth,
24
w. cease from troubling, 51
w. devoureth the man, 134
w. flee when no, 40
w. for the day of evil, 46
w. for their iniquity, 77
w. have inclosed, 178
w. He turneth upside, 220
w. in his pride, 178
w. is snared, 149

w. live, become old, 134
w. man is loathsome, 261
w. man travaileth, 240
w. messenger, 70
w. not be unpunished, 262
w. regardeth not to know,
183
w. shall be cut off, 261
w. shall be turned, 111
w. shall fall by, 142
w. spring as the grass, 146
w. watcheth righteous, 50
w. will He destroy, 195
warn the w., 187
way of the w. is, 262
way of the w. is as, 172
way of the w. prosper, 134
when the w. perish, 52
when w. beareth rule, 114
woe unto the w., 195
years of the w., 87
wickedly
all that do w., 141
God will not do w., 76
have dealt w., 39
have done w., 206
have done w., 42
sinned, we have done w.,
39
still do w., 257
we have done w., 39
wickedness
bands of w., 85
fall by his own w., 142
forgotten the w., 122
have committed w., 39
heart from w., 204
I have done no w., 4
land become full of w., 31
pleasure in w., 113
plowed w., 143
remember all their w., 47
return thy w., 208
reward his w., 194
tents of w., 127
that He should do w., 76
to work w., 76
treasures of w., 47
turn from his w., 262
turn from their w., 121
turn not from his w., 187
w. burneth as the fire, 77
w. of these nations, 253
w. proceedeth, 47
w. which thine heart, 40
whoredoms and thy w.,
130
wide
open thine hand w., 29
widow
city become as a w., 54
oppress not the w., 37
plead for the w., 262
wife a w., 49

widows
  judge of the w., 262
  let thy w. trust in, 262
wife
  after his neighbour's w.,
    133
  children of married w., 31
  covet thy neighbor's w., 4
  goest to take a w., 137
  knew Hannah his w., 88
  man and his w., 130
  prudent w. from the Lord,
    133
  w. a widow, 49
  w. looked back, 41
  w. of his youth, 156
  w. of thy youth, 156
  was thy w., 53
  whoso findeth a w., 156
  with his father's w., 132
wild
  brought forth w. grapes, 63
  w. ass bray, 37
wilderness
  crieth in the w., 44
  die in the w., 58
  dwell in the w., 156
  fall in this w., 50
  forty years in the w., 78
  habitations of the w., 168
  laid wait for us in w., 72
  scapegoat into the w., 219
  than die in the w., 86
  w. a pool, 258
  w. like Eden, 138
  wander in the w., 78
will
  according to His w., 103
  teach me to do Thy w.,
    171
  w. of mine enemies, 178
willing
  w. and obedient, 172
  with a w. mind, 62
wind
  belly with the east w., 252
  bringeth forth the w., 198
  chaff before the w., 72
  east w. brought locusts,
    180
  images are w., 129
  inherit the w., 85
  laboured for the w., 49
  observeth the w., 147
  raiseth the stormy w., 168
  sown the w., 69
  stubble before the w., 260
  w. that passeth away, 91
  wings of the w., 235
windows
  w. in heaven, 230
wine
  but not drink the w., 94
  drink thy w. with, 89

drunken, but not with w.,
    67
flesh, and a flagon of w.,
    27
leave my w., 8
love is better than w., 152
love than w., 152
loveth w. and oil, 181
new w. mourneth, 233
new w. the maids, 191
not drink w. of them, 63
put away thy w., 3
w. and new w. take away,
    151
w. is a mocker, 151
w. mixed with water, 130
w. nor strong drink, 58
w. that maketh glad, 151
w. unto those that be, 151
w. when it is red, 151
w. with a song, 233
whoredom and w., 151
winepress
  trodden the w., 7
wing
  moved the w. or, 40
wings
  goodly w., 12
  healing in his w., 15
  make themselves w., 73
  mount up with w., 19
  oh that I had w., 74
  shadow of Thy w., 106
  shadow of Thy w., 217
  w. of the wind, 235
  w. shall tell, 192
winneth
  w. souls is wise, 233
winter
  summer and w., 221
  w. is past, 221
wipe
  w. Jerusalem as a man w.,
    60
wiped
  reproach shall not be w., 4
wipeth
  w. a dish, 60
  w. her mouth, 4
wisdom
  according to his w., 183
  ancient is w., 6
  apply our hearts unto w.,
    149
  beginning of w., 87
  bringeth forth w., 215
  by thy great w., 62
  corrupted thy w., 38
  despise the w. of thy, 5
  destitute of w., 89
  earth in riches and w., 259
  fools despise w., 68
  get w., 144
  give me now w., 96

glory in his w., 23
good in His sight w., 22
greatness of thy w., 205
he that is void of w., 161
I have put w., 263
in w. hast Thou made, 167
is their w. vanished, 5
knowledge of w. be unto,
    264
Lord giveth w., 263
Lord, that is w., 87
man that findeth w., 119
man's w. maketh, 265
poor man's w., 5
price of w., 263
say unto w., 264
simple, understand w., 250
spirit of w., 159
teach thee w., 121
the world by His w., 46
this is your w., 34
understanding hath w., 250
w. and might are His, 237
w. and thy knowledge, 38
w. better than weapons,
    257
w. builded her house, 264
w. crieth without, 263
w. excelleth folly, 89
w. giveth life, 264
w. hath seven pillars, 264
w. is an house builded, 3
w. is better than, 237
w. is better than rubies,
    264
w. is found, 250
w. is good with an, 264
w. is much grief, 264
w. is the principal, 250
w. of God in him, 263
w. of the prudent, 192
w. shall die, 161
w. shall perish, 195
w. strengtheneth, 237
w. than gold, 259
w. unto the wise, 97
want of w., 130
world by His w., 46
years should teach w., 79
wise
  art a w. man, 166
  be a w. man or a fool, 133
  be w. and refuse it not, 5
  begetteth a w. child, 31
  bread to the w., 28
  by w. counsel thou, 256
  dieth the w. man, 52
  ear of the w., 144
  eyes of the w., 24
  fool is counted w., 90
  fools, when will ye be w.,
    130
  He taketh the w. in, 47
  he that is w., 155

heart of the w., 69
heart of the w., 90
I will be w., 265
instruction to a w. man, 5
is a w. son, 172
let not the w. man glory, 23
lips of the w., 69
make thyself over w., 38
making w. the simple, 35
men are not always w., 6
poor and a w. child than, 5
rebuke a w. man, 47
rebuke of the w., 48
refraineth lips is w., 227
should a w. man utter, 252
simple is made w., 68
strengtheneth the w., 237
that are w. hearted, 263
that they were w., 58
toward a w. servant, 8
unto counsel is w., 5
w. and understanding, 32
w. in his own conceit, 90
w. in his own conceit, 38
w. in their own eyes, 38
w. in thy latter end, 5
w. king scattereth, 146
w. man feareth, 77
w. man is strong, 237
w. man keepeth it in, 192
w. man mad, 154
w. man than an hundred, 48
w. man will hear, 121
w. man's eyes are in, 90
w. man's heart, 63
w. men die, 164
w. men lay up knowledge, 144
w. men turn away wrath, 9
w. more than of the fool, 202
w. more than the fool, 179
w. shall inherit glory, 96
w. son heareth, 47
w. son maketh a glad, 31
w. son maketh a glad, 31
w. to do evil, 112
w. woman buildeth, 123
walketh with w. men, 36
ways, and be w., 62
whoso is w. and will, 100
winneth souls is w., 233
wisdom of their w., 195
wisdom unto the w., 97
with w. men shall be w., 36
words of the w., 117
wiser
    sluggard is w., 38
    will be yet w., 5
witch
    suffer a w. to live, 265

witchcraft
    sin of w., 199
with
    his God be w. him, 255
    I am w. you, saith, 108
    Lord is w. you, 82
    Lord was w. him, 191
    w. him is an arm, 237
    w. thee, saith the Lord, 72
    w. us is the Lord, 237
    while ye be w. Him, 82
withdraw
    w. thy foot from, 125
wither
    w. as the green herb, 260
withered
    w. like grass, 56
withereth
    grass w., 109
    it is cut down, and w., 155
withhold
    good thing will He w., 213
    w. not good, 115
withholden
    thought can be w., 222
withholdeth
    w. corn, 25
within
    terror w. shall destroy, 60
without
    sword is w., 50
    sword w. and terror, 60
witness
    be an unrighteous w., 36
    be not a w. against thy, 124
    countenance doth w., 118
    false w. will utter, 28
    Lord be w. between, 6
    not bear false w., 177
    stone shall be a w., 202
    w. against the sorcerers, 265
    w. delivereth souls, 124
    w. is in heaven, 108
    w. shall not testify, 26
    w. that speaketh lies, 12
witnesses
    false w. are risen, 178
    false w. did rise up, 135
    mouth of two w., 26
    w. against yourselves, 31
    ye are My w., 244
wives
    lie with thy w., 125
wizards
    seek after w., 235
woe
    from our head: w., 212
    w. be to the shepherds, 43
    w. be unto the pastors, 148
    w. is me, 9
    w. is me for I, 86
    w. is me now, 224

w. that are wise, 38
w. to him that buildeth, 114
w. to him that increaseth, 47
w. to him that is alone, 43
w. to the bloody, 47
w. to the rebellious, 16
w. to thee, O land, 148
w. to them that devise, 47
w. unto him that, 121
w. unto him that buildeth, 43
w. unto him that giveth, 67
w. unto him that saith, 129
w. unto the foolish, 84
w. unto the wicked, 195
w. unto them for, 16
w. unto them that call, 112
w. unto them that decree, 114
w. unto them that draw, 230
w. unto them that rise, 67
w. unto them that seek, 64
w. unto you that desire, 141
w. w. unto thee, 66
wicked, w. unto me, 2
wolf
    w. also shall dwell, 10
    w. and the lamb, 24
woman
    adultery with a w., 4
    barren w. to keep house, 88
    be called w. because, 265
    born of a w., 155
    brawling w. in a wide, 156
    but a w. that feareth, 17
    contentious w. are alike, 166
    find a virtuous w., 156
    found; but a w. among, 154
    hand of a w., 253
    keep thee from evil w., 154
    lips of a strange w., 4
    Lord make the w., 87
    made He a w., 45
    man born of a w., 149
    man put on w.'s garment, 246
    means of a whorish w., 191
    serpent said unto the w., 136
    slay both man and w., 10
    so is a fair w., 17
    than with an angry w., 156
    tongue of a strange w., 154
    virtuous w. is a crown, 156
    w. among the daughters, 137

w. buildeth her house, 123
w. forget her sucking, 37
w. is a narrow pit, 191
w. of sorrowful spirit, 30
w. shall be a curse, 4
w. shall not wear, 246
w. slew him, 125
w. that travaileth, 243
w. whom Thou gavest, 20

womankind
mankind, as with w., 123

womb
died I not from the w., 58
estranged from the w., 17
fruit of the w., 31
fruit of the w., 10
grave; and the barren w., 52
made me in the w., 24
mother's w., 2
mother's w. naked, 52
of the w. to see, 59
out of the w., 58
out of the w. I, 20
shut up her w., 30
son of her w., 37
sons in my w., 9
them a miscarrying w., 49
w. to the grave, 224

women
became as w., 45
childless among w., 200
custom of w., 157
love of w., 93
shall become as w., 126
singing w., 6
strength unto w., 154
w. childless, 200

won
harder to be w., 91

wonderful
hast done w. things, 185
love to me was w., 93
many are Thy w. works, 184
name shall be called W., 159
w. works to the children, 184

wonderfully
fearfully and w. made, 46

wonders
praises, doing w., 15
w. in heaven and in, 56
w. in the deep, 172

wondrous
all His w. works, 232
talk of Thy w. works, 136
w. works of God, 167

wood
bears out of the w., 194
brass as rotten w., 237
fire and the w., 167
fire, and this people w., 69

hands, w. and stone, 129
hewers of w., 194
saith to the w. Awake, 129
w. and stone, 129
w. devoured, 256
where no w. is, 113
yokes of w., 26

wool
eat them like w., 60

word
by the w. of the Lord, 46
despiseth the w., 172
dry bones, hear the w., 208
every w. that proceedeth, 157
good is the w., 109
hath spoken this w., 57
hear the w. of the, 76
hear the w. of the, 121
hear the w. of the Lord, 59
hear ye the w., 187
hear ye the w., 258
His w. do I hope, 109
His w. was in my tongue, 135
if the w. of the Lord, 14
in awe of Thy w., 4
Lord gave the w., 187
not a w. in my tongue, 100
not add unto the w., 220
not failed one w., 45
perform His w., 102
rejected w. of the Lord, 41
show the w. of God, 209
Thy w. have I hid, 35
to seek the w. of the, 95
w. fitly spoken, 69
w. is a lamp, 73
w. is true, 221
w. is very nigh, 35
w. let him speak My w., 67
w. of God forever, 109
w. of the Lord, 35
w. of the Lord, 170
w. of the Lord, 255
w. of the Lord, 201
w. of the Lord, 53
w. of the Lord, 190
w. of the Lord from, 140
w. spoken in due season, 5
w. that God putteth, 135
w. that I shall speak, 190
where w. of a king is, 15

words
according to thy w., 6
add not unto His w., 221
afraid of their w., 44
attend to my w., 117
believed not their w., 205
break me in pieces with w., 78
do not My w. do good, 34
ear trieth w., 248

famine of hearing the w., 85
for his w., 66
forcible are right w., 124
hasty in his w., 198
hear thy w. but, 65
heard these w., 233
hearkened unto the w., 65
heed unto all w., 48
know of these w., 222
known by multitude of w., 90
let the w. of my mouth, 185
let these my w., 185
let thy w. be few, 127
make an end of w., 131
multitude of w., 234
My w. upon this city, 66
not afraid of the w., 70
obeyeth not the w., 45
pleasant w. are, 234
spareth his w., 252
sweet are Thy w., 136
that my w. were written, 23
trust not in lying w., 64
w. are not heard, 5
w. in thine heart, 35
w. of a talebearer, 113
w. of Job are ended, 71
w. of my mouth, 234
w. of that prophet, 83
w. of the Lord, 171
w. of the righteous, 24
w. of the wise, 117
w. smoother than butter, 69
w. were softer than oil, 69
w. without knowledge, 130
w. without knowledge, 130
wearied the Lord with w., 78
will make My w. fire, 69
wisdom of thy w., 5

work
according to his w., 142
and do all thy w., 216
bring every w. into, 54
devise iniquity, and w., 47
do thy w., 216
doers of the w., 255
doeth the w. deceitfully, 68
my w. with my God, 81
rested from all His w., 216
shalt not do any w., 216
time for Thee Lord to w., 111
w. a w. in your days, 230
w. is perfect, 97
w. of errors, 129
w. of His hands, 74
w. of men's hands, 129
w. of men's hands, 129

w. of men's hands, 129
w. of nought, 129
w. of righteousness, 215
w. of the hands, 17
w. of their hands, 142
w. of their hands, 101
w. of Thy hand, 46
w. say of him that made, 56
w. shall be rewarded, 212
w. shall be rewarded, 213
w. that they must do, 147
w. wickedness, 76
worship the w., 128
workers
  from the w. of iniquity, 146
  w. of iniquity, 53
  w. of iniquity, 60
  w. of iniquity do, 146
  w. of iniquity shall be, 262
  where w. of iniquity, 47
worketh
  profit hath he that w., 189
  that w. deceit shall not, 64
  w. righteousness, 218
  w. signs and wonders, 56
working
  razor, w. deceitfully, 20
workman
  hands of a cunning w., 17
  w. made it therefore, 130
works
  according to Thy w., 99
  all His wondrous w., 232
  commit thy w. unto, 239
  declare the w. of, 61
  fulfil your w., 173
  holy in all His w., 111
  how manifold are Thy w., 167
  many are Thy wonderful w., 184
  rejoice in his own w., 3
  righteous in all His w., 97
  see the w. of the Lord, 172
  talk of Thy wondrous w., 136
  their w. are nothing, 129
  w. among all nations, 76
  w. of His hands are, 111
  w. of the Lord are, 168
  w. to the children, 184
  with w. of your hands, 191
  with w. of your hands, 98
  wondrous w. of God, 167
world
  established the w., 46
  established the w., 46
  judge the w., 140
  judge the w., 141
  punish the w., 77
  set the w. upon, 68
  w. and all things, 187

w. and they that dwell, 68
w. is Mine, 103
worm
  I am a w. and no man, 174
  man, that is a w., 155
  man, which is a w., 155
  w. is spread under, 52
  w. shall eat, 60
  w. shall feed sweetly, 51
  w. Thou art my mother, 51
worms
  like w. of the earth, 126
  w. cover thee, 52
  w. destroy this body, 51
  w. shall cover, 51
wormwood
  drunken with w., 20
worship
  Him shall ye w., 97
  w. and bow down, 268
  w. Him, all ye gods, 123
  w. the Lord in beauty, 268
  w. the work, 128
worth
  wicked is little w., 124
worthy
  show himself a w. man, 142
  w. of death, 26
  w. to be praised, 55
  w. to die, 67
wound
  w. and I heal, 102
  w. for w., 141
wounded
  a w. spirit who, 57
  cast down many w., 4
  He was w. for our, 159
woundeth
  He w. and His hands, 102
wounds
  bindeth up their w., 233
  faithful are the w., 48
  multiplieth my w., 240
  talebearer are as w., 113
wrath
  anger, and forsake w., 8
  day of the Lord's w., 98
  day of w., 259
  fierceness of His w., 91
  fool's w., 136
  hypocrites heap up w., 3
  in My w. I smote, 37
  king's w. is as, 9
  pour out my w. upon, 98
  provoke Me unto w., 98
  sentest forth Thy w., 199
  slow to w., 176
  turneth away w., 8
  w. for His enemies, 98
  w. is against, 8
  w. is against all, 16
  w. is cruel, 9
  w. is upon all, 66

w. killeth the foolish, 8
w. of a king, 9
w. of the Almighty, 98
w. of the Lord, 65
w. remember mercy, 9
w. shall be kindled, 128
wicked is w., 79
wise men turn away w., 9
wretchedness
  not see my w., 224
write
  w. it before them, 122
  w. the vision and, 33
writer
  pen of a ready w., 234
written
  adversary had w., 3
  all that is w. therein, 220
  w. in this book, 128
  w. with a pen, 178
  w. with the finger, 243
  w. with the righteous, 72
  words were now w., 23
wrong
  chambers by w., 43
  doest me w., 257
  seen my w., 143
  to do them w., 106
wrongeth
  w. his own soul, 264
wrongfully
  enemies w. rejoice, 72
wroth
  w. with all, 41
wrought
  hath God w., 15
  w. for My name's sake, 99

Y

year
  seventh y. let it rest, 48
years
  days of our y. are, 149
  days of the y., 162
  forty y., 78
  hundred y. old, 87
  Jacob served seven y., 152
  ninety y. old, 87
  number of His y., 145
  restore to you the y., 91
  six y. thou shalt sow, 48
  spend our y., 149
  stricken in y., 6
  threescore y. and ten, 149
  unto thy days fifteen y., 37
  walked forty y., 78
  y. in pleasure, 191
  y. in Thy sight, 179
  y. of many generations, 79
  y. of the wicked, 87
  y. of thy life, 5
  y. shall have no end, 75
  y. should teach wisdom, 79

yesterday
  are but as y. when, 179
yield
  land shall y. her increase,
    170
yielding
  y. pacifieth, 192
yoke
  bear the y., 176
  unaccustomed to a y., 64
yokes
  broken the y., 26
  make them y. of iron, 26
young
  breasts are like two y., 17
  calf and the y. lion, 10
  gently with the y. man, 36
  glory of y. men is, 79
  roar like y. lions, 6
  spare ye not her y., 10
  suck to their y., 30
  y. and now am old, 1
  y. children ask bread, 85
  y. children despised me,
    220
  y. lions roar, 6
  y. man and the virgin, 60
  y. man, in thy youth, 268

y. men cheerful, 191
y. men shall see visions, 67
younger
  elder serve the y., 88
  they that are y., 6
  y. brother shall be, 88
youth
  childhood and y. are,
    268
  children of the y., 222
  days of thy y., 97
  days of thy y., 79
  evil from his y., 76
  husband of her y., 54
  not but a y., 10
  rejoice in thy y., 268
  sin of his y., 260
  sins of my y., 91
  trust from my y., 124
  wife of his y., 156
  wife of thy y., 156
  y. even unto this day, 39
  yoke in his y., 176

Z

zeal
  z. for the Lord, 269

Zion
  build up Z., 139
  comfort Z., 139
  daughter of Z., 220
  daughter of Z., 140
  earth, is mount Z., 139
  law go forth of Z., 140
  Lord dwelleth in Z., 140
  Lord hath chosen Z., 139
  Lord hath founded Z., 139
  loveth the gates of Z., 139
  not the Lord in Z., 59
  return, and come to Z., 92
  shall be as mount Z., 19
  shall yet comfort Z., 56
  singing unto Z., 101
  standard toward Z., 218
  strength, O Z., 203
  when we remembered Z.,
    123
  which is Z., 138
  Z. shall be redeemed, 139
  Z. shall go forth, 35
  Z.'s sake will I not, 139